W9-CLB-670

DIFFERENTIATING INSTRUCTION IN INCLUSIVE CLASSROOMS

The Special Educator's Guide

DIANE HAAGER
California State University, Los Angeles

JANETTE K. KLINGNER
University of Colorado at Boulder

Boston ▪ New York ▪ San Francisco
Mexico City ▪ Montreal ▪ London ▪ Madrid ▪ Munich ▪ Paris
Hong Kong ▪ Singapore ▪ Tokyo ▪ Cape Town ▪ Sydney

Executive Editor: *Virginia Lanigan*
Series Editorial Assistant: *Scott Blaszak*
Senior Editorial-Production Administrator: *Beth Houston*
Editorial-Production Service: *Walsh & Associates, Inc.*
Photo Researcher: *PoYee Oster*
Executive Marketing Manager: *Amy Cronin Jordan*
Composition and Prepress Buyer: *Linda Cox*
Manufacturing Buyer: *Andrew Turso*
Cover Administrator: *Kristina Mose-Libon*
Electronic Composition: *Modern Graphics, Inc.*

Copyright © 2005 Pearson Education, Inc.

For related titles and support materials, visit our online catalog at www.alongman.com.

All rights reserved. No part of the material protected by this copyright notice may be reproduced or utilized in any form or by any means, electronic or mechanical, including photocopying, recording, or by any information storage and retrieval system, without written permission from the copyright owner.

To obtain permission(s) to use material from this work, please submit a written request to Allyn and Bacon, Permissions Department, 75 Arlington Street, Boston, MA 02116 or fax your request to 617-848-7320.

Between the time Website information is gathered and then published, it is not unusual for some sites to have closed. Also, the transcription of URLs can result in typographical errors. The publisher would appreciate notification where these errors occur so that they may be corrected in subsequent editions.

Library of Congress Cataloging-in-Publication Data

Haager, Diane.
Differentiating instruction in inclusive classrooms : the special educator's guide / Diane Haager, Janette K. Klinger.
p. cm.
Includes bibliographical references and index.
ISBN 0-205-34074-1
1. Students with disabilities—Education—United States. 2. Inclusive education—United States. 3. Individualized instruction—United States. I. Klingner, Janette K. II. Title.

LC4019.H32 2005
371.9'046—dc22 2004050599

Printed in the United States of America
10 9 8 09

Photo Credits: Page 1, © Richard Hutchings/Photo Researchers; 24, © 2004 Laura Dwight; 50, © SIU/Visuals Unlimited; 97, © Ellen Senisi/The Image Works; 151, © David Young-Wolff/Photo Edit; 195, © David Lassman/Syracuse Newspapers/The Image Works; 238, © LWA-Dann Tardif/CORBIS; 289, © Elizabeth Crews/The Image Works; 331, © Jonathan Nourok/Photo Edit; 390, © Mark Richards/Photo Edit; 431, © Paul Barton/ CORBIS

CONTENTS

CHAPTER THREE
ASSESSMENT-BASED DECISION MAKING 50

CHAPTER FOUR
INSTRUCTIONAL APPROACHES FOR INCLUSIVE CLASSROOMS 97

CHAPTER FIVE

FACILITATING SOCIAL AND BEHAVIORAL COMPETENCE FOR STUDENTS WITH DISABILITIES IN INCLUSIVE SETTINGS 151

CHAPTER SIX

READING INSTRUCTION FOR STRUGGLING READERS IN INCLUSIVE ELEMENTARY CLASSROOMS 195

PREFACE

When we were fellow doctoral students at the University of Miami, studying the dual fields of reading and learning disabilities, we discovered that we shared similar backgrounds in teaching and learning. We had both worked as special educators across a range of ages and settings. We had worked in urban schools with students of diverse backgrounds and cultures. We were both strong advocates for our students. Assisting their families in navigating the complicated web we call special education was important, as was ensuring that our students reached their highest potential in acquiring the skills needed to be successful both socially and academically. We both started our teaching careers at a time when the field of learning disabilities was quite young. The research base on effective teaching strategies for students with learning and behavior disorders was in its infancy. We found that we were often flying by the seat of our pants, using a trial-and-error process to figure out how to maximize our effectiveness as special educators. We often turned to the related fields of reading and psychology for guidance in developing effective teaching strategies. Over time, experience became our best teacher. Seeing a student with very severe reading disabilities pick up a book and read, after months and even years of intensive teaching, remains one of our greatest joys.

Today's special educator must have more skill and knowledge than ever before. Increasing demands for accountability and pressure to improve academic achievement for students with disabilities necessitates a high level of expertise for special educators. As the laws that govern special education increasingly call for instruction and services to take place in the general education setting, special educators must also have a high degree of flexibility. Within a single day, special educators may find themselves going into several different general education classrooms to serve their students. These classrooms are likely to represent a range of ages and curricula and an array of teaching styles on the part of the general education teachers. Special educators, then, must have a rich repertoire of approaches and strategies as well as the professional savvy to work collaboratively with different types of people.

The past ten years have been an exciting time to be in special education. The research base has grown by leaps and bounds. We now have a science of pedagogy that undergirds our profession. National and state initiatives call for teachers to implement practices that are research-validated. A climate of social justice in our culture has also led to an increased emphasis on making general education curriculum and experiences accessible to students with disabilities. It is no longer sufficient to ensure the learning of students with disabilities—we must also ensure that it takes place in a way that maximizes students' membership and participation in the mainstream culture of the school. *Inclusion* is the term used to describe the process of ensuring the success of students with disabilities in the general education environment.

AUDIENCE AND PURPOSE

This book is for current and future special education teachers who will serve students with disabilities either full- or part-time in the general education classroom. Recent statistics in special education indicate that would be nearly 90 percent of special education teachers. The primary purpose of this book is to serve as a textbook for graduate or advanced undergraduate courses in special education. This book is also appropriate as a resource book for special and general education teachers, school administrators, related service providers, and anyone interested in effective methods for inclusion. While most textbooks on inclusion focus on the *general education* teacher, this book is intended to be a guide for the *special educator.* It includes methods for teaching students from kindergarten through high school graduation and beyond. It also includes ideas and strategies for collaboration with general education teachers, parents, and other professionals. Because many students with high-incidence disabilities experience challenges in reading and writing, a significant portion of the book is devoted to methods for developing literacy in elementary and secondary students with disabilities.

In this book, we focus on the high-incidence disabilities: learning disabilities, behavior disorders, and mild mental retardation. Inclusion presents unique challenges for these students, whose disabilities are not usually visibly evident to teachers and classmates. It is often hard for them to understand why these students have difficulty with reading, writing, or mathematics. Facilitating their involvement in academic classroom activities requires planning and collaboration between the general and special education teachers. These students are often behind their general education peers in academic skills and need intensive, remedial instruction. Balancing the general education curriculum and their individual learning needs requires great skill and collaboration. We believe that social and emotional development must occur simultaneously with academic learning. This book includes information about facilitating social competence in inclusive settings.

This text takes a balanced approach to inclusion, emphasizing the importance of basing decisions about students' academic and social goals on assessment data and then determining on an individual basis how and where services will take place. The book integrates theory and pedagogy by illustrating important concepts and constructs with realistic examples and practical ideas that can be readily implemented. Putting research-validated methods into practice is a central theme of this book.

FOCUS OF THE BOOK

This book begins with the foundational knowledge needed to be an effective special educator in an inclusive setting. Chapter 1 provides an overview of the issues and importance of inclusion. Here we define the role of the special educator in an inclusive general education classroom and the larger community of the school. This role is at times delicate and sensitive, at others assertive and bold. Effective inclusive special educators operate with a solid understanding of laws, pedagogy, collaboration, and practical methodology. In Chapter 2, we describe the nature and characteristics of students with high-incidence disabilities. Though most teacher education programs provide an overview course of the characteristics associated with various disabilities, we feel it is important for inclusion specialists to have depth of knowledge about the three high-incidence disability categories of learning disabilities, behavior disorders, and mild mental retardation. In this chapter, we provide knowledge about the characteristics, eligibility criteria and procedures, and prevalence of these disabilities. We include narrative vignettes from the perspective of the students, parents, and teachers.

The next three chapters set the stage for implementing research-validated instruction in inclusive classrooms. Chapter 3 focuses on assessment. Assessment is integral to the successful operation of an inclusive program of special education and different types and purposes of assessment are used in inclusive settings across elementary and secondary settings. This chapter provides information, strategies, and practical examples of assessment. Later chapters build on the foundation of assessment provided here. Chapter 4 provides a broad base of instructional methods as they apply across subject areas. Special educators working in an inclusive setting must be knowledgeable about both general and special education methodology. This chapter covers the research behind the methods as well as practical examples of strategies as they might be implemented in an inclusive setting. The most often cited reason that general education teachers oppose inclusion is behavior problems. Chapter 5 offers an in-depth look at facilitating social and behavioral competence in students with disabilities. In this chapter, we emphasize a positive and proactive approach to classroom and behavior management. All students in inclusive settings will benefit when their teachers anticipate problems and organize classroom structures and routines that get students engaged in learning before problems occur. This chapter also includes methods and strategies for dealing with more serious individual behavioral issues.

The next few chapters focus on specific methods and strategies for teaching academic content. The majority of students with high-incidence disabilities experience academic difficulty in the basic areas of reading, writing, and mathematics. Effective special educators are specialists in teaching basic academic skills. In an inclusion setting, the special educator serves as a consultant, helping to make adaptations and modifications in the general education setting. Chapter 6 focuses on the development of beginning reading skills and the research base of teaching reading. No subject has been as controversial as how best to teach reading. Beginning special educators may find it confusing to go into general education classrooms that represent a wide array of teaching strategies and philosophies of teaching reading. In this chapter, we orient the beginning special educator to a range of approaches that may be present in a whole-class setting and discuss how to support students with disabilities in these contexts. Then, we discuss how to provide explicit instruction for struggling readers in small group or one-to-one settings. Chapter 7 takes a similar approach to writing instruction, first examining methods that are likely to be in place in the general education setting, then discussing strategies for working more intensively with students with disabilities. Chapter 8, contributed by Dr. Margaret Clark, offers an in-depth look at mathematics instruction for students with high-incidence disabilities. This chapter provides research-based approaches in two important areas—explicit skill instruction and cognitive strategy instruction.

The final three chapters focus on working with older students with disabilities in inclusive settings. Chapter 9 offers many ideas and strategies for facilitating students' learning in the content areas of social studies and science. Most students with high-incidence disabilities in upper elementary and secondary settings receive content area instruction in the general education setting. This chapter provides the reader with many ideas for making adaptations and accommodations in content area instruction. Chapter 10 focuses exclusively on secondary settings. Teachers and students face many unique challenges in an inclusive secondary setting. This chapter examines critical issues related to implementing inclusive secondary special education models. Finally, Chapter 11 examines the topic of transition from school-age to adulthood. The authors of this chapter are Dr. Richard Rosenberg, who heads a very successful high school transition program, and Dr. Mary Falvey, a teacher educator. This chapter offers practical, realistic methods for working with secondary students during this important transition period.

SPECIAL FEATURES OF THIS BOOK

This book has a broad **focus on high-incidence disabilities,** covering learning disabilities, mild mental retardation, and emotional disorders. Examples are provided for a diverse array of students, including students from culturally and linguistically diverse backgrounds. This book also covers special education methodology from **elementary to secondary grades,** which reflects the grade-span of the majority of special education teacher education programs. Most chapters include methods and vignettes from both elementary and secondary settings; two chapters are devoted specifically to secondary issues (Chapters 10 and 11). Filled with **real-life descriptions of evidence-based practices,** each chapter includes **vignettes** that bring the realities of the inclusive classroom alive. This text also has a strong emphasis on general education-special education **collaboration,** providing a comprehensive review of collaboration content while contextualizing it in an instructional methods text.

Boxes in every chapter provide analysis of key studies related to topics and issues in inclusive education. Current educational initiatives emphasize the importance of using research-based practices. It is important for prospective teachers to adopt sound practices that are supported by research.

Literacy development is covered in great depth in five chapters (Chapters 4, 6, 7, 9 and 10). Most students with high-incidence disabilities experience significant reading and writing difficulties, and special educators report that they spend most of their instructional time teaching reading and writing. This book provides many activities and methods for teaching reading and writing and methods chapters highlight research-based practices (a key point in the No Child Left Behind Act and Reading First initiatives.)

A focus on **formal and informal classroom-based assessment** is a central focus of this text. Chapter 3 covers assessment in depth and each methods chapter that follows discusses assessment practices specific to the subject matter (e.g., reading or math). This aspect of the text provides a comprehensive review of assessment and ties it to curriculum and instruction from an inclusive standpoint.

Accompanying resources include an Instructors Manual and Test Bank as well as a Companion website (http://www.ablongman.com/haager1e). These resources are designed to support an upper division undergraduate or a graduate level methods course in special education.

ACKNOWLEDGMENTS

This book has been a labor of love through several important phases of our personal and professional lives. Writing a book of this scope takes diligence and determination. It would be impossible to produce a textbook such as this without the help of other very capable and supportive individuals.

First, we would like to thank the many teachers with whom we have worked, in both our teaching and research careers. We have drawn the vignettes and examples in this book from many competent and creative teachers who have served as our inspiration. We would especially like to thank Michelle Windmueller, Mike Jeffers, Kristin Shaw, Romelia Umana, Joyce Duryea, Sallie Gotch, and Ailé Montoya for their ideas and support. We thank the many prospective and practicing teachers who have been in our university classes for allowing us to try out our ideas and for giving us valuable feedback. If you could put the collective classroom experience and practical knowledge of all the above individuals into boxes, it would fill many tall buildings.

We wish to thank all of the children we have taught over the years for inspiring our work and for teaching us how true it is that *all* children can learn. These children could not imagine how much we learned from them.

We certainly want to thank the graduate students who helped us in preparing the book. We would especially like to thank Elizabeth Cramer, Adriana Medina, and Lina Chiappone for their contributions to specific chapters.

Many thanks also go to Virginia Lanigan, our editor, for her longstanding patience and support throughout the writing of this book. In addition, we would like to acknowledge the reviewers of this first edition text for their valuable comments and expertise: Laura Bowden Carpenter, Auburn University Montgomery; Mary-Kay Crane, University of Georgia; Judith J. Ivarie, Eastern Illinois University; Stephanie Kurtts, University of North Carolina at Greensboro; Linda Duncan Malone, Ball State University; Gene Schwarting, Fontbonne College; and Beth Tulbert, University of Utah.

We would like to dedicate this book to our mentor and friend, Sharon Vaughn, who has guided us since we were doctoral students with her wisdom, kindness, and strength. Her friendship throughout the past years has meant more than we can express. In addition, we dedicate this book to the late Candace Bos, who motivated us with her passion and was a constant source of encouragement and support.

Last, we also would like to give a very special thank you to our husbands, Steve Haager and Don Klingner, and our children Emily and Julia Haager, and Heidi Warden, Amy and John Klingner. We deeply appreciate their love, support, and patience over the years.

ABOUT THE AUTHORS

Diane Haager is a researcher and teacher educator in reading and learning disabilities. She is a Professor at California State University, Los Angeles, where she instructs teachers in methods for teaching students with high incidence disabilities. Dr. Haager completed her Ph.D. in Reading and Learning Disabilities at the University of Miami in 1992 after twelve years of public school teaching as a reading specialist and special educator. She has authored numerous articles, books, and book chapters and has directed several funded projects. Her research interests include issues related to effective reading instruction for English language learners and students at risk for reading failure, inclusive education, and professional development. She is a member of the *Reading First National Panel of Experts* for the U. S. Department of Education and is on the editorial review board of three journals in the field of learning disabilities.

Janette K. Klinger is Associate Professor at the University of Colorado, Boulder, in Bilingual Special Education. She was a bilingual special education teacher for ten years before earning a Ph.D. in Reading and Learning Disabilities from the University of Miami in 1994. She has published four books and forty-one articles and book chapters and has been the principal or co-principal investigator on several federally funded grants. Her research interests include reading comprehension strategy instruction, outcomes for students with disabilities in inclusive classrooms, professional development that enhances the sustainability of evidence-based practices, and the disproportionate representation of culturally and linguistically diverse students in special education. She is the Associate Editor for AERA's *Review of Educational Research* and on the editorial board of six other professional journals. She is the Chairperson of AERA's Special Education Research Special Interest Group and in 2004 received AERA's Early Career Award.

CHAPTER ONE

SPECIAL EDUCATION IN INCLUSIVE SCHOOLS

Much learning does not teach understanding.
—Heraclitus, *On the Universe* (540 B.C.–480 B.C.)

KEY CONCEPTS

- Inclusion means providing special services for students with disabilities in the general education classroom to allow these students to be members of the same community as other children.
- Inclusion support for students with high-incidence disabilities should foster social and academic learning in the general education environment.
- Federal law directs schools to specify what types of services and support students with disabilities need to be educated in the general education environment.
- Collaboration among general and special education personnel and with families of children with disabilities is an essential ingredient for successful inclusion.
- Inclusion of students with disabilities in the general education environment enriches the diversity of a school community and provides opportunities for students to accept individual differences as a natural part of life.
- Administrative support is important to the success of an inclusive school model.

FOCUS QUESTIONS

1. Why is it important for students with disabilities to be included in the general education classroom?
2. How does the special education teacher's role change in an inclusive setting?
3. Is it possible to provide individualized instruction for students with disabilities in an inclusive setting?
4. What does the law say about inclusion?
5. Does inclusion facilitate both social and academic success for students with disabilities?

FRONT STREET ELEMENTARY SCHOOL

Toby, a special educator, and Anita, a fourth-grade teacher, are teachers at Front Street Elementary School, a small school in a working-class neighborhood on the periphery of a large urban area. Together they developed and implemented a collaborative model for inclusion of special education students into Anita's class last year. This year, other teachers will join in on a voluntary basis and work with them in developing inclusive classrooms. The principal has asked Toby and Anita to share some of their experiences with the teachers, administrators, and staff in today's faculty meeting as they begin the school year. Here are some excerpts of their meeting. (Note: We use teachers' first names here rather than surnames because in a school environment, teachers are usually on a first-name basis. We wanted to capture their conversations as best we could.)

Toby:

The important thing for me is that our students made progress last year. It's hard to know if they made more progress than they would have if they hadn't been included in Anita's class, but I'm sure they didn't make less progress. That's all I needed to know. The other benefits made it totally worth it to me. To see them work with the other kids and to see them raise their hands to answer questions—that was amazing to me. I've mainstreamed lots of kids. This wasn't the same. These kids really felt like they were a part of the class. That was important to us as we began to think about how to put together this inclusive class. Of course the bottom line is always whether they are learning or not, but we also wanted to be sure the kids felt like they were truly a part of the class. To be honest, that was the hardest part for me. It was hard to give up the feeling that they were MY kids. I had to train myself to say OUR kids.

Anita:

I think because Toby and I worked as a team we were able to go beyond mainstreaming. In the past, I felt like no matter how hard I tried to get the resource kids involved, they never seemed to feel like they belonged. They would say things like, "My teacher says . . . " and I knew they were talking about their special ed. teacher, not me. I didn't hear that last year. They knew they could count on Toby for help but they came to me, too.

Toby:

Planning is critical. We made a plan at the beginning of the year, and we just had to stick with it. We had weekly meetings and had a system of daily communication. We worked out what I would be responsible for and what she would do. Once we got into the routine, we were fine. When we hit bumps along the way, we just said, "Okay, let's deal with it," and we would figure out what to do.

Anita:

At first, I was a little worried about having to share my planning with someone. I'm used to doing my own thing and not having to tell anyone about it. I thought it would slow me down to have to plan with Toby. I knew her as the "expert," and I wasn't sure I wanted her telling me what to do in my own classroom. It wasn't that way at all. I learned a great deal from Toby and from the kids. Toby didn't come in and flaunt her expertise. She was always happy to share her ideas and knowledge, but she tried to figure out how they would fit in my class. She always let me make the final decision on things related to the lessons and activities. I realized I was an expert, too—an expert on how things work in my class. We really had a great deal to teach each other.

Toby and Anita are an example of collaborative consultation at its best. Because they planned their collaborative structure as well as their service delivery program, they were able to avoid many roadblocks experienced by others. They recognized at the outset that they needed a system of communication, a decision-making structure, and goals to make inclusion work for them. Their participation was voluntary and, in fact, was initiated by them. Their principal was happy with the existing special education program, but was open to new ideas and was highly supportive from the start.

Students walk into classrooms with a variety of backgrounds and personal experiences. What students bring to the classroom helps us to determine their learning needs. Students whose skills and knowledge match closely with the curriculum tend to do well. Others need additional support and experiences to assist them in meeting grade-level expectations. Students with disabilities also come to school with a diverse set of skills, knowledge, and learning needs. Often, their disabilities pose a significant challenge to meeting grade-level expectations and they fall behind their peers in learning. Recent changes in the federal law specify that students with disabilities must, to the greatest extent possible, progress in the general curriculum. As teachers, we must be prepared to help all students meet expectations in school. We must have a repertoire of teaching strategies to address all kinds of learners. Though students may come to school with different sets of knowledge and experience, our nation has the same expectation for all: that school is a place for students to learn the essential skills necessary to be successful in our society.

The idea of holding students to grade-level standards may invoke an image of a teacher in front of the class plowing through a prescribed curriculum regardless of whether students are learning. We may all remember a teacher in our past who went right through the planned math lessons (or history, science, poetry, etc.) despite the fact that very few students actually understood the content. Some would maintain that this is necessary to "keep students on track" with prescribed learning standards. However, we believe the opposite approach is necessary if we are to truly succeed with all students. Though it is essential to move through the curriculum and maintain high standards for learning, teachers must be constantly aware of students' learning and must be equipped with strategies for addressing the needs of students who may be struggling. The age-old practice of "teaching to the middle" only addresses the needs of the few students who are truly in the middle in terms of knowledge and skills.

Pull-out model Pulling students with special needs out of the general education classroom for special services such as special education.

Pull-in model Bringing special services and personnel into the general education classroom so that students do not have to leave their teacher and classmates while receiving services.

Special education was designed to address the specific needs of students with disabilities in our public schools. This often means removing students from the general education classroom to a special class, where teachers and specialists provide instruction tailored to students' individual needs. However, this **pull-out model** of removing students from the general classroom also means removing them from the social milieu of the school. Students with disabilities may miss out on rich and interesting learning experiences that occur in the general classroom. Increasingly, schools are adopting a **pull-in model** wherein students with disabilities receive all or some of their special services in the general education classroom.

Inclusion means bringing special services into the classroom to allow students with disabilities to be members of the same community as other children. It is an attractive special education model because it is a positive approach to the issues of discrimination against and isolation of individuals with disabilities. Inclusion provides opportunities for encouraging an appreciation of diversity among all students and teachers (Coots, Bishop, Grenot-Scheyer, & Falvey, 1995; Villa & Thousand, 1995). Inclusion has been the focus of much debate in recent years. Some believe it is fundamentally wrong to exclude children with disabilities (e.g., Gartner & Lipsky, 1987; Stainback & Stainback, 1991; Will, 1986), while others fear the demise of special education (e.g., Fuchs & Fuchs, 1994a, 1994b; Kauffman, 1995; Kauffman & Hallahan, 1995). In the midst of public debates, we have seen a great increase in the number of schools adopting inclusive models for providing special education services. Box 1.1 provides a teacher's point of view on inclusion.

BOX 1.1

FROM THE HEART OF A BEGINNING TEACHER

*Ailé Montoya**

Dear Journal,

It has been a while since I have written, but something has been bothering me lately. Most of the time I feel frustrated in this ESE (Exceptional Student Education, pull-out) setting. I find that some students should be mainstreamed into the regular setting. They have good reading and writing skills but are not mainstreamed either because their behavior is not perfect or there is a sense of fear that they will not do well and it will affect their self-esteem. I understand that concept and feeling, but I believe that if the appropriate accommodations were made, these students would be successful in the regular education classroom. When I mention books on tape, for example, I am told they are only for students who cannot read at all. They don't understand that such an accommodation can benefit both those who are mainstreamed and those who are not. And those who are mainstreamed may need it later or may need it now but are compensating through listening. Behaviors can be modified and assignments can be, too. We now live in the twenty-first century, where computers can be used to help students read and write. So as a result, there are days where I feel that I am not doing enough nor trying my best and I'm letting my kids down by not providing them the best education possible. I feel discouraged.

Why be reluctant to mainstream students for fear of failure? Teddy Roosevelt once said, in his famous speech, "It is hard to have failed, but it is harder to never have tried." So, why not try and allow students to be in the regular education setting? As it is now, students are simply being kept behind without giving them a chance to experience possible success.

Today I received a quote by George Eliot in my mail. She wrote, "What do we live for, if not helping each other?" What a great quote that truly is . . . I thought I would share. For those educators who teach students with disabilities—thanks for reaching out to the world with a helping hand.

*Ms. Montoya is a first-year teacher who teaches middle school students with high-incidence disabilities. She herself has a severe reading disability that was not diagnosed until college. At first her teachers had thought she was behind from confusion learning English as a second language (Spanish is her home language). She eventually learned to compensate for her difficulties with reading by developing excellent listening comprehension skills and an outstanding memory.

APPROPRIATE, INDIVIDUALIZED EDUCATIONAL SUPPORT: OUR PHILOSOPHY OF INCLUSION

High-incidence disabilities Disabilities that occur with the highest frequency, including learning disabilities, behavior disorders, and mild mental retardation.

This book primarily addresses services for students with **high-incidence disabilities**, or those that occur with most frequency, including learning disabilities, behavior disorders, and mild mental retardation (In Chapter 2 we talk more about high-incidence disabilities). The issues regarding inclusion for these students differ from other types of disabilities. For a student who is deaf or hard of hearing, it is usually obvious to a teacher or classmates what types of supports are necessary to facilitate learning. Likewise, when a student with a physical disability uses a wheelchair, the teacher and classmates can readily implement changes in the physical space to accommodate needs. However, the disabling characteristics of students with high-incidence disabilities are usually not readily visible. A student struggling to learn to read may appear "slow" to other students when asked to read aloud in class. A student with a poor attention span may strike a teacher as intentionally misbehaving. Students with high-incidence disabilities are a very heterogeneous population whose needs can vary widely from one another. This heterogeneity makes it essential to tailor an inclusive program to students' individual needs and characteristics.

Many people talk about inclusion in terms of *place,* with all services occurring in the general education classroom. We believe that place is less important than substance. We prefer to describe inclusion as *a set of services and supports for students,* with the purpose being to maximize students' learning of the core curriculum and social development along with their nondisabled peers. For most students with high incidence disabilities, the general education classroom setting is the optimal place when appropriate supports and services are provided and the school and classroom climate are accommodating of their learning needs. However, we also recognize that students' needs and classroom situations may vary, making it more advantageous to provide instruction or other services outside of the classroom setting. In this situation, we encourage teachers to ensure that the student maintains a strong sense of belonging to the general education classroom and that the student does not miss essential learning experiences.

Special educators working in inclusive settings face the daily challenge of having to balance subject area support with skill development. Teachers must work together to help students to be successful in content area classes. This often means crafting adaptations and providing specialized support. Failing to do so contradicts the federal mandate to ensure students' progress in the core curriculum. However, providing systematic and intensive instruction in basic skills (reading, writing, and mathematics) is also essential. Students must develop basic skills in order to become independent in their content-area learning and to develop important life skills. It is important to strike a balance between content support and skills development. Too much focus on skills instruction, ignoring content area support, leads to segregated programs as we have had in the past and excludes students from access to the core curriculum, building important knowledge bases in subject areas, and being included in classes with their peers. To a certain extent, basic skills can be taught within the context of supporting students in content area classes. However, we believe that it is also important to provide direct instruction for a short period of time each day for skills development.

INCLUSION: MEETING STUDENTS' INDIVIDUAL NEEDS

In our thinking, school must be a place where all students learn. Accountability is a buzzword that resurfaces in education from time to time. We are hearing the message from state and federal standards, local school district initiatives, and popular media that we must be responsible for the learning of *all* students. Currently, schools are adopting accountability procedures to ensure that we do not fail children by sending them out into the adult world lacking in academic skills. This principle also applies to students with disabilities, and we must also be accountable for ensuring that these students meet their learning goals. However, we have the additional responsibility of ensuring that students with disabilities are included as integral members of the school community. The special educator's role has been changing as classrooms and schools change. A special educator's primary role is—and has always been—to address the individual learning needs of students who experience particular difficulty. The special attention you will give to these students is necessary for their success. However, it is also your responsibility to facilitate your students' success in being a member of the general school and classroom environment, to help them to fully benefit from normal social and academic experiences. An inclusive approach to providing special education allows students to function within the normal parameters of the school and classroom environments. To further define and discuss our vision of inclusion, we address it from three perspectives: educational, social, and legal.

An Educational Perspective: Facilitating Student Learning

Most general education classrooms are filled with learning opportunities. Teachers' lesson plans, with learning objectives, are only a portion of what students learn. Ideas are generated as teachers and students engage in interactive discussions. While students work on projects, engage in activities, or complete assignments, teachers provide ongoing feedback and additional instruction. In a general education classroom, students learn from teachers, activities, and other students. Students develop language skills, social skills, and general knowledge of the world around them. When we remove students with disabilities from this scenario to provide specialized instruction, there is a cost that must be weighed against the benefits. The cost is that they miss out on the richness of the learning that occurs in the classroom arena.

Some proponents of inclusion believe that it is unwise to pull a student out of the classroom for special education services. They advocate for *full inclusion*, in which all services are brought to the child and the child is never removed from the general education classroom. However, we take a more moderate stance on this issue. We believe that there are times when it is beneficial to take a student or a small group out of the classroom to provide intensive instruction or assessment or to remove the child from the distractions of the classroom. *How* services are provided is more important than *where* they are provided. Having an inclusive way of thinking and ensuring that all students feel they are integral members of the class are much more important than rigidly adhering to the notion of keeping students in the classroom. For some students with learning or attention problems, it is helpful to take them to a quiet space to provide additional instruction on a concept or lesson or intensive remedial instruction in basic skills. It is important for the classroom teacher and the special education teacher to carefully plan how and when this will occur so students will not miss key information or experiences. There may be a time when the classroom teacher and the special education teacher are both pulling students aside for additional assistance. Or there may be times when students are doing independent seatwork or when many students are out of the room for special activities.

A primary role of the special educator working in an inclusive setting is to assist the classroom teacher in implementing adaptations to enable students with learning difficulties to be successful in the core curriculum and classroom activities. The special education teacher, instructional assistant, or other support personnel may go into the classroom to provide extra support for one or more students who are likely to experience difficulty.

When appropriate supports and adaptations are provided, students with learning difficulties are able to grasp grade-level material.

We believe that an inclusive classroom provides important learning experiences for students with disabilities. We must carefully orchestrate individualized instruction and special education services to enable students to fully benefit from the general education classroom. We must also provide appropriate supports and adaptations to enable students to keep up with the content and pace of the general classroom.

A Social Perspective: Inclusion as a Process

Many students with learning and behavior problems have social difficulties as compared to their peers (Elbaum, 2002; Haager & Vaughn, 1997; Vaughn & Haager, 1994a, 1994b; Vaughn, Elbaum, Schumm, & Hughes, 1998). Students with high-incidence disabilities are more likely to have difficulty with peer acceptance, self-concept, and social skills. This does not mean that *all* students with disabilities have social problems—in fact, for some students, this is their area of strength. Inclusive education is most effective when it promotes both social and academic growth.

Many assert the social benefits of educating students with disabilities alongside nondisabled peers as the primary reason for adopting an inclusive model. Ensuring that individuals with disabilities are part of the social fabric of our society is often stated as the goal of inclusion. Inclusion provides an arena in which students with disabilities develop the skills necessary for building friendships and learning to function in society. It also provides opportunities for students without disabilities to learn to accept and include individuals who are different into their normal life routines and ways of thinking. These certainly are important social outcomes of inclusive education.

For students with learning disabilities and other high-incidence disorders, both social and academic outcomes are important. Overemphasizing the social aspects of inclusion marginalizes the primary goal of ensuring students' academic progress. For students with more severe disabilities, who have often been relegated to the fringe of society, social development is an important and reasonable rationale for inclusion. For these students, developing friendships and social skills is a primary goal, as is teaching others to accept their physical and cognitive limitations.

For students with mild to moderate disabilities, who typically have no visible signs of difference, facilitating their social integration is more complicated than one would think (Klingner, Vaughn, Schumm, Cohen, & Forgan, 1998; Vaughn et al., 1998). Their disabilities often impact their language and social skills in subtle ways. Their academic limitations often make them stand out in normal classroom routines and activities. Despite the fact that inclusive classrooms provide greater social opportunities for students, inclusion does not eliminate the social difficulties of students with learning disabilities (Vaughn et al., 1998).

To promote students' social growth in an inclusve classroom, teachers must take steps to ensure success. The most critical factor is creating a classroom and school environment that is highly accepting of students' differences. Just as schools make explicit efforts to foster cultural awareness, we must also be explicit in our efforts to foster acceptance of learning differences. Imagine a student with limited reading skills being asked to read aloud a passage in class and stumbling over the difficult words. The typical response of other students might be to chuckle under their breath or become impatient and correct the student loudly. We can probably all recall a struggling stu-dent being embarrassed in class by such experiences. This type of social interchange does little to promote social acceptance. To promote the social inclusion of students with such difficulties, teachers must *anticipate* such situations and take preemptive steps. For example, the teacher may be selective in the types of reading aloud expected of students. This would avoid the situation. However, this does not teach the other students how to respond appropriately to students' limitations. It is also important to make it acceptable for students to have different skill sets and to appreciate each others' strengths and limitations. One teacher we know has made it an ordinary occurrence for students to need help from time to time. In this teacher's class, the student reading aloud in the situation described above might have felt free to ask for help, or a neighbor student might have readily provided the difficult word without missing a step in focusing on the lesson. There would have been little or no chuckling because all students feel safe in needing help. For example, during math the teacher typically provides a brief whole-class lesson then the students are expected to complete a seat assignment. At the conclusion of the whole group instruction, the teacher matter-of-factly asks a few students to come to her table for more intensive help and assigns peer helpers for others. It is part of the classroom routine for students to help other students and the stigma of needing help is diminished. Another critical factor is explicit instruction in social skills, particularly those skills necessary to function in the normal classroom routine. Students need opportunities to practice appropriate social skills as well as ongoing guidance and support.

Legal Foundation for Inclusive Practices

The 1997 version of the federal legislation for special education, the Individuals with Disabilities Education Act (IDEA), strengthened the legal basis for inclusive education. The original law, enacted in 1977, maintained provisions for placing students with disabilities in the least restrictive environment (LRE), or as close as possible to a regular classroom placement. Several court challenges over the years have helped to shape the meaning of LRE as well as the procedures for ensuring compliance. The recent amendments to this act make specific reference to educating students with disabilities in the regular education environment:

> To the maximum extent appropriate, children with disabilities, including children in public or private institutions or other care facilities, are educated with children who are not disabled, and special classes, separate schooling or other removal of children with disabilities from the regular educational environment occurs only when the nature or severity of the disability of the child is such that education in regular classes with the use of supplementary aids and services cannot be achieved satisfactorily. [Sec. 1412(A)(5)(A)]

Furthermore, the law directs schools to make explicit statements as to the services required to facilitate a student's involvement in and progress in the general education curriculum as well as participation in extracurricular and nonacademic activities alongside children with and without disabilities. The law specifies that, unless the decision-making team (the Individualized Education Program team), comprised of professionals, the parent(s), and the child when appropriate, specifies otherwise, students with disabilities are to be held to the same academic standards and participate in the same district-wide or statewide assessments as other students. Graduation requirements can only be modified by a team decision as specified in a student's Individualized Education Plan (IEP). Each student with disabilities must receive specially designed instruction:

> **(i)** To address the unique needs of the child that result from the child's disability; and
> **(ii)** To ensure access of the child to the general curriculum, so that he or she can meet the educational standards within the jurisdiction of the public agency that apply to all children. [Part 300 Subpart A 300.26(b)]

A school district must make every effort to ensure the student's success in the general education environment and curriculum. Using specially designed instruction, supplementary aids and services, and making adaptations to the curriculum and instruction are the means for accommodating students with disabilities in the general education environment. The means for accomplishing this are to be determined on an individual basis according to the student's assessed needs. Complying with federal mandates to ensure students' access to the general education environment and curriculum is covered throughout all chapters of this book.

ESSENTIAL ELEMENTS OF INCLUSIVE SCHOOLS

Over the past few years, we have worked in several inclusive schools. We have conducted professional development to assist schools in developing inclusive programs, and we have conducted various studies in inclusive schools. From our collective experiences and from the professional literature, we have drawn some common threads that run through these schools. There are school, classroom, and program characteristics that in our opinion are essential for launching and maintaining an inclusive setting.

An Inclusive School Climate

Collaboration. Collaboration is a means to an end. When we go into inclusive schools, we see various forms of collaborative teaming, all focused on the common goal of ensuring learning for *all* students. We see teachers working in pairs or groups. We may see a classroom teacher, a paraprofessional and a special education teacher working together in the same classroom. We may also see a school decision-making team at work that includes teachers, parents, and an administrator. At planning time, we may see a classroom teacher working with a special educator to develop the next week's co-teaching plans, discussing the types of modifications that will be needed by individual students. We may also see a team of people working to solve a specific problem that has arisen. Of course, we will also see individuals working on their own, for no school could run efficiently if everything had

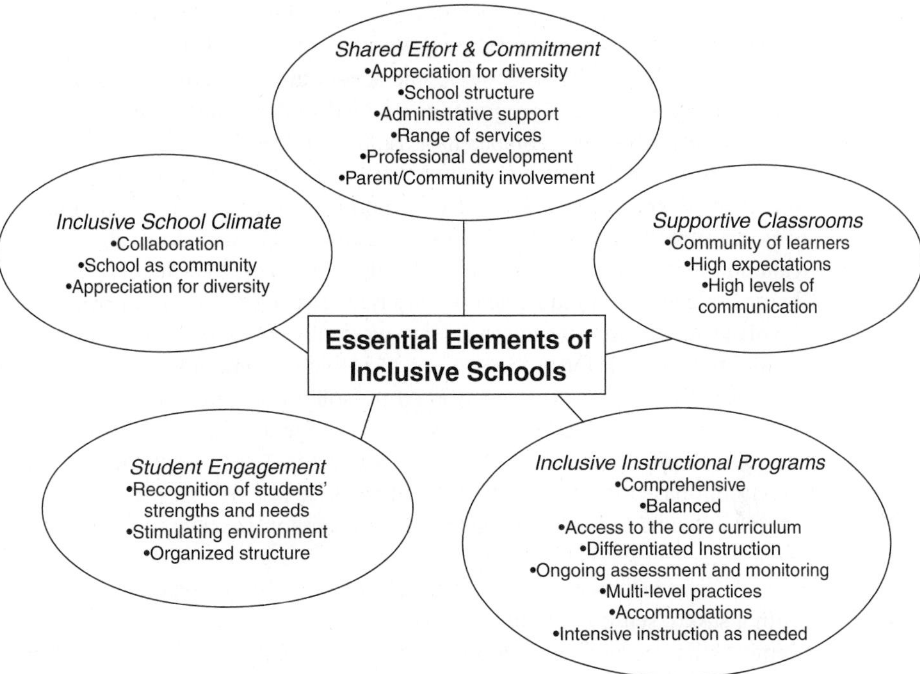

FIGURE 1.1 Essential Elements of Inclusive Schools

to be a team effort. However, individual efforts tend to support the greater aim of the school as a whole. Individuals know that if a situation or problem comes up that is too big for them to handle alone, they have a team to rely on for support.

Inclusive schools embrace collaboration as a key ingredient for day-to-day operation. There must be a "collaborative ethos" that influences school events in large and small ways. It is primarily evident in a pervasive sense of professional respect. It is also evident in the smooth intertwining of participants' efforts. Thus, it is important for those who work in the school (teachers, administrators, parents, and others) to have the professional skills necessary to function in a collaborative team. Collaboration is an essential element of professional development: It is not only important for teachers to know what to do but also to have the tools with which to do it.

School as Community. Most successful schoolwide efforts result in a strong sense of community. We often see in inclusive schools a general positive feeling throughout the school. We have the sense that school is a pleasant place to be for children and their parents, teachers, administrators, and the support staff. People seem to know each other and can tell you what they and other people have been doing. There are school events and activities that draw the school community together. Even so, the primary focus is the business of learning.

Several examples may help to illustrate this point. The first is a school in which one of us worked as a teacher for a few years. Though an outsider's general impression of this school would generally be positive, the school did not have a sense of community. There was a highly visible arts program for talented students, and there were several very effective teachers who were competent at raising children's test scores. However, there were teachers who did not know each other well at all and who only spoke to each other at staff meetings. If you were to ask a teacher about an initiative or program in which he or she was not directly involved, that teacher would know very little about it. Teachers either functioned in isolation or in social groups, or cliques, that mainly served the function of being a place to complain and commiserate. Though there were parents who were highly involved in the arts program, parents were not consistently present or visible in other school functions. Prior to the author's arrival at the school as a special education teacher, the special education program worked in isolation of the general classroom, despite the fact that most of the students were placed in a regular classroom for a portion of the school day. Developing rapport with the classroom teachers and implementing supports for their classroom-based learning were difficult tasks. It was only when other schoolwide reform efforts drew the community together that the author was able to implement inclusive practices.

In contrast, another urban school in which we have worked has evolved into a school with a strong sense of community. There is a schoolwide effort to improve students' academic skills because this is a school with historically low test scores. In this school, parents are integral members of the school community. They serve on the school governance board and participate as volunteers in several capacities. The whole school gathers in the courtyard for a few minutes in the morning for a flag salute, announcements, and a brief word from the principal about focusing on the business of learning. There are ongoing school events that draw the community together. For example, a two-week canned food drive is truly a schoolwide effort with students working to package the food gathered and a team of parents and teachers coordinating the project. A daily bulletin announces how close the school is to its target collection. In addition to serving an important cause, this event is a springboard for a community effort toward a common goal and fosters the sense of being a member of a team effort. People at the school—teachers, students, and parents—feel like they belong at the school.

Shared Effort and Commitment

It is essential for participants to have a shared belief in the value of an inclusive program and make a commitment to see it through. The process of developing a shared vision is a prerequisite to developing a set of procedures for implementation. It is important for teachers, administrators, parents, and support staff to "buy into" the idea of inclusion and to become partners in the effort. At a middle school that launched a schoolwide inclusive program a few years ago, the planning council decided to commit to a three-year implementation. They recognized that significant change takes time and made a commitment to working through the process. At the end of three years they would decide to continue or abandon the idea of inclusion. Meanwhile, they would make a team effort to develop their procedures and practices. In making a three-year commitment, they went through a process of developing buy-in, or shared ownership, of the elements of their inclusive program. All those involved had a voice during the planning stage.

When schools begin an inclusive effort, it may not be a schoolwide effort at first. Very often we see a cluster of teachers within a school launch an inclusive program and then others may join in when they see positive results. Even in smaller groups, participants must develop a sense of shared understanding of what they are trying to accomplish and make a commitment to implementation.

Though a shared vision is essential, we have come to realize that *inclusion* does not necessarily have to be the primary focus of the school. There may be other issues at the forefront, and inclusion may simply be a part of a bigger plan or a larger issue. Inclusion may be one strand of practices designed to reach a more general goal—for example, improving overall achievement or recognizing diversity. Regardless, teachers, parents, students, and administrators must all see inclusion as meeting a need in the school and all must view it as beneficial.

Appreciation for Diversity. We believe that the teachers, administrators, and other staff in successful inclusive schools have a strong appreciation for the richness that student diversity adds to the school and classroom. Today's classrooms are more diverse than ever before. We see diversity in students' cultural backgrounds, language backgrounds, experiential backgrounds and abilities. Students' learning characteristics, including disability, add to the diversity in a school and community. Many teachers, students, and parents who have worked in inclusive schools remark on the positive aspects of learning to understand students who learn differently. Teachers who are equipped with a repertoire of skills and techniques for addressing diverse student needs are most successful in inclusive schools.

School Structure. The school structure, or the organizational and operational procedures, must support learning for *all* students. How the administrators function, how teachers organize and plan instruction, and how support personnel operate are all part of the overarching school structure that makes inclusion and other schoolwide initiatives possible. In such schools, we see a range of options for supporting struggling learners. We see flexibility in the nature and function of support personnel and services. We see students' needs driving decisions about support services. Administrators are skillful at making support personnel available for various functions. For example, one principal makes sure that all instructional assistants are scheduled to be in classrooms during reading and language arts instruction to maximize the possibility of one-to-one and small group instruction for struggling readers. At other times, the assistants may help to free teachers to attend an important meeting or training session.

Another important aspect of school structure is setting expectations for teachers and students. Setting the expectation that *all* students will learn implies a set of expectations for how teachers, support personnel, and students function. Student learning must be the "bottom line" criterion for professional accountability. There must be systematic effort to monitor and evaluate the school's progress toward its goals. There must also be a problem-solving mechanism to handle ongoing issues.

Administrative Support. The principal and other school-based administrators have critical roles in successful implementation of inclusion and other efforts to ensure learning for all (Klingner, Vaughn, Hughes, & Arguelles, 1999). Administrators set the tone for a school's acceptance of change. Teachers readily perceive an administrator's sincerity or lack of sincerity for a particular cause. In order to have a fully functioning inclusive program, the principal must value it in theory and practice. In other words, he or she must not only speak out in support initially but must give ongoing attention to it.

Range of Services. We believe that all students can and must learn. Decisions about what services are needed to ensure learning must be made on an individual basis. The federal law mandates that the educational program for a student with a disability should be determined according to the student's individual needs. To this end, schools must have a range of options available for support services. The law also states that, to the extent possible, students with disabilities should be educated with their nondisabled peers in the general education environment. For many students, this is possible with placement in the regular classroom for the entire day as long as appropriate supports are brought into the classroom. Other students, however, may benefit from being pulled out of the classroom for part of the school day. In our thinking, inclusion is not a *place* but a set of services that maximizes opportunities for students to learn and be with their peers.

It is our experience that not all students with disabilities benefit from a full day of inclusion. For some students, their learning difficulties require more intensive remediation than can be provided in the regular classroom. Often, these students may benefit from a period of intensive remedial instruction but will eventually transition into a more inclusive arrangement. For those students who must be pulled out, every effort must be made to help them feel they are a part of the whole school environment by engaging them socially with their nondisabled peers.

Professional Development. Teachers, administrators, and other staff are most effective when they engage in ongoing professional development, seeing themselves as lifelong learners. In most of the schools in which we have worked, professional development is a priority. Teachers have reported that they feel unprepared for inclusion and would like to have additional training (Dingle, Falvey, Givner, & Haager, 2004; Schumm & Vaughn, 1995a, 1995b; Vaughn, Hughes, Schumm, & Klingner, 1998). We have found that ongoing professional development is critical to successful implementation of inclusive education.

Workshops or single training sessions are not sufficient for developing the repertoire of strategies that teachers need to work in a collaborative inclusive program. There must be a means for ongoing problem-solving and for meeting teachers' individual needs. We believe that effective staff development includes various components: (1) exploration of theory through readings and discussions; (2) demonstrations in actual classrooms; (3) practice under simulated conditions; and (4) coaching and consulting to solve problems and answer questions that arise during implementation (Joyce & Showers, 1995). Teachers should work together to share expertise, provide nonevaluative feedback, help each other master new instructional approaches, adapt teaching models to the needs of students, and develop and refine their classroom skills. Teachers who experience peer coaching exhibit greater long-term retention of innovative instructional strategies and more appropriate use of new teaching models over time (Showers & Joyce, 1996).

Parents and Community. The most effective schools are those in which parents and the community are intricately involved. Furthermore, involvement begins with respect. As practitioners, both of us regularly conducted home visits and created multiple, varied opportunities for parents to participate in school activities. Whether it was by offering a bilingual workshop for parents on how to assist their children with homework (complete with food and childcare), helping parents make tamales or "filhoes" (a Portuguese doughnut) for parent-sponsored luncheons, enlisting parents to serve as volunteer classroom tutors and field-trip chaperones, or talking with parents prior to an IEP meeting to describe what they could expect, we actively involved parents in our special education programs. We sought and valued their input as valuable partners when conducting assessments and designing educational programs. Throughout this book we include recommendations for involving families.

Characteristics of Inclusive Classrooms

Classroom as a Community of Learners. We have noticed a clear and purposeful sense of community in many inclusive classrooms. The teacher, as the classroom leader, sets the tone for accepting all students, including their learning strengths and differences. The teacher also sets the tone for welcoming the special educator and other support personnel as part of the community. Following are several aspects of a classroom as community that we have discerned:

1. There is a clear expectation that *all students will participate* in classroom activities. It is never an option for a struggling student to hang back (as is the natural inclination of many students who view themselves as less capable than others) or to be excluded from an activity. Rather, supports to enable student's participation and involvement occur naturally and fluidly. There may be various forms and levels of participation to suit students' individual needs and capabilities.
2. Students have an *appreciation for diversity*. There is an inherent understanding that students differ in their learning abilities and styles and no stigma is attached to having different skill sets. There is also an open discussion of and appreciation for cultural differences.
3. Students have a *shared responsibility for learning*. In these classrooms we see students helping students as part of the normal routine. Teachers foster student *interdependence* so that students are accountable not only for themselves but for others.
4. Teachers provide *ongoing positive behavior support* for all students. Rather than focus on students' negative behaviors or characteristics, teachers emphasize students' strengths and progress.
5. Classrooms are *student-centered*. Though the teacher is clearly in control and is the central director of activity, students have some opportunity to choose activities and direct their own learning. Teachers consider students' interests and backgrounds in planning.

High Expectations for Student Learning. Many teachers are skillful in establishing a shared understanding that *learning is the order of business*. In these classrooms, learning is valued and is viewed as the primary goal each day. It is important for teachers to set realistic, but challenging, expectations for students (Brophy & Good, 1986). This is especially consequential for students who are at risk for or who are experiencing learning difficulties (Barr & Parrett, 1995; Keogh & Speece, 1996). Adults with learning disabilities reflecting on their early learning experiences often indicate that a particular teacher who challenged them and believed in them made a tremendous impact on their learning (Haager, 1997). Teachers must be persistent in demanding constant progress toward realistic learning goals. We want to push students to their limits, but not beyond. Having high expectations means not giving up on students; if students do not succeed one way, the teacher finds another. The teacher does not take "no" or "I can't" for an answer. Teachers show they care by believing that students can and will succeed. They develop strong and caring relationships with students and perceive of themselves as "tough" and intolerant of students' "messing around" (Garcia, 1998).

High Levels of Communication in the Classroom. We see a great deal of learning going on in classrooms where there is a high level of teacher–student interaction as well as student–student interaction. Of course, we are talking about interactions that are specific to the learning task or topic and not correcting behavior or idle chit-chat. An ongoing instructional dialogue allows advantages for both the teacher and student. For the teacher, it provides a window into the students' understanding of the concepts and skills and provides a basis for adjusting instruction to ensure true learning. For students, it provides an opportunity to engage with and try out a new idea or concept. When students can talk about an idea, they are more likely to fully grasp it. In classrooms with high levels of communication, teachers frequently check with students to make sure they understand instruction and assignments (Bos & Anders, 1992; Garcia, 1998).

Student Engagement in Learning

How teachers organize time and instructional tasks is important. We have worked with teachers who make every effort to maximize students' engagement in meaningful learning. Opportunities to learn are enhanced by efficient use of instructional time, careful scheduling and planning, smooth transitions between activities, and lessons that are focused and uninterrupted. Teachers make sure to fill every spare moment with meaningful activities. For example, when the art teacher is late to arrive, Ms. Brown engages her students in "mental math" activities.

Recognition of Students' Strengths and Needs. We have said that inclusive schools have an appreciation for diversity. At the classroom level, teachers develop an awareness of students' individual strengths and areas of need. One teacher calls it "really knowing my students." In a lesson this teacher is very aware of which students are likely to need close followup and which students may be able to help others. It is not always general academic ability that determines this. Things like student interest and special skills (such as artistic ability, dramatic flair, and spatial ability) influence students' affinity for and success with certain tasks. In an inclusive classroom, students have the opportunity to receive short-term, intensive instructional support when needed.

Stimulating and Rich Classroom Environment. Classrooms that promote active learning tend to be print-rich and learning-rich in terms of the visual display and physical organization. We see interesting and inviting materials placed around the room and students' projects on display. Resources are readily available to students and teachers.

Organized and Systematic Classroom. When classroom teachers and support personnel must work together in the physical space of a classroom, it is important for the classroom to be well managed. Teachers are most comfortable working together when there are systematic routines and activities. It is important for classroom policies and expectations to be clear and well articulated. One teacher described the co-teaching in her classroom as a "well-oiled machine" allowing her and the inclusion specialist to perform their separate but coordinated activities smoothly.

Essential Elements of Inclusive Instructional Programs

Our description of inclusive instructional programs proceeds from elements we consider to be essential for all learners to components specific to learners with special needs.

Comprehensive Instructional Program. An inclusive instructional program must be comprehensive. We define a comprehensive program as one that addresses all content standards for what students should know and be able to do at a given grade level (Simmons & Kameenui, 1998). All students work toward the same standards. These standards serve as curricular guideposts for teachers and provide clear-cut goals for students. Although all students work toward the same standards, clearly students do not all progress at the same rate or in the same way.

Balanced Instructional Program. An inclusive instructional program should be balanced. A balanced program is one in which the teacher strategically selects instructional methods and materials from a large repertoire to ensure that students meet or exceed curricular standards. "Balance" does not mean that all skills and standards receive equal emphasis, but rather that the overall emphasis accorded to the skill or standard is determined by its importance relative to a student's learning needs at a particular time (Simmons & Kameenui, 1998). A balanced approach assures that students learn through a variety of eclectic methods that are skillfully and knowledgeably applied based on students' needs. For example, with a balanced approach to literacy instruction children learn to apply and practice decoding skills with books at their instructional level and also participate in a variety of meaningful experiences with real literature.

Another way to think about a balanced instructional approach is ensuring a sufficient amount of emphasis on both *skills development* and *rich learning experiences in the core curriculum.* Most students with high-incidence disabilities have significant academic skills deficits, so it would be unwise to ignore their need to have systematic explicit skills instruction. Likewise, we want to be sure to provide sufficient experiences in the grade-level standards and content to ensure that students have every opportunity to build their general knowledge.

Access to the Core Curriculum. All students must have access to the core curriculum. Teachers are held accountable for making sure that all students *progress* within this curriculum. Just providing exposure is not enough. For example, this means that all students, including struggling readers, must participate in meaningful, purposeful activities with grade-level text. Whether students listen to tape-recorded books, read with a buddy, or participate in choral reading, they should have access to the same texts and core curriculum as their peers. Ensuring success for students with disabilities is one of the responsibilities (and challenges) shared by the classroom teacher and the inclusion specialist.

Differentiated Instruction. We know that all students do not learn at the same rate and do not come to school with the same set of skills. Classrooms are becoming more and more diverse in terms of students' abilities and backgrounds (Schumm, 1999; Schumm & Vaughn, 1991; Simmons & Kameenui, 1998). This is particularly true in an inclusive classroom where students with disabilities are learning alongside their same-age peers. In a successful inclusive program, curriculum and instruction must be tailored to meet individual needs. A one-size-fits-all approach, in which all students receive the same instruction, regardless of their skills, does not accomplish the goal of ensuring learning for all students (Schumm, 1999). Rather, teachers must differentiate instruction for different types of students. There are several methods for accomplishing this, such as multilevel practices and making accommodations, described next.

Differentiating instruction means ensuring that all students have optimal learning opportunities within the core academic curriculum. The goal is to provide "universal access," or to ensure that all students have access to high-quality learning experiences in the specified grade-level curriculum (e.g., California Department of Education, 1999). To accomplish this, teachers must orchestrate the curriculum, instruction, and activities so that all students have a high level of participation and learn according to their individual needs. Planning in advance for students' special needs is critical to success.

This may seem like a Herculean task for a classroom teacher. This is where you, the inclusion specialist, come in. Inclusion specialists provide both *direct* and *indirect* services to facilitate students' access to learning. You will probably be working directly with students, either one-to-one or within small groups. Through this direct contact with students, you can reteach and review important concepts already covered by the teacher, prepare students with background knowledge for upcoming lessons, or teach basic skills that the teacher will not be able to address in the whole-class instruction. You may also address students' needs indirectly, by providing assistance to the classroom teacher behind the scenes to enable the teacher to provide differentiated instruction when you are not there. Your role may be to assist the classroom teacher in building a repertoire of strategies to provide instruction that simultaneously addresses the needs of different students.

Assessment and grouping are key to providing differentiated instruction within the context of the classroom (California Department of Education, 1999). Conducting ongoing, frequent assessment provides the basis for planning appropriate instruction and placing children in appropriate groups or activities (see Chapter 3 for more information about assessment). *Flexible grouping* means customizing learning groups according to dents' invidual needs and the lesson objectives. Teachers may use heterogeneous when the lesson objectives and lesson format are appropriate for different types of students. Grouping students according to their similar skills allows teachers to provide intensive, focused instruction tailored to a group of students' needs.

Multilevel Instruction. Rather than traditional forms of instruction that "teach to the middle" and expect that some students will fail (as part of the normal curve), the instructional approaches implemented as part of an inclusive instructional program facilitate the successful involvement of all students. A variety of instructional approaches that fit this definition are presented throughout this book, such as Collaborative Strategic Reading, Making Words, and Classwide Peer Tutoring. All of the approaches have in common that students of various achievement levels can participate and experience growth appropriate to their needs. In some cases, as in the above examples, the instructional approach was designed to accommodate different achievement levels in a whole-class context; in other cases, adaptations might be necessary to enable everyone to fully participate.

Accommodations. The federal law mandates that students with disabilities have access to the core curriculum and that their education program ensures that they progress academically. Making accommodations, or *adaptations and modifications,* to the curriculum, instructional activities, or other aspects of the program is the means for accomplishing this mandate. We think of accommodations as making adjustments to the instruction based on a student's individual needs. For example, a student who reads significantly below grade level may be able to participate fully in grade-level social studies classes when the teacher provides the textbook in a taped format. A further accommodation may be to read the test aloud to the student, thus testing his or her knowledge of the content while taking away the reading aspect of the task. Other types of accommodations may involve adjusting a student's seating arrangement, providing additional instruction or practice opportunities, or using an alternative assignment. There are numerous ways to make accommodations, and we discuss this in detail later in this book.

Flexible Grouping Practices. Group lessons are an essential component of effective inclusive classrooms. Teachers who implement grouping effectively use a variety of grouping patterns that are tailored to fit students' strengths and the demands of the curriculum (Flood, Lapp, & Flood, 1992), ranging from whole class to small groups to pairs, depending upon the purpose of the activity. The use of a variety of grouping patterns is referred to as flexible grouping. Groups can consist of students at the same ability level or at mixed ability levels. Both types hold an important place in an inclusive classroom. Small same-ability groups can provide students with the opportunity to receive focused, explicit assistance at the appropriate instructional level. The configuration of these groups should vary on an as-needed rather than a permanent basis. Heterogeneous groups can serve a variety of functions. Students might be grouped together to work at a learning center, complete a group project, prepare a presentation for the class, respond to a reading assignment, or participate in an experiential learning activity. Grouping practices are described in detail in Chapter 4.

Intensive, Systematic Instruction for Students in Need. We know that some students with reading disabilities do not progress in generally well-taught, supportive inclusive classrooms when they are not receiving intensive, individualized instruction (Klingner et al., 1998; Zigmond, Jenkins, & Fuchs, 1995). Thus, instruction above and beyond what their peers receive is essential if they are going to make progress toward catching up. Critical elements of this intensive program include:

- Extra individualized attention
- Intensive direct instruction
- Extensive practice in various contexts
- Precise monitoring
- Careful grouping and pairing
- Modified assignments

Students in the intermediate grades who cannot yet read are in critical need of specialized assistance. This intensive support should be above and beyond the instruction provided within the general education classroom, perhaps in an afterschool tutorial lab or during the school day at a time when it does not conflict with regular class instruction. The assistance students receive should not be a watered-down version of the work in the general education classroom or focusing on isolated drill and practice activities. The most effective intervention for older students is one-to-one tutoring (Torgesen, Wagner, & Rashotte, 1997; Vellutino, 1987). On the other hand, we believe that the most effective instruction is preventive rather than remedial. Early intervention programs designed to prevent problems before they begin are preferable to corrective approaches later on. Thus, teachers in the early grades must provide intensive support for those most in need. Various chapters in this book provide information about how to do this.

Ongoing Assessment and Monitoring. Many teachers think of assessment as synonymous with "testing." We think of assessment as a much broader term to describe an integral part of the teaching process that involves continual monitoring of students' learning. Overton (2002) describes assessment as "the process of gathering information to monitor progress and make educational decisions" (p. 3). Many teachers do a great deal of assessment throughout a typical school year. Good teachers know how to do this in a systematic and easy-to-manage way. This is true for both general and special education teachers, though the nature and purpose of their assessments may differ. In Chapter 3, we examine several types of assessment that are a critical part of ongoing instructional decision making.

An Eclectic Approach. Our task as educators is not to find "one best" approach for all situations and all students, but to learn enough about various approaches to determine what works best when, how, with whom, and under what circumstances. To be effective, teachers must have a large repertoire of teaching approaches at their disposal, along with the knowledge and skills to mix and match different strategies depending on the needs of students and the demands of the learning environment. The ability to creatively and flexibly implement instructional methods requires a deep understanding of the underlying principles that guide each approach, a thorough awareness of how children learn, and a willingness to take risks and try new ways of teaching.

Clearly Defined Roles for Teachers. For a collaborative consultation model to work effectively, it is important for the classroom teacher and the inclusion specialist to be in sync philosophically. Ongoing communication is key. Although the two teachers might not see eye to eye on every aspect of teaching and learning, if they understand the different theoretical perspectives described above and can clearly articulate their reasons for focusing on one approach versus another, an optimal collaborative relationship can be arranged. An example from an actual classroom illustrates how partners can work together in ways that are personally fulfilling and beneficial to their students. In the first example, Juan Carrillo is a fourth-grade teacher and Sallie Rivers is the inclusion specialist. By nature, Mr. Carrillo is business-like, well-organized, and task-oriented. He prefers behavioral approaches such as direct instruction to more collaborative or holistic instructional approaches. For instance, he does not like cooperative learning because he believes that he can explain concepts to students better than their peers. Ms. Rivers, on the other hand, subscribes to both cognitive and constructivist views of teaching and learning more than behaviorist views. She places a high priority on teaching learning strategies to her students with disabilities. She frequently adapts instructional approaches by making them more gamelike to match her teaching style. She values techniques that actively involve everyone and help students feel successful. When these two teachers were first paired together, Ms. Rivers apprehensively confided to one of this book's authors, "I have my work cut out for me." After two years of working with Ms. Rivers, Mr. Carrillo shared with this same author that Ms. Rivers was his favorite of the three inclusion specialists with whom he had worked because "she really got me thinking about different ways to teach. I learned to see my students and myself from a different perspective. I think I grew more from working with her than anyone else." Through communication, these two teachers were able to work our clearly defined roles and responsibilities that took advantage of their individual styles and strengths. In this classroom, it was Mr. Carrillo who was more likely to conduct a task analysis to determine the skills needed by his students to successfully learn a new skill, and Ms. Rivers who was more likely to figure out a way to provide this instruction in a stimulating way that involved everyone. Yet often it is the inclusion specialist who is the expert in conducting task analyses and providing intensive, systematic instruction.

TEACHING STANDARDS

Just fifteen years ago there were no teaching standards. Yet today standards have become the focus of every teacher education program. In 1983, *A Nation at Risk* heightened public concern about the state of education in the United States and brought about a wave of reform initiatives designed to improve U.S. schools. Most of these programs, however, failed to focus on the role of the classroom teacher. Three years later, in 1986, the Carnegie Task Force on Teaching as a Profession issued its report, *A Nation Prepared: Teachers for the 21st Century*. This report recommended the establishment of a National Board for Professional Teaching Standards (NBPTS). The following year, NBPTS was born. "The

NBPTS standards and information about the certification process are available at *www.nbpts.org*.

Since the inception of NBPTS, other organizations have established standards for teachers in various fields. Perhaps the most relevant standards for inclusion specialists are those developed by the Council for Exceptional Children (CEC). CEC has developed a Code of Ethics as well as International Standards for the Preparation of Special Education Professionals, Standards for Professional Practice Professionals in Relation to Persons with Exceptionalities and Their Families, and a Common Core of Knowledge and Skills Essential for All Beginning Special Education Teachers. For more information about CEC standards, visit the Council's website at *www.cec.sped.org*.

REFERENCES

Barr, R. D., & Parrett, W. H. (1995). *Hope at last for at-risk youth.* Boston: Allyn and Bacon.

Bos, C. S., & Anders, P. L. (1992). Using interactive teaching and learning strategies to promote text comprehension and content learning for students with learning disabilities. *International Journal of Disability, Development and Education, 39*, 225–238.

Brophy, J. E., & Good, T. L. (1986). Teachers' communication of differential expectation for children's classroom performance: Some behavioral data. *Journal of Educational Psychology, 61,* 365–374.

California Department of Education. (1999). *English-language arts standards for California public schools: Kindergarten through grade twelve.* Sacramento, CA: Author.

Coots, J. J., Bishop, K. D., Grenot-Scheyer, M., & Falvey, M. A. (1995). Practices in general education: Past and present. In M. A. Falvey (Ed.), *Inclusive and heterogeneous schooling: Assessment, curriculum, and instruction* (pp. 7–22), Baltimore, MD: Paul H. Brookes.

Dingle, M., Falvey, M., Givner C. C., & Haager, D. (2004). Essential special and general education teacher competencies for preparing teachers for inclusive settings. *Issues in Teacher Education, 31(1),* 35–50.

Elbaum, B. (2002). The self-concept of students with learning disabilities: A meta-analysis of comparisons across different placements. *Learning Disabilities Research and Practice, 17*, 216–226.

Flood, J., Lapp, D., & Flood, S. (1992). Am I allowed to group? Using flexible patterns for effective instruction. *The Reading Teacher, 45,* 608–16.

Fuchs, D., & Fuchs, L. S. (1994a). Inclusive schools movement and the radicalization of special education reform. *Exceptional Children, 60*, 294–309.

Fuchs, D., & Fuch, L. S., (1994b). Sometimes separate is better. *Educational Leadership, 52*(4), 22–26.

Garcia, E. (1998). *Understanding and meeting the challenge of student cultural diversity* (2nd ed.). Boston: Houghton Mifflin.

Gartner, A., & Lipsky, D. K. (1987). Beyond special education: Toward a quality system for all students. *Harvard Educational Review, 57*, 367–395.

Haager, D. (1997). Learning disabilities. In J. Wood & A. Lazzari (Eds.), *Exceeding the boundaries: Understanding exceptional lives* (pp. 116–159). Ft. Worth, TX: Harcourt Brace College Publishers.

Haager, D., & Vaughn, S. (1997). Assessment of social competence in students with learning disabilities. In J. Lloyd, E. Kameenui, & D. Chard (Eds.), *Issues in educating students with disabilities* (pp. 129–152). Mahwah, NJ: Lawrence Erlbaum.

Individuals with Disabilities Education Act Amendments of 1997, P.L. 105–17.

Joyce, B., & Showers, B. (1995). *Student achievement through staff development: Fundamentals of school renewal.* White Plains, NY: Longman.

Kauffman, J. M. (1995). Why we must celebrate a diversity of restrictive environments. *Learning Disabilities Research and Practice, 10*, 225–232.

Kauffman, J. M., & Hallahan, D. P. (Eds.). (1995). *The illusion of full inclusion: A comprehensive critique of a special education bandwagon.* Austin, TX: Pro-Ed.

Keogh, B. K., & Speece, D. L. (1996). Learning disabilities within the context of schooling. In D. L. Speece & B. K. Keogh (Eds.), *Research on classroom ecologies* (pp. 1–14). Mahwah, NJ: Lawrence Erlbaum.

Klingner, J. K., Vaughn, S., Hughes, M. T., & Arguelles, M. E. (1999). Sustaining research-based practices in reading: A three year follow-up. *Remedial and Special Education, 20,* 263–274.

Klingner, J. K., Vaughn, S., Schumm, J. S., Cohen, P., & Forgan, J. W. (1998). Inclusion or pull-out: Which do students prefer? *Journal of Learning Disabilities, 31,* 148–158.

National Research Council. (1998). *Preventing reading difficulties in young children* (C. E. Snow & P. Griffin, Eds.). Washington, DC: National Academy Press.

Overton, T. (2002). *Assessing learners with special needs: An applied approach* (4th ed.). Upper Saddle River, NJ: Prentice-Hall.

Schumm, J. S. (1999). *Adapting reading and math materials for the inclusive classroom.* Reston, VA: Council for Exceptional Children.

Schumm, J. S., & Vaughn, S. (1991). Making adaptations for mainstreamed students: General classroom teachers' perspectives. *Remedial and Special Education, 12,* 18–27.

Schumm, J. S., & Vaughn, S. (1995a). Getting ready for inclusion: Is the stage set? *Learning Disabilities Research and Practice, 10,* 169–179.

Schumm, J. S., & Vaughn, S. (1995b). Meaningful professional development in accommodating students with disabilities. *Remedial and Special Education, 16,* 344–353.

Showers, B., & Joyce, B. (1996). The evolution of peer coaching. *Educational Leadership, 53,* 12–17.

Simmons, D. C., & Kameenui, E. J. (1998). Introduction. In D. C. Simmons & E. J. Kameenui (Eds.), *What reading research tells us about children with diverse learning needs: Bases and basics* (pp. 1–17). Mahwah, NJ: Lawrence Erlbaum.

Simmons, D. C., & Kameenui, E. J. (1998). Introduction. In D. C. Simmons & E. J. Kameenui (Eds.), *What reading research tells us about children with diverse learning needs: Bases and Basics* (pp. 1–19). Mahwah, NJ: Lawrence Erlbaum.

Stainback, S., & Stainback, W. (1991). *Curriculum considerations in inclusive classrooms: Facilitating learning for all students.* Baltimore, MD: Paul H. Brookes.

Torgesen, J. K., Wagner, R. K., & Rashotte, C. A. (1997). Prevention and remediation of severe reading disabilities: Keeping the end in mind. *Scientific Studies of Reading, Vol 1,* 217–234.

Vaughn, S., Elbaum, B. E., Schumm, J. S., & Hughes, M. T. (1998). Social outcomes for students with and without learning disabilities in inclusive classrooms. *Journal of Learning Disabilities, 31,* 428–436.

Vaughn, S., & Haager, D. (1994a). Social assessments with students with learning disabilities: Do they measure up? In S. Vaughn & C. Bos (Eds.), *Research issues in learning disabilities: Theory, methodology, assessment, and ethics* (pp. 276–309). New York: Springer-Verlag.

Vaughn, S., & Haager, D. (1994b). Social competence as a multifaceted construct: How do students with learning disabilities fare? In G. R. Lyon (Ed.), *Frames of reference for the assessment of learning disabilities: New views on measurement issues* (pp. 555–570). Baltimore, MD: Paul H. Brookes.

Vaughn, S., Hughes, M. T., Schumm, J. S., & Klingner, J. (1998). A collaborative effort to enhance reading and writing. *Learning Disability Quarterly, 21,* 57–74.

Vellutino, F. R. (1987). Dyslexia. *Scientific American, 256,* 34–41.

Villa, R. A., & Thousand, J. S. (1995). The rationale for creating inclusive schools. In R. A. Villa & J. S. Thousand (Eds.), *Creating an inclusive school.* Alexandria, VA: Association for Supervision and Curriculum Development.

Will, M. C. (1986). Educating children with learning problems: A shared responsibility. *Exceptional Children, 52,* 411–415.

Zigmond, N., Jenkins, J. R., & Fuchs, L. S. (1995). Special education in restructured schools: Findings from three multi-year studies. *Phi Delta Kappan, 76,* 531–540.

CHAPTER TWO

CHARACTERISTICS OF STUDENTS WITH HIGH-INCIDENCE DISABILITIES

The greatest discovery of my generation is that a human being can alter his life by altering his attitudes of mind.

—William James (1842–1910)

KEY CONCEPTS

- Special educators working in inclusive settings often serve students across disability categories, or students with a wide array of educational needs.
- High-incidence disabilities are those that occur most frequently in the population and include learning disabilities, behavior disorders, and mild mental retardation.
- Students with learning disabilities are a heterogeneous group of students, *characterized by* academic difficulties despite adequate intellectual functioning.

- The challenging behaviors of students with emotional and behavioral disorders occur along a continuum of severity. Problem behaviors may be internalizing, characterized by being shy and withdrawn, or externalizing, characterized by acting out. Attention problems represent another type of behavioral difficulty.
- Mild mental retardation is characterized by subaverage intellectual functioning and problems with adaptive, or social, behavior. There are known and unknown causes for this disorder.

FOCUS QUESTIONS

1. What disability categories are included in high-incidence disabilities, and how are they defined?
2. What are the most common characteristics of students with disabilities often served in inclusive classrooms?
3. How many students with disabilities would typically be in an inclusive school setting?

Andrew arrives at school right on time. His mother drops him off on her way to work. As Andrew gets out of the car, he feels the usual uneasy feeling in the pit of his stomach. What is in store for him today? He smiles at his mom to ease her worries. He knows she is worrying about his upcoming report card. He tries to look confident as he waves, for her sake. She has a busy day at work today, he knows. As Andrew walks toward the fifth-grade wing, he sees some boys up ahead greet each other and launch into horseplay. The feeling in his stomach worsens. Andrew wishes they were happy to see him. He feels invisible.

Two years ago, Andrew was tested after almost flunking second grade. He went to a special class in third and fourth grades with Ms. Halley. This year, Ms. Halley is still helping him, but he rarely goes to her room. His teachers and his parents decided he could stay in Ms. Spencer's room all day. She told him the idea is for him to be more a part of Ms. Spencer's class. His fifth-grade teacher seems to really want him to learn, and she and Ms. Halley help him a lot. In this class, they do a lot of things in groups, and Ms. Spencer always makes sure he has a good job in the group. She never asks him to do something he can't. She assigns buddies in the class, and Andrew gets help from other kids—mostly they read aloud to him. She told him he has to do his share of helping, too. Every day, he goes into the first-grade class to help Ms. Charles. He does flashcards with the little kids and listens to them read stories. It makes him feel smart to be able to help them.

Andrew wants to do well in school, and this is what is on his mind. As he walks to his classroom, he goes through a mental checklist. Has he remembered all his homework? Yes, math and language papers, an outline for his social studies report. Has he remembered all his books? Yes, he only had a math book. *"Think about the spelling words, Andrew. You need at least a B this time or Ms. Spencer will give you a D for the term."* The spelling words swim in his head as he looks around at a sea of faces and hurrying children. His homework took him two hours last night. No wonder his mom looked tired. He really needed her help. Someone bumps into him and his homework goes flying. As he picks up the papers, he tries to remember if "receive" is "-ie" or "-ei," resolving to look at his list again before the test. He feels a hand on his shoulder, *"Hey! How ya doing, Andrew? Did you see that dog in front of the school? It was huge!"*

There was Chris, his new friend from class, who sometimes helps him with the social studies readings. Andrew smiles. Maybe it won't be such a bad day after all. *"Yeah, I thought Mr. Warner was going to have a cow trying to catch it."*

Mrs. Turner, Andrew's mother, sighs as she watches him walk toward the school. It was a tough night last night. Andrew just couldn't get through the outline for his social studies report. It was after 9 o'clock when they finished it. Andrew had a great deal of trouble organizing his ideas. He wanted to just start right into writing the report without organizing it first. Ms. Spencer wants the kids to learn to outline before writing. It had taken all her patience, and then some, to keep from just doing the stupid outline for him! She was glad that Ms. Spencer had let him choose a topic he was interested in. It certainly was easier to get him to read the library books. She used to have to read everything to him. Now he seems to be getting a little better at reading. She still has to help him with some of the words, and when he gets fatigued, she reads passages to him. Writing anything is difficult for Andrew. Not only did he have trouble with the outlining, but he made terrible spelling mistakes all the way through. They had done it over three times. She sighs again as she drives away.

Mrs. Turner likes the idea of inclusion. At a parent–teacher conference last week, she learned more about how Ms. Spencer and Ms. Halley work together. She had been concerned that Andrew didn't bring home papers, but learned about the grouping for social studies and science classes and sometimes math. They just don't do a lot of papers. She thinks the groups are a good idea for Andrew. For the first time, Andrew seems to be getting to know some of the kids. She had also thought it was a good idea to use student tutors, but wanted to know if Andrew was embarrassed to be helped by other kids. Ms. Spencer had said it was the norm for students to pair up in her class. Ms. Halley explained her role as co-teacher in the class. Mrs. Turner had known that Ms. Halley comes into the class for at least an hour a day but she learned that quite a bit more goes into the behind-the-scenes work. Ms. Halley and Ms. Spencer do quite a bit of planning and discussing what's best for Andrew and the others. It seems that Andrew gets a great deal of support from the teachers and other students.

Mrs. Turner is glad that Andrew has Ms. Spencer this year, but she worries about the pressure on Andrew. She knows he was smiling for her sake this morning. She could tell how worried he was by how he had played with his breakfast. He wants so much to be like the other kids. Why does he have so much trouble with learning? She and her husband have heard all about learning disabilities. They have been to several parent meetings, and her cousin's son has similar problems. Yet it's still hard to understand what causes all the problems. And why Andrew? Her other son does just fine. As she drives to work, she hopes that Andrew will find something he can do well when he grows up. She thinks he worries too much, and, well, perhaps she does, too. She decides that they should help Andrew develop a hobby, something to do to take his mind off of school. Maybe they should plan a camping trip for the weekend to have some fun together.

Ms. Spencer is hurrying to get the materials ready for today's science project. Each group is measuring and charting the plants they've grown in different light conditions. Her meeting with Ms. Halley went a few minutes late. As she walks toward her room, she sees Andrew waving goodbye to his mother. Her heart goes out to Andrew and Mrs. Turner. She knows they are trying very hard, and, well, she and Ms. Halley are, too. Inclusion is a new experience for Ms. Spencer. She believes in the idea and wants to make it work. So far, she feels it's been worth the extra effort. She has learned a great deal from Ms. Halley and has a new respect for her. She thinks about Andrew and the other three students who are identified for special education. She really has about seven or eight who need extra help, but only Andrew and three others officially receive services. Funny, she has had special education students mainstreamed into her classes for years, but she feels like she is really just now beginning to understand these kids and their learning problems. Andrew happens to be one of her favorites. He works so hard! She loves it when he gets an A. He gets an ear-to-ear grin.

In the meeting, Ms. Halley had shown her his latest math assessment scores. They are keeping a weekly progress chart for each of the special education students. She really likes the performance-based assessment charts that Ms. Halley keeps. She thinks she might like to do it for all her students next year. She vows to spend some time in the summer looking at computer programs that will do charts like this. Andrew's scores have steadily risen. Just today she and Ms. Halley realized that Andrew probably has the skills to work at grade level in math. He certainly has the determination. He always does his homework. They decided to gradually reduce the support he gets for math rather than do it abruptly. This is great news because Ms. Spencer has another student, Marissa, who is failing math and could use Ms. Halley's help. They just started decimals and Marissa is completely lost. Marissa's mind wanders in class, and Ms. Spencer feels she just doesn't reach her. Come to think of it, Marissa's grades have been falling in other subjects, too. The other kids in her group have been complaining that she doesn't do her work. Today she and Ms. Halley had briefly discussed whether Marissa should be referred to the Student Assistance Team. They agreed to watch her for a few days and to look further at her classwork. Maybe she will try to catch Marissa's mother after school and talk with her. As she opens her classroom door, she makes a mental note to talk with Ms. Halley again about attention deficit disorder. Maybe Marissa is having trouble with attention.

WHO ARE THE CHILDREN SERVED IN INCLUSIVE SETTINGS?

Andrew is like many children with learning problems who are served in either special education or inclusive classrooms. Because his learning problems were seriously impacting his academic performance, he was identified in second grade as having a learning disability. Andrew is also *unlike* many other children with learning problems. For example, he doesn't have attention problems like Marissa. Learning disabilities comprise a heterogeneous group of learning disorders that may be manifested differently in different children. Students with learning disabilities make up the largest group served by special education in today's schools. They are also the most likely group of students with disabilities to be included in a general education classroom for at least part of the school day. Students with mild mental retardation or behavior problems, two other special education classifications, or other related disorders are also likely to be found in inclusive classrooms.

In this chapter, we will discuss the various characteristics that are common to these high-incidence disabilities and how they impact the individual and family across the life span. This chapter introduces cross-categorical service delivery and the inclusive classroom. We will also discuss learning characteristics that place other students not identified as disabled, such as Marissa, at risk for learning problems. In an inclusive classroom, these students may also benefit from a built-in support structure to assist students with disabilities. We will learn about prereferral strategies and appropriate assessment practices to prevent misdiagnosis or unnecessary classification and placement. The inclusion specialist and the classroom teacher play important roles in assessment and identification. Because today's classrooms are increasingly diverse, cultural and linguistic considerations in assessment and practice are included as well as a discussion of students with disabilities who are also learning English as a second language.

CROSS-CATEGORICAL SERVICE DELIVERY AND THE INCLUSIVE CLASSROOM

Before inclusive classrooms became widely available in our nation's schools, students like Andrew were served primarily in segregated special education classrooms. At the very least, they would have nonacademic time such as lunch and recess with their same-age peers. Many students with mild disabilities would spend at least part of their day mainstreamed into a general education classroom and would be pulled out of class by a resource teacher for specialized services. For the past twenty-five or more years, it has been standard practice to categorize children with disabilities, organizing services around a categorical framework. Children with like disabilities have been grouped together and educated separately from their nondisabled peers.

In recent years, many have questioned the value and efficacy of a categorical model of special education for most children with disabilities. This traditional model of categorizing and separating special education students from nondisabled students has resulted in special and general education teachers working separately to develop effective instructional strategies and thus two separate systems of education. Some of the early proponents of inclusion argued for eliminating special education as we know it (e.g., Lipsky & Gartner, 1989, 1991; Reynolds, Wang, & Walberg, 1987). Currently, most professionals advocate for maintaining special education and redesigning it as a continuum of services, in which both inclusive and pull-out services are available. In this way, individual needs of children with disabilities are the primary consideration and, to the extent possible, are addressed within the context of educating all children. In inclusive classrooms, labeling, categorizing, and separating children are not as important as providing appropriate educational experiences for all students.

Following is an excerpt of a policy statement from the Council for Exceptional Children (1993).

> Special education takes many forms and can be provided with a broad spectrum of administrative arrangements. Children with special educational needs should be served in regular classes and neighborhood schools insofar as these arrangements are conducive to good educational progress. The Council believes that the goal of educating exceptional children with non-exceptional children is desirable if the individual program is such that it will enhance the exceptional child's educational, social, emotional, and vocational development.
>
> It is sometimes necessary, however, to provide special supplementary services for children with exceptionalities or to remove them from parts or all of the regular educational program. It may even be necessary to remove some children from their homes and communities in order for them to receive education and related services in residential schools, hospitals, or training centers. The Council believes that careful study and compelling reasons are necessary to justify such removal.
>
> The Council charges each public agency to ensure that a continuum of alternative placements, ranging from regular class programs to residential settings, is available to meet the needs of children with exceptionalities. (Available at: *http://www.cec.sped.org/pp/cec_pol.html*)

Cross-categorical approach Grouping students with disabilities by similar educational needs rather than disability categories. A single special education teacher may provide services for students who represent a range of disability categories.

In a **cross-categorical approach** to service delivery, teachers provide support to students of various disability labels. The main rationale for cross-categorical services is that teachers are able to focus on instructionally relevant characteristics of students rather than on their labels. Those strategies that assist one student experiencing difficulty are likely to benefit others as well. Another argument for cross-categorical services for students with disabilities is that of practicality. The number of students served by special education has grown tremendously in twenty years. Schools have struggled to provide adequate services with a categorical model. The number of new special education teachers has not kept pace with the number of new classrooms. In many places, children have been transported away from their home schools to participate in a category-specific special education classroom. A cross-categorical model allows schools more flexibility in arranging services for individual children.

Today's general education classrooms are increasingly diverse. A cross-categorical approach to special education in inclusive classrooms adds to the range of student needs that must be addressed by the general education teacher. However, even without students with disabilities, the idea of "teaching to the middle," or setting uniform expectations for all students, may no longer be realistic in today's classrooms (Schumm, Vaughn, Haager, McDowell, Rothlein, & Saumell, 1995). In reality, the educational needs of students with high-incidence disabilities may be similar to those of other students experiencing learning problems (Reynolds et al., 1987; Stanovich, 1991; Ysseldyke, Algozzine, Shinn, & McGue, 1982). Having a special educator to co-plan, co-teach, assist with referral and identification, and monitor student progress adds resources to the general education classroom that would not normally be available without an inclusive framework.

DEFINITIONS OF HIGH-INCIDENCE DISABILITIES

Many children with disabilities can learn effectively in inclusive classrooms. This book specifically addresses the needs of children with *high-incidence disabilities,* or those disabilities that occur the most frequently: learning disabilities, behavior disorders, and mild mental retardation. There are similarities in the educational needs of these groups of children and the methods and strategies for teaching them in inclusive classrooms. It is quite possible that children with low-incidence disabilities, such as low vision or a hearing loss, may also be able to learn effectively in an inclusive environment with the assistance of disability-specific supports. However, the methods used for providing appropriate supports may be quite different from those for high-incidence disabilities.

Nearly 10 percent of all school-age children, or over 4 million, have disabilities. Of these, over 70 percent fall into the high-incidence categories of learning disabilities, behavior problems, and mild mental retardation. Many more have learning problems but do not qualify for special education. You will find students from all of these categories in both special classes and inclusive settings. In the following sections, we learn about these groups, as well as those students who do not have identified disabilities but seem to need special assistance in the classroom. In each section, we examine the federal definition of the disorder, typical characteristics, and the prevalence of the disorder.

Teachers play important roles in the identification of students with learning disabilities. It is important for teachers to be knowledgeable of characteristics and definitions of disabilities. However, it is also important for teachers to respect diversity and to think of students in terms of their strengths as well as their limitations. It is possible to overidentify and overrefer children who "don't fit the mold." How boring classroom life would be if all students had the same abilities and characteristics! We encourage our readers to use the labels and categories described in this chapter as means of describing and discussing children, but to also think of children in terms of their strengths and to appreciate how individual diversity contributes to the classroom.

Learning Disabilities

Definition: A Controversial Issue. Learning disabilities were defined by Congress when they were included as a category of special education in the Education for All Handicapped Children Act, or PL 94-142. Box 2.1 includes the current federal definition that has remained virtually unchanged since the original 1977 legislation. Prior to 1977, children with learning disabilities were either misdiagnosed as having another disorder such as mental retardation, or they remained unserved or underserved and were thought of as "slow learners" or "brain damaged." This landmark legislation brought learning disabilities into public awareness and public schools scrambled to develop programs and train specialists.

At the time, no one predicted that the federal definition would result in years of controversy and debate. When you examine the wording of the federal definition in Box 2.1, you may agree with many others in the field that it is conceptual in nature and fails to specify recognizable characteristics or definitive criteria for identification, leading to ambiguity and widespread variability in interpretation by state and local education agencies. For example, the term "basic psychological processes" is not defined in the federal regulations, and only 27 percent of the states specify criteria for identifying a processing disorder (Mercer, King-Sears, & Mercer, 1990). Yet, it seems to be a fundamental concept in defining learning disabilities. Professional groups have attempted to resolve the issue by proposing alternative definitions (e.g., National Joint Committee on Learning Disabilities, 1988; Interagency Committee on Learning Disabilities, 1987) but none have successfully eliminated the ambiguity or included widely accepted, specific criteria. Thus, Congress has not adopted an alternative definition to date. Box 2.2 describes recent efforts to reconceptualize the definition and identification process for learning disabilities.

Most states rely on three general criteria for identification of individuals with learning disabilities, as specified in the federal guidelines that accompany the law (U. S. Office of Education, 1977):

1. A significant discrepancy between intellectual ability and academic performance in at least one area of academic functioning listed in the definition.
2. A documented need for services based on achievement below what would be expected for the child's age and/or grade level.

BOX 2.1
FEDERAL DEFINITIONS OF HIGH-INCIDENCE DISABILITIES

LEARNING DISABILITIES

"Specific learning disability" means a disorder in one or more of the basic psychological processes involved in understanding or in using language, spoken or written, that may manifest itself in an imperfect ability to listen, think, speak, read, write, spell, or to do mathematical calculations, including such conditions as perceptual disabilities, brain injury, minimal brain dysfunction, dyslexia, and developmental aphasia.

Terms Not Included: The term does not include children who have learning problems that are primarily the result of visual, hearing, or motor handicaps; of mental retardation or emotional disturbance; or of environmental, cultural, or economic disadvantage. (U.S. Office of Education, 1997; Part B, Section 300.7.c)

EMOTIONAL DISTURBANCE

1. The term means a condition exhibiting one or more of the following characteristics over a long period of time and to a marked degree, which adversely affects educational performance.
   a. An inability to learn that cannot be explained by intellectual, sensory, and health factors.
   b. An inability to build or maintain satisfactory interpersonal relationships with peers and teachers.
   c. Inappropriate types of behavior or feelings under normal circumstances.
   d. A general pervasive mood of unhappiness or depression.
   e. A tendency to develop physical symptoms or fears associated with personal or school problems.
2. The term includes children who are schizophrenic. The term does not include children who are socially maladjusted unless it is determined that they are seriously emotionally disturbed. (U.S. Office of Education, 1997; Part B, Section 300.7.c)

MENTAL RETARDATION

Mental retardation means significantly subaverage general intellectual functioning existing concurrently with deficits in adaptive behavior and manifested during the developmental period that adversely affects a child's educational performance. (U.S. Office of Education, 1997; Part B, Section 300.7.c)

Proposed Alternative Definition. Following is the alternative definition adopted by the American Association on Mental Retardation (AAMR).

Mental retardation is a disability characterized by significant limitations both in intellectual functioning and in adaptive behavior as expressed in conceptual, social, and practical adaptive skills. This disability originates before age 18.

Five Assumptions Essential to the Application of the Definition.

1. Limitations in present functioning must be considered within the context of community environments typical of the individual's age peers and culture.
2. Valid assessment considers cultural and linguistic diversity as well as differences in communication, sensory, motor, and behavioral factors.
3. Within an individual, limitations often coexist with strengths.
4. An important purpose of describing limitations is to develop a profile of needed supports.
5. With appropriate personalized supports over a sustained period, the life functioning of the person with mental retardation generally will improve.

Source: American Association on Mental Retardation (2002).

BOX 2.2

REDEFINING LEARNING DISABILITIES USING A RESPONSE-TO-INTERVENTION MODEL

Many professionals and policy makers in the field have raised concerns about the concept of using a discrepancy-based formula for identifying students with learning disabilities, including under- and overidentification of different groups of students as having learning disabilities, inconsistencies in how the formula is applied, and the denial of assistance to students until upper elementary years (e.g., Speece, Case, & Molloy, 2003; Vaughn & Fuchs, 2003; Vaughn, Linan-Thompson, & Hickman, 2003). Many students show early signs of struggling with academic skills but do not qualify until later grades when the discrepancy between cognitive and academic functioning widens. This essentially denies assistance to students until they have experienced years of failure. Researchers are currently investigating a response-to-intervention model for identifying students with learning disabilities.

Key to a response-to-intervention model is using systematic and ongoing measurement of progress in academic skills for all students. This allows teachers to both identify students who need additional help and monitor progress closely. By tracking students' progress closely, teachers will see that some students respond well to supplemental intervention and do not require specialized services such as special education. Students who do not respond well, or more slowly, may need more intensive, specialized instruction and are likely candidates for consideration of a learning disabilities designation. This moves the focus of identification away from nebulous and hard-to-measure psychological constructs and onto instruction. Students who fail to progress despite adequate opportunities to learn may require special consideration.

Current conceptualizations of a response-to-intervention approach have three tiers of instruction designed to provide appropriate educational support to all students regardless of labels or designations. These tiers are as follows:

Tier One consists of a well-designed, comprehensive core academic program (most current research is focusing on reading). All students receive adequate instruction and are assessed at regular intervals to determine which students are not making satisfactory progress in this tier.

Tier Two is supplemental instruction for students showing early signs of academic difficulty according to systematic progress monitoring assessment. After approximately 10 weeks of instruction, teachers would identify students for supplemental intervention. These students would receive 20 to 30 minutes of supplemental instruction in addition to continuing in the core program. Students are assessed at regular intervals (e.g., every 10 weeks) to determine if they are ready to exit Tier Two, continue, or move on to Tier Three.

Tier Three represents more specialized and intensive instruction for students who have not responded to intervention in Tier Two. After receiving a significant amount of comprehensive instruction in the first tier and supplemental instruction in the second, some students will continue to have difficulty. At this point, teachers may decide to make a referral to special education or another type of service that would provide more intensive, focused, specialized intervention in the third tier.

3. Evidence that the learning disability is not primarily the result of visual, hearing, or motor handicaps, mental retardation, emotional disturbance, or environmental, cultural, or economic disadvantage.

It is important to note that state and local education agencies have the responsibility to operationalize the federal definition and guidelines. Teachers should be knowledgeable of their district's policy and procedures for identifying students with learning disabilities.

Let's examine the factors that qualify Andrew for special education services. Andrew's initial assessment in second grade was multifaceted, using various data sources. Before Andrew was given intellectual and achievement tests, the assessment team ruled out other disorders by testing his vision and hearing and discussing his medical and psychological history with his parents. They were reasonably sure that Andrew did not have another primary disabling condition. Andrew's testing indicated a significant discrepancy between his intellectual functioning (IQ) and academic achievement in several areas. In his district, a discrepancy of two or more standard deviations is used as the criterion. Andrew scored more than two standard deviations below his intellectual functioning in word reading, reading comprehension, math problem solving, written expression, and spelling. Initially, Andrew was placed into Ms. Halley's special education classroom for the maximum amount of time and was mainstreamed for only nonacademic activities such as art and physical education. In third and fourth grades, as Andrew developed more skills, his mainstreaming was increased to include science and social studies classes. Andrew's need for services, the second criterion listed above, was evident in academic scores significantly below his grade level. In second grade, Andrew was virtually a nonreader. He had no decoding skills and recognized very few sight words. His mathematics scores were low but not as low as his reading. He could write very little beyond his name, most of the letters, and a few memorized words.

Characteristics. As a group, individuals with learning disabilities are characterized by heterogeneity. Although there are certain characteristics that are commonly associated with learning disabilities, individuals with this disorder are probably more different from each other than they are different from their peers without disabilities. An individual with learning disabilities may have only one or a few of the typical characteristics. Significant academic difficulty is the central defining characteristic common to all students with learning disabilities served in school programs. By definition, individuals with learning disabilities have significant difficulty in at least one area of academic functioning. According to the federal guidelines and current practices among the states, academic underachievement is the sole criterion for identification. This is considered the outcome, or result, of the underlying learning disability. Typically, individuals with learning disabilities may experience difficulty in any of the following areas: academic skills, cognitive and metacognitive processes, language skills, social competence, and behavior, as described in Table 2.1. Again, it is important to remember that these descriptors may or may not characterize specific individuals with learning disabilities. A multifaceted assessment process is necessary to definitively identify individuals with learning disabilities. Other disorders may co-occur with learning disabilities (as long as they are not considered the primary disabling condition) and often contribute to learning problems: attention deficit-hyperactivity disorder, conduct disorder, medical conditions, physical problems, or emotional difficulties.

Because we tend to focus on the characteristics that cause learning difficulty for an individual student, it is easy to lose sight of the fact that each individual with this disorder is likely to have areas of strength. For example, Andrew, described at the beginning of this chapter, has tremendous difficulty with reading and writing, and this difficulty pervades all

TABLE 2.1 Characteristics Associated with Learning Disabilities

AREA OF FUNCTIONING	CHARACTERISTICS	EXAMPLE
Academic Abilities*	Achievement significantly below expectation for age/grade level and for intellectual ability. Difficulties may occur in one or more academic area: reading, mathematics, writing, spelling.	Difficulty with decoding or sounding out words; difficulty remembering what is read; difficulty learning math concepts, skills, or problem-solving processes; difficulty with handwriting, written expression, grammar, and mechanics; difficulty learning spelling words or in spontaneous spelling during composition.
Language	Significant difficulty with receptive or expressive language abilities, vocabulary, verbal reasoning.	Difficulty with following directions; difficulty with comprehending what is said; difficulty expressing thoughts and ideas verbally; word-finding difficulty in verbal expression; difficulty with new vocabulary; difficulty following logical sequence of ideas.
Cognitive and Metacognitive Abilities	Difficulty with processing information: use of attention, memory, perceptual integration, and self-regulation of learning.	Difficulty with attention to task, difficulty recalling from long-term memory; difficulty with organizing information in memory; poor search-and-retrieval strategies in use of memory; difficulty linking new information with prior knowledge; lack of strategic approach to learning; unaware of when learning breaks down; unaware of task difficulty.
Social Competence	Demonstrates inappropriate or poor social skills; low self-esteem; low peer acceptance; misreads social cues.	Seems awkward or uncomfortable in social situations; uses social skills inappropriately; lacks social skills normal for age group; lacks confidence; self-expectations of failure; left out by peers; ridiculed by peers; withdraws; seems confused in social situations.
Behavioral Characteristics	Demonstrates internalizing or externalizing behavior problems; socially maladaptive behavior.	Withdrawn; depressive; shy; acts out; shows off; class clown; verbally or physically aggressive; lies; cheats; involved in acts of delinquency.

*Note: Academic difficulty is the only area specified by law as a defining characteristic of learning disabilities.

his academic work. Yet, he does have strengths. His teachers recognize that he has become stronger in mathematics. With time, this may develop into a strength for him. Andrew is also sensitive, caring, and quite perceptive of others' feelings, as when he waved to his mother. He has fit well socially into Ms. Spencer's class and does not exhibit any serious behavior problems. In fact, Ms. Spencer thinks of him as a model student in terms of his determination and effort. She often gives him classroom responsibilities because he is extremely dependable. Andrew is her "right hand" with the computer stations in her room. He is very good at troubleshooting when students run into problems on the computer.

Andrew has not yet reached adolescence and the many issues that confront adolescents with disabilities, but his mother is already worrying about Andrew's adult life. Though the federal legislation mandates services only through the age of 22, a learning disability is a lifelong disorder. Reading and writing problems head the list of difficulties for adults with learning disabilities (Blackorby & Wagner, 1997; Greenbaum, Graham, & Scales, 1996; Lerner, 2003). The academic and cognitive difficulties that impact learning in the school-age years persist into adulthood (Levin, Zigmond, & Birch, 1985; White, 1992). Other difficulties may also persist into adulthood, such as social, emotional, and language processing difficulties, which impact employment and quality of life (Greenbaum et al., 1996; Hoffman, Sheldon, Minskoff, et al., 1987; McNulty, 2003; Mellard & Hazel, 1992; Smith, 1988). Although followup studies have yielded discrepant results, we can discern a few indicators of the quality of life for adults with learning disabilities. Some evidence suggests that adults with learning disabilities are employed at a rate similar to nondisabled adults, but that they tend to hold unskilled, entry-level work positions and do not advance in status or pay (Haring, Lovett, & Smith, 1990; Shapiro & Lentz, 1991). Approximately 40 percent of students with learning disabilities withdraw from school before high school completion (Mellard & Hazel, 1992). We are likely to see an improvement in the outcome data of the future because transition goals on IEPs and transition services have been mandated since the passage of the Individuals with Disabilities Education Act (PL 101-476) in 1990, resulting in high schools' implementing new transition programs for students with learning disabilities. Colleges, universities, and vocational/technical centers have been developing support services for individuals with learning disabilities. The Americans with Disabilities Act has also brought an awareness of learning disabilities into the workplace, and employers have begun to provide accommodations. It will be interesting to see the results of studies ten years from now.

Prevalence of Learning Disabilities. Students with learning disabilities are by far the largest group of people served in special education programs. This group of students makes up nearly 50 percent of the special education population. In 1975 the Education for All Handicapped Children Act defined this disability, and federal guidelines were developed for providing services beginning in 1977. Soon after, approximately 800,000 students were enrolled in special education programs for students with learning disabilities. In less than twenty years, this number had grown to over 2 million students, or an increase of nearly 120 percent (U.S. Department of Education, 1991). By 2000, nearly 2.9 million students with learning disabilities were served in schools (U.S. Department of Education, 2002). At the same time, the number of students in special education altogether rose only 16 percent. Possibly, the category of learning disabilities began to pick up some of the students who might otherwise have been classified into some other category. In fact, the number of students identified with mental retardation decreased during this time. Other students who would have remained unserved if PL 94-142 had not mandated service were also identified.

Because of differences in specific criteria and procedures from state to state, it is difficult to determine the proportion of the student population classified as having learning disabilities. Generally, the population of students with learning disabilities ranges from 4 percent to 6 percent of the total school population from year to year. Due to recent federal laws that extended special education services to the preschool population and up through the age of 21 years, we may see a continued increase in the number of students identified as having learning disabilities at earlier and later ages, thus increasing the number of individuals with learning disabilities even further.

Emotional or Behavioral Disorders

Definition: When Is a Behavior Problem Serious Enough? The federal law defines *emotional disturbance* as a category of special education (see Box 2.1). Some states distinguish between serious emotional disturbance and behavior disorders, with the difference being one of intensity or severity of the problem. In other states, only those considered to have *serious* emotional disturbance are served by special education and those with behavior disorders do not receive special education. We have labeled this section *emotional or behavioral disorders* to move away from a narrow focus on emotional disturbance and toward a focus on behaviors that characterize students' difficulties along a continuum of severity. Though the federal law uses the term "emotional disturbance," much of the professional literature uses the term "behavior disorders." Box 2.1 includes the federal definition of emotional disturbance as it appears in the federal law. Five descriptive criteria are included in the federal definition. An individual must exhibit one or more of the specified criteria for an extended duration and to a marked degree. As with learning disabilities, there must be a demonstrated need for services; that is, the disorder must adversely affect educational performance. There is also a clause that specifies schizophrenia as an included disorder but social maladjustment as an excluded disorder. A student with a very serious emotional disorder may need intensive intervention that cannot be provided in the general education setting. Such students may be placed in residential schools specializing in intensive behavioral and psychological therapy. Of course, these students would not be placed in an inclusive classroom. However, a student with less serious behavior problems may be. It is in this sense that we think of emotional or behavioral disorders as a high-incidence disability. Therefore, we need to have an understanding of the definition and criteria for identification and be able to discern what is severe and what is not.

This federal definition, too, has suffered from controversy and debate regarding the ambiguity of the wording and the lack of clear guidelines for identifying children with this disorder. For example, what does "over a long period of time and to a marked degree" really mean? Does this vary by age? How do we determine if the condition is adversely affecting educational performance? Some argue that this strictly means academic performance as indicated by test scores or grades. Others argue that social well-being in the classroom is educationally relevant. Yet, by definition, the term does not include social maladjustment. Many find this definition confusing, and school personnel struggle to operationalize it for practical use.

A recent coalition of national organizations proposed eliminating this terminology and replacing it with *emotional or behavioral disorders* to focus more on the behaviors that can be directly assessed and described. The National Mental Health and Special Education Coalition convened to propose an alternative definition (Forness & Knitzer, 1990). As is true for the definition of learning disabilities, their proposal has not yet resulted in a change in the federal definition.

Cultural considerations are another important issue. For instance, African American students, in particular males, are represented in programs for emotional disturbance at rates 1.6 times as great as their white counterparts (Donovan & Cross, 2002). As with other high-incidence disabilities (such as learning disabilities), students are usually identified as having an emotional disturbance after they start school, and by school personnel rather than medical professionals. Some would argue that this identification process is quite subjective (Harry, Klingner, Sturges, & Moore, 2002; Townsend, 2000). These scholars assert that cultural perceptions and misunderstandings are a central aspect of this subjectivity and contribute to the overrepresentation of African American students in special education programs. Often students exhibit behaviors that may be acceptable in their own culture but are perceived as abnormal by teachers. For example, a special education teacher in a predominantly African American elementary school in the South recently recounted an experience in which a group of students was difficult to manage. The students, who were close friends and lived near each other, regularly engaged in raucous verbal bandying. Their comments were always made at someone's expense, in other words, they were "put-downs." The comments would escalate, each one becoming more negative than the previous. The teacher, who was white and middle-class, perceived this as very hurtful and antisocial. However, the students perceived this as a normal interchange between close friends in an informal setting. What was viewed by the teacher as a negative situation may actually have been a misperceived compliment—that the students were comfortable enough in her classroom and in her presence to behave as they did in their neighborhood. The problem was not that the students had emotional or serious behavior problems, but that the students had not learned to distinguish between acceptable behavior at school and that of the playground or their neighborhood. Once the teacher established ground rules for conversation in the classroom, without being vindictive or blameful of the students, they learned to leave their bandying outside.

When is a behavior problem serious enough to warrant special education? To answer this question, let's look at two other students in Andrew's class.

Michael is in Ms. Spencer's class, at least for now. He is new to the school this year, and Ms. Spencer has been collecting data for an upcoming IEP meeting. Early in the year, she began working with the Student Assistance Team and soon after wrote a formal referral because of his continual behavior problems. Michael seems to be fairly bright but he is failing almost every subject. Ms. Spencer knows he can read because this is one activity he will do when he needs to calm down. She sends him to the reading corner to be alone after an outburst and, after a while, he will sometimes pick up a book and read for long periods. He often asks to take a book home with him. Ms. Spencer knows Michael can write, too, because more than once he has written threatening notes to students or to her when he is angry. More than once he has acted on his threats. He has been sent to the office for fighting on the playground numerous times. Michael seems to make enemies easily but has no apparent friends. He seems to alienate everyone he comes into contact with. Ms. Spencer never knows what will set him off, and his outbursts have been too frequent to ignore. He loses control, and she is afraid someone will get hurt. He talks out in class and is very defiant. Ms. Spencer learned early on to avoid confrontation with him. She has spent a great deal of time talking with his mother. His mother is very worried, too. Many of the behaviors Michael exhibits at school are repeated at home. He fights with neighborhood children and with his family. They have tried numerous discipline plans at home to no avail. Ms. Spencer is anxious to have the IEP meeting and proceed with getting him some help. She knows she has patience, but fears that it will run out soon.

Ms. Spencer is also worried about Roberta and has spoken informally with the Student Assistance Team about her. She has seemed very unhappy lately. Roberta is not really having academic problems, although, according to her records, she has never been a strong student. Recently, Roberta has come to school disheveled and has fallen asleep in class a few times. In her work group, she is grouchy and gets into arguments with other students. Some of her group members secretly pleaded with Ms. Spencer to take her out of the group. She changed her group last week and now she is having the same trouble with the new group. Roberta has never been outgoing or particularly exuberant, but she seems depressed now. She does not go out the door for recess with a group of girls like she used to. She drifts off with one or two girls or, more often, by herself. Ms. Spencer tried to talk to Roberta, and, for a moment, Roberta's eyes flickered as if she wanted to talk about something. Then she "clammed up" and shrugged her shoulders. Two phone calls to Roberta's home have been unanswered.

Of course, we cannot definitively analyze these two cases without the complete compilation of information that would occur at an IEP meeting. In fact, Ms. Spencer has not written a referral regarding Roberta at this time. Recently, she informally discussed Roberta with Ms. Halley and the Student Assistance Team. In Ms. Spencer's opinion, the main criterion that the behavior must occur over a long period of time and to a marked degree has not been met in Roberta's case. Roberta's schoolwork is not yet suffering significantly. At the Student Assistance Team's suggestion, she is informally documenting the frequency of Roberta's behaviors (the sleepiness and unkemptness in the mornings, the altercations with her work group, any other depressive behavior) as well as her grades. She will also continue to try to contact Roberta's family. Ms. Halley has agreed to spend a little time with her, too. Ms. Spencer is aware that Roberta's difficulties could be a temporary state due to some type of personal or family stress. However, Roberta could also be developing a serious internalizing behavior problem, or depression, that does not manifest itself outwardly as do Michael's behavior problems. If her problems continue, Ms. Spencer will continue to work with the Student Assistance Team and eventually write a referral. The IEP team will have to decide if it is "to a marked degree" that warrants special education services. In addition, they will have to decide that she meets at least one of the five criteria.

Michael's case is about to go to the IEP team. It will be difficult for the IEP team to determine what constitutes "over a long period of time" or "to a marked degree." Ms. Spencer has anecdotal recordings of outbursts and aggression toward herself and other students over several months. His behavior is certainly inappropriate under normal circumstances and seems to be harmful to others. His educational performance has been adversely affected, as he is failing every subject. Though we have little information from the home environment, his mother has indicated that his problems exist at home, too. We do not have all the information that will be available to the IEP team, but it is likely that Michael will need intensive assistance.

Internalizing behavior problems A broad category of behavior problems characterized by shy and withdrawn behavior patterns. Depression and anxiety would fall into this category. School personnel often fail to detect internalizing behavior problems because these children are often quiet, fading into the background of busy classrooms.

Externalizing behavior problems A broad category of behavior problems characterized by acting out or aggressive behavior. Though aggressive or acting out behaviors can cause problems in a classroom, they are not always indicative of a disability. When these behaviors are extreme or persist over a long period of time, it is a sign of a severe behavior problem that should be addressed by professionals.

Characteristics. Emotional or behavior disorders include a wide variety of characteristics. As with learning disabilities, you would not expect every individual to display every characteristic. Unlike learning disabilities, this area of disorders has somewhat distinct subgroups, though there is no single classification system that is used universally in schools. You can see from Box 2.1 that the federal definition does not describe subgroups, nor does it provide a classification system. The classification systems that exist are drawn from the fields of psychology and counseling. The *Diagnostic and Statistical Manual of Mental Disorders, Fourth Edition* (DSM-IV) (American Psychiatric Association, 1994) provides guidelines for diagnosis used by the psychological and medical communities. Several types of emotional or behavioral disorders are detailed in this manual. Because this is a manual used by psychiatrists, psychologists, medical doctors, and mental health professionals, the descriptors and guidelines are not necessarily relevant to the school setting or high-incidence disabilities.

Of perhaps more educational relevance is to think of behavioral disorders as either **internalizing behavior problems** or **externalizing behavior problems** (Achenbach & Edelbrock, 1978). Internalizing behavior problems include shy and withdrawn behavior, or behaviors directed inward. In contrast, externalizing behavior problems are acting out, or aggressive behaviors that are directed toward others. Using the federal guidelines, the behaviors would have to occur over an extended period of time and to a marked degree in order to qualify the individual for special education services. In addition, the problems would have to affect educational performance.

Avoidance, compulsiveness, sadness, depression, fearfulness, and fantasizing or daydreaming are considered internalizing behavior problems if they are excessive and problematic to the individual. Children with internalizing behavioral difficulties are often not identified in the school setting because of the "squeaky wheel" syndrome—students with more disruptive and attention-seeking behaviors are noticed while children who are quiet and compliant are not. Yet their behavior problems may be serious enough to warrant attention. Being withdrawn, they may avoid social interaction, which would affect their ability to establish and maintain satisfactory social relationships. With internalizing behavioral difficulties, poor educational performance may be an indicator to teachers to examine the difficulties further. Ms. Spencer is wise to give some special attention to Roberta, described above. She seems depressed, troubled, and fearful and seems to be diminishing her social contacts. Her educational performance has been lagging. However, more time is needed to rule out any other underlying cause or a temporary state and to determine the duration and intensity of her difficulties.

Michael is more characteristic of a youngster with externalizing behavioral difficulties. He has demonstrated excessive and intense aggression to the point of causing Ms. Spencer to fear for his or others' safety. He acts impulsively, has violent outbursts, and is confrontational. In other words, his actions are directed at others. His grades are poor. His difficulties appear to exist in the home setting as well as at school. The IEP team will, of course, need to rule out any other underlying factors or causes and determine a need for services in order for Michael to qualify for special education. Whether he qualifies or not, it is clear that Michael and Ms. Spencer need some type of support or intervention in order for him to be successful in an inclusive classroom.

Students with emotional or behavioral disorders may also experience lifelong effects. Followup research on students with identified emotional or behavior disorders is limited, but evidence indicates far-reaching effects. Adolescents and adults with such disorders are more likely to be involved in the judicial system, continue patterns of aggressive behaviors, and may be involved in drug use (Hunt & Marshall, 2001). They are also less likely to be satisfactorily employed as adults or to graduate from high school.

What about problems with attention and hyperactivity? Do these fit into an internalizing and externalizing classification scheme? *Attention deficit-hyperactivity disorder* (ADHD) is thought of as separate from either learning disabilities or serious emotional disturbance and is not recognized by the federal government as a disability. According to federal guidelines, ADHD may co-occur with learning disabilities or emotional disturbance but is not a disability in and of itself. Achenbach and Edelbrock (1981) include impulsivity and lack of self-control, behaviors associated with attention deficit-hyperactivity disorder, as externalizing behaviors. A person with this disorder might instead be inattentive, disorganized, and easily distracted. These are more internalizing than externalizing behaviors. To be consistent with federal guidelines, it is best to think of ADHD as a related condition that may exist along with other disabilities.

Prevalence of Behavior Disorders. About 8 percent of all children with disabilities served by special education, or nearly 470,000 children, are classified as having serious emotional disturbance (U.S. Department of Education, 2002). This figure may be lower than the actual rate, however. Many children who need services may be unserved because their behavior problems are not disruptive or highly noticeable or because their behaviors do not fit well into the criteria used for identification (Henley, Ramsey, & Algozzine, 2001; Hunt & Marshall, 2001). The fact that some states recognize milder behavior disorders as a disability separate from severe emotional disturbance, while others do not, complicates the task of determining the prevalence of emotional/behavioral disorders. The widespread variability in state and local procedures and criteria and the lack of specificity in the federal definition contribute to different rates of prevalence from state to state (Hallahan, Keller, & Ball, 1986; Tharinger, Laurent, & Best, 1986; Wright, Pillard, & Cleven, 1990).

Mild Mental Retardation

Definition: A Matter of Degree. The federal law includes a definition of mental retardation based on definitions proposed by the American Association on Mental Deficiency and has been in use since 1973. Examine the wording of the federal definition of mental retardation in Box 2.1. In 1993, the American Association on Mental Retardation (AAMR, formerly AAMD) proposed an alternative definition to eliminate ambiguous or offensive wording. This definition is also provided in Box 2.1. While it maintains the reference to intellectual functioning, it more clearly specifies what is meant by "adaptive behavior" and "developmental period." The AAMR definition has gained widespread acceptance by state and local service agencies.

Using either the federal or AAMR definition, there are three basic criteria for identifying individuals with mental retardation. First, a person must have subaverage intellectual functioning, usually determined with an IQ test. Second, the individual must have limitations in adaptive skill areas. Third, the characteristics must be present during the developmental period, or during childhood. The definition of mental retardation is one of degree. Just as the definitions of learning disabilities and emotional or behavioral disorders leave room for interpretation or operationalization by state and local education agencies, the definition of mental retardation does not specify to what degree "subaverage intellectual functioning," or "limitations" in adaptive skills must occur to meet the criteria. Even with the improvements included in the AAMR definition, the degree of severity needed to qualify for special education is left open to interpretation. Many states have established the criteria of performance more than two standard deviations below the average of the general population in both intellectual functioning and adaptive behavior. On a standard IQ test, this would be a score of less than 70 points. However, IQ score alone does not qualify a student for services, and for many students an IQ test is biased or culturally inappropriate.

Adaptive behavior Students with mental retardation often display difficulties in adaptive behavior, meaning that they have not developed age-appropriate skills in the areas of communication, social skills, daily living, and self-care.

There must also be a demonstrated limitation in adaptive behavior. **Adaptive behavior** is defined as those skills or actions required to adapt to situational demands of the environment, and include communication, social, daily living, and self-care skills. The key to understanding adaptive behaviors is focusing on what is age-appropriate and contextually appropriate for the individual. Many states have de-emphasized IQ scores or eliminated them completely as a criterion measure due to inherent cultural bias in the tests. In these states, much more emphasis is placed on measurement of adaptive skills. Mental retardation can occur in varying degrees of severity. Mild to moderate mental retardation is considered a high-incidence disability and is the focus of discussion in this chapter. The interested reader may refer to other texts on mental retardation for information about severe and profound retardation.

Renee is in elementary school and is on Ms. Halley's roster. She is in second grade and has received special education services in an inclusive setting since she was 3 years old and in an integrated preschool. Renee was identified as having mental retardation as an infant when she was not meeting typical developmental milestones. In Renee's case, the cause is unknown and may be a result of stress at birth. Renee has evident limitations in intellectual functioning such as difficulty with memory and basic learning tasks. She is learning basic academic skills at a very slow pace and seems to need a great deal of practice and repetition to make progress. Limitations in adaptive skills are evident in her delayed language abilities, daily living skills, impulsive behavior, and social skills. She has some difficulty with the everyday functional demands of the classroom, such as hand-raising and appropriate responding. She often misreads social situations, and her interactions with other students are awkward. Renee does not seem to have difficulty with motor skills as do some other children with mental retardation. She enjoys physical education and excels at running. Though Renee is significantly behind her class in academic skills, she participates fully in class activities with appropriate supports and modifications of the curriculum. Her teachers have helped her to make social connections by carefully selecting group members and facilitating peer support for Renee. The other students have begun to accept her somewhat clumsy communication and readily ask her to join in play activities.

Justin is in a high school special education program serving students with mild-to-moderate disabilities. He also has notable developmental delays that characterize him as having mild mental retardation. Intellectually, he functions significantly below average and has limitations in adaptive behavior as well, such as social skills, daily living skills, and self-direction. Justin functions significantly below average academically and is working toward a modified high school completion certificate. This allows him to focus on adaptive skills and employment skills needed to function in the adult world upon high school completion. Justin spends a part of his day in an inclusive high school program and part in a supported employment program in the community for students with disabilities.

Characteristics. Mental retardation is a disability of degree in another sense as well. This developmental disability affects the individual's general development. Mental retardation occurs across a continuum of severity, affecting the development of cognitive abilities, language skills, academic performance, and motor skills. As the severity of retardation increases, the level impairment in each of these domains increases. Remember that individuals with learning disabilities are heterogeneous with respect to various domains of characteristics (i.e., cognitive, academic, etc.). This is not true for mental retardation. An individual with mental retardation is likely to be affected in all areas of psychosocial functioning.

An impairment of cognitive abilities is a characteristic central to the definition of mental retardation. For identification purposes, we usually think of cognitive abilities from the rather narrow perspective of intellectual functioning. However, cognitive functioning can be thought of broadly as the processes involved in thinking, learning, and using information. Individuals with mild mental retardation are likely to have difficulty with these basic processes, but not as much difficulty as individuals with moderate or severe retardation. Their ability to reason is often limited to simple rather than complex problems or lines of thought. For example, Renee, described in the case study, is assigned to a cooperative learning group in her classroom. Her teachers have assisted the group in defining roles and tasks that allow her to be successful and participate in the group. However, sometimes the group gets excited about a particular project and the group conversation becomes accelerated. It is typical for several consecutive ideas to come tumbling out of their collective minds or for a sequence of activities or steps to be laid out. This leads to confusion for Renee, who has difficulty following a complex sequence of ideas. The special education teacher has been working with Renee's classmates to recognize when Renee becomes frustrated and to be sensitive to her need for simplification and additional explanation. Similarly, Justin experiences limitations in following complex ideas or reasoning. His teachers feel that, in order to be successful in the workplace, Justin must be able to follow more than simple directions. In a workplace environment, he practices completing sets of tasks that become gradually more complex. Justin has been learning a process of verbal rehearsal that allows him to follow several steps involved in a task, but his performance is still slow and requires intense concentration.

In general, learning is affected by a limited capacity to organize, store, and recall information. This affects learning at all age levels for individuals with mild mental retardation. They may need extra assistance to develop the ability to focus attention for learning (Brooks & McCauley, 1984). Cognitive and academic demands increase in the high school setting. In order to provide an inclusive environment for Justin, his teachers have arranged for him to attend regular classes for half of the school day. In history, science, and an elective, he has opportunities to work on academic learning with his same-age peers. The general and special education teachers work collaboratively to make appropriate modifications for him. Each afternoon, Justin goes into the community to learn employment skills in a vocational training program for youth with disabilities. This is also considered an inclusive environment because he works with same-age peers and a job coach in an actual workplace.

Children with mental retardation usually acquire language skills at a slower than average rate. Individuals with mild mental retardation may not be noticeably different from typically developing children by the time they reach the school-age years (Polloway, Smith, Patton, & Smith, 1996), but they may have difficulty learning vocabulary words or be slower in processing language in the classroom. Academic learning is largely dependent on the ability to think and use language. Reading, writing, mathematics, and content area learning are highly dependent on language ability. It is no surprise, then, that youngsters with mild mental retardation often have academic difficulties. Students with mild mental retardation have particular difficulty with abstract, conceptual learning and with memorizing information.

Most individuals with mild mental retardation have no physical or motor characteristics that would identify them to the casual observer. Moderate and severe retardation are often associated with physical conditions such as Down syndrome that lead to differences in physical development and motor skills. Children with mild mental retardation may have difficulty with motor skills such as a clumsy gait or poor handwriting, but this is not necessarily a universal characteristic nor a serious problem.

Significant limitations in adaptive skills is central to the definition of mental retardation. The AAMR definition includes communication, self-care, home living, social skills, community use, self-direction, health and safety, functional academics, leisure, and work skills as adaptive skill areas. The specific skills needed to be competent in these areas may differ at different ages but students may need support and instruction throughout the school years. Justin, described above, has mastered many of the self-care and living skills and work-related skills are an important part of his education at this point in his life. For Renee, communication, self-care, health and safety, and social skills are important. The special education teacher is working closely with the parents to monitor and teach some of these skills.

Prevalence of Mild Mental Retardation. As the number of students identified as having learning disabilities increased from 1977 to 1990, the proportion of students identified as having mental retardation decreased from 26 percent of the special eduation population to 12 percent (U.S. Department of Education, 1991). How do we explain this decrease? The obvious explanation is that as awareness of the characteristics and criteria for learning disabilities increased, children who would have otherwise been classified as having mental retardation were instead classified as having learning disabilities. Many children were misclassified as having mental retardation and were reclassified into the learning disabilities category. Prior to the 1980s, certain ethnic groups were overrepresented in classes for students with mental retardation (Chinn & Hughes, 1987; Mercer, 1973). With increased awareness and sensitivity to this issue, as well as court challenges, identification procedures have been developed to prevent misclassification, and there is less overrepresentation. Another explanation is that the criteria for mental retardation have changed over the years in many states. Many states previously used one standard deviation, or an IQ score less than 85, as the criterion, but now use 70 as a cutoff score. Adaptive behavior assessments have become a more important part of assessment and identification as well, changing the way we assess and identify children.

Approximately 500,000 school-age people are identified as having mental retardation. Of those, about 440,000 have mild mental retardation. We canot begin to estimate how many more students remain unidentified and unserved. Children whose scores fall near the borderline often are not placed into services for various reasons. Availability of resources may be one reason. Serving a student with a tremendous need may be more desirable than serving one whose scores fall at the borderline. Strict adherence to the stand-ard error of measurement may be another reason. School personnel and parents are reluctant to label children, especially when their scores are at the border. Because different schools use different cutoff scores, some children would qualify in one location but not in another.

CULTURALLY AND LINGUISTICALLY DIVERSE EXCEPTIONAL LEARNERS

Jorge speaks Spanish as his first language and in his home with his parents and five younger siblings; he has been identified as having learning disabilities. Jorge is in Irene's third-grade bilingual class, receiving in-class special education support from Beverly, an LD specialist who does not speak Spanish. Jorge's school has not officially implemented an inclusion model, but he stays in his general education class full-time to receive instruction in Spanish. Let's look briefly at Jorge's educational history: During kindergarten and first grade, Jorge attended bilingual classes and was instructed primarily in Spanish. He also received intensive oral instruction in English as a second language (ESL). Although slightly below grade level in reading, he seemed to be progressing satisfactorily; by the end of first grade, he could read at a primer level in Spanish. He did well in math. In second grade, he was again placed in a bilingual class, but this year his teacher taught primarily in English, and Jorge began learning to read in English. He struggled, and his teacher attributed his lack of success to a poor home environment and a lack of parental support. She suspected that his intelligence was quite low (although he continued to perform adequately in math). She reasoned that he needed more time learning in English and that he should be retained and placed in an English-only (mainstream) classroom. His new second grade teacher was alarmed at his low skills and lack of progress and referred him for a special education evaluation in November. Because by now Jorge could speak close-to-fluent oral English in a conversational setting and his classroom teacher assumed he was English dominant, he was tested exclusively in English. On an intelligence test, he scored in the low-average range (full scale IQ = 89; verbal IQ = 76; performance IQ = 102). He qualified for placement as having a learning disability because of his even lower scores on an

English reading test (standard score = 60, pre-primer grade level), and his difficulty following oral directions in English (it was determined he was weak in auditory processing). In January, Jorge began attending the special education resource room one hour a day for help with reading. Beverly, his special education teacher, was soon frustrated with his lack of responsiveness to the intensive, individualized instruction she provided. In April, Beverly attended a district-sponsored workshop on students with learning disabilities who speak English as a second language and determined to ask the school's ESL teacher for assistance with Jorge. Together, they decided to ask the district's bilingual psychologist and a multidisciplinary assessment team to reevaluate Jorge in Spanish. After administering academic and intelligence tests to Jorge in Spanish (as well as English), observing Jorge in a variety of settings, and talking with Jorge's parents, the assessment team confirmed that Jorge had a learning disability that manifested itself in Spanish as well as English. The team concluded that Jorge's intelligence was in the middle-to-high-average range and that he had a reading-related learning disability. Furthermore, the team noted that Jorge had been transitioned to English instruction too soon, before he had been able to build a strong foundation in his native language. Given that Jorge was a stronger reader in Spanish but was making virtually no progress in English reading, after much deliberation the multidisciplinary committee recommended that he return to a bilingual classroom and receive reading instruction in Spanish, with in-class support from the LD specialist. This is where we find Jorge today, in Irene's third-grade bilingual classroom. The results have been remarkable; once Jorge was again taught in Spanish with effective instructional techniques, he began progressing rapidly, and by May he has made almost two years' growth and is reading at a third-grade level in Spanish.

Does Jorge truly have a learning disability? Or were his difficulties due to confusion learning in two languages and a too-early transition into English instruction? Why was Jorge initially tested only in English? What would have happened to Jorge if he had remained in the English-only classroom? These are questions that perplex the well-meaning educators who work with the more than one million ESL students experiencing difficulties in our schools (Baca & Cervantes, 1988).

Jorge in many ways is typical of other language minority youngsters placed in special education programs. Ortiz and Yates (1988) found in a study of 334 Spanish-speaking students diagnosed to have learning disabilities that the majority were referred in the second grade, 45 percent had been retained, and many were considered by their teachers to be dominant in English even though they were from Spanish-speaking homes. Also, it is common for students to experience difficulties when they transition from bilingual to mainstream English classrooms, particularly if the transition is abrupt, and sharp declines in academic performance are typical (Gersten & Woodward, 1995).

The federal definition of learning disabilities states that a person's handicapping condition cannot be due to extrinsic influences such as cultural differences or insufficient or inappropriate instruction, and that these factors should be ruled out before a child is identified as having a learning disability. Yet determining why a child performs as he or she does is difficult. One dilemma facing educators is that the characteristics of individuals learning a second language are similar to behaviors associated with language and learning disabilities (e.g., difficulty following directions, inattention, daydreaming, and slow academic progress in the second language). Many students are misplaced in special education programs because educators cannot tell the difference between second-language factors and true disabilities (Fradd & McGee, 1994; Ortiz, 1984). It is also possible to overlook a disability in a student learning a second language due to problems with testing and the inability to determine whether the learning difficulties result from second language functioning or a real disability.

Ruiz (1995) suggests that there are three profile types of students placed in bilingual special education classrooms, ranging from students with severe language learning disabilities to students with normal abilities. Ruiz emphasizes the role of the instructional context in revealing the upper and lower ranges of students' communicative and academic competence. In other words, the students she observed appeared competent in some settings and incompetent in others, just as Jorge made little progress when learning to read in English and appeared to lack intelligence, yet did well when placed in an effective bilingual classroom.

Another dilemma is that it is very difficult to accurately assess the cognitive ability of bilingual students (Garcia, 1994). In which language should they be tested? When are they proficient enough in English to be tested only with English-language tests? One reason for confusion is that language proficiency tests are themselves fraught with problems (Figueroa, 1989). It is relatively easy to assess basic interpersonal competence, but much more difficult to determine whether a person is ready to use English in cognitively demanding academic situations. Cummins (1984, 1989) estimates that achieving cognitive academic linguistic proficiency (CALP) takes from five to seven years. Yet, ESL students are usually exited from bilingual or ESL programs much earlier than that, and then tested only in English if they are evaluated for possible special education placement. Verbal intelligence tests become much more like language proficiency tests than true intelligence tests; low verbal ability scores could be an indication that students have not achieved full language proficiency rather than that they lack cognitive ability or potential. Also, students may lack familiarity with the content of test items because of cultural differences (Duran, 1989).

Testing in the native language is also problematic. For non-English speakers, three options are available: (a) translating an English test, (b) using an interpreter with an English test, and (c) using a test in the student's native language (Figueroa, 1989). Yet each of these has difficulties. When a test is translated, the difficulty level of individual test items is changed. Using even trained interpreters may compromise results. Although there are many Spanish-language tests, they typically are developed for monolingual Spanish speakers in a Spanish-speaking country (who have had little or no sustained exposure to English). Their validity with Spanish-speaking students in the United States is highly questionable. For these and other reasons, some school districts do not allow the use of standardized intelligence tests when placing students in special education programs (e.g., San Francisco Unified School District in California). Whatever tests or procedures are used, it is crucial that professionals who have been trained in assessing culturally and linguistically diverse populations conduct the evaluations.

In retrospect, Jorge's case seems fairly straightforward because he is clearly dominant in Spanish and has been able to maintain use of his Spanish while learning English. His placement with a bilingual teacher and a support teacher from special education represents the best of collaboration between bilingual and special education. But, what if he had already forgotten much of his Spanish? Many students in our school system have mixed dominance, and even exhibit what has been called *subtractive bilingualism*—they are less than fully proficient in both English and another language (Fradd & McGee, 1994). This can happen when students are transitioned to English too soon and forget much of their native language without fully acquiring English, or when students do not have a chance to adequately build a strong foundation in one language before learning another. Subtractive bilingualism occurs in environments where a student's home language is not valued and maintained. It is students in this situation who seem at greatest risk in our school system and need to be evaluated and taught with expertise. Inclusion classrooms in which special educators, general educators, and ESL specialists collaborate are one way to provide students with an optimal learning environment.

REFERENCES

Achenbach, T. M., & Edelbrock, C. S. (1981). Behavioral problems and competencies reported by parents of normal and disturbed children aged four through sixteen. *Monographs of the Society for Research in Child Development,* 46, 1–82.

American Association on Mental Retardation. (2002). *The AAMR definition of mental retardation.* Available at: *http://www.aamr.org/Policies/faq_mental_retardation.shtml.*

American Psychiatric Association. (1994). *Diagnostic and statistical manual of mental disorders* (4th ed.) (DSM-IV). Washington, DC: Author.

Baca, L., & Cervantes, H. (1988). *The bilingual special education interface.* Columbus, OH: Merrill.

Blackorby, J., & Wagner, M. (1997). The employment outcomes of youth with learning disabilities: A review of findings from the NLTS. In P. Gerber & D. Brown (Eds.), *Learning disabilities and employment* (pp. 57–76). Austin, TX: Pro-Ed.

Brooks, P. H., & McCauley, C. (1984). Cognitive research in mental retardation. *American Journal of Mental Deficiency, 88,* 479–486.

Chinn, P. C., & Hughes, S. (1987). Representation of minority students in special education classes. *Remedial and Special Education, 8*(4), 41–46.

Council for Exceptional Children. (1994). *CEC policy on inclusive schools and community settings.* Reston, VA: Author.

Cummins, J. (1984). *Bilingualism and special education: Issues in assessment and pedagogy.* San Diego, CA: College Hill.

Cummins, J. (1989). A theoretical framework for bilingual special education. *Exceptional Children, 56,* 111–119.

Donovan, S., & Cross, C. (2002). *Minority students in special and gifted education.* Washington, DC: National Academy Press.

Duran, R. P. (1989). Assessment and instruction of at-risk Hispanic students. *Exceptional Children, 56,* 154–158.

Figueroa, R. A. (1989). Psychological testing of linguistic-minority students: Knowledge gaps and regulations. *Exceptional Children, 56,* 145–152.

Forness, S. R., & Knitzer, J. (1990). *A new proposed definition and terminology to replace "Serious Emotional Disturbance" in Individuals with Disabilities Education Act.* Workgroup on Definition, the National Mental Health and Special Education Coalition, National Mental Health Association.

Fradd, S. H., & McGee, P. L. (1994). *Instructional assessment: An integrative approach to evaluating student performance.* Menlo Park, CA: Addison-Wesley.

Garcia, E. (1994). *Understanding and meeting the challenge of student cultural diversity.* Boston: Houghton Mifflin.

Gersten, R., & Woodward, J. (1995). A longitudinal study of transitional and immersion bilingual education programs in one district. *Elementary School Journal, 60,* 310–322.

Greenbaum, B., Graham, S., & Scales, W. (1996). Adults with learning disabilities: Occupational and social status after college. *Journal of Learning Disabilities, 29,* 167–173.

Hallahan, D. P., Keller, C. E., & Ball, D. W. (1986). A comparison of prevalence rate variability from state to state for each of the categories of special educaiton. *Remedial and Special Education, 7*(2), 8–14.

Haring, K. A., Lovett, D. L., & Smith, D. D. (1990). A follow-up study of recent special education graduates of learning disabilities programs. *Journal of Learning Disabilities, 23,* 108–113.

Harry, B., Klingner, J. K., Sturges, K., & Moore, R. (2002). Of rocks and soft places: Using qualitative methods to investigate the processes that result in disproportionality. In D. J. Losen & G. Orfield (Eds.), *Racial inequality in special education.* Boston: Harvard Education Press.

Henley, M., Ramsey, R. S., & Algozzine, R. (2001). *Characteristics of and strategies for teaching students with mild disabilities* (4th ed.). Boston: Allyn and Bacon.

Hoffman, F. J., Sheldon, K. L., Minskoff, E. H., Sautter, S. W., Steidle, E. F., Baker, D. P., Bailey, M. B., & Echols, L. D. (1987). Needs of learning disabled adults. *Journal of Learning Disabilities, 20*, 43–52.

Hunt, N., & Marshall, K. (2001). *Exceptional children and youth* (3rd ed.). Boston: Houghton Mifflin.

Interagency Committee on Learning Disabilities. (1987). *Learning disabilities: A report to Congress*. Bethesda, MD: National Institutes of Health.

Lerner, J. W. (2003). *Learning disabilities: Theories, diagnosis, and teaching strategies*. Boston: Allyn and Bacon.

Levin, E. K., Zigmond, N., & Birch, J. W. (1985). A follow-up study of 52 learning disabled adolescents. *Journal of Learning Disabilities, 18*, 2–7.

Lipsky, D. K., & Gartner, A. (1989). *Beyond separate education: Quality for all*. Baltimore: Paul H. Brookes.

Lipsky, D. K., & Gartner, A. (1991). Restructuring for quality. In J. W. Lloyd, A. C. Repp, & N. M. Singh (Eds.), *The regular education initiative: Alternative perspectives on concepts, issues, and models* (pp. 43–56). Sycamore, IL: Sycamore.

McNulty, M. A. (2003). Dyslexia and the life course. *Journal of Learning Disabilities, 36*(4), 363–381.

Mercer, C. D., King-Sears, M. E., & Mercer, A. R. (1990). Learning disabilities definitions and criteria used by state education departments. *Learning Disability Quarterly, 13*, 141–52.

Mercer, J. (1973). *Labeling the mentally retarded*. Los Angeles: University of California Press.

Mellard, D. F., & Hazel, J. S. (1992). Social competence as a pathway to successful life transitions. *Learning Disability Quarterly, 15*, 251–271.

Mercer, C. D., King-Sears, P., & Mercer, A. R. (1990). Learning disabilities definitions and criteria used by state education departments. *Learning Disability Quarterly, 13*, 141–152.

National Association of State Boards of Education. (1992). *Winners all: From mainstreaming to inclusion*. Alexandria, VA: Author.

National Joint Committee on Learning Disabilities. (1988). *Collective perspectives on issues affecting learning disabilities: Position papers and statements*. Austin, TX: Pro-Ed.

Ortiz, A. A. (1984). Choosing the language of instruction for exceptional bilingual children. *Teaching Exceptional Children, 16*, 208–212.

Ortiz, A. A., & Yates, J. R. (1988). Characteristics of learning disabled, mentally retarded, and speech-language handicapped Hispanic students at initial evaluation and reevaluation. In A. A. Ortiz & B. A. Ramirez (Eds.), *Schools and the culturally diverse exceptional student: Promising practices and future directions*. Reston, VA: Council for Exceptional Children.

Polloway, E. A., Smith, J. D., Patton, J. R., & Smith, T. E. C. (1996). Historic changes in mental retardation and developmental disasbilities. *Education and Training in Mental Retardation and Developmental Disabilities, 31*, 3–12.

Reynolds, M. C., Wang, M. C., & Walberg, H. J. (1987). The necessary restructuring of special and regular education. *Exceptional Children, 53*, 391–398.

Ruiz, N. T. (1995). The social construction of ability and disability: I. Profile types of Latino children identified as language learning disabled. *Journal of Learning Disabilities, 28*, 476–490.

Schumm, J. S., Vaughn, S., Haager, D., McDowell, J., Rothlein, L., & Saumell, L. (1995). General education teacher planning: What can students with learning disabilities expect? *Exceptional Children, 61*, 335–352.

Shapiro, E. S., & Lentz, F. E. (1991). Vocational-technical programs: Follow-up of students with learning disabilities. *Exceptional Children, 58*, 47–59.

Smith, J. O. (1988). Social and vocational problems of adults with learning disabilities: A review of the literature. *Learning Disabilities Focus, 4*, 46–58.

Speece, D. L., Case, L. P., & Molloy, D. E. (2003). Responsiveness to general education instruction as the first gate to learning disabilities identification. *Learning Disabilities Research and Practice, 18*(3), 1147–1156.

Stanovich, K. E. (1991). Conceptual and empirical problems with discrepancy definitions of reading disability. *Learning Disability Quarterly, 14*(4), 269–280.

Tharinger, D. J., Laurent, J., & Best, L. R. (1986). Classification of children referred for emotional and behavioral problems: A comparison of PL 94–142 SED criteria, DSM-III, and the CBCL system. *Journal of School Psychology, 24*, 111–121.

Townsend, B. L. (2000). The disproportionate discipline of African American learners: Reducing school suspensions and expulsions. *Exceptional Children, 66*(3), 381–391.

U. S. Department of Education. (1991). *Thirteenth annual report to Congress on the implementation of the Individuals with Disabilities Education Act*. Washington, DC: U. S. Government Printing Office.

U. S. Department of Education. (2002). *Twenty-third annual report to Congress on the implementation of the Individuals with Disabilities Education Act.* Washington, DC: U. S. Government Printing Office.

U. S. Office of Education. (1977). Assistance to states for education of handicapped children: Procedures for evaluating specific learning disabilities. *Federal Register, 42,* 65,082–65,085.

U. S. Office of Education. (1977). *Federal Register, 42* (163). August 23, 1977.

Vaughn, S., & Fuchs, L. S. (2003). Redefining learning disabilities as inadequate response to instruction: The promise and potential pitfalls. *Learning Disabilities Research and Practice, 18*(3), 137–146.

Vaughn, S., Linan-Thompson, S., & Hickman, P. (2003). Response to instruction as a means of identifying students with reading/learning disabilities. *Exceptional Children, 69*(4), 391–409.

White, W. J. (1992). The postschool adjustment of persons with learning disabilities: Current status and future projections. *Journal of Learning Disabilities, 25,* 448–456.

Wright, D., Pillard, E. D., & Cleven, C. A. (1990). The influence of state definitions of behavior disorders on the number of children served under PL 94–142. *Remedial and Special Education, 11*(5), 17–22.

Ysseldyke, J. E., Algozzine, B., Shinn, M. R., & McGue, M. (1982). Similarities and differences between low achievers and students classified learning disabled. *The Journal of Special Education, 16,* 73–85.

CHAPTER THREE

ASSESSMENT-BASED DECISION MAKING

It is a capital mistake to theorize before one has data.
—Sir Arthur Conan Doyle, *The Adventures of Sherlock Holmes,* 1891

KEY CONCEPTS

- Assessment is an integral part of the instructional process: Teachers assess, plan, teach, then assess for mastery of what was taught as part of an ongoing process, continuously gathering information about students and their learning.
- Various assessment procedures are available, including norm-referenced assessment, criterion-referenced assessment, curriculum-based assessment, curriculum-based measurement, authentic performance-based assessment, portfolio assessment, and observation.
- Identifying students with disabilities and determining their eligibility for special services is complex and governed by a set of guidelines from federal and state laws and educational policies.

- The law requires a comprehensive evaluation that must be sufficient to provide multiple sources of information about the child's functioning and assess all areas of suspected disability: cognitive, academic, behavioral, social, emotional, motor and sensory, health, and communicative functioning.
- The law provides for fair and unbiased assessment as well as due process safeguards for both families and school personnel.
- Traditional assessment practices with culturally and linguistically diverse students have been criticized because of problematic test development procedures and test uses that create bias.
- Though IDEA stipulates that states must develop policies and procedures that ensure the participation of students with special needs in district-wide and statewide assessment programs, with accommodations as necessary, the extent to which students with disabilities actually participate varies widely, from 0 to 100 percent.
- Various accommodations of four general types have been recommended to enable students with disabilities to participate in high stakes testing; these include changes in how the tests are presented, how students are expected to respond, timing, and setting.

FOCUS QUESTIONS

1. What does "all children can learn" mean?
2. How is the assessment process used to make instructional decisions?
3. What is the role of the inclusion specialist in the instructional decision-making process?
4. How is the assessment process used to determine if a child qualifies for special education services?
5. What does federal law stipulate about the assessment and decision-making process for placing students in special education?
6. Why have traditional assessment practices with culturally and linguistically diverse students been criticized?
7. What accommodations are available for students with disabilities when taking high stakes tests?

"All children can learn." We hear this adage frequently, but what does it really mean? How can teachers make it a reality? When Jane doesn't learn the first time we teach her something, we know we shouldn't give up, that we should try another way to reach her and keep trying until she and we are successful. But how do we know she hasn't been successful in the first place, and how do we decide what to try next? Assessment is the key.

Most people think of assessment as "testing," and teachers will say they do a fair amount of testing during a typical school year. Yearly achievement tests and teacher-made tests determine students' grades and mastery of subject matter. Pretests help teachers know what they need to teach. State competency tests provide information about how students compare with others at their grade level.

> **Assessment** The process of gathering information to monitor progress and make educational decisions.

However, testing is only one type of assessment. Overton (2003) describes **assessment** as the process of gathering information to monitor progress and make educational decisions. The assessment process involves four steps: (1) developing an evaluation plan, (2) administering and interpreting the appropriate measures and procedures (e.g., criterion-referenced tests or behavioral assessment techniques), (3) integrating information and making recommendations, and (4) conducting ongoing evaluations to validate or invalidate existing procedures. The assessment should be related to the curriculum areas covered in the general education classroom (Deno & Mirkin, 1980), consider the particular educational setting of the student, and directly relate to the development of an intervention plan. Good teachers do a great deal of assessment throughout a typical school year. This is true for both general and special education teachers, though the nature and purpose of their assessments may differ.

In this chapter, we will see that assessment provides teachers, parents, students, and schools with important information for making curricular and instructional decisions. There are different types of assessment, used for different purposes. We conduct assessment to determine students' educational needs and their eligibility for special education services. Although this is not the primary purpose of this text, we will look at the special educators' role in this type of assessment in an inclusive setting. In this chapter we will also learn what the law says about assessment in special education and consider how the laws may apply in an inclusive setting. We will also learn about assessment for the purpose of monitoring students' progress and making daily instructional decisions. We will see that assessment is critically important to the success of an inclusion model and that it requires collaboration to make it work well. We will learn some basic principles of assessment and see practical ways to implement effective assessment practices. We will also learn to link assessment to curricular and instructional planning.

Ms. Ryan is an elementary special education teacher working in an inclusive school. She has been working collaboratively with the classroom teachers in this school for two years along with one other special education teacher. As an inclusion specialist, she finds it easier than in previous years as a resource teacher to relate the four steps of the assessment process (developing an evaluation plan, administering and interpreting measures and procedures, integrating information and making recommendations, and monitoring performance) to the general education curriculum and the classroom setting. Following are three scenarios in which Ms. Ryan engages in assessment. Though in each scenario Ms. Ryan is conducting or assisting with assessment, each illustrates a different type and purpose of assessment. We will see that these are three typical uses of assessment in an inclusive school, but they are not the only ways that teachers conduct assessment. Though Ms. Ryan is an elementary teacher, we will see later in this chapter that these types of assessment also apply to secondary settings.

The classroom teachers in her school frequently seek Ms. Ryan out as a consultant when they are experiencing difficulty with individual students. She has been a special education teacher for seven years. Today, she is visiting Mr. Rodriguez's fourth-grade class at his request. He has asked her opinion about Sam, a boy in his class. Sam has had consistent difficulty in several subjects for the first two months of school. He does fine in math, but struggles with language arts, social studies, and science—all subjects that require a great deal of reading and written assignments. At first Mr. Rodriguez thought Sam was being lazy or inattentive. He spoke with Sam's parents several times and has learned that Sam spends a great deal of time with his homework and that his parents help him consistently. Mr. Rodriguez suspects that Sam may have a learning disability that hinders his ability to be successful with written work. Though Mr. Rodriguez has worked with the student study team to develop specific interventions for Sam, he hopes that Ms. Ryan might provide some insight into Sam's problems and help him collect some useful information to take back to the student study team.

Ms. Ryan is not a stranger to this classroom. She has four students with identified disabilities included in this class. She comes in daily to co-teach, provide in-class support, and to consult with Mr. Rodriguez. She often works with groups of students or with individuals on class assignments. Therefore, she has already noticed Sam's struggles, and he does not find it unusual that she sits down beside him and offers some assistance with the social studies assignment he is working on. Ms. Ryan appraises Sam's situation. He has completed two of six end-of-chapter questions. His handwriting is awkward and labored. His two responses are minimal and lack the level of detail that Mr. Rodriguez expects. One response is an incomplete sentence and she casually points it out to Sam. He seems unsure as to how to fix it. Ms. Ryan makes a mental note to further investigate his written work in his class portfolio. He may be having difficulty with spelling and mechanics in written expression. She continues her seemingly casual observation.

Ms. Ryan suggests that she help him with the next question to create an opportunity to observe his reading. He reads the question aloud and she directs him to show her where in the chapter the answer can be found. She notices that he reads the question easily and that it is a rather straightforward and simply worded question. Sam seems to struggle with the text organization and does not use the headings to direct him to the right information, possibly indicating difficulties with text structure. Ms. Ryan points out a section and asks him to read aloud. At once, Sam becomes agitated and looks down at his desk. With his head drooping, he reads haltingly and almost inaudibly. Ms. Ryan quickly puts him at ease by redirecting the task to look at a chart with some pertinent information, but she knows she has discovered Sam's "hidden" reading problem. She is not sure how significant Sam's difficulties are, but she now has enough information to guide her and Mr. Rodriguez to a more formal process of assessment. When she finishes with Sam, she goes away and makes notes in the notebook she carries with her, in a section labeled, "Consultation." Figure 3.1 shows a blank page from her Consultation Log.

Consultation Log

Date   Time

Teacher   Student

Purpose of consultation:

Observation/Information Gathered:

Action Needed:

FIGURE 3.1 Consultation Log

Ms. Ryan notes several important pieces of information from her observation of Sam. First, she writes that Sam was on task and trying to complete the assignment. Under a heading of "writing," she notes his awkward handwriting, incomplete sentences, and lack of strategies for revising his response. She writes, "possible problems with mechanics and spelling." Then she makes a "Reading" heading and writes, "may have significant reading problems" and puts a big asterisk next to it. She also notes his difficulty with text structure and strategic reading. She makes a mental note to suggest that she and Mr. Rodriguez examine his portfolio of reading and writing work and that they plan to conduct a more complete assessment of his reading and writing skills. She is sure that Sam needs some intensive and individualized help with his skills, and he may need to be considered for special education services. She leaves a note for Mr. Rodriguez briefly stating what she found and suggests that they meet later in the day to discuss Sam.

Here, we see Ms. Ryan engaged in assessment *for the purpose of identifying specific learning problems.* Ms. Ryan is acting as a consultant for a classroom teacher who may not have the time or expertise to investigate Sam's problems on his own. Her assessment is informal and does not go into depth in this scenario. Her main purpose was to confirm Mr. Rodriguez's hunch that Sam needs special help. She will likely be involved at some later time in collecting more specific and detailed assessment data to assist in identifying Sam's specific needs. One advantage of teaching in an inclusive classroom is that the special education teacher can conduct informal assessment in a much more comprehensive and reliable manner by being present in the classroom on an ongoing basis. Ms. Ryan will be able to observe Sam and investigate his difficulties over a span of time. The opportunity to get to know him and his work habits enhances her ability to understand his learning difficulties. An added advantage is that she can begin to give Sam the help he needs with reading and writing on an informal basis, through consultation with Mr. Rodriguez as well as direct instruction with Sam, whether or not he is eventually identified as having learning disabilities.

Progress monitoring Continuous evaluation of students' performances to determine the extent to which curricular modifications or extra assistance are needed.

Ms. Ryan also provides ongoing **progress monitoring** of the instruction in general education classrooms and evaluates her students' performances to determine the extent to which curricular modifications or extra assistance are needed. Given that her students usually complete the same assignments as their nondisabled classmates, this has become much more important in the inclusion model in comparison with the resource model when assignments had been unrelated to the general education curriculum. She explains that in previous years she had "taught that little class (her special education students) as a whole, but it wasn't really what the teacher (general education) was doing."

Ms. Ryan co-teaches in Ms. Crawford's fourth-grade class during language arts time. Today Ms. Crawford is explaining an assignment after reading aloud a chapter of a literature book. The students have their own copies of the literature book to use as a reference. The assignment is to write each vocabulary word written on the board, draw an illustration of the word, and write a sentence demonstrating its meaning. The students are using the class dictionaries and will complete any work they do not finish in class for homework. They will also write an entry in their reading journals for homework. Ms. Ryan observes Marcel and Tomika, two students on her special education roster, during the reading time and makes some notes in her consultation log regarding Marcel's improved attention. He has refrained from talking aloud during reading, one of his goals. When the students begin their seatwork, she implements adaptations for both students. They will both do only half of the words, and she and the teacher have prearranged which words are most critical. They will do journal entries later with Ms. Ryan's assistance. She quietly explains the modifications to Marcel and Tomika and directs them to begin with the assignment, reminding them that they should spell the vocabulary words correctly since they are copying them, but they need not worry about spelling all the words right in their sentences; the important thing is getting their ideas down. Ms. Ryan wants to see how much they can do on their own. As she roams around providing assistance to several students, she watches Marcel and Tomika as they begin the task. She notices that Marcel begins to talk out and disturb others and she goes to him and taps his shoulder as a silent reminder. She makes a note of it in her log. Tomika begins with the first vocabulary word and, after puzzling over it, asks a classmate to read it for her. Ms. Ryan notes that Tomika is using the peer assistance strategy that she has worked out with the teacher and makes a note in her log about this as well. Later, when she works individually with them, she will praise Marcel for his improvement in paying attention while the teacher read the story and gave instructions. She will tell him that she noticed that he worked well after she reminded him to quiet down. She will also show Marcel the tally mark she made on his goal sheet, a chart that she keeps in her notebook to keep track of classroom behavioral goals, for the reminder that she gave him. She will praise Tomika for using the peer assistance strategy and for asking for help from her classmate only when she needed it. Tomika has a tendency to be overreliant on help. Ms. Ryan has been recording progress toward behavioral goals for these two students for several weeks. Later, when she and Ms. Crawford meet to co-plan, she will share her recorded information so that Ms. Crawford can see the students' improvement in the past few weeks.

This is an example of assessment *for the purpose of ongoing monitoring of progress toward behavioral goals*. Ms. Ryan gathered the assessment data through her observation of Marcel and Tomika. She recorded the data on record sheets that she had prepared for monitoring and tracking classroom behavior. Almost all of the students on her roster have at least one behavioral goal that they have mutually selected in a meeting with their classroom teachers. During her hour-long visit to Ms. Crawford's classroom, Ms. Ryan records the students' behavioral progress. As an inclusion specialist, it is much easier to administer behavioral assessment techniques (e.g., behavior rating scales or observations) than it was when she was a resource teacher because she is now a regular member of the classroom and can observe students in a nonobtrusive manner. Both Marcel and Tomika also have desk charts on which they *self-record* while she is out of the room. Ms. Crawford gives Ms. Ryan updates on the students' progress, but Ms. Ryan primarily relies on Marcel and Tomika to do their own self-monitoring. Ms. Crawford is very happy with this arrangement because she is very busy directing the whole class and would have found this type of behavioral monitoring burdensome. She is aware of their goals and reinforces their good behaviors as much as possible, but the students have been empowered to be their own monitors.

After school, Ms. Ryan goes over the math papers completed by three students in Ms. Mako's third-grade class. They are working on two-digit by one-digit multiplication with regrouping. Ms. Ryan collects classwork completed while she is not in the classroom to analyze her students' performance and to detect any areas where students may need additional support. Ms. Mako has made a few notes for Ms. Ryan and attached them to the papers. She writes that Megan is really struggling with this skill and that it may be that she has not mastered the multiplication facts. She also writes that Kevin did great today with paying attention and Michael had no problems. Ms. Ryan examines the students' papers. Megan appeared to have the process but did not complete the assignment and made simple calculation errors that confirmed Ms. Mako's guess that she does not know all the multiplication facts. Kevin got only 75 percent correct. His errors indicated that he did not have a complete grasp of the regrouping concept. He consistently forgot to write in the regrouped tens. Michael's paper was excellent—95 percent correct. However, his paper was sloppy and disorganized, and it was a challenge to find his answers. Ms. Ryan thought that Ms. Mako was quite patient to try to decipher his paper. Ms. Ryan pulls out her consultation log and writes different notes under each student's name to indicate what types of followup instruction she will need to plan. For Megan, she will arrange daily flashcard study and will send a note home requesting home practice. For Kevin, she will work with him individually tomorrow and arrange for a peer tutor. She makes a note on his behavioral chart about his improvement in paying attention. She will verbally praise him tomorrow and include it in his weekly progress chart sent home on Fridays. For Michael, she will, of course, praise his excellent math work, but will also spend some time with him showing him how to write his math papers in a more organized fashion.

Here we see Ms. Ryan engaging in a type of assessment called *error analysis,* or *assessment for the purpose of guiding instruction.* She is analyzing the students' work to detect specific types of errors in the mathematical processes. She is using this information to plan followup instruction for these students. Through collaboration with Ms. Mako, she is getting even more information. In their co-planning meetings, Ms. Mako and Ms. Ryan have opportunities to discuss the specific needs of these students. The notes that Ms. Mako wrote provided further information for Ms. Ryan's analysis. This process allows Ms. Ryan to be involved in and aware of her students' instruction even when she is not physically present in their classroom. Because of her error analysis on this day, her instruction with these students will be more meaningfully focused the next day. She will work individually with and for each student in the manner that is most appropriate. Much more collaborative evaluation takes place in the inclusion model than in the resource room model. Because instruction takes place in the general education setting it is important that the assessment, instruction, and curriculum needs of the students be familiar to both teachers.

Each of these examples shows Ms. Ryan engaged in assessment, but each is for a different purpose. Think about the types of information Ms. Ryan collected in each situation and how that information was used. In the first two instances, Ms. Ryan was conducting assessment while performing her usual instructional activities of co-teaching, implementing adaptations, and providing direct assistance to students. In the third case, Ms. Ryan was analyzing work samples outside of her instructional time. In each case, the information would be used to make educational decisions. For Sam, the information will assist Mr. Rodriguez and the student study team to make sound decisions about the type of services Sam needs. For the other students, this assessment was part of the daily instructional routine.

As when she was a resource teacher, Ms. Ryan continues to administer the Woodcock Johnson Achievement Tests-III (WJ-III; Woodcock, McGrew, & Mather, 2001) to her students annually to measure overall progress and to assist in writing new or updated Individualized Educational Plans (IEPs). As an inclusion teacher, however, she feels she is more in tune with the classroom assessment procedures used by the general education teacher than she had been previously (e.g., spelling tests, math tests, or a schoolwide, competency-based assessment of basic skills) and is better able to develop criterion-referenced tests that match the general education curriculum. Thus, her evaluations of student progress (other than the WJ-III) are more closely aligned with the curriculum covered in the general education classroom than in those years when she was in the role of a resource room teacher.

ASSESSMENT AS PART OF THE INSTRUCTIONAL PROCESS

Assessment as a Process

Assessment is an integral part of the instructional process. We can think of the instructional process as cyclical. We assess, plan, teach, then assess for mastery of what was taught. Based on these assessment results, we go through the process again, either reteaching the same content or moving on to the next logical topic or skill. Figure 3.2 shows how this process works. Teachers must gather information to plan what, how, and when to teach. Teachers who are creative, observant, and thorough are able to implement assessment practices fluidly as part of the instructional routine. This is true for both general and special education teachers in inclusive and traditional settings. However, the types of assessment activities may differ for these two types of teachers and in these two kinds of settings. General education teachers are primarily concerned with planning for the class as a whole, though may do some individualized instruction, and will more often conduct assessments that give them information about the class's performance and progress. Classroom teachers are also concerned with individual progress and will examine assessment results to identify students who are having particular problems. Special education teachers are primarily concerned with the needs of individual students and will conduct assessments that give them the necessary information to analyze individual students' instructional needs. Special educators are also concerned about how their students do in the context of the class as a whole, and, therefore, are interested in whole-class results. In an inclusive setting, general and special educators readily share their assessment information with each other, or use the same information for different purposes. In inclusive classrooms, instructional decisions are often collaborative decisions, based on shared assessment data.

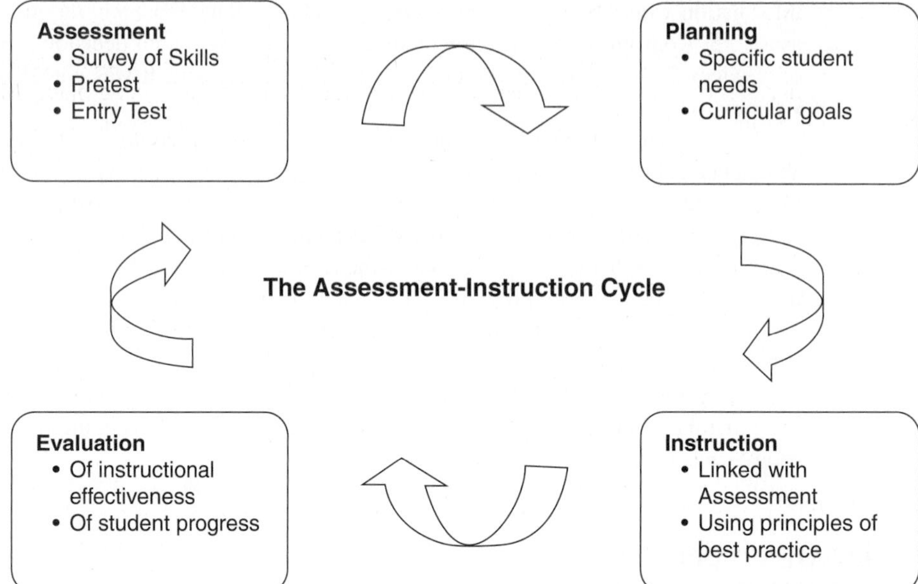

FIGURE 3.2

Assessment as a Decision-Making Tool

Assessment is meaningful when it is used to make informed decisions. Overton (1996) describes assessment as an ongoing process, with teachers continuously gathering information about students and their learning. According to Salvia and Ysseldyke (1998), assessment is "the process of collecting data for the purposes of making decisions about individuals and groups, and this decision-making role is why it touches people's lives" (p. 5). The types of assessment materials and activities used should be determined by the *purpose* of the assessment. If we know what type of decision we need to make, we can decide what process to follow, and what types of materials or activities will be appropriate. When we talk about assessment, we should always speak about *"assessment for the purpose of. . . .* " Later in this chapter, we will discuss several purposes of assessment and specific methods that will optimize our information gathering.

In general terms, the word *assessment* means evaluation. In educational terms, it implies that someone is making a judgment or conducting an evaluation. In classroom-based assessment, the judgment or evaluation is usually done by the teacher. This evaluation could have a dual purpose—to evaluate student progress or performance and to evaluate instructional effectiveness. Though a test may be used as an assessment tool, assessment does not necessarily mean using a test. Teachers use all sorts of information to evaluate students' performance or progress. Direct observation, analysis of students' daily work, and teacher-designed tasks or projects might be used for assessment.

Assessment as a Starting Place

Beginning teachers often find themselves overwhelmed by curricular demands and wonder "Where do I begin to teach?" Assessment provides that starting place. Much of what we teach comes from a set curriculum, often called the "core curriculum," which is usually represented by state or district guidelines or frameworks or by national standards. For example, the National Council of Teachers of Mathematics (NCTM) has issued standards demonstrating a progression of mathematics concepts and skills. Many states or districts have adopted these standards in their own curriculum guides. Teachers wondering where to start can, of course, begin at the beginning of those standards specified for a particular grade level. But, what if the class, or even just a few of the students, has already mastered some of the concepts? Should they relearn them, just to stay in step with the rest of the class? What if one or a few students have not mastered important prerequisite skills of the grade-level curriculum? The special education teacher is concerned with how his or her students fit with the rest of the class with regard to their prerequisite skills. Conducting assessment can assist teachers in determining what to teach. Assessment not only tells teachers in this situation where to begin to teach and what to teach, but also, perhaps, how to group students for instruction or how to individualize instruction within a classroom.

Types of Tests

We describe various assessment procedures throughout this book. For example, in Chapter 5 we describe different reading tests and surveys, in Chapter 7 we present procedures for evaluating students' mathematical abilities, and in the Chapter 4 we discuss methods for assessing behavioral and social skills. In this chapter we provide an overview of different types of assessment instruments and procedures (see Table 3.1).

Norm-Referenced Tests. Standardized, norm-referenced tests are used to assess students' general progress in reading, math, and the content areas; to assess intelligence (i.e., potential for learning); for diagnostic purposes; and as accountability measures (i.e., to evaluate instructional programs, curriculum models, and school and teacher performance). Students' scores are compared with those of a normative sample of students, yielding a standard score that can be compared with other standard scores. These comparisons are used for multiple purposes:

1. To determine eligibility for special education by comparing an individual student's achievement (e.g., in reading) with his or her potential, as assessed by an intelligence test.
2. To assess an individual student's progress by comparing his or her score on an achievement test with his or her score on an equivalent version of the same test, administered at an earlier date.
3. To evaluate how students in one program or setting (e.g., inclusion) are achieving in comparison with students in another setting (e.g., pull-out programs).
4. To assess a student's skills in a specific academic area in greater depth by providing a profile of relative strengths and weaknesses.

TABLE 3.1 Types of Tests

TYPE	DESCRIPTION
Norm-referenced	Published tests administered under standardized conditions (e.g., with computerized answer sheets, timed). Students' scores are compared with those of a normative sample of students.
Criterion-referenced	Students' test scores are compared with pre-determined criterion levels that indicate mastery of the subject matter.
Curriculum-based assessment	Tests are based on actual curriculum materials used in the classroom.
Curriculum-based measurement	Students take frequent, brief tests. Scores are monitored over time to assess progress.
Authentic performance-based	Students perform various real-world tasks, permitting the evaluator to assess their skill level.
Portfolio assessment	Students and teachers select representative work products that they compile into a portfolio.
Observation	Teachers observe students' behaviors and academic functioning, using anecdotal records, scales, or checklists.

Norm-referenced tests are not linked to the curriculum or criterion levels that would indicate mastery of skills or subject matter, and therefore are limited in their usefulness for instructional planning.

Norm-referenced achievement tests provide useful information regarding a student's general academic functioning. When all subtests are used, they provide a thorough overview of a child's strengths and weaknesses. A commonly used battery of achievement tests is the Woodcock Johnson Achievement Tests–III (WJ-III; Woodcock, McGrew, & Mather, 2001). Ms. Ryan administers the WJ to her students once a year to determine how much progress they have made over the previous year. She assesses students using the subtests of Letter Word Identification, Passage Comprehension, Word Attack, Calculation, and Applied Problems (electing not to administer various other subtests, such as Dictation, Writing Samples, Science, Social Studies, and Humanities). The test's standardized scores enable her to estimate how many months growth students have made. She shares this information with parents and general education teachers during each student's annual review. The WJ Achievement Test is also available in a Spanish version, the Batería Woodcock-Muñoz–Revisada: Pruebas de Aprovechamiento (Woodcock, Muñoz, & Sandoval, 1996). Other widely used achievement tests include the Wechsler Individual Achievement Test–2 (WIAT-2; Wechsler, 1999), the Peabody Individual Achievement Test-Revised (PIAT-R; Markwardt, 1989), the Kaufman Test of Educational Achievement (K-TEA; Kaufman & Kaufman, 1997), and the Wide Range Achievement Test-Revision 3 (WRAT-3; Wilkinson,

1993). All of these tests have been described as useful by teachers of students with learning disabilities and behavioral disorders (Overton, 1996, 2003; Pierangelo & Giuliani, 2002).

Diagnostic tests assess students' mastery of specific skills. Like achievement tests, they are useful for determining eligibility for special education and for reevaluation during annual reviews. However, they are more helpful for diagnostic purposes because they provide a detailed profile of a student's performance in a particular subject area. One such diagnostic test is the Woodcock Diagnostic Reading Battery (WDRB; Woodcock, 1997). This test is used to determine an individual's abilities and achievement in five areas of functioning: basic reading skills, reading comprehension, phonological awareness, oral language comprehension, and reading aptitude. Another popular test, the Key Math Diagnostic Test-Revised (Connolly, Nachtman, & Pritchett, 1997), assesses mathematics skills with fourteen subtests in three categories: Basic Concepts, Operations, and Applications. Other diagnostic tests include the Learning Disabilities Diagnostic Inventory (LDDI; Hammill & Bryant, 1998), the Test of Phonological Awareness (TOPA; Torgesen & Bryant, 1994), the Test of Written Language-3 (TOWL-3; Hammill & Larsen, 1996), and the Test of Mathematical Abilities-2 (TOMA-2; Brown, Cronin, & McEntire, 1994).

Criterion-Referenced Tests (CRTs). CRTs measure the extent to which students have mastered a skill based on a preestablished criterion. Unlike standardized tests that compare a student's performance to that of other students, CRTs assess how well a student is making progress toward mastery of specific skills or subject matter. Commercial CRTs are available, or teachers can design their own. One well-known commercial CRT is the Brigance Diagnostic Inventory of Basic Skills-Revised (Brigance, 1999). The Brigance includes a wide range of subtests in different areas, such as reading, math, and spelling. Different inventories are available for younger and older students, from preschool through secondary levels, such as the Brigance Diagnostic Employability Skills Inventory (Brigance, 1995), the Brigance Diagnostic Life Skills Inventory (Brigance, 1994), the Brigance Inventory of Essential Skills (Brigance, 1981), the Brigance Diagnostic Inventory of Early Development-Revised (Brigance, 1991), the Brigance Early Preschool Screen (Age 2–2 1/2) (Brigance, 1990), the Brigance K & 1 Screen-Revised (Brigance, 1992), and the Brigance Preschool Screen (Age 3–4) (Brigance, 1985). A Spanish version of the Brigance Diagnostic Inventory of Basic Skills is also available (Brigance, 1999).

Other CRTs focus on a single subject area, such as various Informal Reading Inventories (IRIs). IRIs generally consist of two main sections, word recognition and passage comprehension. These assessment tools are constructed based on scope and sequence charts in a particular subject area so that the skills they evaluate progress from the easiest to the most difficult. Because of this, CRTs are ideally suited for the purposes of (a) determining the goals and objectives for students IEPs, and (b) evaluating students' progress towards achieving those goals. They are typically given as benchmarks to evaluate progress (e.g., once each grading period), but not more often than that. This is the case with Ms. Ryan and her students. Other assessment approaches are more closely tied to the curriculum and thus are preferable for the day to day monitoring of progress and instructional decision making (e.g., authentic performance-based assessment, curriculum-based assessment, portfolio assessment, and observations).

We recommend the following steps when using a CRT as part of the assessment process:

1. Select the test. Co-teachers in an inclusion classroom might wish to collaboratively select which CRI to use to assess students' progress, or this might be the domain of the inclusion specialist. The classroom teacher can tell from looking at a CRI how well it matches the curriculum and the scope and sequence of skills at that grade level, whereas the inclusion specialist is most likely to know which test would be appropriate for any given student with special needs.
2. Decide on the expected level of mastery. Again, this process can be collaborative. The inclusion specialist is most familiar with the goals and objectives written on the student's IEP (or, in the case of an initial evaluation, with what might be realistic goals and objectives), while the classroom teacher is often the most knowledgeable about grade-level expectations and the minimum student performance standards established by the school district or state.
3. Administer the test. The inclusion specialist most often conducts the actual assessment. Unlike with a standardized test, the directions for administering a CRT do not need to be followed exactly. For example, a student with a short attention span can be allowed frequent breaks.
4. Decide on appropriate instructional goals. This process is best done collaboratively, based on the student's performance on the test as well as expected levels of mastery. Realistic goals are those for which the student already has some skills. For example, if a student answers 5 out of 10 reading comprehension questions correctly, a realistic goal might be for him to answer at least 9 out of 10 questions correctly.
5. Determine short-term objectives. The inclusion specialist has the primary responsibility for this step, but may wish to consult with the classroom teacher regarding acceptable levels of performance. In the case of the student who answered 5 out of 10 comprehension questions correctly, it would be useful at this point to look more closely at the types of questions the student missed. Were all or most of the missed questions of a certain type (e.g., "think-and-search" questions rather than "right-there" questions)? If so, an appropriate short-term objective might be to answer at least 3 out of 5 "think-and-search" questions correctly. Knowledge of how to conduct a task analysis facilitates the process of establishing short-term objectives. Other assessment procedures (e.g., curriculum-based assessment) also provide valuable information.
6. Develop an instructional plan. This step requires knowledge of the student's needs as well as an understanding of the general education curriculum, and thus is best done collaboratively by the inclusion specialist and the classroom teacher. Continuing with the same example, the instructional plan for the student who needs to improve in reading comprehension would include lessons in how to answer "think-and-search" questions. By determining the types of questions or problems that are challenging for a student, the teacher is in a better position to plan appropriate instruction that builds on what the student already knows or can do and provides scaffolded support to help him achieve at a higher level.

Because this entire assessment process has been conducted collaboratively, it is more closely aligned with the general education curriculum than if the special education teacher was operating in isolation. The goals, short-term objectives, and instructional plan developed for this student are appropriate for the student's developmental needs and also consistent with what is required to be successful in the general education classroom.

Curriculum-Based Assessment (CBA). CBA refers to a category of assessment procedures that are based on three essential principles: Test items must be taken from the curriculum, repeated evaluations occur across time, and assessment results are used to formulate instructional plans (King-Sears, 1994). Also, assessment information is recorded on graphs, providing students and their teachers with a visual representation of student progress. These visual displays enhance students' motivation, increase their involvement in the learning process, and facilitate communication with parents and other professionals. The primary purpose of CBA is to systematically assess students' progress toward instructional goals and objectives. Overton (2003) describes CBA as "the very best measure of how much a student has mastered in the curriculum" (p. 299). Ms. Ryan's students include their graphs in their portfolios and enjoy keeping track of their improvement.

CBA has additional purposes. Idol (1989) asserts that it is essential for inclusion specialists to be skilled in conducting curriculum-based assessment procedures as a way to identify learning problems and monitor the effectiveness of instructional interventions, as well as to assess overall progress. Ms. Ryan and the teachers with whom she works find CBA useful for identifying students who may be struggling. By looking at their class profiles, they can quickly see which students are not improving. Whereas the trend lines of most students slant upward, the lines of these students are relatively flat. Also, regular use of CBA for instructional planning can lead to increased learning outcomes because teachers are making better informed decisions (Fuchs, Fuchs, & Hamlett, 1989; Fuchs, Fuchs, Hamlett, & Stecker, 1991). In addition, Ortiz and Wilkinson (1991) recommend CBA as a way to assess the performance of students who are English language learners, in both English and their native language, as an alternative way to determine if students qualify for special education services.

Various forms of curriculum-based assessment have evolved over the years. One of these, curriculum-based measurement, is described in more detail in the next section. Another, precision teaching, is described in Chapter 4 of this book.

Curriculum-Based Measurement (CBM). CBM is a type of CBA that includes a set of standard, simple, short-duration fluency measures of basic skills in reading, spelling, written expression, and mathematics computation (Deno, 1987, 1992; Fuchs & Deno, 1992; Fuchs, Fuchs, Hamlett, Philips, & Bentz, 1994; Marston & Magnusson, 1985). CBM was designed as a formative evaluation tool to monitor students' growth or progress, enabling the teacher to make informed decisions about instructional procedures. Student progress is plotted on equal interval graphs (either manually or with a computerized version of CBM) and presented as individual or class "Skills Profiles" (Fuchs et al., 1994). An equal interval graph is a linear graph in which the distance between lines (e.g., 5 and 10, and 10 and 15) is the same. While numeric data is useful, displaying the data in the form of a graph is easier to interpret and communicate between teachers, parents, students and others (Deno, 1992).

CBM includes the following core testing strategies (adapted from Shinn & Bamonto, 1998):

1. *Reading:* Two procedures have been validated as part of CBM. With one procedure, students read aloud from a basal reader for 1 minute and the teacher keeps track of the number of words read correctly. With the other procedure, students complete a maze reading activity (multiple choice cloze task). The scorer keeps track of the correct number of word choices.
2. *Spelling:* Students write words that are dictated at specified intervals (either 5, 7, or 10 seconds) for 2 minutes. The scorer counts the number of correct letter sequences and words spelled correctly.
3. *Written Expression:* Students write a story for 3 minutes after they are given a story starter (e.g., "Pretend you are playing on the playground and a spaceship lands. A little green person comes out and calls your name . . ."). The scorer counts the number of words written, spelled correctly, and/or correct word sequences.
4. *Mathematics Computation:* Students write answers to computational problems in a set 2- or 3-minute time period. The scorer counts the number of correct digits written.

Performance monitoring charts Charts that depict changes in student performance over time on a single and constant task, allowing for comparison of scores over an extended period of time.

Construction of the graph is relatively straightforward (see Figure 3.3). Student performance typically appears along the vertical axis and time appears along the horizontal axis. The scale displayed on the vertical axis is divided into equal units reflecting a minimum (usually zero) to a maximum level (usually equal to a level slightly above that which has been set as the student's goal) of performance. The choice of units on the horizontal axis typically represents successive days of the school year. Performance is plotted on the graph by placing a mark at the intersection of level of performance and day of the week. It is possible to display two types of scores on the same day, representing correct and incorrect performance. A line is drawn to connect the data values; however, where there is no data as the result of an unplanned absence, the data is not connected. When program changes are made, a vertical line is drawn on the day of change (Tindal, 1990). An alternative is a bar graph on which students would color in their score.

Mastery monitoring charts Charts that depict student mastery of a unit in the curriculum over time. The vertical axis reflects the sequence of objectives of the curriculum, ranging from the earliest unit at the bottom to the highest unit at the top.

Various types of charting options are available. Tindal and Marston (1990) details two types of charts that can be used as illustrated by Figure 3.3. **Performance monitoring charts** depict changes in student performance over time on a single and constant task allowing for comparison of scores over an extended period of time. Advantages for using this method include: (1) The measurement level is always the same, (2) graphs are easily interpreted, (3) charts are easy to organize, and (4) direct comparison to peers is possible. **Mastery monitoring charts** depict student mastery of a unit in the curriculum over time. Rather than depicting student performance levels, the vertical axis reflects the sequence of objectives of the curriculum, ranging from the earliest unit at the bottom to the highest unit at the top. The horizontal axis remains the same as in performance measurement. Mastery monitoring charts have the following advantages: (1) The charting system corresponds closely to traditional instruction models comprising

Line Graph (could be done by computer or by hand)

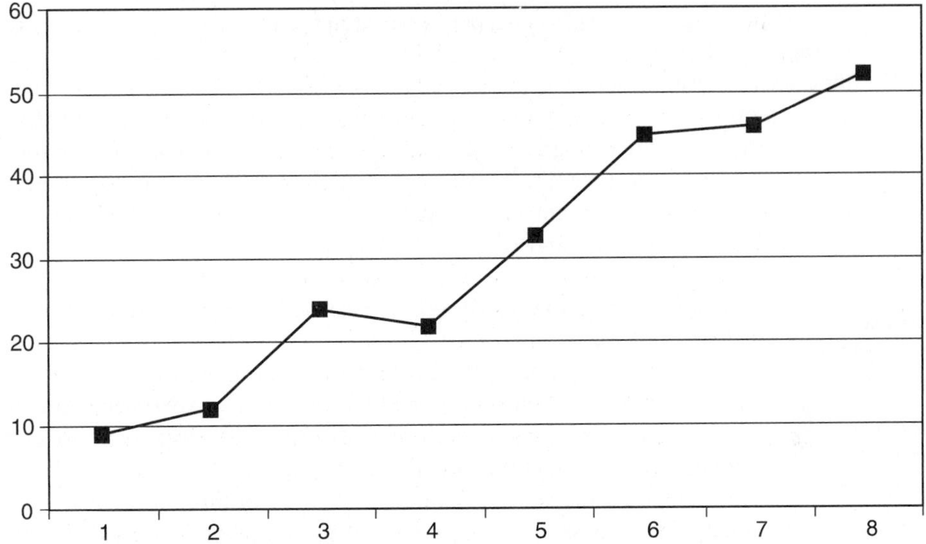

Bar Graph (students could color bars in by hand)

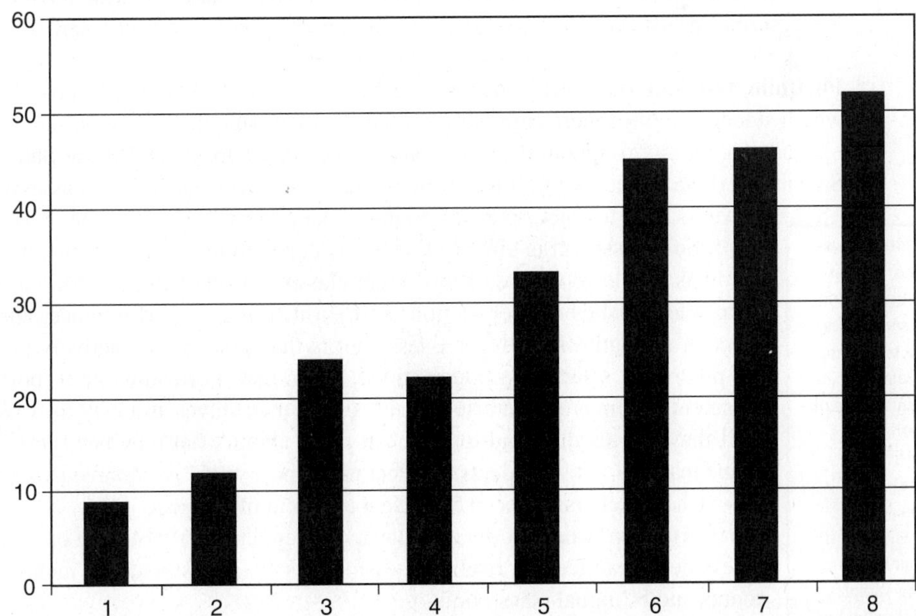

FIGURE 3.3 Carlos's Performance Monitoring Chart for Timed Multiplication Facts Test over Six Weeks

a hierarchy of skills; (2) a close link exists between instruction and measurement; and (3) more information is provided on "what" to teach (Tindal & Marston, 1990).

According to Deno (1992), a performance graph provides several levels of interpretation. First, it provides a reference as to how the student is currently performing. Second, the student's level of performance may be viewed relative to his or her goal. Third, it provides information pertaining to the instructional relevance of a program. Changes in growth before and after program adjustment are easily ascertained, allowing for a formative evaluation of the program. Finally, norm referencing is also possible. Peer performance data enables judgment to be made about the degrees of difference between an individual's performance and that of same-age peers.

Performance-based assessment Providing students with opportunities to demonstrate their mastery of a skill or concept through performance of a task.

Authentic Performance-Based Assessment. The purpose of authentic **performance-based assessment** is to provide students with opportunities to demonstrate their mastery of the curriculum in meaningful ways. A variety of activities are possible, such as designing and performing experiments, conducting investigations, giving presentations and performances, responding to simulations, solving mathematical problems, and developing written or other products (Salend, 2000). Often these are hands-on tasks. Strengths of this approach are that (a) it is directly tied to classroom instruction, (b) it is based on real-life activities, (c) students can use multiple modalities to show mastery, and (d) students can demonstrate mastery in their native language. Authentic performance-based assessments should be embedded at key points during an instructional unit rather than only at the end of the unit, providing teachers with a more systematic and precise understanding of students' progress so that this information can be used when making instructional decisions. We describe specific authentic assessment procedures in the various chapters of this book.

Portfolio Assessment. Portfolio assessment is an ongoing, collaborative process through which students and teachers compile information about students' progress across a range of academic areas throughout the school year (Flood & Lapp, 1989; Pike & Salend, 1995; Salend, 2000; Valencia, 1990). It is a form of authentic performance-based assessment that is well suited for inclusive classrooms. Like other forms of authentic assessment, portfolio assessment is directly tied to the curriculum. Because portfolios contain products that have resulted from actual classroom activities, portfolio assessment clearly establishes the connection between instruction, performance, and assessment. A strength of portfolio assessment is that students are actively involved in the process of selecting products to include in their portfolios. Thus, portfolio assessment becomes an exercise students do for themselves as a way to evaluate how well they are learning and to establish goals about what they need to learn next. Some teachers allow students to select their "best work" to archive in their portfolios. Other teachers prefer to compile a portfolio of "typical" work. Whichever approach is taken, work should be collected at regular intervals. Like other authentic assessment practices, portfolio assessment is ideally suited for inclusive classrooms and bilingual classrooms.

Portfolio assessment A process of collecting student work samples or products that are representative of the student's skills and ability. Portfolios are often used to demonstrate progress over time, such as keeping writing samples throughout an entire school year.

Portfolio assessment is widely used for a variety of subject areas or skills. A student's writing portfolio might include representative writing samples, conference notes, observation records, checklists of skills mastere evaluation checklists (Poteet, Choate, & Stewart, 1996). A reading a reading log, audiocassette tapes of oral reading, a list of books read, jects, assessment checklists, and self-assessments. Portfolios can be IEPs by including work products that indicate progress toward IEP obj writing samples of increasing length and complexity (Swicegood, 1994). Por ment can also be used to track changes in behavioral and social skills. Wesson (1996) documented how a teacher used a portfolio to chronicle the progress of grade boy with a serious behavior disorder. The boy's behavior portfolio included v tapes of his performance during cooperative learning activities, a description of outside-of-school social activities, and a list of narrative observations by the teacher.

Observation. Observations can take various forms, from anecdotal records written in narrative form to checklists and observation scales. Ongoing observation is imperative for monitoring students' progress and making instructional decisions. Inclusion classrooms provide an ideal setting for conducting classroom observations because one teacher can observe students while the other is teaching. Some teachers' observations are informal and others are more structured, such as when completing a checklist for a reading evaluation or a scale designed to indicate social competence. Many of the teachers described in this book record their observations in logs or journals that they carry around with them, keeping anecdotal records of student behaviors. When teachers observe students using specific skills repeatedly over time they check off the skills on a checklist or record sheet and date it to indicated mastery. "Miscue analysis" (Goodman, 1973) is a form of observation that involves watching children while they read, recording their miscues, and making inferences about their reading skills. This procedure is discussed further in the literacy chapter. Many checklists and scales can provide insights into students' social or behavioral development, such as the Social Skills Rating System (Gresham & Elliott, 1990), described in Chapter 5.

Self-Evaluation. Self-evaluation interviews and surveys provide data regarding students' perceptions of their learning needs. Students can evaluate their progress in reading, math, other content areas, and behavioral and social skills, and then set their own goals. This should be done at regular intervals, such as at the beginning of each grading period. Students can also keep track of learning using learning logs in which they record on a daily basis what they have learned, what they do not understand, and what help they need (Atwell, 1987). These are described more fully in Chapter 9.

Modifying Classroom Tests

Many classroom teachers report that they are supportive of testing modifications for students with special needs, although they often find such adaptations to be more desirable than feasible (Gajria, Salend, & Hemrick, 1994; Jayanthi, Epstein, Polloway, & Bursuck, 1996; Schumm & Vaughn, 1991). The inclusion specialist can provide critical support by assisting with the development of user-friendly tests and by helping with accommodations. Tests that are poorly written can adversely affect the performance of all students, not only

gh multiple choice, true-false, matching, and sentence com-
e and are considered more objective than short-answer or
de students with enough of an opportunity to demonstrate
format can be confusing. It is important to write test items
rly with true-false questions, double negatives should be
ns should not include confusing options such as "all of the
ortant to make sure directions are explicit and unambigu-
le.

o plays a significant role in planning for and implement-
ving modifications (adapted from Gajria et al., 1994;
n improve students' ability to demonstrate what they ac-

- Space items on tests sufficiently to reduce interference.
- Provide space on the test for students to respond, rather than on a separate answer sheet.
- Provide items in a predictable hierarchy.
- Administer more tests with fewer items, rather than fewer, longer tests.
- When not testing reading, adjust the reading level of the items or provide assistance with reading when needed.
- Define unfamiliar or abstract words, if their meanings are not being tested.
- Provide models as examples of correctly answered items.
- Change the test setting (e.g., provide a quiet place, away from distractions).
- Allow more time for test completion.
- Allow students to dictate responses.
- Reduce the number of choices on multiply choice tests.

Ms. Ryan helped her students take classroom tests in various ways, depending upon the skills that were being assessed. Given that her students usually completed the same assignments as their nondisabled classmates, this was much more important in the inclusion model in comparison with the resource model when assignments had been unrelated to the general education curriculum. She provided accommodations for students such as simplifying the language on tests, shortening the number of problems on a test, or allowing students to dictate their responses to her rather than write them. Occasionally, Ms. Ryan developed alternative tests for her students, such as spelling tests that consisted of easier words.

Grading Issues

How to grade students with special needs in an inclusion classroom is an important issue with which both general and special education teachers struggle. Applying the same standards of evaluation to all students in a classroom would mean that most students with disabilities would fail. Ms. Ryan helps teachers give grades to the students with disabilities that reflect their effort and progress. She strongly feels that there must be differences between how the students with disabilities and other students are graded and that the extent to which grading procedures are adapted depends upon the needs of the child. She explains, "Whatever they have done, we kind of grade it a little bit different, depending on their skill." For example, in Ms. Mako's class, one student with disabilities is only graded on the initial sounds of the spelling words, whereas another student takes both Ms. Ryan's spelling test and the class spelling test and receives grades for both.

Ms. Ryan develops creative ways of determining grades. For instance, when she prepares alternative assignments (e.g., worksheets with comprehension questions for her students in Ms. Crawford's class), often the entire class completes these, but the grades earned only count as official grades for the students with disabilities. In other words, other students earn a grade in the grade book for answering the comprehension questions listed in the book, whereas the students with disabilities earn their grade by completing the worksheet prepared by Ms. Ryan.

Grading is more complicated in an inclusion model in comparison with a resource model in part because it involves working cooperatively with other teachers. Ms. Ryan put it this way, "Grading used to be easier because I could make decisions by myself—now I need to depend on another teacher." She has learned the importance of grades in the general education classroom and how students compare themselves with others based on the grades they get.

ASSESSMENT FOR THE PURPOSE OF IDENTIFYING STUDENTS WITH DISABILITIES

Identifying students with disabilities and determining their eligibility for special services is an important function of assessment. Assessment for this purpose is complex and governed by a set of guidelines from federal and state laws and educational policies. Formal assessments for determining eligibility for services are usually the responsibility of a professional trained to administer standardized, formal tests. This is usually a school psychologist, but sometimes the special educator conducts academic testing. It is not our intention here to provide the reader with a comprehensive guide to formal assessment for the purpose of determining eligibility. However, special educators must understand their role in this process and must have a working knowledge of the laws and guidelines, the process, and the various tools that are used.

In inclusive schools, special educators are likely to be involved in the identification process. The special educator typically spends a great deal of time in the general education classroom and also engages in consultation with classroom teachers on a regular basis. Thus, the special educator may already be familiar with the students being considered for services. The special educator serves a valuable function in assessment for identification. As in the example at the beginning of the chapter in which Ms. Ryan informally worked with Sam at Mr. Rodriguez's request, the teacher may observe a student and gather informal assessment information. She might also advise a teacher as to whether to pursue a referral. Once the decision to refer a student for a full assessment has been made, the special educator may become involved. Although in some districts achievement as well as ability testing is solely the realm of the school psychologist, in others the special educator may be the person who administers and interprets the achievement tests. When it is suspected that a child has learning disabilities, it is usually recommended that someone other than the child's classroom teacher conduct an observation in the classroom. This role may be given to the special education teacher.

Assessment Tools Used for Comprehensive Evaluations

The law requires that

> **(a)** Each public agency shall ensure that a full and individual evaluation is conducted for each child being considered for special education and related services under Part B of the Act—
>
> **(1)** To determine if the child is a "child with a disability" under §300.7; and
>
> **(2)** To determine the educational needs of the child.
>
> (P.L. 105-17 Final Regulations, Passed March 12, 1999: 34CFR Part 300 Subpart C, §300.320)

This comprehensive evaluation must be sufficient to provide multiple sources of information about the child's functioning and assess all areas of suspected disability. A comprehensive evaluation typically assesses some or all of the following areas, according to the student's individual needs: cognitive, academic, behavioral, social, emotional, motor and sensory, health, and communicative functioning. The term "diagnostic system" is sometimes used to refer to combinations of intelligence, achievement, and other tests. A comprehensive evaluation must be conducted before an initial placement. Prior to the most recent reauthorization of IDEA, a comprehensive evaluation was also required once every three years thereafter as long as the student was receiving special education services. Now the three-year reevaluation is optional. Following is a description of the types of assessment tools typically used in a comprehensive evaluation of students with mild disabilities.

Assessment of Multiple Areas of Functioning

Health Screening. Before an assessment team proceeds with a comprehensive evaluation, it is imperative that the students they are planning to assess undergo a complete health screening by medical professionals. Every screening should include, but not be limited to, an examination of the student's vision, hearing, and physical health. If it should be found that the student needs glasses or a hearing aid, this has important implications for the recommendations made by the multidisciplinary team. Students are sometimes misdiagnosed as having learning disabilities or mental retardation when in fact their difficulties stem from sensory or health impairment. A thorough health screening can avoid misidentification. It is important to consider that difficulties with vision, hearing, or health can lead to learning problems, but these learning difficulties are different than those caused by learning disabilities or mental handicaps, and their treatment and prognosis are different. See Figure 3.4 for a sample Health Screening Form.

Cognitive Functioning. Cognitive functioning is usually assessed using a standardized intelligence test or a cognitive battery (by a school psychologist). The instrument used must

CLARKSVILLE CITY SCHOOLS
Health Screening Evaluation

To be completed by the School Nurse:

Student: ______________________________ School ID: ____________ Date: ______

DOB: ____________________ Grade: ______ Teacher: ________________________

Dental Status: _____Good _____ Needs Care
Comments:

Vision Screening: Date Screened:__________ _____Pass ______Fail

Uncorrected Both eyes 20/ ________ Corrected Both Eyes 20/ ________

Uncorrected Right Eye 20/ ________ Corrected Right Eye 20/ ________

Uncorrected Left Eye 20/ ________ Corrected Left Eye 20/ ________

Near Acuity: ____ Pass ____ Fail

Ocular Alignment: ____ Pass ____ Fail
Comments:

Hearing Screening: Date Screened:__________ _____ Pass ______Fail

	Frequency 500 Hz	1000 Hz	2000 Hz	4000 Hz
Right Ear	_____db	_____db	_____db	_____db
Left Ear	_____db	_____db	_____db	_____db

Comments:

FIGURE 3.4 Health Screening Form

(continues)

Medication:

Medication: __________ Dosage: __________ Frequency: __________

Medication: __________ Dosage: __________ Frequency: __________

Medication: __________ Dosage: __________ Frequency: __________

Physical Conditions/Limitations:

Additional Comments or Concerns:

______________________________ **School Nurse**

Signature

FIGURE 3.4 Continued

be individually administered and must yield composite scores rather than a single general intelligence quotient. The issue of cultural and linguistic bias has led to the diminished use of intelligence tests due to several court cases challenging the validity of intelligence tests for individuals from culturally and linguistically diverse backgrounds (we discuss these issues in more detail later in this chapter). Many states' criteria for the identification of learning disabilities include determining a significant discrepancy between intellectual capacity and academic achievement. In addition, intelligence tests may be used to demonstrate that a student has normal cognitive functioning to rule out mental retardation, although an adaptive behavior scale may serve the same function. This presents many schools with the dilemma of establishing a complex policy of when and if it is appropriate to use intelligence tests and identifying alternative means of assessing cognitive functioning. Many districts are using a cognitive battery, such as the Kaufman Assessment Battery for Children, Second Edition (KABC-II; Kaufman & Kaufman, 2003) or the Woodcock-Johnson III Tests of Cognitive Ability (Woodcock, McGrew, & Mather, 2001c), as alternatives to intelligence tests such as the widely used Wechsler Intelligence Scale for Children, Fourth Edition (WISC-IV; Wechsler, 2003), the Stanford-Binet IV (Thorndike, Hagen, & Sattler, 1996), or the Wechsler Preschool and Primary Scale of Intelligence–Third Edition (WPPSI-III; Wechsler, 2002). For some districts, the test of choice with culturally and linguistically diverse students is the KABC-II because it is considered to be less biased. Some districts also opt to use the Batería Woodcock-Muñoz-III (Woodcock, Muñoz-Sandoval et al., 2004), the parallel Spanish version of the Woodcock-Johnson III Complete Battery (Woodcock, McGrew, & Mather, 2001a). Later in this chapter we discuss the assessment of culturally and linguistically diverse students in much more depth.

Adaptive Behavior. The Adaptive Behavior Scale–2nd Edition (Lambert, Leland, & Nihira, et al., 1993) was designed by the American Association on Mental Retardation (AAMR) as a tool to assess mental retardation. It assesses school-age children's personal and social performance and adjustment—characteristics that are associated with the construct of adaptive behavior. One part of the test evaluates coping skills considered important for personal independence (independent functioning, physical development, economic activity, language development, numbers and time, prevocational/vocational activity, self-direction, responsibility, and socialization). The second part of the scale is concerned with social behavior (social behavior, conformity, trustworthiness, stereotyped and hyperactive behavior, self-abusive behavior, social engagement, and disturbing interpersonal behavior). Other adaptive behavior measures include the Vineland Adaptive Behavior Scale (Sparrow, Balla, & Cicchetti, 1984), Assessment of Adaptive Areas (AAA; Bryant, Taylor, & Pedrotty-Rivera, 1996), and the Adaptive Behavior Evaluation Scale (McCarney & Leigh, 1998).

Academic Achievement. There are several ways to determine a student's academic functioning, including tests, observations, informal assessment tools, and work samples. An IEP team should consider evidence from multiple sources to get a complete analysis of a student's strengths and needs. However, individually administered achievement tests are widely used when conducting assessment to determine a student's eligibility. Though most schools use schoolwide standardized achievement tests, these group-administered tests do not provide in-depth information about an individual's academic skills. When IEP team members suspect that a student has a learning disability, they must follow the federal guidelines for determining eligibility—that is, they must look for a significant discrepancy between a student's cognitive functioning (intellectual capacity) and academic functioning. Academic functioning is often determined using a standardized, individually administered achievement battery such as the Woodcock-Johnson Achievement Tests-III (Woodcock, McGrew, & Mather, 2001). The Batería Woodcock-Muñoz–Third Edition: Pruebas de Aprovechamiento (Woodcock & Muñoz-Sandoval, McGrew, Mather & Schrank, 2004) is the Spanish version of this test. Another achievement test growing in popularity is the Wechsler Individual Achievement Test, Second Edition (WIAT-II; Wechsler, 2001). This achievement battery is appropriate for students in kindergarten through grade 12 and offers comprehensive coverage of the areas of learning specified in the law. Three of the eight subtests—Basic Reading, Mathematics Reasoning, and Spelling—can also be used as brief screening instruments.

When administering standardized achievement tests, it is important to follow strict guidelines so that the validity of the test is not compromised. After all, if a test is administered under different conditions than when it was administered to the individuals who comprised the norming sample, valid comparisons are not possible. These guidelines include:

- Read and use the test manual for standardizing administration procedures.
- Know starting and stopping points.
- Know how much prompting and reinforcement is appropriate for a given test.
- Know the age range for the test.
- Look at the norming population to determine if it reflects a representative sample and includes individuals from diverse backgrounds.
- Review information about the validity and reliability of the test.
- Use the tables and norms appropriately.
- Understand what the norms tell you (e.g., age equivalent scores, grade equivalent scores, standard scores, percentiles, stanines).
- Practice giving and scoring the test prior to use.
- Ask questions, seek help from an experienced person, and attend training session(s).

Behavioral Functioning. Any child referred for a comprehensive evaluation should be assessed for behavioral functioning. The most frequent form of behavioral assessment is direct observation. Behavioral observations can be completed by the classroom teacher, an inclusion specialist, or another trained professional. Students should be observed in several different settings. As discussed at the beginning of the chapter in our description of Ms. Ryan, the inclusion specialist is in an ideal position to conduct behavioral observations in nonobtrusive ways. Behaviors may be observed for frequency, duration, and/or intensity (Overton, 2003). When conducting observations, it is important to be objective, fair, and nonjudgmental. It is also essential to be specific and pinpoint exact problem behaviors. Methods of observing behaviors are described more fully in Chapter 5. We provide an overview here:

- *Anecdotal Recording:* The teacher observes the student and records everything he or she does during a set period of time (e.g., math because this is when the behaviors to be observed tend to occur most frequently for this particular student). It is helpful to also record the *antecedent,* or what happens before the target behavior, and the *consequence,* or what happens immediately after the behavior.
- *Event Recording or Frequency Counting:* The teacher marks or tallies the number of times a specific behavior occurs. This information can be graphed so that students, teachers, and parents can track changes over time.

- *Time Sampling:* The teacher samples the student's behavior at regular intervals (e.g., every 5 minutes) during a set time period. The teacher records only what the student is doing when observed after each interval. This procedure enables the teacher to observe more than one student at a time.
- *Interval Recording:* This procedure is similar to time sampling, except that the teacher simply indicates if a target behavior is occurring or not occurring (e.g., with a + or a –). For example, Ms. Ryan observes Carl and records every 5 minutes if he is in his seat or out of his seat. This method of observation enables the teacher to observe several students at once.
- *Duration Recording:* The teacher records the amount of time a student exhibits a specific behavior (e.g., how long the student is on task).

Other behavioral observation techniques include checklists, rating scales, questionnaires, and interviews. These methods enable the multidisciplinary team to collect information from a variety of sources, asking parents, teachers, and even peers to share their views regarding a student's behavior. Published measures include the ADD-H Comprehensive Teacher's Rating Scale–2nd Edition (ACTERS; Ullman, Sleator, & Sprague, 1991), the ADHD Symptom Checklist-4 (ADHD-SC4; Gadow & Sprafkin, 1997), the Attention-Deficit/Hyperactivity Disorder Test (ADHDT; Gilliman, 1995), the Conners' Parent and Teacher Rating Scales-R (CRS-R; Conners, 1997), and the Spadafore ADHD Rating Scale (Spadafore & Spadafore, 1997).

Social Functioning. There are various ways to measure social functioning. Haager and Vaughn (1997) describe "social competence" as a multifaceted construct with four dimensions: effective use of social skills, absence of maladaptive behaviors, positive relations with others, and accurate/age-appropriate social cognition. Measurement of social functioning should take these dimensions into consideration. It is possible for a student to do well in one area but not others. The purpose of assessment should guide the selection of tools. Keeping anecdotal records of a students' social behavior and interchanges in the classroom is a common practice when a student's placement is in question or a teacher makes a referral to the Student Study Team (or Child Study Team—the schoolwide team where a teacher first shares concerns about a student and is offered prereferral strategies or interventions to try with the student). During the formal assessment process for special education, a school psychologist will often give a social skills rating scale as part of the assessment battery. Examples of such measures include the Vineland Social-Emotional Early Childhood Scales (Vineland SEEC; Sparrow, Balla, & Cicchetti, 1998), the Vineland Social Maturity Scale (Sparrow, Balla, & Cicchetti, 1985), and the Walker-McConnell Scale of Social Competence and School Adjustment, Elementary Version and Adolescent Version (Walker & McConnell, 1995a, 1995b). Other social and behavioral assessments are covered in Chapter 5.

Emotional Functioning. Assessing a student's emotional state is a task for a trained psychologist. The general and special education teachers may play a role in this assessment by providing observational information. One indicator of a child's emotional wellbeing is a self-concept assessment. Self-concept measures include the Culture-Free Self

Esteem Inventories, 2nd Edition (CFSEI-2; Battle, 1992), the Multidimensional Self Concept Scale (Bracken, 1991), the Piers/Harris Children's Self Concept Scale–Revised (Piers, 1986), the Self-Esteem Index (SEI; Brown & Alexander, 1991), the Student Self-Concept Scale (Greshman, Elliot, & Evans-Fernandez, 1995), and the Tennessee Self Concept Scale, 2nd Edition (TSCS:2; Fitts & Warren, 1996).

Sensory and Perceptual Functioning. Sensory and perceptual skills involve the way an individual perceives, processes, and responds to stimuli. These skills include visual perception, visual memory, visual discrimination, visual motor, auditory memory, and auditory discrimination skills. Because the federal definition specifies that LD is "a disorder in one or more of the basic psychological processes" and includes "such conditions as perceptual handicaps," many states include a processing component in their eligibility criteria. Psychoeducational test batteries that assess these skills are designed to provide a detailed description of a student's relative strengths and weaknesses. By better understanding how a student learns, the inclusion specialist and classroom teacher are in a better position to provide appropriate instruction. However, the value of assessing these skills has been questioned in recent years. Tests that provide a detailed profile of a student's perceptual skills were very popular from the 1960s through the early 1980s (e.g., the Detroit Tests of Learning Aptitude, the Beery Test of Visual Motor Integration, or the Illinois Test of Psycholinguistic Abilities), but have since lost favor because their usefulness is considered limited. Current versions of these tests are available: The Detroit Tests of Learning Aptitude, 4th Edition (Hammill, 1998), the Developmental Test of Visual-Motor Integration, 4th Edition (Beery & Buktenica, 1997) and the Illinois Test of Psycholinguistic Abilities, 3rd Edition (Hammill, Mather, & Roberts, 2001). Mather and Kirk (1985) suggested that substantial evidence in support of this type of assessment is lacking because very few students have perceptual problems so severe that they affect learning. During the early years of the field of learning disabilities, a great deal of instructional time was spent trying to remediate students' weak perceptual skills (rather than focusing on their strengths or academic needs). For example, instead of learning to read, students would spend countless hours drawing lines on increasingly narrow pathways across their ditto sheets to improve their visual motor skills, using materials developed by Marianne Frostig. However, research did not support the effectiveness of these techniques. Now assessment results in the area of perceptual functioning are considered more useful for helping teachers understand their students' strengths (Overton, 1996). Sample sensory motor assessment measures include the Quick Neurological Screening Test, II (Sterling, 1998), and the Slosson Drawing Coordination Test for Children and Adults (Slosson, 1996). The Benton Visual Retention Test, 5th Edition (Sivan, 1991) assesses visual memory and the Motor-Free Visual Perception Test, Revised (MVPT-R; Colarusso & Hammill, 1996) and the Developmental Test of Visual Perception, 2nd Edition (DTVP-2; Hammill, Pearson, & Voress, 1993) test visual perception. Tests that focus on auditory discrimination include the Goldman-Fristoe-Woodcock Test of Auditory Discrimination (G-F-WTAD; Goldman, Fristoe, & Woodcock, 1970) and the Wepman Test of Auditory Discrimination, 2nd Edition (ADT-2; Wepman & Reynolds, 1987). The Lindamood Auditory Conceptualization Test (LACT; Lindamood & Lindamood, 1985) and the Test of Auditory Perceptual Skills–Revised (TAPS-R; Gardner, 1996) evaluate auditory perceptual skills.

Oral Language Assessment. Oral language assessment encompasses a wide range of skills. These skills can be clustered into the linguistic categories of phonology (speech sounds), morphology (affixes), semantics (word meanings), syntax (word order), and pragmatics (social context). Oral language skills can also be thought of as receptive (comprehension) or expressive (production). Speech clinicians are responsible for assessing the expressive skills of articulation, voice, and fluency. They might also assess other aspects of a student's language functioning, or other members of the assessment team might conduct these tests. Inclusion specialists sometimes assess students' receptive language vocabulary and oral expressive language.

Many screening devices and standardized tests are available to assist in the assessment of oral language proficiency. The Peabody Picture Vocabulary Test–3rd Edition (PPVT-III; Dunn & Dunn, 1997) measures the student's verbal comprehension skills by presenting sequenced sets of four pictures and asking the student to point to the picture in each set that represents the word stated by the examiner. The Test of Word Finding–2nd Edition (TWF-2; German, 2000) measures word finding, an expressive language skill. In an easel format like the PPVT-III, students are asked to name pictures of nouns, verbs, and categories and complete sentences. Word-finding skills are measured for accuracy and speed. Similar to the TWF-2 are the Test of Adolescent and Adult Word Finding (TAWF; German, 1990) and the Word Finding Referral Checklist (German, & German, 1992). The Test of Early Language Development, 3rd Edition (TELD; Hresko, Reid, & Hammill, 1999) is a measure of the early development of oral language in the areas of receptive and expressive language, syntax, and semantics. The Test of Language Development–Primary: 3rd Edition (TOLD-P:3; Newcomer & Hammill, 1997), Test of Language Development, 3rd Edition: Intermediate (TOLD-I:3; Hammill & Newcomer, 1997), and the Test of Adolescent Language Development (TOAL-3, Hammill, Brown, Larsen, & Wiederholt, 1994) each assesses the language development of students at different age levels. The TOLD-P:3 assesses picture vocabulary, oral vocabulary, grammatical understanding, sentence imitation, grammatical completion, word discrimination, and word articulation. The TOLD-I:3 assesses sentence combining, vocabulary, word ordering, generals, grammatical comprehension. The TOAL-3 assesses students' vocabulary and grammar skills across four dimensions: listening, speaking, reading, and writing. These are standardized tests that compare a student's language abilities in each area to the performance of students in the norming sample. The Test of Basic Concepts–Revised (BOEHM-3; Boehm, 2000) assesses young children's understanding of concepts such as "above," "below," "under," and "over." This instrument measures mastery of basic concepts that are fundamental to understanding verbal instruction and necessary for early school achievement. It is also available in Spanish.

Other tests assess the English language proficiency of students whose first language is not English. These measures range from screening tests, such as the Dos Amigos Verbal Language Scales (Critchlow, 1996), to comprehensive batteries, such as the Woodcock-Muñoz Language Survey (Woodcock & Muñoz-Sandoval, 1993). The Dos Amigos Verbal Language Scales test was designed to reveal the comparative development of a child's English and Spanish and identify the child's dominant language. It also serves as a screening instrument to determine if further evaluation is needed. The more extensive Woodcock-Muñoz Language Survey, English (LS-E) and Spanish (LS-S) (Woodcock &

Muñoz-Sandoval, 1993), provides a broad sampling of proficiency in oral language, as well as in reading and writing. This test measures cognitive-academic language proficiency in English and Spanish and can be used to classify a student's English or Spanish language proficiency. One of the most commonly used language proficiency measures for kindergarten through sixth grade students is the Language Assessment Scales (LAS; DeAvila & Duncan, 1990). Subtests are based on four primary language subsystems: phonemic, semantic, syntactic, and pragmatic, and assess students' pronunciation, vocabulary knowledge, listening comprehension, and storytelling capability. The LAS yields a final score that indicates the student's overall language proficiency. A similar measure is the IDEA Oral Language Proficiency Test (Ballard, Tighe, & Dalton, 1991). This 83-item test assesses the areas of syntax, vocabulary, comprehension, and verbal expression and categorizes students as Non-English Speaking, Limited English Speaking, and Fluent English Speaking. The state of California is currently in the process of developing a new language proficiency test.

Language sampling is the most extensively used technique for language assessment other than the use of standardized tests. Although some individuals collect a language sample from their own interaction with the child, perhaps using pictures as prompts, by far the preferable method is to record the child's speech in a natural setting. Language samples when collected in this way have the advantage of documenting communication in real contexts. De Valenzuela and Cervantes (1998) offer the following recommendations for those collecting and analyzing language samples:

- Collect language samples in natural and multiple contexts.
- Use familiar and culturally appropriate conversation partners.
- Do not attempt to elicit specific language forms.
- Do not pressure for answers during the conversation.
- Videotape or audiotape conversations for later analysis (rather than taking notes).
- Focus on language functions (use) when analyzing samples, not only form and content.
- Use caution when comparing the language performance of culturally and linguistically diverse students to published norms.

What the Law Says about Assessment of Students with Disabilities

You may have already learned some of the basic provisions of relevant federal laws in an introductory course. We have summarized them here to provide a quick review of the special education laws. The Education for all Handicapped Act (PL 94-142), later reauthorized as Individuals with Disabilities Education Act, or IDEA (PL 101-476), governs special education services in public schools. IDEA was most recently reauthorized as PL 105-17 in 1997 and is due to be reauthorized soon. Beginning with PL 94-142, the law protects the rights of students with disabilities and their families. In the IDEA legislation, there are several provisions that apply specifically to assessment practices. The law provides for fair and unbiased assessment as well as due process safeguards for both families and school personnel. Following are provisions of the law that relate directly to assessment.

Informed consent
A signed consent form indicating that a student's parent or legal guardian has given consent to have a student assessed and was fully informed of parental rights, the evaluation activities to take place, any records to be released and to whom, and the nature and purpose of the evaluation.

Informed Consent. The law states that schools must obtain written **informed consent** from parents or guardians to conduct an evaluation of a student and that the parents may revoke their consent at any time. Parents must be fully informed of their rights, the evaluation activities to take place, any records to be released and to whom, and the nature and purpose of the evaluation. Furthermore, parents or guardians must be informed in their native language or primary mode of communication. Due process procedures govern how complaints may be lodged by those involved. Should the parents decide to withdraw their consent after signing the consent forms, they are protected by due process safeguards. Though it is uncommon in practice, the school is also protected by due process and could file a complaint against the parents.

Comprehensive Evaluation. The federal guidelines state that before an initial placement a child must receive a "full and individual evaluation" (Public Policy Unit, Council for Exceptional Children, 1998, p. 15). A multidisciplinary team, with appropriate areas of expertise, must conduct a complete assessment in all areas of suspected disability. In the initial assessment plan, the team should state the specific areas of concern from the areas of cognitive, academic, motor, behavioral, sensory, and communicative functioning. The assessment plan outlines which areas are to be assessed and the assessment tools or sources of information to be used.

Multiple Sources of Information. Federal guidelines specify that "no single procedure can be used as the sole criterion in deciding whether or not a child has a disability. (Public Policy Unit, Council for Exceptional Children, 1998, p. 15). Experts and professional groups have both recommended using multiple data sources when making eligibility decisions. For example, the National Joint Committee on Learning Disabilities (NJCLD) (1998) emphasized that "no single test or battery of tests . . . is sufficient for the diagnosis of learning disabilities" (California Department of Education, 2004, p. 189) (see also the National Commission on Testing and Public Policy, 1990). It is considered "best practice" for a team of qualified professionals to participate in the assessment process using varied assessment tools. Just as a surgeon would not conduct brain surgery without multiple sources of evidence that a tumor exists and is causing imminent harm, it is unthinkable to place a child in a special program based on the results of one test. The possibility for error is just too great. Having a set of results from varied sources enhances the ability of the team to make objective decisions. Furthermore, having multiple sources of information ensures that the multidisciplinary team will have a more complete picture of the individual student's strengths and needs.

Need for Alternative Procedures. Not only is it important to use a variety of assessment tools when evaluating students for possible placement in a special education program, it is also essential to rely on alternative procedures when standardized tests are not considered appropriate (i.e., for students from culturally and linguistically diverse backgrounds) (a description of nondiscriminatory assessment is provided later in this chapter). In their guidelines for using discrepancy formulas for determining whether a student has a learning disability, the state of California adds the following caveat: "When standardized tests . . .

may not be valid, as with Black and Latino/a students, a discrepancy must be 'corroborated by other assessment data which may include other tests, scales, instruments, observations and work samples' (California Department of Education, 2004, p. A-15), as well as information provided by parents and teachers. The specific processes and procedures for implementation of these criteria are to be developed by each special education local plan area." The regulations also specify that "when standardized tests are considered to be invalid for a specific pupil, the discrepancy shall be measured by *alternative means as specified in the assessment plan*" (p. A-15) (italics added), and if the standardized tests do not reveal a severe discrepancy as defined above, the individualized education program team may find that a severe discrepancy does exist, provided that the team documents in a written report that the severe discrepancy between ability and achievement exists as a result of disorder in one or more of the basic psychological processes.

Assessment in All Areas of Suspected Disability. The law states that the evaluation must assess the child in all areas of suspected disability. In the case of mild disabilities, the team may know that the child is experiencing difficulty in school, but may not know to what to attribute the difficulties—cognitive delay, sensory impairment, learning disabilities, social or emotional difficulties, lack of consistent and effective instruction, or other causes. A comprehensive evaluation that includes an assessment of the child's functioning in cognitive, academic, social-emotional, and behavioral domains, as well as an analysis of the instructional setting and the child's instructional history, would be in order, following a screening of the child's vision and hearing. The team may also suspect secondary conditions that occur along with a primary disabling condition. For example, a child with suspected learning disabilities may also have signs of a speech or language disorder that would require an evaluation of speech and language. When the assessment plan is designed, the team must decide all the areas of suspected disability and then plan the comprehensive evaluation accordingly.

Multidisciplinary Team. Students being considered for eligibility for special education services should be assessed by a team of professionals with varied areas of expertise according to the student's individuals needs. The team should include at least one general education teacher (if the child is or will be participating in the general education environment) and one special education teacher (ideally a specialist with knowledge in the area of suspected disability). In addition, the law specifies that placement decisions be made by a group of individuals knowledgeable about the student, the meaning of the evaluation data, and placement options. All areas of suspected disability should be assessed based on evidence obtained during an initial screening and specified in the assessment plan. The team approach diminishes the possibility of subjectivity or discrimination in determining the educational program. Team members use varied assessment tools and sources of information, including information obtained from school records, teachers, counselors, other school personnel, and parents. If a learning disability or emotional/behavioral disorder is suspected, the law requires that at least one team member other than the student's regular teacher observe the child in the classroom setting. This adds objectivity to the evaluation of the child's academic and behavioral performance in the regular classroom. Table 3.2 shows the required and optional team members for cases of suspected mild disabilities and the areas of assessment they would be likely to conduct or information they would provide.

TABLE 3.2 Multidisciplinary Team Members

TEAM MEMBERS	RESPONSIBILITIES AND CONTRIBUTIONS TO THE TEAM
REQUIRED	
parent, guardian, or surrogate parent	to make educational decisions; to provide information regarding child's functioning outside of school
child's teacher	to provide information regarding child's classroom performance and adjustment; to provide performance data, including samples of class work
school administrator as an official representative of the school (or other person with knowledge and authority regarding placement options)	to provide information regarding school structure, resources, and organization; to provide information regarding placement and service options
school psychologist (person conducting assessment, or a qualified replacement who is able to interpret assessment data)	to provide and interpret assessment results; must also be qualified to administer a variety of cognitive, educational, and psychological assessments
special education teacher	to administer and interpret academic assessment; conduct classroom observation and explain findings; to provide information regarding any consultation with classroom teacher; to explain school's special education services
OPTIONAL	
parent advocate (or other representative of parents, at parent's request)	to advise parent(s) prior to, during, and following IEP meeting
school nurse (or other healthcare professional)	to conduct hearing and vision screening, evaluate medical history, refer health issues to appropriate medical resources
speech and language specialist	to provide and interpret results of speech and language evaluation; to recommend appropriate services if need is determined by team
behavioral consultant	to provide and interpret results of behavioral or social assessment; to recommend appropriate services if need is determined by team
school counselor (or representative of community or private counseling agency)	to recommend appropriate school-based or community-based counseling services if need is determined by team; may advise regarding student's scheduling
occupational therapist	to provide and interpret results of fine motor and self-help evaluation; to recommend appropriate services if need is determined by team
physical therapist	to provide and interpret results of gross motor functioning evaluation; to recommend appropriate services if need is determined by team
transition specialist	to provide and interpret results of transition needs evaluation; to recommend appropriate services if need is determined by team
student	to participate in decision-making process

Exclusionary Criteria. Public Law 94-142 (Education for All Handicapped Children Act of 1975), and subsequently the Individuals with Disabilities Education Act (IDEA), included an exclusionary clause stating that a child should not be labeled as learning disabled if the "discrepancy between ability and achievement is primarily the result of environmental, cultural, or economic disadvantage" (U.S. Office of Education, 1977, p. 65083). Many states have further clarified this exclusionary clause. For example, California's Education Code stipulates that, "[t]he discrepancy shall not be primarily the result of limited school experience or poor school attendance" (California Department of Education, 2004, p. A-16). The exclusionary clause is particularly relevant for students from culturally and linguistically diverse backgrounds. Yet evidence suggests that professionals pay little attention to this clause (Harris, Gray, Davis, Zaremba, & Argulewicz, 1988; Ochoa, Rivera, & Powell, 1997). For instance, Ochoa and colleagues surveyed 859 school psychologists who had some experience conducting bilingual psychoeducational assessments. These psychologists indicated that they consider a variety of factors in their efforts to comply with the exclusionary clause, but frequently omit critical factors such as language and number of years of English instruction. Only 6 percent reported asking for the students' home language, and only 1 percent attempted to determine if a discrepancy occurred in both English and the student's home language. These findings show that the majority of school psychologists fail to recognize the significance of language when considering the educational status of LEP and bilingual students. Disregard for the potential influence of language and culture in students' school performance is an unfortunate practice that can have devastating consequences for culturally and linguistically diverse students who might be labeled as disabled when in fact their lack of school success can be attributed to other causes.

Assessment Procedures

Most schools have some type of prereferral team to guide teachers in prereferral interventions and to document students' progress. This team may conduct an initial screening to determine if a formal referral should be made. A parent or an individual student may also initiate a referral. Once a referral has been made, an initial multidisciplinary team will convene to develop an *assessment plan*. The team will specify the suspected areas of disability, assessment tools and procedures to be used, and the personnel who will conduct the assessments. It is at this point that care is taken to select instruments that are nondiscriminatory and valid. Individuals with the appropriate expertise should be selected to administer assessments. A request is sent to parents to inform them of the assessment plan and their parental rights and to secure their informed consent. Once consent is obtained, the assessment may proceed. A date is set for the IEP meeting to review the assessment results and consider the student's eligibility for services. The law specifies that schools make every effort to involve one or both parents in the IEP development and at every step of the referral and placement process. Care should be taken to plan a date and time that is convenient for the parents because placement may not proceed without parental consent.

Assessment That Is Culturally and Linguistically Appropriate

Nondiscriminatory Assessment. Numerous guidelines for conducting nondiscriminatory assessments have been developed in the last few decades (e.g., NJCLD, 1998). Nondiscriminatory assessment is defined as "reducing the chance that a child might be incorrectly placed in special classes and increasing the use of intervention programs which facilitate his [her] physical, social, emotional, and academic development" (Tucker, 1977, p. 109). It is the right of students and their families to have assessments conducted that are free from racial or cultural bias. Federal guidelines specify that evaluations should meet three criteria to be deemed fair and nonbiased:

1. The assessment should be conducted in the student's native language or other mode of communication.
2. Any evaluation material or test should be used for the specific purpose for which it has been validated.
3. A standardized test should be administered by a professional with the appropriate training and expertise to administer it according to the guidelines specified by the test producer.

Problems with Assessment Practices Involving Culturally and Linguistically Diverse Students. Concerns about using standardized tests with students from diverse backgrounds have a long history (Laosa, 1977). Traditional assessment practices with culturally and linguistically diverse students have been criticized because of problematic test development procedures and test uses that create bias (Garcia & Pearson, 1994; Samuda, 1989). The overrepresentation of minorities in special education programs is due in part to bias in testing and referral practices. The following list, adapted from Overton (1996), provides an overview of possible sources of bias in evaluation practices.

1. *Inappropriate content.* Students of culturally or ethnically diverse backgrounds may not have adequate exposure to constructs included in an instrument.
2. *Inappropriate standardization samples.* Minority groups may not have been well represented in the normative sample used to establish the standards for the test.
3. *Examiner and language.* A test conducted in English or an examiner of a cultural or linguistic background different from the student's may cause the student to feel intimidated.
4. *Measurement of different constructs.* Specific constructs in the test may represent a majority culture; tests may only measure the extent to which minority students have absorbed the mainstream white, middle-class culture.
5. *Different predictive validity.* Tests that are used to predict future educational outcomes may not adequately do so for minority students.
6. *Translation of tests in English to other languages.* Translating tests into another language may result in a loss of the original meaning and influence test performance. Translating tests makes the use of the norms for the instrument invalid.

Questionable Standardized Test Assumptions. Standardized tests are based on several assumptions that are questionable when applied to culturally and linguistically diverse students. One premise is that an individual's performance on a test reflects his or her competence or abilities. For example, one might assume that an IQ score of 75 on an intelligence test indicates that an individual has below average intelligence. However, many factors make it difficult to draw conclusions about a person's test performance. It is important to understand that poor performance does not necessarily reflect lack of competence. *Situational factors* can affect how an individual performs. Goodnow (1976) suggested that variations across cultural groups in test performance may be due to different interpretations of the nature of the testing task, what problem is being solved, and how to go about reaching a solution. For example, although speed of completion is highly valued in Western cultures, some other cultures associate intelligence with such characteristics as "slow" and "careful" rather than "quick." We know that students' test performance is affected by speededness, or "the inability of students to complete all of the items included on a test as a result of prescribed time limitations" (Garcia & Pearson, 1994, p. 347). Also, how well children perform in a one-to-one testing situation depends on how much anxiety they feel, how much experience they have had taking tests and how "testwise" they have become, how motivated they are, and how comfortable they feel with the examiner. Referring to African American students, Labov asserted that "the usual assessment situations, including IQ and reading tests, elicit deliberate, defensive behavior on the part of the child who has realistic expectations that to talk openly is to expose oneself to insult and harm" (Cole & Bruner, 1971, p. 869).

> When we systematically study the situational determinants of performance, we are led to conclude that cultural differences reside more in differences in the situations to which different cultural groups apply their skills than to differences in the skills possessed by the groups in question. (Cole & Bruner, 1971, p. 874)

Beyond situational factors, there is the issue of *content validity,* which, as Samuda (1989) explained, assumes "that the test takers have been exposed to and are familiar with the universe of information from which test items are drawn" (p. 28). Yet many culturally and linguistically diverse students have not been exposed to this information. Mercer (1973) and many others (e.g., Hilliard, 1977; Williams, 1974) have argued that this assumption is violated because the tests reflect abilities, skills, and language valued by American "core culture" rather than by the cultures of the students being tested (Mercer, 1973, p. 13).

Another assumption of standardized testing is that skills can be isolated and measured in a decontextualized fashion through the presentation of arbitrary preselected tasks in a controlled situation. Yet we cannot assume that ethnic minority students will be able to perform their skills in a decontextualized situation that is not relevant to their cultural milieu. Indeed, there is ample evidence that cultural differences on cognitive tasks seem to be most pronounced on discrete tasks that occur in isolation. On cognitive tasks where information is embedded in familiar contexts, fewer differences across cultural groups seem to occur. For example, in a study examining memory for spatially organized information, Guatemalan Mayan children performed at least as well as middle-class Salt Lake City children on a contextually organized task that used familiar objects (Rogoff & Waddell, 1982). Similarly, Serpell (1994) compared the performance of Zambian and British children on tests using familiar and unfamiliar materials such as building blocks, wire, and clay. The study found that the Zambian children were superior when building with wire, the British children were superior with blocks, and both groups performed similarly in their handling of clay. In another investigation, Cole, Gay, Glick, and Sharp (1971) studied cultural differences in memory skills and found that, unlike most U.S. white middle-class individuals, Liberian rice farmers performed poorly on recall and semantic organization in standardized memory tasks. However, the Liberian farmers dramatically improved their performance when the tasks were adapted to make them culturally relevant and meaningful (see also Cole, 1990, 1996; Greenfield & Childs, 1977; Saxe, 1988).

In conclusion, sociocultural research suggests that individual cognitive activity must be understood in terms of the social, cultural, and historical processes that provide contexts for people's activities. Thinking does not take place in a vacuum. Assessment of ethnic minority students in special education should be attentive to situational and cultural variables. Sternberg (1998) goes even further in emphasizing that in measuring intelligence we must take into account people, tasks, and situations not only in multicultural measurement, but in *all* measurement.

Linguistic and Cultural Bias. A consistent finding in the research on assessment and diversity is related to linguistic and cultural bias. First, researchers have reported that culturally and linguistically diverse students' test performance is affected by their differential interpretation of questions, lack of familiarity with vocabulary, limited English language proficiency, and issues of language dominance (Garcia & Pearson, 1994). Second, the assessment of culturally and linguistically diverse students is fraught with theoretical misunderstandings and flawed practices. Frequently: (1) language proficiency is not taken into account; (2) testing is done primarily in English; (3) factors related to second language acquisition are misinterpreted as handicaps; (4) home data are not used in the assessment; and (5) the same few tests are used with most children (Figueroa, 1989). Figueroa's (1990) review of the literature on the assessment of bilingual populations suggests that the majority of bilingual groups exhibit the same low verbal IQ, higher nonverbal IQ profile. Unfortunately, diagnosticians and educators often misinterpret the lack of full proficiency in English as a second language as a widespread intelligence deficit (Oller, 1991) or as a language or learning disability (Langdon, 1989). Psychologists have erroneously concluded that bilingualism retards verbal intelligence despite data to the contrary (August & Hakuta, 1997; Hakuta, 1986). We know that determining whether students have acquired full cognitive academic English proficiency rather than only basic interpersonal communication skills is difficult (Cummins, 1984) and that even students who have demonstrated English fluency on oral language measures may not be ready to be assessed at higher cognitive levels in English.

Assessment experts have not yet adequately determined how to differentiate between normal second language learning influences and disabilities (Gonzalez, Brusca-Vega, & Yawkey, 1997; Ortiz, 1997). We do not yet know definitively when a child whose primary language is not English is ready to be tested only in English (Figueroa, 1989; Ortiz, 1997).

No test of language proficiency has yet been developed that can adequately answer this question. Even children who demonstrate English proficiency on language assessment measures still typically demonstrate a low Verbal IQ and high Performance IQ profile. Indeed, "[e]very test given in English becomes, in part, a language or literacy test" (American Educational Research Association, American Psychological Association, & National Council on Measurement in Education, 1985, p. 73). If a child was transitioned prematurely, for example, from a bilingual or English as a Second Language program to a regular classroom, this is likely to have a negative impact on achievement and also depress scores on tests of intelligence. Linguistic minority students are often moved to English-only programs when they have developed superficial basic interpersonal communicative skills after one or two years, but prior to their development of the cognitive academic language proficiency required for demanding learning tasks, which often takes from five to seven years (Cummins, 1984). Authors such as Trueba (1989) have challenged the practice of blaming low achievement on low IQ and factors related to language and culture, looking further at the context within which underachievement occurs in our society. These arguments are equally applicable to speakers of African American Vernacular English (AAVE) or other varieties of English (Hilliard, 1977; Taylor & Lee, 1987). How can we know the extent of the impact, not only of structural differences between standard and nonstandard varieties, but also of the issues of power involved in their use?

Predictive Validity. Intelligence tests tend to underestimate the potential of culturally and linguistically diverse students (Rueda, 1997), thus raising questions about their predictive validity with these students. A case in point is the longitudinal study of a subgroup (60%) of the 2,100 students from the tri-ethnic norming sample for the System of Multicultural Pluralistic Assessment (SOMPA) (Mercer, 1979; Figueroa & Sassenrath, 1989; Valdez & Figueroa, 1994). Students' GPA, standardized reading scores, and standardized math scores in 1982 were compared with their 1972 Full-Scale WISC-R scores. Students who achieved at higher levels than predicted by their IQ scores were considered to be "overachievers," whereas those students who achieved at lower levels than predicted were considered to be "underachievers." Findings indicated that Latino students who in 1972 had scored at or below the mean on the WISC-R were *more* likely than their Anglo counterparts to show above-expected school grades and achievement, thus placing them in the overachiever category. Interestingly, among the Latino groups, those students with more Spanish in the home were more likely to be overachievers than students from English/Spanish homes (who in turn were overrepresented in the underachiever category). Valdez and Figueroa (1994) concluded that the data strongly suggested that decisions based on IQ can lead to inaccuracies in decision making for Latino pupils, particularly students who come from homes where Spanish is spoken.

The Challenge Ahead

Several alternative procedures have been recommended as having potential for conducting linguistically and culturally sensitive assessments, such as portfolios and authentic assessment procedures, dynamic assessment, learning potential assessment, testing-the-limits approaches, targeted rather than global tests, mediated assessment, evaluation of the zone of proximal or potential development, and assessment via assisted learning and transfer (Brown, Campione, Webber, & McGilly, 1992; Dent, Mendocal, Pierce, & West, 1991; Figueroa, 1989; Gonzalez, Brusca-Vega, & Yawkey, 1997; Haywood, 1988; Rueda, 1997; Sternberg, 1998). Moll (1990) suggests looking for the cultural, linguistic, and social resources (funds of knowledge) that students and their families bring to the school setting and using these as strengths upon which to build problem-solving abilities rather than deficits. Similarly, Garcia and Ortiz (1988) and Ortiz (1997) developed a compilation of questions, issues, and accommodations that should be considered with English language learners during prereferral and referral processes. Some of these accommodations include (1) the use of support systems other than special education (e.g., consultants or problem-solving teams); (2) the inclusion of individuals with expertise in language acquisition and diversity issues on referral committees; (3) the use of students' native language in the assessment process; (4) the verification of the language and professional skills of interpreters; and (5) the training of professionals to use interpreters, to use multiple formal and informal measures to compare students' performance in their first and second language and against peers from the same cultural group, to establish the students' language dominance and proficiency, and to document the disability in the students' dominant language. Keogh (1998) notes that assessment must take into account the characteristics both of the students and of the classroom environments in which they are taught. She asserts that focusing exclusively on individual psychometric and educational assessments is not enough, that the content of assessment must be broadened and that "psychologists should spend time in classrooms" (Keough, 1998, p. 314).

HIGH STAKES TESTING AND ACCOMMODATIONS FOR STUDENTS WITH SPECIAL NEEDS

With the school reform efforts of the 1980s, dating back to the publication of "A Nation at Risk" in 1983, our country has increasingly turned to large-scale achievement tests as a way to hold schools and students to high standards of accountability and "raise the stakes." President Clinton's 1997 proposal to create voluntary national tests in reading and mathematics brought even more attention and controversy to this issue. President Bush made such tests part of his campaign platform and in 2002 authorized the "No Child Left Behind Act" with increased accountability one of the principal components of the act. **High stakes testing** continues to increase. These tests can have important consequences for individual students. Their results are commonly used for such crucial decisions as whether students should be admitted to advanced academic programs, promoted to the next grade level, or allowed to receive a high school diploma (National Research Council, 1999).

High stakes testing The use of standardized achievement tests for schoolwide, district-wide, or statewide measurement of students' academic progress. Tests are increasingly being used as a way to hold schools and students accountable to high standards.

Many students with disabilities have been exempt from taking large-scale achievement tests. Though IDEA stipulates that states must develop policies and procedures that ensure the participation of students with special needs in district- and statewide assessment programs, with accommodations as necessary, surveys have indicated that the extent to which students with disabilities participate varies widely, from 0 to 100 percent (Elliott, Erickson, Thurlow, & Shriner, 2000;

Gronna, Jenkins, & Chin-Chance, 1998; Vanderwood, McGrew, & Ysseldyke, 1998). In some cases, teachers and administrators have been unaware of or unwilling to make accommodations for students. Or they may have kept their students with disabilities from taking high stakes tests because they have been concerned that these students' scores could bring down the school's average and reflect poorly on the performance of that school. Others have been concerned that taking large-scale achievement tests will be too stressful for some individuals with special needs. Such tests may increase the dropout rate of students with disabilities.

Yet there are many reasons for including students with disabilities in large-scale assessment programs. Only when all students are included in large-scale assessment programs can accurate aggregate data be compiled. Comparisons across schools, districts, and states are not accurate if some sites include all students and others do not (Vanderwood et al., 1998). Also, individual scores provide potentially valuable information to teachers, parents, and students. Students who do not participate in testing programs may be shortchanged in other ways as well. The following is a true story (other than the name of the school, which is a pseudonym).

Centennial Elementary had a strong inclusion program that was considered a model in its school district. Yet the state began implementing new statewide achievement tests and then "grading" schools based on their test scores. Teachers in schools with high grades are rewarded with pay bonuses, and teachers in schools with low grades were told they might have their pay decreased. As the school began to gear up for the "testing season," the administrators and teachers decided to pull the students with LD out of their third and fourth grade inclusion classrooms so that the classroom teachers could focus their attention on the students whose scores on the achievement tests would "count." After all, some of the students with LD were not even going to take the tests, and the scores of the students with LD who did take the tests would not be included in the school's average. The students with LD were then placed in a resource room with 34 students—more students than had been left behind in their regular classrooms. The teachers and administrators did not feel proud of what they had done—yet they seemed to have reconciled that because the students with LD would not be part of the statewide testing, they were expendable.

Recent federal laws such as Goals 2000 and Title I of the Improving America's Schools Act of 1994 have mandated that all students with disabilities should be included in large-scale assessments (National Research Council, 1999). However, as of yet, this is not happening in most states, in part due to confusion about how to carry out the mandate. The 1997 amendments to IDEA include several provisions designed to increase the participation of students with disabilities in high stakes testing:

- States must develop policies and procedures that ensure the participation of students with special needs in district-wide and statewide assessment programs, with accommodations as necessary.

- Any adaptations or accommodations that a student requires should be note[illegible] student's IEP. If the IEP team determines that a student should not particip[illegible] a particular statewide or district-wide test, the IEP should include a statement explaining why the test would not be appropriate and what alternative methods of assessment will be used.
- States must develop alternative assessment procedures for those students who cannot participate in general state- or district-wide testing.
- States must have policies and procedures in place to ensure the proper recording and reporting of assessment results, particularly concerning the performance of students with disabilities.

Thurlow, House, Scott, and Ysseldyke (2000) noted that states have been actively working to change their participation and accommodation policies to meet new mandates.

Accommodations

Various accommodations of four general types have been recommended to enable students with disabilities to participate (Thurlow, Ysseldyke, & Silverstein, 1995):

1. Changes in how the tests are presented (e.g., providing taped versions for students with reading disabilities, supplying large-print forms, simplifying the language of the tests, allowing a teacher to read the test and/or turn the pages, offering prompts and feedback).
2. Changes in how students are expected to respond (e.g., using another person to write down a student's responses, providing computer assistance on tests not otherwise administered by computer, changing response formats such as circling rather than filling in the bubbles, allowing verbal rather than written responses).
3. Changes in timing (e.g., allowing students extra time to complete a section of a test, or spreading a test over several shorter time blocks).
4. Changes in setting (e.g., administering the test to students in a small group or individually, or in another room that is smaller and/or free from distractions).

Yet accommodations themselves can be problematic or even misused. Some special educators may "overaccommodate," thinking they are only helping their students. If too much help is provided, it is not possible to obtain an accurate representation of the student's achievement. We know very little about the impact of these accommodations on the validity of test scores (McDonnell, McLaughlin, & Morison, 1997; Thurlow et al., 1995). One possible solution to this problem is to tag or flag tests that have been taken with accommodations. This flagging would warn the person using test results that the meaning of the score is uncertain and that caution should be taken when interpreting test results. Yet flagging raises legal, policy, and ethical concerns (McDonnell et al., 1997) because doing so identifies the individual as having a disability. This in turn raises questions of confidentiality and possible stigma. A number of research studies are now exploring viable alternatives, such as new response formats and computerized testing. Other means of enhancing students' performance on standardized tests include teaching test-taking skills, increasing motivation, and improving the test-taking environment.

Modifications for College Entrance Exams

Both the Scholastic Assessment Test (SAT) and the American College Test (ACT) allow special accommodations for students with documented disabilities. Students who meet eligibility requirements can request the following accommodations in advance: extended time, large type, alternative test forms, a reader or recorder, audiocassette tapes with a written form, a magnifying glass, or a four-function calculator.

Modifications on GED Tests

The Test of General Educational Development (GED) was designed to assess the knowledge and skills acquired in a four-year high school program or its equivalent. Students with disabilities who have not graduated from high school (i.e., have dropped out of school) can opt to take this test if they believe they have met high school graduation criteria. Students who wish to take the exam cannot be enrolled in a public school at the time they take the test and are usually over 18. Students with disabilities may complete an "Application for Special Testing." Possible modifications include (General Education Development Testing Service, 2000):

- Audiocassette edition (with large-print reference copy)
- Large-print edition
- Braille edition
- Extended time
- Use of a scribe
- Use of a talking calculator or abacus
- Supervised frequent breaks
- Use of a private room
- One-on-one testing at a health facility or candidate's home
- Vision-enhancing technologies
- Use of video equipment
- Sign-language interpreter
- Other accommodations as warranted by candidate's need

For more information, visit the American Council on Education's website at *www.acenet.edu* and click on "GED" and then "Accommodations for Disabilities."

REFERENCES

American Educational Research Association, American Psychological Association, & National Council on Measurement in Education. (1985). Testing linguistic minorities. *Standards for educational and psychological testing.* Washington, DC: American Psychological Association.

Atwell, N. (1987). *In the middle: Writing, reading, and learning with adolescents.* Portsmouth, NH: Heinemann.

August, D., & Hakuta, K. (Eds.). (1997). *Improving schooling for language-minority children: A research agenda.* Washington, DC: National Academy Press.

Brown, A. L, Campione, J. C., Webber, L. S., & McGilly, K. (1992). Interactive learning environments: A new look at assessment and instruction. In B. R. Gifford & M. C. O'Connor (Eds.), *Changing assessments: Alternative views of aptitude, achievement, and instruction* (pp. 121–211). Boston: Kluwer.

California Department of Education. (2004). *Eligibility criteria.* Retrieved April 28, 2004, from California special education laws and regulations database: *http://eit.otan.dni.us/speced/laws_search/searchDetailsLaws.cfm?id=744&keywords=eligibility%20criteria*

Cole, M. (1990). Cognitive development and formal schooling: The evidence from cross-cultural research. In L. C. Moll (Ed.), *Vygotsky and education* (pp. 89–110). Cambridge, UK: Cambridge University Press.

Cole, M. (1996). *Cultural psychology: A once and future discipline.* Cambridge, MA: Harvard University Press.

Cole, M., & Bruner, J. (1971). Cultural differences and inferences about psychological processes. *American Psychologist, 26,* 867–876.

Cole, M., Gay, J., Glick, J., & Sharp, D. W. (1971). *The cultural context of learning and thinking.* New York: Basic Books.

Cummins, J. (1984). *Bilingualism and special education: Issues in assessment and pedagogy.* San Diego, CA: College Hill.

Deno, S. (1992). The nature and development of curriculum-based measurement. *Preventing School Failure, 36,* 5–10.

Deno, S. L. (1987). Curriculum-based measurement, program development, graphing performance, and increasing efficiency. *Teaching Exceptional Children, 20,* 41–47.

Deno, S. L., & Mirkin, P. K. (1980). Data based IEP development: An approach to substantive compliance. *Teaching Exceptional Children, 12*(3), 92–97.

Dent, H., Mendocal, A., Pierce, W., & West, G. (1991). The San Francisco Public Schools experience with IQ testing: A model for non-biased assessment. In A. G. Hilliard (Ed.), *Testing African American students: Special re-issue of The Negro Educational Review* (pp. 146–162). Morristown, NJ: Aaron Press.

De Valenzuela, J. S., & Cervantes, H. T. (1998). Procedures and techniques for assessing the bilingual exceptional child. In L. Baca & H. Cervantes (Eds.), *The bilingual special education interface* (3rd ed.). Upper Saddle River, NJ: Prentice-Hall.

Elliott, J. L., Erickson, R. N., Thurlow, M. L., & Shriner, J. G. (2000). State-level accountability for the performance of students with disabilities: Five years of change? *Journal of Special Education, 34,* 39–47.

Figueroa, R. A. (1989). Psychological testing of linguistic-minority students: Knowledge gaps and regulations. *Exceptional Children, 56,* 145–152.

Figueroa, R. A. (1990). Assessment of linguistic minority group children. In C. R. Reynolds & R. W. Kamphaus (Eds.), *Handbook of psychological and educational assessment of children; Vol. 1. Intelligence and achievement.* New York: Guilford.

Figueroa, R. A., & Sassenrath, J. M. (1989). A longitudinal study of the predictive validity of the System of Multicultural Pluralistic Assessment (SOMPA). *Psychology in the Schools, 26,* 5–19.

Flood, J., & Lapp, D. (1988). A reader response approach to the teaching of literature. *Reading Research and Instruction, 27,* 61–66.

Fuchs, L., & Deno, S. (1992). Effects of curriculum within curriculum-based measurement. *Exceptional Children, 58,* 232–243.

Fuchs, L., Fuchs, D., & Hamlett, C. (1989). Effects of instrumental use of curriculum-based measurement to enhance instructional programs. *Remedial and Special Education, 10,* 43–52.

Fuchs, L. S., Fuchs, D., Hamlett, C., Philips, N., & Bentz, J. (1994). Classwide curriculum-based measurement: Helping general educators meet the challenge of student diversity. *Exceptional Children, 60,* 15–24.

Fuchs, L. S., Fuchs, D., Hamlett, C. L., & Stecker, P. M. (1991). Effects of curriculum-based measurement and consultation on teacher planning and student achievement in mathematical operations. *American Educational Research Journal, 28,* 617–641.

Gajria, M., Salend, S. J., & Hemrich, M. A. (1994). Teacher acceptability of testing modifications for mainstreamed students. *Learning Disabilities Research and Practice, 9,* 236–243.

Garcia, G. E., & Pearson, P. D. (1994). Assessment and diversity. In L. Darling-Hammond (Ed.), *Review of research in education, 20,* 337–391. Washington, DC: American Educational Research Association.

Garcia, S. B., & Ortiz, A. A. (1988). *Preventing inappropriate referrals of language minority students to special education.* Silver Spring, MD: National Clearinghouse for Bilingual Education.

General Educational Development Testing Service. (2000). *Accommodations for disabilities.* Retrieved September 23, 2000, from General Educational Development Testing Service Online: *http://www.acenet.edu/clll/ged/disability-accom-TT.cfm*

Gonzalez, V., Brusca-Vega, R., & Yawkey, T. (1997). *Assessment and instruction of culturally and linguistically diverse students.* Boston: Allyn and Bacon.

Goodman, K. (1969). Analysis of oral reading miscues: Applied psycholinguistics. *International Reading Association, V,* 9–29.

Goodman, K. (1973). *Miscue analysis: Applications to reading instruction.* Urbana, IL: National Council of Teachers of English.

Goodnow, J. J. (1976). The nature of intelligent behavior: Questions raised by cross-cultural studies. In L. B. Resnick (Ed.), *The nature of intelligence.* Hillsdale, NJ: Erlbaum.

Greenfield, P. M., & Childs, C. P. (1977). Weaving, color terms and pattern representation: Cultural influences and cognitive development among the Zinancantecos of Southern Mexico. *Inter-American Journal of Psychology, 11,* 23–48.

Gresham, F. M., & Elliott, S. N. (1990). *SSRS: Social Skills Rating System.* Circle Pines, MN: AGS Publishing.

Gronna, S. S., Jenkins, A. A., & Chin-Chance, S.A. (1998). Who are we assessing: Determining state-wide participation rates for students with disabilities. *Exceptional Children, 64,* 407–418.

Haager, D., & Vaughn, S. (1997). Assessment of social competence in students with learning disabilities. In J. Lloyd, E. Kameenui & D. Chard (Eds.), *Issues in educating students with disabilities* (pp. 129–152). Mahwah, NJ: Lawrence Erlbaum.

Hakuta, K. (1986). *Mirror of language: The debate on bilingualism.* New York: Basic Books.

Harris, J. D., Gray, B. A., Davis, J. E., Zaremba, E. T., & Argulewicz, E. N. (1988). The exclusionary clause and the disadvantaged: Do we try to comply with the law? *Journal of Learning Disabilities, 21,* 581–583.

Haywood, H. C. (1988). Dynamic assessment: The Learning Potential Assessment Device. In R. L. Jones (Ed.), *The psychoeducational assessment of minority group children: A casebook* (pp. 39–64). Berkeley, CA: Cobb and Henry.

Hilliard, A. G. (1977). The predictive validity of norm-referenced standardized tests: Piaget or Binet? *The Negro Educational Review, 25,* 189–201.

Idol, L. (1989). The resource/consulting teacher: An integrated model of service delivery. *Remedial and Special Education, 10,* 38–48.

Jayanthi, M., Epstein, M. H., Polloway, E. A., & Bursuck, W. D. (1996). A national survey of general education teachers' perceptions of testing adaptations. *Journal of Special Education, 30,* 99–115.

Keogh, B. (1998). Classrooms as well as students deserve study. *Remedial and Special Education, 19,* 313–314.

King-Sears, M. E. (1994). *Curriculum-based assessment in special education.* San Diego, CA: Singular.

Langdon, H. W. (1989). Language disorder or language difference? Assessing the language skills of Hispanic students. *Exceptional Children, 56,* 160–167.

Laosa, L. M. (1977). Nonbiased assessment of children's abilities: Historical antecedents and current issues. In T. Oakland (Ed.), *Psychological and educational assessment of minority children* (pp. 1–20). New York: Brunner/Mazel.

Marston, D., & Magnusson, D. (1985). Implementing curriculum-based measurement in special and regular education settings. *Exceptional Children, 52,* 266–276.

Mastropieri, M. A., & Scruggs, T. E. (2000). The effectiveness of mnemonic instruction for students with learning and behavior problems: An update and research synthesis. *Journal of Behavioral Education, 10,* 163–173.

Mather, N., & Kirk, S. A. (1985). The type III error and other concerns in learning disability research. *Learning Disabilities Research, 1*(1), 56–64.

McDonnell, L., McLaughlin, M., & Morison, P. (Eds.). (1997). *Educating one and all: Students with disabilities and standards-based reform.* Washington, DC: National Academy Press.

Mercer, J. (1973). Labeling the mentally retarded. Berkeley: University of California Press.

Mercer, J. (1979). *System of Multicultural Pluralistic Assessment (SOMPA): Technical manual.* San Antonio, TX: Psychological Corporation.

Moll, L. C. (Ed.). (1990). *Vygotsky and education: Instructional implications and applications of sociohistorical psychology.* Cambridge, UK: Cambridge University Press.

National Commission on Testing and Public Policy. (1990). *From gatekeepers to gateway: Transforming testing in America.* Chestnut Hill, MA: Boston College.

National Joint Committee on Learning Disabilities. (1998). Operationalizing the NJCLD definition of learning disabilities for ongoing assessment in schools. *Learning Disability Quarterly, 21,* 182–193.

National Research Council. (1999). *High stakes: Testing for tracking, promotion, and graduation.* Washington, DC: National Academy Press.

Ochoa, S. H., Rivera, B. D., & Powell, M. P. (1997). Factors used to comply with the exclusionary clause with bilingual and limited-English-proficient pupils: Initial guidelines. *Learning Disabilities Research & Practice, 12,* 161–167.

Oller, J. W., Jr. (1991). Language testing research: Lessons applied to LEP students and programs. In *Proceedings of the first research symposium on limited English proficient students' issues: Focus on evaluation and measurement: Vol. 2* (pp. 42–123). Washington, DC: U.S. Department of Education, Office of Bilingual Education and Minority Language Affairs.

Ortiz, A. A. (1997). Learning disabilities occurring concomitantly with linguistic differences. *Journal of Learning Disabilities, 30,* 321–332.

Ortiz, A. A., & Wilkinson, C. Y. (1991). Assessment and intervention model for the bilingual exceptional student (AIM for the BESt). *Teacher Education and Special Education, 14,* 35–42.

Overton, T. (1996). *Assessment in special education: An applied approach* (3rd ed.). Upper Saddle River, NJ: Merrill.

Overton, T. (2003). *Assessing learners with special needs: An applied approach* (4th ed.). Upper Saddle River, NJ: Merrill.

Pierangelo, R., & Giuliani, G. A. (2002). *Assessment in special education: A practical approach.* Boston: Allyn and Bacon.

Pike, K., & Salend, S. J. (1995). Authentic assessment strategies: Alternatives to norm-referenced testing. *TEACHING Exceptional Children, 28*(1), 15–20.

Poteet, J. A., Choate, J. S., & Stewart, S. C. (1996). Performance assessment and special education: Promises and prospects. In E. L. Meyen, G. A. Vergason, & B. J. Whelan (Eds.), *Strategies for teaching exceptional children in inclusive settings* (pp. 209–242). Denver, CO: Love.

Public Policy Unit, Council for Exceptional Children. (1998). *IDEA 1997: Let's make it work.* Reston, VA: Author.

Rogoff, B., & Waddell, K. J. (1982). Memory for information organized in a scene by children from two cultures. *Child Development, 53,* 1224–1228.

Rueda, R. (1997). Changing the context of assessment: The move to portfolios and authentic assessment. In A. J. Artiles & G. Zamora-Duran (Eds.), *Reducing the disproportionate representation of culturally diverse students in special and gifted education* (pp. 7–25). Reston, VA: Council for Exceptional Children.

Salend, S. J. (2000). Strategies and resources to evaluate the impact of inclusion programs on students. *Intervention in School and Clinic, 35,* 264–270, 289.

Salvia, J., & Ysseldyke, J. E. (1998). *Assessment* (7th ed.). Boston: Houghton Mifflin.

Samuda, R. J. (1989). Psychometric factors in the appraisal of intelligence. In R. J. Samuda & S. L. Kong (Eds.), *Assessment and placement of minority students* (pp. 25–40). Toronto, Canada: C.J. Hogrefe.

Saxe, G. B. (1988). The mathematics of street vendors. *Child Development, 59,* 1415–1425.

Schumm, J. S., & Vaughn, S. (1991). Making adaptations for mainstreamed students: General classroom teachers' perspectives. *Remedial and Special Education, 12,* 18–27.

Serpell, R. (1994). The cultural construction of intelligence. In W. J. Lonner & R. S. Malpass (Eds.), *Readings in psychology and culture* (pp. 157–163). Boston: Allyn and Bacon.

Shinn, M. R., & Bamonto, S. (1998). Advanced applications of curriculum-based measurement: "Big ideas" and avoiding confusion. In M. R. Shinn (Ed.), *Advanced applications of curriculum-based measurement.* New York: Guilford.

Sternberg, R. J. (1998). All intelligence testing is "cross-cultural." In R. J. Samuda et al. (Eds.), *Advances in cross-cultural assessment* (pp. 197–215; 274–285). Thousand Oaks, CA: Sage Publications.

Swicegood, P. (1994). Portfolio-based assessment practices. *Intervention in School and Clinic, 30,* 6–15.

Taylor, O. L., & Lee, D. L. (1987). Standardized tests and African-American children: Communication and language issues. *Negro Educational Review, 38,* 67–80.

Thurlow, M. L., House, A. L., Scott, D. L., & Ysseldyke, J. E. (2000). Students with disabilities in large-scale assessments: State participation and accommodation policies. *The Journal of Special Education, 34,* 154–163.

Thurlow, M. L., Ysseldyke, J. E., & Silverstein, B. (1995). Testing accommodations for students with disabilities. *Remedial and Special Education, 16,* 260–270.

Tindal, G. A. (1990). Classroom-based assessment: Evaluating instructional outcomes. Upper Saddle River, NJ: Merrill/Prentice-Hall.

Tindal, G. A., & Marston, D. B. (1990). *Classroom-based assessment: Evaluating instructional outcomes.* Upper Saddle River, NJ: Merrill/Prentice-Hall.

Trueba, H. T. (1989). *Raising silent voices: Educating the linguistic minorities for the 21st century.* New York: Newbury House.

Tucker, J. A. (1977). Operationalizing the diagnostic-intervention process. In T. Oakland (Ed.), *Psychological and educational assessment of minority children* (pp. 91–111). New York: Brunner/Mazel.

U.S. Office of Education. (1977). Definition and criteria for defining students as learning disabled. *Federal Register.* Washington, DC: U.S. Government Printing Office.

Valdez, G., & Figueroa, R. A. (1994). *Bilingualism and testing: A special case of bias.* Norwood, NJ: Ablex.

Valencia, S. (1990). A portfolio approach to classroom reading assessment: The whys, whats, and hows. *Reading Teacher, 43,* 338–40.

Vanderwood, M., McGrew, K., & Ysseldyke, J. E. (1998). Why we can't say much about students with disabilities during educational reform. *Exceptional Children, 64,* 359–370.

Wesson, C. L., & King, R. P. (1996). Portfolio assessment and special education students. *Teaching Exceptional Children, 28,* 44–48.

Williams, R. L. (1974). The problem of match and mismatch in testing Black children. In L. P. Miller (Ed.), *The testing of Black students: A symposium* (pp. 17–30). Englewood Cliffs, NJ: Prentice-Hall.

Assessment Measures

Criterion Referenced Tests

Brigance, A. (1981). *Brigance Diagnostic Inventory of Essential Skills.* N. Billerica, MA: Curriculum Associates.

Brigance, A. (1985). *Brigance Preschool Screen (Age 3–4).* N. Billerica, MA: Curriculum Associates.

Brigance, A. (1990). *Brigance Early Preschool Screen (Age 2–2 1/2).* N. Billerica, MA: Curriculum Associates.

Brigance, A. (1991). *Brigance Diagnostic Inventory of Early Development-Revised.* N. Billerica, MA: Curriculum Associates.

Brigance, A. (1992). *Brigance K & 1 Screen-Revised,* N. Billerica, MA: Curriculum Associates.

Brigance, A. (1994). *Brigance Diagnostic Life Skills Inventory.* N. Billerica, MA: Curriculum Associates.

Brigance, A. (1995). *Brigance Diagnostic Employability Skills Inventory.* N. Billerica, MA: Curriculum Associates.

Brigance, A. (1999). *The Brigance Diagnostic Assessment of Basic Skills-Revised (Spanish version).* N. Billerica, MA: Curriculum Associates.

Brigance, A. (1999). *Brigance Diagnostic Inventory of Basic Skills-Revised.* N. Billerica, MA: Curriculum Associates.

Norm-Referenced Achievement Tests

Kaufman, A., & Kaufman, N. (1997). *The Kaufman Test of Educational Achievement.* Circle Pines, MN: American Guidance Service.

Kaufman, A., & Kaufman, N. (2003). *Kaufman Assessment Battery for Children* (2nd ed.). Circle Pines, MN: American Guidance Service.

Markwardt, F. (1989). *The Peabody Individual Achievement Test-Revised.* Circle Pines, MN: American Guidance Service.

Wechsler, D. (1999). *The Wechsler Individual Achievement Test–2.* San Antonio, TX: Psychological Corporation.

Wechsler, D. (2001). *The Wechsler Individual Achievement Test* (2nd ed.). San Antonio, TX: Psychological Corporation.

Wechsler, D. (2002). *Wechsler Preschool & Primary Scale of Intelligence* (3rd ed.). San Antonio, TX: Psychological Corporation.

Wechsler, D. (2003). *Wechsler Intelligence Scale for Children* (4th ed.). San Antonio, TX: Psychological Corporation.

Wilkinson, G. (1993). *The Wide Range Achievement Test-Revision 3.* Wilmington, DE: Jastak Associates.

Woodcock, R. W., McGrew, K. S., & Mather, N. (2001a). *Woodcock-Johnson III Complete Battery.* Itasca, IL: Riverside Publishing.

Woodcock, R., McGrew, K., & Mather, N. (2001b). *Woodcock-Johnson Tests of Achievement-III.* Itasca, IL: Riverside Publishing.

Woodcock, R. W., McGrew, K. S., & Mather, N. (2001c). *Woodcock-Johnson III Tests of Cognitive Ability.* Itasca, IL: Riverside Publishing.

Woodcock, R. W., & Muñoz-Sandoval, A. (1996). *Batería Woodcock-Muñoz-Revisada: Pruebas de Aprovechamiento.* Itasca, Il: Riverside Publishing.

Woodcock, R. W., & Muñoz-Sandoval, A., McGrew, K., Mather, N., & Schrank, F. (2004). *Batería Woodcock-Muñoz* (3rd ed.). Itasca, IL: Riverside Publishing Company.

Diagnostic Tests

Brown, V., Cronin, M., & McEntire, E. (1994). *Test of Mathematical Abilities–2.* Austin, TX: Pro-Ed.

Connolly, A., Nachtman, W., & Pritchett, F. (1997). *Key Math Diagnostic Test-Revised.* Circle Pines, MN: American Guidance Service.

Hammill, D., & Bryant, B. (1998). *Learning Disabilities Diagnostic Inventory.* Wood Dale, IL: Stoelting.

Hammill, D., & Larsen, S. (1996). *Test of Written Language-3.* Austin, TX: Pro-Ed.

Torgesen, J., & Bryant, B. (1994). *Test of Phonological Awareness.* London: The Psychological Corporation.

Woodcock, R. W. (1997). *Woodcock Diagnostic Reading Battery.* Itasca, IL: Riverside Publishing.

Tests of Cognitive Functioning

Kaufman, A., & Kaufman, N. (1983). *Kaufman Assessment Battery for Children.* Circle Pines, MN: American Guidance Service Inc.

Thorndike, R., Hagen, E., & Sattler, J. (1996). *Stanford-Binet Intelligence Scale-Fourth Edition.* Itasca, IL: Riverside Publishing.

Wechsler, D. (1989). *Wechsler Preschool & Primary Scale of Intelligence-Revised.* San Antonio, TX: Psychological Corporation.

Wechsler, D. (1991). *Wechsler Intelligence Scale for Children, Third Edition.* San Antonio, TX: Psychological Corporation.

Woodcock, R. W., & Johnson, M. B. (1989/90). *Woodcock-Johnson Psychoeducational Battery-Revised, Tests of Cognitive Ability.* Itasca, Il: Riverside Publishing.

Woodcock, R. W., & Muñoz-Sandoval, A. (1996). *Batería Woodcock-Muñoz-Revisada.* Itasca, IL: Riverside Publishing.

Adaptive Behavior

Bryant, B. R., Taylor, R. L., & Pedrotty-Rivera, D. (1996). *AAA Assessment of Adaptive Areas.* Austin, TX: Pro-Ed.

Gallagher, R. (1983). *Keystone Adaptive Behavior Profile.* Indianapolis, IN: Prentice BS.

Lambert, N., Leland, H., & Nihira, K. (1993). *Adaptive Behavior Scale–Second Edition. School Edition.* San Antonio, TX: Psychological Corporation.

McCarney, S., & Leigh, J. (1998). *Adaptive Behavior Evaluation Scale.* Columbia, MO: Hawthorne Educational Services.

Sparrow, S. S., Balla, D. A., & Cicchetti, D. V. (1984). *Vineland Adaptive Behavior Scale.* Circle Pines, MN: AGS Publishing.

Behavioral Functioning

Conners, C.K. (1997). *Conners' Parent and Teacher Rating Scales-R.* Austin, TX: Pro-Ed.

Gadow, K., & Sprafkin, J. (1997). *ADHD Symptom Checklist-4.* Stony Brook, NY: Checkmate Plus.

Gilliman, J. (1995). *Attention-Deficit/Hyperactivity Disorder Test.* Wood Dale, IL: Stoelting.

Spadafore, G., & Spadafore, S. (1997). *Spadafore ADHD Rating Scale.* Novato, CA: Academic Therapy.

Ullman, R., Sleator, E., & Sprague, R. (1991). *ADD-H Comprehensive Teacher's Rating Scale*, Second Edition. Wood Dale, IL: Stoelting.

Social Functioning

Sparrow, S., Balla, D., & Cicchetti, D. (1985). *Vineland Social Maturity Scale.* Circle Pines, MN: AGS Publishing.

Sparrow, S., Balla, D., & Cicchetti, D. (1998) *Vineland Social-Emotional Early Childhood Scales.* Circle Pines, MN: AGS Publishing.

Walker, H. M., & McConnell, S. R. (1995a). *Walker-McConnell Scale of Social Competence and School Adjustment, Adolescent Version.* Belmont, CA: Wadsworth.

Walker, H. M., & McConnell, S. R. (1995b). *Walker-McConnell Scale of Social Competence and School Adjustment, Elementary Version.* Belmont, CA: Wadsworth.

Emotional Functioning

Battle, J. (1992). *Culture-Free Self Esteem Inventories, Second Edition.* Austin, TX: Pro-Ed.

Bracken, B. (1991). *Multidimensional Self Concept Scale.* San Antonio, TX: Psychological Corporation.

Brown, L., & Alexander, J. (1991). *Self-Esteem Index.* Lutz, FL: Psychological Assessment Resources.

Fitts, W., & Warren, W. (1996). *Tennessee Self Concept Scale*, Second Edition. Princeton, NY: Educational Testing Service.

Greshman, F., Elliot, S., & Evans-Fernandez, S. (1995). *Student Self-Concept Scale.* Circle Pines, MN: AGS Publishing.

Piers, E. V. (1986). *Piers/Harris Children's Self Concept Scale-Revised.* Los Angeles, CA: Western Psychological Services.

Sensory and Perceptual Functioning

Beery, K., & Buktenica, N. (1997). *Developmental Test of Visual-Motor Integration, 4th Edition.* River Grove, IL: Follett Educational.

Colarusso, R., & Hammill, D. (1996). *Motor-Free Visual Perception Test, Revised.* Wood Dale, IL: Stoelting.

Gardner, M. (1996). *Test of Auditory Perceptual Skills–Revised.* Austin, TX: Pro-Ed.

Goldman, R., Fristoe, M., & Woodcock, R. W. (1970). *Goldman-Fristoe-Woodcock Test of Auditory Discrimination.* Circle Pines, MN: American Guidance.

Hammill, D. D. (1998). *Detroit Tests of Learning Aptitude.* Fourth Edition. Austin, TX: Pro-Ed.

Hammill, D. D., Mather, N., & Roberts, R. (2001). *Illinois Test of Psycholinguistic Abilities, 3rd Edition.* San Antonio, TX: Psychological Corporation.

Hammill, D. D., Pearson, N. A., & Voress, J. K. (1993). *Developmental Test of Visual Perception* (2nd ed.). Wood Dale, IL: Stoelting.

Lindamood, C., & Lindamood, P. (1985). *Lindamood Auditory Conceptualization Test.* Wood Dale, IL: Stoelting.

Sivan, B. A. (1991). *Benton Visual Retention Test,* Fifth Edition. San Antonio, TX: The Psychological Corporation.

Slosson, R. (1996). *Slosson Drawing Coordination Test for Children & Adults.* East Aurora, NY: Slosson Educational Publishers.

Sterling, H. (1998). *Quick Neurological Screening Test, II.* Wood Dale, IL: Stoelting.

Wepman, J., & Reynolds, W. (1987). *Wepman Test of Auditory Discrimination*, Second Edition. Los Angeles, CA: Western Psychological Services.

Oral Language Assessment

Ballard, W., Tighe, P., & Dalton, E. (1991). *IDEA Oral Language Proficiency Test.* Brea, CA: Ballard & Tighe.

Boehm, A. (2000). *Test of Basic Concepts-Revised (BOEHM-3).* San Antonio, TX: The Psychological Corporation.

Critchlow, D. (1996). *Dos Amigos Verbal Language Scales: An English-Spanish Aptitude Test.* Novato, CA: Academic Therapy.

DeAvila, W., & Duncan, S. (1990). *Language Assessment Scales.* Monterey, CA: CTB McGraw-Hill.

Dunn, L. M., & Dunn, L. M. (1997). *Peabody Picture Vocabulary Test-III.* Circle Pines, MN: American Guidance Service.

German, D. J. (1990). *Test of Adolescent and Adult Word Finding.* Austin, TX: Pro-Ed.

German, D. J. (2000). *Test of Word Finding* (2nd ed.). Austin, TX: Pro-Ed.

German, D. J., & German, A. E. (1992). *Word Finding Referral Checklist.* Chicago, IL: Word Finding Materials.

Hammill, D. D., & Newcomer, P. L. (1997). *Test of Language Development-Intermediate, Third Edition.* Austin, TX: PO-Ed.

Hammill, D. D., Brown, V. L., Larsen, S. C., & Wiederholt., J. L. (1994). *Test of Adolescent Language Development and Adult Language, Third Edition.* Austin, TX: Pro-Ed.

Hresko, W., Reid, D. K., & Hammill, D. (1999). *Test of Early Language Development* (3rd ed.). San Antonio, TX: Psychological Corporation.

Newcomer, P. L., & Hammill, D. D. (1997). *Test of Language Development-Primary* (3rd ed.). Austin, TX: Pro-Ed.

Woodcock, R. W., & Muñoz-Sandoval, A. (1993). *Woodcock-Muñoz Language Survey, English (LS-E) and Spanish (LS-S).* Itasca, IL: Riverside Publishing.

CHAPTER FOUR

INSTRUCTIONAL APPROACHES FOR INCLUSIVE CLASSROOMS

The mediocre teacher tells. The good teacher explains. The superior teacher demonstrates. The great teacher inspires.

William A. Ward

KEY CONCEPTS

- Teachers should have a large repertoire of teaching approaches at their disposal, along with the knowledge and skills to "mix and match" different strategies depending on the needs of students and the demands of the learning environment.
- Teachers should use a variety of methods to increase students' involvement and participation in the general education environment, such as response cards, Think-Pair-Share, Numbered Heads Together (and other cooperative learning techniques), hands-on learning activities, choral responses, and wait time.

- Learning centers can provide multilevel instruction in an inclusive classroom—centers might be used as an integral part of an overall instructional plan or thematic unit, or to provide supplemental optional experiences.
- Thematic units allow teachers to integrate academic content with the development of basic skills using a variety of methods that capitalize on students' prior knowledge, interests, and strengths.
- Teachers who implement flexible grouping effectively use a variety of grouping patterns that are tailored to fit students' strengths and the demands of the curriculum, ranging from whole class to small groups to pairs, depending upon the purpose of the activity.
- Cooperative learning provides academic and social benefits for students with and without disabilities, as well as English language learners and culturally diverse populations.
- Many strategies have been developed to help students with learning disabilities and other students with special needs become more efficient, active learners (e.g., in reading comprehension, writing, math problem solving, and content area learning).
- With direct instruction, skills are explicitly taught in small sequential steps, students are active participants in lessons, students have opportunities for guided practice, and the teacher provides immediate feedback.
- Technology can provide teachers with many options for enhancing teaching and learning in inclusive classrooms—computers, tape recorders, and other specialized assistive devices can provide ongoing assistance for students both in and out of the classroom.

FOCUS QUESTIONS

1. Describe the characteristics of an effective special education teacher.
2. What can the teacher do to motivate reluctant students?
3. How can teachers make sure they are giving clear assignments and that students with disabilities understand their directions?
4. What are the benefits of cooperative learning and peer or cross-age tutoring for students with disabilities?
5. Describe how flexible grouping might be put into practice in a classroom with both a general education and an special education teacher.
6. What should the special educator know about direct instruction as an instructional method for inclusive classrooms?
7. Describe various ways that technology can help teachers and students in an inclusive classroom.
8. What does IDEA stipulate about assistive technology?

In this chapter we describe various instructional approaches that, when well-implemented, can be appropriate and effective in heterogeneous inclusive classrooms. Keep in mind as you learn about these approaches that your task is not to find the best approach for all situations and all students, but to learn enough about various approaches to determine what works best when, how, with whom, and under what circumstances. We believe that it is important for teachers to have a large repertoire of teaching approaches at their disposal, along with the knowledge and skills to "mix and match" different strategies depending on the needs of students and the demands of the learning environment. It is important to be able to adjust the pace and content of instruction as students' needs and interests vary and to be able to take advantage of "teachable moments." The ability to creatively and flexibly implement instructional methods requires a deep understanding of the underlying principles that guide each approach, a thorough awareness of how children learn, and a willingness to take risks and try new ways of teaching.

We begin this chapter with a description of effective teachers and continue with sections on motivating students, selecting instructional materials, and giving classroom assignments. Next, we discuss ways to increase student participation. Learning centers, thematic units, and grouping practices (including cooperative learning and tutoring) follow. We next describe scaffolded instruction and learning strategies, followed by behavioral approaches such as direct instruction, precision teaching, and mastery learning. We finish with a discussion of technology.

EFFECTIVE TEACHERS

Are effective teachers born or made? Certainly there is no one mold from which all successful teachers emerge. Yet, it does appear that there are some characteristics shared by effective teachers—they love teaching and seeing their students learn. In a summary of the research on effective teaching, Zigmond (1996) describes five qualities of effective teachers in Box 4.1.

Understanding How Children Learn

Rather than adhere strictly to one theoretical perspective, we believe there is much to be learned from various branches of psychology about educational theory. Like the proverb of the blind men who each examined a different part of an elephant and argued in favor of his own perspective without realizing that each was accurately depicting his own small piece, in the field of education it seems we sometimes enthusiastically jump on the bandwagon of one theoretical perspective or another and decry every instructional approach that does not fit tightly within that perspective. Three theoretical approaches are described in this chapter—behavioral psychology, cognitive psychology, and sociocultural theory. Each has had an enormous impact on instructional practices in both general and special education. How do these three models differ? To some extent they can be placed along a continuum, with behaviorist approaches at one end of the spectrum and constructivist approaches at the other. Behaviorist approaches are more specific and bottom-up, or part-to-whole, whereas constructivist approaches are more

BOX 4.1

WHAT MAKES AN EFFECTIVE TEACHER?

- **Effective teachers have memorable personalities.** Effective teachers share some or all of several personality traits—they are friendly, cheerful, sympathetic, virtuous, enthusiastic, humorous, fair, democratic, responsive, understanding, kind, stimulating, alert, responsible, poised, and confident.
- **Effective teachers are academically able and have a strong knowledge of the subject matter they are teaching.** They know enough about the subject matter they are teaching to differentiate between what is important and what is incidental or peripheral.
- **Effective teachers have deep knowledge of general and specific pedagogy.** They know how best to teach specific subject matter; how to present information clearly; how to inspire, excite, and motivate students to learn; and how to evaluate students' learning. In addition, effective teachers know children and their developmental stages and how these influence what can be taught and what will be learned. They have an extensive repertoire of pedagogical practices.
- **Effective teachers can translate knowledge of subject matter and knowledge of pedagogy into practice.** They can create environments that facilitate learning, they use time efficiently, and they can provide positive, constructive feedback to their students. They ask questions that their students are likely to be able to respond to correctly, and they use classroom management strategies that keep students actively participating and appropriately engaged. Effective teachers teach classes that are so exciting, engaging, well-planned and well-paced that students can't help but learn what is being taught!
- **Effective teachers understand that learning is a lifelong process.** They are reflective about their practice and approach their work in a collegial, problem-solving manner.

general and top-down, or whole-to-part. Cognitive approaches fall somewhere in the middle.

Behavioral Psychology. *Behavioral psychology* is based on the premise that the environment greatly influences behavior. According to behavioral psychologists and educators who subscribe to this theory, learning is defined as *measurable* change in *observable* behavior (Haring & Phillips, 1972; Lovitt, 1983; Skinner, 1974). Behavioral psychologists are much more concerned with what individuals *do* than what they *think*. The antecedents and consequences of behavior (i.e., what happens immediately before and after a correct or incorrect response) are important aspects of the learning process. Thus, rewards for appropriate behavior, such as praise and/or tangible reinforcers, figure heavily into this perspective.

Applied behavioral analysis is a term often used to describe behavioral approaches. Applied behavioral analysis focuses on the systematic analysis of the observable behaviors of individual learners (Lovitt, 1975). Hallahan, Kauffman, and Lloyd (1999) noted that perhaps the greatest contributions of applied behavioral analysis are its emphasis on empirical verification of outcomes and its recommendations that teachers collect objective data about pupil performance. During the lesson planning process, teachers clearly specify the behavioral objectives of a lesson (what students will be able to do as a result of instruction). These objectives are then linked to assessment procedures. Student progress data are used to determine the effectiveness of the lesson and to guide instructional decision making.

All behavioral approaches include *task analysis*. "Task analysis is the process of isolating, describing and sequencing all the necessary subtasks which, when the child has mastered them, will enable him to perform the objective" (Bateman, 1971, p. 33). When conducting a task analysis, the teacher lists the competencies or steps required to successfully complete a task, asking him- or herself, "What does the student need to know how to do?" The purpose of task analysis is to make overt the steps of a process that are usually covert. Even though they might not be obvious, even seemingly simple tasks such as reading a word or solving an addition problem require the completion of a series of connected discrete tasks. Prerequisite skills are determined by working backwards from the desired skill, building a hierarchy of subskills. The teacher then teaches the student the easiest skill that he or she is unable to perform without assistance. We believe that the ability to conduct task analyses is an essential characteristic of a special education teacher and that when teachers have difficulty differentiating instruction, it is often this ability they are lacking.

Much of what we know about effective teaching comes from a behavioral orientation. Research reviews on effective teaching (Christenson, Ysseldyke, & Thurlow, 1989; Englert, Tarrant, & Mariage, 1992; Good & Brophy, 1994; Rosenshine & Stevens, 1986) reported the following elements as contributing to positive student outcomes: setting goals and objectives; providing feedback; monitoring student progress; teaching to mastery; using explicit step-by-step teaching methods; ensuring high rates of success; providing multiple opportunities for students to practice what they have learned; and using a variety of demonstration, modeling, and practice presentation formats. The teacher has a great deal of responsibility for ensuring that the environment is structured to provide optimal learning experiences for students.

Methods based on behavioral theories are described throughout this book. Instructional approaches based on the behavioral model include Direct Instruction, Precision Teaching, and Mastery Learning. Behavior modification and operant conditioning are described in Chapter 5. Curriculum-based assessment and curriculum-based measurement are described in Chapter 3.

Cognitive Psychology and Information Processing Theory. In contrast to behavioral psychologists, cognitive psychologists assert that learning involves the formation of mental associations that result in an internal, mental change but not necessarily a behavioral change. Cognition and learning are active processes and require purposeful activity. Knowledge is organized—beliefs, attitudes, and emotions are associated and interconnected. Learning is the process of relating new information to previously learned information (background knowledge). The cognitive system has a built-in limited capacity. Thus, resources spent on lower level tasks will be unavailable for higher level processing (e.g., a student who struggles to identify words while reading will have difficulty comprehending what has been read [LaBerge & Samuels, 1974]). Expert learners, as compared with novices (a) are strategic (i.e., they use strategies to facilitate learning, such as rehearsing or chunking information to be remembered), (b) are motivated, (c) are metacognitively aware, and (d) use self-regulating practices. Many of the instructional approaches that have emerged from cognitive psychology are based on the principle that strategic behaviors can be taught with positive outcomes for students with learning difficulties (Flavell, 1992; Palincsar & Brown, 1984).

To apply cognitive strategies, the learner must use "executive" or "metacognitive" processes that require an active, reflective awareness of the approaches needed to solve problems (Wong, 1986). Metacognition, loosely translated, means "to know what you know" or "thinking about thinking." Metacognition involves (a) understanding the task to be performed, (b) selecting the strategies needed to accomplish the task, and (c) self-monitoring the performance of the task (Palincsar & Brown, 1987). From cognitive psychology, we know that students with disabilities are often inactive learners who lack strategies for planning and monitoring their own learning. Pressley (2000) summarizes many of the strategies that research indicates can help inefficient learners. Both Chapters 6 and 7 explain specific strategies and strategy instruction models that can be used to help students become more strategic learners.

Grounded in cognitive psychology, information processing theory attempts to describe how sensory input is perceived, transformed, reduced, elaborated, stored, retrieved, and used (Swanson, 1987, 1993). These processes are highly interactive. According to this model, the first step in learning is to receive input through the sensory receptors (e.g., ears, eyes). The input then proceeds to the sensory store where it can receive attention. If the learner is attending to other stimuli instead of this input (e.g., a neighboring student who has dropped a pencil), the information will be lost before it can proceed to the next level. If the learner attends to the new input, the next step will be to detect the salient features of the stimuli, applying prior knowledge and the context of the learning environment to assist with this process. Once the new input has been perceived in this way, it can move to the working or short-term memory. At this point, the new information will stay in the short-term memory store only for a short period of time before fading (about 15 seconds) unless the learner takes active steps to remember it. Different strategies that can keep information operative in our short-term memory include rehearsing (repeating it aloud to ourselves), chunking (grouping it, as we do with phone numbers when we cluster the numbers into two groups), and elaborating (Bos & Vaughn, 2001). For the information to be retrievable at a later time, it must be moved to and stored in long-term memory. One efficient way to do this is to relate the new information to knowledge that is already present in long-term memory. Throughout this procedure, it is the executive functioning system, or metacognition, that coordinates the process.

Instructional approaches based on cognitive psychology emphasize metacognitive processes and the active engagement of the student in the learning process. Unlike behavioral approaches, cognitive approaches may not include precise direct measurement of student progress in acquiring component skills. A cognitively oriented specialist would be less concerned with the rate of performance and more concerned about whether the student can apply learning strategies and demonstrate an understanding of underlying concepts.

Sociocultural Theory. According to sociocultural theory, thinking and learning are social processes. Meaning-making is rooted in social interaction, not just "in the head." Thus, cognitive development occurs when concepts first learned through social interactions become internalized and made one's own. Teaching and learning occur in settings where "more competent others" provide "guided participation" to the learner in a joint productive activity (Vygotsky, 1986). Learners develop higher mental functions by interacting with others within their "zone of proximal development," defined as the "distance between a child's actual developmental level as determined through independent problem-solving and potential development as determined through problem-solving under adult guidance or collaboration with more capable peers" (Vygotsky, 1978, p. 86). The adult or more competent other assists the learner by "scaffolding instruction," or providing temporary, adjustable support (Tharp & Gallimore, 1988). Meaningful learning is situated in the context of everyday teaching/learning settings and in everyday problem-solving activities (genuine, holistic activity). These settings and activities vary by culture, SES, and other factors (Diaz, Moll, & Mehan, 1986; Moll, 1990).

An accurate model of sociocultural theory can be found in the way children acquire language. First language acquisition is embedded in everyday meaningful activity (e.g., eating, dressing, playing) and is rarely the direct focus of instruction. No tests or drills are provided, but frequent monitoring is available. The adult adjusts his or her language to be appropriate to the child's level (assisting performance through scaffolding).

The constructivist view of learning is closely associated with the sociocultural perspective. Several basic tenets of constructivism follow, with clear implications for educating students with learning disabilities (adapted from Poplin, 1988):

1. The child engages in the "whole" task, not discrete bits, and the whole is greater than the sum of its parts (e.g., H_2O, or water, is more than two separate molecules of hydrogen and one of oxygen).
2. Learning involves a process of going from whole to part to whole with accurate parts being secondary to an understanding of the whole.
3. Two or more learning experiences transform one another and the structure of present knowledge; thus, learning is not merely additive, it is transformative.
4. Instruction is best derived from student interest and talent and not from deficits or curriculum materials.
5. The assessment of student development, interests, and involvement is more important than the assessment of student performance on subskills.
6. Good teaching is interactive rather than unidirectional.
7. Real-life activities provide better educational experiences than contrived ones.
8. Errors are a necessary part of learning and should not be penalized.
9. Goals of instruction should be more life-related (e.g., literacy) than school-related (e.g., worksheet completion).
10. Reflection, the creation of questions, and interpretation are more critical than "correct" or "right" answers to prepared questions.
11. Problems in learning are the result of interactions of personalities, interests, development, expectations, and previous experiences.
12. Passion, trust, and interest are paramount—subjectivity surrounds learning.

How can each of these theoretical perspectives fit together and complement one another as part of a comprehensive program? How is it possible to draw from such apparently distinct frameworks when designing an instructional curriculum? These questions will be answered throughout this chapter as we present a variety of strategies and techniques for teachers to implement in their classrooms. For example, let's say we want to teach our students how to apply reading comprehension strategies. We note that Maria is confused about how to find the main idea in a paragraph. We scaffold instruction for Maria within her zone of proximal development by first modeling the process for her and then guiding her with leading questions that enable her to identify the most important who or what in the paragraph, and then say the most important idea about the who or what. We have first modeled the whole process for Maria and then broken the task into discrete parts. Next, Maria participates in a discussion with her peers about the main ideas in other paragraphs, practicing her new skill. In this example, we have drawn from sociocultural theory by scaffolding instruction at an appropriate instructional level and recognizing the importance of talking with one's peers as a way to enhance learning. We have drawn from behavioral psychology by breaking a task into its component parts and providing instruction through modeling, direct instruction (albeit brief), and opportunities for practice. We have drawn from cognitive psychology by recognizing the importance of teaching a strategic process for determining the main idea of a paragraph as a way to help one understand and remember what was read.

Getting Started—Motivating Students

The first step in motivating students is to create a positive, caring classroom atmosphere. Teachers should hold high expectations, but at the same time voice frequent approval for small gains made toward achieving major objectives. Praise, when used effectively, can be a powerful way to motivate students (Brophy & Good, 1986). Establishing clear, realistic goals is another way to motivate students. Teachers can help students set their own short- and long-term goals and help them monitor progress toward meeting those goals. Allowing students to make their own choices can also be a powerful motivator. Motivation is further enhanced when learning is personally relevant (Good & Brophy, 1994) and related to real-life objectives (Adelman & Taylor, 1983). Students appreciate when teachers use lesson openers that catch their attention and capture their imagination. They crave excitement and variety. Yet perhaps the most effective way to motivate students is through SUCCESS—this is particularly true for students with learning difficulties who have experienced failure and frustration in the past.

How the Special Education Teacher Can Help Motivate Students. Certainly the inclusion specialist plays a key role in motivating students by assuring that instruction is at an appropriate level and suited to the needs of individual students. This requires careful monitoring of each student and co-planning with the GE teacher to assure that students' needs and interests are considered when planning and preparing lessons. The inclusion specialist can further motivate students by being available to assist when they "get stuck" and need encouragement or further explanation.

Selecting Instructional Materials

Selecting appropriate instructional materials is an important aspect of teaching in inclusive classrooms. Many factors must be considered when choosing books, supplies, and other learning tools. These include students' needs, students' interests, and cultural diversity (Olson & Platt, 1996). Well-selected materials help facilitate the individualization of instruction for learners with special needs. In a school or classroom with a co-teaching model, we advise that special education and general education teachers select materials together. Whether textbooks and other materials are selected by a schoolwide committee, grade-level committees, or teachers for their own class, by combining the complementary perspectives of inclusion specialists and general education teachers, the most appropriate choices can be made. While the inclusion specialist checks for qualities that will facilitate learning for students with special needs, the general education teacher can focus on matching curriculum requirements and meeting whole-class needs.

Students' Needs. As an inclusion specialist, you will be working with students with a wide range of needs and abilities. Thus, instructional materials should (a) be adaptable to a variety of levels; (b) include supplemental materials such as manipulatives, games, visuals, and computer software; (c) have varied entry levels; and (d) allow for monitoring of student progress (Olson & Platt, 1996).

When selecting *textbooks,* look for such features as outlines, lists of key concepts, highlighted key terms, a glossary, review sections in each chapter, and a teacher's edition that includes transparencies, games, and a variety of motivating enrichment and review activities. Choose books that are well-organized and have (a) clear, easy-to-follow directions; (b) only one new concept presented at a time; (c) sufficient opportunities for practice and review in various response modes; (d) relatively low readability levels; and (e) vocabulary that is not overly sophisticated or unnecessarily difficult. Reading materials should have well-formed, interesting passages that are conducive to the application of reading comprehension strategies. Such material is characterized by advance organizers that help students predict what they will be learning, one well-developed main idea in a paragraph, text that helps students connect new information with previously learned material and real-life experiences, and clear definitions of key vocabulary terms in context.

Students' Interests. Materials should be age appropriate, interesting, user friendly, related to real life, and addressing a wide range of topics. Students of all ages are motivated by functional materials that relate to real life (e.g., driver's license or job application forms, menus and order forms for restaurant role-playing).

Cultural Diversity. Instructional materials should include representation from a wide range of cultural groups so that students may learn to recognize, understand, and appreciate differences and similarities among peoples. Underrepresentation seems to occur most often with minority groups, women, people with disabilities, and older persons (Gollnick & Chinn, 1990). Ensuring that the classroom library contains books that cover a wide variety of topics, genres, and cultures is one way to guarantee wide representation. Another is to select textbooks that are sensitive to cultural issues and offer fair and accurate depictions of historical events and the contributions of persons from various ethnic groups.

Giving Clear Assignments

Much can be done to help special education students understand expectations and complete tasks in a timely, efficient manner. Clear, explicit instructions help reduce confusion about classroom assignments by eliminating ambiguity. If information is presented at too fast a rate or too abstract a level of conceptualization, student attention may decrease and students may become "lost" in the content. If this occurs, slow down the rate of presentation, include more visual organizers or media, or include more concrete examples (Scruggs & Mastropieri, 1992). The inclusion specialist can provide additional support, including: (a) models of appropriately completed assignments, (b) timelines for anticipated completion (including due dates for drafts of papers), (c) suggested due dates for completion of various components of projects, (d) dates and times when extra-help sessions will be provided for those interested, and (e) the criteria for acceptable performance on the assignment (Scruggs & Mastropieri, 1992).

When asked how best to give assignments, students with and without learning disabilities and their teachers concurred with the above suggestions and added a few more. They noted that good assignments include (Rademacher, Schumaker, & Deshler, 1996):

1. Clear, well-organized directions so students will know how to do the work.
2. An understood purpose so students will understand how completing the assignment will benefit their learning.
3. A set of product evaluation criteria so students will know how their finished work will be judged.
4. Optimal challenge so students will not be bored or frustrated.
5. Personal relevance factors that relate assignment completion to the social, learning, behavioral, and cultural characteristics of students' lives.
6. Assignment completion feedback so students will know what they did correctly and what they need to do to improve their work.
7. Format variety that differs from the traditional worksheet.
8. Available resource lists necessary for doing the work.
9. Creative expression opportunities so students can use their imaginations in some way.
10. Interpersonal or social actions that include opportunities to work with others.
11. Completion time considerations that include giving students time to work in class.
12. Student choices that allow for options within the dimensions of the assignment itself and how it is to be completed. (p. 167)

REACT. This routine helps students become actively involved during assignment explanations (Rademacher, Schumaker, & Deshler, 1996). The acronym helps students remember to: **R**ecord the assignment explanations; **E**xamine the requirements and choices offered by the teacher; **A**sk questions to better understand the directions; **C**reate a written goal for improving or matching past performances on similar assignments; **T**arget a time to begin, finish, and evaluate the assignment for quality before turning it in to the teacher.

Teaching Study Skills. Study sessions are beneficial for students with learning disabilities and can help everyone in the class. Such sessions might include: (a) the best ways to review and study a particular textbook, (b) how to take class notes, (c) effective highlighting and outlining procedures, (d) ways to prepare for tests, (d) methods of organizing class notebooks and assignment books, and (e) how to be prepared for class (Scruggs & Mastropieri, 1992). These skills might be taught during regular class time or by the inclusion specialist during special sessions or "study workshops" for students with disabilities and all interested others. See Chapter 9 for more information about note taking and study skills.

Increasing Participation

Mr. Collins teaches in a heterogeneous classroom with thirty-four students. He is concerned because he cannot call on every student who raises his or her hand to answer a question, and he is aware that many students do not even bother to raise their hands. He is not sure if his students understand the principles he is teaching or not. He does not know if they have tuned out, turned off, or are too shy to volunteer an answer. He is like so many teachers who try to obtain student participation by posing a question and then calling on one or two students to respond. He is one of the majority of teachers who usually call on the high-achieving students most likely to know the correct answer (Maheady, Mallete, Harper, & Saca, 1991). Rosenshine and Stevens (1986) identify three errors teachers typically make when questioning students: (a) asking a general question such as "Do you understand?" and then assuming, if there are no questions, that everyone understands; (b) calling only on volunteers, who usually know the answers, and then assuming everyone else knows the answers, too; and (c) asking only a few questions before moving on.

Many alternatives to the one-student-at-a-time method are available. Because research has established a clear relationship between active student participation and academic achievement (Fisher & Berliner, 1985; Greenwood, Delquadri, & Hall, 1984), the more frequently students participate the better. Response cards, Think-Pair-Share (and other share-with-a-partner methods), Numbered Heads Together (and other cooperative learning techniques, described later in this chapter), hands-on learning activities, choral responses, and wait time can all dramatically increase student involvement.

Response cards Cards, signs, small dry-erase or chalkboards, or other items that all students in the class simultaneously hold up in response to questions or problems posed by the teacher.

Response Cards. **Response cards** are cards, signs, small dry-erase or chalkboards, or other items that all students in the class simultaneously hold up in response to questions or problems posed by the teacher (Cavanaugh, Heward, & Donelson, 1996; Heward, Gardner, Cavanaugh, Courson, Grossi, & Barbett, 1996). This technique has several advantages. Not only do response cards dramatically increase participation (Heward, 1994), they also provide visual cues that reinforce learning, enable students to learn correct responses by watching others, and provide teachers with an ongoing way to immediately assess students' understanding. This is particularly important in classrooms that include students with special needs. When the GE teacher is teaching, the inclusion specialist can easily focus on the learners who are struggling and monitor their understanding, noting where they might benefit from further instruction. Cavanaugh and colleagues

(1996) successfully used response cards in a high school earth science class that included students with learning disabilities, students with mental retardation, and students with behavioral disorders.

Response cards can be developed for any curriculum area or lesson content and can take many forms. Preprinted cards are preferable when students need only choose among a few responses. Write-on cards are best for lessons with a large number of different answers or where creativity is encouraged. Write-on cards tend to be more difficult than preprinted cards because they require higher levels of recall. The following descriptions were adapted from Heward and colleagues (1996).

1. Preprinted response cards—students select and hold up a card from their own personal set in response to a question or problem. Examples:
   - Yes/No cards
   - True/False cards
   - Colors
   - Traffic signs
   - Planets
   - Science terms
   - Before/After
   - Punctuation marks
   - Letters that correspond with multiple choice answers
2. Preprinted "pinch" response cards—instead of a set of different cards, each student has a single card with multiple answers in clearly marked sections. In response to a question, the student holds up the card with the thumb and forefinger pinching the portion of the card that displays his or her answer. Brightly colored clothespins also can be used as pinchers. Examples:
   - Math operations
   - The parts of an orchestra
3. Preprinted response cards with built-in movable pointers—the student simply moves the pointer so that it indicates the answer. Examples:
   - A clock with movable hands
   - A wheel and a pointer for displaying parts of speech
4. Write-on response cards—Students mark or write on blank index cards or boards that can be erased. Examples:
   - Spelling words
   - Math problems

Response cards can be combined with other approaches and adapted to serve many purposes in the classroom. Heward and colleagues (1996) provide some general suggestions for using response cards:

- Model several question-and-answer trials so that students can practice how to use the response cards.
- Response cards are likely to be more effective when used to provide students with many opportunities to respond within a short period of time (e.g., 5 to 10 minutes) rather than sporadically over a longer period.

- Maintain a lively pace during the response card portion of the lesson.
- Provide clear cues when students are to hold up and put down their cards (e.g., "Cards up" and "Cards down").
- When you see only correct responses, provide quick, positive feedback (e.g., "You're right!") and move on to the next question. If you see only a few incorrect responses, state the correct answer (e.g., "Yes, the word 'playful' is an adjective") and move on. This is where it is important for the inclusion specialist to note who needs more assistance.
- When there are more than a few incorrect responses, state the correct answer and then repeat the same question later.
- Remember that students benefit from watching others. Make sure students understand that it is not cheating to look at classmates' cards.
- With preprinted response cards, put answers on both sides of the cards so students can see what they are showing when they display a card.
- Begin instruction on new content with a small set of fact/concept cards and gradually add more as students improve.
- With write-on response cards, limit responses to one or two words and encourage students to write in large, legible letters.

Note: Rather than holding up response cards, students can simply use "thumbs up" or "thumbs down" hand signals for yes/no, true/false, and other dichotomous questions.

Think-Pair-Share (McTighe & Lyman, 1988). For increasing student involvement and peer interaction during lessons that involve higher level, creative thinking, this is an effective technique. Students are first encouraged to think individually (and silently) about an issue for 1 to 2 minutes. Then students turn to a partner and share their opinions about the topic. Finally, the teacher invites pairs to share their ideas with the entire class. An adaptation of this method would be to have students note a few thoughts in learning logs during the 2-minute "think" period. This option provides a tangible record of learning.

Hands-On Learning Activities (Experiential Learning). Hands-on or experiential learning uses personal experiences to engage the learner in the discovery of new knowledge. Students learn by doing. Typically, the teacher creates or selects an experience to introduce a new concept or unit and to motivate students (or to wrap up a unit as a culminating activity). The experience becomes a springboard to discussion, analysis, and followup activities (such as using the Language Experience Approach following a field trip). See Chapters 6, 8, and 9 for more detailed examples of experiential learning.

Choral Responses. Choral responses, or when a small group or pair of students responds in unison, can lessen students' intimidation and embarrassment and increase their engagement. Kamps, Dugan, and Leonard (1994) effectively used this technique with groups of students that included children with autism and mental disabilities. Courson and Heward (1988) found that choral responding was a helpful technique when used by paraprofessionals working with small groups of students with special needs. Like other techniques suggested for students with disabilities, this method has also been recommended for use with English language learners (Tam & Scott, 1996).

Wait Time. Wait time is a simple but effective technique for increasing participation and improving learning outcomes when asking questions that involve higher level thinking, particularly with students with learning disabilities and students learning English as a second language who may benefit from extra time to think before responding to a teacher's question (Brice & Roseberry-McKibben, 1999; Olson & Platt, 1996; Watson, Northcutt, & Rydele, 1989). When teachers increase the amount of time they wait before calling on students to 3 to 5 seconds, students respond with longer answers, volunteer answers more frequently, and initiate more questions. In a review of wait time research, Tobin (1987) noted that increasing wait time enhanced achievement in all content areas with all levels of students, from kindergarten through twelfth grade.

Creating Multilevel Learning Centers

Learning centers Stations set up at various locations around the room that provide a variety of activities to reinforce initial teaching, clarify concepts, and provide enrichment.

Learning centers can be an excellent way to provide multilevel instruction in inclusive classrooms. They have been used effectively with adolescents with learning disabilities and behavior disorders as part of a career awareness curriculum (Schirmer & George, 1983), to help students with learning disabilities develop problem-solving skills (Carlson & Tully, 1985), and in a first-grade inclusive classroom to foster literacy through art, drama, music, science, and movement activities (Berghoff, 2000).

Centers are stations set up at various locations around the room that provide a variety of experiences to reinforce initial teaching, clarify concepts, and provide enrichment (Cooper, 1981). They should include activities at multiple levels. Learning centers might be used as an integral part of an overall instructional plan or thematic unit, or they might provide supplemental optional experiences. Centers should contain: (a) a name or theme, (b) clear, complete directions, (c) a variety of materials for completing designated activities, (d) some alternative assignments for students, and (e) methods for assessing and recording students' progress. Centers can be organized by subject areas (e.g., creative writing, fractions, listening), interests (e.g., sports, archaeology), or integrated themes. For example, a center on fractions might include activities such as these (Olson & Platt, 1996):

- Follow a recipe that requires measuring solids and liquids.
- Compute distances around the school.
- Solve real-life problems that require fractions (e.g., dividing a pizza so that everyone gets an equal amount).

Learning centers are ideal for heterogeneous classrooms that include students with disabilities because they accommodate many different levels of functioning and interest. Students can work independently on tasks appropriate to their needs, at their own pace, or with a small group. Because there are two teachers in the room, the inclusion specialist can provide extra assistance to those students most in need while the GE teacher monitors general classroom activity.

Scheduling. Various methods can be used to help organize and streamline the process of determining who will work in which centers and when, such as (a) a rotational system that involves having students move from center to center at times specified by the teacher(s); (b) contracts that allow students some choice in selecting centers, (c) assigning students to centers based on their needs and interests, and (d) a self-selection process that uses pocket charts and name cards. Center pocket charts can work well—the center pocket chart lists current learning centers in a column on the left. Next to the name of each center is a numeral indicating the number of students permitted in that center at any one time. Pockets follow, in a row. Each student in the class has his or her own name card. When students enter in the morning, they remove their name cards from the pockets and take them to their seats (the names that remain provide the teacher with a quick indication of who is absent that day). At a designated time, the teacher asks the students to choose the center in which they would like to work during Center Time. If a special activity has been set up or everyone is required to complete a particular task, the teacher asks the students who have not yet had an opportunity to work in that center to place their cards first.

Record Keeping. Record keeping is an essential aspect of the learning center approach. An effective record keeping system helps the teacher monitor students' completion of center activities, evaluate progress, and make informed planning decisions. Records can be discussed by general education and special education teachers during collaborative consultation sessions, and by teachers and students during individual conferences. Recording devices such as contracts and checklists also help students take more responsibility for getting their work finished. Depending on the age of the students and the purposes of the centers, contracts might apply to a week or cover a longer period of time. See Figure 4.1 for a contract that a first-grade teacher used with her students during a thematic unit on dragons (adapted from Slaughter, 1993).

Checklists offer another easy way to provide structure to the record-keeping process. Children can simply check off the centers they have completed. A checklist might include additional space for feedback from the teacher(s) or self-evaluation. Figure 4.2 for an example (adapted from Olson & Platt, 1996).

Using Thematic Units

Thematic unit An instructional unit organized around a theme or topic. The theme approach enables students to develop a shared understanding and build on prior knowledge.

Thematic units organize instruction around a theme or topic. The theme approach allows teachers to integrate academic content with the development of basic skills using a variety of methods. As defined by Fredericks, Meinbach, and Rothlein (1993), a thematic unit is "multidisciplinary and multidimensional; it knows no boundaries. It is responsive to the interests, abilities, and needs of children and is respectful of their developing aptitudes and attitudes . . . well-developed thematic units establish systematic connections across all subject areas" (p. 6). When instruction across the curriculum is related to a central theme, students have the opportunity to develop deep knowledge and become "experts" in a particular area. They are able to make associations and see connections between what they learn in math, reading, science, social studies, and other subjects. Thematic units make the teaching of a crowded curriculum more efficient (Shanahan, Robinson, & Schneider, 1995). Opportunities for extra practice within a meaningful context are built into the approach. Thus, thematic units are ideal for students with special needs (Lewis, 1993;

Dragon Unit Contract

Name ______________________ Date ______________________

I finished the word-to-picture matching game.

I have read the pocket chart story and put the red cards in place.

The special project I worked on was: castle model ____________

papier-maché dragon ____________

diorama ____________

I have read these books:

____

____

____

Here are some interesting words I found in the stories I read:

____

____

I listened to these tape-recordings: *The Knight and the Dragon* ____________

"Leviathan" ____________

The name of the dragon story I wrote is:

____

____

I have copied "Dragon Smoke" neatly. ____________

I would like to know more about knights, ladies, castles, and dragons. This is my question:

____

____

FIGURE 4.1 Example of a Contract

Palincsar, Parecki, & McPhail, 1995; Salend, 1998; Swicegood & Parsons, 1991) as well as English language learners (Enright & McCloskey, 1988; Peregoy & Boyle, 1997; Rupp, 1992).

Thematic methods enable the curriculum to be adapted for students with special needs because students' interests, strengths, and performance levels can be considered

Learning Center Checklist

Name ________________________________

Directions: Put check marks next to the centers you worked in each day.

	Days				
Centers	Monday	Tuesday	Wednesday	Thursday	Friday
Measurement					
Writing					
Geography					
Science					
Reading					

Feedback from the teacher:

Measurement ________________________________

Writing ________________________________

Geography ________________________________

Science ________________________________

Reading ________________________________

Goals for next checklist:

____

____

Discussed on (date) ____________________

Teacher ____________________ *Student* ____________________

FIGURE 4.2 Example of a Checklist

when planning and implementing the approach. Also, students are able to participate and contribute in a variety of ways and feel successful. Lewis (1993) has used thematic units with students with learning disabilities for more than a decade. She found that students who were unable to grasp concepts through more traditional methods learned through a thematic approach. Their motivation and endurance for academic tasks improved, along with their performance. Swicegood and Parsons (1991) effectively used this approach with high school students with learning disabilities. Palincsar and colleagues (1995) taught a thematic literature-based unit in an upper elementary, self-contained class for students with learning disabilities.

Thematic units can be designed in a variety of formats, depending on the length and type of unit. They can last for a few days or for several weeks. Weekly themes are often used with younger children who have shorter attention spans. Monthly or block themes provide extended periods of time for accomplishing the goals of a thematic unit. Cyclical themes are more abstract and cover longer periods of time, such as a quarter.

Planning a Thematic Unit. Some teachers plan thematic units alone or in collaboration with other teachers. Frequently, teachers involve students in the planning process. The first step is to identify a central topic. Students might suggest topics during a brainstorming session, or ideas might emerge while the class is studying another subject. A theme can center around a holiday, current events, student interests, and/or a topic identified in the grade-level curriculum.

Once a topic has been selected, the next step is to plan the unit. Again, the class can brainstorm ideas about what they would like to learn about the chosen topic. The teacher might write students' ideas on the board, an overhead transparency, or large sheets of butcher paper using a semantic web to cluster similar ideas together. Or he or she might ask students to answer two questions: "What do we already know about the topic?" and "What would we like to learn?" (as in a K-W-L chart [Ogle, 1986]).

It is important for the teacher to determine the objectives of the unit with the help of students. During this step, the entire class can again brainstorm ideas, or a class committee might work with the teacher to come up with a list of objectives.

After objectives have been determined, the next step in planning a thematic unit is to decide which learning activities and materials will be incorporated. Students can be included in this stage of the process as well, going to the library or media center to collect books and other resource materials, inviting community members to visit the class, and planning field trips. Students might help set up learning centers. After completion of the unit, students should also be included in the evaluation process, asking "What went well?" "What suggestions do we have for improving this unit?" and "What would we like to do differently next time?" See Figure 4.3 for an example of a two-week thematic unit for sixth-grade students.

Combining Thematic Units and Learning Centers

By combining thematic units with learning centers, students are provided with opportunities to develop communication skills, organizational skills, problem-solving techniques, and multiple intelligences. When students at Lowell Elementary School in Albuquerque, New Mexico, were studying the human body, they became particularly intrigued with the heart. They then helped their teacher plan a two-week thematic unit on the heart that included six learning centers:

- **Listening Center:** While reading along, students listened to a tape-recorded book about taking a pulse. After reading the book, students found a friend's pulse.

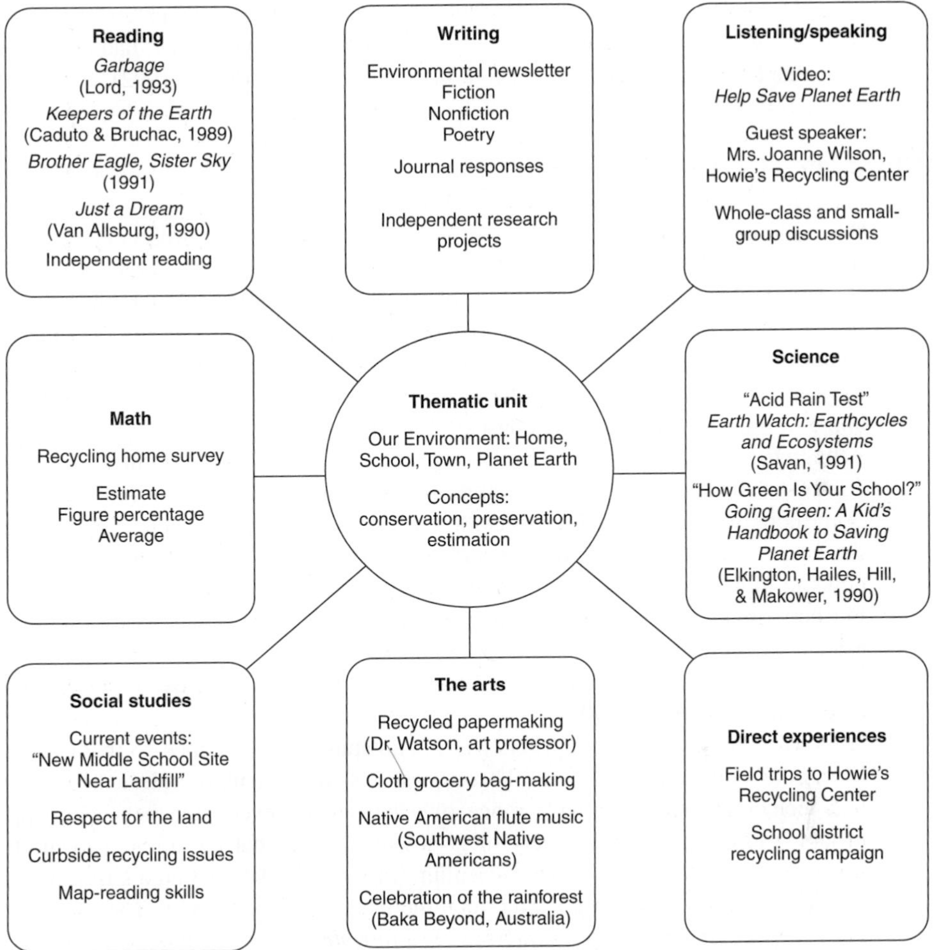

FIGURE 4.3 Two-Week Environmental Thematic Unit: Home, School, Town, Planet Earth

Source: From Heller (1997). With permission.

- **Pulse Rate Center:** Using stethoscopes, students recorded their partner's heartbeat in three situations: after standing, after hopping, and after jogging. They then recorded and compared results.
- **Model Center:** Using a large plastic model of the human trunk, students worked together to identify the heart and its main parts, taking the model apart and putting it back together again.
- **Pumping Heart Center:** At the sink, students cupped their hands together in a basin of water and squeezed them together to find out how the heart pumped blood.
- **Circulation Center, Part A:** Students read a short passage that explained how blood circulates. They then colored a diagram illustrating this process.

- **Circulation Center, Part B:** Students followed the blood's path through the body by walking through a large chart of the circulatory system that had been placed on the floor. It showed a large heart, veins, and arteries. (Rupp, 1992)

GROUPING PRACTICES

The trend in education is toward heterogeneous or mixed-ability grouping practices rather than the homogeneous or same-ability grouping practices that were prevalent for decades (Barr & Dreeben, 1991; Flood, Lapp, Flood, & Nagel, 1992). Clustering students based on perceived ability level was the primary grouping strategy for most of the previous century. Until the advent of whole language instruction, almost all children were taught to read in the high group, a middle group, or the low group. Yet research indicates that ability grouping has negative consequences for students placed in low groups (e.g., Allington, 1980, 1983; Goodlad, 1984; Hiebert, 1983; McGill-Franzen & Allington, 1990)—students rarely escape low group placement and receive differentiated instruction (more drill and isolated practice, less of a focus on comprehension and higher level thinking), so that they fall further and further behind (Shannon, 1985). Even for students in higher groups, research has indicated mixed results (Barr, 1989; Slavin, 1987). Furthermore, homogeneous grouping practices often lower the motivation and self-esteem of low achieving students (Oakes, Gamoran, & Page, 1991) and can result in social stratification in which students from minority groups are overrepresented in low-ability tracks (Oakes, 1990).

What alternatives do teachers have? Can students be grouped so that everyone can learn in an optimal environment? These questions are particularly relevant for classrooms that include students at a wide range of achievement levels. Teachers who implement grouping effectively use a variety of grouping patterns that are tailored to fit students' strengths and the demands of the curriculum (Flood et al., 1992), ranging from whole class to small groups to pairs, depending upon the purpose of the activity. The use of a variety of grouping patterns is referred to as *flexible grouping*.

Flexible grouping Groups that are created, modified, and dissolved as the need arises—they are not permanent.

Flexible Grouping. With **flexible grouping** there are no permanent, fixed groups (Unsworth, 1984). Groups are created, modified, and dissolved as the need arises. Inclusion classrooms are ideally suited for flexible grouping practices because there are two teachers who can juggle instruction. Thoughtful, thorough planning and monitoring thus become critical to the success of flexible grouping. Some teachers start out intending to use flexible grouping but fall into a pattern of whole-class-only instruction, followed by individual practice (Vaughn, Bos, & Schumm, 1997). Although whole-class instruction is appropriate for some objectives, for many other purposes it is not the preferable grouping procedure. While thinking about how to most effectively teach a lesson or meet an instructional objective, it is important to consider many factors, such as the variables described by Flood and colleagues (1992) (see Figure 4.4). Also, see Figure 4.5 for an example of how flexible grouping patterns might be put into practice in a classroom with both a GE teacher and a special education teacher.

Flexible Grouping Variables

1. **Possible bases for grouping students:**
   - The type of task or activity
   - Students who need to develop the same skill (this may be the whole class or a few individuals)
   - Students who share the same interest
   - Students with complementary work habits
   - Students with prior knowledge of content (may be placed together or spread as experts among several groups)
   - Students with prior knowledge of strategies
   - Students with certain social skills (students may be placed in groups because of leadership, problem-solving, or other social skills)
   - Random (e.g., numbering off and putting all of the "ones" in the same group)
   - Students' choice
2. **Possible formats for groups:**

Composition:	Leadership:
Individuals	Teacher-led
Dyads	Student-led
Small groups (3–5)	Cooperative
Larger groups (6–10)	
Half-class	
Whole class	

3. **Possible materials for groups:**
   - Same materials for all groups
   - Different levels of materials with a similar theme
   - Different topics within an overall theme
   - Different themes

FIGURE 4.4 Example of the Use of Grouping in the Classroom

Whole-Class Instruction. Keeping the whole class together can be appropriate for a variety of reasons, such as building classroom community, establishing classroom routines, introducing new units of study, introducing new skills or concepts, conducting whole-class discussions, listening to guest speakers, and viewing educational videos (Vaughn et al., 1997). Although whole-class instruction can be easy to plan, organize, and manage, there are drawbacks to this approach, particularly when it becomes the predominant teaching mode. The pace and content of the lesson might be too easy for some students and too challenging for others. Attending to individual needs can be difficult (however, see the "Increasing Participation" section of this chapter for ways to meet students' needs at a range of levels while teaching the whole class). When whole-class instructional procedures are implemented in an inclusion class, the inclusion specialist plays a crucial role in helping to adapt materials and assignments.

Same-Ability Small Groups. Although we do not advocate the widespread or long-term use of set same-ability groups, we do believe that there are situations in which same-

ACTIVITY	GE TEACHER BEHAVIORS	SE TEACHER BEHAVIORS	STUDENT BEHAVIORS	BASIS FOR GROUPING	FORMAT
1. Morning Message	Leads students in reading Morning Message	Monitors participation and performance of SE students; assists as needed	Read, listen	Task/activity	Whole class
2. Morning News	Listens, probes, encourages	Listens, probes, encourages	Share, listen, interact	Task/activity	Whole class
3. Shared Reading Experience	Observes students, listens to story	Reads a Big Book *	Listen to story	Task/activity	Whole class
4. Story Mapping Explained	Explains Story Mapping*	Observes and notes who needs more instruction	Listen, ask and answer questions	Task/activity	Whole class
5a. Story Mapping Completed		Explains, demonstrates story mapping; assists students in completing a story map	Listen, ask and answer questions; complete a story map	Students who need same skill	Small group
5b. Story Mapping Completed	Monitors, assists individual students		Complete a story map	Task/activity	Individual
6. Independent Reading Time	Monitors, assists individual students	Conducts individual conferences*	Read	Task/activity	Individual and pairs (for Buddy Reading)
7. Centers	Monitors, assists students	Assists students, provides intensive instruction at the Alphabet Center	Complete activities at literacy-related centers	Student choice and students who need same skill	Small groups
8. Readers' Theater	Monitors, assists students	Monitors, assists students	Prepare and practice Readers' Theater	Interest/work habits	Small groups

*Indicates that general and special education teachers may switch roles.

See Chapter 6 for more information about these activities.

FIGURE 4.5 Sample Flexible Grouping Patterns in a First-Grade Inclusion Class

ability groups are the preferable approach. For example, during Writers' Workshop, students are pulled into small groups to receive instruction on an as-needed basis, as identified by their teachers through mini-conferences and an examination of their work products. At times a group might consist of the lowest readers in the class who all need to work on word recognition skills. What differentiates these same-ability groups from the leveled groups of previous years, however, is their temporary nature and the fact that many other types of grouping arrangements are used throughout the school day (e.g., based on interest or heterogeneous cooperative learning groups). Thus, students do not become locked into a low-ability group or made to feel isolated from the other students in the class. A good rule is to keep groups of students who need extra help small so that students can receive the intensity of instruction they need (Good & Brophy, 1994). When the objective of the instruction has been met, the group is disbanded.

Mixed-Ability Small Groups. Heterogeneous groups can serve a variety of functions and can be based on many configurations. Students might be grouped together to work at a learning center, complete a group project related to a thematic unit, prepare a presentation for the class (e.g., through Readers' Theater), complete a followup assignment, discuss a reading assignment (e.g., in a literature response group), or participate in an experiential learning activity (e.g., conduct a science experiment). Groups might be student- or teacher-selected, depending upon the nature of the task. A common type of mixed-ability small group is the *cooperative learning group.*

COOPERATIVE LEARNING

Cooperative learning When students work together to accomplish shared goals—each student is responsible for his or her own learning and the learning of others in the group.

Cooperative learning is another effective technique for inclusive classrooms (McMaster & Fuchs, 2002). Cooperative learning requires working together to accomplish shared goals—it is the instructional use of small groups so that students work together to maximize their own and each other's learning. Within cooperative learning groups, students are given two responsibilities: to learn the assigned material and to make sure that all other members of their group do likewise (Johnson & Johnson, 1989). Students discuss the material to be learned with each other, help each other to understand it, and encourage each other to do their best. They learn collaborative skills at the same time they are mastering content material. Cooperative learning is ideal for classrooms that include students with learning disabilities (McMaster & Fuchs, 2002; Putnam, 1993), English language learners (Kagan, 1986; Richard-Amato, 1992), and culturally diverse populations (Cohen, Lotan, Scarloss, & Arellano, 1999). In a cooperative setting, all participants benefit from diversity: It is the differences among members—differences in their talents, skills, perceptions, and thoughts—that make a cooperative group powerful (Johnson & Johnson, 1993).

Benefits of Cooperative Learning

1. The achievement levels of all students increase. Although the largest gains usually occur among students at the struggling, undermotivated end of the spectrum, there

are benefits for all students (Johnson & Johnson, 1993). Klingner and colleagues (Klingner, Vaughn, Hughes, Schumm & Elbaum, 1998) found that it was the high-achieving students in heterogeneous, inclusive classrooms who showed the greatest gains when using cooperative learning and peer tutoring techniques.

2. Students tend to feel more positive about themselves and to be better adjusted psychologically when they are part of a cooperative classroom structure (Johnson & Johnson, 1993).
3. Students seem to accept differences more readily and are less likely to stereotype others when they are members of the same cooperative team working toward a common goal and sharing successes (Johnson & Johnson, 1993).

Elements of Cooperative Learning

Cooperative learning is not just placing students in a group and telling them to work together. Nor is it having students sit side by side and having the one who finishes first help the slower student. Cooperative learning consists of planned and organized heterogeneous groupwork. Group work seems to function more smoothly and be more effective when it is well-structured with a clear purpose and well-defined responsibilities (Gillies & Ashman, 2000; Klingner & Vaughn, 2000). According to Johnson and Johnson (1989), the following five basic elements must be included for a lesson to be cooperative:

Positive interdependence A characteristic of cooperative learning when students feel that their work benefits others in the group and that their teammates' work benefits them.

1. The first is ***positive interdependence***, or, in other words, when students feel that their work benefits others in the group and that their teammates' work benefits them. Everyone is responsible for helping everyone else learn. One way teachers can structure positive interdependence is by assigning complementary roles to students.
2. For the benefits of cooperative learning to be maximized, there must be considerable *face-to-face, promotive interaction* among students. Group members need to encourage, support, help, and assist each other's efforts to learn. It is important for students to learn to explain their reasoning to each other.
3. The third element is *individual accountability*. This exists when student performance is assessed regularly. Group members need to know who needs more help in completing an assignment. Group members should perceive that they must fulfill their responsibilities in order for each individual and the group to be successful. One way to achieve this is to require students to certify that each group member can correctly explain the answers, and then to randomly select one member of the group to explain the group's answers.
4. Fourth, *social skills* such as encouraging and checking must be taught. Learning groups are not productive unless members are skilled in cooperating with each other. Cooperative skills include leadership, decision making, trust building, communication, and conflict resolution.
5. Finally, at the end of each cooperative learning session, students should *evaluate* their group's functioning by answering two questions: What is something each member did that was helpful for the group? and What is something each member could do to make the group even better tomorrow?

Different Types of Cooperative Learning Groups

Johnson and Johnson (1989) describe three types of cooperative learning groups: small groups, base groups/support groups, and informal groups or partners.

1. *Small groups* are carefully structured formal cooperative learning groups, consisting of about four students of varying ability and achievement levels. These groups typically stay together for about six weeks. Let students know from the onset how long they will be together. Students can write parting letters to each other when they change groups.
2. *Base groups/support groups* are long-term groups of about three students that last for a year or more. The purpose of these groups is primarily to provide peer support. It is especially important for students with special needs to know they are members of an ongoing, permanent group. Students can check in with each other at the beginning of class.
3. *Informal groups or partners* can change frequently. These ad hoc groups of two or three students can be as informal as "turn to your partner and discuss the following question."

Assigning Students to Small Groups.

Step 1: *Rank-order students.* List all of the students in your class, starting with the highest achiever and finishing with the lowest achiever. To determine achievement levels, use pretest scores, recent test scores, past grades, or best guess.

Step 2: *Select the first group.* Choose the top, bottom, and two middle students from your class list. Assign these students to group one, unless they (a) are all of the same sex, (b) they do not reflect the ethnic composition of the class, (c) they are worst enemies, or (d) they are best friends. If any of these are the case, readjust the group by moving up or down one student on the list.

Step 3: *Select the remaining teams.* To produce the second group, repeat Step 2, using the reduced list. Continue until all students have been assigned to a group. If there are a few students left over, distribute them so that you have one, two, or three 5-member groups.

Implementing Cooperative Learning

1. Start out slow. Begin with nonacademic tasks in nonthreatening situations, and then expand. Possible initial activities might include discussions or art activities. Many ideas for implementing group work and teambuilding are available (e.g., see Breeden & Mosley, 1991; Ellis & Whalen, 1990; Hill & Hill, 1990).
2. *Develop social skills.* Teachers need to carefully define and model appropriate group behaviors; the behaviors should then be practiced by the class, using simulation and role-playing, and continually monitored and reinforced (Goodwin, 1999). Teach one social skill at a time, posting each behavior on a chart for reference as it is learned. Some of the skills students need to learn are how to listen attentively, ask clarifying

questions, take turns speaking, provide positive feedback, and resolve conflicts. See Boxes 4.2 and 4.3 for more information on teaching social skills.

3. *Teach leadership roles.* As with social skills, leadership roles need to be taught explicitly, through modeling and practice. Leadership roles will vary depending on the requirements of the learning task and the type of cooperative learning structure applied.
4. *Teach students how to ask for help.* Just as leadership roles should be taught, it benefits students to learn how to request assistance from their peers. Wolford, Heward, and Alber (2001) used modeling, role playing, feedback, and praise to teach this skill to middle school students with learning disabilities.
5. *Stick with it!* It takes time for a class to adjust to cooperative group structures. After all, students have been accustomed to competitive and individualistic work styles for a long time. You may want to begin by having students work in pairs, and then in groups of three, and then in larger groups. It is easier to cooperate with one other person than many. In Box 4.4 we list ways to encourage your students.

BOX 4.2

TEACHING SOCIAL SKILLS FOR COOPERATIVE GROUP WORK

Students need help learning how to work together in cooperative groups. Most children do not have well-developed social skills and need to be taught these skills just as they are taught math or science or reading. Ellis and Whalen divide the social skills needed to work in cooperative groups into three categories: Basic Group Skills, Functioning Skills, and Higher Order Thinking Skills.

Basic Group Skills are those fundamental skills without which a group can't get anything done:

- getting into groups quietly
- bringing necessary materials with you
- staying with your group until the task is done
- talking in quiet voices
- listening to each other
- knowing your task(s) or roles
- taking turns

Functioning Skills enable group members to work together efficiently and effectively:

- contributing your ideas
- supporting your viewpoint with evidence
- asking for help when you need it
- encouraging others to contribute
- complimenting others' contributions
- checking for understanding
- staying on task

Higher Order Thinking Skills improve group members' understanding of the material being learned and enhance thinking skills (these skills are more advanced than Functioning Skills):

- asking for clarification
- providing clarification
- building on another's ideas
- paraphrasing another's ideas to show you understand
- coming to a consensus
- synthesizing several ideas
- evaluating the group's work

Source: Adapted from Ellis & Whalen (1990), pp. 40–45.

BOX 4.3
TEACHING A SOCIAL SKILL

You don't need to teach all of the above skills at once. Pick a starting point that depends on the existing level and needs of your class. If students don't yet know Basic Group Skills, start there, then move to Functioning Skills when students are ready.

Ellis and Whalen (1990) recommend the following six-step process for teaching a social skill:

1. **Define the skill in explicit terms students can understand.** For example, "When I say, 'Get into your groups quickly and quietly,' I mean that you should pick up the materials you will need and walk directly to your work area without any talking."
2. **Help students see the need for the skill.** Ask students why they think the skill is important. Describe what happens when the skill isn't used, for example, "Yesterday you spent almost 5 minutes getting into your groups and ready for work. That cut short your working time, and many of you weren't able to finish." For variety, set up role-playing scenarios that demonstrate when a particular skill isn't used.
3. **Have students describe the skill**. Record their description and keep it in view. You might want to use a T-chart to describe what the skill looks like and sounds like.

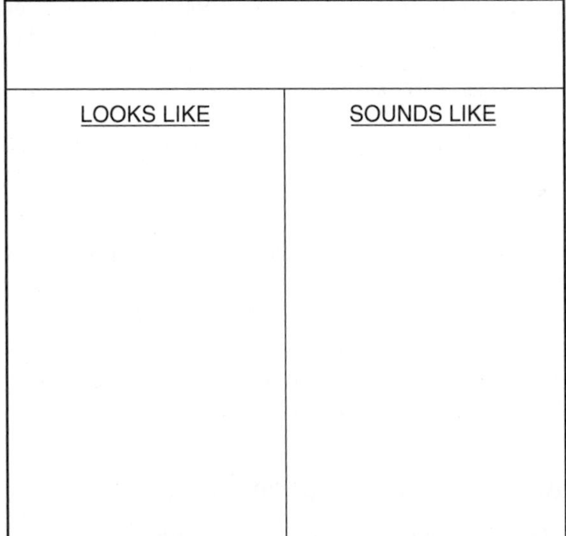

FIGURE 4.6 T-chart

4. **Have students practice the skill**. For example, "Let's practice getting into our groups. I'm going to watch the clock and see how quickly you can do it this time."
5. **Discuss and reinforce students' efforts**. For example, "That time you took just 25 seconds. That's a big improvement."
6. **Follow up by having students practice as often as needed**. For example, "We haven't practiced getting in our groups for a while, and I've noticed that we are starting to take longer and we're getting noisier again. Let's take a few minutes to look over our T-chart and see what it should look like and sound like when we move into our groups."

BOX 4.4

COOPERATIVE COMMENTS: TWENTY WAYS FOR STUDENTS AND TEACHERS TO SAY "GOOD COOPERATIVE WORK!"

1. I really like that comment.
2. Everyone is participating—great!
3. Great discussion—we/you shared lots of ideas.
4. We/You are doing a good job taking turns.
5. Everyone is listening to each other—great.
6. Great explanation—it helped me understand.
7. We/You are a smart group!
8. We've/You've accomplished a lot today.
9. Excellent answer to the question.
10. Great question—it really got me thinking.
11. Creative problem solving!
12. That's an interesting point of view.
13. Very good job getting the gist—you really found the most important idea.
14. Great cooperation—we/you helped each other a lot.
15. Very good job reading.
16. You made this tough assignment look easy.
17. This group is really organized—each person is doing his or her job.
18. Very good job talking in quiet voices.
19. Thank you for helping me.
20. Super cooperative behavior!

Remember . . .
Be specific.
Be positive.
Reinforce interpersonal skills.
Reinforce desired behaviors.

Source: Adapted from Breeden & Mosley (1991), p. 27.

6. *Plan the cooperative activity carefully.* The activity should be organized so that students must cooperate in order to successfully complete the activity and planned so that everyone has a role that will enable him or her experience success.
7. *Include opportunities for individuals and groups to assess their performance.* It is important for students to take the time to evaluate how well they have worked together. See Figure 4.7 for a sample evaluation form.

Challenges Associated with Cooperative Learning

Three of the most common problems associated with cooperative learning are (a) the fears and anxieties of lower-achieving, shy, and/or special education students; (b) higher-achieving students' concerns that their grades will be negatively affected; and (c) passive uninvolvement by students. Some suggestions for dealing with these difficulties follow.

When some students are fearful and anxious about participating in a cooperative learning group, the following steps may help alleviate their anxiety:

1. Explain clearly the procedures that the group will follow.
2. Give students structured roles so that they understand their responsibilities. Even if a student cannot read, he or she can listen carefully and summarize what the group is saying, provide leadership, or help to keep the group on task. There is always some way a student can contribute to group work.

Peer- and Self-Evaluation Skill Building Checklist

Name of Evaluator ______________________________

Group ______________________________

1. Who contributed ideas and information? ____________ Did I? ____
2. Who kept the group on task? ____________ Did I? ____
3. Who listened and paid attention? ____________ Did I? ____
4. Who coordinated or gave directions? ____________ Did I? ____
5. Who summarized ideas? ____________ Did I? ____
6. Who kept the group lively, relaxed? ____________ Did I? ____
7. Who was prepared with assignments? ____________ Did I? ____
8. Who encouraged/supported others? ____________ Did I? ____
9. Who asked for others' opinions? ____________ Did I? ____
10. Who accepted others' opinions? ____________ Did I? ____
11. Who gave reasons for their ideas? ____________ Did I? ____
12. Who helped others? ____________ Did I? ____
13. Who paraphrased ideas? ____________ Did I? ____
14. Who led the group to consensus? ____________ Did I? ____
15. Who helped solve disagreements? ____________ Did I? ____

Source: (Adapted from Glasgow, 1997)

FIGURE 4.7 Sample Evaluation Form

3. Coach students in the behaviors and social skills needed within the cooperative group. Pretraining in social skills and monitoring how well the skills are being implemented will increase students' confidence.
4. Pretrain low-achieving students in the academic skills needed to complete the group's work. Try to give students a source of expertise that the group will need.

When higher achieving students are anxious that the lower achieving student will lower the overall performance of their group, the following procedures might alleviate their concerns:

1. Pretrain higher-achieving students in helping, tutoring, teaching, and sharing skills. Many teaching skills, such as the use of praise and prompting, can easily be taught to students.

2. Make the academic requirements for the lower achieving students reasonable. Ways in which lessons can be adapted so that students at different achievement levels can participate in the same cooperative groups are to (a) use different criteria for success for each member; (b) vary the amount each group member is expected to master; (c) give group members different assignments (e.g., lists of spelling words, or math problems), and then use the average percentage worked correctly as the group's score; and (d) use improvement scores rather than total correct scores.
3. Emphasize that everyone is different and that the group's success depends on utilizing the unique abilities and viewpoints of everyone in the group. Prior to initiating groupwork, teachers should explicitly state that, "No one will be good at everything; everyone is good at something."

When some students are not participating in their groups, are not paying attention to the group's work or are saying little or nothing, the teacher may wish to:

1. Train other group members in how to actively involve these students.
2. Assign a role to the passive, uninvolved student that is essential to the group's success. Choose activities that draw upon different students' abilities and match task requirements to students' competencies.
3. Reward the group for full participation. This will encourage other group members to develop strategies for increasing the passive member's involvement.
4. Implement a token system such as "talking chips" to encourage participation (or to inhibit domination by other students). Each student in the group is provided with the same amount of chips. When a student contributes to the group's discussion, he or she spends a chip. Each group member is expected to spend all of his or her chips (but not more). Chips can be redistributed once they have all been spent.
5. "Jigsaw" materials so that each group member has information the others need.

Peer and Cross-Age Tutoring

Students have been helping students for centuries (for historical reviews, see Allen, 1976a; Goodlad & Hirst, 1989). Tutoring has been shown to benefit both tutors and tutees and to provide academic and social benefits (for comprehensive reviews, see Allen, 1976a; Cohen, Kulik, & Kulik, 1982; Cook, Scruggs, Mastropieri, & Casto, 1986; Devin-Sheehan, Feldman, & Allen, 1976; Goodlad & Hirst, 1989; Jenkins & Jenkins, 1987). Peers, older students, and community volunteers can all be recruited to assist with tutoring programs.

Tutoring has been implemented effectively in inclusive classrooms across a range of subject areas with students with mental retardation (Mastropieri, Scruggs, Mohler, Beranek, Spencer, Boom, & Talbott, 2001; Mortweet, Uthey, Walker, Dawson, et al., 1999), students with behavior disorders (Coleman & Vaughn, 2000), students with learning disabilities (Cook et al., 1986; Fuchs, Fuchs, Hamlett, & Appleton, 2002; Fuchs, Fuchs, Mathes, & Simmons, 1997; Mastropieri et al., 2001; Scruggs & Richter, 1988; Woodward, Monroe, & Baxter, 2001), and culturally and linguistically diverse students with disabilities (Harper, Maheady, Mallette, & Karnes, 1999). As with cooperative learning, students should be taught the skills they need to be effective tutors and tutees. For example, Bentz and Fuchs (1996) successfully taught students how to help their peers with learning disabilities during mathematics. Also, students with disabilities should be given the opportunity to serve as tutors as well as tutees (Vaughn, Gersten, & Chard, 2000).

Cross-age tutoring When one student provides instructional support to a younger student.

Cross-age tutoring is when older students help younger students. Numerous cross-age tutoring programs have been implemented with students with LD as tutors or tutees in a variety of contexts. Scruggs and Richter (1988) conducted a meta-analysis of cross-age tutoring studies with students with LD and reported that although much of the research indicates that children with LD can and do learn in tutoring situations, the specific circumstances under which tutoring is most effective are still not understood. Cook and colleagues (1986) conducted a similar meta-analysis of studies that included behaviorally disordered and students with mental handicaps as well as students with LD. They noted that (a) tutoring programs were generally effective, (b) academic gains for tutors and tutees were greater on criterion-referenced measures than norm-referenced measures, (c) tutees generally gained more that tutors, and (d) tutor and tutee gains on self-concept ratings were small, while gains on attitude measures were larger, especially for tutors.

More recent studies have also produced positive findings for both tutors and tutees. These studies have evaluated a variety of tutoring conditions, such as (a) academically at-risk college athletes tutoring first- and second-grade students with LD in reading and writing (Juel, 1991), (b) students with LD tutoring younger students in basic addition facts (Beirne-Smith, 1991), (c) upper elementary boys with LD who had received social skills training tutoring second-grade boys in spelling (Trapani & Gettinger, 1989), and (d) high school students with LD tutoring primary-grade students in reading, primarily to improve the academic and social deficits of the high school tutors (Schrader & Valus, 1990). Using students with behavioral disorders and students with LD as tutors, Scruggs and Osguthorpe (1986) compared cross-age with peer tutoring, and found that academic gains (in word attack skills) were exhibited with both conditions, but that attitudinal gains were only observed with the cross-age tutoring group. In a study of the effects of tutoring on the attitudes of elementary-aged students with LD, Eisermann (1988) found that those who tutored tended to experience the greatest attitudinal improvements.

Tutoring can benefit tutors because it becomes a "source of power for the powerless" (Malamuth, Turcotte, & Fitz-Gibbon, 1981, p. 118) and can relieve feelings of anonymity that become common when a child moves from elementary to secondary school. Because tutors feel needed by the students they are helping, they gain a sense of purpose and participation often lacking in their lives. Many previously unmotivated and uncooperative students appear to develop positive attitudes towards themselves and school because they are placed in responsible roles (Allen, 1976b; Goodlad & Hirst, 1989). As explained by Allen, enactment of a role produces changes in self-concept, attitudes, cognition, and behavior in a direction consistent with the expectations associated with the role. In a study in which truant junior high students with LD tutored younger students with LD, significant gains were made on a measure of locus of control (defined as an individual's ability to conceptualize the relationship between his or her own behavior and the outcome of events); also, truant behaviors decreased (Lazerson, Foster, Brown, & Hummel, 1988).

These research results have important implications for inclusion classrooms. In a setting where students with LD frequently receive assistance from their peers, they can be encouraged to help younger students who are less knowledgeable. Even students who are struggling with their own classwork can be helped to instruct students in lower grades. This was the case with Andrew, the fifth-grade student with LD introduced in Chapter 2, who regularly tutored first-grade students in reading, boosting his self-esteem and receiving reinforcement in essential reading skills.

OTHER TYPES OF INSTRUCTION

Scaffolded Instruction

Scaffolded instruction When a teacher (or a more competent other) provides the assistance necessary for a student to achieve success—this support is gradually withdrawn as the student becomes more proficient and able to accomplish the task on his or her own.

According to sociocultural theory, it is through **scaffolded instruction** (Bruner, 1975; Englert, Berry, & Dunsmore, 2001; Larkin, 2001; Mariage, 2001; Roller, 1996; Tharp & Gallimore, 1988; Winn, 1994) that the teacher (or a more competent other) provides the support necessary for students to achieve success. This support is gradually withdrawn as students become increasingly more proficient and accomplish the task on their own. As noted by Tharp and Gallimore (1988), "scaffolding does not involve simplifying the task; it holds the difficulty level constant, while simplifying the child's role by means of graduated assistance from the adult/expert" (p. 33). In scaffolded instruction, the expert first models the task. The learner then attempts the task, with the expert providing cueing, assistance, and additional modeling as required. Eventually, the learner is able to complete the task without assistance. Throughout this process, the dialogue between the expert and the novice is the means by which support is provided and adjusted. Scaffolding can be an effective way to teach thinking and problem-solving strategies to students with learning disabilities in inclusive classrooms (Gersten, 1998; Swanson, 1999).

Beed, Forsyth, and Roller (Roller, 1996) have conceptualized the scaffolding process as six levels or actions taken by the teacher when teaching a learning strategy or problem-solving procedure. In the following adaptation of these six levels, Ms. Kelly (the inclusion specialist from Chapter 6) helps a student (Oscar) learn a strategy for figuring out the meaning of unknown words by rereading the sentence the word is in, or the sentences before and after, looking for context clues:

1. At first, the teacher assumes total responsibility for using the strategy (or solving the problem). Here, Ms. Kelly teaches a strategy for figuring out a difficult word, using a think-aloud procedure to model how to use context clues.

   Ms. Kelly: *Uh oh, here is a word I don't understand, "paddies." Let me reread the sentence to see if there are any clues. It says, "U.S. troops fought in the jungles and rice paddies of Vietnam." I don't see any clues that tell me exactly what the word means. Let me see what happens if I read the sentence without the word, "U.S troops fought in the jungles and rice ______."* Well, it has to be a place, because it is where they fought. And it must have to do with rice. I'll bet it's a place where they grow rice. That makes sense.

2. Second, the teacher invites the student's participation.

   Ms. Kelly: *Would you like to read? Tell me when you get to a word you do not understand.*

Oscar reads and stops at the word "embassy."

3. Third, the teacher cues the use of a specific strategy. Here, Ms. Kelly reminds Oscar of the strategy for figuring out difficult words and helps him apply the strategy. Note how his participation has increased.

   Ms. Kelly: *Embassy. Yes, that's a difficult word. Reread the sentence it is in and look for clues to help you figure it out.*

   Oscar: *"The United States opened a new embassy."*

   Ms. Kelly: *Does that help much?*

   Oscar: *I can tell it's something the United States opened, but I'm not sure what.*

   Ms. Kelly: *Let's reread the sentences before and after.*

   Oscar: *"President Clinton decided to form new ties with Vietnam. In August, the United States opened a new embassy in Hanoi, Vietnam's capital. Many U.S. companies are opening offices in Vietnam as well." Well, maybe it's a kind of office.*

   Ms. Kelly: *Good. What kind of office? Is it run by U.S. companies?*

   Oscar: *No, I don't think so.*

   Ms. Kelly: *Right, what gave you that clue?*

   Oscar: *It says "as well," and that sort of means "also." I think it must be an office run by the United States government. Is that right?*

   Ms. Kelly: *Yes. Excellent job figuring out that word.*

4. Fourth, the teacher cues general strategy use. When Oscar gets to the next difficult word, Ms. Kelly prompts him to use a strategy.

   Ms. Kelly: *What can you do to try and figure out that word?*

   Oscar: *Reread the sentence it's in, and maybe the sentences before and after, looking for clues?*

5. Fifth, the teacher reinforces the child's independent use of the strategy. When Ms. Kelly observes Oscar stopping to reread a sentence on his own, without prompting, she acknowledges this.

   Ms. Kelly: *I notice that you remembered to reread the sentence, looking for clues. Excellent.*

6. Finally, the teacher builds metacognitive awareness (an understanding of why, when, and how to use the strategy). Ms. Kelly builds Oscar's metacognitive awareness by asking him to teach the strategy he has learned to another student. (Explaining to others is one way of firming up one's thoughts.)

Over time, Ms. Kelly will probably need to review use of the strategy with Oscar. With scaffolding, the objective is always to give the student sufficient help to be successful and to gradually decrease the amount of assistance provided until the student can perform the task independently. In the above example, Oscar learned quickly how to use a new word clarification strategy. Sometimes scaffolding takes much longer, requiring more assistance from the teacher.

Strategy Instruction

Many strategies have been developed to help students with learning disabilities and other students with learning problems become more efficient, active learners (Clark, 2000). For the most part, these are based on the principles of cognitive psychology, although one of the best known approaches to strategy instruction, Reciprocal Teaching (Palincsar & Brown, 1984; described in Chapter 6), also has a firm grounding in sociocultural theory. Strategies have been designed to help students with reading comprehension, writing, math problem solving, and content area (science and social studies) learning. See Chapters 7, 8, and 9, related to each of these subject areas, for descriptions of specific strategies. Among the most extensively researched strategies are those designed to help students improve their memory.

Memory. Memory deficits are common among students with learning disabilities. However, often problems that appear to be caused by poor memory skills are actually the result of difficulties attending to task (see Chapter 5 for ways to help students with attentional problems). For students who genuinely have short- and long-term memory deficits, there are various strategies that can help (adapted from Scruggs & Mastropieri, 1992):

1. ***Intensify instruction for later recall.*** Highlight important points on the chalkboard or overhead projector and have students repeat key information many times in various contexts. Direct questioning of information to be remembered can help recall (Brophy & Good, 1986). This can take careful planning on the teachers' part to assure that the most important concepts have been identified before the lesson. The inclusion specialist can serve an important role in helping students improve their recall by meeting with students after the presentation of new information and asking them to repeat or explain key information.
2. ***Use external memory systems when appropriate.*** In some circumstances students may be allowed to use external memory aids to support learning. A calculator, for example, can help students who have difficulty remembering math facts. Due dates for assignments, important phone numbers, and a schedule of classes can all be written down and kept in a place where they are easily retrieved. Some teachers allow students to bring an index card with key information when taking a test; other teach-

ers would consider this cheating. Thus, before encouraging the use of an external memory tool, teachers should find out when they can and cannot be used appropriately.

3. ***Use mnemonic strategy instruction.*** **Mnemonic techniques** involve forming strong associations between new information and information already in the learners' knowledge base. One mnemonic strategy is the keyword technique. A keyword is a common word already in the students' vocabulary that sounds like all or part of a target word that needs to be learned. For example, to remember that most common frogs belong to the *Ranidae* family, students are given the keyword *rain* because it sounds like the first part of Ranidae and is easy to picture. Students then are shown (or develop themselves) a picture of a *frog* sitting in the *rain*. When later asked about Ranidae, students are able to retrieve the acoustically similar word "rain," think of the picture of the frog in the rain, and provide the correct response, "frog." Mnemonic techniques have been found to be effective for improving the memory of students with mild disabilities in a variety of settings, including inclusive classrooms, and across a wide range of content areas. They are among the most powerful interventions in special education (Mastropieri & Scruggs, 1989; Mastropieri, Scruggs, & Fulk, 1990; Mastropieri, Sweda, & Scruggs, 2000; Scruggs & Mastropieri, 1992). Specific mnemonic techniques can be used to improve recall in any content or skill area—see Chapters 6, 7, and 8 for a variety of specific techniques.

Mnemonic technique A memory strategy that involves forming strong associations between new information and information already in the learners' knowledge base.

4. ***Promote effective encoding.*** Teachers should do all they can to enhance the meaningfulness, familiarity, and concreteness of the content they are teaching. Active involvement promotes retention more than passively listening to a presentation. With new terminology, vocabulary, or names of unfamiliar places or people, teachers should ask students to attend to the *acoustic properties* of the new words (i.e., what they sound like). Such acoustic encoding can improve later recall of the new word.

Behavioral Models of Learning

The following instructional approaches share **task analysis**, the teaching of subskills, active involvement by students, precise curriculum-based measurement of progress, immediate feedback, and the need for students to master content before proceeding to the next level.

Task analysis A systematic procedure for determining the steps followed by a competent person when performing a task.

Task analysis refers to a systematic procedure for determining the steps followed by a competent person when performing a task (Mager, 1997). Doing a task analysis means answering the question, "What would someone need to know or be able to do to be successful at this endeavor?" For example, before someone can successfully bake chocolate chip cookies (the target skill), he or she must know how to use an oven, make the dough, and spoon the dough onto a cookie sheet (all prerequisite skills). Each of these steps also requires a fund of knowledge and skills. For example, to make the dough, one must know how to read a recipe, measure ingredients, and mix ingredients (which probably requires knowing how to use an electric mixer).

Being able to do a task analysis is an important skill for a special education teacher. Once she or he has determined what a student *can* do, it is through task analysis that he or she determines what the student still needs to learn to become competent in a particular skill, and in what order. The first step when conducting a task analysis is to list the steps that are followed to perform a skill. This can be done through brainstorming and then arranging all prerequisite skills into a hierarchy. Once prerequisite skills have been determined, these can be used to write learning objectives for the student (Mager, 1997).

For example, let's take a look at the steps needed to solve a two-digit subtraction problem that requires borrowing (regrouping). If we first brainstorm, we might think of "knowing how to subtract a one-digit number from a number between 10 and 19," "being able to tell if a one-digit number is greater or less than another number," "knowing that if the top number is less than the bottom number, borrowing is required," "knowing how to borrow by regrouping, moving 10 from the 10s place to the 1s place," "knowing that when we move the 10 over, we indicate this be writing a '1' to the left of the number in the one's place (e.g., so that '1' becomes '11')," "knowing that when we regroup by moving 10 over, we need to cross out the number in the 10s place and replace it with a number that is 10 less (e.g., so that the '3' in '31' becomes '2' when the '1' becomes '11')," "knowing which is the 1s place and which is the 10s place," "knowing that we 'take away' or subtract the lower number from the number on top," "understanding that the numeral in the 10s place, let's say '1', actually represents '10'," and "knowing that we start solving a problem on the right, or, in other words, by subtracting the number in the 1s place." This process has yielded several steps that are not necessarily in order. Once we have finished brainstorming, we can arrange our list so that the easiest steps are presented first, as follows (note that the order might vary somewhat):

- Knowing that we "take away" or subtract the lower number from the number on top (when the problem is written vertically).
- Knowing which numeral is in the 1s place and which is in the 10s place.
- Knowing that we start solving a problem on the right, or, in other words, by subtracting the number in the 1s place.
- Being able to tell if a one-digit number is greater or less than another number.
- Knowing that if the top number is less than the bottom number, borrowing is required.
- Understanding that the numeral in the 10s place, let's say "3," actually represents "30."
- Knowing how to borrow by regrouping, moving 10 from the 10s place to the 1s place.
- Knowing that when we move 10 over, we indicate this be writing a "1" to the left of the number in the one's place (e.g., so that "1" becomes "11").
- Knowing that when we regroup by moving 10 over, we need to cross out the number in the 10s place and replace it with a number that is 10 less (e.g., so that the "3" in "31" becomes "2" when the "1" becomes "11").
- Knowing how to subtract a one-digit number from a number between 10 and 19.

We could go back even further on our hierarchy and include such skills as "being able to read numbers and understand their value" and "being able to write numerals." Understanding all of the steps required to successfully solve a problem enables the teacher to pinpoint when and where a student is getting stuck. For example, if the student often mistakenly subtracts the upper number from the lower in a problem, this skill must be taught before moving on to other components of the task. The inclusion specialist should become an expert in task analysis to be able to provide students with help at the appropriate level.

Direct instruction An instructional approach where skills are taught in small sequential steps, students are active participants in the lesson, and immediate feedback is provided.

Direct Instruction. With **direct instruction**, skills are taught in small sequential steps, students are active participants in the lesson, and immediate feedback is provided. Direct instruction is based on behavioral psychology and therefore emphasizes observable behaviors, precise measurement, and the antecedents or consequences that influence behavior. A meta-analysis of twenty-five experimental studies that compared direct instruction with other methods of teaching reading, math, language, spelling, writing, health, and social skills to students with mild, moderate, and severe disabilities found that 53 percent of the aca-demic and social outcomes favored direct instruction (White, 1988, cited in Hocutt, 1996). In a different meta-analysis, direct instruction and strategy instruction were found to be the most powerful techniques for teaching students with learning disabilities (Swanson, 1999). Research suggests that when the teacher provides step-by-step instruction and students are provided with many opportunities to respond to questions during the lesson, direct instruction can be very effective for students with disabilities and also for low-achieving students who might be referred for special education (Gersten, Carnine, & Williams, 1982; Gersten, Woodward, & Darch, 1986; Swanson, 1999). In a survey of effective teachers of students with reading disabilities, teachers reported using direct instruction embedded in a context of meaningful reading and writing activities (Rankin-Erickson & Pressley, 2000). In general, the greater the needs of students, the more direct instruction they received.

Not everyone agrees on how to define direct instruction. Many researchers and theorists use the term to refer to a set of teaching behaviors specified in the effective teaching literature where teachers follow a prescribed format, as follows (adapted from Rosenshine & Stevens, 1986):

1. Begin a lesson with a short review of previous prerequisite learning.
2. Begin a lesson with a short statement of goals.
3. Present new material in small, sequential steps, with student practice after each step.
4. Directly and explicitly lead the instruction of pupils.
5. Ascertain when each student has achieved a mastery level before moving on to the next level.
6. Teach to specific objectives.
7. Give clear and detailed instructions and explanations.
8. Provide a high level of active, teacher-directed practice for all students.
9. Ask many questions, check for student understanding, and obtain responses from all students.
10. Guide students during initial practice.
11. Provide constant, systematic feedback and corrections.
12. Provide explicit instruction and practice for independent seatwork exercises.

When providing an intensive small group lesson on a particular skill, the inclusion specialist may wish to incorporate these principles of direct instruction outlined by Rosenshine and Stevens (1986).

The term "direct instruction" has also been more narrowly defined as referring to a prescribed set of curriculum materials that include *Reading Mastery* (Engelmann & Bruner, 1997), and *Corrective Reading* (Engelmann, Hanner, & Haddox, 1980). These materials incorporate very specific scripts that the teacher is to read word for word when conducting a lesson on a particular topic.

Many special education researchers now agree that an optimal instructional program includes some elements of direct instruction, along with cognitive strategies (Swanson, 1999). In their review of research syntheses, Vaughn and colleagues (2000) noted that there are common instructional principles that should be considered "exemplars of best practice" (p. 99), regardless of instructional domain and in virtually all areas of academic learning (see Box 4.5).

> **Precision teaching** A technique for providing individualized instruction that is precisely tailored to the particular needs of each student. It requires the close monitoring of student learning through the daily administration of curriculum-based assessment measures and the charting of student progress.

Precision Teaching. **Precision teaching** is a technique for providing individualized instruction that is precisely tailored to the particular needs of each student. It is an assessment tool as well as an instructional method and has been used effectively with students with disabilities in both special education and mainstream settings (Jenkins, Deno, & Merkin, 1979; Wesson, 1991; White, 1986). Precision teaching calls for the close monitoring of student learning through the daily administration of curriculum-based assessment measures and the charting of student progress. Like direct instruction, it originated in the behavioral school of psychology (Lindsley, 1971, cited in Bender, 1996). Although not appropriate for every educational goal, it can be used effectively for reinforcing many lower-level academic skills, such as math computation skills. Five guiding principles underlie precision teaching (Lindsley, 1971, cited in Bender, 1996):

1. The learner knows best: If a student is progressing, the teaching method is appropriate. If the student is not progressing, some other procedure must be tried.
2. Progress is observable: The focus should be on directly observable behaviors in order to obtain a clear, unambiguous picture of progress.

BOX 4.5
CRITICAL FINDINGS FROM LD INTERVENTION RESEARCH

Critical factors in instructional interventions include:

- Control of task difficulty (i.e., sequencing examples and problems to assure high levels of student success)
- Teaching students in small interactive groups of six students or less
- Directed response questioning (e.g., self-questioning strategies, question generation, metacognitive skills)

Source: Adapted from Vaughn, Gersten, & Chard (2000).

3. Frequency should be the measure of behavior: The focus in precision teaching is on the frequency or rate of correct responses.
4. A standard chart should be used for measuring success: Charting has numerous advantages over merely saving work products.
5. A description of environmental conditions is essential: A teacher must understand the effect of the learning environment on the student's behavior and be able to construct the appropriate antecedent and consequent conditions that shape behavior. Thus, knowing what a child can do (prerequisite behaviors) facilitates the decision-making process.

Implementing precision teaching. Certain steps are outlined by Bender (1996) for initiating a precision teaching project. First, pinpoint the behavioral objective for the project (i.e., exactly what you would like the student to do, under what conditions, at what rate, by when). This objective can be developed by asking the student what he or she wants to work on, or you may select an objective based on a curriculum-based assessment measure (and the student's IEP). It is important for the student to "buy into" the objective and take responsibility for learning. Second, prepare graph paper for tracking the student's progress and worksheets that include only the specific type of problem stipulated in the objective. You will also need a timer. Next, establish an "aim line." To do this, time the student's performance for three days, and then use that information to establish an appropriate aim. Finally, select a 3- to 5-minute instructional warm-up activity directly related to the objective (e.g., flash cards for math facts). The student is now ready to begin. Have the student complete the warm-up activity and one timed exercise. Check the student's work (or teach the student how to check his or her own work) and discuss the results with the student. Ask the student if he or she would like to try to do better and allow a second trial. Chart the best time. Once the student is familiar with this procedure, he or she may do the graphing. Continually encourage the student by pointing out successes. If after three days the student has shown no progress, something about the procedure must be changed. The warm-up activity might be altered, an easier, prerequisite task might be selected, or a tangible reward might be added. Once the student can attain the "aim level" for three consecutive days, he or she should move to the next skill in the sequence (e.g., move from regrouping with two-digit numbers to regrouping with three-digit numbers).

Although we have described the precision teaching procedure with an individual, it can easily be implemented with a group of students. One option is to implement various instructional approaches (other than precision teaching) during 45 minutes of a 60-minute time block, and then use precision teaching during the last 15 minutes of the period. Students are provided with individual worksheets, tailored to their specific objectives, and then timed as a group while they complete their work. Both the GE and SE teachers in an inclusion class can then help students correct their work and chart their progress.

Mastery learning An instructional approach based on the premise that all students are capable of learning the basic concepts and skills of a subject if they are given appropriate instruction—students must demonstrate mastery of a skill and/or concept before proceeding.

Mastery Learning. **Mastery learning** is based on the premise that all students are capable of learning the basic concepts and skills of a subject if they are given appropriate instruction (Bloom, 1971). While students do learn at different rates, all can learn if provided with sufficient time and the proper learning conditions.

Rapid learners may spend most of their time working on self-selected objectives that allow them to pursue special interests related to a topic. Learners who are slow to master the first few units often begin to speed up as they experience learning success, many for the first time. Guskey, Passaro, and Wheeler (1995) recommend applying mastery learning in general education classrooms as a way to help at-risk students with learning disabilities. They found that students in a mastery learning program improved their own scores on standardized tests, and outperformed similar students in a more traditional program.

Implementing Mastery Learning.

1. Divide the material to be learned into instructional units (much as textbooks are divided into chapters).
2. Identify a common core of learning objectives for each unit.
3. Provide initial instruction in the unit.
4. Administer a *formative* evaluation or quiz, not as part of the grading process, but to provide feedback to the students and teacher(s) about what material was learned well and what requires further instruction.
5. Offer corrective activities to students who would benefit from additional time and practice learning the material (make sure that these are interesting, motivating activities and *not* skill and drill worksheets). Use a variety of instructional approaches to teach target objectives.
6. Following the corrective work, administer a second formative evaluation to verify mastery.
7. Provide enrichment activities for students who have mastered unit objectives following the first or second formative evaluations.
8. Do not move on to a new unit until mastery (usually 85 percent correct on a unit test) has been achieved.

During mastery learning, the inclusion specialist plays a key role by determining appropriate instructional objectives for students with disabilities, designing a variety of instructional activities that fit students' needs and interests and providing intensive tutoring when necessary. Ms. Kelly and Ms. Carey implement mastery learning when teaching content area concepts (i.e., in science, math, and social studies) using a teach, test, teach, retest format, but they also apply mastery learning principles when assessing performance-based objectives. For each assignment they establish minimal criteria that all students must meet. When students turn in an assignment, the teachers do not merely apply these criteria in order to come up with a grade. They evaluate whether each student has mastered the assignment's objectives. Students who have successfully completed all aspects of the assignment move on to another activity. Students who have not met the pre-established criteria are shown what they need to do to improve and given another chance. Students who have met all requirements receive an A or a B and move on to a related activity (or help others). Students who are missing components or need to improve their writing receive assistance and are encouraged to keep working on their project until they have met the criteria to earn an A or a B. Mastery learning, when applied in this way, provides a structure for scaffolding instruction within a student's zone of proximal development and a bridge between behavioral and sociocultural theoretical perspectives.

TECHNOLOGY

Recent advances in technology have led to an array of options for providing support for students with high-incidence disabilities in the general education classroom. Computers, tape recorders, and other specialized assistive devices provide ongoing assistance for students both in and out of the classroom. In this section of the chapter, we first describe how *instructional technology* can help teachers teach. Then we define and give examples of *assistive technology* for students. We discuss the benefits and drawbacks of instructional software and provide guidelines for evaluating software and web resources for their appropriateness for students with disabilities.

Instructional Technology

Multimedia A computer-based environment that utilizes multiple media (e.g., graphics, motion video, text, and sound) to deliver instruction.

Technology can provide teachers with wonderful tools for enhancing teaching and learning in inclusive classrooms. Special education as well as general education teachers can use technology to augment their teaching, increase their productivity, and foster higher levels of student achievement. The term ***multimedia*** is frequently used to refer to a computer-based environment that utilizes multiple media (e.g., graphics, motion video, text, and sound) to deliver instruction (Poole, 1997). Multimedia applications can be used by the teacher as teaching and demonstration tools or to provide students with an individual learning station or tutor (Wissick, 1996). Although multimedia programs can be a considerable asset in the classroom, Wissick cautions that without a knowledgeable teacher to facilitate instruction, students with disabilities will not be able to benefit from such programs. Thus, it is our belief that the special education inclusion teacher must become knowledgeable about available resources and adept at using technology to assist his or her students.

Edyburn (2000) offered several suggestions for teachers who would like to make better use of technology for instructional purposes. We adapted some of these ideas and describe them next.

1. Use a screen capture tool (e.g., Screen Thief 98, Flash-It, Snapz Pro) to take a picture of an image on your computer screen. You can paste this image into a handout to show students what they can expect to see as they complete an assignment on the computer.
2. Use a digital camera to obtain images that are instructionally relevant for your students. Create a digital library of your images so you can copy and paste them into your instructional materials.
3. Create a web page, for example, using TrackStar (http://scrtec.org/track/). This free, easy-to-use tool enables teachers and students to create web pages with links and descriptions—a valuable alternative to written reports for students and a helpful management resource for teachers who want to make web pages for their students.

4. Use the World Wide Web (WWW) to conduct web searches using specialized and innovative search tools such as Google (http://www.google.com), Ask Jeeves (http://www.aj.com), or The Gateway to Educational Materials (http://www.thegateway.org), and web browser add-ons such as Alexa (http://www.alexa.com). Use these to find relevant information in less time. Provenzo's (1998) *The Educator's Brief Guide to the Internet and the World Wide Web* is an excellent resource for helping teachers learn to navigate the WWW. Be aware that school districts vary in their policies concerning students' access to the web; therefore, before proceeding, it is important to find out what local restrictions or supervision requirements might be in place.

Assistive Technology

Assistive technology
Devices and services that enhance the performance of individuals with disabilities by enabling them to complete tasks more effectively, efficiently, and independently than otherwise possible.

What is assistive technology? **Assistive technology** refers to *devices* and *services* that enhance the performance of individuals with disabilities by enabling them to complete tasks more effectively, efficiently, and independently than otherwise possible (Blackhurst, 1997). An assistive technology *device* is any item, piece of equipment, or product that is used to increase, maintain, or improve the functional capabilities of a child with a disability. Some devices make life easier for all individuals, such as computers for word processing and calculators, while other devices are designed specifically for individuals with special needs. Although historically assistive technologies have been intended for students with low-incidence disabilities (e.g., print magnification systems for individuals with visual impairments), they can also be helpful for students with learning disabilities (Bender, 2001). However, the profession has been slow to recognize the need to integrate state-of-the-art technology into special education programs and services for students with high-incidence disabilities (Edyburn, 2000).

An assistive technology *service* is any support that directly assists a child with a disability in the selection, acquisition, or use of an assistive technology device (Edyburn, 2000). The term includes (a) the evaluation of the needs of a child with a disability; (b) the acquisition of assistive technology devices; (c) the selection, design, customization, adaptation, and maintenance of assistive technology devices; (d) coordination with other therapies, interventions, or services; (e) training or technical assistance for a child with a disability; and (f) training or technical assistance for professionals or other individuals who provide services to, employ, or are otherwise substantially involved in the major life functions of that child.

What the Law Says. The 1997 IDEA reauthorization stipulated that the IEP team *must* consider each student's need for assistive technology. Students with all types of disabilities qualify, regardless of level of severity. Yet IEP teams typically are not ready to implement this statute—individuals who serve on IEP teams still have little or no experience with assistive technology decision making and school districts are unprepared to provide such supports (Zabala, Blunt, Carl, et al., 2000). Cook and Hussey (1995) noted that we lack clearly articulated principles for how to make decisions concerning who should receive what type of assistive technology. Essential questions for members of an IEP team should be: How do we recognize the limitations of instructional or remediation strategies (other than assistive technology) for enabling a student to achieve at a specified level of performance? When do we decide that assistive technology can be utilized to enable the individual to achieve at a higher level of performance? In other words, how do we decide who needs a calculator? A laptop computer? And who doesn't (where do we draw the line)? Common errors of IEP teams include (a) considering assistive technology only for students with severe disabilities; (b) not having anyone on the team who is knowledgeable about assistive technology; (c) not using a consistent decision-making process that is based on data about the student, environment, or tasks; (d) limiting consideration of assistive technology to those items that are familiar to team members or readily available in the district; (e) failing to consider access to the general education curriculum and IEP goals in determining if assistive technology is required; and (f) if assistive technology is not needed, failing to document the decision-making process (adapted from Zabala et al., 2000). As a member of the IEP team, the special education teacher has a responsibility to become informed about assistive technology and what options should be available for students.

Zabala and colleagues (2000) created the SETT framework to help IEP teams gather and organize data to enhance assistive technology decision making (see Figure 4.8). Chambers (1998) has also developed guidelines for IEP teams.

The Student	What does the student need to do? What are the student's current abilities? What are the student's special needs?
The Environment	What materials and equipment are currently available? What is the physical arrangement? Are there special concerns? What is the instructional context? Are there likely to be changes? What supports are available to the student? What resources are available to the people supporting the student?
The Tasks	What activities take place in the environment? What activities support the student's curriculum? What are the critical elements of the activities? How might activities be modified to accommodate the student's special needs? How might technology support the student's active participation in those activities?
The Tools	What no-tech, low-tech, and high-tech options should be considered when developing a system for a student with these needs and abilities doing tasks in these environments? What strategies might be used to increase student performance? How might these tools be tried with the student in the customary environments in which they will be used?

FIGURE 4.8 Joy Zabala's SETT Framework: Questions to Ask at IEP Meetings

Assistive Technology Toolkits. Edyburn (2000) suggests that teachers put together assistive technology toolkits to support students with special needs in inclusive settings. A technology toolkit is a collection of technology devices and resources for meeting the needs of students with high-incidence disabilities. Technology toolkits have become increasingly popular in recent years (Caverly, Peterson, & Mandeville, 1997; Edyburn & Gardner, 1999). Although personal toolkits that enhance productivity can benefit all students, they particularly have important implications for special education as a way to help students with disabilities achieve high standards.

What should be included in a technology toolkit? In any given year, teachers are likely to have students in their classrooms who struggle with reading, writing, mathematics, organizational skills, and study skills. Thus, in a "best case scenario," a multitude of resources would be available. In Box 4.6 we provide a wealth of suggestions, including the addresses of many helpful websites.

Like teachers, students can utilize the WWW for support and research (Oliver, 1997). However, we advise caution when turning students loose to work on computers. They must be monitored carefully to ensure that learning is taking place. This is true for all students, but particularly students with learning disabilities and students with behavioral disorders who may lack organizational skills or can be overstimulated, frustrated, and overwhelmed by the many choices available (Bender, 2001). It can be tempting to "surf" the web and not spend enough time at any one site for understanding to occur. Lab sheets or sets of directions (e.g., scavenger hunts) provide structure for students. Another concern is that the Internet is largely unregulated and students might inadvertently (or otherwise) go to sites with objectionable material. There are different ways to control this. AOL allows for access to certain sites to be blocked. Various sites provide monitoring services, such as Cyber Patrol (http://www.cyberpatrol.com/), Net Nanny (http://www.netnanny.com/), SurfWatch (http://www.surfwatch.com/), and the Global School Network's Guidelines and Policies for Protecting Students (http://www.gsn.org/web/).

Universal Design for Learning

Universal design for learning A proactive approach to adapting the curriculum so that it is appropriate for all learners. Materials are developed from the beginning to include built-in accommodations for students with special needs (rather than adding them on later as an afterthought).

Universal design for learning is a proactive approach to adapting the curriculum so that it is appropriate for all learners. Curriculum developers and teachers plan for diversity and design lessons that provide access to a wide range of students with and without disabilities. In other words, materials are developed from the beginning to include built-in accommodations (rather than added on after the fact), particularly in digital media. Technological advances in three arenas have facilitated universal design for learning: new cognitive neuroscience research tools, new digital multimedia learning tools, and new network technologies (www.cast.org). The "universal" in universal design does not mean having a one-size-fits-all solution for everyone. Rather, it is the opposite, reflecting an awareness of the uniqueness of each learner and the need to accommodate differences in a way that maximizes every student's ability to progress (Rose & Meyer, 2002; also see http://www.cast.org). Through universal design for learning, students are provided with (a) information in multiple formats and media, (b) a choice of pathways for responding, and (c) varied means of engagement.

BOX 4.6

ASSISTIVE TECHNOLOGY TOOLKITS

READING

For students who experience reading difficulties, a text-to-speech scanner and speech output software (e.g., Wynn, eReader, Kurzweil Reader) enable students to place the textbook on the scanner and have the information scanned into the computer and then spoken to them using the computer's digitized speech synthesizer. Access to the Internet and specialized search tools such as Ask Jeeves for Kids (http://www.ajkids.com) could help students with limited reading skills locate the factual information they need to complete assignments in content-area classes. If a student has difficulty reading content-area textbooks, tools such as The Reading Pen (Wiscom) and the Speaking and Spelling and Handwriting Ace (Franklin) enable the user to enter an unknown word and hear a definition.

WRITING

Many students with disabilities have trouble with their fine motor skills, which results in either poor handwriting or a writing pace that is extremely slow. For some of these students, typing may enable them to work much more quickly. For students who have trouble writing and are constantly being sent back to edit and correct work, having the paper saved on a disk enables them to make changes without constantly having to rewrite the paper in its entirety. For students who experience difficulty with written expression, a technology toolkit can offer handheld spelling checkers, predictive word processors, talking word processors, an electronic thesaurus, prewriting software, concept mapping software, graphic writing environments, telecommunications, desktop publishing tools, web publishing, and video production tools.

For students who have trouble coming up with ideas and organizing their thoughts during the planning stage of the writing process, the software products Kidspiration (for grades K-5) and Inspiration (grade 6 through adult; Inspiration Software) offer concept mapping that can be useful for this purpose.

The toolkit might include a word prediction word processor (e.g., Co:Writer) for students whose keyboarding skills are slow or limited. Co:Writer (Don Johnston) utilizes artificial intelligence techniques to predict the word that is being entered so as to speed the text production process.

Voice input products such as ViaVoice (IBM), Dragon Dictate (Dragon Systems), and Voice Xpress (Lernout & Hauspie) enable users to dictate their ideas and have the computer do the typing for them. Speech output products such as Write:OutLoud (Don Johnston), Wynn (Arkenstone), and eReader (CAST) allow students to listen to what they have written.

Core tools for publishing during the final phase of the writing process include clip art, Microsoft Publisher (Microsoft), and either HyperStudio (Havas Interactive) or PowerPoint (Microsoft). Both HyperStudio and PowerPoint have support features that allow the user to publish a slide show to the web. When reports take the form of a web page, tools such as TrackStar (http://scrtec.org/track/) simplify the process.

MATHEMATICS

Just as the word processor is the basic tool for writers, the calculator is the fundamental tool for anyone working with numbers. Students who struggle with mathematical calculations can obtain assistance from computer-based calculators such as Big:Calc (Don Johnston) or Online Calculators (http://www-sci.lib.uci.edu/HSG/RefCalculators.html). For students who need additional support, MathPad (InfoUse) can be valuable. Products such as Number Concepts 1 & 2 (Intellitools) support new math curricula by offering math manipulatives, direct instruction, and computation support in an electronic environment.

ORGANIZATIONAL SKILLS

Organizational difficulties are a problem for many students with and without disabilities. Personal planning systems, such as DayRunner (http://www

(continues)

BOX 4.6 CONTINUED

.dayrunner.com) and FranklinPlanner (http://www.franklincovey.com) can greatly enhance personal productivity. When an individual has regular access to a computer, computer-based day planners such as AnyDay (http://www.anyday.com) and My Yahoo! (http://my.yahoo.com) also may be useful. The Palm Pilot (http://www.palm.com) is a popular portable form of personal-productivity technology. Information is entered with a stylus. At the end of the day, the information can be synchronized with a software version on the computer. Remembering important deadlines or events is another element of being organized. Remind U-Mail (http://calendar.stwing.upenn.edu) is a free service that allows users to create a calendar of important events and set a schedule for the system to automatically send an email message with a reminder notice. Mr. Wake-Up (http://www.mrwakeup.com) is another reminder system, part of a family of products from iPing.com. Users register for this free system and, via a web page, enter their wake-up message, a delivery date and time, and a phone number. At the designated time, Mr. Wake-Up calls and speaks the wake-up message or reads the day's headlines, weather forecast, or other information. The rest of the iPing.com family includes Ms. Reminder, Mr. Notify, Ms. Follow-up, Dr. Dose, and Mr. Dollar. Users can elect to have their messages delivered via telephone, cell phone, pager, email, or personal digital assistant.

STUDY SKILLS

An important component of helping students improve their academic performance involves direct instruction in effective study-skill strategies. At the K-12 level, Lynne Anderson-Inman has validated a series of computer-based study skill strategies and made her materials available through her website as downloadable resources (http://npip.com/CBSS/sampler.htm). Many colleges have designed websites to support students by providing a comprehensive collection of strategies, tools, and resources for fostering effective study skills. Two excellent sites are The Study Strategies Home Page from the University of Minnesota Duluth (http://www.d.umn.edu/student/loon/acad/strat/) and Study Guides and Strategies from St. Thomas (http://www.iss.stthomas.edu/studyguides/).

Among the variety of websites that have been created to help students with their homework are Yahoo! Reference (http://dir.yahoo.com/reference/index.html); Study-WEB (http://www.study-web.com/); John December's List of Essential Resources (http://www.december.com/cmc/info/); High School Hub (http://www.highschoolhub.org/hub/hub.htm); The Writer's Center: Resources for Writers and Teachers (http://www.colostate.edu/depts/WritingCenter/tools.htm); Dave's Math Tables (http://www.sisweb.com/math/tables.htm); and Schoolwork.Org (http://www.schoolwork.org/index.html).

Source: Adapted from Edyburn (2000).

Instructional Software

A number of software programs have been developed specifically for students with learning disabilities (Bender, 2001). For example, Anderson-Inman, Knox-Quinn, and Horney (1996) developed a series of computer-based instructional strategies to support secondary students with learning disabilities in learning study skills. Research has found that this type of multimedia instruction for students with learning disabilities and students at risk for learning problems can be quite effective (MacArthur, Ferretti, Okolo, & Cavalier,

2001; Shiah, Mastropieri, & Scruggs, 1995; Torgesen & Barker, 1995; Woodward & Rieth, 1997).

Well-designed software is motivating and user friendly. It allows students to progress at their own pace, repeat lessons as needed, receive immediate feedback, learn corrective strategies, and practice for automaticity. Yet not all software is created equal. Neuman (1991) found that students with disabilities faced many barriers when using commercial software programs, such as difficulty understanding directions and reading what was on the screen. Students generally approached software programs in a competitive manner. They figured out ways to get out of reading and to work around barriers (e.g., by resetting programs to avoid penalties). The savvy teacher knows how to select the most appropriate programs for his or her students. In the next section, we provide guidelines for evaluating software and web-based programs.

Evaluating Educational Software and Websites for Special Education. Because many educational software publishers provide little information about the development of their products, educators generally are on their own when it comes to selecting programs for students with disabilities (Higgins, Boone, & Williams, 2000). Higgins and colleagues suggest taking into consideration the following guidelines:

- The software's intended use and whether it can help the educator achieve objectives.
- Software content and whether it supplements and complements teacher-led instruction.
- The instructional presentation and whether the software meets the principles of universal design (i.e., multiple representations of content, multiple means of expression and control, and multiple forms of engagement).
- Ease of use by teacher and student.
- Documentation and support provided.
- Technical adequacy.

Also, it is important that self-correcting software include strategies for how to find correct answers rather than merely providing answers without such guidance. Higgins, Boone, and Williams also stress that educators should not rely solely on adult opinion—students must also be involved in the software evaluation process and offer input re: ease of use, appeal, technical support provided, appropriateness of instructional level, and educational outcomes.

Many programs include "bells and whistles" and offer a stimulating video game-like format that might not be suited for students with special needs. For some students, auditory and visual embellishments can be distracting and counterproductive (Okolo, 1993). Thus, it is important to find a balance between game-like features that make a software program appealing and appropriate content that facilitates learning. Most importantly, as Wissick and Gardner (2000) note, teachers should base their choices on a solid theoretical framework about what works.

Accommodating Students with Special Needs. To maximize the benefits of multimedia instruction, students with disabilities should not be left to their own devices but should receive assistance as needed. Wissick and Gardner (2000) provide accommodation ideas matched to features of multimedia instruction as well as potential challenges for students with learning disabilities. They suggest that special education teachers do the following:

- When students have memory or attention deficits, provide advance organizers and activate prior knowledge.
- For students who typically do not take advantage of guides or help features provided by the software program, select programs that offer guided tours before allowing learner control. Also, review options for seeking assistance and encourage the use of help features.
- For students who have trouble with web navigation because they are impulsive and make unnecessary moves without sufficient information, provide the context and structure for exploration and confirm that students are clear about the lessons' objectives (or allow students to set their own objectives).
- When students have a hard time staying focused long enough to gain worthwhile information or discover important relationships, provide a variety of examples and non-examples with and without technology. Encourage students to review and confirm their ideas.
- For students who tend to be passive learners, seek programs that are engaging and focus on student interests as well as curriculum objectives. Provide instructional scaffolds (support) to maintain involvement.
- When students are overwhelmed by the multitude of choices presented to them to the extent that they focus on navigation rather than content, provide concrete examples of navigation that can be posted by the computer.
- When students have trouble understanding navigation metaphors or icons, review and discuss organization first and provide additional examples related to the navigation metaphors.
- When students have gaps in relevant prior knowledge, provide direct instruction before allowing students to work independently.
- When students have problems seeing relationships and patterns, have students keep journals of their observations and discuss patterns and relationships with them.
- When students lack the metacognitive skills to monitor what is needed to perform the task, present options to students and have them suggest the best alternative for their work. Have students decide which aspects of a program most assist their learning.

REFERENCES

Adelman, H. S., & Taylor, L. (1983). Classifying students by inferred motivation to learn. *Journal of Learning Disabilities, 22,* 234–244.

Allen, V. L. (1976a). *Children as teachers: Theory and research on tutoring.* New York: Academic.

Allen, V. L. (1976b). Children helping children: Psychological processes in tutoring. In J. R. Levin & V. L. Allen (Eds.), *Cognitive learning in children: Theories and strategies* (pp. 241–290). New York: Academic.

Allington, R. L. (1980). Poor readers don't get to read much in reading groups. *Language Arts, 57*(8), 872–75.

Allington, R. L. (1983). Fluency: The neglected reading goal. *The Reading Teacher, 36,* 556–561.

Anderson-Inman, L., Knox-Quinn, C., & Horney, M. A. (1996). Computer-based study strategies for students with learning disabilities: Individual differences associated with adoption level. *Journal of Learning Disabilities, 29,* 461–484.

Barr, R. (1989). The social organization of literacy instruction. In *Cognitive and social perspectives for literacy research and instruction: The thirty-eighth yearbook of The National Reading Conference.* Chicago: The National Reading Conference.

Barr, R., & Dreeben, R. (1991). Grouping students for reading instruction. In R. Barr, M. Kamil, P. Mosenthal, & P. D. Pearson (Eds.), *Handbook of reading research* (Vol. 2, pp. 885–910). White Plains, NY: Longman.

Bateman, B. D. (1971). *The essentials of teaching.* Creswell, OR: Otter Ink Press.

Beirne-Smith, M. (1991). Peer tutoring in arithmetic for children with learning disabilities. *Exceptional Children, 57,* 330–337.

Bender, W. N. (1996). *Learning disabilities: Characteristics, identification, and teaching strategies* (3rd ed.). Boston: Allyn and Bacon.

Bender, W. N. (2001). *Learning disabilities: Characteristics, identification, and teaching strategies* (4th ed.). Boston: Allyn and Bacon.

Bentz, J. L., Fuchs, L. S. (1996). Improving peers' helping behavior to students with learning disabilities during mathematics peer tutoring. *Learning Disability Quarterly, 19,* 202–215.

Berghoff, B. (2000). New ways of thinking about assessment and curriculum. *Focus on Exceptional Children, 32*(7), 1–12.

Blackhurst, A. E. (1997). Perspectives on technology in special education. *Teaching Exceptional Children, 29*(5), 41–48.

Bloom, B. S. (1971). Mastery learning. In J. H. Block (Ed.), *Mastery learning: Theory and practice*. New York: Rinehart and Winston.

Bos, C., & Vaughn, S. (2001). *Teaching students with learning and behavioral problems* (5th ed.). Boston: Allyn and Bacon.

Breeden, T., & Mosley, J. (1991). *The middle grades teacher's handbook for cooperative learning*. Nashville, TN: Incentive Publications.

Brice, A., & Roseberry-McKibben, C. (1999). Turning frustration into success for English language learners. *Educational Leadership, 56*(7), 53–55.

Bridges, D. L., & DeVaull, F. L. (1999). Now that we have it, what do we do with it? Using the Web in the classroom. *Intervention in School and Clinic, 34*(3), 181–187.

Brophy, J., & Good, T. (1986). Teacher behavior and student achievement. In M. Wittrock (Ed.), *Handbook of research on teaching* (pp. 340–370). New York: Macmillan.

Bruner, J. (1975). The ontogenesis of speech acts. *Journal of Child Language, 2,* 1–19.

Carlson, J., & Tully, P. (1985). Learning-by-doing centers: A program to foster problem-solving skills of learning disabled students. *Teaching Exceptional Children, 17*(4), 305–309.

Cavanaugh, R. A., Heward, W. L., & Donelson, F. (1996). Effects of response cards during lesson closure on the academic performance of secondary students in an earth science course. *Journal of Applied Behavior Analysis, 29*(3), 403–406.

Caverly, D. C., Peterson, C. L., & Mandeville, T. F. (1997). A generational model for professional development. *Educational Leadership, 55*(3), 56–59.

Chambers, A. C. (1998). *Has technology been considered? A guide for IEP teams.* Reston, VA: Council for Exceptional Children.

Christenson, S. L., Ysseldyke, J. E., & Thurlow, M. L. (1989). Critical instructional factors for students with mild handicaps: An integrative review. *Remedial and Special Education, 10,* 21–31.

Clark, F. L. (2000). The strategies instruction model: A research-validated intervention for students with learning disabilities. *Learning Disabilities: A Multidisciplinary Journal, 10*(4), 209–217.

Cohen, E. G., Lotan, R. A., Scarloss, B. A., Arellano, A. R. (1999). Complex instruction: Equity in coopera-tive learning classrooms. *Theory into Practice, 38*(2), 80–86.

Cohen, P. A., Kulik, J. A., & Kulik, C. C. (1982). Educational outcomes of tutoring: A meta-analysis of findings. *American Educational Research Journal, 19,* 237–248.

Coleman, M., & Vaughn, S. (2000). Reading interventions for students with emotional/behavioral disorders. *Behavioral Disorders, 25,* 93–104.

Cook, A. M., & Hussey, S. M. (1995). *Assistive technologies: Principles and practice.* St. Louis, MO: Mosby.

Cook, S. B., Scruggs, T. E., Mastropieri, M. A., & Casto, G. C. (1986). Handicapped students as tutors. *The Journal of Special Education, 19,* 483–492.

Cooper, A. (1981). Learning centers: What they are and aren't. *Academic Therapy, 16,* 527–531.

Courson, F. H., & Heward, W. L. (1988). Increasing active student response through the effective use of paraprofessionals. *Pointer, 33*(1), 27–31.

Devin-Sheehan, L., Feldman, R. S., & Allen, V. L. (1976). Research on children tutoring children: A critical review. *Review of Educational Research, 46,* 355–385.

Diaz, S., Moll, H., & Mehan, H. (1986). Sociocultural resources in instruction: A context-specific approach. In C.E. Cortes & California Office of Bilingual Education (Ed.), *Beyond language: Social and cultural factors in schooling language minority students* (pp. 299–343). Los Angeles: California State University, Evaluation Dissemination, and Assessment Center. (ERIC Document Reproduction Service No. ED 304 241)

Dodge, B. (2001). FOCUS: Five rules for writing a great WebQuest. *Learning & Leading with Technology, 28*(8), 6–9, 58.

Edyburn, D. L. (2000). Assistive technology and students with mild disabilities. *Focus on Exceptional Children, 32*(9), 1–24.

Edyburn, D., & Gardner, J. (1999). Integrating technology into special education teacher preparation programs: Creating shared visions. *Journal of Special Education Technology, 14*(2), 3–17.

Eisermann, W. D. (1988). Three types of peer tutoring: Effects on the attitudes of students with learning disabilities and their regular class peers. *Journal of Learning Disabilities, 21*, 249–252.

Ellis, S. S., & Whalen, S. F. (1990). *Cooperative learning: Getting started.* New York: Scholastic.

Engelmann, S., & Bruner, E. C. (1997). *Reading mastery.* Chicago, IL: Science Research Associates.

Engelmann, S., Hanner, S., & Haddox, P. (1980). *Corrective reading*. Chicago, IL: Science Research Associates.

Englert, C. S., Berry, R., & Dunsmore, K. (2001). A case study of the apprenticeship process: Another perspective on the apprentice and the scaffolding metaphor. *Journal of Learning Disabilities, 34,* 152–171.

Englert, C. S., Tarrant, K. L., & Mariage, T. V. (1992). Defining and redefining instructional practice in special education: Perspectives on good teaching. *Teacher Education and Special Education, 15,* 62–86.

Enright, D. S., & McCloskey, M. L. (1988). *Integrating English: Developing English language and literacy in the multilingual classroom.* Reading, MA: Addison-Wesley.

Fisher, C. W., & Berliner, D. S. (Eds.). (1985). *Perspectives on instructional time*. New York: Longman.

Flavell, J. H. (1992). *Cognitive development* (3rd ed.). Saddle River, NJ: Prentice-Hall.

Flood, J., Lapp, D., Flood, S., & Nagel, G. (1992). Am I allowed to group? Using flexible patterns for effective instruction. *The Reading Teacher, 45*, 608–616.

Fredericks, A. D., Meinbach, A. M., & Rothlein, L. (1993). *Thematic units: An integrated approach to teaching science and social studies.* New York: HarperCollins.

Fuchs, D., Fuchs, L. S., Mathes, P. G., & Simmons, D. C. (1997). Peer-assisted learning strategies: Making classrooms more responsive to diversity. *American Educational Research Journal, 34,* 174–206.

Fuchs, L. S., Fuchs, D., Hamlett, C. L., & Appleton, A. C. (2002). Explicitly teaching for transfer: Effects on the mathematical problem-solving performance of students with mathematics disabilities. *Learning Disabilities Research & Practice, 17,* 90–106.

Gersten, R. (1998). Recent advances in instructional research for students with learning disabilities: An overview. *Learning Disabilities Research and Practice, 13,* 162–170.

Gersten, R., Carnine, D. W., & Williams, P. (1982). Measuring implementation of a structured educational model in an urban setting: An observational approach. *Educational Evaluation and Policy Analysis, 4,* 67–79.

Gersten, R., Woodward, J., & Darch, C. (1986). Direct instruction: A research-based approach to curriculum design and teaching. *Exceptional Children, 53,* 17–31.

Gillies, R. M., & Ashman, A. F. (2000). The effects of cooperative learning on students with learning difficulties in the lower elementary school. *Journal of Special Education, 34,* 19–27.

Glasgow, J. N. (1997). Let's plan it, map it, and show it! A dream vacation. *Journal of Adolescent & Adult Literacy, 40*, 456–467.

Gollnick, D. M., & Chinn, P. C. (1990). *Multicultural education in a pluralistic society* (3rd ed.). Englewood Cliffs, NJ: Merrill/Prentice-Hall.

Good, T. L., & Brophy, J. E. (1994). *Looking in classrooms* (6th ed.). New York: HarperCollins.

Goodlad, J. I. (1984). *A place called school.* New York: McGraw-Hill.

Goodlad, S., & Hirst, B. (1989). *Peer tutoring: A guide to learning by teaching.* New York: Nichols.

Goodwin, M. W. (1999). Cooperative learning and social skills: What skills to teach and how to teach them. *Intervention in School and Clinic, 35*(1), 29–33.

Greenwood, C. R., Delquadri, J., & Hall, R. V. (1984). Opportunity to respond and student academic achievement. In W. L. Heward, T. E. Heron, D. S. Hill, & J. Trap-Porter (Eds.), *Focus on behavior analysis in education* (pp. 58–88). Columbus, OH: Merrill.

Guskey, T. R., Passaro, P. D., & Wheeler, W. (1995). Mastery learning: In the regular classroom: Help for at-risk students with learning disabilities. *Teaching Exceptional Children, 27,* 15–18.

Hallahan, D. P., Kauffman, J. M., & Lloyd, J. W. (1999). *Introduction to learning disabilities* (2nd ed.). Boston: Allyn and Bacon.

Haring, N. G., & Phillips, E. L. (1972). *Analysis and modification of classroom behavior: How to achieve skill in managing behavior and provide effective instruction for all children in the classroom.* Upper Saddle River, NJ: Prentice-Hall.

Harper, G. F., Maheady, L., Mallette, B., & Karnes, M. (1999). Peer tutoring and the minority child with disabilities. *Preventing School Failure, 43*(2), 45–51.

Hearne, D., & Stone, S. (1995). Multiple intelligences and underachievement: Lessons from individuals with learning disabilities. *Journal of Learning Disabilities, 28,* 439–448.

Heller, M. F. (1997). Reading and writing about the environment: Visions of the year 2000. *Journal of Adolescent & Adult Literacy, 40,* 332–341.

Heward, W. L. (1994). Three "low-tech" strategies for increasing the frequency of active student response during group instruction. In R. Gardner III, D. M. Sainato, J. O. Cooper, T. E. Heron, W. L. Heward, J. Eshleman, & T. A. Grossi (Eds.), *Behavior analysis in education: Focus on measurably superior instruction* (pp. 283–320). Monterey, CA: Brooks/Cole.

Heward, W. L., Gardner III, R., Cavanaugh, R. A., Courson, F. H., Grossi, T. A., & Barbetta, P. M. (1996). Everyone participates in this class: Using response cards to increase active student response. *Teaching Exceptional Children, 28,* 4–10.

Hiebert, E. H. (1983). An examination of ability grouping for reading instruction. *Reading Research Quarterly, 18,* 231–235.

Higgins, K., Boone, R., & Williams, D. L. (2000). Evaluating educational software for special education. *Intervention in School and Clinic, 36*(2), 109–115.

Hill, S., & Hill, T. (1990). *The collaborative classroom: A guide to cooperative learning.* Portsmouth, NH: Heinemann.

Hocutt, A. M. (1996). Effectiveness of special education: Is placement the critical factor? In D. Terman (Ed.), *The future of children: Special Education.* Los Altos, CA: David and Lucille Packard Foundation.

Jenkins, J., Deno, S., & Mirkin, P. (1979). Measuring pupil progress toward the least restrictive environment. *Learning Disabilities Quarterly, 2,* 81–92.

Jenkins, J. R., & Jenkins, L. M. (1987). Making peer tutoring work. *Educational Leadership, 44,* 64–68.

Johnson, D. W., & Johnson, R. T. (1989). Cooperative learning: What special education teachers need to know. *The Pointer, 33,* 5–10.

Johnson, D. W., & Johnson, R. T. (1993). Foreword. In J. W. Putnam (Ed.), *Cooperative learning and strategies for inclusion* (pp. xiii–xiv). Baltimore, MD: Paul H. Brookes.

Juel, C. (1991). Cross-age tutoring between student athletes and at-risk children. *The Reading Teacher, 45,* 178–186.

Kagan, S. (1986). Cooperative learning and sociocultural factors in schooling. In California State Department of Education, *Beyond language: Social and cultural factors in schooling language minority students* (pp. 231–298). Los Angeles: California State University, Evaluation, Dissemination and Assessment Center.

Kagan, S. (1990). *Cooperative learning resources for teachers.* San Juan Capistrano, CA: Resources for Teachers.

Kamps, D. M., Dugan, E. P., & Leonard, B. R. (1994). Enhanced small group instruction using choral responding and student interaction for children with autism and developmental disabilities. *American Journal on Mental Retardation, 99*(1), 60–73.

Klingner, J. K., & Vaughn, S. (2000). The helping behaviors of fifth-graders while using collaborative strategic reading (CSR) during ESL content classes. *TESOL Quarterly, 34,* 69–98.

Klingner, J. K., Vaughn, S., Hughes, M. T., Schumm, J. S., & Elbaum, B. (1998). Academic outcomes for students with and without learning disabilities in inclusive classrooms. *Learning Disabilities Research & Practice, 13,* 153–160.

LaBerge, D., & Samuels, S.J. (1974). Toward a theory of automatic information processing in reading. *Cognitive Psychology*, 6, 293–323.

Larkin, M. J. (2001). Providing support for student independence through scaffolded instruction. *TEACHING Exceptional Children, 34*(1), 30–34.

Lazerson, D. B., Foster, H. L., Brown, S. I., & Hummel, J. W. (1988). The effectiveness of cross-age tutoring with truant, junior high school students with learning disabilities. *Journal of Learning Disabilities, 21,* 253–255.

Lewis, M. E. B. (1993). *Thematic units and strategies in learning disabilities: A textbook for practitioners.* San Diego, CA: Singular.

Lovitt, T. C. (1975). Applied behavior analysis and learning disabilities. Part II: Specific research recommendations and suggestions for practitioners. *Journal of Learning Disabilities, 8,* 504–518.

Lovitt, T. C. (1983). Notes on behavior modification. *Journal of Special Education, 17,* 361–364.

Lyman, L., & Foyle, H. C. (1990). *Cooperative grouping for interactive learning: Students, teachers, and administrators.* Washington, DC: National Education Association.

Lyman, R. (1981). The responsive classroom discussion. In A. S. Anderson (Ed.), *Mainstreaming digest.* College Park: University of Maryland.

MacArthur, C. A., Ferretti, R. P., Okolo, C. M., & Cavalier, A. R. (2001). Technology applications for students with literacy problems: A critical review. *The Elementary School Journal, 101,* 273–301.

Mager, R. F. (1997). *Preparing instructional objectives.* Atlanta, GA: Center for Effective Performance.

Maheady, L., Mallete, B., Harper, G. F., & Saca, K. (1991). Heads together: A peer mediated option for improving the academic achievement of heterogeneous learning groups. *Remedial and Special Education, 12*(2), 25–33.

Malamuth, N. M., Turcotte, S. J. C., & Fitz-Gibbon, C. T. (1981). Tutoring and social psychology. *The Journal of Educational Thought, 15,* 113–123.

Mariage, T. V. (2001). Features of an interactive writing discourse: Conversational involvement, conventional knowledge, and internalization in "Morning Message." *Journal of Learning Disabilities, 34,* 172–196.

Mastropieri, M. A., & Scruggs, T. E. (1989). Constructing more meaningful relations: Mnemonic instruction for special populations. *Educational Psychology Review, 1*(2), 83–111.

Mastropieri, M. A., Scruggs, T. E., & Fulk, B. J. M. (1990). Teaching abstract vocabulary with the keyword method: Effects on recall and comprehension. *Journal of Learning Disabilities, 23,* 92–96, 107.

Mastropieri, M. A., Scruggs, T. E., Mohler, L. J., Beranek, M. L., Spencer, V., Boon, R. T., & Talbott, E. (2001). Can middle school students with serious reading difficulties help each other and learn anything? *Learning Disabilities Research & Practice, 16,* 18–27.

Mastropieri, M. A., Sweda, J., & Scruggs, T. E. (2000). Putting mnemonic strategies to work in an inclusive classroom. *Learning Disabilities Research & Practice, 15,* 69–74.

McGill-Franzen, A., & Allington, R. L. (1990). Comprehension and coherence: Neglected elements of literacy instruction in remedial and resource room serv-ices. *Journal of Reading, Writing, and Learning Disabilities, 6,* 149–180.

McMaster, K. N., & Fuchs, D. (2002). Effects of cooperative learning on the academic achievement of students with learning disabilities: An update of Tateyama-Sniezek's review. *Learning Disabilities Research & Practice, 17,* 107–117.

McTighe, J., & Lyman, F. T., Jr. (1988). Cueing thinking in the classroom: The promise of theory-embedded tools. *Educational Leadership, 45,* 18–24.

Moll, L.C. (Ed.). (1990). *Vygotsky and education: Instructional implications and applications of sociohistorical psychology.* Cambridge, UK: Cambridge University Press.

Mortweet, S. L., Utley, C. A., Walker, D., Dawson, H. L., Delquadri, J. C., Reddy, S. S., Greenwood, C. R., Hamilton, S., & Ledford, D. (1999). Classwide peer tutoring: Teaching students with mild mental retardation in inclusive classrooms. *Exceptional Children, 65,* 524–536.

Nelson, K. (1995, July/August). Nurturing kids' seven ways of being smart. *Instructor,* 26–34.

Neuman, D. (1991). Learning disabled students' interactions with commercial software: A naturalistic study. *Educational Technology, Research and Development, 39*(1), 31–49.

Oakes, J. (1990). *Multiplying inequalities: The effects of race, social class, and tracking on opportunities to learn math and science.* Santa Monica, CA: RAND.

Oakes, J., Gamoran, A., & Page, R. (1991). Curriculum differentiation: Opportunities, consequences, and meanings. In P. Jackson (Ed.), *Handbook of research on curriculum.* New York: Macmillan.

Ogle, D. M. (1986). K-W-L: A teaching model that develops active reading of informational text. *The Reading Teacher, 39,* 564–570.

Okolo, C. M. et al. (1993). A retrospective view of computer-based instruction. *Journal of Special Education Technology, 12*(1), 1–27.

Oliver, K. M. (1997). Getting online with K-12 internet projects. *TechTrends, 42*(6), 33–40.

Olson, J. L., & Platt, J. M. (1996). *Teaching children and adolescents with special needs* (2nd ed.). Englewood Cliffs, NJ: Merrill/Prentice-Hall.

Palincsar, A. S., & Brown, A. L. (1984). Reciprocal teaching of comprehension-fostering and comprehension-monitoring activities. *Cognition and Instruction, 1,* 117–175.

Palincsar, A. S. & Brown, A. L. (1987). Enhancing instructional time through attention to metacognition. *Journal of Learning Disabilities, 20,* 66–75.

Palincsar, A. S., Parecki, A. D., & McPhail, J. C. (1995). Friendship and literacy through literature. *Journal of Learning Disabilities, 28,* 503–510, 522.

Peregoy, S. F., & Boyle, O. (1997). *Reading, writing, and learning in ESL* (2nd ed.). White Plains, NY: Longman.

Poole, B. J. (1997). *Education for an information age.* New York: McGraw-Hill.

Poplin, M. (1988). The reductionist fallacy in learning disabilities: Replicating the past by reducing the present. *Journal of Learning Disabilities, 21,* 389–400.

Pressley, M. (2000). What should comprehension instruction be the instruction of? In M. L. Kamil, P. B. Mosenthal, P. D. Pearson, & R. Barr (Eds.), *Handbook of reading research: Volume III* (pp. 545–561). Mahwah, NJ: Lawrence Erlbaum.

Provenzo, E. F. (1998). *The educator's brief guide to the Internet and the World Wide Web.* Larchmont, NY: Eye on Education.

Putnam, J. W. (1993). *Cooperative learning and strategies for inclusion: Celebrating diversity in the classroom.* Baltimore, MD: Paul H. Brookes.

Rademacher, J. A., Schumaker, J. B., & Deshler, D. D. (1996). Development and validation of a classroom assignment routine for inclusive settings. *Learning Disability Quarterly, 19,* 163–177.

Rankin-Erickson, J. L., & Pressley, M. (2000). A survey of instructional practices of special education teachers nominated as effective teachers of literacy. *Learning Disabilities Research & Practice, 15,* 206–225.

Richard-Amato, P. A. (1992). Peer teachers: The neglected resource. In P. A. Richard-Amato & M. A. Snow (Eds.), *The multicultural classroom: Readings for content-area teachers* (pp. 271–284). White Plains, NY: Longman.

Roller, C. M. (1996). *Variability not disability: Struggling readers in a workshop classroom.* Newark, DE: International Reading Association.

Rose, D. H., & Meyer, A. (2002). *Teaching every student in the digital age: Universal design for learning.* Alexandria, VA: The Association for Supervision and Curriculum Development.

Rosenshine, B., & Stevens, R. (1986). Teaching functions. In M. Wittrock (Ed.), *Third handbook of research on teaching* (pp. 376–391). New York: Macmillan.

Rubado, K. (2002). Empowering students through multiple intelligences. *Reclaiming Children and Youth, 10*(4), 233–235.

Rupp, J. H. (1992). Discovery science and language development. In P. A. Richard-Amato & M. A. Snow (Eds.), *The multicultural classroom: Readings for content-area teachers* (pp. 316–329). White Plains, NY: Longman.

Salend, S. J. (1998). Using an activities-based approach to teach science to students with disabilities. *Intervention in School and Clinic, 34*(2), 67–72, 78.

Schirmer, T. A., & George, M. P. (1983). Practical help for the long-term learning disabled adolescent. *Teaching Exceptional Children, 15*(2), 97–101.

Schrader, B., & Valus, A. (1990). Disabled learners as able teachers: A cross-age tutoring project. *Academic Therapy, 25,* 589–597.

Scruggs, T. E., & Mastropieri, M. A. (1992). Classroom applications of mnemonic instruction: Acquisition, maintenance, and generalization. *Exceptional Children, 58,* 219–229.

Scruggs, T. E., & Osguthorpe, T. T. (1986). Tutoring interventions within special education settings: A comparison of cross-age and peer tutoring. *Psychology in the Schools, 23,* 187–193.

Scruggs, T. E., & Richter, L. (1988). Tutoring learning disabled students: A critical review. *Learning Disability Quarterly, 11,* 274–286.

Shanahan, T., Robinson, B., & Schneider, M. (1995). Integrating curriculum. *The Reading Teacher, 48,* 718–719.

Shannon, P. (1985). Reading instruction and social class. *Language Arts, 62,* 604–613.

Shiah, R., Mastropieri, M. A., & Scruggs, T. E. (1995). Computer-assisted instruction and students with learning disabilities: Does research support the rhetoric? *Advances in Learning and Behavioral Disabilities, 9,* 162–192.

Skinner, B. F. (1974). *About behaviorism.* New York: Vintage Books.

Slaughter, J. P. (1993). *Beyond storybooks: Young children and the shared book experience.* Newark, DE: International Reading Association.

Slavin, R. E. (1987). Ability grouping and student achievement in elementary schools: A best-evidence synthesis. *Review of Educational Research, 57,* 293–336.

Swanson, H. L. (1987). Information processing theory and learning disabilities: An overview. *Journal of Learning Disabilities, 20,* 3–7.

Swanson, H. L. (1993). An information processing analysis of learning disabled children's problem solving. *American Educational Research Journal, 30,* 861–893.

Swanson, H. L. (1999). Instructional components that predict treatment outcomes for students with learning disabilities: Support for a combined strategy and direct instruction model. *Learning Disabilities Research and Practice, 14,* 129–140.

Swicegood, P. R., & Parsons, J. L. (1991). The thematic unit approach: Content and process instruction for secondary learning disabled students. *Learning Disabilities Research and Practice, 6,* 112–116.

Tam, B. K. Y., & Scott, M. L. (1996). Three group instructional strategies for students with limited English proficiency in vocational education. *Journal for Vocational Special Needs Education, 19*(1), 31–36.

Tharp, R. G., & Gallimore, R. (1988). *Rousing minds to life: Teaching, learning, and schooling in social context.* New York: Cambridge University Press.

Tobin, K. (1987). The role of wait time in higher cognitive level learning. *Review of Educational Research, 57*(1), 69–95.

Torgesen, J. K., & Barker, T. A. (1995). Computers as aids in the prevention and remediation of reading disabilities. *Learning Disability Quarterly, 18,* 76–87.

Trapani, C., & Gettinger, M. (1989). Effects of social skills training and cross-age tutoring on academic achievement and social behaviors of boys with learning disabilities. *Journal of Research and Development in Education, 22,* 1–9.

Unsworth, L. (1984). Meeting individual needs through flexible within-class grouping of pupils. *Reading Teacher, 38*(3), 298–304.

Vaughn, S., Bos, C. S., & Schumm, J. S. (1997). *Teaching mainstreamed, diverse, and at-risk students in the general education classroom.* Boston: Allyn and Bacon.

Vaughn, S., Gersten, R., & Chard, D. J. (2000). The underlying message in LD intervention research: Findings from research syntheses. *Exceptional Children, 67,* 99–114.

Vygotsky, L. S. (1978). *Mind and society: The development of higher mental processes.* Cambridge, MA: Harvard University Press.

Vygotsky, L. (1986). *Thought and language.* Cambridge, MA: The MIT Press.

Watson, D. L., Northcutt, Z. & Ridele (1989). Teaching bilingual students successfully. *Educational Leadership, 46*(5), 59–61.

Wesson, C. L. (1991). Curriculum-based measurement and two models of follow-up consultation. *Exceptional Children, 57,* 246–256.

White, O. R. (1986). Precision teaching—precision learning. *Exceptional Children, 52,* 522–534.

White, W. A. T. (1988). A meta-analysis of the effects of direct instruction in special education. *Education and Treatment of Children, 11*(4), 364–374.

Whittaker, C. R., Salend, S. J., & Duhaney, D. (2001). Creating instructional rubrics for inclusive classrooms. *Teaching Exceptional Children, 34*(2), 8–1.

Winn, J. A. (1994). Promises and challenges of scaffolded instruction. *Learning Disability Quarterly, 17,* 89–104.

Wissick, C. A. (1996). Multimedia: Enhancing instruction for students with learning disabilities. *Journal of Learning Disabilities, 29,* 494–503.

Wissick, C. A., & Gardner, J. E. (2000). Multimedia or not to multimedia? That is the question for students with learning disabilities. *Teaching Exceptional Children, 32*(4), 34–43.

Wolford, P. L., Heward, W. L., & Alber, S. R. (2001). Teaching middle school students with learning disabilities to recruit peer assistance during cooperative learning group activities. *Learning Disabilities Research & Practice, 16,* 161–173.

Wong, B. Y. L. (1986). Metacognition and special education: A review of a view. *Journal of Special Education, 20,* 9–29.

Woodward, J., Monroe, K., & Baxter, J. (2001). Enhancing student achievement on performance assessments in mathematics. *Learning Disability Quarterly, 24,* 33–46.

Woodward, J., & Rieth, H. (1997). Historical review of technology research in special education. *Review of Educational Research, 67,* 503–536.

Zabala, J., Blunt, M., Carl, D., Davis, S., Deterding, C., Foss, T., Hamman, T., Bowser, G., Hartsell, K., Korsten, J., Marfilius, S., McCloskey-Dale, S., Nettleton, S., & Reed, P. (2000). Quality indicators for assistive technology services in school settings. *Journal of Special Education Technology, 15*(4), 25–36.

Zigmond, N. (1996). What makes an effective teacher? *CEC Today, 3*(4), 12.

CHAPTER FIVE

FACILITATING SOCIAL AND BEHAVIORAL COMPETENCE FOR STUDENTS WITH DISABILITIES IN INCLUSIVE SETTINGS

If you want one year of prosperity, grow grain.
If you want ten years of prosperity, grow trees.
If you want one hundred years of prosperity, grow people.

—Ancient proverb

KEY CONCEPTS

- Many behavioral problems can be prevented with effective instruction and a proactive approach to classroom management.

- A positive, supportive environment helps *all* students and includes many opportunities for students to experience success and for their needs to be met.
- Mildly disruptive behaviors can be curtailed with techniques such as *planned ignoring, proximity control, signal interference, humor,* and *logical consequences.*
- Many students in special education lack social competence and experience difficulties with peer acceptance, accurate and age-appropriate social cognition, maladaptive behaviors, and poor social skills.
- A comprehensive program for managing disruptive behavior in inclusive classrooms should include social skills instruction, self-control training, a model for problem solving, and stress management.
- Students who are experiencing difficulties should be observed in various settings and at different times of the day for the purpose of analyzing the environmental factors that affect their behavior.
- A problem-solving approach focuses on helping students develop alternative, more appropriate behaviors and take responsibility for their actions.
- Building positive relationships with students is *the* key to effectively managing the most difficult and challenging students.
- Various techniques can be applied in the classroom to help students who demonstrate the characteristics of hyperactivity, inattention, distractibility, impulsivity, and disorganization associated with ADD and ADHD.
- Students who exhibit aggressive behavior may have poor impulse control, low frustration tolerance, difficulties dealing with stress, and limited insight into the feelings of others.
- *Functional Behavior Assessment*, *Behavior Intervention Plans*, and *Positive Behavioral Supports* view systems, settings, and students' lack of skill as parts of the "problem" and work to change those.
- The most effective schools have put in place proactive, schoolwide programs for facilitating a positive climate and maintaining discipline.

FOCUS QUESTIONS

1. How can the inclusion specialist help the classroom teacher prevent inappropriate behavior?
2. What can the inclusion specialist do when students exhibit mildly disruptive behaviors?
3. What should the inclusion specialist do to help students develop social competence?
4. What actions should the inclusion specialist take for students who are exhibiting ongoing behavioral problems?
5. What does it mean for the inclusion specialist to be a "relationship specialist" or a "therapeutic teacher"?
6. How can inclusion specialists support the needs of students with ADHD?
7. What can the inclusion specialist do to help aggressive students?
8. Describe an effective schoolwide plan for preventing and dealing with inappropriate behavior.

In a survey of teachers who had several years of experience with inclusion, being able to manage behavioral difficulties was identified as one of the most important skills for a special education teacher to have (Haager, Givner, & Dingle, 1998). Behavior problems can erupt in even the most well-managed classroom, though many times such problems can be prevented with careful, proactive planning. Students with disabilities often experience more social or behavioral difficulties than their nondisabled peers (Haager & Vaughn, 1995), so it is important for the inclusion specialist to acquire specific techniques and skills for preventing and managing difficult behaviors. Having students with challenging behavior problems, especially attention disorders or hyperactivity, is probably the number one reason many general education teachers resist an inclusion model. It is important to address these issues at the outset of inclusion with a clear, yet flexible, plan. The inclusion specialist's role includes supporting the students and teachers; providing direct intervention; serving as liaison between students, teachers, and parents; connecting with various support services; and serving as a consultant. All teachers must know how to manage a classroom, but a special educator must have specialized knowledge in behavior management, from managing the classroom environment to handling the most difficult individual behaviors.

In this chapter, you will learn important assessment and teaching skills for developing positive social behaviors and diminishing negative behaviors in your students within the general education environment. Collaboration between a general and special education teacher can be a real advantage when it comes to managing difficult behaviors in an inclusive setting. You will see that being positive and proactive is the best approach to smooth classroom management. "An ounce of prevention is worth a pound of cure" is one adage that you should take to heart. Classrooms that run smoothly, keep students engaged in meaningful learning, promote cooperation and peer support, and operate with firm guidelines and clear expectations are less likely to be disrupted by troublesome behavior. First we will examine schoolwide and classwide approaches to *proactive* classroom management. Next, we will see how special education teachers can promote healthy social competence by teaching social skills and providing appropriate support for students with disabilities. Then, we examine individual interventions for students experiencing serious difficulties. Managing severe behavior problems requires depth of knowledge and skill. This is often covered in an entire course in teacher education programs, but we provide some helpful guidelines and resources here to demonstrate how this fits into the role of the special educator in an inclusive setting. Collaboration with families is a theme that runs throughout the chapter. Let's look at two teachers who learned to manage difficult behaviors.

When Nancy Grace first started teaching, her greatest fear was that her classroom management skills would be insufficient. Would she be able to maintain control of her class? What if things got out of hand? Thus, she was relieved when she was initially assigned to teach small groups of students with LD in a pull-out program. Each student would have a general education teacher who would be responsible for the majority of the school day. But right before Thanksgiving she got a call from a district administrator asking her to take over a self-contained class for students with learning, emotional, and behavioral problems at a nearby school. The special education teacher who had begun the year with this class had quit in frustration because she just couldn't handle the students' challenging behaviors. There were eleven students in all, and a teaching assistant assigned to help. Ms. Grace would be responsible for these students for the entire school day. Was she ready? She wasn't sure.

Ms. Grace prepared exciting lessons for the first day with her new students, thinking that she would keep them too busy to fool around. However, she was unprepared for just how much they would test her. They already felt "successful" for having scared away one teacher, and she was to be their next victim. She immediately met with the families of all of the students, just to get to know them. This impressed her students—no teacher had done that before. As the days and then weeks passed, she communicated frequently with parents, inviting them to the classroom and stopping by their homes after school. She shared whatever she could about what students were doing well (rather than starting out talking about problems). She asked parents what their concerns were and what insights they could offer about their children. When she really needed parents' help as difficulties arose, they were ready and willing to provide support as best they could because she had laid the groundwork for parent collaboration (but many of them were frustrated, too). She immediately implemented a token economy system (described later in this chapter) and put each student on an individual behavioral contract. Every student had one or more goals to work on, decided upon by mutual agreement in a conference that included only Ms. Grace and the individual student. She made it her policy to "catch them being good" and provide genuine positive reinforcement whenever possible. She really cared about each of her students, and this came through loud and clear. She and the students together came up with rules for the classroom, with clear consequences for infractions. She implemented a consistent schedule so that students would always know what was expected of them. She spent a great deal of time preparing lessons and materials so that when students arrived, their assignments and activities were ready and they could transition smoothly from one activity to the next. She tried to make learning fun, while at the same time not overstimulating. Students learned to trust her. They learned what she expected—what was acceptable behavior and what was not. The principal marveled at the job she was doing and how well her students behaved when she was with them. However, she still received notes from the occasional substitute teacher to the effect that hers was "the worst class" in which the teacher had ever subbed. And she felt like she could never let down her guard, even for a moment—she always had to be "on." So when the opportunity came at the end of the year to return the following fall to her position as a resource teacher for students with LD, she jumped at the chance. It had been a stressful and challenging year, but a rewarding one. She remained close to her students, maintaining contact with them and their families over the years. And she never forgot what she learned about teaching students with emotional and behavioral problems—about the importance of working closely with families, providing positive reinforcement, providing structure and clear expectations, taking one step at a time, and most of all, caring. She learned to love her students, and they loved her.

Barry Moss works as a special education teacher at West Hills Middle School, in a working-class suburb of a large city. He has taught for five years, only two of which have been in special education. Barry's principal calls him a "natural-born" teacher—someone who has a knack for teaching. Barry has picked up many ideas from fellow teachers and from his university classes, but often he uses ideas that just come to him spontaneously. He is known for being very effective with the most hard-to-reach students. When the school moved to an inclusion model two years ago, Barry led the planning team. He insisted that even the students with the most challenging behaviors should have a chance at being included. He had a personal motivation for making this work—his own teenage son had serious emotional and behavioral difficulties and had spent most of his school career in segregated programs. When he had been moved into general education classes in high school, Barry's son had experienced devastating social difficulties because he was not equipped for the "real world" of school. Barry believed his son should have had more opportunity to develop important social skills when he was younger. Barry was determined to avoid this with the West Hills program. Many teachers at West Hills were doubtful, but went along with the plan. Barry assured them he would give these students special attention. The planning team developed a back-up plan in case things did not work out. The special education department set up a separate special education program, called the "Intensive Support Program," that could be used in either short- or long-term situations for both academic or social reasons. Students could be assigned to this program for varying amounts of time and for varying durations.

Barry developed a system for monitoring students in the general education classroom. A weekly checklist provided information about students' academic performance (grades, participation, and homework) as well as their behavior and social skills. He worked collaboratively in several general education core classes. However, he was not in every class with every student. For those students who had the most significant challenges, it was necessary to enlist teachers' support in monitoring behavior and participation across classes on a daily basis. For a few students, Barry collected daily reports. Barry and the teachers identified those students who would likely need intensive behavioral support. It was helpful that Barry knew his students and their parents well. He met with each student to help establish learning and behavioral goals and developed a discrete daily reporting system that was easy for the classroom teachers to manage and would provide ongoing information to the students, teachers, and parents. Barry met at least every two weeks with the teachers during departmental meetings. Informal discussions about specific students took place when he co-taught in various classrooms or during passing periods. Though they had a good system, there were still students who had serious difficulties, just as in any middle school. Having an ongoing history of monitoring and working with students made it easier to manage the more serious episodes.

A PROACTIVE APPROACH

When you identify the instructional needs of students within the context of the classroom and make curricular adaptations both in content and instructional delivery, you can greatly reduce the occurrence of student misbehavior.

—Daniels, 1998, p. 26

Proactive approach An approach to classroom management that involves anticipating problems *before* they start and successfully preventing them from happening.

Good instruction is the best form of classroom management. Throughout this book we have promoted strategies that actively involve all students in appropriate learning activities. Such instruction keeps students engaged, motivated, and productive. Thus, we advocate a **proactive** rather than problem-oriented **approach** to classroom management. We know that the most effective teachers anticipate problems *before* they start and successfully prevent them from happening.

Tips for Successful Classroom Management

Jacob Kounin was the first classroom management researcher to conduct a detailed analysis of the relationship between teacher and student behaviors (Charles, 1996). He collected several thousand videotaped hours of teachers considered to be extremely effective in managing their classes and also teachers with pervasive management problems. What he found was surprising. There were no substantial differences in how the teachers dealt with misbehaviors *after* they had occurred. How the teachers differed was in their ability to *prevent* discipline problems. Successful teachers were better prepared and organized. They transitioned smoothly from one activity to another and monitored their pacing. They stimulated students' interest and maintained their involvement. The more effective teachers also seemed to have more classroom awareness—they constantly scanned the classroom and anticipated potential problems (Jones & Jones, 2003; Kounin, 1970). Brophy and Evertson (1976), well known for their research on effective teaching, noted, "Our data strongly support the findings of Kounin (1970). . . . the key to successful classroom management is prevention of problems *before* they start, not knowing how to deal with problems after they have begun" (p. 127). Kounin's principal concepts include (adapted from Charles, 1996):

1. *"Withitness":* Kounin used this term to refer to teachers "with eyes in the back of their head"—teachers who always seem to be aware of everything going on in their classrooms. He believed this to be a particularly powerful teacher trait.
2. *Overlapping:* This term refers to a teacher's ability to pay attention to more than one event in the classroom at a time, or "multiprocessing" (e.g., working with a small group while also attending to the rest of the class). Like "withitness" this is an important teacher characteristic.
3. *The ripple effect:* This is when a teacher's words or actions directed at one student tend to spread and also affect the behavior of other students (e.g., when a kindergarten teacher says, "I see Suzie sitting nicely," and then all of the other students sit up a little straighter). This can work very well in the primary grades, but typically has little effect with older students.
4. *Momentum:* This is when teachers have a good sense of pacing and timing—they start lessons without wasting time and keep lessons moving, speeding up or slowing down as necessary.
5. *Smoothness:* This not only refers to the steady progression of lessons, but also to the teacher's ability to stay focused and not go off on tangents while presenting information. One concept builds on another in logical fashion as the lesson develops.
6. *Group alerting:* This term refers to the teacher's ability to quickly and efficiently get students' attention whenever necessary.
7. *Student accountability:* This term refers to a teacher's efforts to keep students engaged and involved in a lesson, noticing when students might be tuning out and taking steps to redirect them and hold them accountable for their learning.
8. *Satiation:* This is when a teacher is in tune with students and sensitive to when they are getting bored or frustrated with a topic or activity.
9. *Valence:* This is when the teacher is able to rekindle interest when it lags. This phrase refers to how teachers keep lessons interesting, using a variety of presentation styles and materials.

Although Kounin's principles are very helpful when thinking about how to effectively manage a general education classroom to minimize misbehaviors, he offers little guidance about what to do once students have misbehaved or how to work with students with emotional and behavioral disabilities. There were no inclusion specialists in the classrooms in which Kounin observed. Yet we think Kounin's principles are important. Certainly "two heads are better than one" and having a second teacher in the classroom can only help with "withitness" and "overlapping." Being in tune with students and their needs is central to classroom management. The inclusion specialist is in an ideal position to pay particular attention to those students most likely to tune out, turn off, or become frustrated and take positive steps to renew their interest or provide assistance so that they can be successful. As we will discuss in more depth later in this chapter, frustration is often a precursor to more disruptive behaviors, and it is imperative to pick up on early signs that a student is feeling this way.

Positive Classroom Climate

As we have discussed elsewhere in this book, general and special education teachers play an important role in establishing a positive, supportive environment for *all* students. Teachers set a powerful example for students through their own words and actions. When they encourage risk-taking, reward effort, accept mistakes, emphasize that everyone is different with their own unique strengths, and do not tolerate teasing or abuse, they are promoting these attitudes in others. Following is a list of characteristics of a positive classroom climate (Abrams & Segal, 1998; Kauffman, 1997):

- Warm, caring atmosphere where differences are valued and students feel comfortable expressing their feelings.
- Order, structure, and consistency.
- Well-organized and predictable environment.
- Clear and realistic expectations.
- Students experience success academically and socially.
- Curriculum capitalizes on students' interests and talents.
- Teachers skilled in interpreting the communicative intent of students.
- Students are given choices and have input into classroom decisions.
- Students are able to interact socially with others in positive ways.
- Students' psychological needs are met (i.e., belonging, safety, competence, and self-esteem).
- Positive teacher–student relationships.
- Frequent positive feedback.

Positive Feedback

An essential element of a positive classroom climate is positive feedback. Being able to provide appropriate, supportive comments to students is an important and valuable teacher skill. This helps to promote enthusiasm and self-confidence in students. It is also important for teachers to provide honest feedback when students fumble with a task. When criticism occurs in an environment where positive comments abound, and when criticism is specific to the task at hand and nonjudgmental, it is not demoralizing to students. Experienced teachers say they tell students what they did right, then help them with what they did wrong.

Praise. Praising well is an art and a skill—as well as a powerful tool in the classroom. Providing appropriate praise means being observant and noticing when a child is making an effort and is showing progress. With some kids, it's easy to "catch them being good" and not hard to come up with words to acknowledge their accomplishments. However, with other students this can be more of a challenge. Yet it is precisely these more difficult students who are most in need of your positive attention. Think of progress as occurring in small steps. Notice when students are trying. This can seem almost impossible at first, but really does get easier over time and can become second nature with enough experience. We have known teachers who always seem to see the glass as "half-full" rather than "half-empty" when interacting with students—this is the kind of teacher we should all strive to be. Students view such teachers as supportive and encouraging.

As much as possible, positive feedback should be personal (include the student's name), immediate, descriptive, specific to the task, genuine, and age-appropriate. Here are some examples of positive teacher feedback:

> "Excellent problem-solving, Maria. You used the new problem-solving strategy you learned and got five answers right."
>
> "Great job, Alex. You remembered to capitalize the first word in every sentence."
>
> "Marcus, you're really trying hard—I noticed you kept your hands to yourself while waiting in line to get a drink of water."
>
> "This is the best you've done, Michael. You should show this to your father!"

These comments are much better than a generic "*Good job.*" Sincerity is also important—don't say, "*I like your story!*" if it is full of blood and guts and you don't really mean it. Words of appreciation, such as, "*Thank you, Marcella. I really appreciate your help!*" also can go a long way. Teaching the child to reward herself through positive self-talk is also valuable (e.g., "*You did very well staying in your seat today. How do you feel about that?*"). As another guideline, remember that positive feedback should far outweigh negative feedback. Note that praise can be written as well as verbal—positive notes to students and "happy-grams" home to parent(s) are very powerful.

Effectively using positive feedback fosters students' confidence and self-esteem and encourages further effort. It also builds trust between you and the student and helps in establishing rapport. Canter believes that being able to give appropriate praise is what most clearly distinguishes the more effective from the less effective teacher (Charles, 1996).

Interventions for Surface Behaviors

Surface behaviors Mildly disruptive behaviors not deemed serious or chronic.

Even in the most exciting classroom learning environment, students may forget rules or become mildly disruptive. The following techniques are recommended for disruptive behaviors not deemed serious or chronic (**surface behaviors**). For each, we discuss the role of the inclusion specialist.

1. *Planned Ignoring:* This requires patience! The principle is simple: Ignore undesirable behavior and reward appropriate behavior. It works best when you decide ahead of time which behaviors you will ignore. The classroom teacher and inclusion specialist should discuss which behaviors (and which students) to ignore. For example, you may decide that you will ignore Trini when she shouts out an answer and reward her for remembering to raise her hand (by acknowledging her efforts and sometimes calling on her). Be forewarned that sometimes a student's misbehavior will initially escalate as the student tries even harder to get your attention.

2. *Proximity Control:* This simply means moving closer to a student as he begins to engage in an inappropriate behavior, such as talking to a neighbor when he should be paying attention to a lesson. No talking is involved, though the teacher might place his hand on the student's shoulder. It might be the classroom teacher or inclusion specialist who uses this technique. When there is a second teacher in the room, she might pull up a chair and sit next to the student. This also allows her to assess the situation and determine if the student needs a more intensive intervention.

3. *Signal Interference:* Here the teacher uses a signal to indicate that an inappropriate behavior is occurring. The teacher and student or students decide ahead of time what the signal will be. A signal might be used for the entire class, such as when the noise level is getting out of hand and the teacher flicks the lights off and on. A signal might also be used with an individual student for a specific target behavior (decided upon with the student), such as a quick hand clap to remind a student to stay in her seat. This is an excellent strategy for the inclusion specialist to use with students with special needs and can be part of a larger behavioral plan.

4. *Defusing Tension through Humor:* This one works great if you can do it! Humor is a powerful tool for keeping students engaged and motivated. However, humor must be used very carefully—teachers should avoid sarcasm, belittling students, or in any way making students the butt of jokes. Similar to using humor is not taking students' pranks too seriously (not overreacting or taking personally their minor disruptions). This might be called being a "good sport" as a teacher. One of the most effective middle-school inclusion specialists we know, Aile Montoya, explains that she is able to use humor because she remembers all too well what it is like to be 13 or 14 and "just want to have fun." So rather than get angry with her students, she occasionally joins in. Once her students got off task and made paper airplanes. She brought them back to the lesson by showing them a new "really cool" model and had them write messages on the planes with one or more vocabulary words. It is important to use good judgment in this. Occasional diversions may serve the purpose described here of "reining students in," but too much diversion will disrupt the pace or focus of learning. It is best to think of this tactic as serving the purpose of "comic relief."

5. *Logical Consequences:* As much as possible, consequences for inappropriate behavior should "make sense" and seem like a natural response. Good teachers often connect the consequence to the deed. For example, if a student walks in the classroom noisily, she should be asked to come in again quietly. If a student turns in a sloppy assignment (and you know he can do better), require that he do it over. If a student throws food at other students during lunch, she can be required to eat by herself the following day.

SOCIAL COMPETENCE

Developing Social Competence

Many students in special education experience social difficulties (Kavale & Forness, 1995; Mastropieri & Scruggs, 2000). These difficulties might be addressed within a classwide social skills program or individually. For students with emotional disturbance, the development of social skills might be a primary concern. Other students with high-incidence disabilities may experience social difficulties as well. It is important to address social difficulties directly and without hesitation to ward off more serious consequences later. As an inclusion specialist, you may be responsible for addressing IEP goals related to the development of social skills.

Developing **social competence** is critical to success in today's world. Consider how important it is to get along well with others in the workplace. People who are successful adults move easily into and out of social situations, adjusting their own behavior to fit the social circumstances. They can read others' responses and feelings and can initiate social interaction. Transition programs that prepare high school students with disabilities for adult life often include social skills training. However, it is important to intervene much earlier than high school when students with disabilities experience social difficulties.

Social competence The ability to get along with others and move easily into and out of social situations, adjusting one's behavior to fit the social circumstances. The ability to read others' responses and feelings and initiate social interactions.

Sharon Vaughn and colleagues define ***social competence*** as a multifaceted construct with intertwined components that interact to produce effective social behaviors (Haager & Vaughn, 1995; Vaughn & Haager, 1994a, 1994b; Vaughn & Hogan, 1990; Vaughn, Haager, Hogan, & Kouzekanani, 1992). The four components (illustrated in Figure 5.1) are peer acceptance, accurate and age-appropriate social cognition, absence of maladaptive behaviors, and effective social skills. We can see that having social skills, or being able to respond appropriately in a social situation, is only one piece of the puzzle. All components are important for social competence. We define the components here, but keep in mind that it is the combination of these elements that yields social competence.

1. *Peer Acceptance.* Having the positive regard of others, whether it is family, friends, classmates, teachers, or colleagues is probably the truest measure of social success for most people. Peer acceptance begins early in a child's school career. As early as kindergarten, students with learning disabilities were found to have low peer acceptance (Vaughn et al., 1992). Childhood peer rejection has been linked with serious social difficulties later in life, such as dropping out of school, criminal involvement, and adult maladjustment (Parker & Asher, 1987). For school-age children, experiencing positive peer regard means having ready access to peer support or even friendship. Difficulty with peer relations is not always detected by typical assessment practices, or even by discerning teachers or other school personnel. It is best assessed through the peers themselves. Later we describe simple techniques for sociometric assessment of peer relations.

Social cognition The ability to understand and interpret social situations and to self-evaluate one's own social circumstances. This includes self-evaluation, social perceptions, and social problem solving.

2. *Social Cognition.* **Social cognition** is "the ability to understand and interpret appropriately the behavior of self and others" in an accurate and age-appropriate

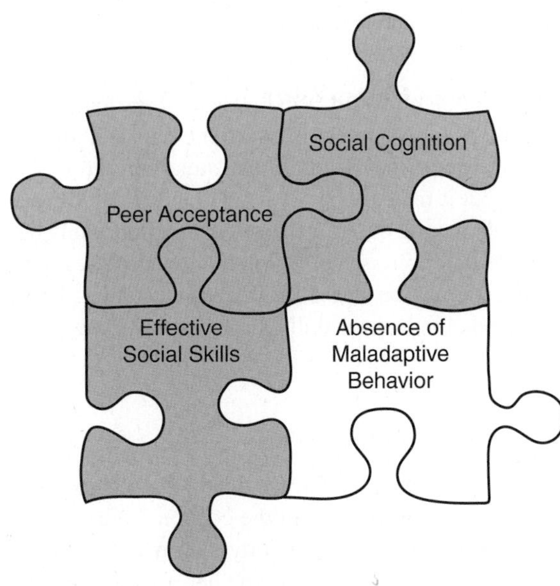

FIGURE 5.1 Model of Social Competence: The Components of Social Competence Work Together to Produce Effective Social Functioning
Source: Adapted from Vaughn & Hogan, 1990.

manner (Vaughn & Haager, 1994, p. 560). It is the most difficult area of social competence to assess, but it is at the heart of interventions for social difficulties. To teach students to use social skills effectively, we must teach them how to interpret social situations, monitor their own and others' behaviors, and to make good social decisions. These all fall within the cognitive domain. We can estimate a student's social cognition by examining such characteristics as self-concept, social perceptions, and social problem solving.

3. *Absence of Maladaptive Behaviors.* In Chapter 2, we described *adaptive behavior* as skills necessary for adapting to situational demands of the environment, including effective communication and social adjustment. The key to understanding adaptive behaviors is focusing on what is age- and contextually appropriate for the individual. Certain behaviors might be socially acceptable at one age but inappropriate at another. For example, very young children often hug each other or hold hands during play time, but in adolescence too much physical contact can be seen as abnormal or promiscuous. We can classify maladaptive behavior problems into two categories: A youngster exhibiting *internalizing behavior* would seem withdrawn or anxious, while an individual with *externalizing behaviors* would seem to be acting out or aggressive. Other maladaptive behaviors may just be inappropriate for the situation. Students with high-incidence disabilities often exhibit challenging behaviors that affect their learning. For students with emotional disturbance, this would be a primary focus of their educational program. Though by definition behavior is not the primary area of difficulty for students with learning disabilities, as many as 30 to 60 percent experience serious behavioral difficulty (Hallahan, Kauffman, &

Lloyd, 1996). Maladaptive behavior is a fundamental concern for students with mental retardation as well.

4. *Effective Use of Social Skills.* Teachers and parents often focus on the development of social skills when a student is experiencing social difficulties. We assume that if an individual has difficulty navigating social situations, he or she needs to learn new skills. This may be true, but it may not be the whole picture. Being socially competent in this domain means not only having the skills to interact appropriately but also knowing *when* and *under what conditions* to exercise skills. Instruction must be contextualized so that students have opportunities to practice new skills in a social setting. There are many curricular programs available for teaching social skills. In selecting a program, the teacher should make sure it is age-appropriate and includes the social skills of greatest concern.

Assessing Social Competence

For the purposes of assessment, we need to measure each of the components separately, but interpretation should occur in the context of the larger social picture. For example, a student may be experiencing difficulty with peers but have a well-developed set of social skills. The student may not be applying her social skills appropriately in peer situations, or other physical or emotional characteristics may be interfering with her peer interactions. It is important to gather information from multiple data sources because any given assessment tool provides only a snapshot of this complex set of skills and cognition (Haager & Vaughn, 1997). Furthermore, assessment over time gives the most accurate depiction of an individual's social competence.

Assessment of Peer Acceptance. Simple sociometric techniques are often used by teachers to assess peer acceptance, but these procedures must be handled with sensitivity. There are two main ways to conduct sociometric assessment. Both should only be used when students have had some time to get to know each other, well after the beginning of the school year. The first is a *peer nomination* procedure. This involves asking students to confidentially name or write down the names of three students in the class they like best and the three students they like the least. Some teachers prefer to omit the "like least" prompt to avoid negative repercussions, but it is very helpful information if handled thoughtfully. Students who receive a high number of positive nominations would be considered "popular" or to have a high level of peer acceptance. Likewise, students who receive a high number of negative nominations would be considered "rejected" or to have a low level of peer acceptance. It is important to think carefully about how you phrase the question to students. Asking students to name the students they "like best" might get a different response than naming students they would most like to "work with" in a group. Students with reading or writing difficulties might not be thought of as attractive group partners but might be socially desirable because of other qualities. Confidentiality is extremely important. When asking students to write classmates' names, it is helpful to seat students so they cannot see each others' responses or to put folders or dividers up to block students' views. Conducting peer nominations may be easier in small groups where the teacher can monitor student-to-student interaction closely.

A *peer rating* procedure is another way to assess peer acceptance (Haager & Vaughn, 1997; Vaughn & Haager, 1994). The teacher would prepare a roster of student names in the class with a rating scale (1–4) next to each student's name. Students are instructed to circle a number to indicate "how much do you like" each student in the class. A "1" rating indicates "not at all," "2" indicates "not much," "3" indicates "pretty much" and "4" indicates "very much." For young children, it is helpful to practice using nonpersonal items: "How well do you like chocolate cake? Spinach?" It is also helpful to point out that people have different likes and dislikes. One might love spinach while another hates it. Figure 5.2 shows a sample peer rating scale. Again, taking steps to ensure students do not discuss or share their ratings is important. Peer ratings can be collected very quickly and are informative in determining which students would benefit from social intervention. It is also

Name ____________________ Date __________

Directions: Please circle the number that best represents how you feel about each person in the class. Cross out your own name.

1 = not at all
2 = not much
3 = pretty much
4 = very much

Name	How well do you like . . . ?			
1. Briana	1	2	3	4
2. Charles	1	2	3	4
3. Deon	1	2	3	4
4. Francesca	1	2	3	4
5. Gabriella	1	2	3	4
6. Josh	1	2	3	4
7. Julie	1	2	3	4
8. Linda	1	2	3	4
9. Marvin	1	2	3	4
10. Sasha	1	2	3	4

Note: Student would cross out his or her own name and rate only other students.

FIGURE 5.2 Sample Peer Rating Scale Used in an Upper Elementary Classroom

helpful to conduct peer ratings early and later in the school year to see how students' social status might change as a result of social skills instruction. To tally scores, total the rating for each student using a simple grid like the one in Figure 5.3. For simplicity, the grid was configured for a small class of ten students, but it typically includes the whole class. Figure each individual's average acceptance rating using the following formula:

$$[(\#\ 4s\ received \times 4) + (\#\ 3s\ received \times 3) + (\#\ 2s\ received \times 2) + (\#\ 1s\ received \times 1)] \div [total\ number\ of\ ratings\ received]$$

An average rating of 3.0 or higher means a student is well-liked by her peers, like Briana in the example. An average rating of 2.0 or lower would indicate social problems, such as Marvin in the example. It is important to note that this technique is sometimes used in middle or high schools, but additional issues complicate the procedure. Because students change classes, the peers they most identify with may not be in the same classroom. A classroom-based peer rating would tell you specific information about the students in your classroom during that period, but would not provide a comprehensive picture of an individual student's peer acceptance in the larger student body.

Compute individual scores using the formula:

$$[(\#\ 4s\ received \times 4) + (\#\ 3s\ received \times 3) + (\#\ 2s\ received \times 2) + (\#\ 1s\ received \times 1)] \div [total\ number\ of\ ratings\ received]$$

Briana's score is $[(3 \times 4) + (4 \times 3) + (2 \times 2) + (0 \times 1)] \div 9 = 3.1$, a fairly high rating indicating positive peer acceptance. Marvin's score is $[(1 \times 4) + (2 \times 3) +$

	Ratings Received									
Ratings Given	Briana	Charles	Deon	Franc.	Gabi	Josh	Julie	Linda	Marvin	Sasha
Briana	X	2	3	4	3	3	4	2	1	3
Charles	3	X	3	3	2	4	2	2	3	3
Deon	3	4	X	3	3	3	2	3	4	3
Francesca	3	2	3	X	4	3	4	3	2	4
Gabi	4	1	2	4	X	4	2	3	1	3
Josh	2	3	4	2	2	X	2	1	3	1
Julie	4	3	2	3	4	3	X	2	1	4
Linda	2	3	4	4	4	4	3	X	2	3
Marvin	3	3	4	3	4	4	3	3	X	2
Sasha	4	3	3	3	4	3	3	2	1	X

FIGURE 5.3 Sample Grid for Scoring Peer Ratings

$(2 \times 2) + (4 \times 1)] \div 9 = 2.0$, a fairly low rating indicating possible peer acceptance difficulties.

Assessing Social Cognition. Social cognition is the ability to understand and interpret social situations and to self-evaluate one's own social circumstances. This includes self-evaluation, social perception, and social problem-solving. The most typical method of assessing this domain is to use a measure of self-concept, such as the Piers-Harris Children's Self-Concept Scale (Western Psychological Services), but for teaching purposes, it is easier to use informal techniques. Teachers may interview students or their parents, use sentence-completion tasks, analyze students' drawings or writings, or use direct observation to determine students' self-perceptions. Role-playing or hypothetical situations can be used to examine students' social problem-solving skills.

Assessing Social Behavior. To assess social skills and maladaptive behavior, teachers and other professionals often use rating scales. There are a number of widely used behavioral checklists. Following are some widely used checklists and their publishers:

- *Walker-McConnell Scale of Social Competence*, Pro-Ed Publishers
- *Child Behavior Checklist,* University of Vermont Center for Children, Youth and Families (available at http://www.ASEBA.org)
- *Burk's Behavior Rating Scales,* Western Psychological Services
- *Social Skills Rating System,* AGS Publishing
- *BASC: Behavior Assessment System for Children*, AGS Publishing

Teachers often use informal checklists or direct observation to determine a student's particular social strengths and needs. Teachers should consider what the most important social skills are and then develop a simple checklist to mark whether the desired behavior is observed. Adaptive behavior scales are also used to examine students' social behaviors. We describe several adaptive behavior scales in Chapter 3. Lerner describes several indicators of social competence difficulties that teachers should watch for:

1. Poor social perception
2. Lack of judgment
3. Difficulties in perceiving how others feel
4. Problems in socializing and making friends
5. Problems in establishing family relationships

These are general characteristics to watch for that might indicate a need to conduct further assessment and observation.

IMPROVING STUDENTS' SOCIAL SKILLS

Later in this chapter we describe schoolwide programs. In addition, there are several social skills training programs that can be used in the classroom setting. Some are designed for whole-class implementation while others may be used with individuals or small groups. Teachers should be aware of the age group targeted for a particular product before purchasing costly materials. One inexpensive and widely used set of materials is the *Skillstreaming* series. There are three programs: for preschool through grade 1, for elementary age, and for adolescence (Goldstein & McGinnis, 2002; McGinnis & Goldstein, 2002a, b). Table 5.1 lists the social skills taught for each age group.

TABLE 5.1 Social Skills Included in *Skillstreaming* Series

PRESCHOOL—GRADE 1	ELEMENTARY AGE	ADOLESCENCE
GROUP I BEGINNING SOCIAL SKILLS	**GROUP I CLASSROOM SURVIVAL SKILLS**	**GROUP I BEGINNING SOCIAL SKILLS**
1 Listening	1 Listening	1 Listening
2 Using Nice Talk	2 Asking for Help	2 Starting a Conversation
3 Using Brave Talk	3 Saying Thank You	3 Having a Conversation
4 Saying Thank You	4 Bringing Materials to Class	4 Asking a Question
5 Rewarding Yourself	5 Following Instructions	5 Saying Thank You
6 Asking for Help	6 Completing Assignments	6 Introducing Yourself
7 Asking a Favor	7 Contributing to Discussions	7 Introducing Other People
8 Ignoring	8 Offering Help to an Adult	8 Giving a Compliment
GROUP II SCHOOL-RELATED SKILLS	9 Asking a Question	**GROUP II ADVANCED SOCIAL SKILLS**
9 Asking a Question	10 Ignoring Distractions	9 Asking for Help
10 Following Directions	11 Making Corrections	10 Joining In
11 Trying When It's Hard	12 Deciding on Something to Do	11 Giving Instructions
12 Interrupting	13 Setting a Goal	12 Following Instructions
GROUP III FRIENDSHIP-MAKING SKILLS	**GROUP II FRIENDSHIP-MAKING SKILLS**	13 Apologizing
13 Greeting Others	14 Introducing Yourself	14 Convincing Others
14 Reading Others	15 Beginning a Conversation	**GROUP III SKILLS FOR DEALING WITH FEELINGS**
15 Joining In	16 Ending a Conversation	15 Knowing Your Feelings
16 Waiting Your Turn	17 Joining In	16 Expressing Your Feelings
17 Sharing	18 Playing a Game	17 Understanding the Feelings of Others
18 Offering Help	19 Asking a Favor	18 Dealing with Someone Else's Anger
19 Asking Someone to Play	20 Offering Help to a Classmate	19 Expressing Affection
20 Playing a Game	21 Giving a Compliment	20 Dealing with Fear
GROUP IV DEALING WITH FEELINGS	22 Accepting a Compliment	21 Rewarding Yourself
21 Knowing Your Feelings	23 Suggesting an Activity	**GROUP IV SKILL ALTERNATIVES TO AGGRESSION**
22 Feeling Left Out	24 Sharing	22 Asking Permission
23 Asking to Talk	25 Apologizing	23 Sharing Something
24 Dealing with Fear	**GROUP III SKILLS FOR DEALING WITH FEELINGS**	
25 Deciding How Someone Feels	26 Knowing Your Feelings	
	27 Expressing Your Feelings	

TABLE 5.1 Continued

PRESCHOOL—GRADE 1	ELEMENTARY AGE	ADOLESCENCE
26 Showing Affection **GROUP V ALTERNATIVES TO AGGRESSION** 27 Dealing with Teasing 28 Dealing with Feeling Mad 29 Deciding If It's Fair 30 Solving a Problem 31 Accepting Consequences **GROUP VI DEALING WITH STRESS** 32 Relaxing 33 Dealing with Mistakes 34 Being Honest 35 Knowing When to Tell 36 Dealing with Losing 37 Wanting to Be First 38 Saying No 39 Accepting No 40 Deciding What to Do	28 Recognizing Another's Feelings 29 Showing Understanding of Another's Feelings 30 Expressing Concern for Another 31 Dealing with Your Anger 32 Dealing with Another's Anger 33 Expressing Affection 34 Dealing with Fear 35 Rewarding Yourself **GROUP IV SKILL ALTERNATIVES TO AGGRESSION** 36 Using Self-Control 37 Asking Permission 38 Responding to Teasing 39 Avoiding Trouble 40 Staying Out of Fights 41 Problem Solving 42 Accepting Consequences 43 Dealing with an Accusation 44 Negotiating **GROUP V SKILLS FOR DEALING WITH STRESS** 45 Dealing with Boredom 46 Deciding What Caused a Problem 47 Making a Complaint 48 Answering a Complaint 49 Dealing with Losing 50 Being a Good Sport 51 Dealing with Being Left Out 52 Dealing with Embarrassment 53 Reacting to Failure 54 Accepting No 55 Saying No 56 Relaxing 57 Dealing with Group Pressure 58 Dealing with Wanting Something That Isn't Yours 59 Making a Decision 60 Being Honest	24 Helping Others 25 Negotiating 26 Using Self-Control 27 Standing Up for Your Rights 28 Responding to Teasing 29 Avoiding Trouble with Others 30 Keeping Out of Fights **GROUP V SKILLS FOR DEALING WITH STRESS** 31 Making a Complaint 32 Answering a Complaint 33 Being a Good Sport 34 Dealing with Embarrassment 35 Dealing with Being Left Out 36 Standing Up for a Friend 37 Responding to Persuasion 38 Responding to Failure 39 Dealing with Contradictory Messages 40 Dealing with an Accusation 41 Getting Ready for a Difficult Conversation 42 Dealing with Group Pressure **GROUP VI PLANNING SKILLS** 43 Deciding on Something to Do 44 Deciding What Caused a Problem 45 Setting a Goal 46 Deciding on Your Abilities 47 Gathering Information 48 Arranging Problems by Importance 49 Making a Decision 50 Concentrating on a Task

Source: Goldstein & McGinnis (2002); McGinnis & Goldstein (2002a, b).

MANAGING DISRUPTIVE BEHAVIOR IN INCLUSIVE CLASSROOMS

Dealing with discipline takes time. In an inclusion classroom that includes students with behavioral, emotional, and/or social problems, students misbehave for a variety of reasons. Sometimes when children act out, they are trying to get attention—perhaps they want their peers' attention, or maybe they are seeking ours. They have decided at some level that negative attention is better than no attention at all. Other students are responding more to an internal need or drive. In any case, they are sending a message that they need our help. To accommodate for a range of students' behaviors, it is important to have a comprehensive plan in place.

A comprehensive program should include social skills instruction, self-control training, a model for problem solving, and stress management. The first step generally should be to analyze the classroom environment and factors related to a student's disruptive behavior. Next, we recommend meeting with the student to come up with a behavioral plan. At the same time, it is important to actively teach alternative behaviors as part of a preventative curriculum. Relationship building is another essential aspect of effective classroom management. Some of the methods we discuss below and others are described later in this chapter. But first we present some common myths about effective classroom management in today's schools (see Figure 5.4). Many new teachers (as well as those with more experience) profess to believe in at least some of these myths, yet these beliefs can get in the way of success.

Analyzing Environmental Factors That Influence Students' Behavior

Once it has become apparent that a student is experiencing ongoing difficulties, the first step should be to observe the student in various settings and at different times of the day. The purpose of these observations is to analyze the environmental factors that affect the student's behaviors. Students' behaviors vary depending upon the context they are in and are affected by many factors. Analyzing a student's behavior systematically and specifically can provide many insights into why, when, where, and how a student is experiencing difficulty. These insights then become very useful when developing a behavioral plan for the student. This is a valuable role for the inclusion specialist. Jones and Jones (2003) suggest first asking the following questions to guide decision making:

1. Could this misbehavior be a result of inappropriate curriculum or teaching strategies? Look at group size, group configuration, cultural and linguistic barriers or differences, access to equipment, materials, and resources.
2. Could this misbehavior be a result of the student's inability to understand the concepts being taught?
3. Could this misbehavior be a result of the student's underlying disability?
4. Could this misbehavior be a result of other factors?
5. Are there causes of misbehavior that the teachers can control?

Myth 1: "Just be consistent!"
If this becomes your motto, it's likely you'll focus on trying to treat everyone the same, with the same consequences, all of the time. This sounds logical, even democratic, but it is an overly simplistic view of classroom management that doesn't take into account the complexities of teaching your most challenging students. A better rule is "Just be fair!" Consistency is important in classroom management, but not at the expense of reaching all students. Powell et al. (2001), advise, "Your success in negotiating acceptable behavior will depend largely on your ability to identify and affirm the needs of your students" (p. 154).

Myth 2: "I can out-tough them."
Being firm, with tough consequences, can work for a while to keep the lid on your most unruly students. But this can also create a hostile learning environment—you aren't diffusing your classroom of negative influences, but merely putting "a temporary lid over a volatile situation that will soon be blown off by the anger, rage, hostility, and even violent behavior of students who have already experienced similar heavy-handed treatment in other classes and at home" (Powell, et al., 2001, p. 154). Be firm and have high expectations for classroom behavior, but focus on building relationships with your students and being fair.

Myth 3: "All they need is love!"
At first this appears to be the opposite of "I can out-tough them." It is great to show true concern and affection for your students, but don't fall into the trap of thinking that they will all reciprocate in kind, demonstrating angelic classroom behavior once they realize they love you. Love and concern are a *start,* but you'll also need mental energy, a tough skin, practical intuition, time, and commitment. The causes of the diverse problems that prompt all the negative personal, social, and academic behaviors of difficult students are deeply rooted—their behavior will not change overnight.

Myth 4: "Grades will motivate unruly students to change their behaviors."
Have you ever heard (or been tempted to say yourself), "You'd better behave, or I'll give you an F"? Unfortunately, many of the hardest to teach students have already ceased caring about grades, learning, or anything related to school. There are better ways of interacting with students who are insolent, noncaring, and disrespectful of authority. On the other hand, it is true that some students would be mortified at the thought of receiving a poor grade—but not the student you're most likely trying to reach with this threat.

Myth 5: "These are not my students!"
General education teachers have used this one for years—claiming that they are not really responsible for their special education students with learning and behavioral problems, e.g., "I'm an English teacher (or a math teacher or a third-grade teacher or . . .) and these students belong to special ed!" This belief goes back to the days of homogeneous classrooms where all students were working at grade level (another myth). The reality is that today's classrooms are increasingly diverse and every student is the classroom as well as the special education teacher's responsibility. As an inclusion specialist, you'll want to discuss this with your co-teachers and assure them that you are there to help.

Myth 6: "Don't ask the principal for help with the tough kids."
We remember feeling like this when we first started teaching—we thought that if we asked for help it meant we weren't doing a good job. We were both teaching in a self-contained class for students with behavioral, emotional, and learning disorders who seemed to always be trying to push the limits. And like the other myths, there is a kernel of truth in the statement. It is true that you don't want to run to the office with every minor problem. Some principals do convey the message to teachers that it would be a sign of weakness to resort to referring students to the office. Yet, on the other hand, the most effective behavior management models are schoolwide and include support from the principal, assistant principal(s), counselors, and other specialists as part of a systematic, proactive plan. The important point is to use this option judiciously. Handle the problems you can and use the school's resources when necessary.

Source: Adapted from Powell, McLaughlin, Savage, & Zehm (2001).

FIGURE 5.4 Myths of Managing Tough Behavior in Today's Inclusive Classrooms

Next, Jones and Jones (2003) recommend using a form such as Figure 5.5 to guide a systematic observation of the student. We believe that this form is particularly useful for the inclusion specialist to use to identify environmental factors that may be influencing a student's behavior. Note that this procedure is quite similar to Functional Behavior Assessment, described later in this chapter.

Part I Student's Misbehavior(s)
1. Describe misbehavior(s)
a. b. c.
2. How frequent is each type of misbehavior?
a. b. c.
3. What time of day does it occur?
a. b. c.
4. In what physical surroundings?
a. b. c.
5. With which peers or adults?
a. b. c.
6. In what kinds of activities is student engaged before misbehavior occurs?
a. b. c.

FIGURE 5.5 Form for Analyzing Environmental Factors

Part II Teacher (or Other) Actions
1. What does the teacher do when student misbehaves?
a. b. c.
2. How does the student respond?
a. b. c.
3. Under what conditions are the teacher's actions most successful?
a. b. c.
4. Under what conditions are the teacher's actions least successful?
a. b. c.
Part III Student Motivation
1. What responsibilities (assignments, tasks) is student asked to complete?
a. b. c.
2. What types of positive reinforcement (praise, encouragement, rewards) does student receive?
a. b. c.
3. How does student respond to positive reinforcement?
a. b. c.

FIGURE 5.5 Continued

(continues)

4. What types of negative reinforcement does student receive?
a. b. c.
5. How does student respond to negative reinforcement?
a. b. c.
Part IV When Student Is Not Misbehaving
1. Describe positive behaviors.
a. b. c.
2. How frequent is each type of positive behavior?
a. b. c.
3. What time of day does each behavior occur?
a. b. c.
4. In what physical surroundings?
a. b. c.
5. With which peers or adults?
a. b. c.

FIGURE 5.5 Continued

6. In what kinds of activities is the student engaged before positive behavior occurs?
a. b. c.
Part V Additional Questions
1. How does student relate to the group (physical aggression, verbal aggression, passivity, withdrawal, other behaviors)? 2. What does the student enjoy doing (hobbies, interests, school subjects)? 3. What does the student do well (hobbies, interests, school subjects)? 4. Are there any reasons to suspect health or physical disabilities?

FIGURE 5.5 Continued

Mr. Schmitt, an inclusion specialist, used this form to observe Carla, a student who was frequently aggressive with her peers, hitting and pinching them. The results of the observation surprised everyone. All but two of Carla's assaults occurred during the language arts block, which consisted of almost two hours of small group and independent work. Furthermore, an in-depth analysis of Carla's reading showed that she was struggling with her assignments and only completed them with 24 percent accuracy. It appeared that before Carla attacked one of her peers she showed other signs of frustration and often sought assistance from her peers (but using inappropriate methods, such as grabbing their paper or looking over their shoulder). Observations indicated that she had a very low rate of positive contact with her peers. Based on this observation, the following interventions were initiated: First, together Mr. Schmitt and the classroom teacher altered the level of work Carla was asked to complete. Second, the teacher recruited two students to serve as peer tutors when Carla needed assistance. Third, Carla was taught how to ask for help in appropriate ways. The teacher also taught Carla other social skills and worked with the entire class on how to be supportive of each other.

Problem-solving approach An approach to classroom management that focuses on developing alternative, more appropriate behaviors. It also helps students take responsibility for their actions.

A Problem-Solving Approach

One technique for dealing with classroom disruptions is to implement a **problem-solving approach**. The strength of this approach lies in its focus on developing alternative, more appropriate behaviors. It also helps students take responsibility for their actions. A problem-solving model can be used for two students who seem to be having trouble getting along or for an individual child who is exhibiting ongoing problematic behavior. This technique is especially well-suited for an inclusion class where there are two teachers and one can focus on helping students learn appropriate ways to handle problems. However, it will not be sufficient by itself for students with behavior disorders and/or social skills deficits who still have a great deal of difficulty evaluating their own behavior and its effect on others. Other individualized methods, as described elsewhere in this chapter are needed.

The following steps are recommended by Glasser, known for his positive, problem-solving approach to classroom management in *Schools without Failure* (1969) (adapted from Jones & Jones, 1995):

1. Be warm and personal and willing to become emotionally involved: "I'm glad you're here and I care about you as a person and a learner."
2. Focus on the present behavior: "What did you do?" Sometimes a question such as "If a video camera had taped what happened, what would it show?" is easier for the student to answer.
3. Encourage the student to make a value judgment: "Is this behavior helping you?" "Is it helping others?" "Is it against a rule?"
4. Work out a plan: "What can you do differently?" "What do you need me to do to help?" "Do you need any assistance from others?"
5. Ask the student to make a commitment: "Are you going to stick with this?"
6. Follow up: "Let's check later and see how the plan is working."
7. Be encouraging but do not accept excuses: "It's OK. Let's keep trying. I trust that you can develop a plan that will work." "I know things happen, but you made a plan. Do you need to change your plan?"

Note: See Jones and Jones (2003) for more information about students' problem solving, conflict management programs, class meetings, schoolwide programs, and more.

Building Effective Relationships with Students with Special Needs (and All Students)

The successful inclusion specialist must also become a "relationship specialist." Experts such as Powell, McLaughlin, Savage, and Zehm (2001) assert that building positive relationships with students is *the* key to effectively managing the most difficult and challenging students. Effective relationship specialists genuinely care about each of their students—they believe that deep down their students want to do well. They recognize each student's unique qualities, talents, and special gifts. When you can connect with your most troubled students in this way, your classroom becomes a haven—an inviting, welcoming, supportive place to learn, grow, and connect with others in positive ways.

What does a helping relationship look like? First, it is important to recognize that as a teacher your relationship with your students is a professional one. You are not their big brother, big sister, or buddy. You should be genuinely respectful of your students, and your goal should be that they look up to you as their trusted teacher (mentor, guide). Characteristics of effective relationship specialists include (adapted from Powell et al., 2001):

1. *Empathy:* Being able to genuinely empathize or "be in" your students' pain, disappointment, frustration, and negative life experiences goes a long way toward building relationships. It shows that you understand their feelings of abandonment, depression, and loss. You care, and you are not judging them negatively for their failures and disappointments.
2. *Advocacy:* "Being for" your students adds another important dimension to your relationships with them. This is especially important with those most challenging students who already have a history of alienating those who try to help them. These students take the longest to develop trust and will test your resolve. Initially, they might respond with disbelief, but don't let their distrust put you off. Just keep letting them know you genuinely care and will do all you can to help them.
3. *Support:* "Being with" your students is another element of a caring relationship. This means letting students know you are there to help, but also recognizing their independence and separateness. Providing support means conveying, "I know you have the ability to be successful and I am here to help." Supporting means recognizing effort and acknowledging even small steps towards improvement.

The Helping Process

Zehm and Kottler (1993) describe a process that can be used to help your most troubled students. Note that this is different than the process used to come up with a plan for improving within-classroom behavior and should only be implemented by inclusion specialists who feel comfortable getting involved at this level. You may be the person the student most trusts and feels comfortable talking to, yet your best course of action might be to refer the student to a professional psychologist or therapist. For this model to work most effectively, it is important to work closely with other professionals as needed, such as the school psychologist, counselor, and/or school nurse.

Assessment. Just as assessment is important as part of the instructional cycle, it also is valuable as the first stage of the helping process. This requires the careful observation of students and meeting individually with them to discuss your observations. During these conferences it is important that you give them your undivided attention so that you can listen attentively (e.g., meet with them during lunch or before or after school rather than when others are in the room). Valuable skills include *attending, listening, focusing,* and *observing*.

Exploration. This involves the mutual exploration of students' feelings, frustrations, and motivations for the purpose of helping them better understand what is going on in their lives. The teacher's role is not to judge but to be a sounding board. Important skills include *reflecting feelings, responding to content, probing, questioning,* and *showing empathy.*

Understanding Motivations. Once students have begun to explore their feelings, you can help them begin to understand why they feel and react as they do. With the student's permission, you may want to seek the assistance of a counselor or other mental health support person with expertise in recognizing the underlying causes of self-destructive behavior. Your goal isn't to solve students' problems for them, but to help them better understand themselves so that they can become more in control of their own lives. Valuable skills include *interpreting, confronting, challenging, giving information, and self-disclosing.*

Action. Once students better understand the reasons they react as they do, they are in a better position to take action and assume responsibility for making changes in their lives. At this point they have a better understanding of what they can and cannot control (e.g., they can't fix their parents' troubled marriage or cure a boyfriend's alcoholism, but they can understand that they are not responsible for these conditions). It is not your place to offer advice, but to support them as they decide upon a course of action, with realistic goals to which they can commit. Your role is to be encouraging and also to monitor how the student is doing once he begins a plan. Important skills include *goal-setting, role-playing, reinforcing, making decisions, and monitoring.*

STRATEGIES FOR ATTENTION-DEFICIT HYPERACTIVITY DISORDER (ADHD)

The classroom environment is very important and can greatly affect the performance of students with ADHD (Yehle, 1998). Imagine that you are taking a very important test—you've prepared for it and you're feeling confident. But the person next to you is chewing gum and keeps snapping it, and this is driving you crazy. Then you notice that someone else looks like he might be cheating—he keeps looking at the inside of his left arm, and you can't be sure but you think you see something written there. The fluorescent lights are humming intermittently. The woman in front of you is wearing a brightly colored orange, magenta, and yellow blouse that distracts you. Outside someone starts mowing the lawn. The test proctor is circulating around the room and her heels keep clicking on the floor as she walks, "click, click, clickety-click." You know that you need to focus and you try to plug your ears and just look at the test in front of you, but you're really having a hard time concentrating. And just when you've read the short passage about which you're now supposed to answer comprehension questions, a cell phone rings (even though everyone had been instructed to turn them off), and you feel like you forget everything you've just read. You want to scream. . . . How could this be prevented? What can the inclusion specialist do? Figure 5.6 lists some strategies can help (Carbone, 2001; Yehle, 1998).

Token Economy

With a token economy, students earn "tokens" that they trade for prizes or rewards about once a week (Minner & Knutson, 1980). Tokens might be plastic counters, play money, stickers, or tally marks on a chart. Some schools have funds to pay for such reinforcers. Students earn tokens throughout the week for appropriate, on-task behavior (e.g., completed assignments, staying in seat). Some teachers do not believe in token economies, thinking that they are too materialistic and that students should be able to work for less tangible rewards. We agree that certainly in an ideal world this would be the case . . . but in

Difficulty 1—Hyperactivity
What can you do to help the student who often fidgets with hands or feet, squirms in her seat, or leaves her seat when she is expected to remain sitting? These strategies can help increase on-task behavior:
1. Incorporate movement into classroom activities (e.g., role playing, demonstrations, and other active responses). Be as interactive as possible. 2. Provide short breaks during long class sessions. 3. Provide frequent teacher monitoring (feedback and supervision). 4. Seat the child in the front row (or at a front table) and close to your desk, but include her as part of the regular class seating. Preferably, she should be in a low traffic area and have her back to the rest of the class to keep other students out of view (except during collaborative group work). 5. Surround the child with well-behaved, attentive classmates. 6. Remove the child from potentially distracting areas, such as windows and the pencil sharpener. 7. For children who sometimes get overstimulated, designate a quiet, distraction-free area of the room where a child can go to complete work or settle down (such as a cubicle). 8. If possible, have a few "free" desks students can move to when they are feeling restless or need a change. 9. Encourage collaboration with peers; implement peer tutoring and cooperative learning techniques. 10. Define the student's workspace when engaging in large-group activities, such as with carpet squares for each child, or using masking tape to designate where to sit. 11. Avoid ridicule and criticism. Remember, children with hyperactivity have difficulty staying in control. Avoid publicly reminding students on medication to "take their medicine."
Difficulty 2—Impulsivity
What can you do with the student who often blurts out answers before questions have been completed, has difficulty waiting his turn, or interrupts or intrudes on others? These students also often have trouble with test-taking, particularly on multiple-choice formats, and have poor planning skills. Typically, they fail to read or follow directions carefully. These strategies help:
1. Provide positive reinforcement when it is apparent the student is attempting to control his impulsivity. 2. Implement group rewards (reinforcement for cooperation, helping and supporting one another). 3. To help students with following directions, provide oral and written versions. ■ Maintain eye contact during verbal instruction. ■ Make directions clear and concise. Be consistent with daily instructions. ■ Give directions one at a time and simplify complex directions. Avoid multiple commands. ■ Check for understanding—ask students to paraphrase what you've said. ■ Repeat instructions in a calm, positive manner, if needed. ■ Help the students feel comfortable with seeking assistance (most children with ADD will not ask for help). Gradually reduce the amount of assistance, but keep in mind that these children will need more help for a longer period of time than the average child. 4. Implement a token economy, set specific goals for improvement, and reinforce students' progress (see the description and example below).

FIGURE 5.6 Strategies for Supporting Students with ADHD

(continues)

Difficulty 3—Inattention and Distractibility
What can you do when the student is easily distracted by extraneous stimuli, often seems not to be listening, even when spoken to directly, fails to pay close attention to details, or makes careless mistakes? These strategies help:
1. Become aware of environmental stimuli and what is most distracting to your student(s). Teachers are no longer told to remove all superfluous visual and auditory stimuli from the classroom as in years past (so that classrooms for distractible students had bare, soundproof walls and/or students worked in unadorned cubicles). Limit the most distracting stimuli. 2. Try not to place students near air conditioners, high traffic areas, heaters, or doors or windows. 3. Some stimuli can be positive. Use color and other novel qualities to highlight important task features (rather than unimportant) for those students who are sensitive to and attracted by visual novelty. For example, you can use colored chalk to emphasize key vocabulary words. 4. Moderate background noise in the classroom can be more conducive to helping students attend to task than quiet conditions (i.e., music). Silence itself can be a distraction. 5. Include in your instruction novel and interesting tasks that can successfully compete with potential distractions for students' attention. 6. Arrange furniture and design the classroom layout for smooth transitions and ease of movement from one area of the classroom to another or from desks to a group area. 7. Use an overhead projector, PowerPoint, and other visuals that capture and hold students' attention. However, distracting elements should be kept to a minimum. 8. Set up a listening center in the classroom. Students can listen to prerecorded instructions or homework assignments, as well as books-on-tape, music, etc. 9. Allow students to wear headphones just to filter out extra noise OR so that they can listen to background music to help them concentrate. 10. Begin your lesson with an attention grabber (e.g., when beginning a unit on Japan enter the classroom wearing a kimono). 11. Indicate that you will be covering essential information by telling students you are about to tell them something particularly important. Highlight, underline, or color code key words in written versions. 12. Avoid abrupt or unexpected transitions, changes in schedule, disruptions, and physical relocation. Monitor students closely on field trips. 13. Give extra time for certain tasks. Students with ADD may work slowly. Do not penalize them for needing extra time. 14. Keep in mind that children with ADD are easily frustrated. Stress, pressure, and fatigue can break down their self-control and lead to poor behavior.
Difficulty 4—Disorganization
What can you do for the student who often has difficulty organizing tasks and activities and loses things (such as homework!)? The student also might have a great deal of difficulty with planning, particularly for long-term assignments.
1. Directly teach organizational skills (e.g., start a "clutter club" with direct instruction in how to organize notebooks, provide assistance, frequently check students' notebooks, and provide positive reinforcement for progress).

FIGURE 5.6 Continued

2. Help students plan ahead how they will schedule their time to complete long-term assignments and when they will study for exams, etc.; monitor their execution of the plan.
3. Model organizational skills in a routine manner—this helps students learn predictable classroom routines and also to set their own routines. At the end of each class, have all students write their homework assignments in a planner just for that purpose. The inclusion specialist should check and initial the planner each day.
4. Set up the physical classroom to help all children keep their belongings in a set, clearly designated place. If space permits, each child can have a bin in which to store his or her materials.
5. Provide individual student mailboxes—homework and notes home can be put in a child's mailbox. As a classroom routine, have students check their mailboxes at the end of the day, right before they leave.
6. Provide (or ask students to supply) different colored folders or notebooks for the different content areas or their different classes.
7. Ask parents to establish set times and routines for homework, to review students' completed homework, and check students' planners/assignment notebooks each night and initial them.

FIGURE 5.6 Continued

reality a token economy can be very effective for helping children who have not yet developed an intrinsic or internal reward system. A token economy can be a wonderful motivator for students, even when other approaches have failed. We suggest using it in combination with other approaches that *teach* children appropriate behaviors and help them monitor them (e.g., "five-minute charts" on desks).

Ms. Grace used an effective token economy system in her class. Every student had a point card taped to the corner of his or her desk. When Ms. Grace first started using a token economy, her tokens were little round stickers that she carried around in her pocket and periodically gave to students to put on their charts. Yet these stickers were sometimes lost or stolen. Later she used a simpler procedure—a ballpoint pen in a color that no one else in the class was allowed to use (e.g., purple). As students worked and she circulated around the room, she marked points on students' charts. Occasionally, she would ask a student to do the job, "Marcia, everyone is working so well. Will you please give everyone two points?" Students rarely tried to manipulate this system (e.g., by giving themselves or friends extra points), but Ms. Grace was vigilant about keeping her eye out for such transgressions. Every Friday after all other work was completed students counted up how many points they had earned. While classmates played learning games, worked at centers, completed assignments, or had free reading or writing time, one or two students at a time "cashed in" their points. Small toys were stored in a treasure box that the teacher kept locked during the week. Additional prizes included "no homework," "extra time on an assignment," and "free-time" passes. It was Ms. Grace's policy not to use candy in her room as a reinforcer, but she did have various kinds of healthy snacks available, such as juice boxes, granola bars, cereal bars, raisins, nuts, fruit rollups, popcorn, and trail mix (all in sealed packages). At the beginning of the year she had sent home a letter to all of her students' parents (in English and Spanish) explaining this system and asking if there were any food items their children shouldn't eat (e.g., peanuts because of a food allergy). As students "spent" their points, they applied addition and subtraction skills. Sometimes Ms. Grace had students first trade their points for play money. Then when they spent their money on prizes they also were reinforcing money skills (e.g., making change).

Students earned points in various ways. First, there were points awarded to everyone in the class at the same time for working well or following directions. There were points awarded to groups or pairs of students for cooperating well together and helping each other and points for individual accomplishments (e.g., a task completed, a goal met). Points awarded for individual accomplishments were a very important aspect of the token economy system. Every student had individualized goals he or she was working on, decided upon in consultation with the teacher. For some students this goal might be to bring their homework in every day, remember to bring all materials to class, get started quickly on an in-class assignment, follow directions the first time, stay in one's seat, remember to raise one's hand during group discussions, or not use any "put-downs" or verbally aggressive behavior (criticisms of self or others). For some students, this individualized goal was monitored by taping a second small paper chart to the student's desk with a set period of time (e.g., a day, or an hour, or length of time of one class session) broken into smaller time segments (e.g., a 60-minute block of time divided into 5-minute segments). For example, Michael's goal was to stay in his seat except when given permission to get up. Because he liked dragons, the teacher used a dragon stamp to fill a 5-minute space on his chart whenever he was successful. If not, she marked the space with an X. At the end of the day, Michael was awarded points for how many dragons he had earned, and then this paper chart was sent home for his parents to sign (possibly along with a brief note written on the back). These individual goals were very much like behavior contracts. Possible steps to follow when using a token economy in this way:

1. Teacher and student identify problem behavior (e.g., frequently out of seat).
2. Teacher (with student's input) identify target behavior that will earn tokens for the student (e.g., staying in seat).
3. Teacher posts appropriate behavior on chart or on student's desk.
4. Teacher and student select reinforcers to exchange for tokens OR student can wait and "spend" them at the class store.
5. Teacher explains rules of the token economy system to the student.
6. Teacher checks for understanding by asking the student to explain the system.
7. Teacher initiates the system.
8. Teacher and student evaluate how well the system is working (e.g., perhaps staying in his seat for 10 minutes at a time before receiving a reward is just too much time for Michael—thus, the teacher decides to reward him every 5 minutes he is successful).

Behavioral Contracts

Behavioral contracts can be an excellent way to help students focus attention on specific goals, either academic or behavioral (Bender, 2001). Together in consultation the student and teacher develop the contract:

- Brainstorm and prioritize possible goals the student might work on.
- Select one (e.g., turn in all homework).
- Select an acceptable success rate (e.g., five days in a row).
- Say how this will determined (e.g., teacher checks the homework).

Behavior contract A pact between a student and a teacher, mutually agreed upon, that outlines a goal a student will work for, how success will be determined, what kind of support the student will receive, and a reward for successful attainment of the goal.

- Decide what the prize will be once this goal has been accomplished (e.g., ten extra tokens to spend at the classroom store).
- Specify how the teacher (or others) will help (e.g., checking the student's homework log each afternoon to make sure all assignments are recorded accurately).

See Figures 5.7 and 5.8 for two examples.

CELEBRATE!!!

I will ______________________________

____

______________________________.

My teacher will help by

______________________________.

To celebrate I will be able to

______________________________.

Date__________ My Name______________________

Teacher______________________

FIGURE 5.7 Sample Behavior Contract for Grades K-6

Behavior Contract

I, ________________________, hereby promise to do the following:
(Name)

____

____

____.

I will receive support from ________________________ who will

____

____.

As acknowledgement of my accomplishments, I will be rewarded by

____

____.

Date______________ Signature ________________________

Teacher____________________________

FIGURE 5.8 Sample Behavior Contract for Secondary Students

AGGRESSIVE BEHAVIOR

Poor impulse control Difficulty controlling one's impulses or desires—impulsive, compulsive.

Low frustration tolerance Difficulty coping with frustration or annoyance. Quick to feel frustrated, discouraged, or aggravated.

Students who exhibit aggressive behavior are often lacking in social skills. They may have **poor impulse control**, **low frustration tolerance**, and experience difficulties dealing with stress. They often have limited insight into the feelings of others and misinterpret social cues and mistakenly assign hostile intent to others' actions. They may feel threatened and become defensive even when no real threat initially existed. They often are experiencing a great deal of frustration—frustration does not always result in aggression, but aggression is always preceded by frustration. These students are typically confused and frightened by their lack of self-control during stressful situations. Possible sources of frustration (over which teachers have some control):

- Disorganized or inconsistent teachers
- Failure
- Boredom
- Lack of positive reinforcement
- Irrelevant, uninteresting curriculum
- Overuse of punishment
- Feelings of powerlessness and lack of control over the environment

Johns and Carr (1995) describe stages of frustration that teachers should be aware of so that they can respond appropriately to students' behaviors:

- *Anxiety Stage*: Student shows nonverbal signs, such as sighing or putting his or her head down. Teacher should respond with active listening and nonjudgmental talk.
- *Stress Stage*: Student shows frustration through minor behavior problems, such as tearing up or crumpling paper, or pencil tapping. Teacher should use proximity control, provide assistance with assignments (e.g., check the difficulty level), and/or boost students' interest and motivation.
- *Verbal Aggression (Defensive) Stage*: Student argues and complains. Teacher should briefly and matter-of-factly remind the student of rules and expectations, use conflict resolution techniques, and encourage the student to ask for help.
- *Physical Aggression Stage*: Student has lost control and begun to threaten others, throw objects, or hit others. Teacher should remind student that he or she still has choices, escort the student from the class, seek help from other staff, protect the safety of other students, and restrain the student if necessary.
- *Tension Reduction Stage*: Student releases tension through crying or verbal venting. Teacher shows empathy and helps student gain insight into feelings and behavior.

Many teachers have difficulty dealing with student frustration and stress. Common teacher reactions include irritability, fear, counteraggression, negative thinking, fatigue, and avoidance (Abrams & Segal, 1998; VanAcker, 1993). When teachers respond in these ways they are more likely to overreact to minor problems and get into power struggles with students, potentially escalating the frequency and severity of aggression in the classroom.

"Therapeutic teachers," on the other hand, are able to create positive environments that tend to reduce rather than increase students' frustration levels. Therapeutic teachers are somewhat like the "Relationship Specialists" discussed earlier. "To be therapeutic, teachers must listen, talk, and act in ways that communicate respect, caring, and confidence, both in themselves and their students" (Kauffman, 1997, p. 519). Characteristics of therapeutic teachers include (adapted from Abrams & Segal, 1998):

- They themselves have good mental health.
- They communicate respect, caring, and confidence in self and others.
- They exhibit and model self-control.
- They establish trust and rapport with students.
- They are aware of the stages of frustration.
- They understand frustration and anxiety in students.
- They are quick to pick up on escalating tension and able to de-escalate tension in the classroom.
- They do not resort to threats or confrontations during stress. They respect students' dignity.
- They display enthusiasm and positive expectations.
- They are aware of individual student's needs, interests, values, and talents.
- They display effective stress-coping skills.
- They create a positive classroom climate.

Preventing Aggressive Behavior and Violence

Zero tolerance policies Strict discipline policies enacted to curtail school violence by providing harsh consequences (such as expulsion) to first offenders as well as others.

Schools and communities typically respond to aggressive and violent behaviors with reactive strategies that are punitive (e.g., corporal punishment, suspension, expulsion, incarceration). These approaches have not been effective (Skiba & Peterson, 2000; Townsend, 2000). Furthermore, they are disproportionately applied to African American students, particularly males (Harry & Anderson, 1995; Townsend, 2000). Yet widespread advocacy for policies such as **zero tolerance** and "adult time for adult crime" are on the rise, even though they actually may exacerbate youth aggression and violence (Leone, Meyer, Malmgren, & Mersil, 2000). For example, research indicates that youth who are transferred to adult jails are more likely to be rearrested for increasingly serious crimes compared to youth in juvenile facilities (Mendel, 2002). In contrast, evidence is accumulating that more integrative, proactive approaches are effective in preventing youth aggression and violence. A common thread runs through effective prevention models: Instead of waiting for aggressive behaviors to occur and then reacting with harsh punishment, educators proactively teach the academic and social skills necessary for success in school and life. In their approach to prevention, Nelson, Crabtree, Marchand-Martella, and Martella (1998, p. 4) emphasize that "disruptive behavior is primarily a socialization problem, not a sickness." Some of the characteristics of proactive, instructional models for preventing youth aggression and violence are (adapted from Skiba & Peterson, 2000):

- Including all youth in school and community programs.
- Providing a full continuum of educational opportunities.
- Reinforcing appropriate behaviors across environments, people, and contexts.
- Promoting academic and social success.
- Establishing partnerships that include shared responsibilities.

Through teaching, modeling, guiding, and reinforcing appropriate skills, schools can provide a context for youth to learn and use appropriate behaviors instead of aggressive and violent ones.

Alternatives to Suspension. Townsend (2000) recommends that schools examine their discipline data and consider more culturally responsive instructional and management strategies, such as enhancing relationships with students, encouraging participation in extracurricular school activities, implementing culturally relevant pedagogy, developing family and community partnerships, and building cultural bridges. Khalsa (1999) suggests the following alternatives to suspension (adapted to include plans for teaching the student alternative behaviors).

- *Extended Time Out:* This might take place in another classroom, the counseling office, or the principal's office. The student might complete a behavioral plan during this time, and/or be given work to do.
- *Loss of Privileges:* The child can be put on a "frozen list" or "on restriction"—he or she loses privileges for an extended period of time. This might mean not eating in the cafeteria; not participating in field trips, assemblies, and other special activities; or not having "free time" in the classroom. This works best when it is a natural consequence (e.g., not eating in the cafeteria because of pushing others in line).
- *Saturday Detention:* This is used at some schools with much success. The student should have work to complete and also come up with a behavioral plan.
- *Parent Shadow Day:* The parent is required to attend school for all or part of the day with the student and shadow him or her (i.e., follow the student from class to class). The parent then can participate in the development of a behavioral plan for the student.
- *In-School Suspension:* The student completes his or her detention in school, perhaps in the counselor's office or the principal's office. The student should have work to complete during this time, as well as a behavioral plan.

Functional behavior assessment A long-term strategy to reduce inappropriate behavior, teach more appropriate behavior, and provide contextual supports through an evaluation of the specific antecedents and consequences associated with inappropriate behavior.

Functional Behavior Assessment and Behavior Intervention Plans

Functional behavior assessment and behavior intervention plans are helpful techniques for reducing aggressive and other inappropriate behaviors for students with behavioral disorders. Also, federal and state regulations now usually require the use of functional behavior assessment. Unlike traditional behavioral management, which views the individual as the problem and seeks to "fix" him or her through negative enforcement and other "assertive" policies, Functional Behavior

Assessment (FBA; also called Functional Assessment and Functional Analysis), Behavior Intervention Plans, and positive behavior support view systems, settings, and lack of skill as parts of the problem and work to change those. These approaches are long-term strategies to reduce inappropriate behavior, teach more appropriate behavior, and provide contextual supports necessary for successful outcomes (Conroy, Clark, Gable, & Fox, 1999).

The inclusion specialist and others identify the specific antecedents and consequences associated with inappropriate behavior. They collect additional data about the time, setting, and situation within which the behavior occurred. Through careful data collection, they gain useful insights into the purpose behind students' behaviors that can help them modify the student's environment and teach alternative behaviors. The information garnered through a FBA is then used to develop a *Behavior Intervention Plan (BIP)* as part of a system of *Positive Behavioral Support (PBS).* The inclusion specialist is in an ideal position to lead these efforts. Typically, an FBA and corresponding behavior plan are only used with students with identified behavioral disorders as part of the IEP process (see Boxes 5.1 and 5.2.

SCHOOLWIDE PROGRAMS

The most effective schools have put in place proactive, schoolwide programs for facilitating a positive climate and maintaining discipline. It is important that the entire community, including school personnel, parents or caregivers, and social service agencies, support the learning of students with serious emotional and behavioral disorders. The proverb "it takes a village to raise a child" is especially true for students with special needs. The system of care should be culturally competent, with agencies, programs, and services that are responsive to the cultural, racial, and ethnic differences of the populations they serve. The National Agenda to Improve Results for Children and Youth with or at Risk of Serious Emotional Disturbance emphasizes seven interdependent strategic targets as important for enhancing outcomes for such students (Osher & Hanley, 1996). They recommend (a) expanding positive learning opportunities and results (b) strengthening school and community capacity to serve students in the least restrictive environment appropriate (c) valuing and addressing diversity (d) collaborating with families (e) promoting appropriate assessment (f) providing ongoing skill development and support, and (g) creating comprehensive collaborative systems.

Similarly, Skiba and Peterson (2000) suggest several components that should be included in a school's plan for preventing and responding to youth aggression and violence:

1. Conflict resolution/social instruction
2. Classroom strategies for preventing and responding to disruptive behavior
3. Parent involvement
4. Screening to identify students who are at-risk for school failure
5. School- and districtwide data systems
6. Crisis and security planning
7. Schoolwide discipline and behavioral planning
8. Functional assessment and individualized behavior plans

BOX 5.1
FUNCTIONAL BEHAVIOR ASSESSMENT

WHY CONDUCT A FUNCTIONAL ASSESSMENT?

Often, the *function* (or purpose) of a student's behavior is not inappropriate—instead, it is the behavior itself that is judged unacceptable (Fitzsimmons, 1998). In other words, it is how the child goes about getting his needs met that is wrong. For example, if the IEP team determines through an FBA that a student is seeking attention by acting out, they can develop a plan to teach the student more appropriate ways to gain attention, thereby fulfilling the student's need for attention with an alternative or replacement behavior that serves the same function as the inappropriate behavior. At the same time, strategies may be developed to decrease or even eliminate opportunities for the student to engage in inappropriate behavior.

CONDUCTING A FUNCTIONAL ASSESSMENT

Several key steps are common to most FBAs:

1. *Verify the seriousness of the problem.* Many classroom problems can be eliminated by the consistent application of effective classroom management strategies. Only when these strategies have not resulted in significant improvement on the part of the student should school personnel go forward with an FBA.
2. *Define the problem behavior in concrete terms.* School personnel need to pinpoint the behavior that is causing learning or discipline problems and to define the behavior in terms that can be measured and recorded. For example, a problem behavior described in abstract terms might be "Mark is aggressive." A concrete description would be "Mark hits other students during recess when he does not get his way."
3. *Collect data on possible causes of problem behavior.* Ask key questions such as: Is the problem behavior linked to a skill deficit? Is there evidence to suggest that the student does not know how to perform the skill? Does the student have the skill but for some reason not perform it consistently? The student herself may provide additional information about what, in each context, contributes to problematic behavior. Common *functions* for school-based behavioral problems include gaining teacher or peer attention, escaping or avoiding specific tasks or persons, expressing frustration, or gaining access to specific desirable items.
4. *Analyze the data.* Identify possible stimulus-response patterns, predictors, consequences, and likely function(s) of the problematic behavior. A behavior pathway chart can be developed by sequentially arranging information about the antecedents to the behavior, the behavior itself, and consequences of the behavior that might be leading to its maintenance.
5. *Formulate and test a hypothesis.* After analyzing the data, establish a plausible explanation (hypothesis) regarding the function of the behaviors in question. This hypothesis should predict the general conditions under which the behavior is most and least likely to occur as well as the consequences that maintain it. Then take steps to alter one or more of the relevant conditions affecting the behavior. If the behavior remains unchanged following this environmental manipulation, reexamine the hypothesis with a view to altering it.

Source: Fitzsimmons (1998).

BOX 5.2
BEHAVIOR INTERVENTION PLANS

The student's behavior intervention plan should include positive strategies, programs or curricular modifications, and supplementary aids and supports required to address the behaviors of concern. It is helpful to use the data collected during the FBA to develop the plan and to determine the discrepancy between the child's actual and expected behavior. Intervention plans should address both the source of the problem and the problem itself and foster the expression of needs in appropriate ways. Scott and Nelson (1999) suggest the following steps:

1. **Determine an appropriate replacement behavior**. After the inappropriate behavior has been objectively defined and its function identified, select an alternative, appropriate replacement behavior. A replacement behavior should be readily acceptable to others in the environment (socially valid) and serve the same function as the inappropriate behavior. For example, if a student's inappropriate behavior is reinforced by teacher attention, then the replacement behavior also should result in teacher attention. School personnel should agree on what constitutes an appropriate replacement behavior given the specific data (e.g., persons, settings, conditions) gleaned from the FBA. O'Neill, Horner, Albin, Sprague, Storey, and Newton (1997) suggest identifying a primary (i.e., long-term) replacement behavior along with several short-term replacement behaviors. These short-term behaviors are taught, modeled, and reinforced to assist the student in learning the primary replacing behavior and achieving written behavioral goals and objectives.
2. **Determine when the replacement behavior should occur**. Once a replacement behavior is identified, explicitly teach the student to use the new skill. This is accomplished by determining the conditions under which the new behavior will serve the same function as the old. It is important to teach the specific conditions under which the replacement behavior should be used. Help the student distinguish between the conditions in which the replacement behavior is likely to achieve the desired outcome and those under which reinforcement is unlikely to occur. Identify and teach positive examples as well as examples of non-use.
3. **Design a teaching sequence**. Teach social and behavioral skills through a planned sequence of instruction as part of ongoing school routines. The plan should include examples and non-examples of when, where, and with whom to display the replacement behavior, what the student will gain by exhibiting the new behavior, and the circumstances in which the replacement behavior is not likely to be reinforced. Actually reinforcing the replacement behavior during the examples may make this clearer.
4. **Manipulate the environment to increase the probability of success**. Based on the FBA data (e.g., specific settings, people, times, tasks), arrange the student's environment so that reinforcing each instance of the replacement behavior is likely. Implement procedures to increase the likelihood that the student will use the replacement behavior at the appropriate time so that reinforcement can be delivered. Prompts, cues, and pre-correction strategies may increase the likelihood of replacement behaviors. As a general rule, use the least intrusive prompts necessary to predict success.
5. **Manipulate the environment to decrease the probability of failure**. Also analyze the environment to identify and remove barriers that might prevent the replacement behavior from being demonstrated under the appropriate conditions. For example, if a student is unlikely to engage in a replacement behavior when seated next to a particular peer, then

we also know that reinforcement will be unlikely. We can increase the likelihood of success by separating the student from the peer during the initial stages of intervention so that the student is more likely to receive reinforcement for appropriate replacement behavior.

6. **Determine how positive behavior will be reinforced**. The goal of this step is to provide natural (functionally equivalent and naturally occurring) reinforcement for replacement behaviors. Initially, reinforcement should be immediate and consistent. But over time, reinforcement can be delivered on a more natural schedule. At this point, reinforcement for displays of the replacement behavior will vary by type (e.g., verbal or tangible reinforcement) and schedule (e.g., reinforcement every second display of the replacement behavior).
7. **Determine consequences for instances of problem behavior**. Even the most appropriate BIP will not immediately negate the student's history of reinforcement for prior inappropriate behavior. Therefore, the behavior intervention plan should include consequences for inappropriate behavior and strategies for their use. This step clearly establishes a distinction between outcomes for the replacement behavior as opposed to the consequences of inappropriate behavior. Such a clear distinction increases the chances that the replacement behavior will be used more often, since the function of that behavior is being reinforced.
8. **Develop a data collection system**. Collect data to determine whether the replacement behavior has been effective in decreasing the frequency, duration, or intensity of the targeted inappropriate behavior. Data should be collected before intervention to provide baseline information and during intervention. Comparing baseline and intervention data facilitates evaluation of intervention effectiveness. School personnel should carefully select a data collection method that best matches the settings in which the behavior intervention plan will be implemented.
9. **Develop behavioral goals and objectives**. To assess overall effectiveness and positive changes in the student's behavior, school personnel should write measurable behavioral goals and objectives related to the replacement behavior. These student-specific behavioral goals and objectives provide standards for evaluating whether changes in the frequency, duration, and/or intensity of the target and replacement behaviors have met objective criteria. O'Neill and colleagues (1997) provide examples of measurable and objective behavioral goals.

Source: Adapted from Scott & Nelson (1999).

EVALUATING THE PLAN

IEP teams should include two evaluation procedures in an intervention plan: one procedure designed to monitor the consistency with which the management plan is implemented, the other designed to measure changes in behavior. In addition, IEP teams must determine a timeline for implementation and reassessment and specify how much behavior change is required to meet the goal of the intervention. Assessment completion should be within the time lines prescribed by IDEA. If a student already has a behavior intervention plan, the IEP team may elect to review and modify it, or they may determine that more information is necessary and conduct an FBA. IDEA states that a behavior intervention plan based on an FBA should be considered when developing the IEP if a student's behavior interferes with his or her learning or the learning of classmates. To be meaningful, plans must be reviewed at least annually and revised as needed. However, the plan may be reviewed and reevaluated whenever any member of the child's IEP team feels it is necessary (Gable, Quinn, Rutherford, & Howell, 1998; Quinn, Gable, Rutherford, Nelson, & Howell, 1998).

Positive Behavior Support (PBS)

Positive Behavior Support A schoolwide model that includes a broad range of systemic and individualized strategies for achieving important social and learning results while preventing problem behavior.

Perhaps the most promising schoolwide model is that of **Positive Behavior Support** (PBS). According to the Center on Positive Behavioral Interventions and Support (Sugai & Horner, 2002a), PBS refers to "a broad range of systemic and individualized strategies for achieving important social and learning results while preventing problem behavior" (p. 130). The goal of PBS is to enhance the capacity of schools to educate all students by establishing an effective continuum of PBS systems and procedures. Particular attention is given to students with challenging behaviors. PBS isn't meant to be an "add on." Rather, schools are asked to consider ways of "working smarter by doing less, but harder" and replacing previous programs with PBS (Sugai & Horner, 2001, p. 2; Turnbull, Edmonson, Griggs, et al., 2002).

Research has demonstrated that PBS benefits children with and without disabilities through an environment that is conducive to learning by all. Students learn more about their own behavior, learn to work together, and support each other as a community of learners. Sugai and Horner (2002b) found that over 500 U.S. schools across 13 states actively implement schoolwide PBS. They note that in schools using PBS, office discipline referrals decrease (40 to 60% reduction), and the quality of the referrals improves by combining (a) proactive efforts to teach, monitor and acknowledge appropriate behavior and (b) predictable and consistent consequences for problem behavior. Furthermore, as behavior improves, academic gains are experienced, and more time is directed toward academic instruction.

Schools that adopt a schoolwide PBS approach establish a full continuum of behavior supports. This continuum is characterized by (a) an emphasis on prevention, (b) an increasing intensity of intervention for increasing intensities of problem behavior, and (c) a provision of basic proactive programming (primary prevention) for all students. Sugai and Horner (2002a) describe support at the following four levels:

- Schoolwide support: Procedures and processes are put in place that are intended for *all* students, staff, and settings. All students and staff members are taught the schoolwide expectations and receive regular and frequent opportunities to practice them and to be positively acknowledged when they use them. Total staff commitment to managing behavior is essential for the plan to work.
- Specific setting support: A schoolwide leadership team guides the systemic adoption and sustained use of research-validated practices. The team oversees all development, implementation, modification, and evaluation activities. The team monitors specific settings that exist within the school environment, and in settings where problem behaviors occur, the team develops strategies that prevent or minimize their occurrence.
- Classroom support: Teachers structure learning opportunities through processes and procedures in individual classrooms. This classroom support should parallel the PBS features and procedures that are used schoolwide. Most contacts between teachers and students should be prosocial (positive and preventive) rather than corrective and punishing (i.e., five to eight positives for every negative interaction). Procedures in-

clude functional assessment strategies, social skills instruction, self-management training, and direct instruction.

- Individual student support: Students who present the most significant behavioral challenges receive immediate, relevant, effective, and efficient responses. There must be processes and procedures for high-intensity, specially designed, and individualized interventions for the estimated 3 to 7 percent of students who present the most challenging behavior. Collaboration with families and social service agencies is important.

Nelson and colleagues (1998) illustrate this multitiered model to meet the needs of all students in Figure 5.9.

Sugai and Horner (2001) recommend implementing schoolwide PBS by attending to the following seven guiding principles:

1. **Do less, but do it better and longer**. Because schools have finite resources, they should start by carefully examining local resources and existing capacity. Investments must (a) be made in a small, finite number of schoolwide initiatives; (b) reflect a redirection from reactive and to more preventive efforts; (c) be directed toward increasing local behavioral competence; and (d) emphasize modification of practices and procedures so that the best results are achieved with maximum efficiency.
2. **Invest in what works.** Schools must focus on evidence-based and conceptually sound practices and processes. Many examples of effective positive behavioral

STUDENT TYPE	INTERVENTION APPROACH
Typical	**Schoolwide Interventions (Preventive and Remedial)** ■ Effective teaching practices ■ Schoolwide discipline plan ■ Schoolwide classroom management plan and strategies
At-Risk (Developing or exhibiting disruptive behavior patterns)	**Targeted Interventions (Preventive and Remedial)** ■ Intensive instruction and counseling in skills for school and life success (e.g., anger management, self-control, conflict resolution) ■ Consultant-based 1-to-1 interventions ■ Intensive academic interventions (if applicable)
Target (Exhibits disruptive behavior patterns)	**Intensive Comprehensive Interventions (Remedial)** ■ Connection of children and caregivers to community-based social service agencies ■ Coordination of school services with social service agencies

Source: Adapted from Nelson et al. (1998).

FIGURE 5.9 Prevention and Remediation Levels to Meet the Needs of All Children

interventions already exist, and the highest priority should be directed toward their adoption and sustained use.

3. **Invest in clear and durable results.** Schools should have a clear idea of what they want to achieve before identifying and selecting a specific practice or procedure.
4. **Attend to individual and cultural differences.** The efficiency of every effective practice or procedure can be improved by accommodating those characteristics that make each student, teacher, family member, school community, etc., unique (e.g., disability, ethnicity/race, language, culture, neighborhood).
5. **Make informed decisions using existing data as much as possible**. Schools can't afford to make uninformed decisions about curriculum adoptions, intervention adjustments, or problem features. Efficient procedures and routines must be established to take advantage of naturally occurring data sources (e.g., office discipline referrals, attendance patterns, behavioral incidence reports).
6. **Work together.** Team-based efforts are the most efficient and effective means of problem solving, securing agreements, mustering supports, and enhancing implementation fidelity. Sustained implementation is more likely if initiatives are not linked to a single individual.
7. **Invest in enhancing local competence.** Schoolwide implementation efforts are vulnerable to short-term implementation if procedural and process expertise is not established within.

For more information, see the following websites:

OSEP Center on Positive Behavioral Interventions and Supports, http://www.pbis.org

Rehabilitation Research and Training Center on Positive Behavioral Support, http://www.rrtcpbs.org

Center for Effective Collaboration and Practice, http://www.cecp.air.org

Behavior Advisor, http://www.BehaviorAdvisor.com

For information on other schoolwide approaches, see Anderson and Matthews (2001); Fitzsimmons (1998); Mehas, Boling, Sobieniak, Sprague, Burke, & Hogan (1998); Nelson et al. (1998); Turnbull et al. (2002); and White, Algozzine, Audette, Marr, & Ellis (2001).

REFERENCES

Abrams, B. J., & Segal, A., (1998). How to prevent aggressive behavior. *TEACHING Exceptional Children, 30*(4), 10–15.

Anderson, J. A., & Matthews, B. (2001). We CARE . . . for students with emotional and behavioral disabilities and their families. *TEACHING Exceptional Children, 33*(5), 34–39.

Bender, W. N. (2001). *Learning disabilities: Characteristics, identification, and teaching strategies* (4th ed.). Boston: Allyn and Bacon.

Brophy, J., & Evertson, C. (1976). *Learning from teaching.* Boston: Allyn and Bacon.

Carbone, E. (2001). Arranging the classroom with an eye (and ear) to students with ADHD. *TEACHING Exceptional Children, 34*(2), 72–81.

Charles, C. M. (1996). *Building classroom discipline* (5th ed.). White Plains, NY: Longman.

Conroy, M. A., Clark, D., Gable, R. A., & Fox, J. J. (1999). Building competence in the use of functional behavioral assessment. *Preventing School Failure, 43*(4), 140–144.

Daniels, V. I. (1998). How to manage disruptive behavior in inclusive classrooms. *TEACHING Exceptional Children, 30*(4), 26–31.

Fitzsimmons, M. (1998, November). *Functional behavioral assessment and behavior intervention plans.* ERIC/OSEP Digest E571. Reston, VA: ERIC Clearinghouse on Disabilities and Gifted Education. *http://www.ericec.org/digests/e571.htm.*

Flannery, K. B., O'Neill, R. E., & Horner, R. H. (1995). Including predictability in functional assessment and individual program development. *Education and Treatment of Children, 18,* 499–509.

Gable, R. A., Quinn, M. M., Rutherford, Jr., R. B., & Howell, K. W. (1998). Addressing problem behaviors in schools: Use of functional assessments and behavior intervention plans. *Preventing School Failure, 42*(3), 106–119.

Glasser, W. (1969). *Schools without failure.* New York: Harper and Row.

Goldstein, A. P., & McGinnis, E. (2002). *Skillstreaming the adolescent: New strategies and perspectives for teaching prosocial skills.* Champaign, IL: Research Press.

Haager, D., Givner, C., & Dingle, M. (1998, April). *A validation of teacher competencies for general and special education teachers in inclusive schools.* Paper presented at the the Annual Meeting of the American Educational Research Association, San Diego, CA.

Haager, D., & Vaughn, S. (1995). Parent, teacher, peer, and self reports of social competence of students with learning disabilities. *Journal of Learning Disabilities, 28,* 205–215, 231.

Haager, D., & Vaughn, S. (1997). Assessment of social competence in students with learning disabilities. In J. Lloyd, E. Kameenui, & D. Chard (Eds.), *Issues in educating students with disabilities* (pp. 129–152). Mohwak, NJ: Lawrence Erlbaum.

Hallahan, D. P., Kauffman, J. M., & Lloyd, J. W. (1996). *Introduction to learning disabilities.* Boston: Allyn and Bacon.

Harry, B., & Anderson, M. G. (1995). The disproportionate placement of African American males in special education programs: A critique of the process. *Journal of Negro Education, 63,* 602–619.

Johns, B. H., & Carr, V. G. (1995). *Techniques for managing verbally and physically aggressive students.* Denver: Love.

Jones, V. F., & Jones, L. S. (1995). *Comprehensive classroom management: Creating positive learning environments for all students* (4th ed.). Boston: Allyn and Bacon.

Jones, V., & Jones, L. (2003). *Comprehensive classroom management: Creating communities of support and solving problems* (7th ed.). Boston: Allyn and Bacon.

Kauffman, J. M. (1997). *Characteristics of emotional and behavioral disorders of children and youth* (6th ed.). Upper Saddle River, NJ: Prentice-Hall.

Kavale, K. A., & Forness, S. R. (1995). *The nature of learning disabilities.* Hillsdale, NJ: Lawrence Erlbaum.

Khalsa, S. S. (1999). *The inclusive classroom: A practical guide for educators.* Glenview, IL: Good Year Books.

Kounin, J. (1970). *Discipline and group management in classrooms.* New York: Holt, Rinehart and Winston.

Leone, P. E., Mayer, M. J., Malmgren, K., & Meisel, S. M. (2000). School violence and disruption: Rhetoric, reality, and reasonable balance. *Focus on Exceptional Children, 33*(1), 1–20.

Mastropieri, M. A., & Scruggs, T. E. (2000). *The inclusive classroom: Strategies for effective instruction.* Upper Saddle River, NJ: Merrill.

McGinnis, E., & Goldstein, A. P. (2002a). *Skillstreaming in early childhood: Teaching prosocial skills to the preschool and kindergarten child.* Champaign, IL: Research Press.

McGinnis, E., & Goldstein, A. P. (2002b). *Skillstreaming the elementary school child: New strategies and perspectives for teaching prosocial skills.* Champaign, IL: Research Press.

Mehas, K., Boling, K., Sobieniak, S., Sprague, J., Burke, M. D., & Hagan, S. (1998). Finding a safe haven in middle school. *TEACHING Exceptional Children, 30*(4), 20–23.

Mendel, R. A. (2002). *Less hype, more help: Reducing juvenile crime, what works—and what doesn't.* Collingdale, PA: DIANE Publishing.

Minner, S., & Knutson, R. (1980). Using classroom token economies as instructional devices. *Teaching Exceptional Children, 12,* 167–169.

Nelson, J. R., Crabtree, M., Marchand-Martella, N., & Martella, R. (1998). Teaching good behavior in the whole school. *TEACHING Exceptional Children, 30*(4), 4–9.

O'Neill, R. E., Horner, R. H., Albin, R. W., Sprague, J. R., Storey, K., & Newton, J.S. (1997). *Functional assessment and program development for problem behavior* (2nd ed.). Pacific Grove, CA: Brooks/Cole.

Osher, D., & Hanley, T. V. (1996). Implications of the National Agenda to Improve Results for Children and Youth with or at Risk of Serious Emotional Disturbance. *Special Services in the Schools, 10*(2), 7–36.

Parker, J. G., & Asher, S. R. (1993). Friendship and friendship quality in middle childhood: Links with peer group acceptance and feelings of loneliness and social dissatisfaction. *Developmental Psychology, 29,* 611–621.

Powell, R. R., McLaughlin, H. J., Savage, T. V., & Zehm, S. (2001). *Classroom management: Perspectives on the social curriculum.* Upper Saddle River, NJ: Prentice-Hall.

Quinn, M. M., Gable, R. A., Rutherford, R. B., Jr., Nelson, C. M., & Howell, K. W. (1998, January). *Addressing student problem behavior: AN IEP team's introduction to functional behavioral assessment and behavior intervention plans.* Available from the Center for Effective Collaboration and Practice, 888.457.1551. Email: center @air-dc.org, Website: http://www.air-dc.org/cecp/ceep .html.

Scott, T. M., & Nelson, C. M. (1999). Functional behavioral assessment: Implications for training and staff development. *Behavioral Disorders, 24,* 249–252.

Skiba, R. J., & Peterson, R. L. (2000). School discipline at a crossroads: From zero tolerance to early response. *Exceptional Children, 66,* 335–347.

Sugai, G., & Horner, R. (2001). *School climate and discipline: Going to scale: A framing paper for the National Summit on the Shared Implementation of IDEA.* Arlington, VA: Council for Exceptional Children.

Sugai, G., & Horner, R. (2002a). Introduction to the special series on positive behavior support in schools. *Journal of Emotional and Behavioral Disorders, 10,* 130–135.

Sugai, G., & Horner, R. (2002b). The evolution of discipline practices: School-wide positive behavior supports. *Child & Family Behavior Therapy, 24,* 23–50.

Townsend, B. L. (2000). The disproportionate discipline of African American learners: Reducing school suspensions and expulsions. *Exceptional Children, 66,* 381–391.

Turnbull, A., Edmonson, H., Griggs, P., Wickham, D., Sailor, W., Freeman, R., Guess, D., Lassen, S., McCart, A., Park, J., Riffel, L., Turnbull, R., & Warren, J. (2002). A blueprint for schoolwide positive behavior support: Implementation of three components. *Exceptional Children, 68,* 377–402.

VanAcker, R. (1993). Dealing with conflict and aggression in the classroom: What skills do teachers need? *Teacher Education and Special Education, 16*(1), 23–33.

Vaughn, S., & Haager, D. (1994). Social competence as a multifaceted construct: How do students with learning disabilities fare? *Learning Disability Quarterly, 17*(4), 253–266.

Vaughn, S., Haager, D., Hogan, A. & Kouzekanani, K. (1992). Self-concept and peer acceptance in students with learning disabilities: A four- to five-year prospective study. *Journal of Educational Psychology, 84,* 43–50.

Vaughn, S., & Hogan, A. (1990). Social competence and learning disabilities: A prospective study. In H. L. Swanson & B. Keogh (Eds.), *Learning disabilities: Theoretical and research issues* (pp. 175–191). Hillsdale, NJ: Lawrence Erlbaum.

White, R., Algozzine, B., Audette, R., Marr, M. B., & Ellis, Jr., E. D. (2001). Unified Discipline: A school-wide approach for managing problem behavior. *Intervention in School and Clinic, 37*(1), 3–8.

Yehle, A. K. (1998). An ADHD success story: Strategies for teachers and students. *TEACHING Exceptional Children, 30*(6), 8–13.

Zehm, S., & Kottler, J. (1993). *On being a teacher: The human dimension.* Newberry Park, CA: Corwin Press.

CHAPTER SIX

READING INSTRUCTION FOR STRUGGLING READERS IN INCLUSIVE ELEMENTARY CLASSROOMS

Reading is to the mind what exercise is to the body.

—Joseph Addison, in the *Tatler*, 1709–1711, no. 147

KEY CONCEPTS

- Teachers of struggling readers must have a depth of knowledge and skills in the art and science of teaching reading. Teachers must be tenacious and persistent and have a high level of professionalism to succeed.
- Reading is a complicated process that cannot be explained by any one theory. Teachers must understand multiple theories to know how reading develops in children and apply these theories to practice.

- Two important national panels have identified a body of research-validated practices for reading instruction that should form the core of instruction.
- The special education teacher working as an inclusion specialist must be able to work within a classroom-based reading program while also providing specialized instruction for individual students.
- Students just beginning to develop literacy skills are at the *emergent literacy* stage. Emergent literacy skills include conventions of print, the purpose of print, the functions of print, and phonological awareness.
- Phonemic awareness, an awareness of the individual sounds of language, is an important precursor to word recognition and often an area of difficulty for struggling readers. Phonemic awareness activities should be part of instruction for many children, but especially for struggling readers.
- The alphabetic principle, or knowing that words are made up of sounds that are represented by letters, is an essential building block for reading.
- Children need to develop a solid foundation of word recognition skills, including sight memory and decoding, to develop fluency in reading.
- Phonics instruction should be explicit, systematic, and sequential.
- Reading intervention for at-risk readers should focus on the "big ideas" of reading, according to students' needs as determined by assessment. The big ideas include phonological awareness, the alphabetic principle, fluency with connected text, vocabulary, and comprehension.

FOCUS QUESTIONS

1. What does it take to become an effective reading teacher for students with reading-related disabilities?
2. How does reading develop in children? Is the process different for students with reading-related disabilities?
3. How does the special education teacher serving as an inclusion specialist work within the reading program of the general classroom?
4. How does the inclusion specialist provide sufficient individualized reading instruction in an inclusive setting?
5. What are research-based practices in reading and how are they applied in an inclusive setting?
6. What role does assessment play in teaching reading to students with disabilities?

Most children learn to read in the primary grades and increasingly read to learn, or use their reading skills as tools for learning, as they progress through school. Yet for students with reading-related disabilities, the process of learning to read is prolonged, many students struggle throughout their school years and even into their adult lives (Haager, 1997; Shaywitz, Shaywitz, Fletcher, & Escobar, 1990; Stanovich, 1986). The students we focus on in this book—students with learning disabilities, emotional disturbance, and mild mental retardation—may struggle for dissimilar reasons, but they follow similar developmental processes and require similar teaching techniques in learning to read. There is a body of research that outlines what constitutes effective reading practice, no matter whether the learner has a disability (Moats, 1999a), and what constitutes good special education lies more in the intensity and focus of that instruction (Moats, 2002).

In this chapter, we provide a variety of teaching strategies and methods and encourage teachers to try them with students. Effective special educators have a repertoire of strategies to use, making adjustments or changes along the way based on student performance. They also have a wealth of knowledge about the reading process and how students learn so they can fine-tune instruction for individual students. Key to making good instructional decisions is a well-developed assessment routine that provides continuous diagnostic information about students' progress. In addition, the special education teacher who serves as an inclusion specialist must artfully work within and around the reading/language arts instruction of the general education classroom. This may entail blending into the activities that are occurring, assisting the classroom teacher with literacy instruction, consulting with the teacher, and, most importantly, providing specialized instruction for specific students to ensure their learning needs are met. In this chapter, we use the terms *special education teacher* and *inclusion specialist* interchangeably to communicate that there may be nuances to the special educator's role in teaching reading in an inclusive setting.

It would be impossible to write a chapter that would teach you, a current or future special education teacher, exactly how to teach reading. Much of what effective reading teachers know about teaching reading comes from applying theory and research to first-hand experiences with children. Information from courses, workshops, professional books, and textbooks is extremely valuable, especially when you can immediately try out ideas with your students. This is what we hope you will do—try out the information and ideas from this chapter with students. Try them again and again, changing something here, adding something there, until you feel comfortable with them and include them in your repertoire. Some of the ideas will not suit you or your students. These you should file away until you someday need a fresh idea. Most of all, we hope that you will find the accomplishment of teaching a nonreader to read as thrilling as we have. We believe it is one of the greatest rewards of being a special education teacher.

In this chapter we first provide an overview of the reading process. Then we discuss reading instruction in three sections addressing beginning reading in the primary grade classroom, reading instruction in the intermediate grades, and then how to provide intensive remedial instruction for students with special needs. We do not specifically describe secondary classrooms here because we do this in a later chapter.

What do teachers need to know about reading? First, the foundation of knowledge that all elementary teachers should have includes:

- *Knowledge of the sequence of skills,* or scope and sequence of reading.
- *Knowledge of the reading process,* or how children acquire literacy.
- *Skills in effective instruction and assessment.*

Special educators who will teach children with severe reading difficulties must have additional skills, knowledge, and personality characteristics that include:

- *Knowledge of the assessment-instruction cycle,* with continuous monitoring of student progress in specific skills.

- *Skill in individualizing instruction,* or matching the instruction to students' needs. It is your job as a special educator to find the right intervention for each individual.
- *Skills in scaffolding instruction,* or facilitating student progress through ongoing support, building students' skills gradually and steadily.
- *Skills in motivating students.* It is a known fact that repeated failure leads to lack of motivation. Students may express this in various ways. Some are defiant or resistant to the idea of reading, others are passive and withdrawn. Teachers must be sensitive to the student's attitude and feelings about reading and work consistently and patiently to convince the student to view himself or herself as capable of learning to read. This may take time and careful, artful crafting of the student's reading experiences.
- *Tenacity as a teacher.* This means not giving up when the going gets tough, being able to come up with new ideas and approaches when learning bogs down, persevering with a student or method when it takes a long time to see visible progress, and maintaining a positive attitude.
- *A sense of urgency.* Teachers must never be complacent when teaching students who are seriously behind in their reading skills. It is important for these students to establish as quick a rate of learning as possible if they are going to catch up with their grade-level. Of course, we don't recommend pushing students to the point of frustration, but we have seen overly nurturing teachers who allow students to languish at low skill levels. This does the student a disservice.

Finally, what skills and knowledge must a special educator have to teach and support struggling readers *in an inclusive setting*? Typically, special educators have pulled students from their mainstream classes during scheduled reading and language arts instruction. However, with the current emphasis on maximizing the general education experience of students with disabilities, the inclusion teacher will provide some or all of students' reading instruction in the general education classroom. Therefore, inclusion specialists must also have interpersonal skills that are conducive to effective collaboration and instruction:

- *Being unobtrusive,* or having an ability to move in and out of whole-class instruction. Literacy instruction comprises a significant portion of a school day, and inclusion teachers may spend only a portion of that time in the general classroom. When the class becomes accustomed to the routine of an additional teacher coming in and working with groups or individual students, the disruption is minimal.
- *Professional communication skills.* It is very important for the inclusion specialist and the classroom teacher to engage in ongoing planning to orchestrate their separate but coordinated roles during literacy instruction. Each must have an awareness of the other's teaching agenda. With teachers' busy schedules and routines, inclusion teachers must be efficient and respectful in carrying out their responsibilities, making sure to communicate regularly with the classroom teacher.

- *Interpersonal skills.* Adjectives we have heard used to describe effective inclusion specialists include: *sensitive, considerate, nonjudgmental, supportive, adaptable, respectful,* and *flexible.* The inclusion specialist must move effectively in and out of various classrooms where teachers may have very different teaching styles. As one inclusion specialist advised, "The main thing is she [an inclusion teacher] has to be a very flexible teacher. And be able to take into consideration how the other teacher is going to feel. It's like a marriage, it has to be with two compatible people who can talk things out" (Klingner & Vaughn, 2002).
- *Sense of responsibility,* for the learning, mastery, and personal welfare of each student with disabilities. If students are not keeping up or do not understand a lesson, rather than blaming them, the inclusion teacher feels compelled to figure out a way to enhance their learning.

HOW DO CHILDREN LEARN TO READ?

Overview of the Reading Process

What is reading? A few years ago, two avid readers shared their views with us. Six-year-old John explained, "Reading is a trip. It's a chance to go somewhere you want to go. Like, let's say you want to go to Australia, you find a book about Australia and read it, and it's like taking a trip there." Michael, a beginning fifth-grader, described reading as "watching TV in your head, only better." He explained that he prefers reading to TV because he likes having the freedom to imagine characters and events "the way you want them." Being able to imagine is important to Michael, and he obviously finds pleasure in the printed word. Years later, John and Michael still find great pleasure in reading. They view reading as an adventure and being able to imagine what is in the book is an important part of the thrill of reading. Michael recently said that some of his high school peers look at reading as too much work but he still prefers reading to movies or television because it provides an opportunity to think about the underlying message while you are reading.

Why do John and Michael have such positive views of reading? Probably it is because both are able to get quickly to the *meaning* of the text. Both John and Michael are able to make meaning from print, the ultimate goal of reading. The mechanics, or nuts and bolts of processing the print, come easily, automatically, to these two readers. Many students with reading-related learning disabilities do not arrive at this point so readily. For them, the process of reading is a day-by-day struggle and the end goal is farther from sight. How did John and Michael get to this point? What are the skills and processes involved in being able to "take a trip" with a book or "see a TV show in your mind"?

Not everyone agrees about just what is involved in the process of reading. Historically, the reading process has been described by many different theories. Three of the most well-known of these are the "bottom-up," "top-down," and "interactive" views of reading.

Gough's (1985) theory states that reading is primarily a "bottom-up" process. Bottom-up theorists viewed reading as beginning with the print on the page and then moving to the reader's brain as the text is decoded. Marks on the page, or letters, form patterns, words, sentences, paragraphs, and whole texts that are translated by the reader into meaning through the brain's information processing system. The bottom-up philosophy underlies a skills-based approach to reading instruction that was predominant through the 1960s, 1970s, and into the 1980s. Phonics was emphasized, as was the importance of developing automaticity (being able to process text quickly and automatically). Recent movements have brought about a return to emphasizing phonics, or word-level reading skills.

Top-down theorists, on the other hand, believe that reading proceeds from the brain to the print on the page (Goodman, 1967, 1985; Goodman & Goodman, 1977; Smith & Goodman, 1971). This view emphasizes that reading is a search for meaning that relies more on syntactic and semantic knowledge than graphic information. Goodman (1967) refers to reading as a "psycholinguistic guessing game" that results from the interaction between language and thought. Efficient reading involves selecting the fewest, most productive cues necessary to produce "guesses" that are correct the first time. The reader verifies these guesses by sampling the printed text. The whole language approach to reading is based on this theory.

The interactive theory emphasizes that reading does not just occur from the bottom up or the top down but is recursive (Rumelhart, 1977). This model stresses that reading is a nonlinear process. Information from syntactic, semantic, lexical, and orthographic sources simultaneously converges in the brain's "message center," where it is stored until it can be confirmed or disconfirmed. Our interpretation of what we read depends on the context in which the text is embedded and our own experiences and expectations. We shift back and forth between attending to the text and what is in our mind. Stanovich (1980) modified this theory somewhat when he developed the *interactive compensatory model* of reading, incorporating his knowledge of skilled and unskilled readers. Stanovich explained that readers compensate for a weakness in one processing area by overly relying on another knowledge source.

More recently, other theories have influenced reading instruction. *Activity theory* focuses on the motives and goals of any endeavor. Thus, reading is conceptualized as not just a complex series of psychological operations, but as a goal-oriented activity (see Roller, 1996). Children must not only learn how to read, but also why. *Reader response theory* emphasizes the importance of the reader's interpretations and reactions in making meaning from text (Flood & Lapp, 1988). *Schema theory* underscores the role of prior knowledge in affecting our processing of print (Anderson & Pearson, 1984). According to this theory, new knowledge is integrated into existing schemata, or concepts that exist in prior knowledge. Knowledge is developed through personal experience in which the learner constructs meaning.

Reading is certainly a complicated process that is not easily explained by any one theory. Comprehension, or making meaning from text, is at the heart of reading. We also believe that "skilled readers use only as many cues as necessary to recognize words, but they possess highly developed decoding skills and employ them flexibly" (Harris & Sipay, 1990, p. 485). This requires a solid foundation of basic word reading skills as well as fluency with the language and its structure. Furthermore, students need abundant strategies for deriving meaning from text. The following principles are not mutually exclusive but together explain the various facets of the multidimensional reading process:

1. Reading requires automaticity with the code, being able to move from the alphabetic code to the pronunciation of the word with ease (LaBerge & Samuels, 1974).
2. Reading is an active search for meaning (Goodman, 1968). The reader constructs meaning by continually comparing and checking possible interpretations of text with past experiences and present understandings.
3. Reading is an interpretive process (Flood & Lapp, 1988; Rosenblatt, 1978). The reader constructs meaning while responding in a personal, individualized manner to what is read.
4. Reading is a strategic process that draws upon a variety of strategies to aid comprehension and memory (Paris, Wasik, & Turner, 1991). Strategies such as predicting, confirming, evaluating, organizing, and integrating information are applied flexibly as the expert reader interacts with text.
5. Reading is an interactive process that relies on many types of knowledge (Rumelhart, 1977; Stanovich, 1980).
   - **a.** Orthographic knowledge (knowledge of spelling patterns).
   - **b.** Phonological knowledge (knowledge of the sound system).
   - **c.** Syntactic knowledge (knowledge of word order and the functions of words).
   - **d.** Semantic knowledge (word-meaning knowledge).
   - **e.** Visual-graphic knowledge (knowledge of the conventions of print, word length, and word configuration).
   - **f.** Pragmatic knowledge (an understanding of the rules that govern language use in different contexts).
   - **g.** Prior knowledge (the necessity of relating new information to what is already known—this is also called schema theory [Anderson & Pearson, 1984].
6. Reading involves processing information in the most efficient way possible. Because the human mind has a limited capacity for storing information in short-term memory and for processing new input, tradeoffs must occur. If the brain's limited processing abilities are focused on lower-level subprocesses (e.g., word recognition), there is less available for executing higher-level subprocesses (e.g., reading comprehension) (LaBerge & Samuels, 1974; Swanson, 1987).
7. Reading as a language learning activity is socially mediated (Vygotsky, 1986; Wertsch, 1985). Knowledge is first constructed while an individual interacts with others and then is internalized.
8. Reading is a purposeful, goal-oriented activity (Roller, 1996).

Characteristics of Proficient Readers

Fully proficient readers possess a wide repertoire of interrelated skills, strategies, and attitudes. We do not advocate a piecemeal approach to reading instruction that teaches these behaviors in isolation; however, we do believe that it is important for teachers to be knowledgeable about the many aspects of reading that should be addressed in a comprehensive, balanced reading program.

Reading Attributes. The *skilled reader* has a large sight vocabulary, uses a variety of strategies to decode words, reads aloud with accurate phrasing and expression, and self-corrects miscues.

The *comprehending reader* has an extensive vocabulary, effectively uses context to grasp meaning, understands both literal and figurative language, and uses prior knowledge to aid understanding. A good comprehender also detects the interrelationship of words and ideas, understands main ideas, recollects significant details, notes cause-effect relationships, makes intended inferences, and anticipates outcomes. The good comprehender also reads critically and is able to understand the author's intent; distinguish between fact, opinion, and inference; identify errors in reasoning and extrapolate from what is read to reach new ideas and conclusions.

The *functional reader* locates information using various information sources such as an index, table of contents, dictionary, encyclopedia, and the Internet. The functional reader also understands various types of technical and subject-specific text; reads maps, graphs, and charts; follows technical directions; uses text features such as headings, subheadings, marginal notes, and other study aids; organizes information in such forms as note-taking, highlighting, and outlining; and uses appropriate study habits.

The *recreational reader* displays an interest in reading and enjoys reading as a voluntary, leisure-time activity. The recreational reader selects appropriate reading material, seeks information or pleasure from reading, and refines literary judgment by appreciating the style and beauty of language (adapted from Harris & Sipay, 1990).

Reading Disabilities

Experts suggest that reading disability is the principal cause of failure in school (e.g., Carnine, Silbert, & Kameenui, 1997; Kaluger & Kolson, 1978; Mercer, 1997). Failure to learn to read is associated with numerous long-term consequences including academic failure (e.g., Fletcher & Lyon, 1998; Simmons & Kameenui, 1998). The term "dyslexia" is often used to refer to severe difficulty in learning to read and is commonly used by medical specialists. However, most educators prefer the term "severe reading disability." Though specific causes are unknown, several factors are related to reading disabilities (adapted from Mercer, 1997):

1. **Physical/neurological** (Bakwin, 1973; Hinshelwood, 1917; Orton, 1937).
2. **Environmental** (e.g., inadequate instruction, environmental factors) (Adelman, 1989; Heilman, Blair, & Rupley, 1994).
3. **Psychological** (e.g., auditory processing difficulties, visual processing difficulties, language disorders) (Kirk, Kirk, & Minskoff, 1985; Samuels, 1973).
4. **A combination of interacting factors** (Rosner, Abrams, Daniels, & Schiffman, 1981).

Figure 6.1 describes these characteristics.

Students with reading disabilities need two types of reading experiences: success with grade-level text and systematic instruction at their instructional level. For students with high-incidence disabilities, their instructional level is usually below their grade level. In traditional pull-out models of special education, students with serious reading difficulties have typically had limited experiences with grade-level text, reading mostly from easy-to-read texts and missing out on the literature of the general education classroom. An

READING HABITS

Tense, insecure, loses place, makes lateral head movements, holds reading material too close.

WORD RECOGNITION ERRORS

Omissions, insertions, substitutions, reversals, mispronunciations, transpositions, unknown words, slow choppy reading.

COMPREHENSION ERRORS

Difficulty recalling basic facts, sequence, and the main ideas. Difficulty using information from the story in analytical, reflective, or interpretive tasks.

MISCELLANEOUS INDICATORS

Word-by-word reading; strained, high-pitched voice; inadequate phrasing; ignored or misinterpreted punctuation.

Source: Adapted from Mercer (1997).

FIGURE 6.1 Characteristics of Reading Disabilities

Core literature Literature selections that form the core of the language arts curriculum at a particular grade level.

Decodable text Reading passage or text that has a controlled vocabulary, including only text that students could decode given their skill level and sight vocabulary.

inclusive classroom is an ideal setting for accomplishing one of the most important mandates of IDEA: access to the core curriculum. In the area of reading, this means helping students to participate in reading the **core literature**, or grade-level text that forms the core of the language arts curriculum. The special educator should work with the classroom teacher to make appropriate accommodations for students with disabilities so they can have positive and meaningful experiences with the reading material of the regular class. We believe this is doubly important because of the cultural literacy, vocabulary development, and general world knowledge that students obtain from experiences with literature. Yet, students must also have appropriate and plentiful instruction in texts they are able to read, or **decodable texts**. Reading decodable text provides opportunities to practice valuable word reading skills, thus enhancing automaticity with the code and facilitating comprehension (Chard, Simmons, & Kameenui, 1998; Juel, 1991).

IMPORTANCE OF RESEARCH IN READING

No topic in education has been more controversial than how to teach reading. The question remains for policy makers and teachers: Whose research do we listen to? Many would characterize the reading field as being caught in a great debate of whether to teach using holistic methods, such as whole language, or skills-driven approaches that include phonics. Proponents for both sides cite research evidence that validates their idea of best practice. Several states, the most notable being two of the larger—Texas and California—have been reforming teaching practices statewide based on research evidence indicating a core of effective practices, including systematic instruction in the alphabetic code. State standards and assessment systems have been developed to reflect current research (California Department of Education, 1999; Texas Education Agency, 1997). We would agree with a recent *New York Times* article that there is more consensus across the two camps than is readily apparent in public debates (Rothstein, 2001). We support a balanced, comprehensive approach to teaching reading that includes both systematic instruction in basic skills and rich experiences with language and literature. Reading teachers must continually upgrade their skills through ongoing professional development while being discerning about trendy ideas that come along. Beware of practices that are "validated" by "experts" who fail to provide a convincing research base to back up their claims.

Throughout this book we emphasize research-based practices, but in no area is it as important as in teaching reading. In fact, two separate national panels of experts in reading were recently commissioned to systematically review the enormous body of research on reading and make recommendations for practice. The National Research Council formed the Committee on Prevention of Reading Difficulties in Young Children. This group reviewed all the relevant research and made its recommendations for primary grade instruction in a report published in 1998 (Snow, Burns, & Griffin, 1998). The National Reading Panel subsequently reviewed the research on specific topics related to reading practice and developed a set of instructional guidelines (National Reading Panel, 2000). We see from these reports that there is now some convergence among the wide body of reading research on what practices are and are not effective. As a recent article stated in its title, "Teaching Reading IS Rocket Science," the main point is that effective practices in teaching reading are now well documented (American Federation of Teachers, 1999). Public awareness of this converging evidence on what is effective in teaching reading has led to state and national initiatives promoting the use of research-validated practices. Lawmakers and educational agencies are providing opportunities for professional development for teachers, and large-scale training efforts are leading to transformation of how teachers implement reading instruction. What is critical, however, is how these research-based practices play out in the hands of real teachers outside of experimental conditions.

A COMPREHENSIVE APPROACH TO LITERACY INSTRUCTION

As an inclusion specialist responsible for teaching struggling readers, you must be able to promote meaningful literacy experiences for students in a supportive learning environment while providing the high level of explicit instruction needed for such students to gain important skills and strategies. A focus on the complete literacy event does not mean that traditional skills are unimportant. "Rather these skills are situated within a holistic context that is intimately linked with goals and conditions of reading" (Roller, 1996, p. 34). As noted by Harris and Graham (1996), there have been problems for students with and without disabilities receiving whole language instruction when skills have not been explicitly taught. Many parents and educators have voiced concerns about those students who have not learned to read "naturally" by the first or second grades and whose spelling remains "inventive" long past the early grades. "Students who face challenges in terms of learning, behavior, social and emotional development, or some combination of these areas may face greater difficulty in developing fluency and automaticity with skills and strategies than do their peers" (Harris & Graham, 1996, p. 136). Because of the challenges these children face, many seem to require extensive, explicit instruction to develop essential skills and strategies. We do *not* advocate the wholesale return to a skills-based approach. Rather, we support *explicit instruction that is bolstered by meaningful, purposeful reading experiences and is grounded in sound instructional methodology*. Read about how two special educators support reading instruction in two different types of classrooms.

THE INCLUSION TEACHER SUPPORTING READING INSTRUCTION IN THE PRIMARY-GRADE CLASSROOM

There is nothing quite like the thrill of helping someone to read for the first time. Ms. Sousa still remembers when long ago, while she was in high school, she tutored a young neighbor, Jerry, a first-grader, who was having difficulty learning to read. Ms. Sousa enjoyed thinking of new ways to help Jerry practice the sight words he was learning. But it was frustrating, too. It seemed as if he would know a word one day, but forget it the next. Then one day Ms. Sousa thought of asking Jerry to make up a story about his new puppy. Jerry was excited at the prospect. As he dictated his story and read the words Ms. Sousa was writing, he finally understood what reading was all about. Reading was just saying the words someone had written, and *he* could read them himself. Ms. Sousa will never forget when Jerry's face lit up as he exclaimed, "I can read this all by myself!" It was at that moment that Ms. Sousa decided she wanted to be a teacher, and she wanted to help children like Jerry.

Ms. Sousa is now a special education teacher, teaching at Humphrey Elementary School, a diverse school that implements an inclusive model. Ms. Sousa co-teaches with Ms. DaVoll almost all day in a kindergarten/first-grade combination classroom. The school made a commitment to early intervention for at-risk students and carefully placed students in this class that might benefit most from having a classroom teacher and special educator working closely together. Several of the students in the class are being monitored because they are showing early signs of academic difficulty. The principal considers these two teachers to be very effective, and they have reputations for being successful with at-risk students. As an inclusion specialist, Ms. Sousa is very involved in the identification of students with special needs. She works closely with students already identified as having disabilities and also with struggling students not identified. She tries various early and prereferral interventions to help students experiencing difficulty get back on track.

This heterogeneous classroom includes four students with identified disabilities (two with learning disabilities, one with mild mental retardation, and one with a behavioral disorder), six low-achieving students whom the school is watching closely as possible candidates for a special education referral (three of these are English language learners), nine average-achieving children, and seven high-achieving students.

Ms. Sousa and Ms. DaVoll exemplify a successful primary grade inclusion model where the general and special education teachers work fluidly and cooperatively through co-teaching and consultation. The administrators and other teachers feel it is a good investment of the school's resources for Ms. Sousa to spend most of the day in this kindergarten/ first-grade classroom. The teachers are pleased with being able to identify students in need of special education at such an early age and feel Ms. Sousa's work with the at-risk students is invaluable. Ms. Sousa performs other duties in the later part of the afternoon such as consulting with primary-grade teachers regarding specific students, assisting with assessment for IEPs, meeting with parents and conducting IEP meetings.

In order to know how to support students with disabilities in an inclusive setting, the inclusion teacher must understand the nature and structure of classroom reading instruction. There are a variety of programs and approaches used in today's primary grade classrooms. Some schools implement a specific commercial or "homegrown" district reading program schoolwide. However, other schools allow classroom teachers to choose their own program. Some teachers are eclectic and pull from several different resources. As an inclusion teacher, you may find yourself adapting to multiple approaches as you go from classroom to classroom. In this section, we will review several instructional approaches used in primary grade classrooms so you can become familiar with them. First, let's visit Ms. Sousa and Ms. DaVoll again to see how their classroom is set up. Both teachers have a strong belief in a whole language approach, but insist on providing daily systematic, explicit skills instruction, especially for those students who are struggling readers. After that, we'll visit another school using a code-emphasis reading program throughout the entire school. This program is scripted and teacher directed and requires the full reading/language arts time block.

Ms. Sousa and Ms. DaVoll have worked hard to set up a learning environment that allows their students to flourish. Since Ms. Sousa is assigned almost full-time to Ms. DaVoll's classroom, they had the opportunity to collaborate extensively as they planned the year's instruction. They spent much time examining their underlying beliefs about teaching and learning and established guiding principles that provide the foundation for the psychosocial environment in their room. They have given great attention to organizing the physical environment to efficiently use all available space and to make sure their room is warm and "user friendly." They have also co-planned a schedule that they feel maximizes students' involvement in literacy-related experiences.

THE PSYCHOSOCIAL ENVIRONMENT

Ms. Sousa and Ms. DaVoll strongly believe that all children can learn and will learn in their classroom. They have established an active community of learners where everyone feels successful and *is* successful. Each student believes he or she has something of value to contribute and that he or she is accepted and respected. Students are encouraged to take risks and to support the risk-taking of their peers. As a student in a similar program noted, "Here everybody is equal. We can all read books and talk about them with each other. Some people might take longer to read a book but everybody does it and everybody has something to say. We all get more ideas" (Short & Klassen, 1993, p. 67). Variability is a naturally occurring phenomenon in this classroom. Ms. Sousa and Ms. DaVoll post the following expectations in their classroom:

- Everyone is a reader.
- Reading is a tool for learning.
- Reading is a way to "hear" stories.
- Everyone participates during reading time.
- There are different ways to participate.
- We respect everyone's choice to participate as he or she chooses.

THE PHYSICAL ENVIRONMENT

The co-teachers organized their classroom around a rug that they use for shared story reading, circle time, discussions, and other activities. Students' desks are clustered in groups of four or five and are used for individual and group work. Learning centers are set up around the room. Bulletin boards relate to learning centers or exhibit children's work and display theme-related pictures and information (e.g., about dolphins and whales) or the classroom rules. Labels and environmental print signs abound.

THE DAILY SCHEDULE

Ms. Sousa and Ms. DaVoll teach language arts using a literacy block and like the flexibility allowed by this way of scheduling:

8:30 Arrival—Interactive Journals

8:45 Opening Activities and Circle Time

> Pledge of Allegiance, Morning Message, Morning News/Sharing
>
> Students set a goal for what they wish to accomplish that day

9:00 Literacy Block

> Whole class *shared reading experience,* with a whole-class *mini-lesson* (15 minutes).
>
> *Independent reading time* and *small-group skills lessons* (30 minutes): Students read quietly to themselves or with a partner for 15 to 25 minutes and share with a partner. Teachers conduct small-group skills lessons for 10 to 15 minutes and hold individual conferences.
>
> *Center time* (30 minutes). Note: On Fridays special activities are substituted for center time (e.g., the performance of a play by students in the class or a cooking activity accompanied by a whole-class language experience story).

10:15 Recess

10:25-11:00 Writing Workshop (and Spelling/Making Words)

The rest of the day is devoted to other subject areas, but the teachers integrate as much literacy instruction as possible into these subjects. In addition, there is an Afterschool Literacy Lab for at-risk first graders. Students are identified by assessment scores and teacher referral and attend for a half hour three days per week.

The two teachers provide an integrated curriculum that revolves around thematic units. Literacy instruction occurs in meaningful and authentic contexts. Every day the teachers read to their students and students read by themselves, to each other, and to the teachers. Students read and discuss a Morning Message, Morning News, Big Books, predictable books (also called patterned books), children's literature, and stories they have themselves composed. Students work at learning centers, at their desks independently, in pairs, or in groups of four. Students are involved in a modified version of Reading Workshop, Making Words, Writer's Workshop, Journal Writing, and the Language Experience Approach. Cross-age tutors and parent volunteers periodically come into the room to read with students.

In many ways the literacy curriculum in this classroom is similar to that of the Early Literacy Project (Englert, Rozendal, & Mariage, 1994), an exemplary program for special education students. With certain students, they provide critical elements of an intensive early literacy program in addition to the opportunities for learning provided to all. These include:

- extra individualized attention
- intensive direct instruction
- extensive practice in various contexts
- precise monitoring
- careful grouping and pairing
- modified assignments

MS. SOUSA'S ADVICE FOR NEW TEACHERS

Why is Ms. Sousa such a successful teacher? Why do students thrive under her tutelage? When asked in a recent interview if she had any advice for upcoming teachers, this was her response:

"Always look for ways to help your students be successful and grow. All children can learn, but it takes knowing every child really well to have a thorough understanding of what each one can do by himself or herself, what each can do with assistance, and what is beyond current capabilities. This is always on my mind when I'm teaching; it's sort of like I keep a mental file for every child where I keep track of what he or she has already accomplished and what I think that child is ready to learn, and then I adjust my assistance accordingly. I also keep in mind things like if some students are easily frustrated or if they respond well to a challenge. Every child is different. I don't tell children answers or do their work for them—I'm always trying to figure out how to help them do it by themselves. When a child asks for help, my first response is usually, 'How can you figure it out?' But then I might give clues. For example, let's say someone has just asked me what a word is in a book she is reading. I'd probably ask, 'How can you figure it out?' She might respond, 'Reread the sentence and see what makes sense.' Then, if she still doesn't know the word, I might say, 'What is the first sound in the word?' or 'What does the picture remind you of?' depending on the word, the context, and what I think the child needs to learn. So not only do I need to know the child really well, but I also need to know the reading process in detail so I know what kind of help to provide."

INCLUSION IN A CODE-EMPHASIS READING CLASSROOM

Now we will visit a classroom that is very different from Ms. DaVoll's and Ms. Sousa's whole-language environment. Mr. Snow is a special educator at Terrace Elementary School, an urban school where students are primarily English-language learners (ELLs). The school is situated in an older neighborhood in a large city where many people are recent immigrants to the United States. Most of the parents do not speak English, and Spanish is the predominant language used at home. The primary-grade classrooms provide intensive English immersion in addition to the regular curriculum. The school has undergone significant change in the past two years in an effort to raise achievement scores as part of a district-wide initiative. The district has adopted a skills-oriented, code-emphasis, structured reading program, and the primary-grade teachers are mandated to use the program. They have undergone extensive training in the reading program. The reading program requires 2 or more hours per day of whole-class instruction as well as an additional 30 to 60 minutes for breaking into groups. The whole-class instruction is scripted, with explicit instructions for teachers. During group time, students work on independent writing or reading and complete various reading tasks related to the lesson of the day, or work with a teacher or paraprofessional for reading intervention to improve specific skills. Intervention is guided by ongoing assessment.

Mr. Snow goes into five primary grade classrooms. He serves students with disabilities who have IEPs as well as a number of children who are at risk for reading failure but have not been formally identified by an IEP team. These students are under consideration by the school's Student Study Team for possible retention or special education placement. Because Mr. Snow goes into five primary-grade classrooms and sees all the at-risk students, he works closely with the Student Study Team to monitor students' progress so the team can make careful decisions. They are hoping to reduce the number of students needing special education by providing early intensive reading intervention. The five classrooms where Mr. Snow works stagger their group time so he can be there to provide intervention to his students. Small group instruction is also provided by the classroom teacher and may include the at-risk students. An afterschool intervention program provides another opportunity for supporting at-risk students. Three primary-grade students with disabilities are placed with a special education teacher in a pull-out program for all or part of the day. These students are not part of the inclusion program because their reading skills are so delayed or their behavior problems so severe that they cannot function in the same activities as the rest of the class. In this way, the school provides a continuum of services to meet the needs of students with various disabilities.

The physical environment in these classrooms allows for whole-class instruction on a rug near the whiteboard and at children's seats. The seats are arranged in a U-shape so the teacher can move easily from desk to desk. There are three kidney-shaped tables for pulling groups of students for directed lessons. There is a listening station where children listen to taped stories from their reading program to provide extra practice in building reading fluency. There is a classroom library where children may select books to take home or to read in the afternoon when their assignments are complete. Each classroom has a word wall with high frequency words. In addition, there is a great deal of environmental print in each classroom. Some of it is generated through the directed lessons in the reading program to reinforce phonics or grammatical concepts learned. Some reflects children's own writing or group-generated stories from morning circle time.

The teachers are attentive to the psychosocial environment, but it is not a central focus. The main focus in these classrooms is on the business of learning. Students in these classrooms are learning English at the same time they are learning to read in English. Teachers realize this is a tall order, and they integrate as much language development as possible throughout the day. Following are central themes observed in these classrooms:

- The classroom must be a safe environment to experiment with English. Students are encouraged to try to express their ideas in English and are not overcorrected. Oral language activities and vocabulary development are integrated throughout the curriculum.
- English is the primary language of instruction, and Spanish is used strategically to support learning. Teachers provide instruction in English, but when students become confused or seem lost, teachers may explain a concept or directions in Spanish.

- Reading/language arts instruction must occur in an uninterrupted block of time. Nothing else is scheduled from 8:00 to 11:00 AM.
- Teachers must maximize students' engagement in learning. Transitions between activities must be efficient. Teachers must be well prepared to keep activities flowing.

The school has made an investment in starting children out with solid literacy instruction in the primary grades. Title I money is used to provide paraprofessionals for reading/language arts instruction. Each classroom teacher has a paraprofessional to work with students during their independent work time. Mr. Snow also has a paraprofessional who moves among the five classrooms with him. The teachers stagger their independent work times so the paraprofessionals and Mr. Snow can spend 30 to 45 minutes in each classroom. During independent work time, there may be as many as four adults—Mr. Snow, the classroom teacher, and two paraprofessionals—working with small groups of students or individuals. They believe this level of intensity is important for ensuring success in an urban school. Mr. Snow is well trained in the structured reading program used at the school. He uses the reading program and supplemental sources. He consults closely with the classroom teachers to plan activities that coordinate and reinforce the lessons taught each day. He works with students in small groups or individually on their IEP reading-related goals, but draws on the basic reading program so students will not be confused by too many approaches or divergent materials. When the reading program does not provide enough extra practice with concepts, or when students' needs are not met by the reading program, he supplements with materials from other sources.

In two years of implementation, the achievement scores at the school have risen steadily. Some of the teachers struggled with the drastic change from a more student-oriented approach as in Ms. Sousa's and Ms. DaVoll's school to a more teacher-directed program. Teachers at Terrace Elementary feel they don't have enough time for child-centered literacy strategies such as writer's workshop or free-reading time. Their children have less opportunity to discover literature and set personal learning goals. The teachers are developing ways to integrate language and literacy development into other subjects throughout the day, but this is a constant challenge. Most of them believe it has been worth it to institute the structured reading program. Their achievement scores are approaching the national average and students are excited about learning. However, teachers are seeking ways to better nurture students' language and literacy growth.

EARLY READING CURRICULUM

Emergent Literacy

Clay (1979) identified four abilities that are prerequisites for becoming a successful reader. First, children must have receptive and expressive proficiency with oral language. They must be able to follow verbal directions and have some understanding of a story as it is read to them. Second, children's visual perception skills should be adequately developed to attend to and analyze complex visual cues. Third, children need to begin to understand the concept of words, that the names of things and the words they use when speaking can be represented by a series of graphic marks called letters. Fourth, children must have enough motor control to follow a line of text. They must know the order in which to read print on a page (in English, from left to right and top to bottom).

Emergent literacy Awareness of print and language and their function in society. Includes phonological awareness, understanding of print concepts and basic language skills.

Gunn, Simmons, and Kameenui (1998) describe **emergent literacy** as including the following kinds of knowledge: conventions of print, the purpose of print, the functions of print, and phonological awareness. Emergent readers develop an awareness of how print works in their world and the sounds of our language. Through exposure to books and language in their surroundings, children gradually become familiar with many aspects of reading and develop prerequisite language and literacy skills.

Phonological awareness Understanding the different ways that language can be broken down and manipulated, such as rhyming, syllabication, and phonemic awareness.

Phonological awareness. **Phonological awareness** is an important prerequisite to learning to read. It is a language skill rather than a reading skill. We think of it as a building block for reading. People often confuse the terms "phonological awareness" and "phonemic awareness." They are related but are not the same. *Phonological awareness is knowledge of the sound structure of spoken language.* This means understanding the different ways that language can be broken down—into words, rhymes, syllables, and phonemes. *Phonemic awareness is the understanding that words contain individual sounds, or phonemes, and the ability to manipulate these sounds.* We can think of phonological awareness as a set of skills, the umbrella in Figure 6.2, that includes the subskills of rhyming, word awareness, syllable awareness, and phonemic awareness.

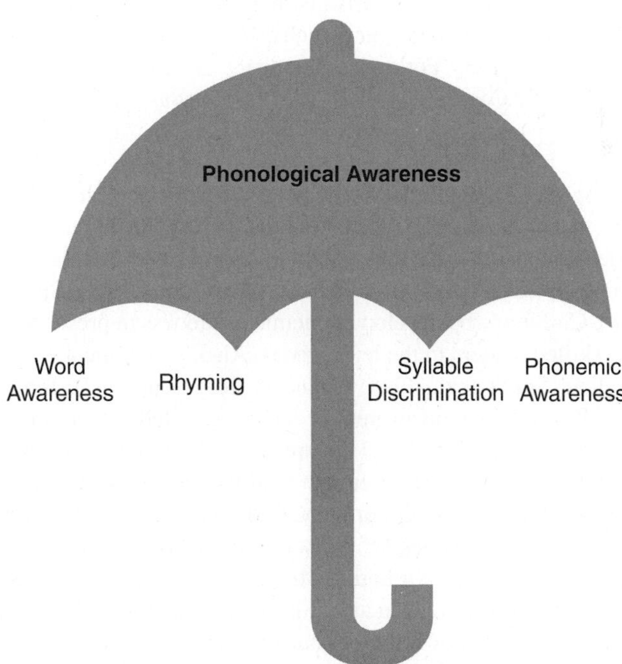

FIGURE 6.2 Phonological Awareness and Its Components

Following are some ideas for promoting phonological awareness. It is important to note that these are *language* skills and do not involve the use of text. Teachers often jump into using letter tiles or writing words and letters on the board to teach these skills, but these are auditory tasks that require no text:

Word awareness Understanding "word boundaries," or where one word ends and another begins.

Rhyming Ability to recognize and produce rhymes.

Phonemic awareness Understanding that words can be broken down into single sounds, or phonemes, and the ability to manipulate the sounds.

1. **Word awareness** means understanding "word boundaries" or where one word ends and another begins. For example, when young children learn the pledge of allegiance, they often confuse the word boundaries and think of "pledge-allegiance" as one word. To help children acquire this skill, teachers might have children stomp their feet, one stomp per word, along with a song or rhyme. Using Big Books and pointing word by word also helps children to understand this concept.
2. **Rhyming** is an important emergent reading skill. Children must learn to recognize rhyme (e.g., Does "man" rhyme with "pan"?) as well as to produce rhymes (Can you say a word that rhymes with "car"?).
3. Awareness of syllables is also an auditory task that can be learned at a young age. Having children clap the syllables in their names and other familiar words is a typical activity.
4. Promoting **phonemic awareness** is the most important aspect of the phonological awareness. This means understanding that words can be broken down into single sounds, or phonemes, and being able to manipulate them. Most beginning reading programs have phonemic awareness activities embedded within language arts instruction. There are also several supplemental phonemic awareness programs such as *Phonemic Awareness Activities for Young Children* (Adams, Foorman, Lundberg & Beeler, 1998) and *Ladders to Literacy* (O'Connor, Notari-Syverson, & Vadasy, 1996). The next section provides sample activities and ideas for phonemic awareness.

Developing Phonemic Awareness. Understanding that the words of our language are made up of individual sounds, or phonemes, is probably the most important building block for developing early reading skills for several reasons. First, we know that it is a powerful predictor of later reading outcomes (see Adams, 1990; Smith, Simmons, & Kameenui, 1998). Children who develop phonemic awareness in preschool and kindergarten are likely to be skilled readers in the later grades. Also, phonemic awareness lays the foundation for decoding (Smith et al., 1998; Wagner & Torgesen, 1987). Table 6.1 explains the skills that are included phonemic awareness and a suggested developmental sequence.

Phonemic awareness skills are critically important in early reading. In kindergarten-age children, these abilities predict reading achievement independently from letter knowledge, vocabulary, and IQ (Bradley & Bryant, 1985; Share, Jorm, Maclean, & Matthews, 1984; Torgesen, Wagner, & Rashotte, 1994; Wagner, Torgesen, Laughon, Simmons, & Rashotte, 1993). Thus, it appears that phonological awareness plays a key role when acquiring the alphabetic principle (the understanding that spoken words are composed of sounds represented by letters in our writing code) and helps when learning to read (Ehri, 1989; Gough, Juel, & Griffith, 1992; Share & Stanovich, 1995). We have been encouraged in recent years by research indicating that phonological awareness can be taught

TABLE 6.1 Development of Phonemic Awareness

SKILL	EXAMPLE
Onset Recognition	*"Dog" begins with the sound /d/. Which picture begins with the same sound as "dog"?* (show student picture cards)
Onset-Rime Segmenting and Blending	*Students separate onsets (beginning sounds) from the rime (end unit of a single syllable word).* pine = /p/ - /ine/; make = /m/ - /ake/ *Students blend words from onsets and rimes:* /b/ + /ike/ = bike
Phoneme Segmenting	*Tell me the sounds in the word "pot."* /p/ /o/ /t/
Phoneme Blending	*I'll say the sounds and you tell me what word I am saying:* /v/ /a/ /n/ van
Phoneme Deletion	*Say the word "hat" without the /h/:* /at/
Phoneme Substitution	*Change the p in "pan" to a /r/ sound.* ran

to those students who have not already acquired it on their own. When young children with and without disabilities have been taught phonological blending and segmenting in controlled experiments, they have demonstrated gains in reading acquisition greater than those of control group students (Ball & Blachman, 1991; Cunningham, 1990; O'Connor, Jenkins, & Slocum, 1995; O'Connor et al., 1996; Torgesen, Morgan, & Davis, 1992).

Concepts of print Awareness of the communicative function of print in the world.

Concepts of Print. Many children develop **concepts of print,** or an awareness of the functions of print in the world, prior to entering school. From early experiences with books and other print media, children learn that the visual symbols connect with the spoken word. For example, when young children play-act, they may pretend to be a waiter or waitress and take the orders of their customers, writing scribbles on a pad of paper. The child cannot read or write formal print and the scribbles may be meaningless to others, but the child has the notion of how writing represents a concrete object or idea, that is, the food ordered. Awareness of print is a prerequisite skill for word reading (Chard et al., 1998; Sulzby & Teale, 1991). Through experience, children develop other concepts of print such as learning that text reads from left to right and top to bottom and what and where a title is.

Several classroom activities are designed to promote print awareness. Print is a natural and necessary part of our lives. In many homes, we read not only books, magazines, newspapers, and labels, but also messages. Classroom teachers conduct different kinds of whole-class activities to help children understand the function of print in our world and to connect children's use of language with print. Following are examples of print awareness activities:

1. The Morning Message. Notes left on refrigerators, grocery lists, and phone messages emphasize the importance and prevalence of print as a form of communication. The classroom "morning message" is a way to reinforce this perception (Crowell, Kawakami, & Wong, 1986; Farnan, Flood, & Lapp, 1994). Rather than passing along information verbally, the teacher writes a brief daily message in a predictable format on the board to be read by students (with help) and discussed during morning opening activities (e.g., "Today is October 29, 2005. We will have a special visitor from the fire department today.") As students become familiar with the format, words can be deleted to encourage students to predict words that make sense.
2. Morning News. During Morning News (Englert et al., 1994), selected students relate a personal experience to their teachers and the class. With the assistance of the class, the teacher acts as a scribe and writes down each student's story. Classmates ask questions and offer suggestions that might be incorporated into the recorded version of the story. All students have an equal opportunity to participate.

The inclusion teacher must be able to assess students' knowledge of print awareness. This is usually done through ongoing observation. The special educator may also conduct an assessment by asking the student to perform certain tasks and noting the student's response. Figure 6.3 provides a simple checklist for teachers to use to assess students' knowledge of print concepts.

Alphabet Awareness and Alphabetic Principle. Children who are read to in their early years develop an awareness of letters in print. They may recognize some letters and point them out in signs as they drive in a car with their parents. Whether they learn at home, in preschool, or when they begin formal schooling, children learn the alphabet and become aware of the function of letters in print. We call this *alphabetic awareness*. Eventually, children learn that *words are made up of sounds which are represented by letters,* or the **alphabetic principle**. Learning letter-sound correspondence is fundamental to learning to read phonetically. Some call this "grapheme-phoneme" correspondence (Chard et al., 1998). The next step is learning to see the letters, say the sounds, and then *blend* the sounds to make a whole word. Phonics instruction encompasses this process and we discuss this in the next section.

Alphabetic principle Understanding that words are made up of sounds, which are represented by letters; understanding letter-sound correspondence.

Table 6.2 illustrates typical emergent literacy development activities included in kindergarten reading programs.

Word Recognition Instruction

Word recognition Being able to pronounce a word from print using either decoding strategies or sight memory.

Once children have a foundation of emergent literacy development, it is time for beginning reading instruction. It is important to note that some of the pre-reading skills discussed above continue to develop once formal reading instruction begins. One goal of early reading instruction is **word recognition**, or being able to pronounce a word from print. This may involve using the alphabetic code or recog-

Concepts of Print

Student Name ______________________________

Use any children's book for this assessment. Ask the child to point out different features of the book or its text. Mark the student's responses as correct or incorrect.

Features of Books

1. _____ Identifies book cover
2. _____ Identifies book title
3. _____ Identifies book author
4. _____ Identifies illustrator
5. _____ Identifies beginning and end of book
6. _____ Can point out direction for reading (left-to-right orientation)

Features of Text

7. _____ Identifies a sentence on a page
8. _____ Identifies the beginning and end of a sentence
9. _____ Identifies a capital letter
10. _____ Can point out punctuation such as period, comma, question mark
11. _____ Can point out a single word
12. _____ Can point out individual letters within words

Ask the following question and record the student's response:
"What are books for?"

FIGURE 6.3 Concepts of Print Checklist

Decoding Using the alphabetic code, or letter-sound correspondence and/or word structure, to arrive at the correct pronunciation of a word.

nizing a word from memory. Using the alphabetic code, or letter-sound correspondence, to arrive at the correct pronunciation of a word is called **decoding** (Cunningham & Stanovich, 1997). It is actually "phonological recoding," meaning that children "recode" strings of letters into the sounds they represent, store them in short-term memory, and blend them into connected sounds to make words (Ehri, 1991; Chard et al., 1998). Phonics instruction encompasses all of this—teaching the letters and sounds, letter combinations, rules that govern pronunciation, and how to blend sounds into words. The goal is *automaticity,* or being able to process the letters and sounds almost automatically, with little effort.

TABLE 6.2 Typical Emergent Literacy Instructional Activities Included in Basal Reading Programs

CONCEPTS	TYPICAL ACTIVITIES
Read-aloud	Various read-aloud activities, familiarizing students with books and their features
Oral language	Language concepts, vocabulary, background knowledge, listening comprehension
Phonemic awareness	Games and oral activities focusing on words and phonemic elements, segmenting and blending, syllabication, rhyming,
Letter recognition, sound–symbol relationships	Isolating letters and sounds, using pictures and known symbol words to associate sounds with letters
Writing	Tracing, copying, printing, handwriting, composing, journals
Print awareness	Exposure to print in various forms and media

Source: Adapted from Snow, Burns, & Griffin (1998).

Guidelines for Phonics Instruction. Phonics instruction has an increasing presence in today's elementary classrooms. In past years, it was embedded in more holistic reading and writing experiences. With recent evidence that fluent, automatic decoding skills are characteristic of skilled readers (e.g., Fletcher & Lyon, 1998; Foorman, Francis, Fletcher, Schatschneider, & Mehta, 1997), schools and districts have demanded that teachers include systematic explicit phonics instruction in the primary grades. What constitutes good phonics instruction? Following are general guidelines adapted from Moats (1999b):

1. *Teach speech to print, not print to speech.* "Teach children a sound, then anchor the sound to a grapheme (letter, letter group, or letter sequence)" (p. 241) to avoid confusion of letters that make multiple sounds. Many reading programs teach the other way around—teaching a letter and then the sound it makes. However, when students encounter counterexamples, words in which the letter has an alternate sound, it leads to confusion. Moats further suggests teaching high-utility/low-complexity consonant and vowel units first and moving gradually to less common and more complex graphemes.

2. *Teach explicitly and systematically.* Teach in a logical order, going from simple to complex, and teaching predictable and common letter-sound combinations before variant letter-sounds. Moats suggests teaching no more than one linguistic concept at a time. Furthermore, she recommends following introduction of the letter-sound with experience reading it in words, sentences, and passages. Explicit instruction leaves little to chance. It means contolling the learning situation so that there is no confusion about what the concept is. Systematic instruction means moving sequentially through a series of skills and providing regular, planned instruction. Teachers should use "decodable books" that contain the phonic elements taught to provide students with opportunities for practice of learned concepts.

3. *Teach pattern recognition, not rule memorization.* The linguistic patterns in written English come from its historical roots. There are too many rules, many obscure and little used, to remember them all. We learn spelling patterns from consistent exposure to and practice with them. Moats suggests, for example, explaining to students that "aw" and "au" are two ways to spell the /aw/ sound and giving extensive examples of words containing these patterns.

4. *Encourage active, constructive exploration of words and sounds.* Good teachers find multiple ways for students to be actively engaged and responding during instruction. This principle holds true for phonics instruction. Activities that lead to students' reflection on word patterns and how words are similar and different from others leads to internalizing the concepts. Furthermore, when students write words, manipulate letter tiles, or use hand movements, they are engaged and attentive. Having to select, classify, and consciously manipulate sounds and letters leads students to become active decision makers in the decoding process.

5. *Anticipate, prevent, and correct confusions.* Teachers need to have depth of knowledge about the language structure to anticipate where students may experience difficulty and craft the experience to avoid confusion. For example, some consonant pairs are similar in how the sounds are produced and are easily confused in children's writing—such as /p/ and /b/, as in "pest" and "best." A savvy teacher may provide an activity that purposefully contrasts these sounds, such as having children sort picture cards into two piles, one for words beginning with /b/ and one for /p/.

6. *Provide corrective feedback.* As children are reading and writing, it is important for teachers to provide immediate, specific feedback to avoid prolonged confusion. When a student misreads a word, for example, due to confusion about a phonics element (e.g., reading "net" for "neat," misreading the vowel sound), the teacher should give *specific* feedback rather than just correcting the whole word. The teacher might point out the "ea" letter combination and inquire about its sound to point out exactly where the child experienced trouble in the word.

7. *Move from the known to the new, building on students' prior knowledge about word patterns.* As your students develop some knowledge of the code, you can build on what they already know. For example, students often pick up the letter sound for the letter that begins their own name or those of peers. They may also recognize letters from their own experiences, environmental print, or known sight words. For example, most students have seen a stop sign on the way to school. The teacher might this out when teaching the letter "s."

Some general guidelines to keep in mind are:

- Phonics instruction should be *systematic,* occurring in a set routine during specified blocks of time daily.

- Phonics instruction should be *sequential*. We recommend purchasing a phonics program that follows a sequence similar to the one in Figure 6.4 below. A good phonics program will organize the skills sequentially so that instruction continually builds on students' existing knowledge.
- Phonics instruction should be *explicit*. Though it is good to reinforce phonics concepts throughout the entire reading/language arts instructional block, there must be a portion of time set aside for explicit, intentional instruction in phonics concepts.
- Phonics instruction must have ongoing *review* built in. Students should have opportunities to decode words containing previously learned concepts.

Phonics Sequence. Figure 6.4 shows a sample scope and sequence for teaching phonics concepts. When looking for a reading program or supplemental materials to teach phonics, this would be a good sequence to follow.

Sight Words. Reading is more efficient when we learn to recognize high-frequency words by sight rather than having to decode them sound by sound. These words are accessed from long-term memory, and we use the visual representation of the word to retrieve it. About 50 percent of the words young children encounter in typical reading passages come from the 100 most frequently used words (Calkins, 2001). Knowing these words automatically enables the reader to focus more attention on the words that must be decoded through letter-sound correspondence. Many of the sight words are not decodable, but have irregular spelling patterns. Teachers often call them the "irregular" words. With frequent and consistent practice, children will become fluent with these words in their reading and writing. A common classroom activity for teaching sight words is the use of a "word wall." Teachers pull words from reading passages and post them on the wall, usually alphabetically, for constant daily practice. We recommend "doing" the word wall rather than "having" a word wall—teachers who visit the wall in daily instruction, using it for practice and instruction, find their students learn the words.

Automaticity
Being able to process the reading of words automatically, with ease.

Automaticity is a related concept. When students can read a word with **automaticity**, it means they can read automatically or with ease, which leads to fluent reading and comprehension. According to Snow and colleagues (1998), students need to move beyond the initial level of reading to achieve fluency; this depends on sufficient practice with different texts. For a fluent reader, the process of reading a written words takes only a fraction of a second (LaBerge & Samuels, 1974). More than twenty years of research have demonstrated the important connection between the development of phonemic representations and fluent reading (Naslund, 1997). Beginning readers must have sufficient practice with decodable text, or text that they can read with ease, to develop automaticity. Providing many consistent opportunities for your students to read text that is easy for them will help your students build automaticity.

Shared Reading Experiences in the Primary Grades

The inclusion teacher must be aware of different types of classroom activities in order to figure out how to fit in with inclusion support. It is important for the inclusion teacher to know how to move in and out of various whole-class activities to provide support for the struggling readers. Sometimes it is important to stay back and observe the instruction and how individual students respond in order to know how to reinforce it later. Other times, it

Note: This chart only includes decoding concepts. This is not a comprehensive scope and sequence for *all* early reading skills. Sight word instruction, comprehension, and other important skills would be included in a comprehensive scope and sequence.

PREPRIMER:

Sound-symbol associations:

Consonants: b, c /k/, d, f, g /g/, h, j, l, m, n, p, r, s, t, w

Morphemes (word parts): Inflectional endings "s" (plurals—*dogs*) and "ed" *(called)*

PRIMER:

Sound-symbol associations:

Consonants: k, v, y, z

Consonant digraphs: ch, sh, th

Consonant blends: pl, st, tr

Short vowel sounds: a, e, i, o, u (i.e., as at the beginning of the words *apple, elephant, igloo, octopus, umbrella*)

Spelling patterns: ight, all

Generalizations:

- In vowel-consonant (vc) words, the vowel sound is usually short (e.g., *at, in, on, up*).
- In consonant-vowel-consonant (cvc) words, the vowel sound is usually short (e.g., *cap, net, him, mop, nut*).

Context clues: Using semantic and syntactic cues to recognize unknown words

Morphemes:

Inflectional endings "s" (third person singular verbs—*eats*), "d" (*liked*), "es" (*boxes*), "s" (possessive—*Tom's*), "er" (comparative—*faster*)

Suffix "er" *(farmer)*

FIRST GRADE:

Sound-symbol associations:

Consonant: x

Consonant digraphs: wh /w/, kn /n/, wr /r/, ck /k/

Consonant blends: br, cr, dr, fr, gr, bl, cl, fl, sl, sc, tw, ld, nd

FIGURE 6.4 A Sample Scope and Sequence for Acquiring Decoding Skills.*

(continues)

Short vowels: y

Long vowels: a, e, i, o, u, y

Vowel digraphs: ay, ea (as in *eat* and as in *head*), ee, oa, ow (as in *row*)

Vowel diphthongs: oi, oy, ow (as in *cow*)

Spelling patterns: alk, eigh

Generalizations:

- In the initial position, "y" represents a consonant sound, in other positions, a vowel sound.
- In consonant-vowel-consonant-silent "e" (cvce) words, the initial vowel sound is usually long (e.g., *game, bite, hope, cube*).
- In consonant-consonant-vowel-consonant (ccvc) words, the vowel sound is usually short (e.g., *clap, sled, trip, frog, plum*).
- In two-syllable words where each syllable is formed from a cvc pattern, the vowel sounds are usually short (e.g., *butter, happen*).

Morphemes:

Inflectional endings "ing" *(walking)* and "est" *(fastest)*

Compound words: A longer word composed of two known shorter words

Contractions: not = n't *(doesn't),* will = 'll *(I'll)*

SECOND GRADE:

Sound-symbol associations:

Consonants: c /s/, g /j/

Consonant digraphs: ph /f/, tch /ch/, gn /n/, mb /m/, dge /j/

Consonant blends: gl, pr, qu, sk, sm, sn, sp, sw, scr, sch, str, squ, thr, lk, nk

Vowel digraphs: ai, oo (as in *look* and as in *too*), ey, ew, ei, ie, ue

Vowel diphthongs: ou, au, aw

Schwa (as the initial sound in *ago*)

r-controlled vowels: ar, er, ir, or, ur, oor (as in *door* and as in *poor*), ear (as in *year, earn, bear, heart*), our (as in *hour* and as in *four*)

Spelling pattern: ough (as in *through, though, thought, rough*)

Generalizations:

- When "'c" is followed by "e," "i," or "y," it usually represents a soft sound (as in *cent*).
- A single vowel letter at the end of an accented syllable usually represents its long sound.

FIGURE 6.4 Continued

- A single vowel letter followed by a single consonant (other than “v”) and a final “e” usually represents its long sound and the “e” is silent.

Morphemes:

Inflectional endings: “s” (*boys’*), “en” (*beaten*)

Prefix: “un”

Suffixes: “ful,” “fully,” “ish,” “less,” “ly,” “ness,” “self,” “y”

Contraction: have = ’ve (*I’ve*)

Recognizing words with spelling changes made when adding suffixes (when the final “e” is dropped—*hide/hiding,* “y” is changed to “i”—*baby/babies,* and a final consonant has been doubled—*sit/sitting*)

THIRD GRADE

Sound-symbol associations:

Consonant blends: spl, spr, ng

Morphemes:

Prefixes: “dis,” “ex,” “im,” “in,” “post,” “pre,” “re,” “sub,” “super”

Suffixes: “or” (as in *actor*), “ous,” “tion,” “sion,” “ment,” “ty,” “al,” “able”
Contractions: are = ’re *(they’re),* would/had = ’d *(I’d)*

* This scope and sequence chart provides a rough approximation of when many students acquire these decoding skills. Although the skills at earlier levels tend to be easier and are usually acquired before the skills at higher levels, it is not essential that they be learned in this order. This list can be used as a source for objectives and/or a checklist to determine what needs to reviewed or taught.

Source: Adapted from Harris & Sipay, 1990.

FIGURE 6.4 Continued

is necessary to intervene during instruction, sometimes providing prompts or reminders to students to help them stay focused or to provide immediate feedback. Depending on the teaching assignment and instructional arrangement, the general classroom teacher and the inclusion specialist may co-teach, swapping roles of delivering whole-class lessons and roaming around to provide individual support.

All students must have an opportunity to practice and integrate their newly acquired reading skills. Shared reading provides an occasion for students to interact with each other and the teacher about books. The primary goal of the shared reading experience is for children to learn to love books and stories. Students also learn that print conveys meaning. This is a type of activity in which students with disabilities may be able to participate without intervention or support. The teacher is doing the reading, so students’ lack of decoding skills will not be readily apparent. The inclusion teacher may want to revisit the books read during whole-class instruction later with individuals or small groups to provide the basis for individualized instruction in basic reading skills.

The shared reading experience has been found to be superior to round-robin reading in reducing young children's oral reading errors, improving their fluency, increasing their vocabulary acquisition, and improving their reading comprehension (Eldredge, Reutzel, & Hollingsworth, 1996). Other studies have also found that young children's word recognition abilities improve when they are assisted to read materials they are unable to read independently (Bridge, Winograd, & Haley, 1983; Eldredge & Quinn, 1988). Supported reading seems to have its greatest impact on the poorest readers (Eldredge et al., 1996).

Another way of giving students practice in reading is through the use of learning centers. Examples from a kindergarten classroom are described in Box 6.1.

BOX 6.1

CENTER-BASED LEARNING

Many teachers develop centers for moving small groups of students through learning activities. A teacher may have several centers set up, each with a specific purpose or learning objective. The special educator may need to provide individualized support for students with disabilities as they move to centers, and may need to modify activities to meet students' needs.

Following are examples of centers from a kindergarten classroom.

- The *classroom library* contains not only a wide array of books (about 500 including multiple copies), but also colorful beanbag chairs that invite students to put their feet up with a good book.
- The *listening/recording center* contains recorded versions of many stories and other books. Some of these are commercial materials; others have been recorded by students, teachers, and parents. Students assigned to this center might listen to a story or they might record a story (typically, the center is used for listening/reading along during independent reading time and for recording stories during center time).
- The *alphabet center* has one or two activities in this center that change frequently and are designed to reinforce the sounds and letters introduced or reviewed in other contexts.
- The *production center* includes props and materials for creating various types of theatrical reenactments of stories students have read.
- The *computer center* allows students to create their own stories, cartoons, or movies, and play learning games.
- The *writing/publication center* contains all of the supplies needed to publish books (including paper, construction paper, tagboard, and contact paper for bookcovers, staplers, and even an old sewing machine).
- An *art/illustration center* is adjacent to the writing/publication center. It includes various types of paper, markers, colored pencils, oil pastels, scissors, old magazines (for cutting out illustrations), tape, and glue. Occasionally, the teachers add watercolors and paintbrushes.

During center time, the teacher may post a schedule on the wall to indicate groups' movement through the centers. Teachers usually assign students to centers, but students can request a particular center, and occasionally the teacher may declare a free-choice day.

INCLUSION SUPPORT IN INTERMEDIATE-GRADE CLASSROOMS

In the intermediate grades of elementary school, students are expected to further develop their reading and writing skills. Increasingly, students use reading and writing as tools for learning in every subject. The volume of vocabulary learning increases as content area learning introduces technical terminology, and literature selections include sophisticated vocabulary. Comprehension, too, is an important focus of the intermediate grades. To facilitate inclusion, the special educator must be well-versed in vocabulary and comprehension strategies to help students with disabilities to be successful in the general education curriculum. Let's examine how an inclusion teacher works in an intermediate inclusion classroom.

Ms. Kelly, a special educator, and Mr. Carey, a general education teacher, co-teach for three hours in a fourth/fifth-grade inclusion classroom. Their class includes nine students with disabilities (seven with learning disabilities, five of whom have reading disabilities, one with an emotional/behavioral disorder, and one with mild mental retardation), eight low-achieving students, and ten average-achieving students. Ms. Kelly is a veteran special education teacher who is respected in her school and district as a specialist in literacy instruction.

Ms. Kelly and Mr. Carey strongly support an integrated constructivist curriculum for the intermediate grades, but they also believe they must provide extensive, explicit instruction in fundamental reading and writing skills. They have a two-hour literacy block but do not believe that literacy is only taught during this time period. Their students read and write throughout the day, beginning by reading the Word of the Day when they first enter the room and finishing by writing one thing they learned that day and one question left unanswered on a "What I Learned Today" card.

During the literacy block, the first half hour is a whole-class lesson featuring introduction of the passage students will read in groups, preteaching of important vocabulary words, review of previously learned comprehension or word analysis skills, and an explanation of a specific skill or strategy to be taught in the day's lesson. Following the whole-class discussion, Mr. Carey divides the class into groups. The groups remain stable throughout an instructional unit over several weeks, but will change as a result of end-of-unit assessments or in conference with Ms. Kelly about specific students. There are three groups.

During the next hour, there are three 20-minute periods for group work. The largest group is composed of average and above-average readers. These students typically read a passage and then spend 15 to 20 minutes with Mr. Carey to go over the day's lesson. Ms. Kelly does not work with this group but may help individuals as needed. Mr. Carey discusses vocabulary and comprehension strategies with the group and answers any questions, then the group works in pairs or independently on assigned reading work. The group may check back in with Mr. Carey at the end of the hour to report progress or clear up any questions. The other two groups consist of students with disabilities and other students who are likely to need more direct assistance and support. Ms. Kelly works with one group for 20 minutes and then with the other group. Mr. Carey also works with these two groups in 20-minute blocks. The two lower performing groups then receive 40 minutes of small group instruction, 20 with each teacher, and have 20 minutes of paired or independent work time. Because Ms. Kelly only sees two groups, she has an additional 20 minutes to pull aside individual students who need additional assistance completing assignments or assessment.

The final half hour of the reading block varies in format. Sometimes Mr. Carey pulls the whole class back together to go over decoding, vocabulary, or comprehension strategies. Sometimes the students have a writing assignment related to the story and both teachers rotate around to provide individual support. During this final half hour, Mr. Carey and Ms. Kelly usually grab a few minutes to confer with each other and make any adjustments to the next day's plans. Ms. Kelly keeps a plan book that outlines what her responsibilities are for the week and makes notes about her consultation with Mr. Carey.

Including students with disabilities in reading instruction in the intermediate grades provides a rich and stimulating learning environment for students with disabilities. However, it poses challenges when the reading material or vocabulary words are too difficult for students who struggle with reading. Whether the class is tackling tough subject matter or rich literature, it takes great sensitivity and skill to ensure that these students can participate meaningfully in activities with their peers. Following are some suggestions for helping students with reading-related disabilities to have meaningful learning experiences along with the general education class.

Making Difficult Books Accessible

As noted by Fielding and Roller (1992), some students do not want to read the books they can read and cannot read the books they want to read. Many children are quite self-conscious about the level of their books and do not want to appear to be reading "baby" books. Yet, a supportive and noncompetitive classroom environment, in which students regularly select books of a wide range of difficulty levels, can do much to remove the stigma of reading "easy" books (Fielding & Roller, 1992).

When a student is motivated to read a certain book and has a purpose for reading, such as finding out information about a selected topic, reading a too-hard book can be a rewarding and successful experience. All students, even those with severe reading disabilities, should be able to participate in shared activities with grade-level literature. There are various approaches to this (Roller, 1996). The following are listed in order from the easiest for students to the most challenging:

- *Tape-recorded books* allow the student to read along while listening to a recording of a book. Many audiobooks are available commercially or from Recordings for the Blind, an organization that provides recorded print material for students with learning disabilities.
- *Partner reading* is technique in which a more able reader is paired with a less able reader. The stronger reader reads the text orally, and the second reader chimes in and reads along when able, following along with his or her finger.
- *Choral reading* is similar to partner reading, except that it involves a group of students reading a passage in unison.
- *Rereading* of a familiar text develops reading rate and word-recognition accuracy (Dowhower, 1987, 1989). When a student has already listened to a book and is familiar with its content and vocabulary, reading the book independently becomes easier.

- *Paired reading* is when two readers take turns reading a passage or story. The more able reader reads first, followed by the less able reader. The more able reader assists the second reader as needed. Classwide Peer Tutoring, described below (Fuchs, Fuchs, & Mathes, 1997), includes a highly structured version of paired reading.
- *Preceding difficult books with easier books* on the same topic or theme is another way of making books accessible to students (Roller, 1996). Students learn key vocabulary and concepts making it easier when reading about similar information in a harder book.

Improving Fluency and Strengthening Word Recognition Skills

An important goal of literacy instruction is improving students' reading fluency. Once a student has read fluently and understands that reading should sound like spoken language, he or she is ready to extend reading fluency to an increasingly wider range of materials. Rhodes and Dudley-Marling (1988) described two techniques for helping students with reading disabilities develop fluency: assisted reading and repeated reading.

Assisted reading provides students with a model of what fluent text should sound like while at the same time increasing their understanding of the material (Bos, 1982). The technique requires the teacher or another fluent reader to read a text aloud smoothly and evenly while the student reads along. The reading of the text should not be interrupted to discuss individual words—the goal is for the student to experience the text as a coherent whole. Repeated reading simply means that the student reads the same text over and over until he or she can read it fluently.

Peer-Assisted Learning Strategies (PALS; Delquadri, Greenwood, & Whorton, 1986; Fuchs, Fuchs, & Mathes, 1997). PALS is a supplemental reading activity that is ideal for large, heterogeneous, inclusive classrooms. One average or high reader is paired with a lower student for a period of about four weeks. To pair students for PALS, teachers would use oral reading fluency scores to rank students in the whole class from highest to lowest. Splitting the list in half, so there is a more fluent group and a less fluent group, teachers would pair the highest from each group, the second-highest from each group, and so on, until the lowest from each group is paired. Each pair has a more fluent and less fluent reader but the gap between them is not large. Reading materials are geared to the level of the lower reader. Pairs engage in partner reading and take turns in the roles of reader and coach. Students work with a carefully developed script that helps them to follow a sequence of activities and to provide specific feedback in constructive ways. Students earn points as they successfully complete activities. Activities include Partner Reading, Retelling, Paragraph Shrinking, and Prediction Relay.

With Partner Reading, the stronger reader reads aloud for 5 minutes. The weaker reader then reads the *same* text aloud for 5 minutes. Whenever either reader makes a mistake (i.e., says the wrong word, leaves out a word, adds a word, or waits longer than 4 seconds), the other student, as the coach, says, "Stop, you missed that word. Can you figure it out?" The coach then waits 4 seconds, and if the reader has not correctly read the word, says, "That word is ____. What word?" After the reader repeats the word, the coach replies, "Good. Read the sentence again." After the weaker reader has read for 5 minutes, for 1 or 2 minutes he or she sequences the main ideas that have been read. The first (stronger) reader asks, "What did you learn first?" and then "What did you learn next?"

The next activity, Paragraph Shrinking, requires the stronger reader to read for 5 minutes, stopping after each paragraph to summarize what has just been read. The weaker reader then reads and summarizes paragraphs for an additional 5 minutes, continuing with new text rather than rereading the same text as the stronger reader. To prompt the summarization, or "shrinking" of each paragraph, the coach says, "Name the who or what. Tell the most important thing about the who or what. Say the main idea in 10 words or less."

For Prediction Relay, the stronger reader continues with new text, first making a prediction about what will happen next, then reading a half page, then stopping to check whether the prediction came true, then summarizing that half page, then predicting what will happen on the next half page, and finally continuing to read and repeating the whole process. When 5 minutes have elapsed, the weaker reader has a turn to predict, read, check, summarize, predict again, just as the first reader did, and also for 5 minutes.

PALS for Students with Special Needs. PALS has been used successfully in inclusion classrooms (Vaughn, Hughes, Schumm, & Klingner, 1998). No adaptations are needed for most students with disabilities; however, it is important to make sure the reading materials are at a level that can be read by the student. For emergent readers who cannot independently read text, PALS can be adapted by having the first reader read each sentence and the non-reader repeat the sentence immediately afterward.

Improving Critical Thinking Skills

Dialogical-Thinking Reading Lessons (D-TRLs) (Commeyras, 1993). D-TRLs promote reasoning and critical thinking as students learn to debate on behalf of their point of view. D-TRLs encourage students to (a) engage in reflective thinking as they decide what they believe about a story-specific issue, (b) return to the text to verify or clarify information, (c) consider multiple interpretations, (d) identify reasons to support their interpretations, and (e) evaluate the acceptability and relevance of alternative interpretations. Commeyras has used this approach effectively with students with LD (1991), and found that it "led students who struggle to read to engage with text in ways that are associated with proficient reading and thinking" (Commeyras, 1993, p. 487).

A D-TRL lesson is composed of two phases, the reading phase and the discussion phase. During the reading phase, students may read an entire story or chapter on their own. Or, to support students who might find this difficult, the teacher might use a guided reading approach, silently reading one page at a time and summarizing after each page. The discussion phase involves many steps. It begins when the teacher introduces the day's central question and two hypothesized conclusions and writes these on the board or a transparency.

D-TRL for Students with Special Needs. Students with learning disabilities have used this approach successfully (Commeyras, 1991). Yet some modifications may make it easier for certain students. To simplify D-TRL, concentrate on identifying reasons to support the two hypothesized conclusions rather than identifying *and* evaluating reasons. Some students might benefit from the teacher's modeling of this procedure (e.g., selecting different reasons rather than restating those already suggested). Starting with shorter passages simplifies the task for students, as does providing page numbers that indicate where reasons are located. Once students have become proficient at identifying reasons, then they can move on to evaluating them.

Enhancing Comprehension

Successful comprehenders have developed metacognitive awareness and are able to monitor their understanding and use various strategies to remediate problems and improve their comprehension. However, many students with high-incidence disabilities have difficulty with comprehension. Their lack of knowledge about when and how to apply strategies prevents them from using their abilities to their full advantage (Baker & Brown, 1984; Pressley, El-Dinary, & Afflerbach, 1995). Many strategies have been developed to improve the understanding, storage, and retrieval of complex information (Mastropieri & Scruggs, 2002; Pressley, Brown, El-Dinary, & Afflerbach, 1995; Scruggs & Mastropieri, 2003; Swanson & Hoskyn, 2000). In this section we describe Transactional Strategies Instruction, Reciprocal Teaching, and Story Mapping because they have been applied extensively with narrative text. Note that these approaches share many overlapping features.

Transactional Strategies Instruction (Pressley, El-Dinary, Gaskins, Schuder, Bergman, Almasi, & Brown, 1992). This is a long-term approach to comprehension strategies instruction. These authors identified the characteristics of effective strategy instruction:

1. Strategy instruction is ongoing and integrated with other forms of instruction.
2. Teachers make explicit the connection between active, strategic thinking and academic success.
3. Effective strategies instruction emphasizes the flexible application of a repertoire of strategies rather than the use of single strategies in isolation.
4. Teachers introduce strategies one at a time and provide opportunities for practice with authentic texts. Teachers explain strategies, model their use, and provide hints and additional explanations as needed.
5. Much of strategy instruction occurs in small groups. Students learn to think aloud as they read, apply strategies, and discuss what they are learning. Students react, interpret, and offer alternative points of view.
6. Students learn that people make meaning from what they read based on their own experiences and evaluations of text. The meaning that emerges from a group is the synthesis of the reactions from all the persons in that group.

Through modeling, think-alouds, and coaching, students are taught to use various strategies to monitor their comprehension and solve problems while reading children's literature ("just like good readers do"). Students learn to ask themselves various questions as they read.

Reciprocal Teaching. This strategy was designed by Palincsar and Brown (1984; Palincsar, 1986; Palincsar, Brown, & Martin, 1987) to improve comprehension for students who are adequate decoders but poor comprehenders. Students learn to use four comprehension strategies that are representative of the kinds of activities successful readers engage in while interacting with text: prediction, summarization, question generation, and clarification. The strategies are not learned and practiced in isolation but are taught in the context of reading for real purposes. Lessons are teacher-directed at first, with a great deal of modeling and prompting. As students develop proficiency applying the strategies, the teacher gradually turns control over to students and they lead discussions about text content. A more detailed description of the four strategies follows.

1. *Predicting*: Students find clues in the structure and content of a passage that suggest what might happen next. Predicting activates prior knowledge and also motivates students to continue reading to determine if their predictions were correct. Students learn to use a story's title to make initial predictions and then to use clues in the unfolding story to make additional predictions as they continue to read.
2. *Clarifying*: Students learn to discern when there is a breakdown in comprehension and take steps to restore understanding. Clarifying assures that the passage will make sense to the reader. Students are instructed to be alert to occasions when they do not understand the meaning of what they are reading. They learn that when this occurs they should process the text again. Students learn that if a word does not make sense they should try to define the word by reading the sentences before and after the word looking for context clues. If, after rereading the passage they still do not understand, they are instructed to request assistance.
3. *Summarizing*: Students use one or two sentences to tell the most important ideas in a passage in "their own words." They learn to include only the most important ideas and to leave out unimportant details. Summarizing can improve understanding and help students remember what they have read. Students are instructed to find the topic sentence in a paragraph. If they cannot find a topic sentence, they are taught to make up their own by combining sentences they have underlined as containing the most relevant ideas in the paragraph. Students learn to locate the most important details that support the topic sentence and to leave out information that is unimportant or redundant. Finally, they are instructed to restate the main idea and supporting details in their own words.
4. *Question Generating*: Students learn to construct questions about important information in the text rather than about unimportant details. Through question generation students self-test their understanding of the text and identify what is important in the story. Students are instructed to select important information from the text and use the words "who," "how," "when," "where," and "why" to begin their questions. They learn to ask about main ideas in the passage as well as important details. Students are encouraged to ask questions that involve higher level thinking skills rather than only literal recall.

To implement Reciprocal Teaching, the teacher first explains why it is important to learn comprehension strategies—to become better, more "strategic" readers. Comprehension strategies are the tactics that good readers use automatically to help them understand what they read. Following these purpose-setting statements, the teacher models the entire process of reading a passage and applying comprehension strategies. By demonstrating how to use all of the strategies on the first day, the teacher helps students get "the big picture" and understand the entire strategic reading process.

On the second day, the teacher again models the complete process of reading a passage and applying the strategies, providing students with the support necessary to implement the strategies and participate in a text-related discussion. On subsequent days, students are encouraged to take turns leading discussions in the role of "teacher," with the amount of support provided gradually decreasing as students become more proficient in leading discussions and applying the strategies. By about the eighth day of strategy instruction, it is likely that students will require minimal assistance. They have learned not only why, but also how and when to implement the strategies.

Comprehension strategies for expository text are covered in more detail in Chapter 9. Chapter 10 includes further information about literacy instruction in secondary schools.

PROVIDING INTENSIVE INTERVENTION FOR STRUGGLING READERS

The special educator, or inclusion specialist, must not only be well versed in various classroom practices but must also know how to make the most of short blocks of one-to-one or small group instruction. To minimize the student's loss of important shared experiences in the general classroom, you will probably allot only 20 to 30 minutes per day per group (or individual) to providing intensive reading intervention. This does not mean students are only getting a small amount of instructional time. We can assume they are learning a great deal from the general classroom. In this section we describe techniques for providing intensive instruction. This may occur at a table somewhere in the general education classroom, or you may pull the students out into a quiet room. Where the services take place matters less then the quality of the services provided.

Hit the "Big Ideas" of Reading

In a 20- to 30-minute intervention period, it is important to cover the most essential early reading skills. Gunn, Simmons, and Kameenui (1998) refer to the "big ideas" of emergent reading, or the basic building blocks. If students develop these foundational skills in the early stages of reading, they are more likely to develop into fluent readers. They identify four big ideas for emergent reading:

- Knowledge of the conventions and purposes of print
- Knowledge of the connection between oral and written language
- Phonological awareness
- Knowledge of letter-sound relationship

Beyond emergent reading and into the early reading skills covered in first through third grade reading levels, the big ideas would include five elements:

- Phonological awareness
- Alphabetic principle

- Fluency with reading connected text
- Vocabulary development
- Comprehension development

Because students are engaged in many different kinds of literacy experiences within the whole-class instruction, we want to be sure to devote the intervention session to the bare essentials. Focusing on the big ideas provides the foundational building blocks for your students to be successful in reading. Be sure to cover the essential skill areas of phonological awareness, letters and sounds (including blending), and reading words in connected text, while leaving some time at the end for language development and/or reading comprehension.

Starting Out with Beginning Readers

The Language Experience Approach (LEA) has been used successfully with emergent readers for many years (Allen, 1976; Ashton-Warner, 1963; Fry, 1977; Stauffer, 1980; Sulzby & Teale, 1991). We have found this to be an excellent way to get *nonreaders* started with beginning reading instruction. For students who have experienced failure in their initial reading experiences, it helps them to experience immediate success. It also shows the student how language and print connect intimately in the reading act.

LEA is a whole-to-part, constructivist approach that has been widely recommended for students with learning disabilities (Bender, 1996; Bos & Vaughn, 1994; Klingner & Nares, 1984) and for students acquiring English as a second language (Dixon & Nessel, 1983; Hudelson, 1989; Peregoy & Boyle, 1993; Rigg, 1986, 1989). Thus, it is appropriate for diverse, inclusion classrooms. LEA can be applied with an individual child, a small group of children, or an entire class. The student(s) dictate a story about an actual experience to a teacher, a teaching assistant, a parent volunteer, or a tutor. Next they copy the story (or trace it), illustrate it, and read it over and over. Thus, children's actual language becomes their reading material. This has several advantages: The students are familiar with all of the vocabulary used in the story, as well as the content and context of the story. They are motivated to read the story silently and to others; it is based on their interests and prior knowledge. They develop awareness of the connection between reading and writing: Written words are recorded speech, intended to convey meaning that can be read by others. Many students who have experienced difficulty learning letters and sounds in isolation (going from part to whole or letters to words) excel when they use this approach. Students are able to memorize their own story words, then they learn that a certain letter makes the sound at the beginning of a favorite word (e.g., "p" for "Power Rangers"). When they see the letter, they think of the word, and then they are able to make the association between symbol and sound.

Organizing Intervention Instruction: Working in Small Groups

Intervention is best when it is systematic, explicit, and intensive. This is provided through individual instruction or within a small homogeneous group. Using diagnostic assessment (covered in the next section), the inclusion specialist can place students into groups with similar needs and IEP goals. This is where the "specialness" of special education comes into play. Within small groups, the intervention specialist provides the specialized instruction tailored to specific students and the skills they need most. For instance, in one of the classrooms served by Mr. Snow described earlier in the chapter, one group of students has a critical need for developing phonemic awareness skills, while another group is working primarily on letter-sound skills, including blending. In both groups, Mr. Snow will hit all the big ideas, but he will emphasize or spend more time on the specific skills needed by the groups. The groups overlap—two students participate in both groups because they are weak in both skill areas, and they seem to be benefiting more from the small-group instruction than from the whole-class activities. This maximizes their services from special education while still allowing them to be included in the general education classroom.

Interestingly, recent studies have shown that one-to-one tutoring is *not* necessarily more effective than small groups of about three students (Elbaum, Vaughn, Hughes, Moody, & Schumm, 2000; Polloway, Cronin, & Patton, 1986; Thurlow, Ysseldyke, Wotruba, & Algozzine, 1993). It is likely that the discussion among members of a small group related to the lesson content provides more of a forum for students to be actively engaged in the learning process than does one-to-one instruction. When students *talk* about something with their peers, they think about and process the information. A group provides a lively atmosphere for practicing skills.

Planning ahead is essential. The inclusion teacher is often moving from class to class and may need to carry materials from room to room. It is also important to plan *with* the classroom teacher to ensure that the intervention instruction not only meets the students' individual needs, but also complements what is going on in the classroom. Another important aspect of planning is to plan *where* to conduct intervention. A small table in a corner or in the back of the room will pull children away from the main stream of activity and avoid distractions.

Scheduling is another important organizational issue. As the inclusion teacher organizes the special education services within the general education classroom(s), it is important to be both flexible and firm. First, the inclusion teacher must be willing to work around the events and activities planned for the general education classroom. Though classroom teachers generally follow a schedule, particularly for reading/language arts instruction, special events and activities sometimes make it necessary for the inclusion teacher to make scheduling changes. Also, specific needs may arise for individual students, and the inclusion teacher may want to make adjustments to give certain groups more or less time. However, it is also necessary to be firm in ensuring that all students with IEPs receive their full services. If changes to the schedule become too frequent, it is important for the inclusion teacher to advocate for maintaining consistency and quality in the special education services.

Special education teachers have a serious responsibility for accountability. It is important to keep detailed records of the services you provide to your students. Mr. Snow, who travels from room to room, keeps a log of his activities organized by classroom. He keeps a binder with a section for each class. Within each section, there is a separate page for each student on his roster. He notes the lesson objectives, activities, assessment conducted, consultation with the classroom teacher, and any other notes. Ms. Sousa, who works in only one classroom, keeps a joint lesson plan book with Ms. DaVoll. She keeps a separate column in the book to record any activities specific to the students with IEPs.

Ongoing Diagnostic Assessment

Diagnostic assessment Assessment to determine students' specific areas of strength and need.

In conducting intervention, it is important to know exactly what your students can and cannot do in terms of basic reading skills. Just as a doctor gathers information in order to know how to treat a patient, so must an intervention specialist conduct **diagnostic assessment** to determine students' specific reading skills. Chapter 3 contains information and guidelines for using assessment in an inclusive model. Here we want to show how assessment supports and guides reading intervention for students with disabilities.

There are many informal assessment tools available that can be used to guide intervention. These informal assessment tools should be used for two purposes: a) to identify students in need of additional instruction on specific skills, and b) to conduct ongoing monitoring of students' progress.

Benchmarks Predetermined levels of skill that indicate sufficient progress toward a goal.

For these purposes, you will need assessment tools that provide information about how a student is doing relative to a certain standard or goal. **Benchmarks** are predetermined levels of skill that indicate sufficient progress toward a goal. To identify students in need of intervention in a particular aspect of reading, we look for students who fall below the benchmark. Furthermore, to monitor progress, we look for students to reach the benchmark. Once they do, we go on to the next set of goals and begin to measure progress toward higher standards. The assessments you select should reflect your school's or district's curriculum or standards for grade-level instruction.

Just as intervention should be organized around the essential early reading skills, so assessment should focus on phonological awareness (and especially phonemic awareness), letter-sound relationships, and reading fluency. We recommend conducting frequent assessment in these areas for the two purposes mentioned above. Frequent skill checks provide up-to-the-minute snapshots of students' progress in these areas.

For detailed information about students' daily instructional needs, teachers use *diagnostic* assessment tools such as checklists, skills surveys, and daily work samples. Phonics checklists are often included in commercially available informal reading inventories such as Bader (2001) and Ekwall and Shanker (2000). Many teachers have gathered informal checklists from various published and teacher-made sources. A good phonics checklist would ask students to read words containing sounds being assessed while the teacher checks off sounds read correctly. A phonemic awareness assessment would give oral tasks, such as phoneme blending or segmenting and the teacher would mark students' responses on a score sheet. Assessing letter-sound knowledge might be done with letter tiles or cards while the teacher marks on a score sheet. By examining the students' correct and incorrect responses, the teacher can plan instruction targeted at specific needed skills. Figure 6.5 shows an assessment system used in beginning reading to identify students for intervention and to guide instruction.

In recent years, many schools have used an assessment system called *Dynamic Indicators of Basic Early Literacy Skills,* or DIBELS, to identify students at risk for reading failure and for ongoing progress monitoring (Kaminski & Good, 1996). DIBELS was designed for use in kindergarten through fifth grade and consists of several subtests or tasks, each of which has been shown to be predictive of later reading outcomes. The predictive nature of the scores allows school personnel to identify students in need of intervention *before failure sets in.* Prevention of reading difficulty is much more desirable than remediation in later grades.

DIBELS is designed to assess students' fluency with fundamental reading skills. The DIBELS subtests represent constructs organized in a progression of foundational skills of early reading. These skills are prerequisite to reading success (Good, Kaminski, & Hill, 2000). The skill areas assessed are phonological awareness, alphabetic principle (letter-sound relationships), and fluency with connected text. The score for each task reflects the number of correct responses given in a timed minute. Each subtest takes only a minute, so an individual student can be assessed in 5 to 7 minutes, depending on how many subtests are given.

DIBELS has established benchmarks—levels that indicate sufficient progress with a particular skill such as phonemic awareness. The benchmarks have been established through several years of field testing.

The DIBELS materials are available free of charge online at *http://dibels.uoregon.edu.* The website shows the subtests given at different grades, the constructs measured, and the time period given.

FIGURE 6.5 Dynamic Indicators of Basic Early Literacy Skills

REFERENCES

Adams, M. J. (1990). *Beginning to read: Thinking and learning about print.* Cambridge, MA: MIT Press.

Adams, M. J., Foorman, B. R., Lundberg, I., & Beeler, T. (1998). *Phonemic awareness in young children: A classroom curriculum.* Baltimore, MD: Paul H. Brookes.

Adelman, H. S. (1989). Beyond the learning mystique: An interactional perspective on learning disabilities. *Journal of Learning Disabilities, 22,* 301–304.

Allen, R. V. (1976). *Language experiences in communication.* Boston: Houghton Mifflin.

American Federation of Teachers. (1999). *Teaching reading is rocket science: What expert teachers of reading should know and be able to do.* Item No. 39-0372. Washington, DC: Author.

Anderson, R. C., & Pearson, P. D. (1984). A schema-theoretic view of basic processes in reading comprehension. In P. D. Pearson (Ed.), *Handbook of reading research* (pp. 255–291). New York: Longman.

Ashton-Warner, S. (1963). *Teacher.* New York: Bantam Books.

Bader, L. (2001). *Bader reading and language inventory and readers passages* (4th ed.). Englewood Cliffs, NJ: Prentice-Hall.

Baker, L., & Brown, A. L. (1984). Metacognitive skills and reading. In P. D. Pearson (Ed.), *Handbook of research research* (pp. 491–572). New York: Longman.

Bakwin, H. (1973). Reading disability in twins. *Developmental Medicine and Child Neurology, 15,* 184–187.

Ball, E., & Blachman, B. (1991). Does phoneme awareness training in kindergarten make a difference in early word recognition and developmental spelling? *Reading Research Quarterly, 26,* 49–66.

Bender, W. N. (1996). *Teaaching students with mild disabilities.* Boston: Allyn and Bacon.

Bos, C. S. (1982). Getting past decoding: Assisted and repeated readings as remedial methods for learning disabled students. *Topics in Learning and Learning Disabilities, 1,* 51–75.

Bos, C. S., & Vaughn, S. (1994). *Strategies for teaching students with learning and behavior problems* (3rd ed.). Boston: Allyn and Bacon.

Bradley, L., & Bryant, P. (1985). *Rhyme and reason in reading and spelling*. Ann Arbor: University of Michigan Press.

Bridge, C., Winograd, P., & Haley, D. (1983). Using predictable materials versus preprimers to teach beginning sight words. *The Reading Teacher, 36,* 884–891.

California Department of Education. (1999). *English-language arts standards for California public schools: Kindergarten through grade twelve*. Sacramento, CA: Author.

Calkins, L. M. (2001). *The art of teaching reading*. New York: Longman.

Carnine, D. W., Silber, J., & Kameenui, E. J. (1997). *Direct instruction reading* (3rd ed.). Upper Saddle River, NJ: Merrill.

Chard, D. J., Simmons, D. C., & Kameenui, E. J. (1998). Word recognition: Research bases. In D. C. Simmons & E. J. Kameenui (Eds.), *What reading research tells us about children with diverse learning needs: Bases and basics* (pp. 141–167). Mahwah, NJ: Lawrence Erlbaum.

Clay, M. M. (1979). *Reading: The patterning of complex behavior.* Portsmouth, NH: Heinemann.

Commeyras, M. (1991). *Dialogical-thinking reading lessons: Promoting critical thinking among "learning disabled" students.* Unpublished doctoral dissertation, University of Illinois, Champaign.

Commeyras, M. (1993). Promoting critical thinking through dialogical-thinking reading lessons. *The Reading Teacher, 46,* 486–493.

Crowell, D., Kawakami, A., & Wong, J. (1986). Emerging literacy: Reading-writing experiences in a kindergarten classroom. *The Reading Teacher, 40,* 144–149.

Cunningham, A. (1990). Explicit vs. implicit instruction in phonemic awareness. *Journal of Experimental Child Psychology, 50,* 429–444.

Cunningham, A. E., & Stanovich, K. E. (1997). Early reading acquisition and its relation to reading experience and ability ten years later. *Developmental Psychology, 33* (6), 934–945.

Delquadri, J. C., Greenwood, C. R., & Whorton, D. (1986). *Exceptional Children, 52,* 535–542.

Dixon, C. N., & Nessel, D. (1983). *Language experience approach to reading (and writing).* Hayward, CA: Alemany.

Dowhower, S. L. (1987). Effects of repeated reading on second-grade transitional readers' fluency and comprehension. *Reading Research Quarterly, 22,* 389–406.

Dowhower, S. L. (1989). Repeated reading: Research into practice. *The Reading Teacher, 42,* 502–507.

Ehri, L. C. (1989). The development of spelling knowledge and its role in reading acquistion and reading disability. *Journal of Learning Disabilities, 22,* 356–365.

Ehri, L. C. (1991). Development of the ability to read words. In R. Barr, M. L. Kamil, P. B. Mosenthal, & P. D. Pearson (Eds.), *Handbook of reading research* (Vol. 2, pp. 383–417). New York: Longman.

Ekwall, J. L., & Shanker, E. E. (2000). *Ekwall/ Shanker Reading Inventory* (4th ed.). Boston: Allyn and Bacon.

Elbaum, B., Vaughn, S., Hughes, M. T., Moody, S. W., & Schumm, J. S. (2000). A meta-analytic review of the effect of instructional grouping format on the reading outcomes of students with disabilities. In R. Gersten, E. Schiller, J. S. Schumm, & S. Vaughn (Eds.), *Issues and research in special education* (pp. 105–135). Hillsdale, NJ: Lawrence Erlbaum.

Eldredge, J. L., & Quinn, W. (1988). Increasing reading performance of low-achieving second graders by using dyad reading groups. *Journal of Educational Research, 82,* 40–46.

Eldredge, J. L., Reutzel, D. R., & Hollingsworth, P. M. (1996). Comparing the effectiveness of two oral reading practices: Round-robin reading and the shared book experience. *Journal of Literacy Research, 28,* 201–225.

Englert, C. S., Rozendal, M. S., & Mariage, M. (1994). Fostering the search for understanding: A teacher's strategies for leading cognitive development in "zones of proximal development." *Learning Disability Quarterly, 17,* 187–204.

Farnan, N., Flood, J. & Lapp, D. (1994). Comprehending through reading and writing: Six research-based instructional strategies. In K. Spangenberg-Urbschat & R. Pritchard (Eds.), *Kids come in all languages: Reading instruction for ESL students* (pp. 135–157). Neward, DE: International Reading Association.

Fielding, L., & Roller, C. (1992). Making difficult books accessible and easy books acceptable. *The Reading Teacher, 45,* 678–685.

Fletcher, J., & Lyon, G. R. (1998). Reading: A research-based approach. In W. Evers (Ed.), *What's gone wrong in America's classrooms* (pp. 49–90). Stanford, CA: Hoover Institution Press.

Flood, J., & Lapp, D. (1988). A reader response approach to the teaching of literature. *Reading Research and Instruction, 27,* 61–66.

Foorman, B. R., Francis, D. J., Fletcher, J. M., Schatschneider, C., & Mehta, P. (1997). The role of instruction in learning to read: Preventing reading failure in at-risk children. *Journal of Educational Psychology, 90,* 1–15.

Fry, E. B. (1977). *Elementary reading instruction*. New York: McGraw-Hill.

Fuchs, D., Fuchs, L. S., & Mathes, P. G. (1997). Peer-assisted learning strategies: Making classrooms more responsive to diversity. *American Educational Research Journal, 34*, 174–206.

Goodman, K. S. (1967). Reading: A psycholinguistic guessing game. *Journal of Reading Specialist, 6*, 126–135.

Goodman, K. S. (1968). The psycholinguistic nature of the reading process. In K. S. Goodman (Ed.), *The psycholinguistic nature of the reading process* (pp. 13–26). Detroit, MI: Wayne State Press.

Goodman, K. S. (1985). Unity in reading. In H. Singer & R. B. Ruddell (Eds.), *Theoretical models and processes of reading* (3rd ed., pp. 813–840). Newark, DE: International Reading Association.

Goodman, K. S., & Goodman, Y. M. (1977). Learning about psycholinguistic processes by analyzing oral reading. *Harvard Education Review, 47*, 317–333.

Gough, P., Juel, C., & Griffith, P. (1992). Reading, spelling, and the orthographic cipher. In P. Gough, L. Ehri, & R. Treiman (Eds.), *Reading acquisition* (pp. 35–48). Hillsdale, NJ: Lawrence, Erlbaum.

Gough, P. B. (1985). One second of reading. In H. Singer & R. B. Ruddell (Eds.), *Theoretical models and processes of reading* (3rd ed., pp. 661–686). Newark, DE: International Reading Association.

Gunn, B. K., Simmons, D. C., & Kameenui, E. J. (1998). Emergent literacy: Instructional and curricular basics and implications. In D. C. Simmons & E. J. Kameenui (Eds.), *What reading research tells us about children with diverse learning needs: Bases and basics.* Mahwah, NJ: Lawrence Erlbaum.

Haager, D. (1997). Learning Disabilities. In J. Wood & A. Lazzari (Eds.), *Exceeding the boundaries: Understanding exceptional lives* (pp. 116–159). Ft. Worth, TX: Harcourt Brace.

Harris, A. J., & Sipay, E. R. (1990). *How to increase reading ability: A guide to developmental and remedial methods* (9th ed.). New York: Longman.

Harris, K. R., & Graham, S. (1996). Memo to constructivists: Skills count, too. *Educational Leadership, 53*(5), 26–29.

Heilman, A. W., Blair, T. R., & Rupley, W. H. (1994). *Principles and practices of teaching reading* (8th ed.). Upper Saddle River, NJ: Merrill/Prentice Hall.

Hinshelwood, J. (1917). *Congenital word blindness.* London: H. K. Lewis.

Hudelson, S. (1989). Write on: Children writing in ESL. Englewood Cliffs, NJ: Prentice-Hall Regents.

Juel, C. (1991). Cross-age tutoring between student athletes and at-risk children. *The Reading Teacher, 45*, 178–186.

Kaluger, G., & Kolson, C. J. (1978). *Reading and learning disabilities* (2nd ed.). Columbus, OH: Merrill.

Kaminski, R., & Good, R. H., III. (1996). Toward a technology for assessing basic early literacy skills. *School Psychology Review, 25*(2), 215–227.

Kirk, S. A., Kirk, W., & Minskoff, E. (1985). *Phonic remedial reading drills.* Novato, CA: Academic Therapy Publications.

Klingner, J. K., & Nares, I. (1984, January). *Intervention strategies for working with LEP/NEP students with learning disabilities.* Paper presented at the annual meeting of the California Association for Bilingual Education, San Francisco, CA.

Klingner, J. K., & Vaughn, S. (2002). The changing roles and responsibilities of an LD Specialist. *Learning Disability Quarterly, 25*, 19–31.

LaBerge, D., & Samuels, S. J. (1974). Toward a theory of automatic information processing in reading. *Cognitive Psychology, 6*, 293–323.

Mastropieri, M. A., & Scruggs, T. E. (2002). *Effective instruction for special education* (3rd ed.). Austin, TX: Pro-Ed.

Mercer, C. D. (1997). *Students with learning disabilities* (5th ed.). Upper Saddle River, NJ: Merrill.

Moats, L. C. (1999a). *Teaching reading IS rocket science: What expert teachers of reading should know and be able to do.* Washington, DC: American Federation of Teachers.

Moats, L. C. (1999b). Teaching decoding. In *Read all about it!* (pp. 237–248). Sacramento, CA: California State Board of Education. (Reprinted from *American Educator,* pp. 42–49, 95–96.)

Moats, L. C. (2002). *Preventing and treating reading, spelling and writing difficulties by using research-based practices.* Keynote address, Council for Learning Disabilities, Denver, CO.

Naslund, J. C. (1997). Automaticity and phonemic representations: Perceptual and cognitive building blocks for reading. *Reading & Writing Quarterly: Overcoming Learning Difficulties, 13*, 147–164.

National Reading Panel. (2000). *Reports of the Subgroups. Teaching children to read: An evidence-based assessment of the scientific research literature on reading and its implications for reading instruction.* Washington, DC: Author.

O'Connor, R., Jenkins, J., & Slocum, T. (1995). Transfer among phonological tasks in kindergarten: Essential instructional content. *Journal of Educational Psychology, 2,* 202–217.

O'Connor, R., Notari-Syverson, A., Vadasy, P. F. (1996). Ladders to literacy: The effects of teacher-led phonological activities for kindergarten children with and without disabilities. *Exceptional Children, 63,* 117–130.

Orton, S. T. (1937). *Reading, writing, and speech problems in children.* New York: W. W. Norton & Company.

Palincsar, A. S. (1986). The role of dialogue in providing scaffolded instruction. *Educational Psychologist, 21,* 73–98.

Palincsar, A. S., & Brown, A. L. (1984). The reciprocal teaching of comprehension-fostering and comprehension-monitoring activities. *Cognition and Instruction, 1,* 117–175.

Palincsar, A. S., Brown, A. L., & Martin, S. M. (1987). Peer interaction in reading comprehension instruction. *Educational Psychologist, 22,* 231–253.

Paris, S. G., Wasik, B. A., & Turner, J. C. (1991). The development of strategic readers. In R. Barr, M. L. Kamil, P. Mosenthal, & P. D. Pearson (Eds.), *The handbook of reading research, Volume II* (pp. 609–640). New York: Longman.

Polloway, E. A., Cronin, M. E., & Patton, J. R. (1986). The efficacy of group versus one-to-one instruction: A review. *Remedial and Special Education, 7,* 22–30.

Pressley, M., Brown, R., El-Dinary, P. B., & Afflerbach, P. (1995). The comprehension instruction that students need: Instruction fostering constructively responsive reading. *Learning Disabilities Research and Practice, 10,* 215–224.

Pressley, M., El-Dinary, P. B., & Afflerbach, P. (1995). The comprehension instruction that students need: Instruction fostering constructively responsive reading. *Learning Disabilities Research and Practice, 10,* 215–224.

Pressley, M., El-Dinary, P. B., Gaskins, I., Schuder, T., Bergman, J., Almasi, L., & Brown, R. (1992). Beyond direct explanation: Transactional instruction of reading comprehension strategies. *Elementary School Journal, 92,* 511–554.

Rhodes, L. K., & Dudley-Marling, C. (1988). *Readers and writers with a difference: A holistic approach to teaching learning disabled and remedial students.* Portsmouth, NH: Heinemann.

Rigg, P. (1986). Reading in ESL: Learning from kids. In P. Rigg & D. S. Enright (Eds.), *Children and ESL: Integrating perspectives.* Washington, DC: Teachers of English to Speakers of Other Languages.

Rigg, P. (1989). Language experience approach: Reading naturally. In P. Rigg & V. G. Allen (Eds.), *When they don't all speak English: Integrating the ESL student into the regular classroom.* Urbana, IL: National Council of Teachers of English.

Roller, C. (1996). *Variability not disability: Struggling readers in a workshop classroom.* Newark, DE: International Reading Association.

Rosenblatt, L. M. (1978). *The reader, the text, the poem: The transactional theory of the literary work.* Carbondale, IL: Southern Illinois University Press.

Rosner, S. L., Abrams, J. C., Daniels, P. R., & Schiffman, G. B. (1981). Dealing with the reading needs of the learning disabled child. *Journal of Learning Disabilities, 14,* 436–448.

Rothstein, R. (2001, September 5). Consensus in reading war if sides would only look. *New York Times* [On-line serial]. Available: NYTimes.com. Retrieved September 19, 2003.

Rumelhart, D. (1977). Toward an interactive model of reading. In S. Dornic (Ed.), *Attention and performance VI.* Hillsdale, NJ: Lawrence Erlbaum.

Scruggs, T. E., & Mastropieri, M. A. (2003). Science and social studies. In H. L. Swanson, K. R. Harris, & S. Graham (Eds.), *Handbook of learning disabilities*. New York: Guilford.

Share, D., Jorm, A., Maclean, R., & Matthews, R. (1984). Sources of individual differences in reading acquisition. *Journal of Educational Psychology, 76,* 1309–1324.

Share, D. L., & Stanovich, K. E. (1995). Cognitive processes in early reading development: Accommodating individual differences into a model of acquisition. *Issues in Education, 1,* 1–57.

Shaywitz, S. E., Shaywitz, B. A., Fletcher, J. M., & Escobar, M. D. (1990). Prevalence of reading disability in boys and girls: Results of the Connecticut Longitudinal Study. *Journal of the American Medical Association, 264,* 998–1002.

Short, K., & Klassen, C. (1993). Literature circles: Hearing children's voices. In B. Cullinan (Ed.), *Children's voices: Talk in the classroom* (pp. 66–85). Newark, DE: International Reading Association.

Simmons, D. C. & Kameenui, E. J. (1998). Introduction. In D. C. Simmons & E. J. Kameenui (Eds.), *What reading research tells us about children with diverse learning needs: Bases and basics* (pp. 1–19). Mahwah, NJ: Lawrence Erlbaum.

Slaughter, J. P. (1993). *Beyond storybooks: Young chil-*

dren and the shared book experience. Newark, DE: International Reading Association.

Smith, F., & Goodman, K. S. (1971). On the psycholinguistic method of teaching reading. *Elementary School Journal, 71,* 177–181.

Smith, S. B., Simmons, D. C., & Kameenui, E. J. (1998). Phonological awareness: Research bases. In D. C. Simmons & E. J. Kameenui (Eds.), *What reading research tells us about children with diverse learning needs: Bases and basics* (pp. 61–127). Mahwah, NJ: Lawrence Erlbaum.

Snow, C. E., Burns, M. S., & Griffin, P. (1998). *Preventing reading difficulties in young children.* Washington, DC: National Academy Press.

Stanovich, K. E. (1980). Toward an interactive-compensatory model of individual differences in the development of reading fluency. *Reading Research Quarterly, 16,* 32–71.

Stanovich, K. E. (1986). Matthew effects in reading: Some consequences of individual differences in the acquisition of literacy. *Reading Research Quarterly, 21,* 360–406.

Stauffer, R. G. (1980). *The language-experience approach to the teaching of reading* (2nd ed.). New York: Harper & Row.

Sulzby, E., & Teale, W. (1991). Emergent literacy. In R. Barr, M. L. Kamil, P. B. Mosenthal, & P. D. Pearson (Eds.), *Handbook of reading research* (Vol. 2, pp. 727–757). New York: Longman.

Swanson, H. L. (1987). Information processing theory and learning disabilities: An overview. *Journal of Learning Disabilities, 20,* 3–7.

Swanson, H. L., & Hoskyn, M. (2000). Intervention research for students with learning disabilities: A comprehensive meta-analysis of group design studies. In T. E. Scruggs & M. A. Mastropieri (Eds.), *Educational interventions: Advances in learning and behavioral disabilities* (Vol. 14, pp. 1–153). Oxfork, UK: Elsevier Science/JAI.

Texas Education Agency. (1997). *Texas essential knowledge and skills for English language arts and reading* (Texas Administrative Code, Title 19, Part II, Chapter 110). Austin, TX: Author.

Thurlow, M. L., Ysseldyke, J. E., Wotruba, J. W., & Algozzine, B. (1993). Instruction in special education classrooms under varying student-teacher ratios. *The Elementary School Journal, 93,* 305–320.

Torgesen, J., Morgan, S., & Davis, C. (1992). Effects of two types of phonological awareness training on word learning in kindergarten children. *Journal of Educational Psychology, 84,* 364–370.

Torgesen, J. K., Wagner, R. K., & Rashotte, C. A. (1994). Longitudinal studies of phonological processing and reading. *Journal of Learning Disabilities, 27,* 276–286.

Vaughn, S., Hughes, M. T., Schumm, J. S., & Klingner, J. (1998). A collaborative effort to enhance reading and writing. *Learning Disability Quarterly,* 21, 57–74.

Vygotsky, L. S. (1986). *Thought and language.* Cambridge, MA: MIT Press.

Wagner, R. K., & Torgesen, J. K. (1987). The nature of phonological processing and its causal role in the acquisition of reading skills. *Psychological Bulletins, 101,* 192–212.

Wagner, R. K., Torgesen, J. K., Laughon, P., Simmons, K., & Raschotte, C. A. (1993). Development of young readers' phonological processing abilities. *Journal of Educational Psychology, 85,* 83–103.

Wertsch, J. V. (1985). *Vygotsky and the social formation of mind.* Cambridge, MA: Harvard University Press.

CHAPTER SEVEN

WRITING INSTRUCTION IN INCLUSIVE CLASSROOMS

It has been said that the two most precious gifts an adult can give a child are roots and wings: a solid foundation coupled with the courage and confidence to pursue big dreams.

—Fletcher, 1993, p. 8

KEY CONCEPTS

- Writer's Workshop includes several components: Prewriting, Drafting, Revising, Editing, Publishing, Mini-lessons, Writing Conferences, and Sharing.
- Students with disabilities benefit from explicit instruction in strategies that help them plan, organize, and revise their writing.
- It is important to teach different genres of writing (e.g., expressive and informative writing, persuasive essays, and narratives).
- Interactive Journals/Dialogue Journals can be a valuable tool in inclusive classrooms, providing students with individualized support at their instructional level.

- Assessment of students' writing should take place regularly, by routinely observing students as they write and by collecting regular writing samples.
- Spelling is a developmental process—children progress through various stages along a continuum as they develop proficiency.

FOCUS QUESTIONS

1. Why should we teach writing using a writing process approach?
2. What are the key components of Writer's Workshop?
3. Why should we teach planning and revising strategies?
4. What are the teachers' roles in a Writer's Workshop inclusive classroom?
5. What does a "community of writers" look like?
6. How can students with disabilities get the support they need as they develop as writers in an inclusive classroom?
7. Do students with disabilities receive individualized instruction in a Writer's Workshop inclusive classroom? Explain.
8. How might Dialogue Journals be implemented in a Writer's Workshop inclusive classroom?
9. How will you provide spelling assistance for students with learning and other disabilities?

Ms. Rivera is a special education teacher working in an inclusion program for the first time. Writing has become her favorite subject to teach. She feels that nothing else is quite like writing for empowering students, for awakening in them the conviction that their thoughts, feelings, and ideas have value, matter to someone, and count for something. Many of her students with learning disabilities previously had thought that writing mostly meant forming letters correctly, capitalizing the first word in a sentence, putting a period or something else at the end of a sentence, and spelling words right. They had experienced too many write-about-what-you-did-last-summer-type assignments and received too many papers back filled with red-ink corrections. When her students realized that writing means being an author, reflecting, creating, informing, and sharing, they truly became inspired. And as they became inspired, they became motivated not only to write more, but to read more, and to learn more. All of Ms. Rivera's students with learning and other disabilities write—a lot. They are an integral part of the community of writers in their classrooms.

Writing is infused throughout the curriculum in Ms. Rivera's classes. Writer's Workshop is the key component of her program, along with writing strategies. Her students write and publish books that they take home or put in the classroom or school library. They write fiction and non-fiction, letters, plays, poetry, newspaper articles, and more. She and her co-teachers teach reading and writing through the content areas, and the content areas through reading and writing, using thematic units. Students use planning routines to enhance their writing. Ms. Rivera's students are engaged in motivating, meaningful activities. They are writing for real purposes in authentic contexts. They are learning.

During the previous summer vacation, Ms. Rivera had attended a district-sponsored two-week workshop on writing. She felt the workshop had been somewhat like a religious experience, inspiring her to try new ways of teaching writing in her classroom. She was anxious for the new school year to begin so that she could put into practice what she had learned. She hoped to implement Writer's Workshop, to use Learning Logs and Interactive Journals, and to try new ways of expanding writing skills. But she was apprehensive, too, because she would be co-teaching for the first time. Instead of pulling all of her students to the resource room for special assistance as she had done for several years, she would be working with most of her students in their general education classrooms, teaching in Ms. Murphy's fourth-grade class for two hours in the morning and in Mr. Wilson's third-grade class for two and a half hours in the afternoon. Mr. Wilson's and Ms. Murphy's teaching styles were quite different. Mr. Wilson had taught full-time for one year. He was quite structured and very well organized. He liked to be in charge in his classroom, managing his students with firmness and fairness. He expected students to work quietly at their seats and discouraged talking among students, even if the talk was task-related. Ms. Rivera knew she would need to be careful not to step on Mr. Wilson's toes and that co-teaching with someone not accustomed to sharing center stage might be difficult. But she also knew that if she and Mr. Wilson didn't learn to work together, her students would have difficulty achieving success in his classroom. During the summer, she had called Mr. Wilson and talked to him about her ideas for teaching writing. At first he was reluctant to give up the English (writing) textbook he had been using and voiced his concern that Writer's Workshop sounded too unstructured and not sufficiently skill-based. Yet he respected Ms. Rivera; some of his students had attended her resource room the year before and had made remarkable progress. Also, he had learned a little about Writer's Workshop in a university class and was curious to find out more. He felt writing had been his weakest subject the previous year, so he agreed to let Ms. Rivera take the lead with writing instruction, and in exchange he offered to take the lead with mathematics, a subject he considered to be a strength.

Ms. Murphy, on the other hand, was a veteran teacher who was quite comfortable with her existing writing program. She was proud that almost all of her fourth-graders usually wrote well-formed, correctly punctuated paragraphs by the end of the year and could write in a variety of genres. Yet Ms. Murphy was concerned that a few of her lowest students never seemed to get past writing a few sentences and that some students clearly did not enjoy writing. Also, fourth grade was the year students took a state-mandated high-stakes writing assessment. Ms. Murphy was a creative, vibrant, effective teacher. Ms. Rivera felt optimistic about working in her classroom and was excited about learning from such an experienced well-respected teacher, but she knew that because Ms. Murphy was somewhat set in her ways, the danger existed that she might be perceived more as a classroom aide than a co-teacher. When the two teachers met before the school year began, Ms. Rivera shared her ideas about teaching writing. At first Ms. Murphy was somewhat reluctant to alter her existing approach. She felt bound by curriculum requirements to teach personal-experience narratives, short stories or plays, poems, reports, and persuasive essays and was worried about covering all of these different types of writing so that students would be prepared for their writing test. Ms. Rivera explained how these are addressed in Writer's Workshop, and Ms. Murphy eventually agreed to give it a try. The two teachers decided to take turns in the lead role. One teacher would direct a discussion or teach a mini-lesson (see the section on Mini-Lessons) while the other would write ideas on the chalkboard or circulate among the students, providing assistance. Both teachers would regularly conference with students about their writing. As the teachers discussed how to co-teach writing, listening to each other's ideas and offering suggestions, they gained increased respect for one another. Their apprehensions lessened and their excitement about the upcoming year grew.

In the following pages we discuss the various approaches for teaching writing implemented by Ms. Rivera and her co-teachers. We present sample lesson plans, as well as other supplemental activities teachers can try in their classrooms. While considering different aspects of writing, we detail the writing difficulties experienced by some students and we offer possible solutions to various potential problems.

The approaches presented in this chapter are appropriate for a wide range of age and ability levels. They are research based. However, some techniques are more applicable to the needs of younger children, and others are more relevant for older students. More information about teaching writing to adolescents with learning disabilities is included in Chapter 9 (e.g., Report Writing).

RATIONALE FOR TEACHING WRITING

Why is writing so important? Reading, writing, listening, and speaking are all interconnected. Together, they form the language arts. Yet their use is not limited to a block of instructional time called "language arts." They are part of every aspect of the curriculum, interwoven throughout the day. Writing and reading are closely related, like two sides of the same coin. Both processes involve creating meaning through print. Writing creates the need to read; we read what we write and are motivated to read what others have written. Writing inspires us to want to know more and to seek out information through print. Reading gives us ideas, broadens our horizons, and motivates us to try new ways of writing. It is no secret that writers become better readers.

Writing and talking are also interrelated. They are both expressive, creative skills. When we want to share our thoughts and our feelings, we can choose to do so through writing or speaking. If we get stuck while writing, we can clarify our thoughts by expressing them aloud. "We find out what we think by seeing what we say" (Cullinan, 1993, p. 3).

The strategies for teaching writing included in this chapter are appropriate and well-suited for heterogeneous, diverse classrooms. Writers' Workshop, strategy instruction (e.g., think sheets, planning sheets), and interactive journals have been recommended by experts in the fields of general education (e.g., Atwell, 1998; Calkins, 1994; Graves, 1983; Ruddell, 1993), special education (Baker, Gersten, & Graham, 2003; Gersten & Baker, 2001; Graham & Harris, 2001; Rhodes & Dudley-Marling, 1988; Zaragoza & Vaughn, 1995), and multilingual/multicultural education (Garcia, 2001; Edelsky, 1986; Johnson & Roen, 1989; Peyton & Staton, 1993). Some are holistic approaches, supported by the theories of Vygotsky (1978, 1986), and based on the idea that learning grows out of personal knowledge and interests. They build upon students' strengths. They are based on the belief that literacy and language learning take place in the context of meaningful activities in a social community that emphasizes interaction and real communication. They provide ways for students to each work at their own level (in their zone of proximal development, or region of receptiveness to instruction) and receive appropriate feedback and intensive instruction suited to their individual needs. (Even in a class with over thirty students!)

BOX 7.1

WHAT THE RESEARCH SAYS ABOUT TEACHING WRITING TO STUDENTS WITH DISABILITIES

Gersten and Baker (2001) conducted a meta-analysis of thirteen studies on writing interventions for students with learning disabilities. All of the techniques designed to improve the expressive writing skills of students with learning disabilities were effective. Findings suggested that three components should be part of any comprehensive instructional program: (a) the steps of the writing process (as in Writer's Workshop), (b) explicit instruction in the critical dimensions of different writing genres, and (c) structures for providing students with extensive feedback from peers and teachers (again, as in Writer's Workshop).

Students with disabilities benefited from "think sheets," prompt cards, and mnemonics to help them as they engaged in the planning, writing, and revising stages of the writing process. Well-developed plans resulted in better first drafts. Also, peer support enhanced editing. Explicit teaching in text structures helped students write persuasive essays, personal narratives, compare and contrast essays, and in other genres. Students benefited from modeling and prompts. Guided feedback from teachers or peers about the overall quality of writing, strengths, and missing elements improved the final product.

WRITER'S WORKSHOP

Writer's Workshop emphasizes the creative, active *process* of writing. In fact, it is also called "The Writing Process Approach" (Zaragoza, 1995). In a Writer's Workshop classroom, *all* children are authors who write, share their work with an audience, revise, edit, and publish books. Writer's Workshop is very appropriate for heterogeneous classrooms because students work at their own levels and receive feedback appropriate to their individual needs. It is an approach ideally suited for co-teaching because students benefit from having two teachers available to provide assistance during writing conferences or through mini-lessons. One teacher can work with a small group of students who need help with a specific skill (using flexible grouping practices), while the other teacher circulates among the remaining students and conducts conferences.

Steps in Writer's Workshop: The Writing Process

The writing process involves many steps. Focusing on one step at a time helps the author not feel overwhelmed by attempting to write a paper that is perfect in every area. Each step develops a different writing subskill. The writing process is generally considered to include five steps: prewriting, drafting, revising, editing, and publishing (Scott & Vitale, 2003). Other components of Writer's Workshop occur at various stages of the process, such as teacher-student writing conferences, mini-lessons, and sharing.

BOX 7.2
THE WRITING PROCESS

1. **Prewriting** This is where you are planning, mapping, and (perhaps) talking with others about your ideas. You select a topic and envision what you want to say.
2. **Drafting** This is where you write quickly, generating ideas. You are writing to think. You don't worry about mechanics.
3. **Revising** This is where you fix up your writing. Here, you write to communicate to others. You think about your audience. Have you said what you intended to say?
4. **Editing** This is where you focus on spelling and punctuation. Here, you are making your writing readable for others.
5. **Publishing** This is where you write your final draft and publish it. You share it with others in some way.

Prewriting. During the first step, prewriting, students select their topics and get ready to write. They rehearse what they will say, thinking about how to start a story, planning the sequence of events, or maybe mulling over a clever ending. The prewriting stage is not limited to the classroom, because when students know they will be writing, they rehearse stories while taking a shower, walking to school, or waiting for the bus. When people write regularly, they develop a heightened consciousness or extra-awareness of potential stories (Calkins, 1994), noticing events or their own feelings from an author's point of view (e.g., "That would make a great story!"). As noted by Thucydides, "Stories happen to those who tell them."

Self-selection of topics is an important component of Writer's Workshop. It is through topic selection that students realize that their own thoughts and experiences have value and learn to think for themselves and to cultivate creativity. When students see that their work and opinions are accepted in a supportive atmosphere, they become more willing to take risks (Zaragoza, 1995). Writing takes on more meaning. Self-selection of topics does not mean that students must think of ideas in isolation. Talking about ideas with others (both peers and teachers) is a valuable component of this step. But even though a classmate or a teacher might suggest an idea, ultimately the choice of what to write about is left up to the author. Following are some suggestions to help students who are having difficulty formulating ideas (adapted from Zaragoza, 1995):

- Think about personal experiences; think about your memories.
- Think about subjects you know a lot about.
- Go to the library (in the classroom, school, or community) and look at the topics of other books.
- Interview others in your class for ideas.
- Discuss possible topics with family members.

- Keep a list of possible topics in your writing folder.
- Look at the idea bulletin board in the classroom.

Thinking of ideas will also become easier when students have read or listened to good children's literature and discussed authors' techniques (e.g, choice of topic, vocabulary, plot, and characters).

This aspect of Writer's Workshop (self-selection of topics) is initially a difficult one for many teachers and students. In fact, it was the first point of contention between Ms. Murphy and Ms. Rivera as they implemented Writer's Workshop in their fifth-grade classroom. The year had begun smoothly, with both teachers enthusiastic about their new writing program. But Ms. Murphy had felt disappointed with students' initial efforts. She was concerned that students seemed to run out of ideas. Their first few books were too short and too shallow. She was worried that students were not being exposed to enough variety. She conveyed to Ms. Rivera her concern that perhaps Writer's Workshop is more appropriate for younger students and that in the fifth grade it might be best to teach different genres of writing by assigning writing formats. Yet Ms. Rivera had anticipated that this could happen. She knew that students who are accustomed to passively receiving assignments from their teachers often initially feel frustrated when faced with the task of choosing their own topics. It can take a while for students to develop self-assurance and confidence in their own creative instincts and to be willing to explore new ways of writing. Ms. Rivera was able to convince Ms. Murphy to wait a little longer. Meanwhile, Ms. Rivera conducted a whole-class mini-lesson about topic selection, talking to the class about options and ways they could "stretch" themselves. She did this by asking the students for their input, and bringing to their attention a few stories written by students in the class. One captivating story, a Halloween mystery, inspired the class to want to learn more about mystery-writing. So the next day Ms. Murphy conducted a mini-lesson on the elements of mysteries (e.g., an unsolved problem, clues, suspects, a resolution). Soon after, most of the class chose to write their own Halloween mysteries. Many students also read mysteries during Sustained Silent Reading time. These endeavors lead to interesting discussions about how authors build suspense with clues and graphic language. Students were challenged to think of surprise endings for their stories. They eagerly anticipated writing time each day and asked if they could have more time to write and hear their peers' stories. Ms. Rivera breathed a sigh of relief; it appeared they were "over the hump." Ms. Murphy enthusiastically agreed to continue with Writer's Workshop and began thinking about other mini-lessons she could conduct about different writing genres.

Once a topic has been selected, another important component of the prewriting stage is planning. Many students with learning disabilities have difficulty organizing their thoughts and planning what they will write (Baker et al., 2003; Englert, 1990; MacArthur, Harris, & Graham, 1994). Whereas some students are able to use their knowledge of text structure to help organize their writing and to develop goals and set plans to achieve these goals, other students lack these skills. Explicit, teacher-directed instruction in prewriting strategies can help unorganized thinkers develop the ability to plan ahead and organize content. Various strategies have been found to be effective for helping students think about what they want to say during the prewriting stage.

BOX 7.3
DIRECT STRATEGY INSTRUCTION

As a supplement to Writer's Workshop, research indicates that explicit, direct instruction in strategies improves the quality and quantity of the writing of students with learning disabilities (Baker, Gersten, & Graham, 2003; De La Paz & Graham, 1997; Englert, 1990; Englert et al., 1995; Graham & Harris, 1989; Graham, Harris, & Larsen, 2001; Hallenbeck, 2002; MacArther, Graham, Schwarz, & Schafer, 1995; Troia & Graham, 2002). Strategy instruction can be provided during 15 to 20 minute mini-lessons in which the teacher works with small groups or the entire class. The targeted strategy is taught to students using a visual such as an overhead transparency, modeling by the teacher using a think-aloud procedure, and guided practice by the students within the context of Writer's Workshop. Strategies have been developed for improving prewriting, revising, and editing. They can take the form of planning sheets, mnemonic devices, or checklists. The goal of strategy instruction is to teach students the skills they need to work independently. To help students internalize and generalize the use of a strategy, it is valuable for them to think about WHAT a strategy is for, HOW to use it, WHEN to use it, and WHY it is important.

MacArthur and colleagues (e.g., MacArthur, Graham, Schwartz, & Schafer, 1995; MacArthur, Schwartz, & Graham, 1991a, 1991b) teach strategies as part of their Computers and Writing Instruction Project (CWIP). Framed within a process approach to writing instruction, their curriculum includes two basic strategies: a planning strategy based on the use of common text structures to generate and organize content and a reciprocal revising strategy for pairs or small groups of students. The planning strategy uses mnemonic devices to help students recall the parts of a story (C-SPACE: C-characters, S-setting, P-problem or purpose, A-action, C-conclusion, E-emotion) or the parts of an essay (TREE: T-topic, R-reasons, E-examples, E-ending). The Student Editor Strategy provides a response structure for peers to follow when providing feedback to a classmate who has just shared a story. (See the examples discussed in the prewriting and revising sections of this chapter.)

De La Paz and Graham (2001) developed a STOP strategy to help students plan persuasive essays. Using the mnemonic STOP, students learn to S-suspend judgment, T-take a side, O-organize ideas, and P-plan as they write.

Troia and Graham (2002) effectively taught a slightly different STOP strategy to students with learning disabilities (Stop, Think of Purposes), along with a LIST strategy (List Ideas, Sequence Them), to help them identify the purpose of a given writing activity and set appropriate goals.

Englert and colleagues (e.g., Englert, 1990, 1992; Englert et al., 1995) developed the Cognitive Strategy Instruction in Writing (CSIW) program to provide a framework for teaching strategies. Like CWIP, CSIW is intended to support teachers as they teach writing through a writing process approach. CSIW relies on think-sheets to make expository text structures visible to students and assist them in their planning, organizing, drafting, editing, and revising activities. Think-sheets help students at each of these stages by activating the writing strategies that students with learning disabilities do not typically employ and by fostering metacognitive awareness of the mental processes involved in writing. Think-sheets also provide a format for teachers to follow when leading classroom discussions about writing strategies. Each think-sheet is color-coded to cue students to where they are in the general writing process. (See the examples included in the sections of this chapter on prewriting and revising.) Hallenbeck (2002) applied the CSIW strategy with adolescents with learning disabilities as a way to help them take responsibility for their own writing.

Martin and Manno (1995) effectively taught a self-management procedure to adolescent writers to help them monitor the completeness and quality of their compositions using a Check-Off Form (see Figure 7.1). The students were taught to write their ideas in the sections under "Write As I Plan" before beginning to write, and to check off each planned element as they included it in their stories.

BOX 7.3 CONTINUED

Write as I Plan	Check Off as I Write
Main Character	
Other Characters	
Setting	
Problem	
Plan (action)	
Ending	

FIGURE 7.1 Check-Off Form

Visual representations such as planning sheets can be very beneficial for students (Baker et al., 2003). They are useful for jotting down a few key ideas and helping students think ahead, and they can be used for expository writing or narratives. The organization sheet is one type of planning sheet (Englert, 1990, 1992). It looks much like the semantic webs used to aid reading comprehension (Pearson & Johnson, 1978), with the topic or title of the story written in a circle in the middle of the page, and then the subtopics or components of the plot written in the surrounding circles.

Ms. Rivera decided to teach the students in both of her classes how to use this type of planning sheet. She included the C-SPACE **mnemonic device** for helping students remember the elements of a story (C-characters, S-setting, P-problem, A-action, C-conclusion, E-emotion)

Mnemonic device A tool that helps students remember key facts or, in the case of writing, the steps to be followed in carrying out a task.

(MacArthur, Schwartz, & Graham, 1991b; MacArthur, Graham, Schwartz, & Schafer, 1995) (see Figure 7.2). Ms. Rivera introduced the planning sheets to the class during a mini-lesson by modeling their application using a think-aloud procedure and demonstrating on an overhead transparency how to fill-in each circle, "Today I feel like writing about a time I felt really embarrassed. It was the day I almost lost my contact lens in a movie theatre when I was twelve. To help me organize my ideas, I'm going to use a planning sheet. First, I write the title in this circle in the middle. I think I'll call it, 'Lost in the Movie Theater.' Then I'll fill in each of the C-SPACE circles. First, I list the *C*haracters, or WHO I want to include in my story. Well, I was there, and Sue, my friend, two people who worked in the theater, and the other people in the audience. Next, I describe the *S*etting, or WHERE and WHEN the story took place. It was in a movie theatre when I was 12. OK, now I state the *P*roblem, or WHAT happened. Let's see, I accidentally dropped a contact lens. Next, I describe the *A*ction. That would be that everybody helped me look for it while the movie was on and the two people who worked in the theater used flashlights. Next, I put the *C*onclusion, or HOW the problem was solved. That would be when Sue found the contact lens on the floor. Finally, I describe my *E*motions, or HOW I felt. At first I was really worried. Then when Sue found my contact lens I was relieved! But I was also really embarrassed. Now I'm ready to write my story, and I have my ideas written down so I won't forget them" (see Figure 7.3). As a followup during another mini-lesson, Ms. Rivera made transparencies out of a few students' organization sheets and asked them to describe what they were thinking as they wrote their plans. She paired up a few students who seemed confused with buddies who helped talk them through the process. She and Ms. Murphy also provided assistance as they circulated among students.

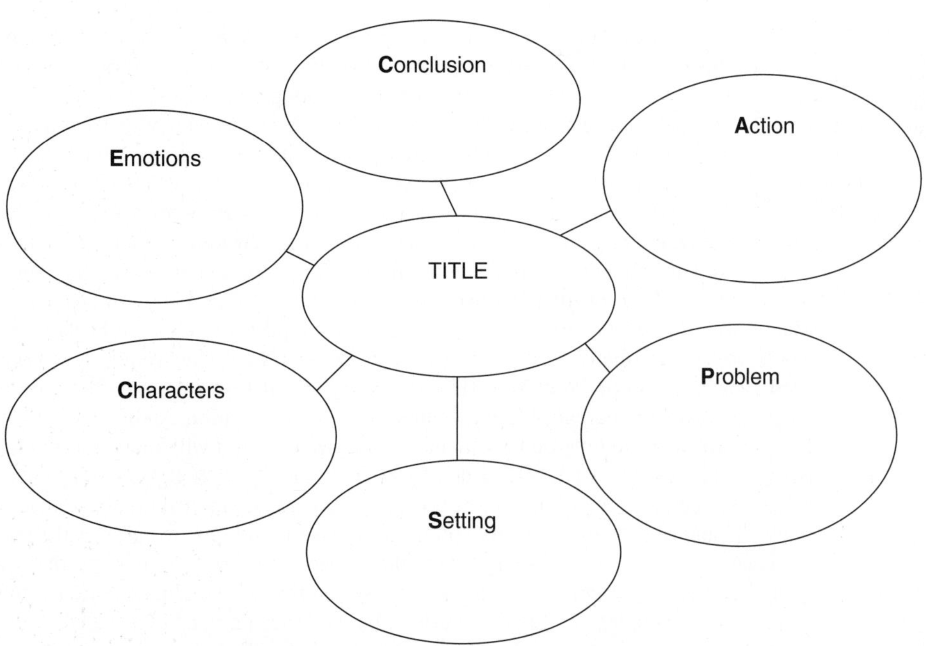

FIGURE 7.2 Blank Expert Organization Form with C-SPACE

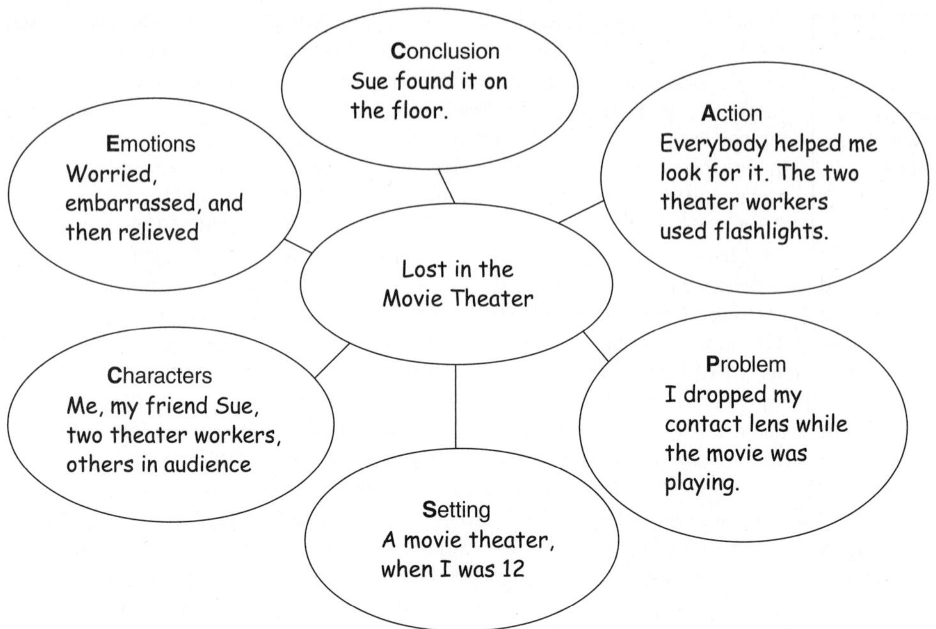

FIGURE 7.3 Filled-In Expert Organization Form with C-SPACE

> **Think-sheets** Cue sheets or planning sheets that remind students how to implement the various steps of the writing process.

In Ms. Murphy's class, Ms. Rivera decided to also teach how to use different **think-sheets** from the Cognitive Strategy Instruction in Writing Project (CSIW; Englert, 1990, 1992; Englert, Garmon, Mariage, Rozendal, Tarrant, & Urba, 1995). These think-sheets were designed to help students plan and organize different genres of writing. Ms. Rivera began by teaching how to use the Planning Think-Sheet (see Figure 7.4). In addition to planning WHAT will be written, students think about WHO they are writing for (i.e., the intended audience), WHY they are writing (e.g., to inform, to persuade, to entertain), and HOW they will group their ideas. Again, Ms. Rivera modeled for students how to complete the form, using a think-aloud procedure and filling in a planning sheet on an overhead transparency: "Let's see, I think I want to write about 'How to Make Little Pizzas.' We are going to be making little pizzas in class on Friday, so I thought I would write down the directions for everyone. Do you think that would be a good topic? So, WHO am I writing for? You! You will be my audience. If I were writing for someone else, say the principal or your parents, I might include different information. And WHY am I writing this? I want to write this to tell you how to make little pizzas so you will know how to do it. My purpose is to inform you. Next, WHAT do I know about my topic? Well, I know a lot because I have made these before. Where should I begin? The ideas are all jumbled up in my head. Let's see, I think I'll start with the ingredients you need to make the pizzas. I'll picture the ingredients in my head, and then list everything on the think-sheet. You need English muffins, pizza sauce, grated cheese, and a topping, like pepperoni. Next, I'll write the steps you follow to make a little pizza. First, you take an English muffin. You put sauce on it, and then cheese. Then you add whatever other toppings you want. I like pepperoni! Finally, you put the pizza on the baking sheet and put it in the broiler oven. You have to watch it carefully. In a few minutes, the cheese melts and gets bubbly, and it's done. Then you use the pot holder to take it out of the oven. You

Name:______________________ Date:______________________

TOPIC:______________________________________

WHO: Who am I writing this for?

____

WHY: Why am I writing this?

____

WHAT: What do I know? (Brainstorm)

____

____

____

____

____

____

HOW: How can I group my ideas?

FIGURE 7.4 Plan Think-Sheet

need to let it cool for just a few minutes. Finally, you can eat it! Have I left anything out? Materials! I probably should include that you need a broiler oven, a pot holder, and a baking sheet. Let's see HOW should I organize my ideas? Well, I think they are organized pretty well already, except that I should put the materials next to the ingredients, and write about that before I list the steps you follow to make the pizzas. The steps seem to be in the right order. What if the steps were all mixed up? Sometimes when we are brainstorming and writing down our ideas for the first time, they are not organized the way we would like them to be. What if I had put as the first step that you take the pizzas out of the oven? That would have been OK while I was thinking about what I know, but then I would have wanted to change the order on my plan sheet before writing. Well, that's it; now I'm ready to write my draft" (see Figure 7.5 filled-in form). After this introduction, Ms. Rivera and Ms. Murphy encouraged students to try completing their own planning think-sheets. They suggested that students seek help from their buddies

Name: Ms. Rivera Date: 9/23/2005

TOPIC: How to Make Little Pizzas

WHO: Who am I writing this for?

You, my students

WHY: Why am I writing this?

To inform you how to make little pizzas

WHAT: What do I know? (Brainstorm)

1. You need English muffins, sauce, grated cheese, and pepperoni.
2. First, you put an English muffin on a baking sheet.
3. Put sauce, cheese, and pepperoni on the English muffin.
4. Put the baking sheet in the broiler oven and turn the oven on.
5. Watch the pizza cook.
6. Use the pot holder to take the little pizza out of the oven when it is done.
7. Let it cool and then EAT.
8. You also need a baking sheet, broiler oven, and pot holder.

HOW: How can I group my ideas?

Ingredients	Materials
English muffins, sauce,	baking sheet, broiler oven,
grated cheese, pepperoni	pot holder

Steps you follow	Eat!
See 3-7 above.	☺

FIGURE 7.5 Filled-In Plan Think-Sheet

when they were stuck. Ms. Rivera then put students' think-sheets on overheads to demonstrate various examples.

Students might wish to develop alternative formats for recording their ideas. Later Ms. Rivera and Ms. Murphy introduced a Compare/Contrast Think-Sheet and an Explanation Think-Sheet (note that the above think-aloud lesson about making little pizzas could also have been demonstrated using this type of think-sheet) (see Figures 7.6 and 7.7) (Englert, 1990). The

What two things are you comparing and contrasting?

On what feature?

Alike?	Different?

On what feature?

Alike?	Different?

On what feature?

Alike?	Different?

FIGURE 7.6 Compare/Contrast Think-Sheet

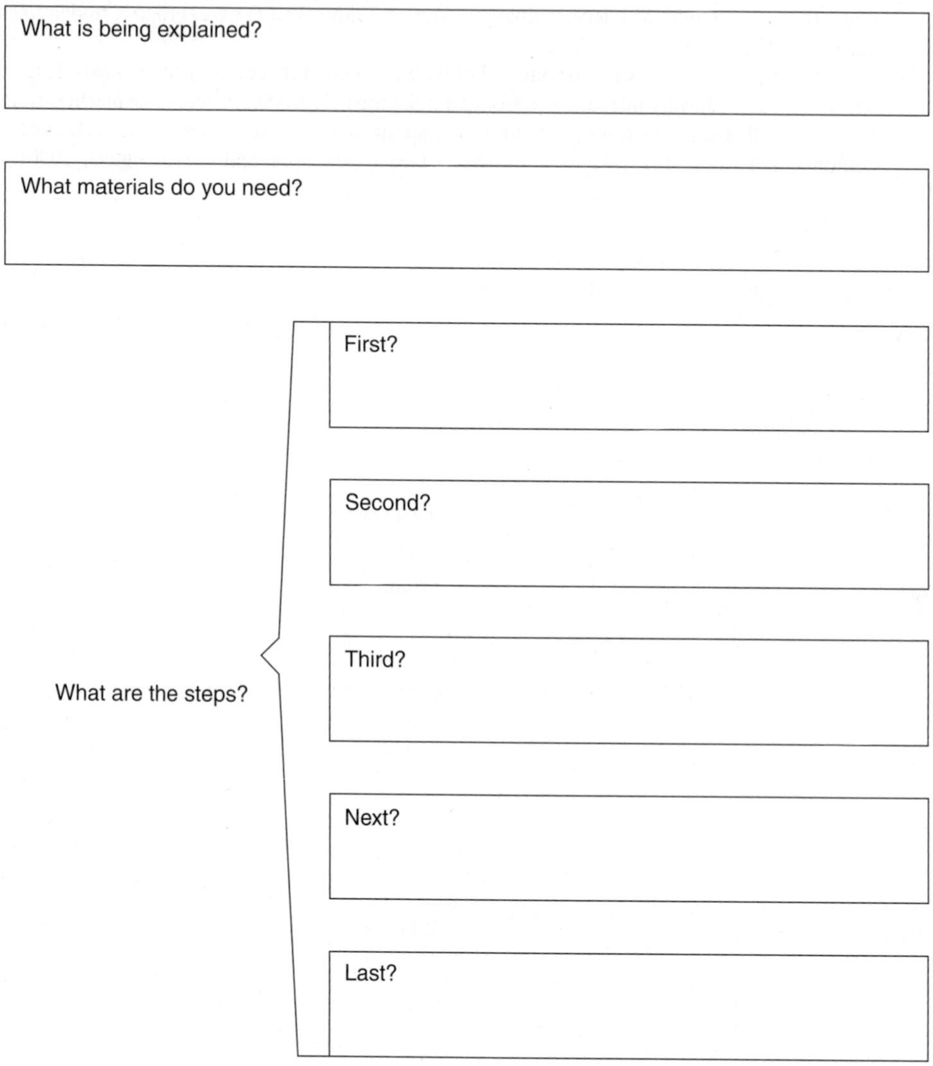

What is being explained?

What materials do you need?

What are the steps?

First?

Second?

Third?

Next?

Last?

FIGURE 7.7 Explanation Think-Sheet

teachers encouraged students to select the form they thought best fit their purpose. By doing this, they were helping students generalize use of the planning strategies.

Ms. Murphy and Ms. Rivera also taught students an organizing structure for planning a five-paragraph, three-point persuasive essay. Their school had just announced that there would be a schoolwide writing contest on the topic, "How to Improve the Cafeteria." The winning essays would be read by their authors over the school's television broadcast system during the Morning Announcements. The teachers decided this would be the perfect time to teach a mini-lesson on essay writing. Ms. Murphy drew a large closed fist on the chalkboard, with the thumb and little finger touching. She explained to students that this fist was to help them remember the parts of an essay: The thumb represents the introductory paragraph that states the topic; the second, third, and fourth fingers symbolize the paragraphs that establish the essay's three main points (or reasons) and provide supporting details; and the little finger represents the concluding paragraph. The thumb and little finger are touching to indicate that the final paragraph restates the information presented in the first paragraph and wraps up the essay. Most students chose to enter essays in the contest, including the students with learning disabilities. They were so excited when one of the essays from their class won first place for the fifth grade!

Drafting. During the second step, drafting, students put their ideas on paper. Students are instructed not to worry about spelling, punctuation, or handwriting. Once students understand that invented spellings are acceptable at this stage of the writing process, their increased confidence leads to more risk-taking and greater productivity. Students learn that crossing out is faster and more efficient than erasing, allowing them to further focus on recording their ideas. Each writer develops his or her own style. Some students quickly fill a page, their momentum building with each new word. Other students are more tentative, trying different opening lines, crossing out, and beginning again. Students should be encouraged to take chances. Students with learning disabilities who have previously felt constrained and frustrated while worrying about spelling or mechanics often "take off" when they realize it is their ideas that matter most. Students might initially need assistance learning to transfer the ideas they have recorded on their planning sheets to their first drafts. Modeling and prompting by the teacher can help.

What about students who cannot yet read or write, other than perhaps a few letters, words, and their name? These students, too, can participate in Writer's Workshop, each at his or her own developmental level. Writing begins when young children explore with a marker, crayon, or pencil, scribbling on their papers. In kindergarten, we start out by giving children paper and writing materials and saying, "You can draw and write." Although students may not have mastered every sound-symbol correspondence, they learn to perceive of themselves as writers. When students tell us about their pictures and what the letters they have written symbolize, "reading" to us, we can help them see that letters and words convey meaning and that the choice of the letter they put down depends on the sound it represents. As students experiment with writing, they progress from using strings of scribbles or random letters to complete spellings that approximate the intended words.

In Mr. Murphy's class, Tamika, a student with learning disabilities, liked to draw elaborate pictures, but hesitated to write letters. She was at an early invented spelling stage, and it was difficult for anyone else to read her few tentative words. Ms. Rivera approached her on the first day of Writer's Workshop and, noticing that she had drawn a picture of an airplane, pointed to the paper and commented, "Now tell me something about this airplane." Ms. Rivera continued to circulate among other students, later returning to Tamika, who had by now written a few words in invented spelling. Their conversation went like this:

Ms. Rivera: "Good, Tamika, you have written something. Tell me what it says."

Tamika: "My daddy went on an airplane."

Ms. Rivera: "The story goes with your picture, great!" (She reinforces this important concept.) "Hmm, your daddy went on an airplane. How do you feel about that?"

Tamika: "Sad. I don't know when he's coming back."

Ms. Rivera: "Yes, that is sad. Do you want to write more about that?"

Tamika then nodded and turned back to her work. Later that week, when Tamika wanted to edit and then publish her story (see the sections on editing and publishing), Ms. Rivera wrote out the story as Tamika dictated it to her. Tamika then copied this dictated version for her final draft and learned to read what she had written. She proudly shared her story with her peers and received their positive feedback.

When Writer's Workshop is used in this way, it is similar to the Language Experience Approach (LEA) (see Chapter 6). One key difference, however, is that with Writer's Workshop students first write their own stories (even if they only draw pictures and a few letters), and then later dictate to the teacher. With LEA, students start out by dictating their stories. A combination of the two methods can benefit emerging writers such as Tamika, who might write a little or draw a picture, then dictate, then write or draw more, and then dictate again.

What about reluctant writers, students who possess some basic writing skills beyond the invented spelling stage but say they do not know how to write or do not want to write (Marchisan & Alber, 2001)? Many students with learning disabilities who have participated in a traditional writing program have experienced failure and have turned off to writing. Perhaps they have been marked down for poor handwriting, or maybe their papers were returned filled with red marks correcting spelling and punctuation errors. They have learned to view being a good writer as synonymous with being a good speller or with having good penmanship and view themselves as "bad" writers because of difficulties in these areas. The major goal with these students is to help them put spelling and handwriting in perspective. Usually, even reluctant writers warm up to writing with time in a Writer's Workshop classroom where the focus is on the fluent expression of ideas rather than on mechanics. Patience and extra encouragement may be sufficient. However, some students may genuinely feel so frustrated and dissatisfied with their efforts to write that more assistance "getting over the hump" is required. The type of aid provided depends on the student's needs. Focus on the student's strengths, what he or she *can* do, what he or she already knows. Build the child's confidence. The following examples provide ideas for helping children with spelling difficulties (see the Spelling section of this chapter for more information):

Students who spell phonetically can be praised for hearing the sounds in words and encouraged to build fluency by writing words as they sound. They should not be concerned with how words should look at this point (there is time for that during the editing stage).

Developing visual memory skills and preparing a word bank of "spelling demons" (words that are not spelled phonetically) should take place during separate mini-lessons or tutoring sessions.

Some students waste time trying to think of easier-to-spell synonyms rather than attempting to write "hard" words. Asking these students to describe orally what they want to say and then to commit to writing these words on paper, no matter how difficult they are to spell, can help. If the students ask for assistance with spelling, reply that they should do the best they can, as quickly as they can (refuse to spell words for students; otherwise, they may get the wrong message that spelling really *is* important at the drafting stage). Sometimes it is helpful for students to underline or circle words that they would like to return to later.

Graves (1983, p. 208) suggests a strategy for helping students focus on meaning that also provides natural spelling support. During a brief conference, ask the student about the topic he or she is considering. As the student talks, perform the role of secretary, writing down key ideas for the student. When the conference ends, hand your notes to the student, saying something like, "If you'd like to use some of these words you were just speaking, here they are."

Rhodes and Dudley-Marling (1996) suggest meeting with a small group of reluctant writers and asking them to each contribute a sentence with "hard words" for the group to write using invented spellings. This explicit practice in using invented spellings can be just the help students need to overcome their fear of attempting difficult words.

Or, as suggested for emergent writers, reluctant writers might profit from a combination of writing and dictating (as used with the Language Experience Approach). Ms. Rivera motivated one disinclined student with learning disabilities (who also had behavioral difficulties) by encouraging him to write a few lines and then letting him dictate the next few to her. She later weaned him from this practice by stretching the amount written between dictations until he felt comfortable writing on his own.

Rhodes and Dudley-Marling (1996) suggest techniques for improving the fluency of students with handwriting difficulties. As with spelling, when students overly focus on handwriting, the flow of their ideas suffers. For students who spend a great deal of time carefully forming letters, conducting races during journal or free-writing time can help (e.g., "How many words can you write in three minutes?"). Or, for students who erase and rewrite a lot, prohibit the use of erasers. For students with motor problems, increased practice (more time spent writing) often improves fluency. Some students who have postural or motor difficulties and are easily fatigued improve when they change the position of their paper, their body, or their grip on the pencil. Try sitting next to the child and writing exactly as he or she is writing to diagnose the problem. Occasionally, a handwriting disability will exist that does not respond to remediation. In such cases, it is probably best to teach the student an alternative way to register ideas. For example, students for whom handwriting is a laborious, time-consuming task might choose to record their thoughts with a tape recorder and then transcribe what they have recorded on the computer. Once students have learned to type efficiently, they can do all of their writing with a word processor.

Special education teachers in inclusion classrooms must constantly be trying to figure out the best way to build on students' strengths and remediate their weaknesses in ways that help them feel successful. In an inclusion classroom, this type of problem solving is enhanced because the special education teacher is part of a team working in the best interests of the students, who can consult with the general education teacher.

Revising. The next step in the writing process, revising, suggests a "re-vision" or "seeing gain" of the piece, this time through the eyes of the intended audience. The author takes a step back from his or her work, trying to see it from a new perspective. This stage of writing can take place after an author has shared with others, or, particularly with experienced writers, it can be a rereading of one's own work as if for the first time. During revising, authors cross out, insert, and move text, reshaping and refining their work. Vivid vocabulary is substituted for over-used words. Extraneous information is deleted. Clarifying details are added. Revising is an interactive process that has an ebb and a flow. First, the author concentrates on getting a phrase or section just right. Then the author steps back and reads the new text, asking the same questions over and over. What have I said so far? Is this what I intended to say? How does it sound? How can I make it better? Will my readers understand? What questions might they have? What comes next? Teachers can ask these same questions during teacher-student writing conferences, modeling this process for students (we will discuss writing conferences in more depth in the next section). Teachers can also remind students to consider possible revisions that were suggested during sharing time. Note that at this stage in the writing process the author is not yet concerned with the mechanics of writing, but is still focusing on ideas.

Ms. Murphy, Mr. Wilson, and Ms. Rivera found that revising was difficult for most of their students. Students who were accustomed to writing only one draft resisted spending the extra time required to revise. Many students seemed genuinely unsure of how to go about changing a draft and were frustrated by the process. Students tended to correct errors rather than add or clarify information. "Maybe my expectations are too high, but I just want them to add more," Ms. Murphy confided. She lamented that students frequently would not follow through on suggestions provided by other students or the teacher after they had shared their work in progress, even when she tried to hold them accountable by saying, "I expect to see this in your writing tomorrow."

The teachers tried various strategies to help improve the revising process. First, Ms. Rivera noticed that many students were unaware of how to take advantage of the word processors in their classrooms. Although many students chose to draft their stories using one of the six computers in the class, most did not know how to delete, add, and move text efficiently. Ms. Rivera conducted mini-lessons for interested students on how to implement these functions. She then asked a few students who were proficient in word processing to assist students who needed help "cutting and pasting" with the computer. MacArthur, Schwartz, and Graham (1991b) recommend using word processors to facilitate the writing process. They suggest that students practice typing using computer tutorials that provide basic lessons in word processing skills. (See the technology section in Chapter 4 for more information.)

Second, Ms. Rivera implemented a buddy system to help with the revising process. Students selected a classmate to serve as a buddy who could take notes when they read their drafts aloud and received feedback from peers and the teacher during whole-class or small group sharing time (see the section on Sharing). This provided students with a written record of suggestions that might be incorporated into their stories. Students also conferred with their buddies as they revised. Before a student could show a revised draft to a teacher, the buddy signed the student's draft indicating that he or she felt that sufficient revisions had been made. Some students may be embarrassed to have a peer read their work and feel discouraged from writing if they know they will have to share. In a supportive classroom room these fears usually can be allayed.

In the fourth-grade class, Ms. Rivera added a feedback sheet (an adaptation of the Student Editor Strategy developed by MacArthur, Schwarz, & Graham, 1991a) for use when peers shared their drafts with a partner or a small group. The steps in the strategy (expressed as directions to the buddy who provides feedback and takes notes) are as follows:

1. LISTEN and read along as the author reads.
2. TELL what you liked best.
3. Make NOTES about:
   CLEAR? Is there anything that is hard to understand?
   DETAILS? Where could more information be added?
4. DISCUSS your suggestions with the author.

Third, Ms. Rivera and Ms. Murphy taught their students revision symbols using an adaptation of the revision think-sheet developed by Englert (1990). The revision think-sheet prompts students to (a) put a checkmark by the suggestions on their feedback sheets that they plan to use, (b) consider how to make their paper more interesting, and (c) make their revisions directly on the first draft (see Figure 7.8).

Name ____________________ Date ____________________

1. What revisions do you plan to make? (Put a √ next to the suggestions on your feedback sheet that you will use.)

2. How will you make your paper more interesting?

____

____

____

3. Go back to your draft and make your revisions on your paper.

Revision Symbols

	Symbol	Example
Add Words	∧	The ∧(little) girl is my sister.
Take Words Out	—	The boy ~~had~~ tried to run.
Change Order	∿	He had go to home.
Add Ideas	↙	The dog is friendly. ← Tell which dog

FIGURE 7.8 Revision Think-Sheet

Ms. Rivera, Mr. Wilson, and Ms. Murphy noticed that students' confidence was increasing and their revisions were improving. More students were choosing to use word processors to draft and revise their stories and were doing so more efficiently. The buddy system provided added support for students during the revising process, and students seemed to really enjoy working together. The feedback sheets and revision think-sheets helped students focus on the components of the task and provided a system of accountability. The teachers observed that there seemed to be carryover—students were incorporating their classmates' suggestions when writing their next pieces. Slowly but surely, students' writing was improving.

Editing. During the next phase of the writing process, editing, students concentrate on spelling, punctuation, grammar, and capitalization. The purpose of editing is to facilitate communication by making the piece of writing easily understandable to others. Editing is also students' last chance to ask, "Does this make sense?"

Most students need help with editing. It is many students' least favorite aspect of writing, and they tend to pay limited attention to editing their work. Students find editing tedious and do not understand its importance. Or they have become overly dependent on teachers or others to correct their work for them. A crucial step in teaching students to become good editors is convincing them of the need to do so (Ferris, 1995). To develop an appreciation for the importance of editing, it is helpful to display writing samples that contain a variety of errors on an overhead projector. First, rather than simply finding and correcting errors, discuss with students how errors hinder their understanding.

Although a few individuals seem to learn the conventions of writing through osmosis, most students require direct, specific instruction in the rules of writing. Mini-lessons, either with the whole class or in small, flexible groups, are essential for helping children learn how to edit. We recommend that you practice editing in front of the entire class, using overhead transparencies of samples of students' writing, increasingly involving students in the process as they become more proficient. Students can be provided with copies of the displayed sample so that they can make corrections at their seats while a teacher or another student edits the same work on the overhead. Wall charts can display proofreaders' marks and various rules (e.g., "When to Use Capitals"). Writer's Workshop provides the ideal framework for teaching about the mechanics of writing within the context of genuine communication. Punctuation rules, for example, become much more meaningful when they are applied to a student's story rather than a list of sentences on a workbook page.

Particularly in a heterogeneous classroom that includes students with high-incidence disabilities (i.e., students with learning disabilities, mental retardation, and emotional disturbance), it is to be expected that students will be working at very different levels. Some students are ready to grasp the intricacies of quotation marks and dialoguing, while other students are still struggling with ending punctuation. Small group mini-lessons with only those students who require further explanation of a specific skill can be very effective here. A co-teaching arrangement is ideal for this type of intensive, individualized instruction.

In Mr. Wilson's class, the co-teachers agreed that at least twice a week Ms. Rivera would conduct small group mini-lessons while Mr. Wilson circulated among the remaining students. For example, on one particular Thursday Ms. Rivera conducted two mini-lessons, the first on capitalization rules and the second on quotation marks. The first group included four of the six students with learning disabilities in the class, as well as three other students Mr. Wilson and Ms. Rivera had decided would benefit from such instruction. The second group was made up of those students who were attempting to include dialogue in their stories and seemed to have mastered the rules for ending punctuation (this group included one student with learning disabilities). Because Ms. Rivera worked with higher achieving students as well as lower achieving students and sometimes taught the whole class, she was not perceived by her students as the learning disabilities teacher, but as everyone's teacher.

Editing can take three different forms: self-editing, peer-editing, and teacher-editing. When students self-edit, they check their own work for errors. When they peer-edit, they check the work of a classmate. Students can be required to seek the assistance of multiple peers before they turn to a teacher—"ask three, then me." Research has shown that peer editing can be a powerful technique for improving the quality of students' writing (Wong, Butler, Ficzere, Kuperis, Corden, & Zelmer, et al., 1994), even more so than teacher-editing.

Whether checking their own work or that of someone else, students can be provided with a mnemonic device or a checklist for this purpose. Students might use a strategy called COPS (Alley, 1988). With the COPS mnemonic device, students question themselves as follows:

C Have I ***capitalized*** the first word and proper nouns?
O How is the ***overall appearance*** of my paper? Have I made any handwriting, margin, or messy errors?
P Have I used end ***punctuation*** and commas carefully?
S Do words look like they are ***spelled*** right?

Or students might use an editing checklist such as the one in Figure 7.9 (adapted from Calkins, 1994):

Despite teaching various mini-lessons related to editing, Ms. Rivera and Ms. Murphy felt frustrated with the way the editing process was being carried out in their class. The teachers had established the requirement that before a draft could be turned in to a teacher for final editing, it must be edited by a peer (and then signed by that peer). Yet peers were signing off papers that still contained many errors. When Ms. Murphy conducted mini-lessons using students' writing samples made into overhead transparencies and asked the class to edit the samples, students were able to find and correct all errors. Yet somehow when students edited on their own, they missed many mistakes. Ms. Rivera and Ms. Murphy discussed this problem in one of their collaborative consultation meetings. It was Ms. Murphy's idea to establish classroom experts in each aspect of the editing process. One table (a grouping of six desks) was designated the capitalization table. Another became the punctuation table, another the spelling table, and another the "Does it make sense?" table. The teachers conducted additional mini-lessons on each specific skill with the students at that table. Then, rather than have one peer edit for all errors, students were required to have their drafts checked and signed off by one person at each of the expert tables. After three weeks, roles rotated and students became experts in another aspect of writing mechanics. This system did improve students' editing, but it was time consuming. After following the procedure for nine weeks, Ms. Murphy and Ms. Rivera decided that students' editing skills had progressed sufficiently to return to a peer-editing routine that required only one peer to check each draft.

Publishing. The last step in the writing process, publishing, involves preparing written work to be shared with others. Not all drafts must be published, and students should be allowed to choose which works will end up in published form. At this stage, students copy their piece in their best handwriting or print what they have written with a word processor and bind it into a book. They learn that legibility is another necessary aspect of effective communication. Students may even wish to publish their work on the World Wide Web. Smith, Boone, and Higgins (1998) describe this process in an article in *TEACHING Exceptional Children.* They relate the story of a middle school student with learning disabilities whose writing expanded and improved when he published on the web.

There are different ways to bind books. The easiest way is to staple stories or reports between folded construction paper covers. Our favorite method takes a bit longer, but is

Author: ______________________

Title: ______________________

Peer Editor: ______________________

Does it make sense?

Spelling?

Punctuation?

Periods, question marks, commas, exclamation marks, quotation marks

Paragraphs?

Capital letters?

FIGURE 7.9 Editing Checklist

well worth the effort. Students' final products look like "real" hardbound books and are ready to be placed in the classroom or school library for sharing. First, attach the book pages together by sewing them down the middle (or stapling them). Be sure to add an extra sheet of folded blank paper to the outside before doing this (it is this extra sheet that gets glued to the cover). The cover itself is made with tagboard (or other sturdy cardboard, cut into two 6" X 9" pieces and 1/4" X 9" strip) and contact paper (one 17" X 12" piece per book). Peel the backing off the contact paper and place it sticky side up on the table or desk. Center the two larger tagboard pieces 1/2 inch apart on the contact paper and press them down to attach. Place the strip between the two larger pieces and prerss it down. Cut the corners off the contact paper, and then fold the top, bottom, and sides of the contact paper over onto the tagboard, pulling gently and smoothing out any wrinkles or air bubbles. Now the cover is ready for the inside pages to be added. Glue one side down at a time, and you are done!

As Zaragoza (1995) emphasizes, you cannot underestimate the power of these book covers. It is through sharing their published "real" books that students feel like "real" authors. Once students have published their first books and understand the full writing process, they are motivated to write more.

Components of Writer's Workshop

Regular Writing Time. Children should have uninterrupted time to write every day, for at least 20 to 30 minutes. When students know that writing is an important part of each day's routine, they learn to anticipate writing time, to mentally rehearse what they might say, and to converse with others about their stories.

When Ms. Rivera overheard three of her students excitedly talking about their stories in the cafeteria, she wished she could tape-record their conversation to share with others who might be skeptical about Writer's Workshop. Two of these students with learning disabilities had been quite reluctant to write at the beginning of the year, complaining that they could not think of anything to say and "writing was boring." Now these same students were engaged in an animated discussion about writing, during their free time.

During writing time, students might choose to work individually or with a co-author. Collaboration is fine; in fact, it can be encouraged. Ms. Rivera and Mr. Murphy found that so many of their students wanted to co-author all the time, however, that the teachers established a rule that students could co-author every other story at the most.

Teacher as Model. In Writer's Workshop, teachers write along with their students for the first 10 minutes or so of writing time, at least once a week. Students see that writing is an activity valued by their teachers. Also, students are able to see the entire process of writing modeled for them. Often students have the notion that good writing simply happens, that authors sit down with their paper and pen (or at the computer) and a finished piece of writing magically appears. When students see that even experienced writers go through the processes of prewriting, drafting, revising, editing, and publishing, they better understand what writing entails, and they tend to feel less frustrated with their own efforts.

Ms. Rivera and Ms. Murphy felt that one benefit of co-teaching was that they were able to model sincere disagreements in front of their class. When they had a difference of opinion (e.g, about the interpretation of a line of poetry or the direction in which a lesson should go), they openly sought the other's point of view. They modeled active listening and compromising for their students. As students witnessed their teachers' constructive efforts to understand each other's ideas, they felt more comfortable offering multiple points of view themselves. This type of discussion is conducive to higher-level thinking and conceptual development (Alvermann, Dillon, & O'Brien, 1987; Harris & Sipay, 1990).

The importance of the teacher's role in modeling the process of providing feedback during whole class or small group sharing or peer conferences cannot by overemphasized. Teacher–student conferences should precede student–student conferences so that children can become familiar with the process and repeat it later with fellow students.

Teacher–Student Writing Conferences. Writing conferences are perhaps the most important component of Writer's Workshop. They provide the opportunity for students to receive one-to-one attention and individualized feedback from a teacher. In a heterogeneous classroom that includes students working at many different levels, this type of feedback is particularly important. Also, conferences provide teachers with the opportunity to assess students' progress and to determine each student's stage of writing development.

To conduct writing conferences, teachers move around the room with a chair, meeting with individual children at their seats to discuss their work. Typical conferences last from 2 to 3 minutes, but they can be as short as 30 seconds when it is sufficient to merely check in or as long as 10 minutes when more in-depth support is required. As Graves (1983) and Atwell (1987) both point out, however, the first few conferences tend to take longer while teachers and students learn what conferencing is all about (i.e., what can and cannot be done in 2 to 3 minutes).

How often should each child meet with a teacher? Conferences can be conducted by appointment as initiated by the student, on a regular conference day, or as needed. When there are two teachers in the classroom rather than one, it is much easier to conduct regular writing conferences.

Ms. Rivera and Ms. Murphy decided that they would hold scheduled conferences with their students three days a week, with each teacher seeing ten to twelve students a day. This permitted each teacher to check in with every child at least once a week and keep tabs on students' progress. Students were able to benefit from both teachers' ideas and knew when to expect their meetings (e.g., "On Mondays I conference with Ms. Rivera and on Wednesdays I conference with Ms. Murphy"). Additionally, teachers met with any student who needed immediate attention. Usually, however, students with questions were directed to seek assistance from another student when it was not their time for a scheduled conference.

Different record-keeping systems are available for keeping track of conferences and students' progress. Some teachers maintain a conference log in a spiral notebook, using dividers to set apart a separate section for each student. Other teachers keep track of students' progress on a sheet that is stapled to the front of each writing folder, enabling students to see the teacher's comments. Different writing skills can be listed on the left side of the paper, with checkmarks in two parallel columns indicating "Things I Can Do" and "Things I Am Learning." Ms. Rivera and Ms. Murphy used another method. They prepared a 5" X 7" index card for every student and used these to document concerns and progress. They organized the index cards into three sets to correspond with their conferencing schedule and kept these in different sections of a file box.

Two types of writing conferences are common in Writer's Workshop—revising conferences and editing conferences. The purpose of revising conferences is to discuss content and help students clarify and refine their thinking. Teachers move from student to student asking general questions such as, "Can you tell me about your story?" "Is there anywhere you are stuck?" "Can you tell me more?" "What do you think you will do next?" Questions such as these are important because they demonstrate the teacher's confidence in the child's judgment and do not take control away from the child. They encourage the student and not the teacher to talk. See Figure 7.10 for specific questions for various problems (adapted from Atwell, 1987).

Sometimes the job of the teacher is simply to respond to the message of the story, however, whether it's with laughter, joy, or sadness. If a story moves us in a certain way, letting the child know how we are feeling might be enough feedback.

PROBLEM	CONFERENCE APPROACHES
The piece is unfocused: It covers many different events, ideas, etc.	Do you have more than one story here? What's the most important thing you're trying to say? What's your favorite part?
There isn't enough information.	I don't understand; can you tell me more about it? What else do you know about your topic?
There's too much information in the piece.	Is all of this information important to your reader? Are there any parts you don't need?
The piece is a list of events and includes little of the writer's reflections.	How did you feel when this happened? What do you think about this? Why is this important to you?
The conclusion is either too sudden or drags on and on.	What do you want your reader to know or feel at the end of your piece? Does this conclusion do it? Where does your piece really end?

FIGURE 7.10 Questions That Can Help with Writing Conferences

Editing conferences are quite different than revising conferences in that they focus on the mechanics of writing. By the time a student meets with a teacher to discuss editing, his or her paper should already have been self- and peer-edited. The paper is just about ready to be published and requires the teacher's stamp of approval. There is insufficient time during editing conferences to teach or reteach new skills, however. This is best done through mini-lessons. But editing conferences do help the teacher decide what should be covered in mini-lessons. When a child needs more assistance with a particular skill (e.g., using dialogue), the teacher might direct the student to seek the assistance of a more knowledgeable peer (e.g., "Manny has used quotation marks in his story. Why don't you ask him to help you with yours?").

Writing conferences provide teachers with the opportunity to spend additional time with those students with learning disabilities who require extra assistance. Although skills are best taught during mini-lessons, writing conferences can be used to reinforce concepts students have already learned. Often students with learning disabilities have trouble transferring skills from one setting or activity to a novel situation. Or they might have difficulty maintaining a skill, forgetting from one day or week to the next. During editing conferences, the teacher can remind students what they have learned (i.e., "Remember how we learned last week to put quotation marks around dialogue?" "Do you remember what quotation marks look like?" "Where should you put them in your story?"). Checking frequently with students with learning disabilities to see how they are progressing is essential.

Sharing. Sharing takes place during various phases of the writing process. The two most common times are before revising and after publishing. Students learn the importance of writing as communication and the necessity of considering one's audience. Sharing at this stage can take place with a peer, in small groups (often called "Response Groups"), or with the whole class (sometimes called "Author's Chair").

Author's Chair provides students with the opportunity to read their drafts in front of the class. Classmates listen, respond to the meaning of the piece, and ask real questions that help the author decide what revisions to make. The author makes the final decision about which questions suggest revisions that are important and relevant to his or her story. It is through sharing one's work that students learn to feel a valued member of the community of writers within their classrooms. Even students with learning disabilities or limited writing skills who have written relatively brief accounts feel the flush of success when they stand in front of their peers and discuss their work.

Mr. Wilson was somewhat skeptical about this at first, fearing that higher achieving students would be too critical of their less proficient peers or inattentive. His fears soon evaporated, however, as he marveled when his lowest student read a few tentative lines ("The Beach. Saturday we got up. We went to the beach. I played in the sand. We came home. It was fun."), and her classmates responded with enthusiasm, telling her they also liked to go to the beach, and asking questions about what she did while at the beach (e.g., "Did you make a sand castle?" "Did you go swimming?"). Ms. Murphy had a similar concern. When Paul, a student with learning disabilities in her class who had only written a few lines, asked to share, she held her breath as she waited to see how classmates who had themselves written several paragraphs would react.

Yet Paul didn't stop after reading his three sentences. Instead, he stood in front of his peers and narrated an elaborate, interesting story about how he had lost and then found his dog (pretending to be reading from his paper). The student next to Ms. Rivera leaned over and whispered to her, "Did he really write all that?" Ms. Rivera just smiled. When Paul had finished, the class clapped and conducted "TAG" (explained below) without mentioning their doubts about whether he had actually written down his story. Ms. Rivera approached him immediately afterwards, congratulated him on a job well done, and offered to help him record the story in writing. Both of these examples illustrate that when students feel nurtured within a supportive environment, they seem to find it easier to help others, each at his or her own level. Everyone should have equal opportunities to share. And as one second grader emphasized, "Be sure to have people clap hands when someone shares" (Zaragoza & Vaughn, 1995, p. 46).

TAG A procedure for providing feedback to an author about a piece of writing. The acronym reminds the listener or reader to "**T**ell what he or she liked, **A**sk questions, and **G**ive ideas."

TAG (Zaragoza & Vaughn, 1995) is an acronym that helps students learn how to give constructive feedback after a classmate has shared a story, report, poem, or essay. "T" means to *tell* what you like; "A" signifies to *ask* questions; and "G" means to *give* ideas (or offer suggestions for improving the piece). Feedback should be provided in the order of the letters in TAG. Particularly at first, teachers play an important role in modeling the procedure for students by telling what they genuinely like, asking relevant questions, and giving ideas that might help students expand or clarify their writing. Students and teachers tend to find TAG very helpful as a framework for guiding the dialogue about a student's work. Students can be provided with a list of possible questions, or they can generate their own list. The following list was suggested by a class of second graders (Zaragoza & Vaughn, 1995):

1. Where did you get that idea? Is your story fiction or nonfiction?
2. What is the main idea?
3. What is your favorite part of the story?
4. What was the problem? How was the problem solved?
5. Who is your favorite character? What are your characters like?
6. What's your setting?
7. What part do you think needs more work?
8. What are you going to do next?
9. Are you going to publish it?
10. Were you trying to write the way a certain author writes?

Response Groups are small student-led groups that allow for more in-depth attention than is possible with the whole class. To run smoothly, Response Groups require extensive instruction and teacher modeling in how to provide positive, constructive feedback. Students can use TAG, the same method of providing feedback suggested for whole-class sharing, or they can implement a slightly more detailed method, such as the feedback sheet described in the Revising section on page 257. As with TAG, students tell what they liked and make suggestions. A peer can take notes (as described in the Revising section). Response groups meet at least twice weekly; each student should get a chance to share every week.

Mini-lessons. Mini-lessons are short (3- to 15-minute) lessons presented by a teacher to the whole class or to small groups. Skills should be drawn from areas of need as perceived by the teacher when evaluating students' work (e.g., during writing conferences). Grade-level curriculum guidelines can help teachers pinpoint what to look for. Mini-lessons use students' writing as models and the writing of other authors (i.e., from books read by students or the teacher to the class). Lessons might cover language conventions, such as punctuation, capitalization, common misspellings, pronouns, verb tenses, or editing skills. They might include literary structures, such as introductions, conclusions, settings, plots, characters, episodes, or dialogue. Or they might discuss style, such as voice or use of descriptive language. A few sample mini-lessons for teaching writing strategies have already been presented in earlier sections of this chapter. Calkins (1994) provides many suggestions for developing mini-lessons within the following categories: early writing, the launch (getting started with writing workshops), topic choice, conferences, classroom procedures, rehearsal and revision strategies, qualities of good writing, and literature.

Writer's Workshop classrooms are characterized by high levels of student input. Yet this does not mean that teachers do not play a key role, also providing extensive input. Many teachers have the impression that because students choose their own topics, have ownership over the writing process (making their own decisions about what to include or not include in a piece), and confer with other students as well as their teachers, Writer's Workshop means that teachers should remain in the background and not provide much input (Calkins, 1994). This is a misconception; teachers *must* take an active role in helping students become better writers. Thus mini-lessons are very important as a way for teachers to provide input and teach writing skills. Yet these lessons should remain just as they sound, as "mini" rather than maxi-lessons. They should be quick and applicable to students' immediate writing needs, placed in the context of their own writing.

Small group mini-lessons focus on specific skills needed by some but not all students in the class. When selecting topics for small group mini-lessons, focus on major patterns of error rather than attempting to correct every single mistake. Look for common error types in students' work. Because not all students make the same errors, flexible grouping is important. Mini-lessons should be provided only for the students in need of a specific skill at a particular time, as demonstrated in their writing. Instruction should be personalized as much as possible. This is one of the features that sets a writing process approach apart from traditional textbook-based writing instruction that teaches one skill or rule at a time to everyone in the class.

Particularly in classes that include students with learning disabilities, teachers must provide intensive, explicit instruction in writing skills and frequent followup lessons that reinforce previously taught competencies. Although many students learn quickly and are able to transfer information learned in one context to another with little or no prompting, students with learning disabilities often require more assistance. Sometimes it is sufficient to remind a student to check whether a rule has been applied (e.g., whether the first letter in each sentence has been capitalized); at other times, a new mini-lesson that teaches a previously taught skill from a different angle is called for (e.g., selecting an overused word such as "good" and brainstorming a list of alternative adjectives, and then looking for examples in their own writing where they have used "good" and substituting different descriptors). Although students with learning disabilities are taught in a general education classroom rather than pulled out for remediation in a resource room, they still require special, individualized instruction. Through mini-lessons and writing conferences, Writer's Workshop and a co-teaching arrangement provide an ideal format for providing this additional support within a meaningful context.

Writing for Multiple Purposes

In a Writer's Workshop classroom, teachers should capitalize on students' efforts to experiment with different writing genres by sharing these pieces with the rest of the class and identifying the type of writing employed (i.e., "Mindy has decided to write a persuasive essay about protecting the manatees"). Yet it is also important that students receive explicit instruction in different writing forms. Reading a variety of types is important as well. During a mini-lesson, one or various types can be presented and briefly discussed, using students' work or books the class is reading as examples. A bulletin board might include an overview of selected types, such as illustrated in Figure 7.11 (adapted from Chittenden, 1995).

The Classroom as a Writing Laboratory

Whether at a writing center, a publishing table, or elsewhere in the class, students need to have easy access to writing and publishing materials, such as pencils, rulers, crayons, scissors, paper, and book covers (or the materials for making covers). Writing folders should contain all complete and in-process drafts, a list of possible topics, possibly a revising checklist, blank planning sheets and feedback forms, an editing checklist, and a spelling list.

PERSUASIVE (Essay, Editorial, Letter)
"This is what I believe and why I think you should believe it . . . "
Purpose: To influence or convince others of one's ideas or beliefs.

NARRATIVE (Story)
"This is what happened . . . "
Purpose: To tell a story; to relate an experience or observation.

INFORMATIVE (Report, Directions)
"This is what I know and how I came to know it."
Purpose: To convey information to others; to explain ideas, facts, or processes.

EXPRESSIVE (Story, Journal Entry, Letter)
"This is what I think, see, feel, and remember . . . "
Purpose: To create, reveal, or clarify ideas or experiences for oneself or others.

FIGURE 7.11 Writing for Multiple Purposes

Student-authored books should be prominently displayed around the classroom. Perhaps a few books can stand upright on a shelf or windowsill. Student-authored books should also be included in the classroom library. Because some of the students in Mr. Murphy's class were bilingual and biliterate, his library included books in Spanish as well as English. A small green sticker on the spine of each indicated it had been written in Spanish (or both Spanish and English). Some of Mr. Murphy's students asked if they could write and publish bilingual books, too, complete with a small green sticker on the outside.

BOX 7.4

PREPARING FOR HIGH STAKES TESTING IN A FOURTH-GRADE INCLUSION CLASSROOM

Sallie Gotch, Inclusion Specialist, Miami, Florida

The writing process is a favorite of our students and we try not to ruin it for them just because we have to prepare for the Florida Comprehensive Assessment Test Writing test (FCAT; Florida's fourth-grade writing assessment). In our school, typically about a third of the students in the inclusion classrooms have learning disabilities or autism. They range from virtually nonreaders to grade level, but with learning deficits. This year, all of our special education students took the state-mandated writing test, and all but one took the test in the regular class setting without modifications. The test is scored 1 through 6 using a rubric, and of our students with disabilities, one scored a 4, several received 3s, and even our nonreader scored a 1.

We find that Writer's Workshop is a great leveler because each child actually works at his or her own pace and can access the skills needed for the writing process. Our techniques are simple and success oriented. We devote the first month of the school year to developing fluency, confidence, and style through free writing. Students choose their own topics, which range from personal narratives through fictitious tales about magical dragons in far away places. We conduct mini-lessons, conferences, and "TAG" (**tell** something you like, **ask** a question about the piece, and **give** a suggestion), so that students can share their work with the class and get feedback from their peers while we model how to critique writing. During that month—and of course thereafter—we revise, add technique, edit, and publish at least one piece of the child's choosing. We keep the rules simple:

1. Authors need silence.
2. Don't worry about spelling.

We talk about how we are interested in ideas first and will consider spelling when we get to editing for publishing so everyone will be able to read exactly what the author meant.

Once the writing process is established, our students learn from each other's best practices and feel safe sharing. They enjoy revising since they get to do it with friends and see that everyone has strengths and everyone is accepting instruction. For our emergent writers, we buddy them with someone who can take dictation, but ONLY after they themselves have marked the paper with their thoughts. Their partner can then write in "dictionary spelling," and they can rewrite and practice with vocabulary that arose from their own internal source. We utilize various techniques for paired sharing including Kagan cooperative structures, appointments (with sticky notes), etc. And we follow the advice that good writing is content (you've got to have something to say) and creativity (say it in the best way possible), rather than practicing a prompt a week with "drill and kill." We do, of course, work together to achieve our best expression with prompted expository and narrative writing, but in a workshop, celebratory setting.

The other day I found five of my last year's fourth-grade students with disabilities and asked them to "quick write" what they remembered liking about Writer's Workshop or that they found helpful in preparing for the FCAT Writing test, and they mentioned among other things: picture writing, access to "tough words," and vivid verbs. They offered their opinions as self-appointed experts unhesitatingly and with joy.

One student wrote: ". . . *Riters werkshop tot me a plentitude of woderfole theins like how to let my emagenashen go wiyold also how to read beter. And last but not lest," he said, "don't were abot spelling." "p.s" he wrote, "You shod try riters werkshop."* I concur.

Some resources we have found useful are:

- *Writing Pictures K-12: A Bridge to Writing Workshop* by Michelle Takenishi and Hal Takenishi ISBN 0-926842-88-9
- *Razzle Dazzle Writing* by Melissa Fournay ISBN 0-929895-48-7
- Kagan Cooperative Structures *www.KaganOnline.com*

INTERACTIVE JOURNALS (DIALOGUE JOURNALS)

Interactive journals are written conversations between students and their teachers (Flores, Garcia, Gonzalez, Hildago, Kaczmarek, & Romero, et al., 1985). Students write in their journals on a daily basis about self-selected topics that are meaningful to them and receive a personal reply from a teacher. Interactive journals are ideally suited for an inclusion class because students can write and receive feedback at their individual levels. Also, students have the opportunity to converse through writing with two teachers.

Journals give children an opportunity to:

1. Experience person-to-person authentic communication with their teachers.
2. Reinforce the concept that writing is communication.
3. Develop fluency in written language (as well as in reading).
4. Apply the skills learned in language, literature studies, reading, writing, and spelling lessons.
5. Develop a close personal relationship through writing.
6. Experiment with language in a meaningful context (this can be especially important for students acquiring English as a second language).

Journals give teachers an opportunity to:

1. Assess students' application of knowledge and skills taught in other areas, and use this information when planning lessons.
2. Model the conventions of standard English in an authentic context (this can be particularly important for English language learners).
3. Learn about each child's background, interests, and ideas. Journals can be a wonderful way to learn about the different cultures represented in your class.
4. Interact on an individual basis with each child, creating a close personal bond.
5. Obtain an easy-to-follow daily developmental record of each child's writing and language development.
6. Resolve problems and disagreements.

Issues in Journal Writing

Getting Started. Journals are most effective when they become part of the daily routine of the classroom (in a positive way) (Peyton & Staton, 1993). They should be introduced as early in the year as possible, as soon as the first day of school. Students who are not yet proficient in English can write in their native language at first. Students who can't yet write can draw pictures. Little preparation is required. Once students have journals, they are ready to start.

To begin, the teacher can simply tell the students that they will be having a conversation in writing, sort of like sending letters back and forth. The only guidelines are that (a) each entry should be dated and (b) invented spellings are OK. The class might brainstorm reasons why interactive journals are important, some possible topics, and even a sample entry for students who may be having difficulty getting started.

What to Write In. Interactive journal writing should be kept separate from other classwork. Each student should have a notebook or computer file only for that purpose. Most teachers use bound notebooks of some sort (spiral notebooks, composition books, or student-made books). Except for with emergent writers who draw many pictures, lined paper seems to work best.

When and How Often to Write. It is essential that journal writing occur regularly to create a true sense of dialogue and to maintain a continual interchange of ideas. When students are accustomed to writing each day, they tend to think about what they will write at other times during the day, and say things like, "I'll write to you about it in my journal." One way to implement interactive journal writing is to give students about 10 minutes to write in their journals when they first arrive in the morning. Students can come in and pick up their journals, read what the teacher has written, and then write their responses. Many students add to their journals throughout the day when/if they have the time and inspiration.

How Much to Write. Most teachers generally do not put restrictions on how much students write in interactive journals. Some students write brief entries; others write very long ones. When students have little to say, try to elicit more dialogue by asking stimulating questions and by writing interesting entries that prompt a response. Some teachers require a minimum of three sentences.

Responding to Students' Entries. Ideally, it would be best to respond to each student every day. Yet finding enough time to respond to every student everyday can be difficult. In an inclusion classroom, half of the class can write to the special education teacher for nine weeks or so while the other half writes to the general education teacher. Then roles can switch. If there is a paraprofessional or student teacher in the room, that teacher can also be part of the rotation. If only one teacher is responding, an alternative would be to answer six or seven students each day, so that each student receives a response at least once a week.

Another adaptation is for students to write to each other, either in brief or extended conversations. Interactive journals can work well with cross-age tutors.

Responses can vary in length, from one or two sentences to a paragraph or, occasionally, more. Research has shown that the type of response affects the quality and amount of students' writing. Garcia, Berry, and Garcia (1990) found that questions that requested elaboration (e.g. "Why," "How," and "What if") elicited richer responses than affirmative responses such as "Very good," "I like that," or "I agree." Yet it is also important for the teacher to share interesting information in addition to asking questions.

A key aspect of interactive journals is that mistakes should not be corrected directly. Accurate usage should be modeled. For instance, if a student writes, "I goed to the prak," one response would be, "What did you do when you went to the park?" Students should be encouraged to express their true feelings, even when they are feeling angry. The opportunity to vent emotions in writing can prevent more inappropriate outbursts. For students with behavioral disorders, this can be a valuable and effective outlet, helping students with externalizing behaviors to keep their emotions under control and students with internalizing behaviors to express their anxieties. The teacher's responses should not be judgmental.

Privacy is an important issue. It is important to assure students from the first day that their journals are private and that their contents will not be shared with anyone else unless there is reason to believe that the student might be in danger in some way or involved in a very serious problem. When students write entries they don't want anyone else to read, they can attach the "off-limits" pages together with a sticker.

Keeping the Dialogue Going. The primary goal of interactive journal writing is communication. Journal writing should be interesting for both the students and the teacher and should not be a tedious chore for either. Sometimes it can take a while to get a conversation going (as in real life). Thought-provoking "real" questions can promote students' thinking and language development.

Evaluation of Interactive Journal Writing. Journal writing should not be the sole means of evaluating students' growth in writing. Yet some teachers do monitor, evaluate, and document students' growth in expressive language and in the mechanical elements of writing (such as handwriting, spelling, punctuation, capitalization, and grammar usage) (but without making direct corrections). Evaluation summaries can be used to demonstrate each child's growth across time.

Adaptations for Students with Special Needs. Particularly for students at beginning levels whose writing is difficult to decipher, it is a good idea to ask students to "read" to you what they have written. You can then respond orally (as well as in writing). Emerging writers who have drawn a picture can explain their drawing. Students should be encouraged to at least record a few letters that represent their message.

Modifications. Rather than writing in a spiral-bound notebook or a composition book, the teacher and students can exchange email messages through their computers. Each person in the classroom can have his or her own personal electronic mailbox and send messages back and forth through the internet. MacArthur (1998) taught students to use speech synthesis and word prediction with their word processors while writing in dialogue journals *and* found that legibility and the percentage of correctly spelled words greatly increased.

Buddy Journals are a variation of interactive journals (Bromley, 1995). Instead of the teachers and students corresponding, peers write back and forth to each other. Bromley effectively used this technique pairing up students acquiring English as a new language and native-English-speaking students.

ASSESSMENT

Evaluating students' progress in writing is best accomplished by routinely observing students as they write and collecting regular writing samples (Graves, 1983; Parker, Tindal, & Hasbrouck, 1991). Graves recommends sitting with individual students as they write and observing how they approach the task. Thus, the teacher can see where the student gets "stuck," whether he or she might benefit from using planning sheets or other such strategies, and what topics might be discussed in writing conferences or a mini-lesson. Students should be observed as they write for a variety of purposes on a variety of topics of their own choosing. Methods for recording students' progress are suggested in the Teacher–Student Writing Conferences section of this chapter.

Writing samples collected at different times can be compared to determine whether they represent improvement. Students' writing should be evaluated by determining if it fulfills two general questions: Does the writing fulfill its purpose (e.g., to inform, persuade, or express feelings)? What does the student know about writing, including writing conventions, that helps fulfill his or her intentions? Thus, assessment of students' writing should examine overall cohesiveness, style, and language use as well as the application of language mechanics. Various scoring rubrics are available to assist with assessing students' writing. Figure 7.12 shows a generic version (adapted from Wiggins, 1998) and Figure 7.13 presents an adaptation of the Mississippi Department of Education Writing Rubrics for Grades 4 and 7 (2003). Many rubrics are available online and can be found by searching for "writing rubrics."

SPELLING

Spelling is a developmental process. Children progress through various stages along a continuum as they develop proficiency (Cummings, 1988; Edwards, 2003; Henderson, 1990; Read, 1975; Templeton & Bear, 1992). The first stage is *prephonemic* spelling. A prephonemic speller has learned that letters represent language, but has not yet developed an awareness of sound-symbol correspondence. Random strings of letters mark this stage. The next point in the process is *phonemic* spelling. Children at this stage have discovered the phonetic principles of spelling and attempt to capture the sounds of words as they write. This stage is characterized by an overreliance on phonetic rules. As students learn to read they notice differences between their own and conventional spelling and enter the *transitional* stage of spelling development. At this point, children increasingly incorporate the visual features of standard English orthography into their spelling. Finally, students become *correct* spellers when they regularly include the visual features of standard English spelling in their writing (although they may still make

Level	*Student should be able to*
1	Use pictures, symbols, or isolated letters, words, or phrases to communicate meaning.
2	Independently produce simple, coherent pieces of writing that include some complete sentences, at least some of which begin with capital letters and end with periods or question marks. Structure sequences of real or imagined events coherently in chronological order. Show an emerging understanding of the rudiments of story structure by establishing an opening, characters, and one or more events.
3	Independently produce coherent pieces of writing using complete sentences, most of which begin with capital letters and end with periods or question marks. Begin to use a wider range of sentence connectives than just "an" and "then" in chronological writing. Write increasingly complex stories that have some detail beyond simple events and have a defined ending. Begin to revise and redraft based on feedback from a teacher or other students, paying attention to meaning and clarity as well as checking for correct usage of grammatical forms such as verb tense and pronouns.
4	Independently produce clear, coherent pieces of writing in which an attempt is made to present the subject in a structured way with a title and separate paragraphs, and in which punctuation is generally accurate. Write stories that have an opening, a setting, characters, a series of events, and a resolution. Organize nonchronological writing in orderly ways using established text structures. Begin using complex sentence structures other than those characteristic of speech (e.g., subordinate clauses). Attempt to independently revise their own writing and talk about the changes made.
5	Independently write in a variety of forms (e.g., stories, letters, instructions, poems), for a range of purposes (e.g., to plan, inform, explain, persuade, entertain). Produce well-organized pieces of writing (e.g., with a clear layout, headings, and paragraphs) in which sentence punctuation is almost always used correctly, and in which simple uses of commas are accurate. Write in Standard English (except in contexts where nonstandard forms are appropriate) and show an increasing differentiation between speech and writing (e.g., using structures that decrease repetition). Show ability to assemble ideas on paper and produce a draft from them and revise as necessary.

FIGURE 7.12 Developmental Rubric for Levels of Writing Ability (adapted from Wiggins, 1998)

Grade 4 Writing Rubric

SCORE 4 The student's writing:

a. is about the topic (fully develops the writing prompt).
b. includes several details that support the topic.
c. is organized (maintains logical sequence).
d. frequently contains interesting words (grade-level vocabulary or above).
e. contains complete sentences.
f. follows punctuation, capitalization, spelling (both correct and phonetic), and usage rules. Two types of errors may occur: (1) those that appear as a consequence of risk-taking and (2) those that do not detract from overall quality.

SCORE 3 The student's writing:

a. is about the topic (partially develops the writing prompt).
b. includes some details that support the topic.
c. is organized (may not maintain logical sequence throughout).
d. contains some interesting words (grade-level vocabulary).
e. contains complete sentences (may have occasional fragments and/or run-on sentences).
f. follows punctuation, capitalization, spelling (both correct and phonetic), and usage rules (Occasional errors occur that may detract from overall quality).

SCORE 2 The student's writing:

a. is about the topic (minimally develops the writing prompt).
b. includes only a few details that support the topic.
c. shows minimal organization.
d. contains only a few interesting words (grade-level vocabulary).
e. contains complete sentences (may have numerous fragments and/or run-on sentences).
f. rarely follows correct punctuation, capitalization, spelling, and usage rules.

SCORE 1 The student's writing:

a. attempts to address the topic (may digress from the writing prompt).
b. includes vague or no details that support the topic.
c. shows no organization.
d. includes no interesting words (below grade-level vocabulary).
e. contains numerous fragments and/or run-on sentences (may contain a complete sentence).
f. does not follow correct punctuation, capitalization, spelling, or usage rules.

SCORE 0 The student's writing:

a. is incomprehensible.
b. is insufficient to score.

Grade 7 Writing Rubric

SCORE 4 The student's response:

a. addresses the specific writing prompt (fully develops the topic).

FIGURE 7.13 Mississippi Department of Education Writing Rubrics for Grades 4 and 7

b. contains a clearly stated main idea (thesis).
c. shows a sense of audience and purpose.
d. contains a minimum of three indented (or clearly delineated) paragraphs.
e. has a clear beginning, middle, and end.
f. has a main idea developed by supporting details that are well elaborated.
g. exhibits logical order and appropriate sequencing of steps or ideas with adequate transitions.
h. contains precise and vivid language (grade-level vocabulary or above).
i. maintains a consistent point of view.
j. contains no errors in grammar usage that detract from the overall delivery. (Grammar/usage includes subject-verb agreement, verb tense, pronoun case and reference, and complete and varied sentences.)
k. may contain a few errors in the correct use of mechanics (i.e., underlining, quotation marks, commas, semicolons, apostrophes, capitalization, and spelling), but errors do not detract from overall delivery.

SCORE 3 The student's response:

a. addresses the specific writing prompt (partially develops the topic).
b. contains a stated or implied main idea (thesis).
c. shows a sense of audience and purpose.
d. contains a minimum of three indented (or clearly delineated) paragraphs.
e. has a clear beginning, middle, and end.
f. has a main idea developed by supporting details, but these are not consistently well elaborated.
g. exhibits some logical order; sequences most steps or ideas with transitions.
h. contains appropriate language, but word choice may be repetitive (grade-level vocabulary).
i. maintains a consistent point of view.
j. may contain occasional errors in grammar/usage that may detract somewhat from the delivery. (Grammar/usage includes subject-verb agreement, verb tense, pronoun case and reference, and complete and varied sentences.)
k. may contain some errors in the correct use of mechanics (i.e., underlining, quotation marks, commas, semicolons, apostrophes, capitalization, and spelling) that may detract somewhat from delivery.

SCORE 2 The student's response:

a. addresses the specific writing prompt (minimally develops the topic).
b. contains a vaguely implied main idea (thesis).
c. shows little regard for audience and/or purpose.
d. may not exhibit indented (or clearly delineated) paragraphing.
e. has a beginning, middle, and end.
f. addresses the main idea with minimal supporting details.
g. exhibits some evidence of organization but does not sequence steps consistently and/or does not use transitions.
h. contains some appropriate language; word choice is repetitive (grade-level vocabulary).

FIGURE 7.13 Continued

(continues)

i. may not maintain a consistent point of view.
j. may contain frequent errors in grammar/usage that may impede communication. (Grammar/usage includes subject-verb agreement, verb tense, pronoun case and reference, and complete and varied sentences.)
k. may contain frequent errors in the correct use of mechanics (i.e., underlining, quotation marks, commas, semicolons, apostrophes, capitalization, and spelling) that may impede communication.

SCORE 1 The student's response:

a. attempts to address the writing prompt (may digress from the topic).
b. does not contain a main idea (thesis) or contains only an implied focus on the topic.
c. shows no regard for audience and/or purpose.
d. may not exhibit indented (or clearly delineated) paragraphing.
e. may lack a beginning, middle, and/or end.
f. contains vague or no details that support the topic.
g. lacks organization; presentation is rambling and repetitive.
h. contains vague and imprecise language (below grade-level vocabulary).
i. does not maintain a consistent point of view.
j. exhibits serious errors in grammar/usage that may severely impede communication (Grammar/usage includes subject-verb agreement, verb tense, pronoun case and reference, and complete and varied sentences.)
k. contains repeated errors in the correct use of mechanics (i.e., underlining, quotation marks, commas, semicolons, apostrophes, capitalization, and spelling) that may severely impede communication.

SCORE 0 The student's response:

a. is incomprehensible.
b. is insufficient to score.

CONDITION CODES

A Blank/Refusal
B Illegible
C Written in a language other than English
D Copy of the prompt
E Off-topic

FIGURE 7.13 Continued

some errors). Children progress through these stages at different ages and speeds. The stages are not discrete, and children may revert to earlier stages when attempting to spell unfamiliar words.

Research indicates that most children with learning disabilities progress through these same stages, but more slowly. The poor spelling of almost all students with learning disabilities looks very much like the spelling of younger, normally achieving students (Edwards, 2003; Gerber, 1986; Nelson, 1980; Worthy & Invernizzi, 1990). Spelling continues to be a roadblock to fluent writing for many students with disabilities, even those who have been taught by a writing-process approach (Jones, 2001). Many students who learned to use invented spelling do not make the transition to standard spelling and find it difficult to self-edit their work because they cannot detect or correct spelling errors. Thus, students with disabilities often benefit from systematic word study. Mercer (1997) indicated that required spelling competencies include the following:

- Auditory discrimination
- Consonants
- Phonograms
- Plurals
- Syllabication
- Structural elements (root words, prefixes, suffixes)
- Ending changes
- Digraphs and diphthongs
- Silent e

In this section we present a model for teaching spelling in heterogeneous, inclusive classrooms within the context of Writer's Workshop. First, we describe two complementary programs for whole-class implementation: *organic spelling* (Sangirardi-Gray & Meltzer, 1993) and *cued spelling* (Topping, 1995). You may decide to use either of these programs or combine features of both. Next, we discuss spelling assessment. Then we present suggestions for providing remedial instruction to students who experience difficulties with spelling. Finally, we introduce Making Words, a supplemental phonics program that can be used with the whole class (in the primary grades) or small groups of students who need this instruction (in the intermediate or middle grades).

Spelling for the Whole Class

Spelling is a curriculum area that is often neglected or mistaught (Gordon, Vaughn, & Schumm, 1993), with the focus on memorizing long weekly lists of words that may have little relevance to students' writing or developmental needs. The goal of spelling instruction should be to spell words correctly in spontaneous writing (not scoring 100 percent on a spelling test, although As on spelling tests are certainly a step in the right direction). Errors in spelling should be viewed as opportunities to explore words and language. Not all students are developmentally ready or able to spell correctly all the words they would like to use in their writing (Sangirardi-Gray & Meltzer, 1993). All students can be taught strategies for compensating with spelling difficulties, however. Dictionaries, spellcheckers, peers, and adults can all provide assistance.

One controversy related to spelling instruction is whether every student should be required to study and learn the same list of spelling words, even in a heterogeneous class that includes students at many different levels. Most teachers persist in this practice, perhaps allowing students with learning disabilities to spell fewer words than their classmates, but still studying the same list. Within the context of a Writer's Workshop classroom, we recommend that students select and learn to spell words from their own writing. This approach individualizes spelling for students and is more motivating and meaningful. A criticism of having students self-select words has been that students tend to avoid including words in their writing that they do not know how to spell (Kerr & Lambert, 1982). Yet this is truer of traditional writing programs than Writer's Workshops where the emphasis is on recording ideas, and students are taught to "not worry about spelling." In fact, research suggests that children's self-selected words are usually longer and more complex than those assigned by the teacher but are retained to at least the same degree (Gettinger, 1985; Michael, 1986).

The first of the following procedures for teaching spelling using an individualized approach was adapted from Sangirardi-Gray and Meltzer.

Organic Spelling. Students begin each week by identifying seven words from their own writing they know they have misspelled, or peers or teachers have indicated are misspelled during editing conferences. (Or students might select from one to three words each day.) Having students first try to find their own spelling errors helps develop editing skills and prevents students from becoming overly dependent on others to correct their mistakes. Most students (at a transitional or correct stage) can sense when a word is wrong because it does not "look" or "sound" right. Yet sometimes students need assistance finding inaccurate words. One technique is to tell the student how many words are misspelled, perhaps specifying the page or paragraph or even the sentence where an elusive word is located if the student is having difficulty finding it. Students who misspell many words in their spontaneous writing are not ready to learn every word they might want to use. For these few students, additional assistance by the teacher selecting appropriate words and looking for patterns in words is necessary. Other suggestions for working with these students are presented later in this section. Students who tend to be excellent spellers and miss few words when writing can select words from their reading they would like to know.

When all students have compiled their weekly seven-word lists, they complete the following activities:

- Make seven index cards with one word written on each.
- Use each word in a sentence on the back of each card.
- Enter the words in personal dictionaries or word banks.
- Study the words at home and with a partner at school.
- Using structured practice activities.
- Give each other individual spelling quizzes every Friday.
- Spell the words correctly in future writing.

When words are still misspelled after practicing them in this way, they can be included on future lists. Practice activities might include manipulating or tracing letter tiles, computer keyboard practice, and writing the words from memory and self-checking for accuracy (Gordon et al., 1993). Merely copying a word over several times is not effective. Other strategies for studying words can be adapted from the cued spelling program.

Cued Spelling. The second whole-class approach, cued spelling (Topping, 1995), has many features of organic spelling. It also gives students greater control over their own learning than traditional methods, includes guided practice with a partner and immediate feedback, and is appropriate for a wide range of age and ability levels. The pairs in cued spelling might be two children working together in school or a parent and child working at home. The procedure includes ten steps (see Figure 7.14): One child chooses a high-

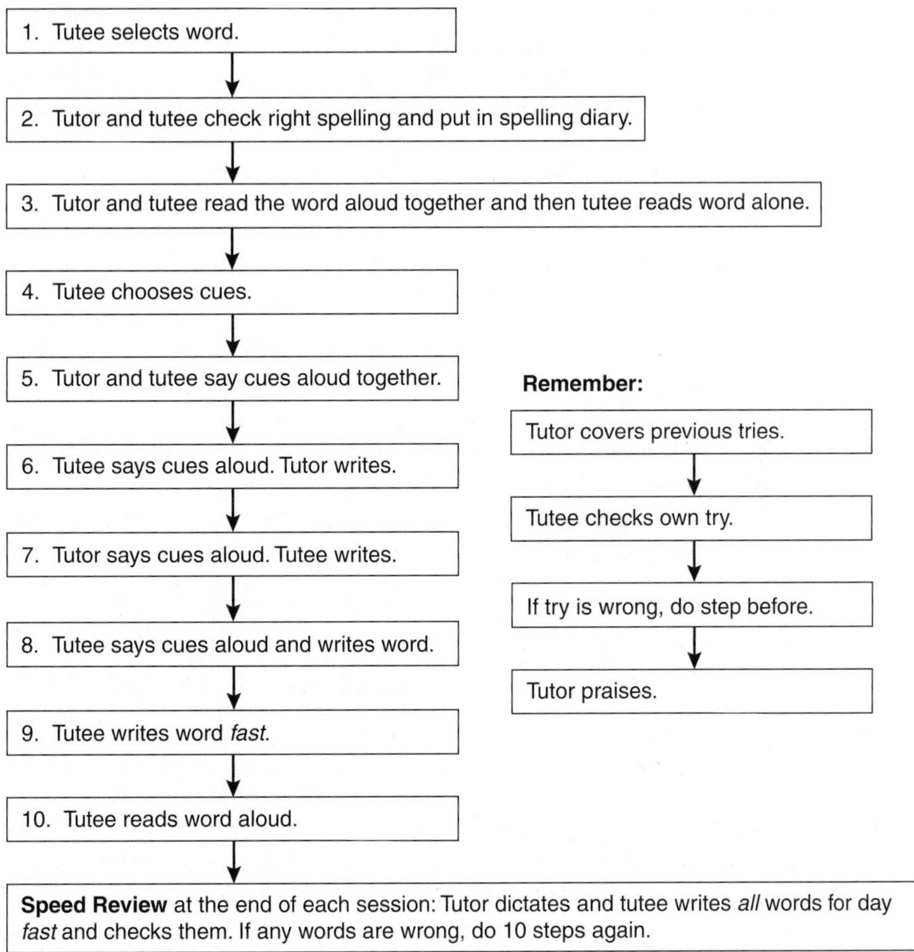

FIGURE 7.14 The Ten Steps of Cued Spelling (adapted from Topping, 1995)

interest target word (Step 1), checks the spelling of the word and enters it in a Spelling Diary (Step 2), practices reading the word (Step 3), selects a strategy or cue for remembering the word (Step 4), practices the cue and writes the word with the partner (Steps 5, 6, and 7), practices with cue and writes the word alone (Step 8), writes the word as quickly as possible (Step 9), and reads the word aloud again (Step 10). At the end of the week, each student writes all of his or her target words as fast and accurately as possible from dictation in random order (writing words quickly promotes generalization and transfer to spontaneous writing). Words spelled incorrectly can be returned to a list of potential target words for possible selection the following week. Cues for remembering words might include phonic sounds, letter names, syllables, or chunks of words (see Figure 7.15). It is important for students to select their own cues. Students typically experiment with different strategies before routinely selecting the cues that are most appropriate for their particular

Rules	Some spellings follow logical rules, such as "*i* before *e*, except after c." Keep rules simple and few in number.
Words in words	Breaking words into smaller parts, such as syllables, helps us remember them. If you can break long words into smaller words, it's even easier to remember them (such as water-fall or class-room).
Fronts and backs	Many words have the same sort of beginning, such as pre-, un-, or tri-. Many words also have the same ending, such as -tion, -ght, or -ous.
Families	Words that have the same start or finish can be put in groups or families (such as rhyming words). Sorting words into families can be a game.
Making pictures	Forming pictures in your mind about a word can help you remember it. Some mind pictures seem really silly, but this is good because if they are funny you will remember them better. For example, you might think of two people getting married (wed) in a **nes** t to help you remember how to spell Wed **nes** day.
Shrink and grow	You can remember a short hard bit of a word or just some initials for each part (like "par" in separate). It can help to "grow" the initials into new words that make a sentence or a saying. For example, "**b**ig **e**lephants **a**ren't **u**gly" can help you remember the first four letters in b-e-a-u-tiful.
Fix and stretch	It helps if you really understand what hard words mean. Talking about the meaning of a word can help fix it in your mind.
Funnies	Think of jokes or other silly things about your spelling words. Funny things are much more likely to be remembered.
Rhyme	Rhyming can be very good for helping you remember, such as "i before *e*, except after *c*."
Chant or sing	Try singing or chanting words or letters (for example, substituting the letters in "could" for the letters in the song B-I-N-G-O, about Bingo, the big black dog).
Highlight	Try highlighting or using a different color to write the hard part of a word, or writing the hard part with bigger or capital letters, like this: stationEry.
Say sounds	Try exaggerating the way you say each of the sounds in a word, such as "be-a-yu-ti-ful" for "beautiful."

Try different strategies to see what works best for you. Some people learn better with one strategy while other people learn better with different strategies. Try thinking of your own ideas, too.

FIGURE 7.15 Cued Spelling: Mnemonic Strategies

learning style. Occasional whole-class mini-lessons related to strategy selection can help with this process. One of the advantages of cued spelling is that it helps students become self-sufficient, self-regulatory strategy users. Also, after participating in a cued spelling program over time, students tend to more readily perceive consistencies in word structures and improve their spelling during free writing.

Assessment in Spelling

Students' spelling skills can be assessed using commercial criterion-referenced tests, such as the The Spellmaster Assessment and Teaching System (Greenbaum, 1987) or Test of Written Spelling, Fourth Edition (Larson, Hammill, & Moats, 1999). These CRTs measure the spelling of phonetically regular and irregular words, as well as knowledge of the structural elements of words. Their purpose is to guide instruction by helping teachers deter-

BOX 7.5
SPELLING INTERVENTIONS FOR STUDENTS WITH LD

Based on a summary of several spelling intervention studies for students with learning disabilities, Gordon, Vaughn, and Schumm (1993) contrasted typical instructional practices that appear ineffective with suggested practices (see Table 7.2). Note that the recommended practices are already included or can be incorporated into the organic and cued spelling programs.

Graham (2000) conducted a review of spelling research and reported that children learn many words incidentally or informally as they read and write, but that good spellers learn many more words this way than poor spellers. On the other hand, many research studies indicate that direct spelling instruction can improve the spelling performance of both good and poor spellers—however, it is unlikely that such instruction is extensive enough to account for all of the growth necessary to become a competent speller. Thus, it is important for classroom teachers to stress both informal *and* formal methods. Graham recommends a balanced approach. He compiled a list of research-based procedures for teaching spelling to students with LD (1999). These include:

- Before studying new spelling words, the student takes a pretest to identify words that need to be studied.
- After studying new spelling words, the student takes a posttest to determine which words were mastered.
- Immediately after taking a spelling test, the student should receive feedback and correct any misspellings.
- The student is taught a systematic and effective strategy for studying new spelling words.
- Study and testing of new words takes place daily.
- Students work together, using cooperative learning methods such as Classwide Peer Tutoring for Spelling (Mortweet, Utley, Walker, Dawson, Delquadri, Reddy, & Greenwood, 1999), to learn new spelling words.
- The number of new words to be mastered varies depending on the capabilities of the student.
- While studying, the student monitors on-task behavior and the number of times words are practiced successfully.
- Spelling words already learned are reviewed periodically to ensure retention.

mine what spelling patterns students already know and what they need to learn. Teacher-created informal spelling inventories (ISI) can serve a similar function. Words might be selected from a commercial spelling series already in use in the classroom, or by creating a list that draws upon a scope and sequence of spelling skills from the school district's curriculum guidelines. Table 7.1 shows a sample ISI (adapted from Jones, 2001).

Additional Support for Students with Learning Disabilities

Spelling is an area of great difficulty for many students with learning disabilities. Students often need explicit instruction to help them progress in spelling. Cued spelling and organic spelling already include several features helpful for students with learning disabilities (i.e., individualized attention, practicing a few words at a time, self-correcting errors, receiving

TABLE 7.1 Informal Spelling Inventory

SPELLING WORDS	SPELLING SKILLS	SPELLING WORDS USED IN SENTENCES
1. ran	Short Vowel /a/	She ran home as fast as she could.
2. let	Short Vowel /e/	Let me try to do it by myself.
3. spill	Short Vowel /i/ and Consonant Blend /sp/	Be careful not to spill the milk.
4. crust	Short Vowel /u/ and Consonant Blends /cr/ and /st/	My favorite part of bread is the crust.
5. drove	Long Vowel V-C-e	We drove for five hours to get here.
6. train	Long /a/ spelled /ai/	Have you ever been on a train ride?
7. field	Long /e/ spelled /ie/	The field was full of flowers.
8. light	Long /i/ spelled /igh/	Please turn on the light.
9. roast	Long /o/ spelled /oa/	Would you like a roast beef sandwich?
10. flew	Long /u/ spelled /ew/	The jet flew high in the sky.
11. moist	Diphthong /oi/	The cake was moist and sweet.
12. mouth	Diphthong /ou/	The dentist looked into his mouth.
13. forest	R-controlled /or/	We saw a deer in the forest.
14. park	R-controlled /ar/	Can we please go to the park?
15. thirsty	R-controlled /ir/	I was so thirsty after my hike.
16. bought	aw /o/ sound spelled /ough/	She bought a new dress.
17. quiet	Digraph /qu/	Would you please be quiet?
18. dodge	/j/ spelled dge/	Let's play dodge ball.
19. bubble	Final /le/	She liked to take bubble baths.
20. kindest	Suffix /est/	He was the kindest person I knew.
Etc.		

TABLE 7.2 Typical Instruction versus Suggested Instruction

	TYPICAL INSTRUCTION	SUGGESTED INSTRUCTION
Error imitation and modeling	Spelling errors are marked as wrong with little or no feedback.	Use error imitation and modeling in response to spelling errors (the teacher reproduces an error prior to showing the correct spelling).
Unit size	Entire word list is presented at the beginning of the week.	Use a reduced unit size (e.g., three words a day).
Modality	Students copy words multiple times.	Writing, tracing letter tiles, and computer key boarding are effective.
Computer Assisted Instruction (CAI)	Spelling is not usually included in CAI.	CAI develops positive attitudes toward spelling practice; spelling errors are decreased through CAI; individual programs are optimal.
Peer tutoring	Peer tutoring is nonexistent or unstructured.	Individual and classwide structured peer tutoring are effective.
Study techniques	Word study is unstructured and incidental.	Individual or group structured word study strategies and self-questioning strategies are effective.

Source: Adapted from Gordon, Vaughn, & Schumm (1993).

immediate feedback, and using strategies to study words during guided practice sessions), but for a few students with learning disabilities, increased teacher-guided instruction might be called for. The following suggestions are adapted from Rhodes and Dudley-Marling (1996).

Instruction for Prephonemic Spellers. Children at this stage have yet to discover that there is a systematic correspondence between oral and written language. Using a Language Experience Approach where students dictate and then read the words they have spoken helps make this connection explicit. Reading predictable books (with the same pattern of words repeated frequently) also helps. Interactive journals are another excellent way for prephonemic spellers to learn that writing is systematic. The teacher's role in modeling the process of writing is key here.

Some students at this stage do have some awareness of sound-symbol correspondence, but do not use it when they spell (Gerber, 1986). Some students might be able to say that "dog" begins with a "d," but then not write a "d" in a story about a dog. Help these students by asking them what they want to write, asking what sounds they hear, and then asking them to write down the letters that represent these sounds. Even a few beginning sounds recorded correctly are worthy of praise. Spend only a few minutes on this activity the first day, during Writer's Workshop, and then return to the student's desk the following day and do the same thing. Once students are accurately writing some sounds, they are moving to the phonemic stage.

Instruction for Phonemic Spellers. Improving the skills of phonemic spellers involves similar strategies, except that the teacher needs to help students examine the words they are trying to spell more carefully. If students are correctly representing only the first sound, they need prompting to listen to other sounds as well. Model saying the sounds in a word aloud while you write down the corresponding letters. Again, brief but frequent lessons such as this should be helpful. Be careful not to give students more information than they can handle at this point. If a student at this stage writes "ran" for "rain," resist the temptation to say, "And I know you can't hear it, but there's an 'i' after the 'a'." This sort of information might be helpful to a transitional speller, but not to a student at the phonemic stage you are helping to hear the sounds in words.

As students progress toward transitional spelling, they will learn more and more conventional spellings from words they encounter frequently in their reading, and become increasingly dissatisfied that their words are not spelled "right." This is a sign of growth. Acknowledge this increased attention to the visual conventions of spelling by saying something like, "You used to spell 'my' as 'mi' and I notice that now you are spelling it 'my' like in books. How did you learn that?" Students who include more conventional spelling patterns in their writing have progressed to the transitional stage.

Instruction for Transitional Spellers. Once students are using transitional spellings, they are ready to edit their own work for spelling errors (at the editing stage of the writing process). Students now have more of a sense that a word "doesn't look right." Once students can locate their own spelling errors, it is important not to overwhelm them by asking them to correct all of their mistakes if there are many. One technique is for you (or a peer editor) to quickly correct the more difficult errors and leave some (say, three) for the student to correct. It is important for students to develop strategies for correcting words by themselves. One method is for the student to try rewriting a misspelled word a number of different ways and then to select the spelling that "looks the best." Using spellcheckers or dictionaries are other options (when the word begins with the correct letter and is not too far off).

The selection of words for spelling practice and the compilation of a word bank (as suggested with organic spelling and cued spelling) is useful for students at the transitional stage. Not all misspelled words should be practiced or added to the word bank, however. The teacher can help students select words during editing conferences by asking, "Which of these words do you think you will want to use again in your writing?"

Helping students conduct "word sorts" where they look for categories of spelling patterns is also useful. Collect unconventional spellings from students' work over time and then categorize the errors, listing the conventional spellings next to the unconventional spellings. Ask students to try to figure out the "rule" that establishes each category. This can be an appropriate topic for mini-lessons.

Many spelling games, such as "Hangman," "Boggle," "Spill and Spell," "Scrabble," and "Word Mastermind," can help students at this developmental stage. Occasional "game days" that incorporate these activities are motivating and educational.

Despite our best efforts, some children seem to remain stuck at the transitional spelling stage. These children need to learn coping strategies for dealing with their spelling difficulties. Asking others (peers or teachers) to proofread their papers and correct spelling errors is an appropriate tactic. In a Writer's Workshop inclusive classroom that values students' different strengths and encourages cooperation and helping one another, this can be a procedure that does not stigmatize the student. Other strategies for helping poor spellers develop writing fluency are discussed in the "Drafting" section of this chapter.

Making Words

As an effective supplement to an existing spelling program and Writer's Workshop, Making Words (Cunningham & Cunningham, 1992; Cunningham & Hall, 1994) was designed as a whole class teacher-guided activity that helps students become more aware of common word patterns and increases their phonemic awareness. It improves spelling and decoding skills. Making Words is intended to supplement rather than replace existing spelling and reading programs. Although it was initially developed for whole-class implementation with primary grade students, it can also be used with groups of intermediate or middle-school students who need practice with common spelling patterns.

During a Making Words lesson (approximately 15 minutes), students form twelve to fifteen words using their own sets of individual laminated letters. The teacher guides students through the lesson by directing them to spell different words, modeling correct spelling using large letters and a pocket chart, and pointing out different spelling patterns. The last word includes all of the letters in that day's set. For example, students might receive the letters "e,u,d,h,n,r,t." After spelling words such as "red," "her," "hut," and "under," students would finish by making the word "thunder." Two books that include Making Words lessons are available: *Making Words: Multilevel, Hands-On, Developmentally Appropriate Spelling and Phonics Activities* (Cunningham & Hall, 1994) and *Making Big Words: Multilevel, Hands-On Spelling and Phonics Activities* (Cunningham & Hall, 1994).

CWPT and the SPELLER Strategy

This instructional model for inclusive classrooms combines spelling and Classwide Peer Tutoring (CWPT; Delquadri, Greenwood, Whorton, Carta, & Hall, 1986—see Chapter 6 for more information about CWPT as a reading technique). The entire class is involved, for about 20 minutes per day, at least three times a week (Keller, 2002). Students "tutor" each other while working in pairs. This approach works well whether all students are assigned the same words, or each student has an individualized list of words. Students write their words on flashcards so that they each have their own set. The method for practicing words follows the steps listed in the acronym SPELLER: **S***pot the word and say it;* **P***icture it with eyes open;* **E***yes closed and visualize it;* **L***ook to see if it's right;* **L***ook away and write it;* **E***xamine it to see if it's right;* and **R***epeat if the word was spelled incorrectly* or **R***eward if it was spelled accurately*. One student in the role of tutor guides his or her partner through these steps for 10 minutes, and then partners switch roles and repeat the process.

REFERENCES

Alley, G. R. (1988). Effects of generalization instruction on the written language performance of adolescents with learning disabilities in the mainstream classroom. *Reading, Writing, and Learning Disabilities, 4,* 291–309.

Alvermann, D. E., Dillon, D. R., & O'Brien, D. G. (1987). *Using discussion to promote reading comprehension.* Newark, DE: International Reading Association.

Atwell, N. (1998). *In the middle: New understanding about writing, reading, and learning* (2nd ed.). Portsmouth, NH: Heinemann/Boynton/Cook.

Baker, S., Gersten, R., & Graham, S. (2003). Teaching expressive writing to students with learning disabilities: Research-based applications and examples. *Journal of Learning Disabilities, 36,* 109–123.

Bromley, K. (1995). Buddy journals for ESL and native-English-speaking students. *TESOL Journal, 4*(3), 7–11.

Calkins, L. M. (1994). *The art of teaching writing* (2nd ed.). Portsmouth, NH: Heinemann.

Chittenden, L. (1995). *Authoring strategies for use throughout the writing process, and when writing for many purposes.* Handout presented at the Zelda Glazer Writing Institute, Miami, FL.

Cullinan, B. E. (Ed.). (1993). *Pen in hand: Children become writers.* Newark, DE: International Reading Association.

Cummings, D. (1988). *American English spelling.* Baltimore, MD: Johns Hopkins University Press.

Cunningham, P. M., & Cunningham, J. W. (1992). Making words: Enhancing the invented spelling-decoding connection. *The Reading Teacher, 46,* 106–115.

Cunningham, P. M., & Hall, D. (1994). *Making words: Multilevel, hands-on spelling and phonics activities.* Carthage, IL: Good Apple.

De La Paz, S., & Graham, S. (1997). Strategy instruction in planning: Effects on the writing performance and behavior of students with learning difficulties. *Exceptional Children, 63,* 167–181.

Delquadri, J., Greenwood, C. R., Whorton, D., Carta, J. J., & Hall, R. V. (1986). Classwide peer tutoring. *Exceptional Children, 52,* 535–542.

Edelsky, C. (1986). *Writing in a bilingual program: Había una vez.* Norwood, NJ: Ablex.

Edwards, L. (2003). Writing instruction in kindergarten: Examining an emerging area of research for children with writing and reading difficulties. *Journal of Learning Disabilities, 36,* 136–148.

Englert, C. S. (1990). Unraveling the mysteries of writing through strategy instruction. In T. E. Scruggs & B. Y. L. Wong (Eds.), *Intervention research in learning disabilities.* New York: Springer-Verlag.

Englert, C. S. (1992). Writing instruction from a sociocultural perspective: The holistic, dialogic, and socialenterprise of writing. *Journal of Learning Disabilities, 25,* 153–172.

Englert, C. S., Garmon, A., Mariage, T., Rozendal, M., Tarrant, K., & Urba, J. (1995). The early literacy project: Connecting across the literacy curriculum. *Learning Disability Quarterly, 18,* 253–275.

Ferris, D. (1995). Teaching students to self-edit. *TESOL Journal, 4*(4), 18–22.

Fletcher, R. (1993). Roots and wings: Literature and children's writing. In B. E. Cullinan (Ed.), *Pen in hand: Children become writers.* Newark, DE: International Reading Association.

Flores, B., Garcia, E., Gonzalez, S., Hidalgo, G., Kaczmarek, K., & Romero, T. (1985). *Holistic bilingual instructional strategies.* Tempe, AZ: Arizona State University.

Garcia, E. (2001). *Understanding and meeting the challenge of student cultural diversity* (3rd ed.). Boston: Houghton Mifflin.

Garcia, E. E., Berry, C., & Garcia, E. (1990). The effect of teacher reaction on student's interactive journal entries. *Early Child Development and Care, 56,* 35–47.

Gerber, M. M. (1986). Generalization of spelling strategies by learning disabled students as a result of contingent imitation/modeling and mastery criteria. *Journal of Learning Disabilities, 19,* 530–537.

Gersten, R., & Baker, S. (2001). Teaching expressive writing to students with learning disabilities: A meta-analysis. *The Elementary School Journal, 101,* 251–272.

Gettinger, M. (1985). Effects of teacher-directed versus student-directed instruction and cues versus no cues for improving spelling. *Journal of Applied Behavior Analysis, 18,* 167–171.

Gordon, J., Vaughn, S., & Schumm, J. S. (1993). Spelling interventions: A review of literature and implications for instruction for students with learning disabilities. *Learning Disabilities: Research and Practice, 8,* 175–181.

Graham, S. (1999). Handwriting and spelling instruction for students with learning disabilities: A review. *Learning Disability Quarterly, 22,* 78–98.

Graham, S. (2000). Should the natural learning approach replace spelling instruction? *Journal of Educational Psychology, 92,* 235–247.

Graham, S., & Harris, K. R. (1989). A components analysis of cognitive strategy instruction: Effects on learning disabled students' compositions and self-efficacy. *Journal of Educational Psychology, 81,* 353–361.

Graham, S., Harris, K. R., & Larsen, L. (2001). Prevention and intervention of writing difficulties for students with learning disabilities. *Learning Disabilities Research & Practice, 16,* 74–84.

Graves, D. H. (1983). *Writing: Teachers and children at work.* Portsmouth, NH: Heinemann.

Greenbaum, C. (1987). *The Spellmaster Assessment and Teaching System.* Austin, TX: Pro-Ed.

Hallenbeck, M. J. (2002). Taking charge: Adolescents with learning disabilities assume responsibility for their own writing. *Learning Disability Quarterly, 25,* 227–246.

Harris, A. J., & Sipay, E. R. (1990). *How to increase reading ability: A guide to developmental and remedial methods* (9th ed.). Boston: Addison-Wesley.

Henderson, E. (1990). *Teaching spelling.* Boston: Houghton Mifflin.

Johnson, D. M., & Roen, D. H. (1989). *Richness in writing: Empowering ESL students.* New York: Longman.

Jones, C. J. (2001). Teacher-friendly curriculum-based assessment in spelling. *TEACHING Exceptional Children, 34*(2), 32–38.

Keller, C. L. (2002). A new twist on spelling instruction for elementary school teachers. *Intervention in School and Clinic, 38*(1), 3–7.

Kerr, M. M., & Lambert, D. L. (1982). Behavior modification of children's written language. In M. Hersen, R. M. Eisler, & P. M. Miller (Eds.), *Progress in behavior modification* (Vol. 13, pp. 79–108). New York: Academic Press.

Larsen, S. C., Hammill, D. D., & Moats, L. C. (1999). *Test of Written Spelling* (4th ed.). Austin, TX: Pro-Ed.

MacArthur, C. A. (1998). Word processing with speech synthesis and word prediction: Effects on the dialogue journal writing of students with learning disabilities. *Learning Disability Quarterly, 21,* 151–166.

MacArthur, C. A., Graham, S., Schwartz, S. S., & Schafer, W. D. (1995). Evaluation of a writing instruction model that integrated a process approach, strategy instruction, and word processing. *Learning Disability Quarterly, 18,* 278–291.

MacArthur, C. A., Harris, K. R., & Graham, S. (1994). Improving students' planning processes through cognitive strategy instruction. In E. C. Butterfield (Ed.), *Advances in cognition and educational practice: Vol. 2. Children's writing: Toward a process theory of the development of skilled writing* (pp. 173–198). Greenwich, CT: JAI Press.

MacArthur, C. A., Schwartz, S. S., & Graham, S. (1991a). A model for writing instruction: Integrating word processing and strategy instruction into a process approach to writing. *Learning Disabilities: Research & Practice, 6,* 230–236.

MacArthur, C. A., Schwartz, S. S., & Graham, S. (1991b). Effects of a reciprocal peer revision strategy in special education classrooms. *Learning Disabilities: Research & Practice, 6,* 201–210.

Marchisan, M. L., & Alber, S. R. (2001). The write way: Tips for teaching the writing process to resistant writers. *Intervention in School and Clinic, 36*(3), 154–62.

Martin, K. F., & Manno, C. (1995). Use of a check-off system to improve story compositions by middle school students. *Journal of Learning Disabilities, 28,* 138–149.

Mercer, C. (1997). *Students with learning disabilities* (5th ed.). Upper Saddle River, NJ: Merrill (Prentice-Hall).

Michael, J. (1986). Spelling categories and strategies. *Reading, 25,* 33–37.

Mississippi Department of Education (2003). *Writing rubrics for grades 4 & 7.* Retrieved August 26, 2003, from *http://www.mde.k12.ms.us/acad/osa/write47.htm#4.*

Mortweet, S. L., Utley, C. A., Walker, D., Dawson, H. L., Delquadri, J. C., Reddy, S., & Greenwood, C. R. (1999). Classwide peer tutoring: An effective spelling instruction procedure for students with educable mental retardation and their typical peers. *Exceptional Children, 65,* 524–536.

Nelson, H. E. (1980). Analysis of spelling errors in normal and dyslexic children. In U. Frith (Ed.), *Cognitive process in spelling* (pp. 475–493). London: Academic Press.

Parker, R., Tindal, G., & Hasbrouck, J. (1991). Progress monitoring with objective measures of writing performance for students with mild disabilities. *Exceptional Children, 58,* 61–73.

Pearson, P. D., & Johnson, D. (1978). *Teaching reading comprehension.* New York: Holt, Rinehart, & Winston.

Peyton, J. K., & Staton, J. (1993). *Dialogue journals in the multilingual classroom: Building language fluency and writing skills through written interaction.* Norwood, NJ: Ablex.

Read, C. (1975). *Children's categories of speech sounds in English.* Urbana, IL: National Council of Teachers of English.

Rhodes, L. K., & Dudley-Marling, C. (1996). *Readers*

and writers with a difference: A holistic approach to teaching struggling readers and writers (2nd ed.). Portsmouth, NH: Heinemann.

Ruddell, M. R. (1993). *Teaching content reading and writing.* Boston: Allyn and Bacon.

Sangirardi-Gray, J., & Meltzer, E. (1993). Organic mechanics: Developing skills through literature and student writing. In B. E. Cullinan (Ed.), *Pen in hand: Children become writers.* Newark, DE: International Reading Association.

Scott, B. J., & Vitale, M. R. (2003). Teaching the writing process to students with LD. *Intervention in School and Clinic, 38*(4), 220–224.

Smith, S., Boone, R., & Higgins, K. (1998). Expanding the writing process to the web. *TEACHING Exceptional Children, 30*(5), 22–26.

Templeton, S., & Bear, D. (Eds.). (1992). *Development of orthographic knowledge and the foundations of literacy.* Hillsdale, NJ: Lawrence Erlbaum.

Topping, K. J. (1995). Cued spelling: A powerful technique for parent and peer tutoring. *The Reading Teacher, 48,* 374–383.

Troia, G., & Graham, S. (2002). The effectiveness of a highly explicit, teacher-directed strategy instruction routine: Changing the writing performance of students with learning disabilities. *Journal of Learning Disabilities, 35,* 290–305.

Vygotsky, L. S. (1978). *Mind in society.* Cambridge, MA: MIT.

Vygotsky, L. S. (1986). *Thought and language.* Cambridge, MA: MIT.

Wiggins, G. (1998). *Educative assessment: Designing assessments to inform and improve student performance.* San Francisco, CA: Jossey-Bass.

Wong, B., Butler, D., Ficzere, S., Kuperis, S., Corden, M., & Zelmer, J. (1994). Teaching problem learners revision skills and sensitivity to audience through two instructional modes: Student-teacher versus student-student interactive dialogues. *Learning Disabilities Research and Practice, 9,* 78–90.

Worthy, M. J., & Invernizzi, M. (1990). Spelling errors of normal and disabled students on achievement levels one through four: Instructional implication. *Annals of Dyslexia, 40,* 138–151.

Zaragoza, N. (1987). Process writing for high-risk and learning disabled students. *Reading Research and Instruction, 26,* 290–301.

Zaragoza, N. (1995). *A teacher's guide to the Writer's Workshop.* Unpublished manuscript.

Zaragoza, N., & Vaughn, S. (1992). The effects of process writing instruction on three 2nd-grade students with different achievement profiles. *Learning Disabilities Research and Practice, 7,* 184–193.

Zaragoza, N., & Vaughn, S. (1995). Children teach us to teach writing. *The Reading Teacher, 49,* 42–47.

CHAPTER EIGHT

TEACHING MATH TO STUDENTS WITH HIGH-INCIDENCE DISABILITIES IN INCLUSIVE SETTINGS

MARGARET D. CLARK
California State University, Los Angeles

Do not worry about your difficulties in Mathematics. I can assure you mine are still greater.
—Albert Einstein (1879–1955)

KEY CONCEPTS

- Many children with high-incidence disabilities struggle to learn mathematics throughout their school career.
- Abstract concepts pose a particular challenge to students with math-related disabilities.
- Explicit instruction and cognitive strategy instruction are both important in teaching students with math-related disabilities.
- Effective math instruction is sequential, building on previously learned concepts, and moves from concrete to abstract representation.

FOCUS QUESTIONS

1. How do high-incidence disabilities affect students with regard to mathematics learning?
2. What constitutes effective mathematics instruction?
3. How can the special educator collaborate, co-teach, and co-plan with a general education teacher?
4. How can students who are behind in mathematics fit into a general education classroom?

Vanessa is a sixth-grade student with a learning disability that impacts her mathematics learning. Mr. Rodriguez, her sixth-grade teacher, observes with some frustration that despite his attempts to provide remedial instruction in basic calculation skills, Vanessa continues to achieve at a level far below that of her classmates, and consequently, has not been able to move on to fractions and decimals. Mr. Rodriguez has sought the help of Ms. Frye, the special education inclusion teacher. He complains with some frustration that Vanessa seems to be making little progress, but rather continues to make the same errors over and over again. Among the patterns of errors in subtraction her teacher notes are her inability to distinguish when she should or should not regroup, ignoring zeros when regrouping, and making calculations from the left to the right. Moreover, her teacher notes she still depends on tally marks, her fingers, or other manipulatives, yet makes a variety of repetitive errors in number facts. Ms. Frye, who currently has no students on her roster in Mr. Rodriguez's class, agrees to come in to observe Vanessa and the class even though it is not on her regular schedule. She will observe Vanessa during two math classes in one week, then she will pull Vanessa out to conduct some informal one-to-one math assessment. Mr. Rodriguez suggests that she observe her in one or two other subject areas just to compare her math performance with other areas.

For many students with high-incidence disabilities in the general education classroom, learning mathematics presents a challenge arguably as great as learning to read. These students' disabilities in cognition, perception, behavior, or attention make learning mathematics a difficult process. This is particularly true given that general education teachers typically give limited attention to concrete presentation of mathematics in their instruction. In fact, many students with and without disabilities struggle with mathematics and often have difficulty generalizing operations to tasks outside those presented in the classroom. There are several factors that contribute to the mathematical difficulties. The mathematics curriculum tends to make rapid shifts from one concept to the next, students have inadequate opportunity to explore concepts and practice skills, and the concepts often seem abstract and unrelated to real life.

As many as 64 percent of students with learning disabilities perform below grade level in math (McLesky & Waldron, 1990; Miller, Butler, & Lee, 1998). Students in other disability categories often struggle with math as well. The majority of math-related struggles first manifest in the elementary years, and in most cases, continue to impact students' learning into the secondary school years (Miller & Mercer, 1997) and often into adulthood (Patton, Cronin, Bassett, & Koppel, 1997). Yet far less attention has been devoted to research on identification and remediation of math-related needs of students with high-incidence disabilities (Rivera, 1997) as compared to students with disabilities in reading.

"I HATE MATH!"

How often do we hear students with math disabilities say this? For many students with such disabilities, their daily math class represents a source of frustration and failure. Concepts elude them, content changes rapidly, numbers have little meaning, and assignments are difficult, if not impossible, to complete. Moreover, what math work they complete generally contains numerous errors; for many students, success is measured by getting to the bottom of the page or the last problem, with little regard for the accuracy of the work done. This pattern of frustration on the part of these students also proves challenging to their teachers: Students appear to lack effort when approaching math tasks and have a tendency to be anxious about mathematics (Lerner, 2000). Students with math-related disabilities tend to have negative attributions for their math achievement, meaning they hold a chronically negative self-perception with regard to math (Kistner, Osborne, & Le Verrier, 1988; Licht, 1983).

Students with high-incidence disabilities typically exhibit a range of difficulties with math, including the inability to recall math facts and overdependence on manipulatives, lack of calculation skills and strategies, and difficulty solving word problems (Bryant & Dix, 2000). Behaviors most frequently identified by these students' teachers include difficulties with multi-step problems, regrouping ("borrowing") and renaming ("carrying") errors, lack of automatic recall of math facts, inability to determine the reasonableness of answers, and the inability to copy and align numbers accurately (Bryant, Bryant, & Hammill, 2000). When such difficulties are not identified and addressed in the early grades, they can persist well into the later school years and often are at the root of continuing failure in mathematics.

Typical math instruction in the general classroom often presents a variety of challenges for students with high-incidence disabilities. Math instruction tends to follow a commercial math book or book-based program, and the frequent changes in topics typical of most of these programs—division one week, geometry the next—fails to afford students sufficiently long periods of gradually more challenging instruction and continued review that they need to successfully master math skills. With a greater emphasis on including students with disabilities in the general education curriculum posted in the 1997 legislation of P.L. 105–17, there is an increased risk that students' basic difficulties will go unidentified or unaddressed as teachers expect these students to move through the curriculum with their nondisabled peers. It is critically important for general and special education teachers to collaborate in implementing a systematic program of assessment and instruction in order to closely monitor and address the specific, sometimes very small-scale, skill needs of these students.

The gap between the skills of students with disabilities and the demands of the curriculum widens as students move into secondary grades. Miller and Mercer (1997) found instruction at the secondary level largely driven by the class textbook. As much as 75 percent to 90 percent of classroom instruction at the high school level is based on these textbooks, with the content of classes largely aligned to the scope and sequence of the chosen book. They suggest that this approach results in superficial coverage of topics, quick introduction of skills, emphasis on textbook rather than life-skills problems, and a push to "get through the book" rather than the decision to slow down, teach part of the curriculum, and assure the learning of all students.

Lerner (2000), examining the characteristics of typical classroom math programs, notes the following shortcomings:

- Lack of connections to students' prior knowledge
- Too rapid introduction of concepts
- Insufficient guided practice to allow students to successfully transition from instruction to independent practice and application of skills
- Insufficient review to assure students retain new learning

These four critical issues, along with the heavy dependence on text materials at the secondary level, can arguably be viewed as a blueprint for failure for many students with high-incidence disabilities in mathematics classes.

Clearly, students with high-incidence disabilities need a stronger system of instructional support in order to be successful in mathematics. This makes the role of the special education teacher—as teacher, as collaborator, and as support provider—a critical one. The purpose of this chapter is to present methods special education teachers can use when teaching mathematics to children with high incidence disabilities in a variety of inclusive settings. It will begin by examining the foundations for effective mathematics instruction. Assessment practices for the purpose of designing appropriate instruction and instructional methodology will be presented, as well as models for providing instruction in a variety of settings. Finally, the chapter will conclude with a short discussion of the use of instructional technology.

At the core of this chapter are four instructional philosophies: (1) that math learning is a gradual, incremental, and sequential process that requires sufficiently long periods of practice to assure mastery of skills; (2) that effective mathematics instruction has as its foundation the strong development of underlying mathematical concepts; (3) that mathematics instruction must continuously emphasize and develop problem-solving skills; and (4) that teachers of mathematics must teach not only to the curriculum but to the specific needs exhibited by their students with math disabilities.

A FRAMEWORK FOR MATH INSTRUCTION

Traditionally, elementary school mathematics instruction has emphasized calculations and word problems, with higher order math skills such as algebra and geometry taught at the secondary level. Following on the heels of the "new math" and "back to basics" movements of the 1960s and 1970s, recent reform efforts have drawn increasing attention to the way in which we teach mathematics to all students (Rivera, 1997). In 1991, the National Council of Teachers of Mathematics released the *Professional Standards for Teachers of Mathematics*. Although at times controversial (Rivera, 1997), in part because of their limited research base, dependence on constructivist learning, and limited attention to disability, the Standards have been widely accepted and form the foundation on which to build a comprehensive program of mathematics instruction for students with disabilities.

In 2000, the NCTM introduced their revised *Principles and Standard for School Mathematics* (NCTM, 2000), comprised of six Principles and ten accompanying Standards for mathematics instruction. The six Principles describe critical issues that affect math instruction, curriculum, assessment and selection of materials:

Content standards Specific elements of mathematics content that students should learn during the K-12 grades.

- Equity: High expectations and strong support for all students.
- Curriculum: Curriculum is coherent, well articulated across the grades, and focused on important aspects of mathematics.
- Teaching: Instruction focuses on what students know as well as what they need to know, providing sufficient challenge and the opportunity to learn well.
- Learning: Students actively build new knowledge on a foundation of prior learning.
- Assessment: Assessment provides information to teachers while supporting learning of new skills.
- Technology: Technology is an essential part of math instruction, enhancing st dent learning.

Process standards Specific mathematical processes that students should learn during the K-12 grades.

In a notable departure from the 1991 Standards, the ten 2000 Standards (see Table 8.1) are divided into two categories: **content standards** that address specific math content and **process standards** that address the processes students use in mathematics. Together, they define what students should learn and do from kindergarten to grade 12. Although the standards do not receive equal emphasis at each grade level, they apply across all grade levels, ensuring uniformity and cohesiveness to

TABLE 8.1 NCTM 2000 Standards for School Mathematics

THE CONTENT STANDARDS	THE PROCESS STANDARDS
■ Number and Operations	■ Problem Solving
■ Algebra	■ Reasoning and Proof
■ Geometry	■ Communication
■ Measurement	■ Connections
■ Data Analysis and Probability	■ Representation

Source: National Council of Teachers of Mathematics. (2000). *Principles and Standards for School Mathematics* (Electronic Edition). Reston, VA: Author.

math instruction. For teachers of students with disabilities, they can help to form a foundation for assessing math skills and assuring a comprehensive program of instruction.

Also useful for determining what skills should be taught are state and school district curriculum guides. Often these publications, as well as many commercial math programs contain a comprehensive scope and sequence of skills that can be reviewed, both to assist teachers' development of appropriate goals and benchmarks and to assure instructional materials adequately teach skills needed by students with math disabilities.

THE DEVELOPMENT OF MATHEMATICS

Early Foundations

Children's math skills develop early, from the time they begin to encounter and manipulate objects in their environment. These early experiences with objects are critical to the formation of concepts on which skills are built. Young children playing with blocks, puzzles, construction toys, toy animals, and even everyday household objects such as pots, pails, and boxes explore and manipulate these objects intuitively. From these explorations, they develop such early math readiness skills as counting, sorting, categorization, seriation, matching, and comparison. From these early skills come the concepts of one-to-one correspondence and number constancy. Lack of these early experiences, either through lack of opportunity or because of deficits in attention, cognitive skills, or perceptual skills may result in children's failing to develop these early skills and result in later difficulties in mathematics. Critical to the development of all these skills is the amount of time parents spend talking with young children about these concepts, allowing them to explore and ask questions about their environment. Without answers to these early math-related questions, children often experience far less success in mathematics.

Similarly, children who do not play with toys such as blocks, construction toys, and puzzles that allow them to experience the relationships between objects in space may fail to develop important directional and positional relationships such as over/under, before/after, front/back, top/bottom, near/far or high/low, and right/left. During the elementary school years, these children may continue to struggle with these concepts.

Consequently, they may not appreciate basic numerical relationships such as the relative position of numbers along a number line (is 5 closer to 4 or 9?) or the order of numbers (does 5 come before 6 or after it?) (Lowenthal, 1998). These children may also have difficulty with spatial orientation tasks, such as arranging written work on a piece of paper, or finding their way around the school campus.

Concepts of time are equally impacted by lack of early experience. Children are expected to learn to tell time to the minute by the early elementary grades, and lack of exposure to such early temporal concepts as now/later, morning/afternoon/evening, and a little while/a long time may impact their ability to tell time.

Mathematics in the Elementary School Years

Students first encounter math instruction and paper-and-pencil math tasks in the early elementary grades. First instruction emphasizes development of numerical concepts, counting, numbers from 10 to 100, place value, one-step word problems, and memorization of basic math facts. Few students with high-incidence disabilities are typically identified during these early years. Consequently, for many students with as-yet-unidentified disabilities, uniformity of instruction and movement through the curriculum tend to be emphasized over instruction that meets the needs of all learners. Students who may later be identified as having learning disabilities often experience difficulty with early math when too early emphasis is placed on calculations rather than on concept development, an even greater challenge for students with cognitive impairments. Seatwork that requires a high level of independence may be challenging for students who have difficulty remaining on task or seated, or for students with learning disabilities, who tend to profit more from closely monitored guided practice.

As these children progress through the elementary years, they are confronted with an increasing number of math competencies: early geometry, advanced computations, estimation, fractions and decimals, probabilities, and perhaps the biggest challenge of all, multistep word problems, which demand not only good basic math skills, but near grade-level reading skills as well. Math skills become increasingly abstract with less and less emphasis placed on conceptual development through the use of concrete materials. Although by middle school most students with high-incidence disabilities have been identified, they may exhibit significant deficits in math as well as reading. When confronted with increasingly difficult instruction, they often continue a pattern of failure established in the early grades, unless a system of appropriate supports is put into place. Happily, with these supports, many students with high-incidence disabilities do flourish in elementary school math.

Mathematics in the Secondary Years

As students with disabilities transition to secondary school, the nature of schooling, and math instruction, changes dramatically. Increasing maturity demands are placed on these students as they cope with departmentalized instruction and a different teacher for each class for the first time. At the same time, emphasis on instructional standards and high-stakes testing increases. By the high school years, graduation requirements and the possibility of college loom large, adding additional pressures to succeed.

Underlying math instruction at the secondary level is the assumption that basic skills have already been mastered (Lerner, 2000). Secondary mathematics increases in difficulty and abstraction, with courses emphasizing one area of instruction, such as algebra or geometry, with limited use of concrete instructional materials. Students with high-incidence disabilities unable to compete in these advanced courses tend to remain in remedial, special education, or basic mathematics courses.

Students with high-incidence disabilities may encounter a variety of difficulties with secondary math. In addition to teaching at a highly abstract level, teachers may provide too few examples to allow students to grasp concepts (Miller, 1996), particularly when they have not developed solid basic skills. Students may have difficulty discriminating among various types of problems (Carnine, 1997), especially when they are confronted with a variety of types of problems on a page. Vocabulary increases in difficulty (e.g., complementary and supplementary angles, rhombus, and polygon) and may be presented too rapidly for these students to learn effectively.

Development of the special education math curriculum at the secondary level must, for the first time, consider more than the demands of the school and the curriculum. Special education teachers of secondary math must not only plan with the needs of the student and the requirements of the curriculum in mind, but must also consider the postsecondary needs of their students. Despite these difficulties, many students with high-incidence disabilities do succeed in math courses and go on to postsecondary education. Others pursue a prevocational course of study. Still others require a program that will allow them to use math in functional applications that foster independent living. The instructional needs of these groups of students vary widely, and an appropriate program of instruction is essential.

MATH ASSESSMENT FOR STUDENTS WITH HIGH-INCIDENCE DISABILITIES

The purpose of assessment is to answer questions about the performance of students and the effectiveness of instruction and to form a basis for sound decision making (Bryant & Rivera, 1997). Thus, assessment data are a critical aspect of effective mathematics instruction. As special educators, we assess for a variety of reasons, including

- Determination of special education eligibility.
- Development of mathematics goals and objectives or benchmarks.
- Development of appropriate math instruction.
- Monitoring student progress toward mastery of math skills.
- Evaluation of instructional and programmatic effectiveness.
- Reviewing attainment of math goals and objectives (Rivera, 1997).

Assessment tools selection is based upon the purpose for which an assessment is used. Some assessments are best used for diagnostic purposes, and others are more effective for the development of goals and objectives, and others are best when charting student achievement and determining mastery. Mathematics is made up of networks of discrete, sequential skills, each skill building on the one before it. For instructional purposes, authentic or curriculum-based assessment tools that align closely to math curriculum materials are the most appropriate for determining mastery and evaluating instruction. These assessments most closely duplicate the tasks students perform on a daily basis and are flexible enough to allow evaluation of a given sequence of skills that a student must master.

Defining Mastery

At this point, it may be useful to briefly discuss what is meant by *mastery* in terms of mathematics and how this relates to mathematics assessment. When IEPs are prepared according to the requirements of P.L. 105–17, they contain a number of long-term instructional goals as well as group of benchmarks or objectives that lead to the attainment of each goal, typically over the course of a year. Each of the skills that take a student from his or her current level of performance to the level of the goal, and its benchmarks, must be mastered before the student has met the goal. Recall criterion levels for attainment of an objective may appear in form such as:

a. *Percentage of accuracy:* Chris will divide three (3) or more digit numbers by one (1) digit with remainder with 80 percent accuracy.
b. *Accuracy across multiple trials:* Vanessa will gather necessary materials for her math assignment on 4/5 instructional days.
c. *Rate:* Frederico will compute 16 out of 20 sums to 10 on a two-minute timed test.

In order to master a skill, a student must demonstrate it:

- Independently (with minimal assistance)
- On a consistent basis (over multiple assessments)
- With a reasonable level of automaticity (speed)
- At a criterion level determined by the teacher and the IEP

The criterion level for a given skill, degree of automaticity, and threshold for mastery are largely arbitrary. Usually, they are set by the teacher based on the needs of the individual student. A useful guideline for determining mastery is when a student can perform a task as described above on five assessments, including three assessments in a row. How, then, do we assess student progress in mathematics and determine if our teaching has been effective?

Preparing an Assessment

Just as teaching takes thought and planning, so does assessment. A teacher selecting assessment tools should consider the reasons for the assessment. Some useful questions a teacher may wish to consider are:

- What is the purpose of the assessment?
- What do I already know about the student's skills and needs?

- What do I need to know?
- What are the components of the instructional task to be assessed?
- What will the assessment tell me about the effectiveness of my teaching?
- What assessment tools will best answer my questions?

Careful selection of math assessment tools allows a teacher to fully answer these questions in a thorough and meaningful way. Not all tools provide the same information, and for instructional purposes, teachers should select tools that allow them to identify and describe *specific* student skills, determine student mastery of instructional objectives, and evaluate the effectiveness of instruction. Similarly, teachers should be mindful of response mode (paper and pencil, oral, demonstration, etc.) when selecting an assessment, to be certain it is appropriate to the task being measured as well as the capabilities of the child.

As you read the next section, consider the following:

Ms. Harris has been providing daily instruction designed to teach a group of students with high-incidence disabilities to identify the operation in a one-step word problem. They have been practicing reading problems, identifying key words that indicate the operation, then determining the operation. She wishes to assess their progress toward mastering the task so she can determine if her students are ready for the next step—setting up the computation. In so doing, she will also be able to see if she has taught the necessary skills completely and effectively or whether there are gaps in her students' knowledge. She will do this by surveying the assessment results for such information as consistent patterns of errors made by the majority of her students. What tools and strategies do you think might best answer her questions?

Selecting Appropriate Assessment Tools

Assessment is far more comprehensive than simply using commercial or even teacher-made tests. Instead, these tests should be thought of as one component of a battery of assessments that can also include observations, student work samples, probes, checklists, and much more. Moreover, not all assessment tools are equally well suited to a given situation, because different assessments provide different kinds of information.

To most effectively assess the students they teach, teachers of students with high-incidence disabilities should continuously enlarge their repertoire of assessment strategies. At times, assessments must be administered in a small-group setting or in the general classroom, creating the need for discreet, quickly administered tools. Often, the most useful assessments for the purpose of tracking progress toward mastery of skills and the effectiveness of daily instruction are the ones a teacher develops in response to a specific assessment situation or during a routine classroom activity such as observing a student performing a task. The results of these assessments, when recorded, provide valuable information about student skills and needs. Something as simple as a question directed to a student performing a task ("Michael, why did you carry the three from the one's place to the ten's place?") can be a form of assessment.

Let us review some of the math assessment tools and strategies available to teachers of students with high-incidence disabilities. The purpose of this review is to determine which assessment tools will allow us to:

- Identify and describe specific student math skills in *instructional* language (i.e., Steven is able to subtract fractions with like denominators).
- Track the level of student attainment of a skill (i.e., Maisha can add a column of 3 to 5 one-digit numbers with 65 percent accuracy)
- Determine the effectiveness of instruction, an instructional program, or an instructional strategy.
- Write or review attainment of goals and benchmarks.

Norm-Referenced Tests. Used primarily for diagnostic purposes, norm-referenced tests such as the *Woodcock-Johnson III* (Woodcock, McGrew, & Mather, 2001), or the *Key Math Diagnostic Inventory* provide overall estimates of student performance. Scores are typically numerical and may include such scores as an estimate of grade-level and/or age-level performance, a percentile ranking, and a standardized score such as a scaled score or normal curve equivalent. These tests are of limited usefulness for instructional assessment because they do not describe specific skill attainment; however, they can be useful when tracking student achievement on a long-term basis, such as from initial IEP to triennial IEP review.

Criterion-Referenced Tests. Criterion-referenced tests such as the *Brigance Comprehensive Inventory of Basic Skills* (Brigance, 1999) are used to assess students' knowledge as compared to a set criterion, or what would be considered mastery. For example, a teacher may select a test that determines whether students can reduce fractions or convert a fraction to a decimal. Criterion-referenced tests survey a variety of skills, allowing a teacher to determine where along a continuum of skills a student falls, such as a survey of addition skills that consists of a group of increasingly more advanced addition problems. These tests are often used to assess students prior to writing or reviewing goals and benchmarks for an IEP. Moreover, these tests can be administered at any point in time. Well-made criterion-referenced tests should contain enough items to effectively assess whether a student has understood math content (Bryant & Rivera, 1997), and teachers should be mindful of the limitations of these tests. Criterion-referenced tests seldom cover all the skills a teacher may need to assess, and they seldom allow a measure of automaticity, or speed. Teachers selecting these tests may need to supplement them and may want to observe students as they complete a task, in order to allow for these limitations. Despite this, criterion-referenced tests can be useful assessment tools for routine assessment tasks.

Curriculum-Based Measurement. Similar to criterion-referenced tests, Curriculum-Based Measurement (CBM) assesses student performance as directly compared to a school curriculum (Fuchs & Fuchs, 1988; Shinn & Hubbard, 1993). Instructional progress toward a year-end goal is regularly assessed to identify skills learned and evaluate the effectiveness of instruction over time (Fuchs, Fuchs, Hamlett, & Alinder, 1989; Fuchs, Fuchs,

Karns, Hamlett, Katzaroff & Dutka, 1998). Assessment items are drawn directly from the curriculum and are selected to track student learning through the year. Characteristics of CBM include:

1. Standardized, but not normed, procedures for administration. Items are drawn from the classroom curriculum, administered under the same conditions, then analyzed in order to make decisions.
2. A focus on long-term curricular goals (such as year-end goals) and measurement of progress toward the end goal.
3. One teacher-developed test (with many versions) of all the skills to be taught over the year.
4. Scoring for achievement of whole skills (can a child solve a subtraction properly?) and discrete skills (did the child regroup correctly?).

Periodic administrations monitor how well and how rapidly the student is progressing through the curriculum and whether expectations for the student should be modified (Rivera & Bryant, 1997). Results of the individual administrations of the assessment are graphed in order to track progress over the school year. CBM is a particularly useful assessment tool for tracking long-term performance, such as toward a given goal on an IEP.

Survey tests Assessments that test students' performance of a set of skills in order to determine a starting place for instruction within a set curriculum sequence.

Probe A test, usually teacher-made, that assesses students' performance in a specific skill set or on a target skill. For example, a teacher may assess a whole class or an instructional group on addition with regrouping to make sure they have mastered the concept before moving on to a more advanced skill.

Authentic Assessment. A variety of other, more informal measures are available to teachers wishing to assess students' progress and mastery of skills. Very closely aligned to daily instruction and the curriculum, many of these assessments are developed by teachers in response to the specific questions they wish to answer. Two of the most effective methods to pinpoint assessment and align it to the curriculum are **survey tests** and **probes**. Survey tests are similar to the survey assessments in CRTs in that they assess a sequence of skills in order to determine where instruction is needed. However, survey tests are "made to order" and can be developed to match closely to the classroom curriculum. Mercer and Mercer (1998) suggest the following steps for constructing a survey test:

1. Select a skill hierarchy that includes the content area to be assessed. This may be drawn from a district curriculum guide or from the school math program.
2. Decide on the range of skills that need to be evaluated.
3. Construct items for each skill within the range selected. Start with the easiest items and construct the test to increase in difficulty.
4. Score the test and interpret the student's performance.

More specific than survey tests, probes are made up by teachers to evaluate whether a student or groups of students are mastering a skill, as well as to identify problem areas of instruction (Mercer & Mercer, 1998). Teacher-made probes, consisting of 10 to 20 items (see Figure 8.1), can assess a single skill (such as math

Name____________________ Date__________

Skill: Sums 10–18 # Correct ___1.10___

1. 6 +5	2. 4 +9	3. 7 +3	4. 8 +4	5. 9 +3
6. 5 +7	7. 9 +2	8. 4 +6	9. 3 +8	10. 7 +6

FIGURE 8.1 Sample 10-Item Probe

facts), or a target skill, and related skills (such as addition of two-digit numbers, with a secondary analysis of fact knowledge).

Student performance on probes leading toward mastery can easily be tracked using a simple grid that can be made up ahead of time and personalized each time a student or group of students start a new skill. Data such as dates of assessments, scores, and levels of mastery can be logged, as can anecdotal notes, the objective toward which the student is working and dates of initiation and completion of the skill and/or the objective.

Other Informal Measures. Informal assessments are not limited to probes and survey tests. Teachers can keep files of student work, observe students, and interview general classroom teachers to gather information about student performance. Performance-based assessments (Fuchs & Deno, 1994) can be used to evaluate student thinking and problem solving. Students are presented with a problem, and the results are scored on a rubric. Finally, student work can be analyzed for errors in order to determine what difficulties students are having. When coupled with interviews with students about their work, these assessments can offer insights into student thinking and learning. Ginsburg (1997) has identified five key areas where students with math disabilities tend to make patterns of errors:

- Symbolism: Many students do not understand what mathematical symbols mean. Often students know what to *do* when the symbols appear, but not what they actually mean.
- Bugs: Computational errors occur due to overapplication of systematic strategies. For example, Ginsburg cites the case of a child who subtracts as follows:

$$\begin{array}{r} 12 \\ -4 \\ \hline 12 \end{array}$$

In this case, although he notes the child may know intuitively that you can't subtract 4 eggs from a carton of 12 and still have 12, a different strategy (always subtract the smaller number from the larger number) has interfered, resulting in the error.

- Beliefs: Students often develop negative or harmful beliefs about what is entailed in learning mathematics. Teachers may focus on right and wrong answers or on getting finished, rather than on understanding concepts and ideas, resulting in misplaced effort on the part of students.
- Rote learning: Much math learning is presented as little more than rote learning. Students learn to use operations, but not to solve problems or develop theories about how math works.
- Lack of connection between the formal and informal: Children often have informal math knowledge, but often are either not encouraged or actually discouraged from using it.

Algorithm A step-by-step problem-solving procedure. In mathematics instruction, students learn established, recursive computational procedures for solving problems.

Singer and Resnick (1992) found that once children learn mathematical **algorithms**, they can no longer use their informal knowledge of math to solve problems. Instead, the algorithm becomes *the* way to compute.

When assessing students with high-incidence disabilities, teachers must dig below the surface and endeavor to find not only what a student can or cannot do, but why. Analysis of student errors and math interviews can provide valuable clues as to how a child thinks about math, and what errors result (see Figure 8.2).

To conclude, what would the best choices for Ms. Harris be? Clearly, a norm-referenced test will not answer her questions. Ms. Harris would probably be best served by developing a probe that specifically targets the skill sequence leading up to the skill she plans to teach next: setting up the computation. It is unlikely a criterion-referenced test will have these interim skills; however, she may be able to use one when she is ready to assess their ability to solve a word problem. Further, Ms. Harris can delve deeper into her students' performance by carefully analyzing the patterns of errors her students make and by asking them questions about their performance. All of these data can come together to give her a more complete picture, not only of her students' progress, but of the effectiveness of her own teaching.

STRATEGIES FOR TEACHING STUDENTS WITH HIGH-INCIDENCE DISABILITIES

Models of Instruction

A variety of instructional models can be implemented to provide high-quality math instruction for students with high-incidence disabilities. A model should be chosen based on

Addition Errors

Problem	Error
265 + 398 = 51513	Student does not rename
(carried 1 1) 473 + 218 = 991	Student renames to both 10s and 100s place

Subtraction Errors

Problem	Error
(4 crossed out to 3; 1 1 above) 427 − 298 = 139	Student regroups from 100s to 10s and 1s
(4 crossed out to 3; 1 above) 460 − 284 = 184	Student treats zero as place holder
591 − 347 = 256	Student subtracts smaller from larger number regardless of position

Multiplication Errors

Problem	Error
(carried 3 4) 396 × 47 = 1772	Student multiplies 1s × 1s, 10s and 100s × 10s
(carried 1 2 / 1 4) 628 × 136: 3768, 20140, 87800 = 111708	Student needs a strategy to manage carried number—adds them in repeatedly.

FIGURE 8.2 Sample Problems with Error Analysis

such factors as whether the grouping is heterogeneous or skill-based, whether the instruction will take place in small instructional groups or in a whole-class setting, and whether the special education teacher is the primary teacher, a co-teacher, or providing support for a few students. Math instruction provides excellent opportunities for exploring various co-teaching models.

Direct Instruction

Direct instruction is an instructional method that allows students to achieve mastery through explicit, carefully planned, and well-structured instruction. Direct instruction integrates teaching techniques into curriculum design, an approach that lends itself to the sequential nature of mathematics. Mathematics programs based on direct instruction follow an ordered plan of instruction based on task analysis of skills to be taught, explicit teaching of skills, and continuous assessment (Carnine, 1997; Carnine & Gersten, 2000). Of equal importance is sufficient practice to allow students to master skills and a focus on essential concepts. The direct instruction approach follows four steps, starting from the student's current level of achievement:

1. Select a target mathematics objective. The objective must be both measurable and observable.
2. Specify the sequence of skills needed to reach that objective.
3. Determine what the student already knows. The student may have knowledge or skills of some aspects of the skill already.
4. Develop a sequence of steps needed to reach the objective.

A substantial body of research has demonstrated the direct instructional approach is an effective method for teaching mathematics (Carnine, 1997). Moreover, for teachers working in inclusive settings, direct instruction lends itself to a variety of groupings: whole-group instruction, small groups in the resource room, and both pull-out groups and center-based rotating groups in the general classroom. There are a few commercial programs that adhere to the direct instruction approach, the most notable being *Corrective Mathematics* (Engelmann & Steely, 2002). This well-known remedial program is for students in grades 4 and up, but is used widely across elementary and secondary grades.

Learning Strategies Approach

Special education teachers working in an inclusive classroom often provide instructional support to a small number of students within a larger general classroom. Various co-teaching models may be followed. One common approach is "floating" or "grazing," in which the general classroom teacher directs the whole-class lesson while the special educator moves from student to student, addressing specific needs and questions, providing on-the-spot assistance with the mathematical concepts and processes. This might possibly be followed with later instruction in the resource room. This model is particularly prevalent at the secondary level. Whatever co-teaching model is followed, it is important for general and special education teachers to make sure students understand the concepts and processes involved in the sometimes rote steps of mathematical problem solving. Special education teachers often take the role of providing strategy instruction for students with disabilities who may get bogged down in the cognitive processes required to follow complex processes.

Cognitive learning strategies help students to master skills and take examinations more effectively through the use of self-talk, quiet discussions, and questioning that focus attention on critical aspects of assigned work. Statements such as "this is where I bring down the zero." "what step did I forget," or "does my answer make sense," actively engage students in thinking about their math tasks (Deschler, Ellis & Lenz, 1996; Montague, 1997). For example, Montague and Bos (1986) developed an eight-step procedure for solving math problems:

1. READ the problem aloud.
2. PARAPHRASE the problem aloud.

3. VISUALIZE the information.
4. STATE the problem aloud.
5. HYPOTHESIZE and THINK the problem through aloud.
6. ESTIMATE the answer.
7. CALCULATE and LABEL the answer.
8. SELF-CHECK by using the self-questioning to ask if the answer makes sense.

Another effective teaching strategy is the Demonstration and Permanent Model approach (Rivera & Smith, 1987; Smith & Lovitt, 1982). This teaching technique provides useful guidelines for students. In this approach, the teacher *demonstrates* how to complete a given problem, such as long division. Once instruction is completed, the problem is written in permanent form where it is easily accessible—the top of a worksheet page, on a large file card, or on an assignment folder. This provides students a readily available *permanent model* to which they can refer when the teacher is unavailable. This strategy is particularly helpful in a setting where students must display some independence or engage in long periods of seatwork.

Remedial Math Programs

A wide variety of structured commercial math programs are available that are designed to teach students with the types of math learning difficulties typical of students with high-incidence disabilities. Some may be targeted for specific disabilities, and many serve a wide range of learning and cognitive levels. Programs such as *Corrective Mathematics* (Engelmann & Steely, 2002), *Connecting Math Concepts* (Engelmann, Carnine, Engelmann & Kelly, 2002), *KeyMath Teach and Practice* (American Guidance Service, 2003), *Mastering Math* (Steck Vaughn, 2003), and others offer teachers a wide range of choice as well as acting as stand-alone instructional programs or resources to supplement general classroom instruction.

THE IMPACT OF SPECIFIC DISABILITIES

General and special education teachers must plan to address a variety of cognitive, learning, and motivational needs of students in their math instruction (Mastropieri & Scruggs, 2000). Teachers of students with high-incidence disabilities might expect to see a variety of disability-specific behaviors. Table 8.2 summarizes the most common factors that affect math learning (Lerner, 2000; Mastropieri, Bakken, & Scruggs, 1991; Miller, 1996; Montague, 1996). However, not all students exhibit all the characteristics identified, nor is this an exhaustive list of mutually exclusive characteristics, and teachers should be prepared to "think on their feet" in response to the needs of these students.

Many children with math-related disabilities have gaps in their learning of mathematics concepts. They often know a process but fail to grasp the concept behind it or fail to understand a basic concept but have a skill that is technically beyond the basic. This is often the result of spotty instruction or experiencing sporadic problems in moving from concrete to abstract. This may often result from the additional challenge their disability creates when

TABLE 8.2 Math Learning Factors Related to Specific High-Incidence Disabilities

LEARNING DISABILITY

1. Poor memory and strategy deficits leading to difficulty conceptualizing, representing and recalling math facts, developing algorithms, and developing and using word problem-solving strategies
2. Difficult-to-remediate patterns of errors based in faulty learning of basic computational rules and procedures
3. Use of immature math vocabulary
4. Impulsive response patterns, particularly to written work
5. Low motivation and poor self-esteem with respect to math
6. History of failure that leads to lack of confidence, and lack of belief in own competence.

MENTAL RETARDATION

1. Slow pace of learning
2. Difficulty with the language of math
3. Difficulty understanding and acquiring concepts, especially abstract concepts of mathematics
4. Difficulty remembering and executing facts and procedures
5. Poor math reasoning

EMOTIONAL DISTURBANCE

1. Lack of motivation
2. Low levels of attention and concentration
3. Acting-out behavior in response to failure
4. Inappropriate or immature classroom behavior
5. Anxiety or depression related to math performance
6. Difficulties with metacognitive processes and memory

trying to learn difficult abstract concepts, particularly without benefit of sufficient opportunity to explore concepts using concrete materials. Or, it may in part stem from the nature of mathematics instruction in the general classroom and the limitations of math texts.

At least in part, students' failure to grasp basic math concepts grows out of a lack of basic math readiness skills: directional and positional concepts (right/left, up/down), object constancy (3 is always 3), number concepts and number words ([picture of four objects] = 4 [numeral] = four [word]) and basic concepts of time (how many minutes?) and quantity (how many crayons?). Further, visual perceptual problems, poor listening skills, and limited organizational and/or unreliable memory skills characteristic of learning disability may add to their difficulty learning underlying concepts.

DESIGNING AND PLANNING EFFECTIVE MATHEMATICS INSTRUCTION IN INCLUSIVE SETTINGS

Effective mathematics instruction is a sequential process. Just as a train needs all the cars connected in order to for the train to move, mathematics requires students to learn sequences of skills effectively in order to make their "math trains" go. Teachers developing math lessons for their students should begin by asking themselves what step their students' understanding has currently reached. Moreover, mastery of conceptual knowledge should be assessed and attained in the same way as skills and should be revisited in later instruction in order to sustain mastery. Gaps in skill learning result in many of the long-term patterns of performance we see among students with high-incidence disabilities.

Levels of Instruction

Effective math instruction should progress from concrete to abstract slowly, affording students ample time to explore and understand concepts and computations before moving to more abstract representations. The National Council of Teachers of Mathematics (1991) recommends three levels of instruction: concrete, semi-concrete, and abstract.

Concrete Instruction. Concrete instruction uses manipulatives, or tangible objects, to represent math concepts and skills. It is often helpful to use real-life materials that help children to relate the math concepts to their own lives. Concrete math instruction is hands-on and should have a strong problem-solving component. As part of concept instruction, a teacher might present a concrete problem to students such as the following (adapted from Cathcart, Pothier, Vance, & Bezuk, 2000) sample lesson.

SAMPLE CONCRETE LESSON ON SUMS

Children learning math facts often do not understand that a whole number (sum) is made up of "parts" or pairs of numbers that combine to form the sum. To help students discover this concept, try the following problem:

MATERIALS:
Ten unifix cubes in each of two colors (for the five example—the number will vary depending on the sum they are exploring)

PROCEDURE:

1. Teacher makes a rod for students showing the sum five is made up of five blue cubes. Say and record on the board or chart paper "five blue cubes make a five rod." Teacher and students together duplicate using five yellow cubes.
2. Teacher asks students, "Can you make a five rod using two colors?" Students experiment with the rods individually or with a partner until they make one five-rod successfully.
3. Teacher asks students, "How many five rods can we make, using the cubes we have?" Once students understand the problem to solve, they continue to use a combination of blue and yellow cubes to make other "five rods" and record their combinations on the on chart paper.
4. To build oral language and thinking skills, students show their rods and charts to the group, explaining why they feel each is a "five rod." The teacher should encourage students to demonstrate how their rod adheres to the rule ("my rod is a five rod because it has three yellow and two blue cubes. There are two colors and five cubes.")
5. The teacher leads students in deducing and establishing a rule for making a "five-rod": They must use a total of five cubes of one or both colors.

Optional: Add a challenge: Ask students to form a square demonstrating all the possible combinations of yellow and blue rods forming five in logical order. They should create a square, as pictured in Figure 8.3.

Semi-Concrete Instruction. Semi-concrete or representational instruction replaces manipulatives with such representations as drawings, pictures, and tally marks. Typical math textbooks contain many of these drawings, particularly when introducing new skills, as do student workbooks and worksheets. Teachers often instinctively draw pictures on the board or scrap paper to help students struggling with specific problems. This is an example of using semi-concrete instruction. The following sample lesson builds on the previous lesson by illustrating a previously learned concept in a semi-concrete form.

MOVING FROM CONCRETE TO SEMI-CONCRETE IN THE LESSON ON SUMS

Moving from concrete to semi-concrete, the sum rods built in the previous activity can later be drawn on graph paper with a large grid (half-inch for visual ease) and labeled with the appropriate sum-rod label ("five rods"). The teacher should point out how the picture represents the

FIGURE 8.3 Unifix Cubes in Rows, Dark Color Descending, Light Ascending

actual rods used earlier. Some students with disabilities need explicit demonstration of how the semi-concrete represents the concrete.

Extension activity: Students can continue to build, then illustrate and label sum rods on gridded paper, matching pairs (2+3 to 2+3). Later explorations in subtraction can begin with the unifix and later the paper sum rods, breaking them apart to determine what happens when one color is taken away.

Abstract Instruction. In this phase, students work solely with numbers and few or no illustrations. The majority of secondary instruction in the general education classroom takes place at the abstract level and the special educator may have to bring in concrete or semi-concrete activities to illustrate the abstract.

MOVING FROM SEMI-CONCRETE TO ABSTRACT IN THE LESSON ON SUMS

In this phase, students must be led to eliminate the use of objects or pictorial representations and rely solely on written or oral numerals. To facilitate this transition, the teacher might show the students how to label their sum rod drawings with the appropriate numerals to represent math facts. This approach juxtaposes the semi-concrete and abstract representations. The teacher then shows students only the abstract representation, or the number facts written traditionally as math problems with numerals and symbols.

Typically, math instruction moves from concrete to semi-concrete to abstract in a more or less linear manner with increasingly less concrete instruction as children progress through the grades. However, for students with disabilities, it may be useful to continue to draw on concrete and semi-concrete strategies as students learn new skills throughout the grades, according to the needs of individual students.

Teachers should also expect students to progress from one level of instruction to the next at varying rates of speed and plan accordingly. In a typical general education classroom, whether elementary or secondary, a special education teacher may have a group of four to six students where three are using semi-concrete representations of a skill, one is using manipulatives, and two are working at an abstract level.

Carnine (1997, 1998) has identified five components for effective math instruction found to be effective for students with learning disabilities. Many are equally useful for students with emotional discorders and mental retardation. These are detailed in Box 8.1.

Planning Math Instruction with General Education Colleagues

For special educators teaching in collaborative models, planning math instruction is often done in collaboration with their general education partners. To varying degrees, special

BOX 8.1

MAJOR COMPONENTS OF EFFECTIVE MATH INSTRUCTION FOR STUDENTS WITH LEARNING DISABILITIES

1. Focus on "big" ideas rather than details.
2. Teach "conspicuous" strategies that are of the right scope to be versatile and useful. Avoid strategies that are too specific or too broad.
3. Make efficient use of time: Do not try to teach too much at a time, but proceed at a comfortable pace. Establish priorities, focus instruction on high priority objectives and approach complex strategies in small steps. Teach clusters of information focused around a central idea.
4. Communicate strategies clearly and explicitly. Model strategies to allow students to see how they are used and provide continuous feedback.
5. Provide ample practice and review to promote retention.

Source: Carnine (1997, 1998).

education teachers may meet with resistance from their general education colleagues, making planning a difficult process. Elementary teachers are typically more willing to plan for students with disabilities than secondary level teachers (McIntosh, Vaughan, Schumm, Haager & Lee, 1993; Schumm & Vaughn, 1995; Schumm, Vaughn, Haager, McDowell, Rothlein, & Saumell, 1995). These studies describe secondary teachers as tending to view specialized planning as unrealistic given their class load and time demands, something that is not surprising to experienced secondary special education teachers. What little planning is done tends to be modifications to the whole-class plan, rather than truly individualized planning (Schumm et al., 1995). Special educators should be prepared to assume a leadership role in establishing and supporting planning when initiating co-teaching or other instructional models that require shared planning. As general educators grow more comfortable with the process, they often will assume greater responsibility for the planning process.

Explicit Teaching of Mathematical Concepts

In order for students with mild disabilities to generalize math calculations to various applications successfully, they need sufficient opportunities to concretely explore and manipulate materials that illustrate the nature of basic mathematical concepts, including the concepts underlying basic calculations. Sufficient instructional time must be assigned to concrete concept development prior to transitions to semi-concrete and abstract learning as well as to calculations and word problems. Teaching these concepts should not be viewed as the first step of a lesson teaching a skill (i.e., step one in a lesson in teaching addition is to teach the concept), but rather the first step along a sequence of instruction leading to a skill (i.e., several days' instruction on the concept, followed by increasingly independent

Manipulatives Concrete, tangible objects are often used in mathematics instruction to make abstract concepts seem real to students. Having trouble with abstract concepts is characteristic of students with high-incidence disabilities. Teachers often use blocks, color tiles, or other objects to illustrate concepts such as counting, adding, or subtracting.

practice). It is a step that may take many days of appropriate instruction and modeling, as well as ample practice, to master.

Unquestionably, the best tool a teacher of these students can have is a collection of math **manipulatives** in sufficient quantity to allow each student the opportunity to experience math concepts hands on. More than just a method to demonstrate how a concept "works," commercial manipulatives such as counters, Cuisenaire rods, unifix cubes, fraction blocks, geoboards, and base-ten blocks, along with such materials as graph paper, centimeter and inch grid paper, and reproduceable venn diagrams, clock faces, and number lines, can be used to teach a wide variety of concepts well into the middle school years. Thornton and Wilmot (1986) recommend using manipulatives to talk through problems, develop a model (such as the unifix cube sum rods), determine and record solutions, and transition from old to new learning. Equally useful are materials adapted from other uses: An 18-inch rule makes an excellent number line, a flannel board with flannel fraction bars or circles can demonstrate fractional concepts, and popsicle sticks can be used to teach place value. It should be noted not all students will work equally well or respond in the same way to a given manipulative—teachers would be well advised to always have a backup plan.

An overhead projector can extend the effectiveness of manipulatives by affording students the opportunity to see their teacher model the same activities in which they engage. An overhead projector can be motivating, and many students will eagerly approach a task when offered the opportunity to do so on an overhead projector. More and more commercial manufacturers are making manipulatives for the overhead, such as the "Calc-u-vue" overhead calculator (Learning Resources), multicolored transparent counters, coin and bill sets, geometric shapes and geoboards, base ten blocks, and attribute blocks.

BOX 8.2
THE TRAVELING TEACHER'S BOX OF MANIPULATIVES

Useful for special education teachers co-teaching in general education classrooms, this collection of manipulatives is versatile enough to use in a variety of grades. They are easily stored in zippered plastic bags and packed into a modestly sized file box:

- Graph paper (6 squares/inch and 4 squares/inch)
- Crayons, markers, and/or colored pencils
- Counters (teddy bear or similar, based on grade level) and chips
- Base ten blocks
- Tangrams and/or attribute blocks
- Three-dimensional geometric shapes (cube, cylinder, etc.)
- Unifix cubes
- Calculators
- 18-inch rulers (to use as number lines)
- Fraction blocks (pie and/or bar)
- Coin and bill sets
- Coin and bill stamps

Strategies for Teaching Early Math Skills. Children with high-incidence disabilities often need remedial instruction in spatial, directional, positional, and quantitative concepts and vocabulary that form the foundation for early math skills. Time should be devoted to experiencing and manipulating objects such as attribute or pattern blocks and unifix cubes, engaging students in activities such as describing characteristics, forming patterns, creating groups, ordering and classifying, and identifying and changing positions of objects throughout the instructional day. Early math activities can be connected to language arts by using stories such as *The Very Hungry Caterpillar* (Carle, 1969) that have math-related content. Science activities can include math by having students make, manipulate and discuss collections of objects relating to content. Application of skills helps students generalize beyond classroom situations. Use of math vocabulary should be encouraged whenever possible.

Student: May I have more pretzels?

Teacher: How many more do you want?

Student: I want three.

Teacher: You want *three more* pretzels? Say it for me.

Student: I want three more pretzels.

Counting and Numeration. Students with disabilities often have difficulty learning counting skills. Counting should be introduced slowly and rhythmically. Counting can easily be introduced alongside quantitative concepts, connecting the concept of number, a numeral, and a number word as well as placing each number word into a sequence of number words.

Students should begin counting with just a few numbers at a time, adding one or two at a time, as they master counting sequences.

Teacher: Count with me: 1, 2, 3, 4

Students: One, two, three, four!

The teacher can then ask one or two students to count on their own, then to count four objects in the environment.

Teacher: Excellent, let's add a *one more* number. Listen to me count: One, two, three, four, five. Now, count with me, slowly. . .

Students: One, two, three, four, *five*.

Teacher: Let's see if we can try counting to five by looking around us. Remember: Five is one more than four. Jeremy, can you count five students for me?

The lesson can then progress to the teacher introducing the concept of five, relating the numeral to the quantity five and encouraging students to identify groups of five objects in the environment and create groups of five objects. Once students are able to count to a given number and identify the corresponding number of objects, the numeral can be introduced and objects labeled. This three-step process—count—identify the quantity—connect a numeral—will allow numbers to take on unique identities rather than just being a sequence of words to be memorized.

Other strategies to help students count include having children clap as they count to regulate flow or count with a group or peer (Mastropieri & Scruggs, 2000). As students become more fluent at counting, they can begin to look for, count, and label numbers of objects in their environment. Together, students and their teacher can create a "number-rich" environment for the students, allowing them to see numbers and quantities on a continuous basis.

One-to-One Correspondence. As part of counting instruction, students can build one-to-one correspondence. Students can count out objects such as three bears, then pair up a second set of objects, such as three popsicle sticks. Students can count the pairs aloud and explain why the pairs go together to the teacher or a partner as part of their matching activity.

Early Geometric Concepts. As students master counting, they should learn to identify simple two-dimensional shapes (such as a circle, square, rectangle and triangle) and to use correct vocabulary for identifying shapes. They should be taught the attributes of each shape ("a triangle has three sides and a square has four sides"). Attribute blocks come in a variety of simple shapes, often in several colors, and three sizes. Students can sort blocks according to shape, learning to attend to critical features of a shape (number of sides) while learning to ignore nonessential attributes (color, size). Opportunities to explain their rationale for sorting and labeling should be a regular part of instruction, as students deduce rules for determining a given shape and make discriminations between shapes. As critical features are learned, students can explore their environment, locating and labeling shapes, and adding to their math diaries.

Addition and Subtraction Concepts. Because these concepts are very abstract, many children learn to add and subtract without ever fully understanding how the underlying concepts work. Teachers may not see how little students understand these concepts until they begin to learn place value and renaming and regrouping, then make a variety of errors. It is important teachers of students with high-incidence disabilities allot sufficient instructional time to building these early skills, setting a comfortable pace, and assessing frequently to be sure their students have a firm grasp on each concept. Students should practice daily, using manipulatives such as unifix cubes to count objects to be added.

Teacher: Everyone, please count out four unifix cubes for me and line them up in front of you, like we did yesterday. (Teacher monitors to be sure students have four and creates a model.)

Teacher: Now, count out two cubes and put them in line next to the four you already have. (Teacher monitors to be sure students line up the two additional cubes and adds two more to the model.)

Teacher: Now how many do we have all together? Count with me! One, two, three, four, five, six. Who can tell me what happened?

Student: We had four cubes, then when we put two more with them, we had six.

Teacher: Yes, we have six cubes altogether. That means that when we have four cubes and add two more cubes we have six cubes.

As the students practice and are able to describe what happened with the cubes, the teacher can simplify the number sentence to "four cubes plus two cubes makes six cubes" and eventually "four cubes plus two cubes *equals* six cubes." This slow approach to introducing not only the concept of addition but the accompanying vocabulary allows children to focus on one or two "big ideas" (Carnine, 1997, 1998) at one time, mastering each before moving to the next. Students can see that the addition process is "part plus part equals whole" (Lerner, 2000) through these manipulations. Later, students can invert the process to learn subtraction, starting with a quantity of cubes or counters, then taking away and determining how may are left, forming subtraction sentences as they progress.

Teachers should be cautious not to assume that students can demonstrate a skill once they have mastered or even fully understand it. Ample instructional time and repeated successful demonstrations are needed before a student has truly mastered a concept.

Teachers should go slowly before introducing paper-and-pencil tasks, transitioning gradually by slowly fading the use of manipulatives. The purpose of manipulatives is to allow students to develop concepts concretely, rather than to quickly move to abstract paper-and-pencil tasks. Once students have developed fluency with manipulatives, a number line can be introduced, and students can be taught to count up (addition) and down (subtraction) to find answers (see Figure 8.4). When first making the transition, teachers should explicitly demonstrate the connection between the addition or subtraction of cubes and the numbers counted on a number line.

Writing Numbers. A variety of tools can be employed to help students learn to write numbers. Students with motor control difficulties are often slow to learn to write numbers, and many students with high-incidence disabilities reverse numbers. Use of models, graph paper to help align numbers and keep size even, dashed lines, and stencils can help students learn to write numbers correctly. Ample practice and feedback and the opportunity to correct errors will help students attend to correct formation of numbers (Mastropieri & Scruggs, 2000).

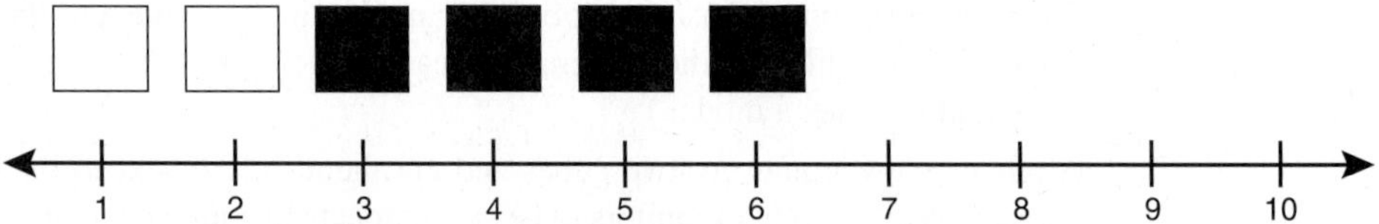

FIGURE 8.4 Number Line with Cubes

Strategies for Teaching Addition and Subtraction Facts. Number facts are one of the biggest challenges students with high-incidence disabilities face when learning math. Great importance is often placed on memorizing addition and subtraction facts quickly in the early elementary grades, and once math instruction moves on to larger number calculations, opportunities to catch up on facts not memorized are seldom available within the math curriculum. For students with cognitive, memory, and attention/concentration deficits, learning number facts can be a herculian task.

Once early addition and subtraction concepts are mastered, students with high-incidence disabilities should begin to learn number facts slowly, and with ample time to practice. Early instruction should emphasize recitation of facts, then slowly introduce paper-and-pencil computations (Mastropieri & Scruggs, 2000). Once students begin paper-and-pencil calculations, manipulatives, including counters and a number line, should be at hand to help students who have not memorized facts yet. Manipulatives can help students transition from oral to written calculations by allowing them to display concrete representations of written problems (see Figure 8.5).

Students with high-incidence disabilities should be taught the commutative property of addition and related fact families to strengthen learning of relationships between addition and subtraction facts. Fact families are groups of four related facts, two addition and two subtraction, such as (4 + 3 = 7; 3 + 4 = 7; 7 – 3 = 4; 7 – 4 = 3). Simple three-sided flash cards can help students see and practice a family.

Bley and Thornton (1989) suggest the following strategies for teaching addition facts:

1. Teach "zero facts." A number plus zero equals the number (3 + 0 = 3; 0 + 3 = 3). (19 facts)
2. Count-up facts for ones, twos, and threes. Starting with the larger number, students count up one, two, or three more. 2 + 5 = (count up two more: 6, 7) 7; 6 + 3 = (count up three more: 7, 8, 9) 9. Students can generally count up and hold a small number of digits such as this in their heads. (45 facts)
3. Teach "doubles" such as 4 + 4 = 8 using visual mnemonics. 4 + 4 is the "spider" fact because there are four legs on each side of a spider, and 5 + 5 = 10 is the "finger" fact, because there are five fingers on each hand. To make these mnemonics more meaningful to students, they can find their own examples of these double phenomena, then create and illustrate small posters that can be kept with their math materials.

Lerner (2000) suggests students spend time "making tens." Students begin by exploring groups of facts that add up to ten, using manipulatives to form groups of ten and recording related number facts. These ten facts can later be used to add long columns of numbers quickly by teaching students to find ten combinations.

Subtraction facts can be more difficult to master than addition facts. Strategies for teaching subtraction facts are largely the inverse of those for addition such as teaching count-backs instead of count-ups on a number line. If fact families are introduced early, students should already be familiar with the relationship between addition and subtraction facts. They should also be taught to use inverse facts to check calculations early: Check addition with subtraction and the reverse. As with addition, ample time to practice facts and work with relationships are crucial to mastery.

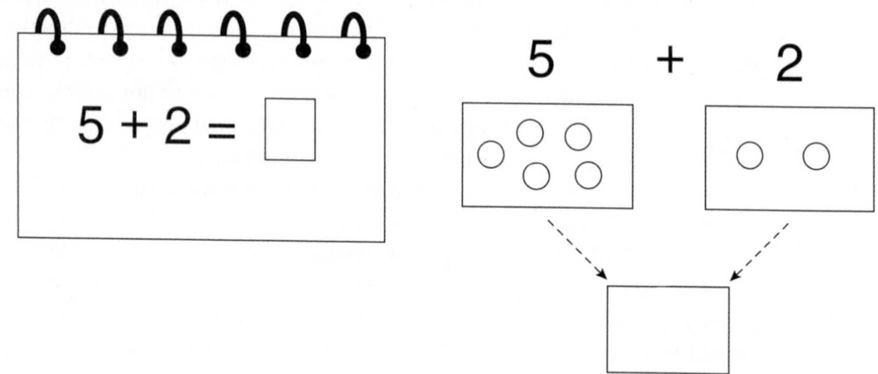

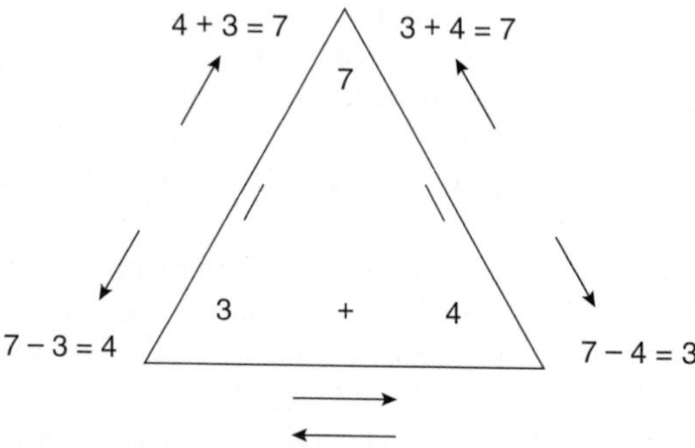

FIGURE 8.5 Flash Cards

Simple practice tools such as flash cards, classroom drills, classroom math games, and computer software such as Math Blaster (Davidson), Math Munchers (MECC), and Math Rabbit (The Learning Company) are useful to help students practice facts and calculations in a variety of ways, avoiding "drill-and-kill." Students can make flashcards themselves to take home and to keep in the desks, using 4" × 6" file cards and crayons or markers.

Once students understand the relationships and properties of addition and subtraction facts, and have begun to master basic number facts, larger number addition and subtraction *without* regrouping can be introduced. An addition/subtraction chart (Figure 8.6) can be used to help students move on to larger number calculations while memorizing facts. These charts are readily available in reproduceable form in a variety of "teacher

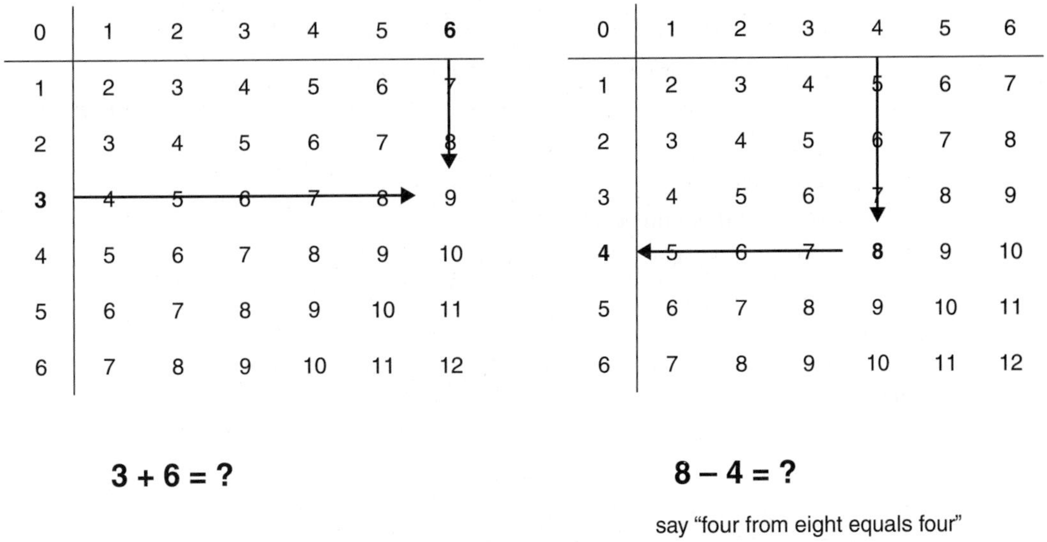

0	1	2	3	4	5	**6**
1	2	3	4	5	6	7
2	3	4	5	6	7	8
3	4	5	6	7	8	9
4	5	6	7	8	9	10
5	6	7	8	9	10	11
6	7	8	9	10	11	12

3 + 6 = ?

0	1	2	3	4	5	6
1	2	3	4	5	6	7
2	3	4	5	6	7	8
3	4	5	6	7	8	9
4	5	6	7	**8**	9	10
5	6	7	8	9	10	11
6	7	8	9	10	11	12

8 – 4 = ?

say "four from eight equals four"

FIGURE 8.6 Addition Chart

helper" books at most educational supply stores and can be stapled or laminated into student folders or laminated onto poster board and distributed to students. These charts have the added benefit of providing students with additional subtle practice with facts. Students can be taught to both add and subtract on what is traditionally called an addition chart.

Place Value and Regrouping/Renaming. Along with number facts, students with high-incidence disabilities face significant difficulty learning place value and the rules for renaming in addition and regrouping in subtraction. To successfully master these skills, students must understand the principle of *exchange* that makes groups of ones become tens and groups of tens become hundreds; this lies at the heart of regrouping and renaming. Students also need to see and understand the meaning of two-digit numbers.

Two types of manipulatives can be used to illustrate these principles. When illustrating simple exchange rules (ten ones for one ten), students can use base ten materials that cannot be broken apart, such as base ten blocks or bean sticks. However, when students must construct their own groupings, they should use manipulatives that can be broken apart and rearranged, such as unifix cubes, colored chips, or bundles of sticks.

Students should begin learning place value by doing simple exchange activities, learning the basic rules of exchange. Teachers can give students base ten blocks and engage in simple exchanges. The teacher in this example has handed various numbers of single base ten blocks to students and has laid several tens blocks in front of the group. She engages them in making exchanges:

Teacher: Lisa, you have ten ones in front of you. What should you exchange them for?

Lisa: One ten.

Teacher: Correct. Please make the exchange.

Lisa: I change ten ones for one ten. (Student changes the base ten blocks.)

Teacher: Jose, you have seven blocks in front of you. Do you have enough to exchange?

Jose: I don't think so.

Teacher: Why don't you think so?

Jose: Because I have to have ten to exchange.

Once students understand the basic principle of exchanging ones for tens, they can learn chip trading. Commercial chip trading games are available, but can easily be made with one die, multicolored chips, and mats (Figure 8.7) drawn on poster board and laminated.

The rules for chip trading are simple:

1. Each color chip has a value: Ones can be red and tens blue (green can be hundreds and so forth as larger values are added).
2. Each student has a chip trading mat and one die.
3. The teacher (or later one student) acts as "banker," holding the containers or piles of chips and making exchanges as they are requested.

100s	10s	1s

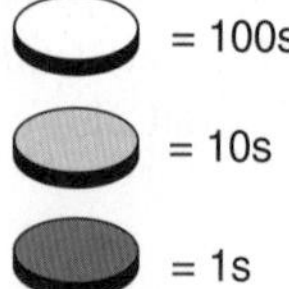

FIGURE 8.7 Chip Trading

4. Students must adhere to one simple rule: They can have no more than nine chips in the ones place. When they have ten or more ones chips, they must exchange ten ones (red) for one ten (blue) chip.
5. Each student in turn rolls the die and asks the banker for as many chips as the number rolled.
6. Beginning with the second roll, students will need to make trades. Chips are handed to the banker, who exchanges them for a higher value chip. If a student misses a trade, the teacher or a buddy can remind a student to make the trade.
7. To reinforce exchanges students can verbalize what they have done ("I trade ten ones for one ten").

As students master the basic chip trading game, larger numbers can be made by adding additional colors of chips to represent the hundreds and thousands places. Chip trading can also be used to transition students from concrete to abstract representations of numbers. One advantage to teacher-made chip trading mats that are laminated is that they allow the teacher or student to write on the mat with wipe-off markers. Once students have mastered the basic exchanges, they can begin to label the chips on their mats, allowing them to see the relationship between two-digit numbers and their values (Figure 8.8).

Students should be taught to make exchanges and play chip trading in reverse to teach subtraction concepts. Students begin with a fixed number of chips in the ones and tens places (for example, 2 tens and 5 ones). Chips must be removed from the ones place

100s	10s	1s
	4	3

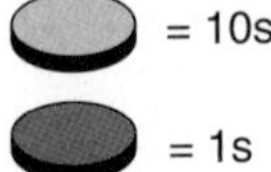

FIGURE 8.8 Chip Trading Mat with Chips Laid Out

based on the roll of the die. If insufficient chips are in the ones place, students must exchange one ten for ten ones.

Finally, chip trading can be used to demonstrate how calculations using regrouping and renaming work. A modified (and laminated) chip trading mat can be made by the teacher. It contains a row of boxes divided into tens and ones for the addend (for addition) or minuend (for subtraction), another row of boxes below it for the second addend or subtrahend separated by a dashed line, and a box for the sum or difference (the "solution" box), separated by a heavy line. Above the addend/minuend row of boxes is a lightly shorter row of boxes, in which exchanged (borrowed or carried) chips can be placed (the "exchange" box). Each box (see Figure 8.9) is large enough to allow students to lay out chips to represent the number in the box.

As students increase in fluency using chip trading, the chips can be replaced by base ten blocks. Somewhat more abstract than chip trading, base ten blocks come with mats that allow students to represent and solve computations using the mats.

Beginning Problem-Solving. Students learning addition and subtraction should begin solving problems relating to these skills as soon as they start working with manipulatives. Teachers can build problem solving into daily instruction, often by simply restating a question ("How do you think we can . . . ?" rather than "This is how we . . ."), and solving problems should be a regular part of skill instruction and practice. Students should have the opportunity to solve problems alone, with a partner, and as a member of a group in order to build collaborative problem-solving skills. Oral presentation of problems can gradually be supplemented, then replaced by written word problems. As teachers provide feedback to students solving problems, they can direct students' attention to key words in problems ("Remember the problem said you should *take away* three"). Additionally, students should be able to discuss and provide rationales for their solutions to problems.

A

100s	10s	1s
	2	6
+	3	5

= 10s
= 1s

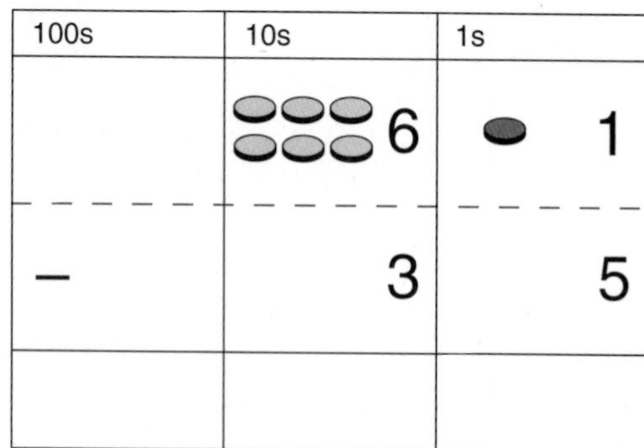

FIGURE 8.9 Modified Chip Trading Mats

BOX 8.3
MORE ADVANCED OPERATIONS WITH CHIP TRADING

USING CHIP TRADING TO MODEL ADDITION WITH RENAMING

1. The teacher, then later the student, writes the problem in the boxes as shown in Figure 8.9A.
2. The correct number of properly colored chips (ones: red; tens: blue) are laid in the boxes with the numbers.
3. The chips in the ones place are gathered together and pushed into the ones "solution" box. The student counts the chips and applies the rule for making a trade. The trade is made, with the tens chip placed in the narrower "exchange" box, and the number of chips (1) in the exchange box recorded—this represents the carried number.
4. The chips in the tens place are gathered together and pushed into the tens "solution" box. The student counts the chips and records the number of chips. (Optional: The answer can be transferred to a worksheet with the same problem.)

USING CHIP TRADING TO MODEL SUBTRACTION WITH REGROUPING

1. The teacher, then later the student, writes the problem in the boxes as shown in Figure 8.9B.
2. The correct number of properly colored chips (ones: red; tens: blue) are laid alongside the minuend numbers.
3. The teacher prompts the student to take the number of chips in the subtrahend from the minuend box, then move the remaining chips to the solution box.
4. If insufficient chips are in the ones minuend box, the student must exchange (borrow) one tens chip for ten ones chips. The number in the tens minuend box is crossed out and the new number recorded in the exchange box. The exchange is made, and the number of chips in the ones minuend box recorded in the ones exchange box.
5. The chips in the ones subtrahend column are removed, and the remaining chips moved to the solution box and recorded. The procedure is repeated in the tens column.

Miller and Mercer (1993b) propose a four-step strategy for teaching word problems, to be used at the concrete, semi-concrete, and abstract levels of instruction:

- Provide an advance organizer.
- Demonstrate the skill, then have students practice.
- Provide a guided practice activity.
- Transition to independent practice.

Recall that guided practice is done under close supervision of the teacher and includes a strong component of feedback. Students can also construct their own problems and exchange them with other students.

Strategies for Teaching Multiplication and Division. Although addition and subtraction of larger and larger numbers will remain a key instructional need well into the elementary years and beyond, students should be taught multiplication and division. Students who have a solid foundation in addition and subtraction have many of the basic skills they need to learn multiplication successfully and have the potential to progress through the multiplication curriculum successfully.

Learning multiplication and division facts requires more sophisticated strategies than learning addition and subtraction facts (Mastropieri & Scruggs, 2000). Students with math disabilities to not readily make connections between what they already know (3 + 3 = 6) and new learning (3 x 2 = 6) (Van Luit & Naglieri, 1999). However, many strategies used to learn addition and subtraction facts can be easily modified and used to teach multiplication and division facts, making explicit connections to earlier learning:

- Teach the commutative property of multiplication.
- Teach fact families (3 x 5 = 15; 5 x 3 = 15; 15 ÷ 5 = 3; 15 ÷ 3 = 5).
- Teach division as the inverse of multiplication.
- Teach students to check calculations with their inverse.
- Teach rules such as the zero rule (0 x any number = 0) and one rule (1 x any number = that number), which can be related to comparable addition rules.

Other useful strategies for teaching facts include

- Connect twos to comparable addition facts (3 x 2 = 3 + 3).
- Teach adding on (4 x 3 = 3 + 3 + 3 + 3).
- Teach students to count by twos, threes, and fives and relate to facts.
- Teach students the relationship between multiplying by 1, 10, and 100 (1 x 3 = 3, 10 x 30 = 30, and 100 x 3 = 300).

These instructional strategies dramatically reduce the numbers of facts to be memorized. Moreover, programs such as Touch Math and software such as Math Blaster (Davidson) can be useful to help students memorize more difficult facts.

Teaching Multiplication and Division Operations. Organization and clarity of steps are critical to student learning of multiplication and division. Students accustomed to approaching math problems from right-to-left must change direction when solving division problems. Problems have more steps, and larger numbers to deal with, and students often have difficulty aligning numbers or will lose their place in the middle of problems.

Graph paper aligns numbers and provides structure to calculations as students learn more complex multiplication and long division, particularly when used from the beginning of instruction. Four squares/inch paper provides adequate room for numbers and allows students to work a problem with room for added arrows, notes, or other cues. As students become more fluent with calculations, they can change to smaller six squares/inch paper and eventually to blank or lined paper. As with addition and subtraction, students need ample practice with multiplication and division to build fluency.

BOX 8.4

FINGER MATH: FINGER NINES

For nines multiplication facts.

- Number the fingers from left pinkie to right pinkie.
- Lower the finger number being multiplied by nine.
- Remaining fingers form tens (to the left of the lowered finger) and ones (to the right of the lowered finger.

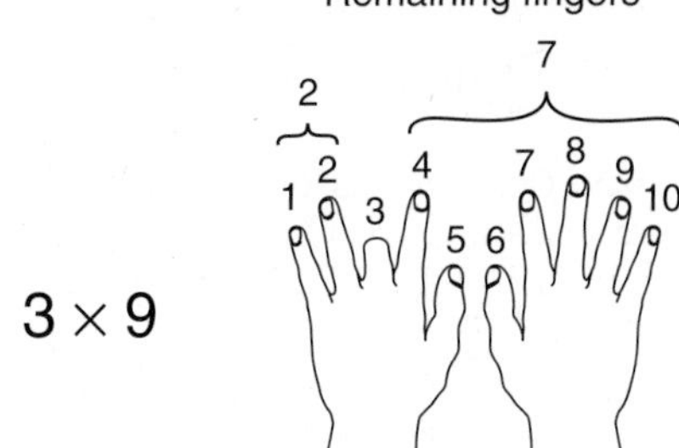

FIGURE 8.10 Fingers Formed to Do Calculation at Left

Multiplication of two or more digits by two or more digits can be particularly difficult for students with math disabilities. Problems increase in abstractness and require a solid understanding of place value. As students progress to multidigit multiplication, it

BOX 8.5

FINGER MATH: LARGE-DIGIT MULTIPLICATION

To speedily calculate 11 x 11 to 15 x 15

To use this strategy, students must:

a. Know 10 x 10 = 100.
b. Be able to differentiate tens and ones place.
c. Know multiplication facts 1x0 to 5x5.
d. Have some ability to do mental math.

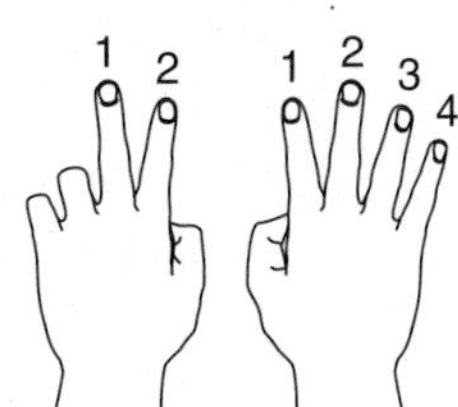

FIGURE 8.11 Fingers Positioned to Do Calculation at Left

- Number each hand 1 to 5 from thumb to little finger.
- Left hand represents the first number, right hand represents second number in the problem.
- On each hand, raise the same number of fingers as numbers in the *ones* place of that hand's number.
- Calculate:
  a. 10 fingers = 100
  b. Count raised fingers by 10s (60)
  c. Add to 100 (160)
  d. Multiply right-hand fingers by left-hand fingers (2 x 4 = 8)
  e. Add to previous (168)

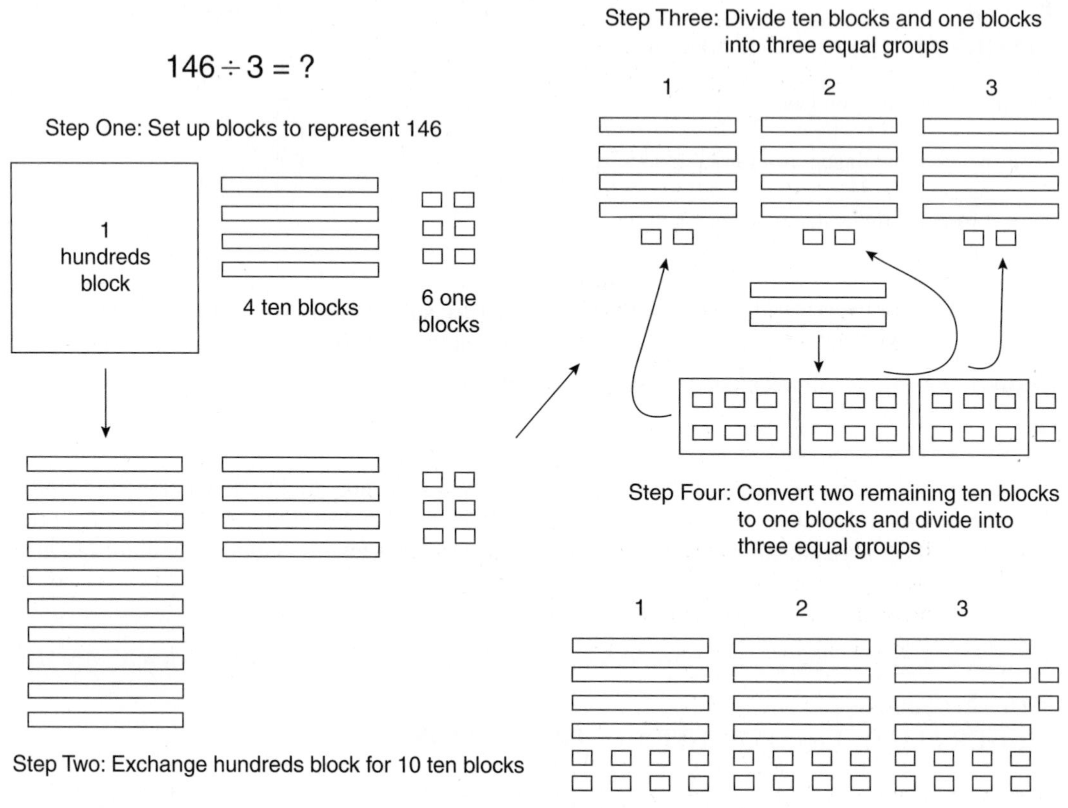

FIGURE 8.12 Division Practice Using Base Ten Blocks

may be advisable to assess students' understanding of place value, providing any needed remediation, before proceeding with instruction.

As with earlier skills, large number multiplication and division should be introduced at the concrete level. Base ten blocks can be manipulated to introduce concepts and practice skills. Ample time should be devoted to practicing multiplication and division of larger numbers before paper and pencil tasks are introduced (see Figure 8.12). As students transition to abstract computations, chip trading activities can be used to reinforce regrouping skills.

Two-digit multiplication problems can be broken down into smaller problems when introduced. The problem 32 x 56 (see Figure 8.13) can be broken into smaller problems and taught step by step:

$$\begin{array}{r} 32 \\ \times\ 56 \\ \hline \end{array}$$

Steps	Calculation	Record
■ Multiply 32 x 6 and record answer.	1. $\begin{array}{r} \scriptstyle 1 \\ 32 \\ \times\ 6 \\ \hline 192 \end{array}$	192
■ Multiply 2 x 50 and record answer.	2. $\begin{array}{r} 2 \\ \times\ 50 \\ \hline 100 \end{array}$	100 +
■ Multiply 30 x 50 and record answer. ■ Sum across responses.	3. $\begin{array}{r} 30 \\ \times\ 50 \\ \hline 1500 \end{array}$	$\begin{array}{r} 1500 \\ \hline 1792 \end{array}$

FIGURE 8.13 Demonstrating Steps at Left

Instruction can be made more concrete by using place value blocks to illustrate each step, particularly multiplication by 50. Gradually the second and third steps can be merged, and then the conventional form of the calculation taught. Color-coding clarifies steps, and colored or numbered arrows guide students as they learn the calculation. A "helper" zero can be placed in the ones place to remind students to use the zero placeholder, then gradually removed.

Using Calculators. More and more, calculators are a viable tool for students with high-incidence disabilities learning mathematics. The availability of low-cost solar calculators make them an everyday tool for most people, meaning that calculator skills become an important aspect of mathematics. Yet debate continues over whether students should use calculators, and if so, when (Smith, 1999). Most textbook publishers include calculator skills, and Smith contends that in our technological age, the argument over calculators seems outdated. For most students with disabilities, calculator skills are essential, particularly if they have long-term difficulties with number facts. Instruction in calculator skills should begin by the middle elementary school years, or as soon as a need becomes apparent, both as an accomodation for students who have not memorized number facts and a means to help students progress through more difficult mathematics.

Solving Multistep Word Problems. As they progress through the math curriculum, students with high-incidence disabilities are confronted with the need to solve multistep word problems. Strategies such as that proposed by Montague and Bos (1996) can easily be modified to be used with multistep problems by coding or numbering each step in a problem, then solving each step separately. For multistep word problems, Shiah, Mastropieri, Scruggs, and Fulk (1994, 1995) suggest the following strategy:

- Read the problem.
- Think about the problem.
- Decide the operation.
- Write the math sentence.
- Do the problem.
- Label the answer.
- Check every step.

As with single-step problems, students should be encouraged to develop and share their own problems, working both alone and with a partner or group to develop collaborative problem-solving strategies.

Fractions and Decimals. Fractions are highly abstract and difficult for most students with high-incidence disabilities to conceptualize. As much as possible, early instruction should emphasize fractions in relation to students' own experiences. Students routinely experience pizza cut in fractions, segments of an orange, and graham crackers that break in half. Materials such as Menu Math (available from Lakeshore Learning Materials) and Fraction Burger (available from Delta Education) teach fractions using common food applications. Fraction terminology (numerator, denominator, equivalent) should be taught slowly, one term at a time. Fraction blocks can be used to illustrate fraction equivalents on the overhead projector, and paper folding allows students to predict fraction equivalents, then test their predictions.

Cooking in the classroom allows students to apply fractional skills to real-life applications. Doubling and tripling recipes allow students to make calculations on fractions and use fraction equivalents. Once fraction skills are mastered, students can learn to make calculations. Perhaps the most difficult skill for students is determining when a fraction should be reduced. Mastropieri and Scruggs (2000) propose a self-monitoring strategy, consisting of a series of questions students can ask themselves:

- Can you divide the denominator by the numerator?
- Are both the numerator and denominator even number? If so, divide by 2.
- Do the numerator and denominator both end in 5 or 0? If so, divide by 5.
- Can you divide both numbers by three?
- Can the fraction be reduced further? Check by repeating steps 1 through 4.

For students who have mastered whole-number calculations, decimals present far less of a challenge than fractions. Moreover, decimals can readily be related to money, always of interest to students from the upper elementary grades on. Students will need ample practice with a number line to grasp the values of decimal numbers. For calculations, graph paper with an added red guide line can help students keep decimal points aligned. For many students, teaching decimal operations, particularly multiplication and division, on calculators will make these operations manageable.

Algebra. Many secondary school students with high-incidence disabilities are able to successfully progress to algebra and learn skills successfully. However, algebra can be a

BOX 8.6
THE STAR STRATEGY

1. **S** earch the word problem.
   a. Read the problem aloud carefully.
   b. Ask yourself the questions "What do I know?" "What do I need to find?"
   c. Write down facts.
1. **T** ranslate the word into an equation in picture form.
   a. Choose a variable.
   b. Identify the operation(s).
   c. Represent the problem with manipulatives* (concrete application).
   Draw a picture of the representation (semi-concrete application).
   Write an algebraic equation.
2. **A** nswer the problem.
3. **R** eview the solution.
   a. Reread the problem.
   b. Ask questions, "Does the answer make sense?" "Why?"
   c. Check answer.

*Maccini and Hughes (2000) recommend use of Algebra Lab Gear.

source of difficulty and anxiety for many of these students, and many have difficulty with algebra (Maccini, McNaughton, & Ruhl, 1999). This is of particular importance with many states now including algebra competencies in state standards and tests (e.g., California State Board of Education, 1997). Students must learn a wide variety of new terminology, as well as skills of problem representation and solution. Basic math is essential to the mastery of algebra, and students must be able to recognize and use basic mathematical terms and skills. Mastropieri and Scruggs (2000) suggest teaching algebraic representation at an early stage of problem solving, thus familiarizing students with basic notation and the concept of an unknown quantity. For example, in the missing addend problem $3 + ? = 7$, the question mark can be replaced with the unknown x, acquainting students with the concept of the unknown quantity.

Very little literature addresses the issues surrounding students with high-incidence disabilities learning algebra, and few interventions have been designed to assist students with the challenges of algebra. What is clear is that students need a sequential instructional sequence that takes them from the concrete to the abstract (Maccini et al., 1999). Moreover, common to most interventions is the use of a mnemonic designed to help students recall steps or procedures. Maccini (1998) integrated many of these principles into the STAR (for Search, Translate, Answer, Review) strategy for algebraic word problems (see Box 8.6).

Strategies such as STAR require careful teaching. The strategy should be taught slowly, allowing students to grasp essential components. In a study validating the STAR strategy, Maccini and Hughes (2000) adapted procedures from Mercer and Miller (1992):

- Provide an advance organizer (identify the skill or concept, and provide a rationale for learning).
- Describe and model.
- Provide guided practice.
- Provide independent practice.
- Give a post-test.
- Provide feedback.

Careful measured instruction will assure students with high-incidence disabilities avoid becoming overwhelmed by the new strategy and the terminology that accompanies it.

Teaching Negative Numbers. Another challege students face is learning positive and negative numbers. Manipulatives such as unifix cubes or algebra tiles can be used to teach these skills. One color cube or tile can represent the zero point, a second positive numbers and a third negative numbers, allowing students to count up and down while adding and removing cubes or tiles. Positive cubes or tiles can be seen to "cancel out" negative cubes or tiles, illustrating concepts. In time, the cubes or tiles can be placed along a number line with positive and negative numbers, allowing to transition to the use of the number line more effectively.

REFERENCES

American Guidance Service. (2003). *Key Math Teach and Practice Program.* Circle Pines, MN: AGS Publishing.

Bley, N., & Thornton, C. (1989). *Teaching mathematics to students with learning disabilities.* Austin, TX: Pro-Ed.

Brigance, A. H. (1999). *Brigance Comprehensive Inventory of Basic Skills-Revised.* North Billerica, MA: Curriculum Associates.

Bryant, B., & Rivera, D. P. (1997). Educational assessment of mathematics skills and abilities. *Journal of Learning Disabilities, 30*, 57–68.

Bryant, D. P., Bryant, B. R., & Hammill, D. D. (2000). Characteristic behaviors of students with LD who have teacher-identified math weaknesses. *Journal of Learning Disabilities, 33*, 168–177.

Bryant, D. P., & Dix, J. (1998). Mathematics interventions for students with learning disabilities. In W. N. Bender (Ed.), *Professional issues in learning disabilities: Practical strategies and relevant research findings.* Austin, TX: Pro-Ed.

California State Board of Education. (1997). *Mathematics content standards for California's public schools: Kindergarten through grade twelve.* Sacramento, CA: Author.

Carle, E. (1969). *The very hungry caterpillar.* New York: Putnam.

Carnine, D. (1997). Instructional design in mathematics for students with learning disabilities. *Journal of Learning Disabilities, 30*, 130–141.

Carnine, D. (1998). Instructional design in mathematics for students with learning disabilities. In D. Rivera (Ed.), *Mathematics education for students with learning disabilities* (pp. 119–138). Austin, TX: Pro-Ed.

Carnine, D., & Gersten, R. (2000). The nature and roles of research in improving achievement in mathematics. *Journal for Research in Mathematics Education, 31*(2), 138–43.

Cathcart, W. G., Pothier, Y. M., Vance, J. H., & Bezuk, N. S. (2000). *Learning mathematics in elementary and middle schools.* Upper Saddle River, NJ: Merrill.

Deschler, D., Ellis, E. S., & Lenz, B. K. (1996). *Teaching adolescents with learning disabilities: Strategies and methods.* Denver: Love.

Engelmann, S., Carnine, D., Engelmann, O., & Kelly, B. (2002). *Connecting math concepts.* DeSoto, TX: SRA/McGraw-Hill.

Engelmann, S., & Steely, D. (2002). *Direct instruction:*

Corrective mathematics. DeSoto, TX: SRA/McGraw-Hill.

Fuchs, L. S., & Deno, S. L. (1994). Must instructionally useful performance assessment be based in the curriculum? *Exceptional Children, 61*(1), 15–24.

Fuchs, L. S., & Fuchs, D. (1988). Curriculum-based measurement: A methodology for evaluating and improving student programs. *Diagnostique, 14*, 3–13.

Fuchs, L. S., Fuchs, D., Hamlett, C., & Alinder, R. (1989). The reliability and validity of skills analysis within curriculum-based measurement. *Diagnostique, 14*, 23–51.

Fuchs, L. S., Fuchs, D., Karns, K., Hamlett, C., Katzaroff, M., & Dutka, S. (1998). Comparisons among individual and cooperative performance assessments and other measures of mathematics competence. *Elementary School Journal, 99*(1), 203–221.

Ginsburg, H. P. (1997). Mathematics learning disabilities: A view from developmental psychology. *Journal of Learning Disabilities, 30*, 20–33.

Kistner, J. A., Osborne, M., & Le Verrier, L. (1988). Causal attributions of learning disabled children: Developmental patterns and relation to academic progress. *Journal of Educational Psychology, 80,* 82–89.

Lerner, L. (2000). *Learning disabilities: Theories, diagnosis and teaching strategies* (8th ed.). Boston: Houghton-Mifflin.

Licht, B. G. (1983). Cognitive-motivational factors that contribute to the achievement of learning disabled children. *Journal of Learning Disabilities, 16*, 483–490.

Lowenthal, B. (1998). Precursors of learning disabilities in an inclusive school. *Learning Disabilities: A Multi-disciplinary Journal, 9*(2), 25–32.

Maccini, P. (1998). *Effects of instructional strategy incorporating concrete problem representation of the introductory algebra performance of secondary students with learning disabilities.* Unpublished doctoral dissertation, Pennsylvania State University, University Park.

Maccini, P., & Hughes, C. A. (2000). Effects of a problem-solving strategy on the introductory algebra performance of secondary students with learning disabilities. *Learning Disabilities Research and Practice, 15*(1), 10–21.

Maccini, P., McNaughton, D., & Ruhl, K. L. (1999). Algebra instruction for students with learning disabilities: Implications from a research review. *Learning Disability Quarterly, 22*(2), 113–126.

Mastropieri, M. A., Bakken, J. P., & Scruggs, T. E. (1991). Mathematics research for individuals with mental retardation: A perspective and research synthesis. *Education and Training in Mental Retardation, 26*, 115–129.

Mastropieri, M. A., & Scruggs, T. E. (2000). *The inclusive classroom: Strategies for effective instruction*. Upper Saddle River, NJ: Merrill.

McIntosh, R., Vaughn, S., Schumm, J. S., Haager, D., & Lee, O. (1993). Observations of students with learning disabilities in general education classrooms. *Exceptional Children, 60*(3), 249–261.

McLesky, J., & Waldron, N. (1990). The identification and characteristics of students with learning disabilities in Indiana. *Learning Disabilities Research and Practice, 5*, 72–78.

Mercer, C. D., & Mercer, A. R. (1998). *Teaching students with learning problems* (5th ed.). Upper Saddle River, NJ: Merrill.

Mercer, C. D., & Miller, S. P. (1992). Teaching students with learning problems in math to acquire, understand, and apply basic math facts. *Remedial and Special Education, 13*(3), 19–35, 61.

Miller, S. P. (1996). Perspectives on mathematics instruction. In D. Deschler, E. Ellis, & B. Lenz (Eds.), *Teaching adolescents with learning disabilities*. Denver: Love.

Miller, S. P., Butler, F., & Lee, K. (1998). Validated practices for teaching mathematics to students with learning disabilities: A review of the literature. *Focus on Exceptional Children, 31*(1), 47–56.

Miller, S. P., & Mercer, C. D. (1993a). Mnemonics: Enhancing the math performance of students with learning disabilities. *Intervention in School and Clinic, 29*, 78–82.

Miller, S. P., & Mercer, C. D. (1993b). Using a graduated word problem sequence to promote problem-solving skills. *Learning Disabilities Research and Practice, 8*, 169–174.

Miller, S. P., & Mercer, C. D. (1997). Educational aspects of mathematics disabilities. *Journal of Learning Disabilities, 30*, 47–56.

Montague, M. (1996). What does the "New View" of school mathematics mean for students with mild disabilities? In M. C. Pugach & C. L. Warger (Eds.), *Curriculum trends, special education, and reform: Refocusing the conversation* (pp. 84–93). New York: Teachers' College Press.

Montague, M. (1997). Cognitive strategy instruction in mathematics for students with learning disabilities. *Journal of Learning Disabilities, 30*(2), 164–177. *Focus on Learning Problems in Mathematics, 8*(2), 7–21.

Montague, M., and Bos, C. S. (1986). Verbal mathematical problem solving and learning disabilities: A review.

National Council of Teachers of Mathematics (NCTM) (1991). Professional standards for teachers of mathematics. Reston, VA: Author.

National Council of Teachers of Mathematics (NCTM) (2000). *Principles and standards for school mathematics* (Electronic Edition). Reston, VA: Author.

Patton, J. R., Cronin, M. E., Bassett, D. S., & Koppel, A. E. (1998). A life skills approach to mathematics instruction: Preparing students with learning disabilities for the real-life math demands of adulthood. In D. Rivera (Ed.), *Mathematics education for students with learning disabilities* (pp. 201–218). Austin, TX: ProEd.

Rivera, D. P. (1997). Mathematics education and students with learning disabilities: Introduction to the special series. *Journal of Learning Disabilities, 30,* 2–19.

Rivera, D. P., & Smith, D. D. (1987). Influence of modeling on acquisition and generalization of computational skills: A summary of research findings from three sites. *Learning Disability Quarterly, 10*(1), 69–80.

Schumm, J. S., & Vaughn, S. (1995). Getting ready for inclusion: Is the stage set? *Learning Disabilities Research and Practice, 10*, 169–179.

Schumm, J. S., Vaughn, S., Haager, D., McDowell, J., Rothlein, L., & Saumell, L. (1995). General education teacher planning: What can students with learning disabilities expect? *Exceptional Children, 61*(4), 335–352.

Shiah, R. L., Mastropieri, M. A., Scruggs, T. E., & Fulk, B. J. M. (1994–1995). The effects of computer assisted instruction on the mathematical problem solving of students with learning disabilities. *Exceptionality, 5,* 131–161.

Singer, J. A., & Resnick, L. B. (1992). Representations of proportional relationships: Are children part-part or part-whole reasoners? *Educational Studies in Mathematics, 23* (3), 231–46.

Smith, C. (1999). Pencil and paper numeracy. *Mathematics in School*, *28*, 10–13.

Smith, D. D., & Lovitt, T. C. (1982). The computational arithmetic program. Austin, TX: Pro-Ed.

Steck-Vaughn Company. (2003). *Mastering math.* Barrington, IL: Harcourt Supplemental Publishers.

Thornton, C. A., & Wilmot, B. (1986). Special learners. *Arithmetic Teacher*, *33*, 38–41.

Van Luit, J. E. H., & Nagleri, J. A. (1999). Effectiveness of the MASTER program for teaching special children multiplication and division. *Journal of Learning Disabilities*, *32*, 98–107.

Woodcock, R. W., McGrew, K. S., & Mather, N. (2001). *Woodcock-Johnson III Complete Battery*. Itasca, IL: Riverside Publishing.

CHAPTER NINE

SUPPORTING STUDENTS' LEARNING IN THE CONTENT AREAS

We live in a society exquisitely dependent on science and technology, in which hardly anyone knows anything about science and technology.

—Carl Sagan (1989)

KEY CONCEPTS

- IDEA specifies that students with disabilities must be provided opportunities to progress in the general education curriculum; content area teachers and inclusion specialists must make sure that the curriculum is accessible, or deliverable, to *all* students.
- The curriculum should be adapted to help make it accessible—the content, evaluation criteria or expectations, materials or textbook, instructional delivery, timing or pacing of instruction, physical environment, type of support provided, and grouping procedures can all be adjusted.
- Vocabulary acquisition is essential for academic growth to occur—content area classes re-

quire the understanding of critical sets of relevant vocabulary terms, yet many students with high-incidence disabilities have limited vocabularies.

- Students can be taught how to use context clues and morphemic analysis to help them figure out words; graphic organizers, such as semantic webs, tree diagrams, word maps, concept maps, and semantic feature analysis, can also be used to teach word meanings.
- Many students with disabilities are poor comprehenders and lack both the metacognitive skills to monitor their reading comprehension and the "fix up" strategies to repair understanding when it breaks down—yet numerous strategies have been developed to improve the understanding, storage, and retrieval of complex information.
- Writing is an essential component of content area classes—learning strategies can help students record observations and experimental data, write research reports, and take notes during class and while reading.
- Students with disabilities should be taught study skills and techniques for remembering key concepts, such as how to study for tests and how to use mnemonic devices.

FOCUS QUESTIONS

1. What can the inclusion specialist do to help content area teachers assure that the curriculum is accessible to all students?
2. Why is "locus of control" an important construct when working with students with disabilities, and what can the inclusion specialist do to help students develop an internal locus of control?
3. What can the inclusion specialist do to help students with disabilities improve their vocabularies and figure out unknown words?
4. Why is it so important to teach comprehension strategies to students with disabilities? What are some of the strategies that students can be taught?
5. What techniques can the inclusion specialist teach students with disabilities to enhance their writing skills in content classes?
6. What study skills and strategies for remembering key concepts should students with disabilities be taught?
7. What should the classroom content area teacher know about how to provide "listener-friendly" lectures?
8. What should the inclusion specialist know about teaching students who are English language learners and also have disabilities?

Booker T. Washington High School is a middle-sized urban high school. Many of the students are English language learners who speak a variety of different first languages. The school recently adopted a modified inclusion model. Students with severe reading disabilities attend small, intensive reading classes taught by a learning disabilities specialist, but are included in all other classes. One inclusion specialist at each grade level works with the students with high-incidence disabilities at that grade level. At Booker T. Washington, Mr. Barnes works with the ninth graders. He teaches the intensive reading classes but does not actually attend students' content area classes. However, he does attend the planning meetings for these classes and provides support in other ways. At Booker T. Washington, all teachers who teach the same subject at a particular grade level meet once a week for collaborative planning. Thus, Mr. Barnes is part of the planning teams for the Physical Science and World History classes that all ninth graders other than those in advanced placement classes must take. At these meetings, Mr. Barnes reviews the material that will be covered in the next week, makes suggestions for how to present the material in ways that will be best for the students with disabilities (e.g., what type of advance organizer or mnemonic device to use), and assists in modifying students' textbooks (the chapters of the World History book are notoriously dense and difficult to read). Because Mr. Barnes knows his students well and understands the curriculum that must be covered, he is able to point out potentially confusing concepts and skills. He brings a notebook to these meetings and jots down areas that he thinks might be problematic for certain students (e.g., "make sure Bryce and Linda can differentiate between the different phases of matter"). In addition, Mr. Barnes holds a "consultation period" once a day. Classroom teachers send students who need extra help, either calling, stopping by ahead of time, or writing a note explaining what the student needs (e.g., "Mike is going to come in this morning to study his vocabulary words for a test third period").

Once a week at an appointed time Mr. Barnes has a conference with each student to discuss how he or she is progressing. Students bring copies of their most recent science or history test, quiz, or assignment that has already been graded. They show Mr. Barnes the class notes they have taken using the forms he provided and taught them to use. Together they go over key vocabulary terms and the semantic maps they have created. They also look at new assignments. Mr. Barnes checks what type of assistance, if any, might be needed, and helps students come up with a plan for completing the assignment. For instance, he has Marcos, Sergio, Grace, and Cynthia each come up with a plan for what they will achieve each day toward the completion of their science projects. Students check off on their planning sheets that they have completed a day's task and show this to Mr. Barnes, checking with him during their reading class, coming in during the consultation period, or dropping in before school. Mr. Barnes makes sure that he is available for the hour before school to provide this type of assistance. Subject-area teachers also know that they can come by before school to discuss students or leave a note. These teachers appreciate that Mr. Barnes has made adequate time in his schedule for ongoing communication about their shared students. Mr. Barnes's students agree that the help they receive from him is invaluable. His efforts help them stay organized, on task, and productive. When they get stuck and don't know how to proceed, he helps them problem-solve next steps. Mr. Barnes feels that his schedule provides an optimal balance between providing intensive skills instruction for those students who need it most, collaborating with classroom teachers, and working with students to provide support in the content areas. Many of the techniques used by Mr. Barnes and his colleagues are described in this chapter.

In a traditional resource program model, many students miss science or social studies instruction because they are removed from their classrooms for supplemental instruction during the time those subjects are taught. Some specialists have rationalized that this is the best time to pull students because learning to read takes priority over content area learning. In some cases, students with disabilities have actually been discouraged from pursuing science (National Research Council, 1993). Many children with disabilities fall behind their peers in content knowledge because they are not in class when instruction takes place. They often leave or return during instruction, miss it altogether, or are present for the instruction but do not understand because adaptations and accommodations are not made to facilitate their learning. In some inclusion models, the special education teacher is *not* present for content area instruction. If she or he works with multiple classes, scheduling is such that the inclusion specialist is in the room for language arts and mathematics instruction, but not science or social studies. Yet students with disabilities often need a great deal of assistance during these two subjects. In this chapter we describe instructional approaches and adaptations that are appropriate for heterogeneous, inclusive classrooms and discuss potential roles for the inclusion specialist.

Although the focus of much of this chapter is on strategies for supporting students' content area learning in the upper grades, we believe that content area reading need not wait until students are proficient readers and should begin in the primary grades (Guillaume, 1998). Content area learning is often the hook to captivate otherwise unmotivated learners. Young children are quite motivated to learn more about the world around them-many children have favorite books about such topics as dinosaurs, space, trucks, and trains. The content areas build motivation and a purpose for reading: We read to know. Content area reading experiences help students develop the abilities to process and analyze information, even at a young age.

Covering the curriculum and providing whole-class instruction are primarily the domain of the classroom teacher. The inclusion specialist also needs to be knowledgeable about these areas in order to be an effective consultant during the planning process. The inclusion specialist's role is to provide expertise in differentiating among whole-class instructional techniques, small group methods, and individual strategies. Because the inclusion specialist knows the students with disabilities well and understands their needs, he or she is usually in the best position to determine which method or strategy would be best under which circumstances. English language learners, who are in the process of learning English while at the same time learning in the content areas, present additional challenges. Fortunately, many of the techniques that are beneficial for students with disabilities are often useful for English language learners, and vice versa (Echevarria & Graves, 1998).

By serving in a co-teaching or consulting role with a content area teacher, the inclusion specialist is an ideal position to facilitate the learning of students with learning disabilities and students with other special needs (Gurganus, Janas, & Schmitt, 1995). First, the inclusion specialist can help the science or social studies teacher plan instruction and gather materials. He or she knows what strategies students have learned or could learn that would help them understand the content they will be covering (e.g, a K-W-L chart or semantic feature analysis—both defined later in this chapter). If any adaptations or accommodations would be helpful for particular students, the inclusion specialist knows this and can work with the content area teacher or other support personnel to provide this assistance. Also, sometimes the inclusion specialist is in the best position to know how subjects might be integrated. For example, Mr. Barnes knows that the "kitchen science" unit currently taught by two of the science teachers links with the concepts they are covering in the ninth grade math class on measurement and calculating fractions. He is able to make this connection explicit for students. The inclusion specialist can provide supplemental instruction for students who might have gaps in their learning from having been pulled out of previous content area classes for supplemental reading and/or mathematics instruction. The inclusion specialist as a co-teacher can provide valuable assistance during hands-on and cooperative learning activities, circulating the room and monitoring student learning. The inclusion specialist can also help design and conduct performance-based assessments. Finally, the inclusion specialist might provide additional instruction and generalization opportunities for students who are experiencing difficulty.

MAKING CONTENT AREA LEARNING ACCESSIBLE THROUGH ADAPTATIONS

Whole-class learning strategies Instructional strategies designed to make the curriculum more accessible to all students.

Individual learning strategies Instructional strategies designed to serve as *additional* instruction to assist students with special learning needs.

Adaptations Specially designed instruction designed to meet the individual learning needs of an eligible student; adapting the content, methodology, or delivery of instruction and to ensure access to the general education curriculum.

There is nothing so unequal as the equal treatment of unequals.

—author unknown

It may not have been the intent of this author to speak about classroom instruction, but the concept does apply. When content area teachers change their goal of instruction from content delivery to student learning, they are faced with the task of making the curriculum accessible, or deliverable, to *all* students. In an inclusive classroom, this means developing lessons and instructional techniques for a diverse array of students. It may mean altering the instruction for some students but not for others. It may mean providing additional instruction for some. Thus far, we have discussed **whole-class instructional strategies** designed to make the curriculum more accessible to all and **individual learning strategies**, which can be viewed as additional instruction for some students, as ways to provide content area learning for students with special learning needs. However, what happens when teachers plan these good instructional practices and they know that a particular student is still not likely to be successful? This is when the classroom teacher and inclusion specialist must work together to develop appropriate **adaptations** for individual students.

The 1997 Amendments to IDEA specify that students with disabilities must be provided opportunities to progress in the general education curriculum as part of their individualized education plan. The term "adaptations" is introduced in the federal law as a means for making adjustments for individuals:

> Specially designed instruction means adapting, as appropriate to the needs of an eligible child, the content, methodology, or delivery of instruction—

a. To address the unique needs of the child that result from the child's disability; and
b. To ensure access of the child to the general curriculum, so that he or she can meet the educational standards within the jurisdiction of the public agency that apply to all children. [Part 300 Subpart A 300.26(b)]

Information about accommodations, modifications, or adaptations should be recorded in a student's Individualized Education Plan (IEP).

Both the IDEA legislation and the Americans with Disabilities Act of 1990 make it clear that schools must make accommodations for individuals with disabilities. Making adaptations, then, is a practical means for making learning accessible to students with disabilities.

Accommodation The act of making learning appropriate and accessible to students with disabilities as needed and, as required by law by making adaptations or modifications.

Modifications Adapting the normal learning expectations so that they are realistic and individually appropriate.

Accommodation, modification, and *adaptation* are all words that are used to describe adjustments teachers make for individual students. Different authors have various conceptualizations of these terms (e.g., Bradley, King-Sears, & Tessier-Switlick, 1997; Vallecorsa, deBettencourt, & Zigmond, 2000). People often use these terms synonymously, and we only point out their differences here because they may cause confusion if people do not have common understandings of the terms. ***Accommodation*** is the act of making learning appropriate and accessible to students with disabilities as needed and as required by law. It could be some type of change in the school, such as wheelchair ramps or special bathroom equipment, or it could be some type of curricular or instructional adjustment. When the IEP team determines that accommodation is necessary for a student to be successful, we may make *adaptations,* or adjustments, to the curriculum, instruction, textbooks, or learning environment. For example, a classroom teacher may give a particular student fewer vocabulary words from the master list. A student may have an adapted test with fewer test items or may have the same test but take it orally in a one-to-one situation with the teacher. The student participates in the same activity and uses the same materials but with slight adaptations. When a student's disability is such that the general education learning expectations are not realistic, the adaptations might be called ***modifications,*** a term that means adapting the normal learning expectations so that they are realistic and individually appropriate. An example of this might be rewriting a worksheet in simpler language or with fewer concepts involved. Another example would be the use of an alternative assignment or test.

Another way to think of these terms is in subsets: A modification is a type of adaptation (one that results in different learning outcomes) and an adaptation is a type of accommodation. Let's use an example to illustrate. Chris is a seventh-grade student with mild mental retardation. Maura is also a seventh-grader who has learning disabilities and has difficulty with written language. The law specifies that the school must make accommodations to allow these students to have access to the general curriculum and be with their nondisabled peers to the greatest extent possible. Physical access is not an issue for either student. Academic adaptations are implemented for both in an inclusive school. This means that both have opportunities to be in the general education classroom with specialized services brought into the classroom. The social studies curriculum presents challenges for both requiring that students learn difficult vocabulary, remember a great deal of detail, and grasp abstract concepts. For Maura, adaptations include extended time to take tests and a reader to assist with written assignments and tests. She listens to audiotapes of the textbook. The teacher and specialist collaborate to shorten the vocabulary list for her. However, she is held accountable to the same learning standards as the other students: She must learn the same content and have the same scores to earn passing grades. These expectations are unreasonable for Chris, who has extreme difficulty with abstract concepts. The teachers have worked out adaptations that result in a modified curriculum for him. During co-planning, the teachers identify the core curricular concepts and develop modified assignments and tests for him. He, too, uses audiotaped textbooks. Vocabulary worksheets have fewer words and a simple fill-in-the-blank format with very literal and concrete wording. His tests are written by the special education teacher and reflect only the core concepts that were identified in the planning process. Both students have appropriate access to the general education curriculum, participate in all group activities and whole-class lessons, and are able to progress to the best of their ability. However, Maura's program involves only adaptations while Chris is provided with modifications.

Reasons for Making Accommodations

Federal law does specify that we must assist students in accessing the core curriculum. The Americans with Disabilities Act also specifies that we must provide reasonable accommodations for individual students. Making adaptations ensures that we are providing reasonable accommodations.

The law is not the only reason for making special accommodations for individual students. Teachers report that when they adjust their teaching for a particular student it often helps other students or improves their teaching in general (Schumm, Vaughn, Haager, McDowell, Rothlein, & Saumell, 1995). Most teachers are willing to make accommodations when they know it will truly make a difference in student learning (Zigmond, 1996).

Elementary and Secondary Perspectives on Making Adaptations. Generally, classroom teachers in the elementary grades are more willing and more able to implement adaptations for individual students than are secondary teachers (McIntosh, Vaughn, Schumm, Haager, & Lee, 1993; Schumm & Vaughn, 1992; Schumm et al., 1995). There are several explanations for this. Elementary teachers generally have smaller class sizes and more flexible schedules than secondary teachers. They have one group of students throughout the entire day rather than one group after another. Elementary teachers tend to have more frequent and regular contact with the special education teachers and other support personnel than do secondary teachers. In addition, secondary teachers, concerned with content delivery, find it difficult to focus on individual student needs except in the scope of instructing and planning for the class as a whole. At the high school level, teachers are responsible for adhering to strict standards for high school completion and often have little room for flexibility. Many secondary teachers feel it is wrong to make adaptations because it fails to prepare the student for the "real world" that lies beyond high school.

How, then, do we reconcile teachers' legitimate concerns about making adaptations with mandates for reasonable accommodations? Inclusive models of providing special education services have helped to inform secondary teachers of their responsibilities and methods for making accommodations. It is helpful for schools to launch schoolwide efforts to provide information and resources to classroom teachers through staff development and training. Ongoing collaboration and consultation between general and special educators alleviates teachers' concerns and leads to workable solutions.

Students' Views of Adaptations. Research regarding students' perceptions of adaptations for students with special needs in inclusive classrooms has been conducted with general education students only (Vaughn, Schumm, Niarhos, & Daugherty, 1993; Vaughn, Schumm, Niarhos, & Gordon, 1993), as well as with combinations of students with and without learning disabilities (Fulk & Smith, 1995; Vaughn, Schumm, Klingner, & Saumell, 1995; Vaughn, Schumm, & Kouzekanani, 1993).

Students consider adaptations to be desirable. Elementary and middle school students with and without disabilities reported positive responses to teachers' adaptations for special learners (Fulk & Smith, 1995; Vaughn, Schumm, & Kouzekanani, 1993; Vaughn, Schumm, Niarhos, & Gordon, 1993). Fulk and Smith (1995) revealed that although students with and without disabilities asserted that many adaptations were acceptable to them, their teachers infrequently enacted adaptations—only 1 in 17 teachers was perceived as providing differentiated work. One student advised, "What she's (teacher) doing with him isn't working. Maybe she should try something new" (p. 415).

The perceptions of middle and high school students regarding the types of adaptations teachers make to meet the special learning needs of students revealed that they overwhelmingly preferred adaptations in their textbooks to assist them in understanding difficult content material (Vaughn, Schumm, Klingner, & Saumell, 1995; Vaughn, Schumm, & Kouzekanani, 1993; Vaughn, Schumm, Niarhos, & Daugherty, 1993). Rationales provided by middle school students centered more around adaptations to make the material interesting, whereas high school students craved adaptations to promote learning (Vaughn, Schumm, Klingner, & Saumell, 1995). Middle and high school students wanted teachers to provide the same tests and homework to all students and to ensure that all students used the same textbooks and materials. Yet these students recognized that many classmates were having trouble keeping up and understanding lessons. Most were willing to have the teacher slow down even if it meant that more capable students might be bored. Middle and high school students were willing to have teachers make adaptations in instructional practices (Vaughn, Schumm, & Kouzekanani, 1993). One student described why he preferred a particular teacher: "Because she (the teacher) helps kids when they need help. When she is teaching a lesson, she sees a person does not understand and she goes and shows them a different way." (p. 551). Interestingly, students who most preferred adaptations were those with higher reading and math scores (Vaughn, Schumm, & Kouzekanani, 1993; Vaughn, Schumm, Niarhos, & Daugherty, 1993).

As noted in Klingner and Vaughn's (1999a) synthesis of students' perceptions, students want everyone to be treated the same, yet they also recognize that learning needs differ—not all students learn in the same way, or at the same speed. Thus, students with and without disabilities value teachers who slow down instruction when needed, who explain concepts and assignments clearly, who teach learning strategies, and who teach the same material in different ways so that everyone can learn. Most students did not perceive instructional adaptations and accommodations to meet the special needs of selected students as problematic. In fact, the majority of students believed that these adaptations and accommodations could facilitate their own learning. Thus, with few exceptions, classroom teachers do not need to be concerned that such instructional adaptations will be perceived negatively by their students with or without disabilities.

Types of Adaptations and Strategies for Implementation

Teachers are most successful with implementing adaptations when several factors are in place. Classroom teachers are more likely to be accommodating of students with disabilities when they have positive, accepting attitudes about such students and they hold a genuine belief that they are able to teach them (McIntosh et al., 1993; Schumm, Vaughn, Haager, McDowell, Rothlein, & Saumell, 1995). In addition, co-planning (collaborative planning sessions involving both the general and special education teachers) is a helpful process for tailoring instruction for individual students (Schumm, 1999; Schumm, Vaughn, & Leavell, 1994). Also, classroom teachers are more likely to implement specific adaptations for individual students in a co-teaching situation (Zigmond, 1996). Without co-planning and co-teaching, general classroom teachers tend to accommodate students with special needs only through whole-class, generalized adaptations (Baker & Zigmond, 1995; Schumm et al., 1995). Time is another critical factor. Teachers need to have time built into their schedule to plan and prepare lessons that can address a diversity of student needs (Schumm & Vaughn, 1992).

Simplicity should be the rule during co-planning. We like to use the KISS maxim: Keep It Sweet and Simple. Teachers are most likely to implement adaptations when they are unobtrusive and fit in with what teachers have planned for the class as a whole and are well integrated into the curriculum (Schumm et al., 1995; Vallecorsa et al., 2000). Teachers should consider the options for what could be adapted and then make their decisions based on both the likelihood of student success and ease of implementation.

Using the KISS principle, teachers would select adaptations that are the least obtrusive and disruptive to the teaching routine while still maximizing the possibility of student success and enabling the student to develop independence. In other words, given a choice of using a peer buddy to read a written assignment to a student or rewriting the worksheet, the teachers would have to weigh the effort involved and the student's needs. For some students, though rewriting is effortful, the teachers may decide to make the investment because several students will benefit from the alternative assignment and it will allow them to work independently. However, using a peer buddy may be a good choice for other students because peers will provide a model for the process and the easier text will be more understandable. Figure 9.1 provides examples of different types of adaptations to accommodate individual learners. Teachers may choose one or a combination of adaptations.

The following steps have been adapted from Schumaker and Lenz (1999) to guide teachers in the process of developing adaptations:

1. *Create a plan for making adaptations.* This entails short-term planning within the context of the "bigger picture" of long-term planning. Teachers make clear decisions as to the responsibilities of each professional involved. Teachers may also involve students in the decision-making process as the "consumer" of the adaptation.

Types of Adaptations and Examples

Adapt the Content

- Learn 10 vocabulary words instead of 25.
- Emphasize key battle names and causes of conflicts in social studies without requiring details such as dates.
- Read and test student on textbook material section by section.
- Teach a related, similar unit of study, such as simple machines in physical science, parallel to the whole-class unit on simple and complex machines and forces of nature.
- Simplify or rearrange the steps in a process.

Adapt the Evaluation Criteria or Expectations

- Teach basic subtraction facts while the class learns subtraction with regrouping.
- Score a writing sample based on student's targeted needs, such as punctuation or paragraph structure, rather than the grade-level criteria.
- Require a lower number of problems or items on an assignment or test.

Adapt the Materials or Textbook

- Eliminate some math problems or chapter questions in a social studies text.
- Provide a study guide or outline emphasizing key points.
- Use a highlighter to mark key concepts.
- Substitute materials, textbooks, or videotapes for assigned text.
- Use audiotaped textbooks or peer readers.
- Use assistive technology, such as the Kurzweil Reader, that will read scanned text.
- Simplify materials by rewriting or restructuring.
- Eliminate superfluous material to shorten reading tasks.

Adapt the Instructional Delivery

- Provide additional preteaching, or preview, of concepts to be covered such as vocabulary words to be covered in a literature selection.
- Make key concepts explicit and review them often.
- Ask questions with reasonable certainty that the individual student will answer successfully.
- Teach the same concept with multiple presentations or modes of instruction.
- Use consistent routines and prompts.
- Reteach for students who need further instruction.
- Provide samples of finished products.

Adjust the Timing or Pacing of Instruction

- Provide additional time for students to read or complete assignments.
- Slow the pace or provide additional explanation.

FIGURE 9.1 Adaptation Choices to Meet Individual Student Needs

Adjust the Physical Environment

- Seat students strategically.
- Provide visual cues or prompts on the wall or student's desk.
- Write assignments on specific spot on board.
- Group students' desks to provide peer support.
- Provide a table for small group work with teacher or support teacher.
- Provide a listening area for audiotaped books.

Adjust the Type of Support Provided

- Provide individual support from the classroom teacher and/or specialist.
- Provide opportunities for peer support such as peer tutoring or partner reading.
- Work with target students in a small group following the whole-group presentation.
- Provide concept maps, outlines, and study guides as advance organizers.
- Allow student to use a word bank or dictionary of words for writing tasks.
- Go over the directions and model tasks individually with target students.
- Check on individual students frequently.

Adjust Grouping Procedures

- Place students in heterogeneous groups for peer assistance and modeling.
- Pair students with a knowledgeable and supportive peer.
- Place students in skills-based groups for direct instruction.

FIGURE 9.1 Continued

2. *Identify and evaluate the demands on the student.* This involves observing the student and evaluating the curriculum and textbooks to understand how to tailor instruction to the individual's specific needs.
3. *Determine the purpose or aim of the adaptations.* The overall goal should be to enable the student to be successful without becoming dependent on the support of teachers and peers. Adaptations should be planned as short-term solutions with the aim of leading the student to full participation or independence in the particular class or subject.
4. *Determine the type of adaptation needed.* In co-planning, teachers must decide whether to adapt the content or the structure for an individual student. Adapting the materials, procedures, or grouping format would all be examples of structural adaptations rather than a curricular adaptation.
5. *Inform the students and parents about the adaptation.* Teachers may want to not only inform the individual student about an adaptation, but also want to have a whole-class discussion about accommodating individual needs. It is important for discussions of this type to be conducted in a sensitive and respectful manner without

indicating specific individuals. Teachers should keep parents informed as well so that they may provide necessary support at home. The student's IEP is an appropriate place to record information about adaptations.

6. *Implement, evaluate, and adjust the adaptations.* Teachers are constantly adjusting their instruction as they see how it works out in practice. The same is true of adaptations. As general and special education teachers carry through with their plans and activities, they often find that they need to do some "fine-tuning." Systematic evaluation of their separate and shared roles and activities allows for such adjustments. Table 9.1 lists some example adaptations grouped by type of student need.

TABLE 9.1 Examples of Adaptations Suitable for Different Types of Student Needs

	ELEMENTARY	SECONDARY
Student has difficulty with organization	■ Establish simple routines. ■ Provide visual cues for ordered steps. ■ Use concept maps to illustrate key ideas. ■ Keep work area clear. ■ Provide prompts at regular intervals for collection of materials. ■ Assist student with notebook, backpack organization.	■ Post assignments on board routinely. ■ Teach student how to record assignments and organize notebook. ■ Use graphic organizers. ■ Use visual prompts to illustrate steps. ■ List materials needed for labs or projects.
Student has difficulty with reading/writing	■ Use audiotaped textbooks. ■ Provide peer or adult assistance with written material. ■ Use manipulatives or media. ■ Simplify or modify materials and tasks. ■ Provide alternatives for demonstration of student skills (e.g., oral book report) ■ Preteach difficult vocabulary.	■ Use audiotaped textbooks. ■ Provide peer or adult assistance with written material. ■ Provide additional time for reading, writing, and tests. ■ Use graphic organizers or study guides. ■ Prioritize and emphasize key concepts.
Student has difficulty with attention	■ Seat student strategically. ■ Provide frequent breaks. ■ Secure student attention prior to giving instructions. ■ Frequently monitor student. ■ Make special effort to engage student.	■ Give student choice in assignments to maximize interest. ■ Seat student strategically. ■ Develop visual prompt or secret cue. ■ Chart and self-record on-task behavior.
Student has difficulty with memory	■ Preteach vocabulary. ■ Simplify and prioritize concepts and vocabulary. ■ Constant review and practice. ■ Provide peer or adult assistance for drill. ■ Use verbal rehearsal.	■ Prioritize and stress key concepts. ■ Verbal rehearsal, drill. ■ Constant review and practice. ■ Use mnemonic techniques. ■ Chunk material. ■ Use concept maps to show relationships between concepts.

INSTRUCTION THAT FACILITATES LEARNING FOR STUDENTS WITH DISABILITIES

We believe that all students are entitled to access the content area curriculum and the reauthorization of IDEA supports that notion. The first principle of the National Science Education Standards emphasizes that "all students, regardless of age, gender, cultural or ethnic background, disabilities, aspirations or interest and motivation in science, should have the opportunity to obtain high levels of scientific literacy" (National Research Council, 1996, p. 20). It is important not to "water down" the curriculum (Ellis, 1997)—too many programs emphasize the memorization of loosely related facts and provide insufficient opportunity to apply newly learned information in meaningful, thought-provoking ways. Thinking skills are erroneously considered by some to come after literacy skills on a hierarchy of learning experiences. Thus, students with reading disabilities are often relegated to rote learning that is frequently decontextualized and relatively meaningless. Accommodations made to help students with disabilities (such as requiring students to learn fewer vocabulary terms or fewer facts) may actually limit students' learning experiences in unnecessary, counterproductive ways. Ellis (1997) recommends that the curriculum be "watered up" for students with mild disabilities (see Figure 9.2).

> **Locus of control** Extent to which an individual attributes success and failure to internal or external factors. People who primarily have an internal locus of control believe that their successes are due to their own efforts and abilities; individuals with an external locus of control believe that their successes are caused by factors external to the self, such as luck.

Locus of Control: What the Student Brings to the Learning Situation

Locus of control refers to the extent to which an individual attributes success and failure to internal or external factors (Slavin, 1994). People who primarily have an internal locus of control believe that their successes are due to their own efforts and abilities, whereas individuals with an external locus of control believe that their successes are caused primarily by luck, other people's actions,

- More emphasis on students' constructing knowledge.
- More depth, less superficial coverage.
- More emphasis on archetypal (universal) concepts and patterns.
- More emphasis on developing understandings of the relationships among content.
- More emphasis on making connections to real-world contexts.
- More student elaboration.
- More emphasis on developing higher-level thinking skills, problem-solving abilities, information-processing skills, and learning strategies.
- More integration across subject areas.
- More authentic assessment tied closely to instruction.

Source: Adapted from Ellis (1997); Gurganus, Janas, & Schmitt (1995).

FIGURE 9.2 Goals of a "Watered-Up" Curriculum

and/or the difficulty of the situation. The possession of an internal locus of control is a powerful predictor of academic achievement (Brookover, Beady, Flood, Schweister, & Wisenbaker, 1979) and students with an internal focus tend to be high achievers. This is due in part to the fact that those who believe that their success is due to their own efforts tend to try harder. In contrast, students with learning disabilities, emotional/behavioral disorders, and mental handicaps frequently have an external locus of control, especially for their successes (Curry & Craighead, 1990; Grolnick & Ryan, 1990; Hagborg, 1996; Tabassam & Grainger, 2002; Wehmeyer & Kelchner, 1996). If they are successful, they tend to believe it is because someone helped them or they were lucky. On the other hand, they tend to have an internal orientation for their failures, believing that they failed because of their own ineptness. This leads to a phenomenon known as **learned helplessness**, a conditioned response that is very difficult to break. These students become passive in learning situations, literally give up, and seem to lack strategies for approaching a task.

Learned helplessness Students who experience failure time after time eventually give up and are unable to try. Characteristic of this psychological phenomenon is a very passive, disengaged approach to learning situations.

One's locus of control can and does change through experience. Thus, students with learning disabilities can be helped to develop a more internal locus of control, or to focus more on effort, through activities that help them become aware of the influence they can exert on various circumstances and their outcomes (Martin, 1996). It is important for students undergoing this kind of training to experience success with their initial efforts. To facilitate this, teachers can provide activities that actively involve students in the manipulation of events and engage them in dialogue to help them clarify their roles. An important goal of the inclusion specialist is to help students feel competent in the content areas. Figure 9.3 presents various strategies that foster the development of an internal locus of control (adapted from Martin, 1996).

Supported Inquiry and Activities-Oriented Instruction

Supported inquiry and activities-oriented instruction are approaches that may have benefits for students with high-incidence disabilities in inclusive settings. We previously

1. Encourage students to evaluate the outcomes of their investigations (e.g., Why did I achieve these results?).
2. Encourage students to try changing variables (e.g., If I change this, what will happen?).
3. Encourage students to suggest additional ways of investigating a given phenomenon.
4. Encourage students to suggest topics for investigation and to set their own goals.
5. Encourage speculation by asking questions (e.g., What do you think will happen?).
6. Encourage students to evaluate their own progress.
7. Encourage cooperative inquiry where each student plays a role.
8. Teach students how to ask each other questions.

FIGURE 9.3 Classroom Strategies during Inquiry-Based Science Learning That Foster the Development of an Internal Locus of Control

Supported inquiry An approach to teaching science or other subject that incorporates the constructivist principle that students are active learners who continually construct and revise their worldview through interactions with the environment and others; this approach involves designing learning experiences that allow students to question and discuss hypotheses.

mentioned the phenomenon of learned helplessness that many students with learning problems experience. Supported inquiry and activities-oriented science instruction facilitate active learning and may combat students' tendency to be passive learners. Mastropieri, Scruggs, and Magnusen (1999) found that adapted activities-based approaches fostered engagement and involvement among students with and without disabilities and led to greater learning. Additionally, these methods were preferred by students. "Science education professionals generally agree that hands-on, inquiry-based science potentially benefits all students, yet there are few specific guidelines for helping students with LD achieve success in general education science classrooms" (Dalton, Morocco, Tivnan, & Mead, 1997, p. 670). Supported inquiry is based on the constructivist principle that students are active learners who continually construct and revise their worldview through interactions with the environment and others. Conceptual change is a complex socio-cognitive process. The principles of supported inquiry include (adapted from Dalton et al., 1997):

1. Provide a safe environment for expressing emerging or divergent views (rationale: students with learning disabilities often avoid participating in classrooms that emphasize finding the one-and-only correct answer as quickly as possible).
2. Design curricula and instruction to focus on a unifying topic using thematic teaching and integrative instruction (rationale: this contributes to a deeper understanding of the concept than is possible when knowledge is accumulated in bits and pieces).
3. Elicit students' alternative conceptualizations and provide opportunities for them to examine conflicting evidence through hands-on experience (rationale: because children are often highly resistant to change, opportunities to manipulate variables themselves increase the likelihood of conceptual learning).
4. Through instructional conversations, use whole-class teaching/coaching to help students revise and elaborate their understandings (rationale: the teacher plays an essential role in helping students reach new understandings).
5. Integrate opportunities for students to work with new material in small peer groups as well as individually and with the whole class (rationale: students develop new conceptual knowledge while collaborating with knowledgeable others).
6. Use multiple modalities to help students explore and examine science concepts and engage in science processes (rationale: students with language difficulties often have strengths in other learning modalities; see Gardner's work on multiple intelligences).
7. Embed assessment at key points during instruction (rationale: to provide teachers with a more systematic and precise understanding of students' strengths and weaknesses at times when such information can inform the instructional decision-making process). Include hands-on performance tasks as well as questions that students respond to by drawing or writing.
8. Provide guidelines and procedures for collaborative science inquiry (rationale: some structure helps students with learning disabilities contribute to their small groups in productive ways).

VOCABULARY

Vocabulary acquisition is essential for academic growth to occur. This is an area that can affect all aspects of learning, but we will discuss it in the context of content area learning here. Content area classes in science, social studies, and mathematics all require the understanding of critical sets of relevant vocabulary terms (Echevarria & Graves, 1998). Yet many students with high-incidence disabilities have limited vocabularies. Vocabulary size and academic achievement are linked (Baumann & Kameenui, 1991). The difference between the number of words known by students with poor vocabularies compared with the number known by students with extensive vocabularies is large, becomes apparent early, and grows over time (Baker, Simmons, & Kameenui, 1994). As early as 1941, Smith found that high-achieving high school seniors knew four times as many words as their low-achieving peers. Studies since then have consistently reported similar results (Graves, 1989; Graves, Brunetti, & Slater, 1982). Furthermore, Simmons and Kameenui (1998) found that 10- and 12-year-old students with learning disabilities had less extensive vocabularies than peers of the same age without disabilities. Not only do students with disabilities typically know fewer words, their understanding of concepts may lack depth. Many factors contribute to differential rates of vocabulary growth. Some students with disabilities suffer from general language deficits that affect their vocabulary learning (Stahl & Erickson, 1986). Others have problems with memory and/or recall (Swanson, 1986). These difficulties are compounded for students who are also English language learners (Echevarria & Graves, 1998).

Many instructional methods designed to improve vocabulary learning have helped students with various types of learning difficulties. However, no single best method of vocabulary instruction has been identified (Beck, McKeown, & Kucan, 2002). We believe special education teachers and content area teachers need to be equipped with multiple teaching strategies. Students learn the majority of new words through **incidental learning** while engaged in everyday experiences with oral and written language (Blachowicz & Fisher, 1996). Students learn many new words from reading and being read to (Eller, Pappas, & Brown, 1988; Elley, 1988) and from context (e.g., from watching ice skating on TV, we learn what a triple lutz is). Yet many students with disabilities are less likely to pick up words incidentally and need help honing this ability. Because of this, we want to be sure to create opportunities for **intentional learning** to help improve students' vocabulary acquisition. Intentional learning occurs when students are provided with systematic, explicit vocabulary instruction. When focusing on vocabulary development with students, it is important to help students build an in-depth understanding of concepts, not just surface level knowledge (Simmons & Kameenui, 1998).

Incidental learning
Acquiring vocabulary words or other knowledge through everyday experiences such as reading, conversation, or television.

Intentional learning
Providing systematic, explicit instruction in vocabulary or other content.

Students in inclusive classrooms who struggle with the numerous difficult vocabulary terms in their content area classes benefit from two kinds of intentional learning for vocabulary development. First, they need help understanding word meaning for specific words in order to be successful in their content coursework. Yet this support will not be sufficient to reduce the gap between students with poor and rich vocabularies. Students also need to become independent with vocabulary learning. Therefore, students must also learn strategies that enable them to learn on their own. In this chapter we present both.

General Guidelines for Vocabulary Instruction

Vocabulary words can be classified as *general* or *technical* (Konopak, 1991; Readence, Bean, & Baldwin, 1998). General words are those with common meanings, such as "change" or "surface." Technical words are specific to a particular subject, such as "photosynthesis." Special education teachers should check students' understanding of both kinds of terms. Content area teachers are concerned with helping students learn novel information and develop conceptual understanding. Students must experience new concepts in a variety of learning situations. This helps students to develop a schemata or conceptual framework that connects the new vocabulary term with prior knowledge. When students have multiple experiences with the same word, they expand their conceptual understanding of it. When students lack the background knowledge and experiences necessary to understand these terms, learning can be quite difficult. Students with special needs require careful, systematic planning and instruction to help them acquire new vocabulary. The focus should be on helping students make connections or associations between new words and previously learned information. It may be necessary to help them build the background knowledge needed to understand a concept. Whenever possible, new terms should be taught in categories rather than as isolated words. Meanings should be made explicit to students through demonstration, visual aids, discussion, and usage in varied contexts. In general, "less is more"—it is preferable to teach fewer words in depth rather than to superficially teach many words (Gersten & Jimenez, 1994). In this way it is more likely they will be retained.

According to Beck, McKeown, and Kucan (2002), words can be thought of according to a Three-Tier Model. Words in Tier 1 are the most basic words like "car," "desk," and "jump." Words in Tier 2 are high-frequency general words that make language use more mature. These are words like "performed," "benevolent," and "capture." Words in Tier 3 are low-frequency words that are more obscure and may be used as technical terms or infrequently as adjectives. Technical words are specific to a particular subject, such as "metamorphic." Beck, McKeown, and Kucan suggest that teachers spend the majority of their time improving students' knowledge of Tier 2 words. They suggest that teachers consider the following questions when selecting words for explicit instruction:

1. *Usefulness of the Word.* Is the student likely to encounter this word again? Will learning this word help the student in describing his or her own experiences?
2. *Relatedness of the Word.* Does the word relate to what the class has been discussing or studying or to a topic of interest to the student?
3. *Connection to Text.* Does the word relate to the reading or connect to big ideas in the reading?

Once vocabulary terms have been selected, many strategies can be used to provide explicit instruction in word meanings for students with learning disabilities.

Guidelines for Explicit Vocabulary Instruction (adapted from Konopak, 1991). Special education teachers use many strategies to provide explicit instruction in vocabulary for content area learning. Several strategies are described in later sections of this chapter. Following are some questions to guide the special education teacher in choosing techniques that will facilitate vocabulary learning:

1. Does the instructional technique help students connect new vocabulary to their background knowledge, building a bridge between old and new information?
2. Does the instructional technique help students develop elaborate word knowledge by providing a variety of opportunities to apply their newly acquired knowledge?
3. Does the instructional technique provide for active student involvement in learning new vocabulary?
4. Does the instructional technique develop students' abilities to acquire new vocabulary independently, becoming more strategic word learners?

Figuring out the Meaning of Unknown Words While Reading

Context Clues. We all encounter unknown words while reading. Successful readers have developed many strategies for figuring out the meanings of words (Jiménez, Garcia, & Pearson, 1995). These strategies are usually applied automatically and quickly. Yet less proficient readers often struggle with unknown words and do not feel equipped to figure them out. Many students have been told to "just skip" the words they do not know (Klingner & Vaughn, 1996)—a technique that can leave them confused and frustrated. Yet even struggling readers can be assisted to learn strategies for determining the meanings of unknown words (Klingner, Vaughn, & Schumm, 1998). The first step in providing this support is to teach students the ways in which content textbook authors provide definitions in context. There are three main types of context clues (Readence, Bean, & Baldwin, 1998):

1. *Definition:* Key terms are often defined in the sentence in which they are introduced, although sometimes definitions appear in previous or subsequent sentences. Definitions are the most common type of context clue in content textbooks (Readence, Bean, & Baldwin, 1998). For example: **Unemployment**, or the number of people without jobs, reached an all-time high. During his last four years in office, Roosevelt talked about **conservation**. By this, he meant the protection and wise use of land and resources.
2. *Description:* Although an explicit definition for the word is not provided, the word is described in such a way that a good guess can be made about its meaning. For example: Many people lived crowded together in cheaply built **tenements**.
3. *Contrast:* The word is compared with another word or concept, often its opposite. For example: Many immigrants lived in **urban** areas while others chose to live in rural areas as farmers.

Often key vocabulary words are written in bold (as in the above examples), underlined, or italicized to draw attention to their importance. Thus, students should be prompted to look for context clues when they see a word so highlighted.

Morphemic Analysis. Many of the long words that students encounter while reading can be broken into smaller parts. These word parts are called *morphemes.* Through this process, students can look for a prefix or suffix in the word and its root (e.g., *historian* = history + ian). Or they can look for smaller words they know (*landform* = land + form). High school students preparing for their college entrance tests are often taught to do this as a test-taking strategy. It is one way for the learner to become independent with vocabulary building.

References. External references provide a third source of information about unknown vocabulary words (Readence, Bean, & Baldwin, 1998). Many students with disabilities benefit from guided practice using these external sources of information. These sources include glossaries, dictionaries, and thesauruses. Glossaries are typically the easiest form of external reference to use because the meaning given will directly apply to its use in the book. Most textbooks include them (usually at the back of the book) and the definitions provided match those used in the book. When the textbook does not include a glossary, students might consult a dictionary. Yet dictionaries can be difficult to use and can lead to misunderstandings. Many students have not been taught how to use guide words and have trouble finding words. Also, most words have multiple definitions—trying to determine the preferable one can be confusing. Increasingly, students are turning to thesauruses rather than dictionaries. Perhaps this is due in part to the inclusion of thesauruses with word processing software.

Mr. Barnes, the secondary teacher described earlier, encourages his students with disabilities to rely on context clues and morphemic analysis in an attempt to figure out challenging words while reading, but not to stop and check an external source until after reading the day's passage. He asks students to keep a log of the difficult words they encounter while reading and jot down a brief definition before proceeding. Once students have completed a chapter (or section of a chapter), he encourages them to verify their definitions using a glossary, dictionary, and/or a thesaurus. Mr. Barnes checks these logs for students at their weekly meetings or during the consultation period. He has found that usually students can detect their own misconceptions using this procedure, but that occasionally he comes across an inaccurate definition that has not yet been clarified.

Teaching Word Meanings

Preteaching vocabulary helps students by providing them with background knowledge that can help them understand the topic they will be studying. Preteaching also indicates to students what information is important and requires their attention while reading. Direct, explicit instruction in short segments can effectively increase students' understanding of new vocabulary (Bos & Anders, 1990; Echevarria & Graves, 1998). First, the teacher says the new term and writes it on the board. The student then says the word and writes it on paper. Next the teacher defines the word and uses pictures, demonstrations, and examples that are relevant to students to convey the meaning of the word. Graphic organizers can also be used to teach word meanings.

Graphic Organizers

There are many types of graphic organizers. Graphic organizers provide a visual or spatial framework for organizing the important conceptual relationships among new vocabulary words. They can be a valuable learning tool for students who are having difficulty understanding a concept because they present key vocabulary terms and indicate the relationships among the terms.

Tree Diagram. Konopak (1991) presents six steps for developing tree diagrams (see Figure 9.4):

1. Select the most important concepts to be learned and identify the vocabulary necessary for learning them.
2. Construct a tree diagram using the concept(s) and vocabulary terms.
3. Evaluate the tree diagram for accuracy and modify as needed.
4. Decide how to present the diagram (e.g., on an overhead transparency or the chalkboard).
5. Refer to the diagram before and during the lesson, revising as needed.
6. Help students develop their own diagrams.

Semantic Map or Web. Semantic mapping is a process of diagramming related concepts from a reading passage or oral lesson (Heimlich & Pittelman, 1986). This is one of the most common methods for vocabulary instruction used by both general and special education teachers. Webs can be completed as a pre- or post-reading exercise. The technique can be used with the entire class to assist students in organizing and understanding the relationships among concepts, but may be particularly helpful for students with comprehension-related learning difficulties. This teaching technique has also been used with English language learners with disabilities (Bos & Anders, 1992; Gallego, Durán, & Scanlon, 1990) with positive results. Semantic mapping has also been recommended as a strategy for improving the content area learning of English language learners by de la Luz Reyes and Molner (1991), Echevarria and Graves (1998), and O'Malley and Chamot (1990).

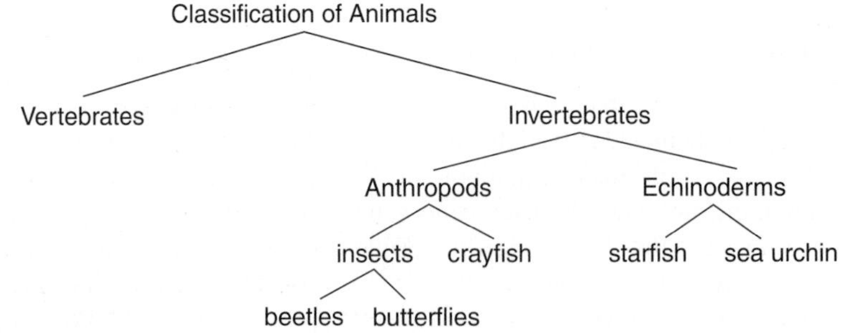

FIGURE 9.4 Tree Diagram

To construct a semantic map (see Figure 9.5), use the following steps (adapted from Readence, Bean, & Baldwin, 1992):

1. Select an important word or topic from the lecture or reading assignment (a semantic map can be constructed *before* or *after* the lesson or reading assignment).
2. Write the word on the chalkboard or overhead projector.
3. Ask students to say (or jot down) as many related words as they can think of, from their own experiences or from their reading of the text.
4. List these words on the chalkboard or overhead projector.
5. Organize the words into an octopus-like diagram.
6. Give names to the various categories. Elaborate by adding new categories or subcategories and related words as appropriate.

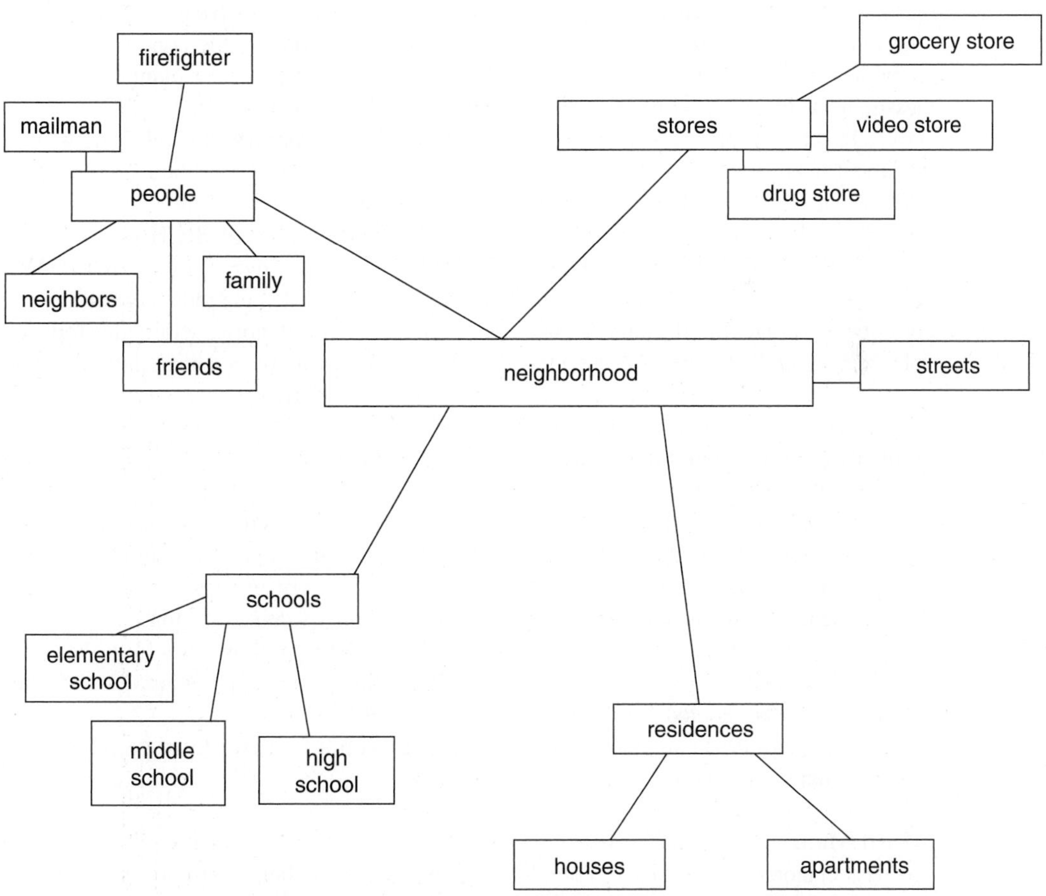

FIGURE 9.5 Semantic Map

7. Perhaps the most important steps in this activity are the discussion and questioning activities that accompany the diagram.

Adaptation. Use rainbow-colored sticky notes to create webs (Ellis, 1997). Students can write their own ideas while working individually, with a partner, or in groups. Once ideas have been written on separate sticky notes, they can be listed in columns, categorized, and mapped at will, and then moved when appropriate. Students can come up with initial maps prior to reading and then change them after reading more easily when using movable sticky notes. This process can facilitate their understanding of the interconnections and relationships among ideas.

Concept Maps. Similar to a semantic map, a concept map provides a graphic representation of the links among various concepts (Konopak, 1991; Martin, 1996). Martin notes that "the concept map is an extremely valuable tool in constructivist science education" (p. 387). There are various ways to prepare concept maps. Martin suggests a method that presents the concepts hierarchically with the most general or inclusive term at the top and the most specific or restricted term at the bottom. Lines connect the concepts indicated how they are related. Concept mapping can be used before a lesson for planning, during a lesson to facilitate learning, or after a lesson as a study aid or assessment tool.

To teach your students how to construct concept maps, try the following activity (adapted from Martin, 1996): First, cut 3x5 index cards in thirds to obtain smaller cards. Provide each student with a set of fourteen cards. Ask students to write the following words on the cards—one to a card: FLOWERS, DAFFODIL, ROSE, ORCHID, COLORS, EASTER, GIFTS, YELLOW, PINK, BIRTHDAYS, VALENTINE'S DAY, HOLIDAYS, PURPLE, NAMES. Tell students to arrange the cards so that (a) the most general topic or prototype is at the top; (b) intermediate terms that represent categories within this topic are placed next, underneath at the same level; and (c) examples are placed next, underneath the category cards. There can be variation in the way students arrange their cards, depending upon their prior experiences and how they perceive the relationships among concepts. Once students have completed this exercise and compared their arrangements with yours, they should write their concept maps on paper. Starting with cards enables students to move terms around until they are satisfied with the organization of their maps. Writing the concept map on paper provides a permanent record that can be used as a study guide or as a way for the teacher to keep track of student learning. One of the advantages to concept maps is they present in visual form a representation of how people perceive information.

Once students have written their maps on paper, they can draw lines to further specify the relationships among concepts. For example, lines connecting examples with their categories can be labeled with "such as" (see Figure 9.6).

Konopak (1991) suggests providing students with a framework for preparing their concept maps (see Figure 9.7).

Word Maps. Word maps are similar to concept and semantic maps except that they are less elaborate and easier to complete (Blachowicz & Fisher, 1996). To create a word map, students think of a synonym, an antonym, an example, and a nonexample for a

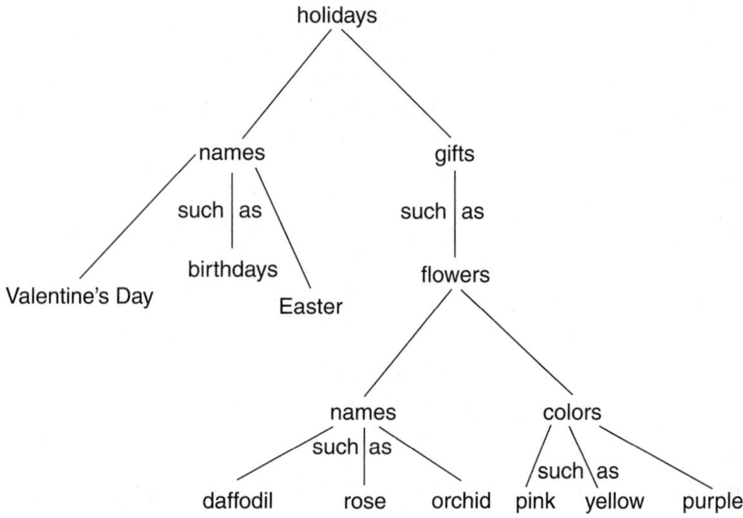

FIGURE 9.6 Concept Map

vocabulary word. These they arrange in boxes or circles with the target word in the middle (see Figure 9.8).

Semantic Feature Analysis. Semantic feature analysis is another process that helps students with disabilities understand concepts (Bos & Anders, 1992). It is a process of categorizing important concepts from a reading passage by summarizing distinct ways in which related concepts are similar and different. A semantic feature analysis can be completed in combination with a semantic map, or as an activity by itself (see Figure 9.9).

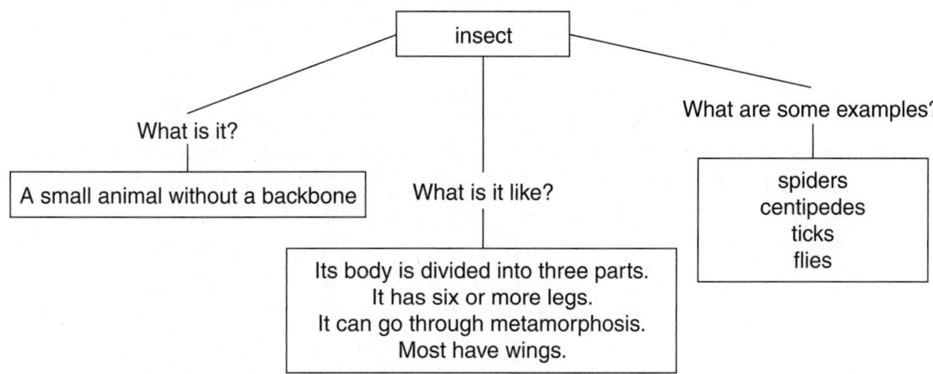

FIGURE 9.7 Framework for Concept Mapping

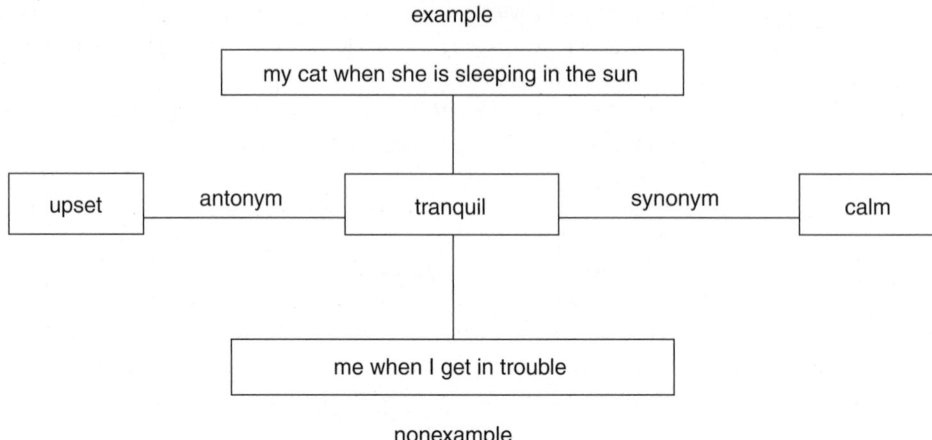

FIGURE 9.8 Word Map

Readence and colleagues (1992) recommend the following steps for conducting a semantic feature analysis:

1. Select a category that consists of two or more items that are similar. Such categories could be things like kinds of animals, elements, foods, or famous historical characters.
2. List the category terms along the left-hand side of the chalkboard or overhead transparency. Try not to use a large number of items the first time you use the procedure.
3. List the features that will be used to describe the terms across the top of the chalkboard or overhead transparency. Students may select the features or you may do it yourself.
4. Students should be guided through the development of the feature chart as they indicate whether each category item possesses a given feature. A plus (+) shows that

TREES

	BROADLEAF	NEEDLELEAF	CONE-BEARING	FRUIT-BEARING	DECIDUOUS	EVERGREEN
Oak	+	–	–	+	+	–
Cypress	–	+	+	–	–	+
Maple	+	–	–	+	+	–
Holly	+	–	–	+	–	+
Pine	–	+	+	–	–	+
Spruce	–	+	+	–	–	+
Apple	+	–	–	+	+	–

FIGURE 9.9 Semantic Feature Analysis

the category item has a feature; a minus (−) indicates that the category item does not have the feature. Every category item must have a plus or a minus for every feature; there should be no blank spots.

5. The final step is to have students make observations about the category items. Give students an opportunity to make generalizations on their own.

Computer Software. Programs such as Inspiration and Kidspiration (Inspiration Software, 2004) help students organize their ideas. Kidspiration was developed for students in kindergarten through the fifth grade, while Inspiration was designed for students in grades 6 through adulthood. Both programs help students organize and categorize information, understand concepts, clarify their thinking, and express their thoughts as they create graphics such as outlines, diagrams, and visual maps. Both programs help students reinforce understanding, integrate new knowledge, and identify misconceptions.

Comprehension Strategies

As students progress through the elementary grades, they must increasingly rely on reading comprehension to learn content area material from textbooks. Though we cover reading comprehension in another chapter, we discuss it here as it applies to helping students acquire content knowledge. Reading comprehension strategies acquired while students negotiate meaning as part of an active, constructive process can improve reading comprehension in general (Dole, Duffy, Roehler, & Pearson, 1991). Many students with learning disabilities are poor comprehenders and lack both the metacognitive skills to monitor their reading comprehension and the "fix-up" strategies to repair understanding when it breaks down (Swanson & Ashbaker, 2000; Torgesen, 1980). Numerous strategies have been developed to improve the understanding, storage, and retrieval of complex, meaningful, and organized information (e.g., Mastropieri, Scruggs, & Graetz, 2003; Paris & Oka, 1989; Pressley, Brown, El-Dinary, & Afflerback, 1995). The effectiveness of these strategies has been documented with students with learning disabilities (for reviews, see Gersten, Fuchs, Williams, and Baker, 2001; Mastropieri, Scruggs, Bakken, & Whedon, 1996; Weisberg, 1988), with English language learners (Hernandez, 1991), and students with behavioral disorders (Babyak, Koorland, & Mathes, 2000). Comprehension strategies are helpful for *all* readers, but are *critical* for students with learning problems. In an inclusive content area class, the general education teacher might teach comprehension strategies to the entire class (perhaps co-teaching with the inclusion specialist). Or the special education teacher might teach specific strategies to those students who would most benefit from this instruction. How do teachers decide who gets help with strategies? This depends on the demands of curriculum, the type of strategy under consideration, and the needs of the students. A multitude of strategies can help improve reading comprehension.

Yet the challenges of such instruction are many, as attested to by those who have tried to adapt strategy instruction for large classrooms (Klingner, Vaughn, Argüelles, Hughes, & Ahwee, in press; Pressley & El-Dinary, 1997; Scanlon, Deshler, & Schumaker, 1996). A key issue is how to achieve a balance between content and strategy instruction so that the academic needs of all students are met. Teaching learning strategies to students with learning disabilities so that their use becomes second nature requires a great deal of expertise and commitment on the part of teachers. Perhaps the best model for how to teach strategies has been developed by Deshler, Schumaker, and colleagues at the University of Kansas Institute for Research on Learning Disabilities (Deshler, Schumaker, Lenz, Bulgren, Hock, Knight, & Ehren, 2001).

The University of Kansas Institute for Research in Learning Disabilities: Learning Strategies.

Strategies Intervention Model (SIM) (Deshler, Ellis, & Lenz, 1996; Tralli, Colombo, Deshler, & Schumaker, 1996). The Strategies Intervention Model was developed to respond to the academic, social, and motivational needs of students at risk for school failure, including students with learning disabilities. The model is based on extensive research and was designed to serve as a guide for secondary program development. The authors define "strategies intervention" as a "system of strategies organized and linked in a manner to help an individual meet specific learning and performance demands that is taught in a strategic manner and is supported in a strategically enhanced environment" (SIM flyer, 1991, p. 1). SIM provides a working model for teaching learning strategies. Once the teacher has learned how to teach strategies using SIM, he or she can select the strategies for use in a particular classroom based on students' needs. SIM includes eight instructional stages. The following description was adapted from Ellis, Deshler, Lenz, Shumaker, and Clark (1991).

STAGE 1: PRETEST AND MAKE COMMITMENTS

The major purpose of Stage 1 is to enable students to *want* to make a commitment to learn a strategy. Students become motivated to learn a new strategy by encountering a demand for the strategy in a content class, developing an awareness for how they perform without the strategy, and realizing that the strategy can help them improve their performance. There are two phases within this stage. In the first phase the teacher provides an introduction to the strategy and administers a pretest (e.g., how to store information from a lecture). During the second phase students review their performance on the pretest and become aware of their deficits. They then make a commitment to learn the strategy. This stage is based on the principle that instruction should be driven by student goals.

STAGE 2: DESCRIBE THE STRATEGY

During this stage the teacher "paints a picture" of what the new strategy entails and how its use will facilitate learning. During an orientation and overview, students learn where and when the strategy is appropriate and when not to use it. Students learn about the overall intent of the strategy as well as the nature and purpose of each component. For example, students should be told that a particular strategy is effective because it helps them transform (e.g., cluster, organize, paraphrase) information into a form that is easier to understand and remember. Students should be encouraged to compare the new strategy with their previous approaches to a learning situation and to set individual goals for learning the new strategy.

STAGE 3: MODEL THE STRATEGY

The modeling stage of strategy instruction is essential for teaching the cognitive behaviors needed to complete a given task. During this stage the teacher "thinks aloud" while actually *using* the strategy. The first step when modeling a strategy is to orient students by reviewing previous learning and sharing expectations regarding student involvement during the lesson. Next the teacher demonstrates the strategy, taking care to explain all of the cognitive activities that make up the strategy. It is important for the teacher to rehearse the "think aloud" process until it becomes fluid and well-organized. The novice may find it difficult to avoid making mental leaps between specific strategy steps. Whereas the application of a strategy may have become second nature to the teacher, for students it is new. Here is an example of one teacher's "think aloud" while demonstrating a strategy for determining the meaning of an unknown word while reading a paragraph about Vietnam. Note that the intent of this strategy is to teach students to reread the sentence that contains the word and look for clues that can help them figure out the word's meaning:

> Uh oh, here is a word I don't understand, "paddies." Hmm, let me see if there are any clues that can help me figure it out. I'll try reading the sentence without the word, "U.S. troops fought in the jungles and rice ___." Well, it has to be a place, because it is where they fought, and maybe it is sort of like a jungle, because it says "jungles and rice paddies." Also, I know it has to do with rice. I'll bet it's a place where they grow rice. That makes sense.

During the final phase of the modeling stage of strategy instruction, students are prompted to gradually perform more and more of the steps of the strategy themselves. The teacher uses scaffolding to provide assistance, requiring students to use the actual words they should say to themselves when using the strategy and providing feedback and prompting to assure success.

STAGE 4: VERBAL PRACTICE

The purpose of this stage is to ensure comprehension and memorization of the processes involved in applying the new strategy. Two phases are involved in this stage: verbal elaboration and verbal rehearsal. During verbal elaboration, students first describe the "big picture" in their own words. Once they clearly understand the overall purpose of the strategy, they are encouraged to describe specific strategy steps, saying what each step is designed to do and why it is an important component of the overall process. During verbal rehearsal, students commit the strategy steps to memory via rote rehearsal until mastery is reached.

STAGE 5: CONTROLLED PRACTICE AND FEEDBACK

Practice is an essential part of learning a new strategy for building fluency and confidence. It is through practice that a strategy becomes internalized and the student makes it his or her own. Thus, the transition from teacher-mediated to student-mediated instruction takes place during this phase. The teacher controls the student's practice using the strategy along three dimensions: (a) the type of instructional materials used, (b) the context within which the strategy is practiced, and (c) the amount of teacher or peer mediation provided. This instructional stage may take place over several days. First the teacher orients students to this stage of strategy learning, prompting them to share what they have already learned about the strategy. Then the teacher provides various opportunities for guided practice and feedback. If necessary, the teacher again models how to implement the strategy. When students have become more proficient in applying the strategy, they are ready for independent practice. It is important for the teacher to continue to monitor performance during this phase of instruction, looking for opportunities for provide individualized, explicit instruction to students about specific strategy components.

STAGE 6: ADVANCED PRACTICE AND FEEDBACK

The real test of students' mastery of a strategy is their ability to apply it to assignments from their content area classes. This stage of instruction marks an important turning point in the overall learning process. Learning shifts from how to perform the strategy to how to apply the strategy to real-life tasks. Yet the students are still in a setting where they can enlist support as needed. As students learn how to proficiently use and adapt the strategy to a wide variety of materials and assignments, the amount and type of teacher mediation should gradually fade.

STAGE 7: POST-TEST AND MAKE COMMITMENTS

The purpose of this stage in the strategy acquisition process is to document students' mastery of the strategy and to promote its generalization. Through post-testing, the teacher and student confirm that the strategy has been acquired. Together they celebrate the student's mastery. Then the student and the teacher make a commitment to generalize the strategy. It is at this point that other teachers (i.e., content area teachers) also affirm their commitment to assist with the student's generalization of the strategy.

STAGE 8: GENERALIZATION

Students do not automatically transfer strategies across content settings (Ellis & Lenz, 1987). Successful generalization requires that they learn to recognize naturally occurring cues that signal an opportunity to apply a strategy. Students must learn to (a) discriminate when to use a particular strategy, (b) develop methods for self-checking to see that the strategy is being used appropriately, (c) experiment with ways to adapt the strategy across settings, (d) use feedback to develop goals and plans to improve performance, and (e) incorporate the strategy and its various adaptations into a permanent problem-solving system. The support of an inclusion specialist and content area teachers is essential to promote students' full generalization of a strategy. The phases of this stage include: the orientation phase, the activation phase, the adaptation phase, and the maintenance phase.

During the *orientation phase,* students reaffirm the importance of applying the strategy in a purposeful manner. Students evaluate the pros and cons of using the new strategy in various contexts, and develop ways to remind themselves to use the strategy in different settings. For example, students can create cue cards that list the steps of a strategy—these can be placed in their textbooks or notebooks. Or students might write affirmations that connect the use of a strategy with success in meeting a particular demand (e.g., "I am a successful writer when I monitor my errors.").

During the *activation phase,* the focus is on enlisting the support of content area teachers. Working collaboratively, the inclusion specialist and other teachers prompt students to apply the strategy to specific assignments to be completed in the class or at home. They assist students in developing a plan to increase strategy usage and in setting daily and weekly goals to use the strategy in a variety of situations. They monitor implementation of the plan and provide feedback regarding the effects of using the strategy across different settings. They might assist the student to develop a chart to record progress related to applying the strategy. Finally, they reinforce progress and success through praise and, in some cases, extrinsic rewards.

The purpose of the *adaptation phase* is to prompt students to explore the applications of a strategy in various contexts. In order to adapt a strategy, students must clearly understand why it is important and how to implement it. With teacher guidance, students should be able to discuss what they are actually doing and thinking about as they implement each step of a strategy. Next, with teacher assistance, students should identify how a strategy can be modified to meet additional demands (e.g., "How can we make paraphrasing work in the social skill of carrying on a conversation?"). Students then write down the strategy modifications and how they will be used.

We feel that being masterful at using a strategy and being able to adapt it is not achieved by a careful, systematic breaking down of the strategy into its component parts. Rather, the ability to adapt the strategy is achieved by internalizing the steps of the strategy and being able to perform them automatically. This reminds us of the analogy of water (the whole—water—is greater than the sum of its parts). Once a strategy has been mastered it becomes more than the sum of its parts. We believe in the importance of task analysis and breaking a strategy into its discrete components for the purposes of initial instruction. Yet we also believe that there comes a point at which the skillful strategy user achieves a higher level of application, where attempting to analyze and break down the steps needed to fulfill the strategy becomes counterproductive.

The purpose of the *maintenance phase* is to ensure that the student continues to use the strategy over time. Students and their teachers jointly develop plans designed to promote long-term use of the strategy. These plans should include goals and procedures for evaluating progress at various checkpoints. As a teacher observes a student using a particular strategy, he or she can provide feedback about barriers that might hinder continued use of the strategy and promote activities that facilitate strategy usage (such as reviewing cue cards and affirmation cards). Finally, the teacher can identify self-reinforcers that can be used in conjunction with successful maintenance of the strategy.

ROLES OF THE SPECIAL EDUCATION AND CONTENT AREA TEACHERS

The special educator's major role is to teach students specific strategies, either in a support class, a before- or afterschool program, or within the general education classroom. Once students have learned various strategies, the special education teacher assists the student in selecting and applying the appropriate strategy for a specific purpose. Other responsibilities include working with content area teachers to create an environment in the content classroom that promotes the use of strategies. This may require modeling usage of the strategies in the content classroom and/or providing content area teachers with short written descriptions of the strategies that explain when to use a strategy, why, and how. The special educator also should evaluate classroom teaching materials, instructional routines, and classroom activities to ensure that sufficient cues are available for the student to identify when to use a specific strategy. The classroom becomes the context in which strategies can be generalized most effectively. The teacher also must promote the student's independent functioning—in other words, instead of tutoring a student in specific subject matter, the specialist can help students set goals and plan how to use specific strategies to facilitate learning. Rather than doing work "for" students, students must be given the tools to work independently (Schumaker, Deshler, & McKnight, 2001).

The role of the content teacher is to deliver instruction in ways that promote the application of strategies and enable students to understand and remember content information. Occasionally the content teacher might also teach a particular strategy to students. To promote the use of strategies, the content teacher should cue students when a specific strategy would be appropriate in a given situation and structure the delivery of content to facilitate the application of the strategy. For this to work effectively, the special educator and the content teacher must work together closely and communicate frequently.

Content Enhancement Model (Boudah, Lenz, Bulgren, Schumaker, & Deshler, 2000; Lenz, Bulgren, & Hudson, 1990). Content Enhancement is an approach to planning and teaching that focuses on the teacher's decision-making process. The teacher thinks deeply about what it is most important for students to know and how to teach this information. The teacher selects central concepts and necessary supporting details and presents these so that they "hang together," using instructional strategies and integrated teaching routines. The components of the Content Enhancement Model include (a) the "reflActive" planning process, (b) powerful teaching devices, and (c) explicit teaching routines.

"ReflActive" planning is based on the premise that teachers should become more reflective as they select, organize, and make decisions about how to provide content area instruction. This reflective process must include consideration of how to meet the needs of individuals at a range of achievement levels, including those students with special needs. The teacher also must be continually active in preparing, using, and evaluating the various instructional methods selected during the planning process. In a co-teaching or consultation model, this planning and evaluating would include the special educator. The goal is to create a curriculum that will enhance learning for *all* students.

The steps of the "reflActive" planning process can be remembered with the acronym "SMARTER" and include

S*electing* critical content outcomes. Consider: What is really critical for all students to understand? What do I want students to still remember at the end of the year? How can I frame this information into critical questions that capture their essence? What are the big ideas that tie all of this information together?

M*apping* the organization of the critical content. Consider: How would I like students to organize this information in their heads? How can I best paraphrase the big ideas in what I am teaching?

A*nalyzing* learning difficulty based on:

quantity	complexity	interest
students' background	relevance	organization

R*eaching* enhancement decisions by selecting powerful teaching devices. Develop an overall instructional plan, select teaching devices, prepare teaching devices, revise the plan as needed.

T*eaching* strategically with explicit teaching routines. During instruction, share plans with students. Develop learning partnerships with students. Communicate the value of using learning strategies.

E*valuating* mastery of the critical content and processes. Consider: How effective were these teaching devices? Did all of the students learn what was intended? Do aspects of the content need to be retaught? Did I spend enough time developing the teaching routine? What do I need to do differently next time?

R*eevaluating* learning outcomes. Review whether students have learned critical information. If they have not, provide additional instruction. Do not compromise these standards—if students have not learned critical information, reteach for mastery.

Powerful teaching devices are instructional tools that the teacher uses to enhance learning. These devices are powerful in that they enable the teacher to (a) focus on a specific point, (b) make learning explicit, (c) prompt elaboration on specific points, and (d) make ideas and relationships concrete. These devices can include graphics, manipulatives, stories, rationales, study guides, and role-play activities. For a device to be effective, it must be well prepared and used within a specific teaching routine.

An explicit teaching routine is created when a teacher selects a teaching device, explains to students how the teaching device will be used to enhance their learning, and then regularly uses the same teaching device as an ongoing part of instruction. Numerous routines have been found to be effective in inclusive classrooms (Schumaker, Deshler, & McKnight, 2001). The Survey Routine is used at the beginning of a unit of instruction to provide an overview of the information that will be learned. The Concept Teaching Routine presents a concept diagram to introduce the major concept in the unit of study. The Advance Organizer Routine uses planning sheets to provide an overview of a lesson. The Verbal Enhancement Routine includes the oral presentation of instructional devices (e.g., analogies or illustrative stories to connect new information to everyday knowledge) to make abstract information more understandable and memorable. The Visual Enhancement Routine relies on visual depictions (e.g., diagrams, tables, concept maps) to make abstract information more understandable and easier to remember. The Comparison Routine involves students in completing a Comparison Table (see Figure 9.10) for the purpose of

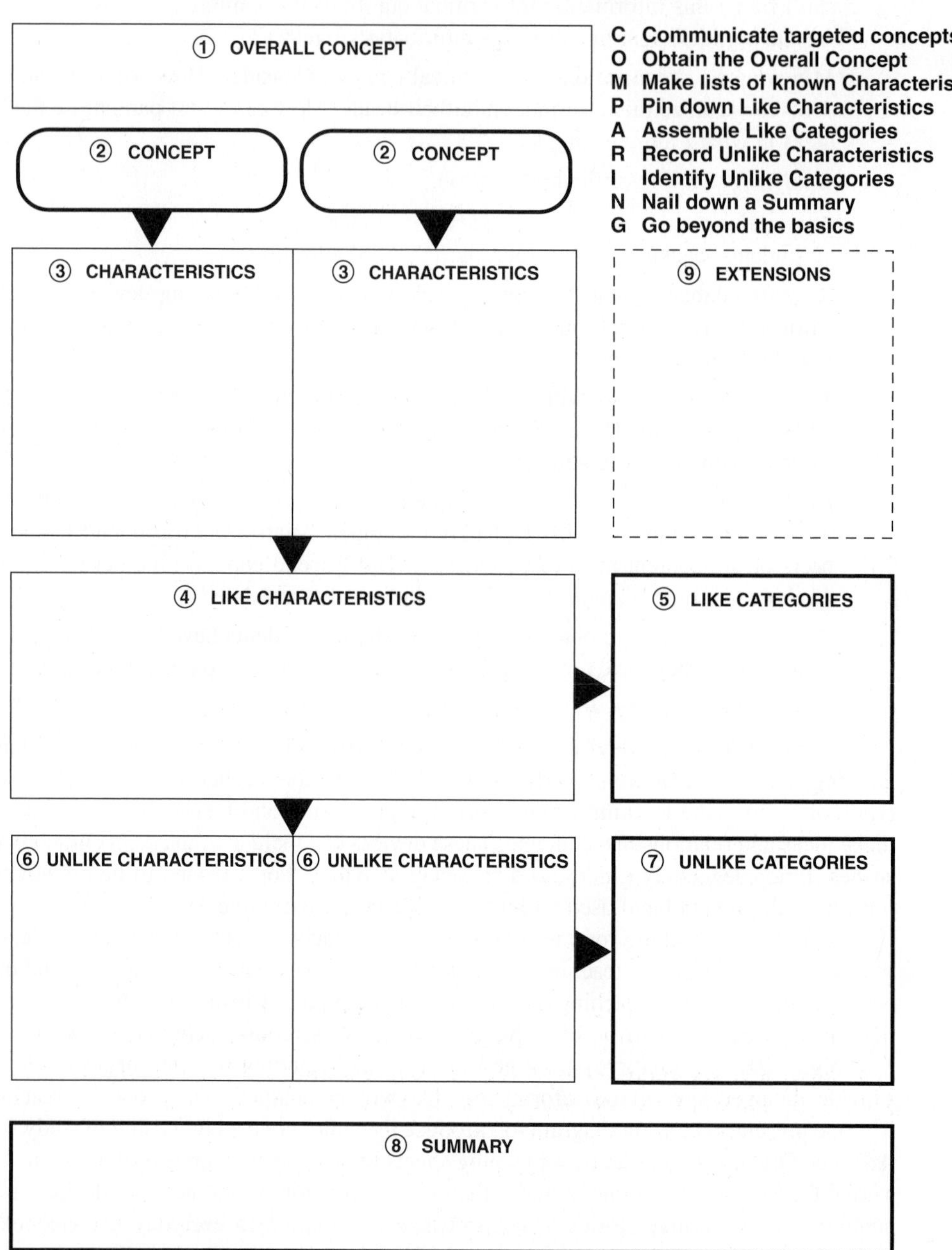

University of Kansas Center for Research on Learning, December 1995.

FIGURE 9.10 Comparison Table

analyzing the similarities and differences between two or more concepts or events in a way that enhances their understanding and retention of the information

Text structure
The way text is organized provides cues to the reader in identifying important concepts and making connections between ideas.

Text-Structure-Based Strategies **Text structure** refers to the way the text is organized to guide readers in identifying key information and making connections between ideas. Text-structure-based strategies help students determine the type of structure used in content area passages and apply appropriate structure-specific strategies (Bakken, Mastropieri, & Scruggs, 1997). Because the structure of expository prose differs from that of narrative text, strategies that students have learned to implement with narrative prose do not necessarily transfer. When students have learned the various text structures typical of expository text, it becomes easier for them to identify the main idea and supporting evidence in a paragraph (Bakken, Mastropieri, & Scruggs, 1997). The ability to understand and make use of expository text structure is important for school success, yet can be problematic for students with disabilities (Dickson, Simmons, & Kameenui, 1995). According to Seidenberg (1989), students with learning disabilities demonstrate less awareness of the different expository text structures than their normally achieving peers. This is probably true for the other areas of high-incidence disabilities as well.

The expository text structures found in science and social studies textbooks include a variety of formats, such as (a) enumeration—a list of facts concerning a single topic, (b) sequence—a series of events that occur over time, (c) compare/contrast—a focus on the similarities and differences between two or more topics, (d) classification—information organized according to categories, (e) generalization—one major idea contained with a few sentences, (f) problem-solution—the statement of a problem followed by its solution, and (g) procedural description—the steps used to carry out a task (Weaver & Kintsch, 1991). Students must not only attend to the information in the text, but also identify the type of text structure used to present it (Englert & Hiebert, 1984).

Compare/Contrast Structure. The compare/contrast text structure focuses on the similarities and differences between topics and is signaled by words such as "like," "different," "in contrast," and "but." The following steps can help students identify this structure (Dickson, Simmons, & Kameenui, 1995):

1. Identify two topics being compared and contrasted.
2. Look for key compare/contrast words such as "alike," "different," "but."
3. Determine the organization of the compare/contrast structure. This can be:
    a. Whole/whole, where the author(s) describe each topic separately, with a different paragraph or set of paragraphs for each.
    b. Part/part, where the author(s) present a feature-by-feature comparison of two topics.
    c. Mixed, where the author(s) might first discuss each topic separately, and then in another paragraph provided a feature-by-feature analysis.
4. Locate the explanation of how the topics are the same.
5. Locate the explanation of how the topics are different.

Interactive Instructional Model. Bos and Anders (1990, 1992) developed the interactive instructional model for text comprehension and content area learning. The model was developed specifically for students with learning disabilities but can benefit other students as well, particularly English language learners (Echevarria & Graves, 1998). It was derived from schema theory (Anderson & Pearson, 1984; Rumelhart, 1980) and emphasizes the importance of activating background knowledge. The model has the dual purpose of developing both content knowledge and strategic knowledge. It relies on semantic feature analysis using relationship maps and relationship charts (see the example in the Vocabulary section) and also incorporates interactive strategic dialogues. To follow the interactive instructional model

1. Make a *brainstorm list* using what you already know about the topic.
2. Make a *clue list* using what the text tells you about the topic.
3. Make a *relationship map* or *relationship chart* to predict how the concepts are related.
4. *Read* to confirm and integrate your understanding and the relationships among concepts.
5. *Review* and *revise* the map or chart.
6. Use the map or chart to *study* for a test or *write* about what you learned.

Students apply these steps while working together in cooperative discussion groups. Like with Reciprocal Teaching (Palincsar & Brown, 1984), as students become increasingly proficient using the strategies, the role of the teacher changes from that of a "mediator" to that of a "facilitator" with the students scaffolding and supporting each other in their cooperative learning groups (Bos & Anders, 1992).

K-W-L. K-W-L (Ogle, 1992) is an easy to implement strategy for increasing students' engagement with expository text. The teacher or students prepare a K-W-L chart on the chalkboard, chart paper, an overhead transparency, or a sheet of paper. The chart is divided into three columns, the first with a K at the top, the second with a W, and the third with an L. Before reading, the teacher and students brainstorm what they already *K*now about the topic they will be studying and record this information in the K column of the chart. This step helps activate prior knowledge and also provides the teacher with useful information about the extent to which students are familiar with a topic or may need additional prior experiences to understand a difficult lesson (e.g., a video). Next, still before reading, students generate questions about *W*hat they would like to learn about the topic and write these questions in the second column. This step helps establish a purpose for reading. Finally, after reading, students record what they *L*earned as a result of the day's lesson in the third column of their charts. A K-W-L chart can provide a springboard for follow-up activities. Students might be motivated to find answers to their questions from the W column that were not addressed in the day's reading. Or students might use the information they recorded in the L column to write a summary of what they learned (Readence, Bean, & Baldwin, 1998). An entire class might generate one K-W-L chart, or small groups or pairs of students might each come up with their own charts.

Mr. Barnes sometimes asks his students with disabilities to complete the K and W columns of a chart before beginning a new topic in their science or social studies classes. This prereading assistance provides them with a preview of what they will be learning. The classroom teachers at Washington High have noted that students' participation in class discussions has increased since Mr. Barnes initiated this activity.

Directed Reading-Thinking Activity. The Directed Reading-Thinking Activity (DRTA) is another strategy for helping students understand content area text (Haggard, 1988). This approach is an "oldie but goodie." Similar in some ways to the predicting strategy included in Reciprocal Teaching (Palincsar & Brown, 1984), it was developed to help students refine their purpose for reading and apply prior knowledge to understanding text. It can also enhance critical thinking. Students first survey the chapter they will be reading by looking at the title, subtitles, headings, illustrations, and diagrams, and skimming the text. They make predictions about what they will learn and write down questions that come to mind while sampling the text. Next students read the chapter and look for answers to their questions. After reading, students develop questions that the text has not answered. Doing so can motivate students to seek additional information through the internet or other reference sources. Like the other instructional approaches described in this section, DRTA helps students become actively engaged in the learning process. Questions can also serve as an advance organizer.

Answering Comprehension Questions. One of the most common activities in content area classrooms is the asking and answering of questions as a way to assess students' comprehension of text. Students with learning difficulties often have problems locating specific information in text. Two strategies that can assist them are Question-Answer Relationships and Text Lookbacks.

Question-Answer Relationships. The Question-Answer Relationships (QAR) strategy (Raphael, 1986) results in improved ability to answer comprehension questions, especially for average and low-average students (Raphael & Pearson, 1985). Students are taught to identify the different kinds of information needed to answer comprehension questions, as well as where to find this information. Questions can be of various types and can occur before, during, or after reading.

Pearson and Johnson (1978) developed a method of classifying questions based on the relationship between the question and the location of its answer. From this classification system Raphael (1982, 1986) developed a strategy for teaching students how to answer different types of questions. This strategy is called Question-Answer Relationships (QAR). QAR helps students by clarifying how they should approach the task of answering questions and also teaches them a way to generate their own questions as a method of monitoring what they read (Swanson & De La Paz, 1998). The first type of answer is referred to as *textually explicit* because it is stated directly in the text. Questions with textually explicit answers are typically the easiest because the reader can search through the text to find the exact words needed for a response. Some teachers refer to these as "right there" answers. The second type of answer is called *textually implicit* because it must be inferred from the text. This kind of response is also called a "think and search" answer because it can be found in the text but is not stated directly. The third type of response is referred to as *scriptually implicit* because it consists of information already in the mind of the reader that he or she brings to the interpretation of the text. Responses of this type are generally elaborative in nature and are also called "on my own" answers. These questions generally require higher level thinking skills. For example:

MACBETH

One of William Shakespeare's most popular tragedies is *Macbeth.* This tragedy tells the story of a man who succumbs to temptation and is confused and incited into committing murder by his wife, Lady Macbeth, as well as the pressure of unusual circumstances. Macbeth is portrayed as a righteous character whose conscience torments him as he debates whether to carry out terrible actions. His vacillation and mental torment allow the audience to feel admiration and sympathy for the tragic hero. The author skillfully shows the audience the murderer's self-inflicted torture and remorseful feelings, which allows the audience to get to know him, but not those characters Macbeth committed terrible acts against. In other words, "the protagonist's degeneration is counteracted by mounting pity" (Lerner, 1963, p. 187). The play portrayed a tragic view of the destruction of a man's potential for goodness and greatness. When the tragedy ends, the hero is dead, his name unsoiled. The message of the tragedy seemed to be that a man's potentially positive actions could be affected by forces and pressures that can lead him to commit negative deeds when he could have just as easily done otherwise.

Textually Explicit (Right There)
Question: What was the title of Shakespeare's tragedy?
Answer: *Macbeth*
Textually Implicit (Think and Search)
Question: Why does Macbeth inspire sympathy from the audience?
Answer: He was a righteous character who is tormented by his conscience.
Scriptually Implicit (On My Own)
Question: Why is it difficult to condemn Macbeth?
Answer: Because Macbeth has some very positive characteristics and we, the readers, are made aware of the pressures and forces that lead him to commit the terrible deeds. In addition, the author purposefully allows the reader to get to know Macbeth's character, but not those who were harmed by him.

TEACHING QAR. Through teacher modeling, students are first shown how to identify question-answer relationships. Next the teacher provides students with sample questions and answers and asks them to classify each one. Once students are proficient at this, the teacher then asks questions and leaves it up to students to supply answers, QAR labels, and the reasons for their choices. Finally, students generate their own questions, making sure that they think of at least one question for each type. Students might work in pairs or groups as well as individually to come up with their questions and answers. Learning the QAR procedure can help students create different kinds of questions as part of CSR's Wrap Up. We have seen even children as young as third grade come up with sophisticated "teacher-like" questions using this procedure.

Once students have learned the QAR strategy, it should be incorporated into the regular classroom routine so that its use becomes automatic. Whether students work in pairs, small groups, or with the whole class, they can regularly say what kind of information they used to derive responses to questions. For students with learning disabilities and others who may have difficulty learning the strategy, the following instructional activities might be helpful: (1) Provide answers and ask students to locate their sources, (2) provide questions and the locations where answers can be found, and (3) ask students to generate and answer their own questions.

TEXT LOOKBACKS. Another procedure for helping students find the answers to comprehension questions is Text Lookbacks (Garner, 1982). This strategy complements the QAR strategy by providing students with guided practice in looking back in a text to find specific information. Being able to quickly skim a passage to find the answer to a question is a valuable skill that can lead to enhanced achievement on comprehension tests (Garner & Hare, 1984). Yet Garner and colleagues found that even when students were told they could look back at what they had already read to find the answer to a question, many thought it was "illegal" to do so. Swanson and De La Paz (1998) recommend using modeling and a think-aloud procedure to show students how to skim a text while looking for explicit information. Students learn to turn back to the section of text where they would be most likely to find the answer and then to look at subheadings, key words, and other clues that help them narrow their search. As students think they are getting closer to finding an answer, they learn to slow down and read more carefully. While teaching this procedure, the teacher should provide many opportunities to practice with different types of text, beginning with short segments and proceeding to longer, more elaborate passages. High-interest materials such as driving manuals can be used along with textbooks.

Collaborative Strategic Reading. Collaborative Strategic Reading (CSR) teaches students to use comprehension strategies while working cooperatively (Klingner & Vaughn, 1999b; Klingner, Vaughn, Dimino, Schumm, & Bryant, 2002). Students of mixed achievement levels apply comprehension strategies while reading content area text in small groups (n=5). Initially, the teacher presents the strategies (preview, click and clunk, get the gist, and wrap up) to the whole class using modeling, role playing, and teacher think-alouds. After students have developed proficiency applying the strategies through teacher-facilitated activities, they are then divided into heterogeneous groups where each student performs a defined role as students collaboratively implement the strategies.

The goals of CSR are to improve reading comprehension and increase conceptual learning in ways that maximize students' involvement. Developed to enhance reading comprehension skills for students with learning disabilities and students at risk for reading difficulties, CSR has also yielded positive outcomes for average and high-achieving students (Klingner & Vaughn, 1996; Klingner, Vaughn, & Schumm, 1998).

Phase I: Teaching the Strategies. Students learn four strategies as part of the CSR Plan for Strategic Reading: Preview, Click and Clunk, Get the Gist, and Wrap Up (see Figure 9.11). Preview is used only *prior* to reading the entire text for that lesson, and Wrap Up is used only *after* reading the entire text for the lesson. The other two strategies, Click and

Before Reading

1. **Preview**
   a. **Brainstorm:** What do we already know about the topic?
   b. **Predict:** What do we think we will learn about the topic when we read the passage?

R E A D (the first paragraph or section)

During Reading

2. **Click and Clunk**
   a. Were there any parts that were hard to understand (clunks)?
   b. How can we fix the clunks? Use fix-up strategies.
      1. Reread the sentence without the word. Think about what would make sense.
      2. Reread the sentence with the clunk and the sentences before or after the clunk looking for clues.
      3. Look for a prefix of suffix in the word.
      4. Break the word apart and look for smaller words.
3. **Get the Gist**
   a. What is the most important who or what?
   b. What is the most important idea about the who or what?

R E A D (Do steps 2 and 3 again, with all the paragraphs or sections in the passage.)

After Reading

4. **Wrap Up**
   a. **Ask questions**: What questions would show we understand the most important information? What are the answers to those questions?
   b. **Review**: What did we learn?

FIGURE 9.11 CSR Plan for Strategic Reading

Clunk and Get the Gist, are used multiple times while reading the text, after each paragraph or section.

PREVIEW. Students preview the entire passage prior to reading each section. The goals of previewing are (a) for students to learn as much about the passage as they can in a brief period of time (2 to 3 minutes), (b) to activate their background knowledge about the topic, and (c) to help them make predictions about what they will learn. Previewing serves to motivate students' interest in the topic and to engage them in active reading from the onset. When students preview before reading, they should look at headings, words that are bolded or underlined, pictures, tables, graphs, and other key information to help them do two things: brainstorm what they know about the topic and predict what they will learn about the topic. Students are given 1 1/2 to 2 minutes to write down everything they already know about a topic in their CSR Learning Logs (see the description of CSR Learning Logs on page 372 in the Materials section). Students then share their responses with one another for about 1 minute. Another 1 1/2 to 2 minutes are provided for students to write down their predictions of what they might learn, followed by 1 minute to share their ideas with one another.

CLICK AND CLUNK. Students click and clunk while reading each section of the passage. The goal of clicking and clunking is to teach students to monitor their reading comprehension and to identify when they have breakdowns in understanding. Clicks refer to portions of the text that make sense to the reader—comprehension "clicks" into place as the reader proceeds smoothly through the text. When a student comes to a word, concept, or idea that does not make sense, "clunk," comprehension breaks down. Reaching a clunk is like running into a brick wall.

Many students with reading and learning problems fail to monitor their understanding when they read. Clicking and clunking is designed to teach students to "pay attention" to when they are failing to understand what they are reading or what is being read to them. The teacher asks, "Does everything you just read make sense? Who has a clunk?" Students know that they will be asked this question and are alert to identify clunks during reading.

After students identify clunks, the class uses "fix-up" strategies to figure out the clunks. On each of the clunk cards is printed a different strategy for figuring out a clunk word, concept, or idea:

1. Reread the sentence without the word. Think about what would make sense.
2. Reread the sentence with the clunk and the sentences before or after the clunk looking for clues.
3. Look for a prefix or suffix in the word.
4. Break the word apart and look for smaller words you know.

GET THE GIST. Students learn to get the gist by identifying the most important idea in a section of text (usually a paragraph). The goal of getting the gist is to teach students to restate in their own words the most important point as a way of making sure they have understood what they have read. Getting the gist can improve students' understanding and memory of what they have learned. Students are taught to get the gist by identifying the most important who or what in the paragraph they have just read and then stating in their own words the most important idea about the who or what. Students are also taught to provide the gist in as few words as possible while conveying the most meaning, leaving out details.

WRAP UP. Students learn to wrap up by formulating questions and answers about what they have learned and by reviewing key ideas. The goals are to improve students' knowledge, understanding, and memory of what they read. Students generate questions that ask about important information in the passage. They learn to use question starters to begin their questions: *who, what, when , where, why*, and *how* ("the 5 Ws and an H"). Students pretend they are teachers and think of questions they would ask on a test to find out if their students really understood what they had read. Other students should try to answer the questions. If a question cannot be answered, that might mean it is not a good question and needs to be clarified. Students are taught to ask some questions about information that is stated explicitly in the passage and other questions that require an answer not right in the passage, but "in your head." Students are encouraged to ask questions that involve higher-level thinking skills rather than literal recall.

To review, students write down the most important ideas they learned from the day's reading assignment in their CSR Learning Logs. They then take turns sharing what they learned with the class. Many students can share their "best idea" in a short period of time, providing the teacher with valuable information about each student's level of understanding.

Phase II—Cooperative Learning Group Roles. Once students have developed proficiency applying the comprehension strategies through teacher-led activities, they are ready to learn the roles they will perform while using CSR in their peer-led cooperative learning groups. Roles are an important aspect of CSR because cooperative learning seems to work best when all group members have an assigned, meaningful task. Roles should rotate on a regular basis so that students can experience a variety of roles and so that everyone takes a turn being the Leader. Students can perform more than one role at a time if necessary. Possible roles include:

Leader: Leads the group in the implementation of CSR by saying what to read next and what strategy to apply next. Asks the teacher for assistance if necessary.

Clunk Expert: Uses clunk cards to remind the group of the steps to follow when trying to figure out a difficult word or concept.

Gist Expert: Guides the group towards the development of a gist and determines that the gist contains the most important idea(s) but no unnecessary details.

Announcer: Calls on different group members to read or share an idea. Makes sure everyone participates and only one person talks at a time.

Encourager: Watches the group and gives feedback. Looks for behaviors to praise. Encourages all group members to participate in the discussion and assist one another. Evaluates how well the group has worked together and gives suggestions for improvement.

Reporter: During the whole-class wrap up, reports to the class the main ideas the group learned and shares a favorite question the group has generated.

Timekeeper: Sets the timer for each portion of CSR and lets the group know when it is time to move on (the teacher might do this instead of students).

MATERIALS.

Cue Sheets. Cue sheets outline the procedures to be followed in cooperative learning groups and provide structure and support for students while they are learning CSR. Each role comes with a corresponding cue sheet that explains the steps to be followed to fulfill that role. Cue sheets seem to help students stay focused and on task and increase their confidence. Students should discontinue use of the cue sheets when they feel secure in carrying out their roles. See Figure 9.12 for an example of a cue sheet.

CSR Learning Logs. CSR learning logs enable students to keep track of learning "as it happens" and provide a springboard for followup activities. Logs furnish an additional way

BEFORE READING	DURING READING	AFTER READING
PREVIEW: S: We know that today's topic is ____________. S: Let's brainstorm and write everything we already know about the topic in our learning logs. S: Who would like to share their best ideas? S: Now let's predict. Look at the title, pictures, and headings and think about what we might learn today. Write your ideas in your learning logs. S: Who would like to share their best ideas?	**READ:** S: Who would like to read the next section? **CLICK AND CLUNK:** S: Did everyone understand what we read? If you did not, write your clunks in your learning log. S: (if someone has a clunk): Clunk Expert, please help us out. **GET THE GIST:** S: Gist Expert, please help us out. S: Now we will go around the group and each say the gist in our own words. **GO BACK AND DO ALL OF THE STEPS IN THIS COLUMN OVER FOR EACH SECTION**	**WRAP UP:** S: Now let's think of some questions to check if we really understood what we read. Remember to start your questions with who, when, what, where, why, or how. Everyone write your questions in your learning log. S: Who would like to share their best question? S: In our learning logs, let's write down as much as we can about what we learned. S: Let's go around the group and each share something we learned. **COMPLIMENTS AND SUGGESTIONS:** S: The Encourager has been watching carefully and will now tell us two things we did really well as a group today. S: Is there anything that would help us do even better next time?

FIGURE 9.12 CSR Leader's Cue Sheet

for all students to participate actively in their groups. Logs can be used for recording ideas while applying every strategy, or only used for some of the strategies (e.g., for writing down clunks and key ideas). Logs might be kept in spiral-bound notebooks or journals made by folding paper in half and stapling on a construction paper cover. A different learning log can be created for each social studies or science unit; these logs provide written documentation of learning and become excellent study guides (see Figure 9.13 for an example). Some special education teachers have even used CSR learning logs to document that students were meeting the objectives on their Individualized Educational Plans (IEPs; Chang & Shimizu, 1997).

Today's Topic ______________________ Date ____________ Name _______________

Before Reading: *PREVIEW*

After Reading: *WRAP UP*

What I Already Know about the Topic	Questions about the Important Idea
What I Predict I Will Learn	What I Learned

During Reading:

CLUNKS

GISTS

FIGURE 9.13 CSR Learning Log

Reading Materials. CSR was designed primarily to be used with expository text found in social studies and other content area textbooks. CSR can also be used with narrative text. You should select reading material with well-formed, interesting passages that are conducive to strategy application. Such material is characterized by (a) clues that help students predict what they will be learning, (b) having one main idea in a paragraph, and (c) providing context that helps students connect information. We recommend that when you begin CSR you use the *Weekly Reader, Scholastic Magazine,* or a similar nonfiction publication that captures students' interest and can be read in a short time.

Timer. A timer is optional. Kitchen timers that students set by themselves can help groups to remain on task and not get excessively bogged down with any one strategy or step in the Collaborative Strategic Reading process. For example, the timekeeper might say, "We have 1 1/2 minutes to write down everything we already know about the topic."

Then the timekeeper would set the timer for 1 1/2 minutes. An alternative is for the teacher to set one timer and direct students in their groups to carry out the strategies for a set period of time. We recommend using this procedure for at least the first few days that students work together in groups so that they can develop an understanding of how the process works. Once groups can function more autonomously, they should be encouraged to do so.

TEACHER'S ROLE MONITORING GROUPS. Once the teacher has taught the strategies and procedures to students and they have begun working in their cooperative learning groups, the teacher's role is to circulate among the groups and provide ongoing assistance. Teachers can help by actively listening to students' conversations and if necessary clarifying difficult words, modeling strategy usage, encouraging students to participate, and modeling a cooperative, helpful attitude. It is expected that students *will* need some assistance learning to work in cooperative groups, implementing the strategies, and mastering social studies or science content.

FOLLOWUP ACTIVITIES. A variety of activities can be used to reinforce key vocabulary and important ideas students have learned from reading the day's passage and also help the teacher to monitor learning. Each group might complete a different followup activity and then share their products with the rest of the class. For example, one group might prepare a semantic map, another a crossword puzzle, another mnemonic devices, another Clunk Concentration, another a Venn diagram, and another theme pictures. Students can also prepare games and activities as homework and practice with them during free time (for more ideas, see Klinger & Vaughn, 1999b).

Concluding Comments. The teachers we have worked with like that once students learn the strategies (preview, click and clunk, get the gist, and wrap up), they can apply them in cooperative groups. They also like the demonstrated gains that students make on their reading achievement tests. Tiffany Royal, an inclusion teacher and expert CSR implementer, told us, "What I like best is that my students learn how to understand what they read while they improve their vocabulary. Also it helps on our end of the year Stanford Achievement Tests." CSR can be used in general education classrooms where students with special needs are included for instruction (Klingner, Vaughn, & Schumm, 1998) as well as in special education settings (Klingner & Vaughn, 1996).

WRITING TO LEARN

Writing is an essential component of content area classes. To be successful, students must be able to record observations and experimental data, write research reports, and take notes during class and while reading. Writing is a means for students to reflect about what they are learning, providing an important bridge between students' prior knowledge and new ideas. The following instructional methods are appropriate for inclusive classrooms.

Learning Logs (Atwell, 1987; Santa & Havens, 1991)

What Are Learning Logs? Logs are spiral-bound notebooks or journals that last a whole year, one for each subject. Students keep track of learning "as it happens." Log entries are informal and brief, usually recorded in less than ten minutes of focused free writing. The teacher poses questions and situations or sets themes that invite students to observe, speculate, list, chart, web, brainstorm, role-play, ask questions, activate prior knowledge, collaborate, correspond, summarize, predict, or shift to a new perspective: in short, to participate actively in their own learning. After writing, children might read aloud their entries in pairs or small groups, or volunteer to share with the entire class. Logs are not for personal writing; they are not interactive journals.

Why Use Learning Logs? Logs are a way to help children think about the world around them, about math, literature, social studies, and science. Through writing learning logs students become active participants in the quest for knowledge. When writing logs, students become more self-directed, more focused, more critical, and more willing to take risks. Teachers' roles change, too—from lecturers to guides, from dispensers of information to facilitators of learning. Learning logs are one way to break the lecture–listen syndrome in the content areas.

How Do You Use Learning Logs? Logs are versatile and can be used in a variety of ways: for example,

1. *Focusing and Activating Prior Knowledge:* Before a lesson or new unit of instruction, teachers might begin by asking students (a) to brainstorm possible topics, (b) to record what they already know, (c) to write down what they predict they might find out, (d) to record what they would like to learn, or (e) to plan what they are going to do.
2. *Gathering:* Observations of all kinds, through listening, smelling, seeing, tasting, and touching, can be recorded in students' logs.
3. *Organizing:* After information is gathered, it must be organized so that it makes sense. Students can use their logs to make comparisons, classify (e.g., "same or different" or "floats or sinks"), or create a web.
4. *Predicting and Elaborating:* Prompts such as, "What do you think will happen next?" or "Pretend that you lived at the time of the Civil War" require students to predict and elaborate, extending their understanding.
5. *Integrating:* Integrating means to put together relevant parts and build meaningful connections between new information and prior knowledge. Summarizing is one way students can assimilate data. When students summarize, they combine information, condense it, select what's important, and discard what is not.
6. *Reflecting and Evaluating:* Some teachers ask students to respond to "process" questions, such as "What did I like or dislike about class today?" "What is not clear about today's work?" It's important to give students time to reflect on their experiences. After a lesson, students can refer back to entries before and/or during the lesson and reflect about they learned.

Research Reports

Oral and written reports are an effective way to individualize instruction because each student can work at his or her own level. However, at its worst, a research paper can amount to little more than a student laboriously copying out of reference books. Yet at its best, a research paper can be the culmination of a student's attempts to become an expert in a topic that interests her so that she can share this expertise with others (Calkins, 1994). Writing a research paper is a complex task that requires students to organize their ideas and record them on paper in a meaningful way. Even for students who do not struggle, the task can be quite bewildering. Do you remember the first time you were asked to complete a research report? Were you able to organize all of the components of the task and complete each step in a timely manner? Or did you procrastinate until the last minute and need "bailing out" by a sympathetic parent? Students with LD can feel overwhelmed, frustrated, and discouraged at the prospect of writing a research paper, not knowing how to begin or which way to proceed. Consequently, students with LD benefit from guided practice through each step of the process (Mastropieri & Scruggs, 1987). We recommend the following steps to writing a research report, as adapted from Mangrum and Strichart (2001) (for other techniques, see Atwell, 1987; Korinek & Bull, 1996; Michaelis, 1992):

WRITING A RESEARCH REPORT

1. Decide on a topic for your report. Select something
   a. that interests you
   b. about which you will be able to find information
   c. you will be able to finish given time limits (don't pick a topic that is either too broad or too narrow), and
   d. your teacher approves.
2. Think of questions you have about the topic—what do you want to know? What might others want to know? List the main research questions you think should be addressed in your report.
3. Locate sources of information for your topic (such as encyclopedias, reference books, magazines, newspapers, books, websites, films, and experts you might interview).
4. Prepare bibliography cards for each source of information you have identified. On each card, write the author, date of publication, title of the article, book or other source, place of publication and publisher's name, and relevant page numbers of the source. Place the cards in alphabetical order by the author's last name. Number the cards (in the upper right-hand corner).
5. Prepare note cards for each source (preferably on cards that are 4 X 6 inches or 5 X 8 inches). Record information in your own words. Number these cards to correspond with the bibliography cards. As an alternative, students might keep notes on a word processor or even a tape recorder.
6. Put the note cards in order so that they correspond with your research questions. Use these to prepare an outline for your paper, using the following format:

TITLE OF YOUR RESEARCH REPORT (YOUR TOPIC)

I. Use Roman numerals for main headings.
  A. Use capital letters for subheadings.
    1. Use Arabic numerals for details.
      a. Use small letters for subdetails.

7. Write a rough draft of your paper. Focus on recording your ideas rather than worrying about spelling and punctuation. Number your pages. Your paper should include the following parts:
  a. The **title** of the research report.
  b. An **introduction** that provides an overview of the topic (like a "sneak preview" to get the reader interested in finding out more).
  c. The **body** that presents the key information of the report (taken from your note cards). Use your outline to help with organization.
  d. The **conclusion** that summarizes what was learned in the paper.

8. Reread the paper at least three times looking for ways to make it better. Revise the paper, using the following checklist:
  a. Does the title reflect the topic of the paper?
  b. Does the introduction clearly introduce the topic?
  c. Does the body contain all of the important facts needed?
  d. Does every paragraph include a main idea?
  e. Does every paragraph and sentence add information to the paper about the topic? (Don't put in extra information about something else.)
  f. Did I choose the best words to explain my ideas? (Avoid overused words such as "good"—think of synonyms that mean the same thing but are more exciting.)
  g. Does the conclusion summarize the important facts in the paper?
  h. Have I corrected all misspelled words?
  i. Have I capitalized all appropriate words?
  j. Have I used correct punctuation (including quotation marks to identify quotations)?

9. Prepare the bibliography—type all of your information sources in alphabetical order using your bibliography cards.

10. Prepare the title page and table of contents. Type the title of your research report on a separate page with your name and the date (and any other information required by your teacher). To prepare a table of contents, write "Table of Contents" at the top and list each of your major headings underneath with the page number on which it begins to the right.

11. Do a final check before turning in your research report. Ask yourself:
  a. Do I have a title page?
  b. Do I have a table of contents?
  c. Do I have an introduction, a body, and a conclusion?
  d. Are all of the pages numbered correctly?
  e. Do I have a bibliography?

Study Skills

Most students can benefit from instruction in study skills or learning strategies (see Figure 9.14). In general, when teaching study skills, you should follow these three steps: (a) assess your students' needs by observing them while performing a task; (b) teach the new study skill or strategy by modeling and describing what you are doing ("thinking aloud"); and (c) provide opportunities for generalization and transfer, prompting students and gradually withdrawing support.

Taking Notes during Lectures. Students in many content area classes spend the majority of their time listening to oral presentations by their teachers (Mastropieri & Scruggs, 1987). Notetaking can be very challenging for any student, but it can be particularly problematic for students with LD who may experience difficulties identifying important information and writing fast enough to keep up with a lecture (Weishaar & Boyle, 1997). After a lecture, students often have a hard time making sense out of what they have written and making meaningful connections between key ideas. Many notes taken by students with disabilities appear incomplete and disorganized. Yet taking notes does much more than provide a study guide that can help students prepare for a test. Notetaking actively involves the student in the learning process, helps the student monitor understanding and identify when breakdowns in comprehension occur, and aids in the encoding of information for long-term memory storage. Notetaking can help students organize information and link new ideas with prior knowledge while applying reading comprehension strategies.

Notetaking is both an art and a complicated skill. It requires simultaneously listening, understanding, identifying and synthesizing main ideas, and retaining ideas long enough to write them down (Strichart & Mangrum, 2001). Students with slow auditory processing, poor listening comprehension, poor auditory short-term memory, and/or poor visual motor skills are clearly at a disadvantage. Yet notetaking can be taught and improved

- ***Skimming*** text for general ideas.
- ***Scanning*** text to look for specific information.
- ***Listening*** for important information.
- ***Notetaking*** skills.
- ***Memorizing*** facts, using mnemonic and other strategies for remembering.
- ***Organizing*** information, including categorizing, mapping, and creating flowcharts.
- ***Questioning*** to increase comprehension.
- ***Problem solving*** to derive conclusions.
- ***Error monitoring*** to correct one's own mistakes.
- ***Test taking*** more systematically and efficiently.

Source: Adapted from Riegel, Mayle, & McCarthy-Henkel (1988).

FIGURE 9.14 Strategies and Study Skills

through direct instruction and guided practice. In this section we describe two notetaking procedures, one by Strichart and Mangrum (2001) and the other by Weishaar and Boyle (1997).

Strichart and Mangrum (2001) present a three-stage notetaking strategy. The three stages of their method explain (a) how to *get ready* to take notes, (b) how to *take notes,* and (c) what to do *after notes* have been recorded.

GET READY

1. Have available all of the materials necessary to take notes (e.g., notebook, learning log, or two-column notetaking sheets, sharpened pencils with erasers).
2. Review notes from previous classes. Seek clarification for anything not understood.
3. Complete all prior assigned readings. Seek clarification for anything not understood.
4. Ask the teacher to specify the purpose(s) of the lecture when this is not clear.

TAKE ROUGH NOTES

1. Take notes on one side of a paper only.
2. Skip lines to show changes in ideas or topics.
3. Write ideas or phrases, not complete sentences.
4. Underline or place an asterisk by information that the teacher identifies as important.
5. Write down information that the teacher writes on the chalkboard or other visual display.
6. Leave blanks for information that is missed (and fill in later by asking the teacher or another student for assistance, or locating the information in the textbook).
7. Don't worry about spelling.
8. Don't try to write down everything—decide what is important and record only that.
9. Make sure your notes are clear and legible.
10. Write notes in your own words.
11. Be alert for cues from the teacher that tell you what is most important (e.g., repeating information, or saying "this is important").
12. Include examples of difficult or abstract concepts in your notes.
13. Make choices that maximize your ability to concentrate (e.g., select a seat close to the front of the room, in the center).
14. Utilize the structure provided by the teacher (e.g., if the teacher says, "first, second, third . . . ," notes should include a list numbered 1, 2, 3).
15. Use common abbreviations to increase speed.
16. Keep notes as concise as possible—don't write down information you already know.

AFTER NOTES STAGE

1. Add important information you remember the teacher saying but did not write down.
2. Review notes to see if anything is unclear or not understood. Clarify this information by checking with the teacher or another student or looking in the textbook or a reference book.

3. In the same manner, locate any information needed to complete blank spaces.
4. Look up key vocabulary terms in a dictionary and record their meanings.
5. Prepare final notes that incorporate information from rough notes and vocabulary definitions. Use these final notes to study for quizzes and tests.

Strichart and Mangrum recommend using notetaking sheets with a two-column format for "Rough Notes" and "Don't Understand," and a separate section for "Vocabulary" (see Figure 9.15).

Weishaar and Boyle (1997) developed a notetaking form and a procedure for teaching how to use it. First, provide students with a notetaking form (see Figure 9.16, adapted from Weishaar & Boyle). Before beginning the lecture, identify the lecture topic and ask students to summarize what they already know about the topic. During the lecture, ask students to cluster together three to seven main points with supporting details from the lecture. Use additional forms as necessary. After the lecture, at the bottom of each page, students should summarize the notes listed on that page and check for understanding.

Name ____________ Class ________ Period ________ Date ________ Page ______

ROUGH NOTES	**DON'T UNDERSTAND**

VOCABULARY

FIGURE 9.15 Two-Column Notetaking Sheet (adapted from Strichart & Mangrum, 1993)

Name ______________________ Date ______________________

Fill in this portion before the lecture begins.

What is today's topic? ______________________

What do I already know about the topic? ______________________

____

____

Fill in this portion during the lecture.

What are the main points of the lecture? (Record information as it is presented. Use as many forms as necessary.) **Highlight or underline** new vocabulary terms.

(1) ______________________

____

(2) ______________________

____

(3) ______________________

____

(4) ______________________

____

(5) ______________________

____

(6) ______________________

____

Fill in this portion after the lecture (or at an appropriate stopping point).

Write a brief summary of the main ideas.

____

____

____

____

____

Source: Adapted from Weishaar & Boyle (1997).

FIGURE 9.16 Notetaking Form

Remembering Information. Students more easily remember information that is meaningful, relevant to their experiences, and of personal interest. Thus, the more the teacher can do this and build on student interest, the better. Students need assistance determining what is most important to remember. When the teacher uses key words and phrases during oral presentations to identify important information and/or highlights important information on visual presentations, it can greatly help students with LD who tend to be disorganized thinkers and may have trouble distinguishing between main ideas and interesting but unessential details.

Mnemonic devices (memory aids) can improve not only students recall of important information, but also their comprehension and affect (Bulgren, Deshler, & Schumaker, 1997; Scruggs & Mastropieri, 1990, 1992). Numerous studies over a period of several years document the effectiveness of mnemonic devices for improving the content learning of students with LD (for a review, see Mastropieri & Fulk, 1990).

With promising results, Bulgren, Deshler, and Schumaker (1997) taught a *Recall Enhancement Routine* that uses these nine mnemonic devices to teachers in inclusive secondary classes. Teachers learned how to target factual information from the curriculum, select an appropriate mnemonic device to facilitate instruction, create the mnemonic device, and teach the device and the corresponding content to their students using the Recall Enhancement Routine. The routine is implemented during a lesson whenever a new mnemonic device is presented to students and involves the following steps:

1. The information to be mastered is explained.
2. The information is written on the chalkboard or an overhead transparency.

BOX 9.1

THE REMEMBERING STRATEGY

1. **Select** the information you want to remember.
   - **Ask** the teacher what is most important.
   - **Examine** your class notes.
   - **Reread** text assignments.
   - **Study** any handouts.
2. **Remember** the information using different memorization techniques.
   - **Visualize** (form a picture in your mind of something you need to remember—be sure to include all of the important parts and how they are connected)
   - **Associate** (group information that goes together, such as "bread and butter")
   - **Apply** (use the information in some way)
   - **Repeat** (read the information to be remembered, say the information with your eyes closed, write the information without looking, and repeat as necessary)
   - **Use mnemonic devices** (memory aids)
3. **Review** using techniques to keep what you want to remember in your memory.
   - **Reread**
   - **Recite**
   - **Rewrite**

Source: Adapted from Strichart & Mangrum (1993).

BOX 9.2

MNEMONIC DEVICES

- *Reconstructive Elaborations*

  Literal Pictures (mimetic reconstructions): Used with familiar, concrete information.

  Symbolic Pictures (symbolic reconstructions): Used with familiar but abstract information. For example, to teach that birds (a familiar item) are warm-blooded (an abstract concept), a picture of a bird lounging in a warm, sunny scene could be depicted (Scruggs & Mastropieri, 1992).

  Keywords (acoustic reconstructions): Used with unfamiliar information. For example, to learn the word *vituperation* (a word meaning "abusive speech"), a good key word would be *viper* because it is acoustically similar to vituperation and can be pictured. The resulting mnemonic picture would be of a viper speaking abusively to someone (Scruggs & Mastropieri, 1992).

  Familiar Associations: Used with unfamiliar information (usually a person's name).

- *Other Mnemonic Devices*

  Acronyms: Formed with the initial letter of successive words (e.g., the names of the five great lakes form the acronym HOMES: Heron, Ontario, Michigan, Erie, Superior).

  Loci: A specific sequence of places is memorized and used to associate ordinal information with each place in a predetermined sequence.

  Pegwords: Each of several pairs of preselected rhyming words is associated with an item in a sequence to facilitate the memory of numbered or ordered information.

  Rhyme: Words in a constructed rhyme represent information to be mastered (e.g., In 1492, Columbus sailed the ocean blue.)

  Code: Mastering strings of numbers (i.e., as in an important date) by substituting letters for the numbers.

Source: Adapted from Bulgren, Deshler, & Schumaker (1997).

3. The teacher cues the students that the information is important to remember and that a mnemonic device will be taught.
4. The teacher reminds students to write the information and the mnemonic device in their notes.
5. The teacher presents the mnemonic device and links it to the information to be learned.
6. At a later time, the teacher and students interactively review the information and the device.

ENGLISH LANGUAGE LEARNERS

Students with LD and other high-incidence disabilities who are also English language learners face an additional challenge. Not only must they struggle to overcome their disability, they also face learning in a language that is not their first language. Typical content area textbooks are not written with English language learners in mind (Boyle & Peregoy, 2001).

The Role of Background Knowledge

All students benefit from accessing prior knowledge as they broach a new topic, but this is especially true for English language learners. Echevarria and Graves (1998) recommend several approaches for enhancing students' background knowledge and helping them connect new information with what they already know. Ask students to brainstorm about their own relevant experiences before beginning a unit or lesson. Having all students jot down a few ideas to share with their classmates improves participation and increases the likelihood that students will contribute to a class discussion. Students' comments can be recorded on an overhead transparency. Provide students with opportunities to expand their experiential knowledge base. Field trips are a great way to provide students with shared experiences that can provide the foundation for extension activities in the classroom (e.g., a trip to a sea aquarium before beginning a unit about marine life). Videos, live demonstrations, direct experiences through hands-on learning, multimedia presentations, websites, and guest speakers can provide further background knowledge. Luis Moll (1990) suggests bringing in experts from the local community to help bridge students' home and school cultures and reinforce the value of what students already know and can do. Pictures, real objects, and other visual aids are also important tools for enhancing students' background knowledge.

CALLA was developed as an instructional program for English language learners who are preparing to participate in mainstream academic content instruction (O'Malley & Chamot, 1990). Because the elements of CALLA are consistent with instructional techniques recommended for students with LD, it is a model appropriate for classrooms that include students with a range of needs. The CALLA model consists of three components: (a) a focus on content subject areas, (b) the development of academic language skills, and (c) direct instruction in learning strategies. CALLA lessons include both teacher-directed and learner-centered activities. Each lesson is divided into five phases: Preparation, Presentation, Practice, Evaluation, and Expansion Activities. These phases are often recursive in that the teacher may wish to go back to earlier phases in order to provide additional instruction.

1. **Preparation:** In this phase, the teacher finds out what students already know about the concepts in the subject to be presented, what gaps in prior knowledge need to be addressed, and what strategies the students already know. The lesson's objectives are explained.
2. **Presentation:** In this phase, new information is presented and explained in English, supported by contextual clues such as demonstrations and visuals. Learning strategies are taught.
3. **Practice:** This phase is learner-centered, as students engage in hands-on practice. The teacher acts as a facilitator during this phase, helping students to assimilate new information and apply learning strategies. Cooperative learning is often implemented during this phase.
4. **Evaluation:** In this phase, the teacher and students check the level of students' performance and understanding.

5. **Expansion Activities:** In this phase, students are given a variety of opportunities to think about and apply the new concepts and skills they have learned. They continue to develop academic language and exercise higher-order thinking skills.

Learning strategies taught in the CALLA model include metacognitive strategies, cognitive strategies, and social and affective strategies:

METACOGNITIVE STRATEGIES

Advance organization (previewing the text)
Advance preparation (rehearsing the language needed for an oral or written task)
Selective attention (focusing on key information)
Self-monitoring (checking one's own comprehension while listening or reading)
Self-evaluation (judging how well one has accomplished a task)
Self-management (seeking or arranging conditions that facilitate one's learning)

COGNITIVE STRATEGIES

Resourcing (using reference materials)
Grouping (classifying words and concepts)
Notetaking (writing down key words and concepts)
Summarizing (making a mental or written summary of key information)
Imagery (using visual images to understand and remember information)
Auditory representation (rehearsing a sound, phrase, or fact to assist with recall)
Elaboration (relating new information to prior knowledge)
Transfer (applying what is already known)
Inferencing (using text information and prior knowledge to guess meanings)

SOCIAL AND AFFECTIVE STRATEGIES

Clarification (eliciting an explanation or verification from a teacher or peer)
Cooperation (collaborating with peers to solve problems)

Sheltered English Techniques for the Mainstream Class

For English language learners, the focus during content instruction should be on learning English as well as content. Students acquire English *through* the new content they are learning. The following instructional practices are beneficial for English language learners with special needs as well as other students (Becijos, 1997; Garcia, 1999; Sullivan, 1992):

- Simplify language by using shorter sentences, emphasizing important nouns and verbs, and avoiding idioms and ambiguous terminology (speaking more loudly does not help).
- Don't "water down" the curriculum, make it more accessible: Use a variety of pictures, charts, diagrams, demonstrations, and realia to illustrate new concepts.

- Provide hands-on learning experiences that make use of all of the senses—allow students to touch, to listen to sounds, and even to smell and to taste.
- When teaching new vocabulary, provide context and link new information with prior knowledge. Build on students' background experiences and interests.
- Provide frequent opportunities to practice new vocabulary in a variety of contexts.
- Provide opportunities to interact with others, exchange ideas, and talk about content.
- Pair or group students with bilingual peers and native English speakers during cooperative learning tasks.
- Increase wait time before calling on students to answer questions in order to allow sufficient time for them to think and frame their responses.
- Respond to the accuracy of the content in a student's response rather than the grammar (instead of correcting a grammatical error, rephrase the student's answer in Standard English).
- Support the student's home language and culture, viewing these as assets.

REFERENCES

Anderson, R. C., & Pearson, P. D. (1984). A schema-theoretic view of basic processes in reading. In P. D. Pearson (Ed.), *Handbook of reading research* (pp. 255–291). New York: Longman.

Atwell, N. (1987). *In the middle: Writing, reading, and learning with adolescents.* Portsmouth, NH: Heinemann.

Babyak, A. E., Koorland, M., & Mathes, P. G. (2000). The effects of story mapping instruction on the reading comprehension of students with behavioral disorders. *Behavioral Disorders, 25,* 239–258.

Baker, J., & Zigmond, N. (1995). Themes and implications from these five cases. *Journal of Special Education, 29,* 163–180.

Baker, S. K., Simmons, D. C., & Kameenui, E. J. (1994). Beginning reading: Educational tools for diverse learners. *Social Psychology Review, 23* (3)372–91.

Bakken, J. P., Mastropieri, M. A., & Scruggs, T. E. (1997). Reading comprehension of expository science material and students with learning disabilities: A comparison of strategies. *Journal of Special Education, 31,* 300–324.

Baumann, J. F., & Kameenui, E. J. (1991). Research on vocabulary instruction: Ode to Voltaire. In J. Flood, J. Jensen, D. Lapp, & J. Squire (Eds.), *Handbook of research on teaching the English language arts* (pp. 604–632). New York: Macmillan.

Becijos, J. (1997). *SDAIE: Strategies for teachers of English learners.* Bonita, CA: Torch Publications.

Beck, I. L., McKeown, M. G., & Kucan, L. (2002). *Bringing words to life: Robust vocabulary instruction.* New York: Guilford.

Blachowicz, C., & Fisher, P. (1996). *Teaching vocabulary in all classrooms.* Englewood Cliffs, NJ: Merrill.

Bos, C. A., & Anders, P. L. (1990). Effects of interactive vocabulary instruction on the vocabulary learning and reading comprehension of junior-high learning disabled students. *Learning Disability Quarterly, 13,* 31–42.

Bos, C. S., & Anders, P. L. (1992). A theory-driven interactive instructional model for text comprehension and content learning. In B. Y. L. Wong (Ed.), *Contemporary intervention research in learning disabilities: An international perspective* (pp. 81–95). New York: Springer-Verlag.

Boudah, D. J., Lenz, B. K., Bulgren, J. A., Schumaker, J. B., & Deshler, D. D. (2000). Don't water down! Enhance content learning through the unit organizer routine. *TEACHING Exceptional Children, 32*(3), 48–56.

Boyle, S. F., & Peregoy, O. F. (2001). *Reading, writing, and learning in ESL: A resource book for K-12 teachers* (3rd ed.). New York: Longman.

Bradley, D. F., King-Sears, M. E., & Tessier-Switlick, D. M. (1997). *Teaching students in inclusive settings: From theory to practice.* Boston: Allyn and Bacon.

Brookover, W., Beady, C., Flood, P., Schweister, J., & Wisenbaker, J. (1979). *School social systems and student achievement.* New York: Praeger.

Bulgren, J. A., Deshler, D. D., & Schumaker, J. B. (1997). Use of a recall enhancement routine and strategies in inclusive secondary settings. *Learning Disabilities Research & Practice, 12,* 198–208.

Calkins, L. M. (1994). *The art of teaching writing* (2nd ed.). Portsmouth, NH: Heinemann.

Coley, J. D., DePinto, T., Craig, S., & Gardner, R. (1993). From college to classroom: Three teachers' accounts of their adaptations of reciprocal teaching. *Elementary School Journal, 94,* 255–266.

Curry, J. F., & Craighead, W. E. (1990). Attributional style in clinically depressed and conduct disordered adolescents. *Journal of Consulting and Clinical Psychology, 58,* 109–115.

Dalton, B., Morocco, C. C., Tivnan, T., & Mead, P. L. R. (1997). Supported inquiry science: Teaching for conceptual change in urban and suburban science classrooms. *Journal of Learning Disabilities, 30,* 670–684.

Deshler, D. D., Ellis, E. S., & Lenz, B. K. (1996). *Teaching adolescents with learning disabilities: Strategies and methods.* Denver, CO: Love.

Deshler, D. D., & Schumaker, J. B. (1993). Strategy mastery by at-risk students: Not a simple matter. *Elementary School Journal, 94,* 153–167.

Deshler, D. D., Schumaker, J. B., Lenz, B. K., Bulgren, J. A., Hock, M. F., Knight, J., & Ehren, B. J. (2001). Ensuring content-area learning by secondary students with learning disabilities. *Learning Disabilities Research & Practice, 16,* 96–108.

Dickson, S. V., Simmons, D., & Kameenui, E. J. (1995). Instruction in expository text: A focus on compare/contrast structure. *LD Forum, 20*(2), 8–15.

Dole, J. A., Duffy, G. G., Roehler, L. R., & Pearson, P. D. (1991). Moving from the old to the new: Research on reading comprehension instruction. *Review of Educational Research, 61*, 239–264.

Echevarria, J., & Graves, A. (1998). Curriculum adaptations. In J. Echevarria & A. Graves, *Sheltered content instruction: Teaching English-language learners with diverse abilities* (pp. 121–149). Boston: Allyn and Bacon.

Eller, R. G., Pappas, C. C., & Brown, E. (1988). The lexical development of kindergartners: Learning from written context. *Journal of Reading Behavior, 20,* 5–24.

Elley, W. B. (1988). Vocabulary acquisition from listening to stories. *Reading Research Quarterly, 24,* 174–187.

Ellis, E. S. (1997). Watering up the curriculum for adolescents with learning disabilities. *Remedial and Special Education, 18,* 326–346.

Ellis, E. S., & Lenz, B. K. (1987). A component analysis of effective learning strategies for LD students. *Learning Disabilities Focus, 2*(2), 94–107.

Englert, C. S., & Hiebert, E. H. (1984). Children's developing awareness of text structures in expository materials. *Journal of Education Psychology, 76,* 65–75.

Fulk, C. L., & Smith, P. J. (1995). Students' perceptions of teachers' instructional and management adaptations for students with learning or behavior problems. *The Elementary School Journal, 95,* 409–419.

Gallego, M. A., Durán, G. Z., & Scanlon, D. J. (1990). Interactive teaching and learning: Facilitating learning disabled students' progress from novice to expert. In J. Zutell & S. McCormick (Eds.), *Literacy theory and research: Analyses from multiple paradigms. Thirty-ninth yearbook of the National Reading Conference* (pp. 311–319). Chicago: National Reading Conference.

Garcia, E. (1999). *Student cultural diversity: Understanding and meeting the challenge* (2nd ed.). New York: Houghton Mifflin.

Garner, R. (1982). Resolving comprehension failure through text lookbacks: Direct training and practice effects among good and poor comprehenders in grades six and seven. *Reading Psychology, 3,* 221–231.

Garner, R., & Hare, V. C. (1984). Efficacy of text lookback training for poor comprehenders at two age levels. *Journal of Educational Research, 77,* 376–381.

Gersten, R., Fuchs, L. S., Williams, J. P., & Baker, S. (2001). Teaching reading comprehension strategies to students with learning disabilities: A review of research. *Review of Educational Research, 71,* 279–320.

Gersten, R., & Jimenez, R. (1998). *Promoting learning for culturally and linguistically diverse students: Classroom applications from contemporary research.* Belmont, CA: Wadsworth Publishing.

Graves, M. F. (1989). A quantitative and qualitative study of elementary school children's vocabularies. *Journal of Educational Research, 82,* 203–209.

Graves, M. F., Brunetti, G. J., & Slater, W. H. (1982). The reading vocabularies of primary grade children of varying geographic and social backgrounds. In J. A. Niles & L. A. Harris (Eds.), *New inquiries in reading research and instruction* (pp. 99–104). Rochester, NY: National Reading Conference.

Grolnick, W. S., & Ryan, R. M. (1990). Self-perceptions, motivation, and adjustment in children with learning disabilities: A multiple group comparison study. *Journal of Learning Disabilities, 23,* 177–184.

Guillaume, A. M. (1998). Learning with text in the primary grades. *The Reading Teacher, 51,* 476–486.

Gurganus, S., Janas, M., & Schmitt, L. (1995). Science instruction: What special education teachers need to know and what roles they need to play. *Teaching Exceptional Children, 27*(4), 7–13.

Hagborg, W. J. (1996). Self-concept and middle school students with learning disabilities: A comparison of scholastic competence subgroups. *Learning Disability Quarterly, 19,* 117–126.

Haggard, M. R. (1988). Developing critical thinking with the directed reading-thinking activity. *Reading Teacher, 41,* 526–533.

Heimlich, J. E., & Pittelman, S. V. (1986). *Semantic mapping.* Newark, DE: International Reading Association.

Hernandez, J. S. (1991). Assisted performance in reading comprehension strategies with non-English proficient students. *Journal of Educational Issues of Language Minority Students, 8,* 91–112.

Inspiration Software. (2004). *Inspiration.* Retrieved on April 25, 2004, from *http://www.inspiration.com/home.cfm*

Jiménez, R. T., Garcia, G. E., & Pearson, P. D. (1995). Three children, two languages, and strategic reading: Case studies in bilingual/monolingual reading. *American Educational Research Journal, 32,* 31–61.

Klingner, J. K., & Vaughn, S. (1996). Reciprocal teaching of reading comprehension strategies for students with learning disabilities who use English as a second language. *Elementary School Journal, 96,* 275–293.

Klingner, J. K., & Vaughn, S. (1999a). Students' perceptions of instruction in inclusion classrooms: Implications for students with learning disabilities. *Exceptional Children,* 23–37.

Klingner, J. K., & Vaughn, S. (1999b). Promoting reading comprehension, content learning, and English acquisition through collaborative strategic reading (CSR). *The Reading Teacher, 52,* 738–747.

Klingner, J. K., Vaughn, S., Argüelles, M. E., Hughes, M. T., & Ahwee, S. (in press). Collaborative strategic reading: "Real world" lessons from classroom teachers. *Remedial and Special Education.*

Klingner, J. K., Vaughn, S., Dimino, J., Schumm, J. S., & Bryant, D. (2002). *From click to clunk: Collaborative Strategic Reading.* Longmont, CO: Sopris West.

Klingner, J. K., Vaughn, S., & Schumm, J. S. (1998). Collaborative strategic reading during social studies in heterogeneous fourth-grade classrooms. *Elementary School Journal, 99,* 3–21.

Konopak, B. C. (1991). Teaching vocabulary to improve science learning. In C. M. Santa & D. E. Alvermann (Eds.), *Science learning: Processes and applications* (pp. 134–146). Newark, DE: International Reading Association.

Korinek, L., & Bulls, J. A. (1996). SCORE A: A student research paper writing strategy. *Teaching Exceptional Children, 28*(4), 60–63.

Lenz, B. K., Bulgren, J., & Hudson, P. (1990). Content enhancement: A model for promoting the acquisition of content by individuals with learning disabilities. In T. E. Scruggs & B. Y. L. Wong (Eds.), *Intervention research in learning disabilities.* New York: Springer-Verlag.

Lerner, L. (1963). *Shakespeare's tragedies: An anthology of modern criticism.* Baltimore, MD: Penguin Books.

Mangrum, C. T., & Strichart, S. S. (2001). *Teaching study skills and strategies to students with learning disabilities, attention deficit disorders, or special needs* (3rd ed.). Boston: Allyn and Bacon.

Martin, D. J. (1996). *Elementary science methods: A constructivist approach.* Albany, NY: Delmar.

Mastropieri, M. A., & Fulk, B. J. M. (1990). Enhancing academic performance with mnemonic instruction. In T. E. Scruggs & B. Y. L. Wong (Eds.), *Intervention research in learning disabilities* (pp. 103–121). New York: Springer-Verlag.

Mastropieri, M. A., & Scruggs, T. E. (1987). *Effective instruction for special education.* Boston: College Hill.

Mastropieri, M. A., Scruggs, T. E., Bakken, J. P., & Whedon, C. (1996). Reading comprehension: A synthesis of research in learning disabilities. In T. E. Scruggs & M. A. Mastropieri (Eds.), *Advances in learning and behavioral disabilities.* Greenwich, CT: JAI Press.

Mastropieri, M. A., Scruggs, T. E., & Graetz, J. E. (2003). Reading comprehension instruction for secondary students: Challenges for struggling students and teachers. *Learning Disability Quarterly, 26,* 103–116.

Mastropieri, M. A., Scruggs, T. E., & Magnusen, M. (1999). Activities-oriented science instruction for students with disabilities. *Learning Disability Quarterly, 22,* 240–249.

McIntosh, R., Vaughn, S., Schumm, J. S., Haager, D., & Lee, O. (1993). Observations of students with learning disabilities in general education classrooms. *Exceptional Children, 60,* 249–261.

Michaelis, J. U. (1992). *Social studies for children* (10th ed.). Needham Heights, MA: Allyn and Bacon.

Moll, L. C. (Ed.). (1990). *Vygotsky and education: Instructional implications and applications of sociohistorical psychology.* Cambridge, MA: Cambridge University Press.

National Research Council, National Committee on

Science Education Standards and Assessment. (1993). *National Science Education standards: An enhanced sampler.* National science Education Standards, 2101 Constitution Avenue, NW HA 486, Washington, DC 20418.

National Research Council. (1996). *National science education standards.* Washington, DC: National Academy Press.

Ogle, D. M. (1986). K-W-L: A teaching model that develops active reading of expository text. *The Reading Teacher, 39,* 564–570.

O'Malley, J. M., & Chamot, A. U. (1990). *Learning strategies in second language acquisition.* Cambridge, England: Cambridge University Press.

Palincsar, A. S., & Brown, A. L. (1984). Reciprocal teaching of comprehension-fostering and comprehension-monitoring activities. *Cognition and Instruction, 1,* 117–175.

Paris, S. G., & Oka, E. R. (1989). Strategies for comprehending text and coping with reading difficulties. *Learning Disability Quarterly, 12,* 32–42.

Pearson, D. P., & Johnson, D. (1978). *Teaching reading comprehension.* New York: Holt, Rinehart & Winston.

Pressley, M., Brown, R., El-Dinary, P. B., & Afflerbach, P. (1995). The comprehension instruction that students need: Instruction fostering constructively responsive reading. *Learning Disabilities Research and Practice, 10,* 215–224.

Pressley, M., & El-Dinary, P. B. (1997). What we know about translating comprehension-strategies instruction research into practice. *Journal of Learning Disabilities, 30*(5), 486–488, 512.

Raphael, T. E. (1982). Question-answering strategies for children. *Reading Teacher, 36,* 186–190.

Raphael, T. E. (1986). Teaching question answer relationships, revisited. *Reading Teacher, 39,* 516–522.

Raphael, T. E., & Pearson, P. D. (1985). Increasing students' awareness of sources of information for answering questions. *American Educational Research Journal, 22,* 217–235.

Readence, J. E., Bean, T. W., & Baldwin, S. (1998). *Content area literacy: An integrated approach.* Dubuque, IA: Kendall/Hunt.

Riegel, R. H., Mayle, J. A., & McCarthy-Henkel, J. (1988). *Beyond maladies and remedies: Suggestions and guidelines for adapting materials for students with special needs in the regular class.* Plantation, FL: A.D.D. Warehouse.

Rumelhart, D. E. (1980). Schemata: The building blocks of cognition. In R. J. Spiro, B. Bruce, & W. F. Brewer (Eds.), *Theoretical issues in reading comprehension.* Hillsdale, NJ: Lawrence Erlbaum.

Santa, C. M., & Havens, L. T. (1991). Learning through writing. In C. M. Santa & D. E. Alvermann (Eds.), *Science learning: Processes and applications.* Newark, DE: International Reading Association.

Scanlon, D., Deshler, D. D., & Schumaker, J. B. (1996). Can a strategy be taught and learned in secondary inclusive classrooms? *Learning Disabilities Research & Practice, 11,* 41–57.

Schumaker, J. B., Deshler, D. D., & McKnight, P. C. (2001). Ensuring success in the general education curriculum through the use of teaching routines. In M. R. Shinn, G. Stoner, & H. M. Walker (Eds.), *Interventions for academic and behavior problems II: Preventive and remedial approaches.* Bethesda, MD: National Association of School Psychologists.

Schumaker, J. B., & Lenz, B. K. (1999). *Adapting language arts, social studies, and science materials for the inclusive classroom.* Reston, VA: The Council for Exceptional Children.

Schumm, J. S. (1999). *Adapting reading and math materials for the inclusive classroom.* Reston, VA: The Council for Exceptional Children.

Schumm, J. S., & Vaughn, S. (1992). Planning for mainstreamed special education students. *Exceptionality, 3,* 81–90.

Schumm, J. S., Vaughn, S., Haager, D., McDowell, J., Rothlein, L., & Saumell, L. (1995). General education teacher planning: What can students with learning disabilities expect? *Exceptional Children, 61,* 335–352.

Schumm, J. S., Vaughn, S., & Leavell, A. (1994). Planning pyramid: A framework for planning for diverse student needs during content area instruction. *The Reading Teacher, 47,* 608–615.

Scruggs, T. E., & Mastropieri, M. A. (1990). Mnemonic instruction for students with learning disabilities: What it is and what it does. *Learning Disability Quarterly, 13,* 271–280.

Scruggs, T. E., & Mastropieri, M. A. (1992). Classroom applications of mnemonic instruction: Acquisition, maintenance, and generalization. *Exceptional Children, 58,* 219–229.

Seidenberg, P. L. (1989). Relating text-processing research to reading and writing instruction for learning disabled students. *Learning Disabilities Focus, 5,* 4–12.

Shakespeare, W. (1980). *Macbeth.* Bevinton, D., Kastan,

D.S., Hammersmith, J., Turner, R.K. (Eds.). New York: Scott, Foresman and Co.

Simmons, D. C., & Kameenui, E. J. (1998). *What reading research tells us about children with diverse learning needs: Bases and basics.* Mahwah, NJ: Lawrence Erlbaum.

Slavin, R. E. (1994). *Educational psychology: Theory and practice.* Boston: Allyn and Bacon.

Stahl, S. A., & Erickson, L. G. (1986). The performance of third grade learning disabled boys on tasks at different levels of language: A model-based exploration. *Journal of Learning Disabilities, 19,* 285–290.

Strichart, S. S., & Mangrum III, C. T. (1993). *Teaching study strategies to students with learning disabilities.* Boston: Allyn and Bacon.

Sullivan, P. (1992). *ESL in context.* Newbury Park, CA: Corwin Press.

Swanson, H. L. (1986). Do semantic memory deficiencies underlie learning disabled readers' encoding processes? *Journal of Experimental Child Psychology, 41,* 461–488.

Swanson, H. L., & Ashbaker, M. H. (2000). Working memory, short-term memory, speech rate, word recognition and reading comprehension in learning disabled readers: Does the executive system have a role? *Intelligence, 28,* 1–30.

Swanson, P. N., & De La Paz, S. (1998). Teaching effective comprehension strategies to students with learning and reading disabilities. *Intervention in School and Clinic, 33*, 209–218.

Tabassam, W., & Grainger, J. (2002). Self-concept, attributional style and self-efficacy beliefs of students with learning disabilities with and without Attention Deficit Hyperactivity Disorder. *Learning Disability Quarterly, 25,* 141–151.

Torgesen, J. K. (1980). Conceptual and educational implications of the use of efficient task strategies by learning disabled children. *Journal of Learning Disabilities, 13,* 364–371.

Tralli, R., Colombo, B., Deshler, D. D., & Schumaker, J. B. (1996). The strategies intervention model: A model for supported inclusion at the secondary level. *Remedial and Special Education, 17,* 204–216.

Vallecorsa, A. L., deBettencourt, L. U., & Zigmond, N. (2000*). Students with mild disabilities in general education settings: A guide for special educators.* Upper Saddle River, NJ: Merrill.

Vaughn, S., Schumm, J. S., Klingner, J. K., & Saumell, L. (1995). Students' views of instructional practices: Implications for inclusion. *Learning Disability Quarterly, 18,* 236–248.

Vaughn, S., Schumm, J. S., & Kouzekanani, K. (1993). What do students think when their general education teachers make adaptations? *Journal of Learning Disabilities, 26,* 545–555.

Vaughn, S., Schumm, J. S., Niarhos, F. J., & Daugherty, T. (1993). What do students think when teachers make adaptations? *Teaching and Teacher Education, 9,* 107–118.

Vaughn, S., Schumm, J. S., Niarhos, F. J., & Gordon, J. (1993). Students' perceptions of two hypothetical teachers' instructional adaptations for low achievers. *The Elementary School Journal, 94,* 87–103.

Weaver, C.A., III, & Kintsch, W. (1991). Expository text. In R. Barr, M. L. Kamil, P. Mosenthal, & P. D. Pearson (Eds.), *Handbook of reading research* (pp. 230–244). White Plains, NY: Longman.

Wehmeyer, M. L., & Kelchner, K. (1996). Perceptions of classroom environment, locus of control and academic attribution of adolescents with and without cognitive disabilities. *Career Development for Exceptional Individuals, 19,* 15–30.

Weisberg, R. (1988). 1980s: A change in focus of reading comprehension research: A review of reading/learning disabilities research based on an interactive model of reading. *Learning Disability Quarterly,* 11, 149–159.

Weishaar, M. K., & Boyle, J. R. (1997). Notetaking for students with mild disabilities. *CEC Today, 4*(5), 12.

Zigmond, N. (1996). Organization and management of general education classrooms. In D. L. Speece & B. K. Keogh (Eds.), *Research on classroom ecologies: Implications for inclusion of children with learning disabilities* (pp. 163–190). Mahwah, NJ: Lawrence Erlbaum.

CHAPTER TEN

INCLUSIVE SECONDARY SETTINGS FOR STUDENTS WITH HIGH-INCIDENCE DISABILITIES

Experience is a hard teacher. She gives the test first and the lessons afterwards.

—Anonymous

KEY CONCEPTS

- Secondary school settings present unique challenges for students and teachers when implementing inclusion due to student, teacher, curricular, and school factors.
- Inclusion is most successful in middle and high schools when there is a schoolwide commitment to establishing an inclusive atmosphere as well as structural change that facilitates accommodating students' individual learning needs.

- Establishing a peer support network is an important element of secondary inclusion.
- Reading and writing difficulties pose great challenges for students with disabilities included in secondary general education classrooms. Adaptations and accommodations are crucial to success.
- It is important for the special education teacher to continue to address secondary students' specific literacy learning needs and not just focus on their content area classes and assignments.

FOCUS QUESTIONS

1. What are the challenges experienced by students and teachers in secondary inclusion programs?
2. How can special education teachers collaborate with numerous general education teachers and adapt to many different classroom structures and styles?
3. How can special education teachers address the literacy learning needs of secondary students?
4. What methods promote success of secondary students with disabilities in secondary classrooms?

Upon entering middle school, most students experience anxiety. Even the most capable students fear getting lost in a big campus, being teased by older students, giving a "dumb" answer, or not "fitting in." The process begins anew when students leave middle school for an even bigger high school campus. From middle school through high school, there is a fine line of distinction between peer support and peer pressure. Social issues and concerns may outweigh academic matters in many students' minds. Most students navigate their way through the challenges as well as successful and enriching school experiences. However, for some students, it may be a more arduous journey.

When students with disabilities enter the secondary school setting, they face many additional challenges. Most students with high-incidence disabilities are included for at least part of the school day in secondary settings, yet the gap between their academic skills and the demands of the classroom widens as they progress through the secondary grades. Reading and writing are the primary vehicles for evaluating students in secondary classes putting most students with disabilities at risk for failure in the secondary general education classroom. What, then, can teachers, parents, and support staff do to help these students achieve academic success? How can teachers make inclusion possible in the secondary setting? How can these students learn alongside their peers?

Secondary schools are contextually different from elementary programs in many ways. Besides the sheer size of secondary schools, there are differences in schedules, structures and routines, and the very nature of instruction. It is clear that an inclusion program at the secondary level must be different from an elementary program. In this chapter, we will examine the tremendous demands and challenges for students and teachers that are unique to secondary settings and other important issues related to inclusion at the secondary level. We will describe what we see as essential components of secondary inclusion programs and methods for supporting students as they navigate their way through middle and high school. We will pay particular attention to methods for improving students' literacy skills in secondary programs because this is the single greatest challenge for teachers and students. We will present various models of secondary inclusion, including a multi-tiered model that we believe provides sufficient academic support while allowing inclusion opportunities in secondary settings. We will also discuss methods for integrating technology to support learning, assessment issues, and methods for involving students and parents as part of the team process.

Let's begin with a look at how two secondary schools have chosen to address their students' academic needs within an inclusive framework. While each school has grappled with similar issues, there are other concerns that are unique to each setting.

MID-CITY MIDDLE SCHOOL

Change is not new to this urban middle school, known in the city as MCMS. Under new leadership, the school has recently undergone significant restructuring to address such urban school issues as falling test scores, violence, poor attendance, and teacher burnout. When Mr. Sarkis came on as a new principal a year ago, almost one-third of the teachers either transferred or retired, and many new teachers were hired. Inclusion of students with disabilities came on the heels of other significant change at this school. Change at MCMS began with a series of meetings involving teachers, parents, administrators, community members, and students. Initially, the purpose of the meetings was to establish a vision and a mission for MCMS. Soon, however, many people were organized into working teams to bring about significant change at all levels of running the school. It was in the initial meetings that the special educators and concerned parents began to consider inclusive education for their students with special needs. Their vision of students with disabilities learning alongside their peers in classrooms equipped to make appropriate adjustments for their learning needs became enveloped in the larger vision of a more caring and personalized urban middle school. A sense of ownership for the educational outcomes of all MCMS students began to take hold of the teachers and support staff at the school.

One of the greatest schoolwide changes was the adoption of a middle school teaming model. Students are heterogeneously grouped into cohorts of 120 to 150 students. Each cohort shares a team of four teachers who teach the core subjects. Except for elective classes, the students do not interact with students or teachers from other cohorts. Each team of teachers meets regularly in joint planning meetings where they discuss individual students, coordinate their plans, and plan special group events. The purpose of this arrangement is to create a "school within a school," where the students can get to know each other, do not get lost in the shuffle, and receive more personalized instruction.

Adopting an inclusive model of service delivery for students with disabilities has been a suitable arrangement for MCMS's teaming model. It provides one more means of personalizing students' instruction within the cohort system. The special educators at the school have become part of a support team that includes three special educators, two Chapter 1 teachers, two ESL teachers, a speech and language specialist, and five instructional aides shared by the various programs. Though each member of the support team performs his or her own function independently, the students and classroom teachers have become accustomed to the members of this support team coming into their classes or pulling individual students out. Students and teachers are aware that these specialists provide support as needed, and little stigma is attached to the need to receive special help. It has become part of the classroom and school routine.

One special educator is assigned to each of three grades. These specialists attend the team meetings for that grade level and plan collaboratively with the classroom teachers. At these meetings, they plan the logistics of providing support for students on their roster including scheduling, assessment, and specific types of instructional support. They also assist in planning modifications and adaptations for individual students. Special educators coordinate any other special services such as speech and language therapy or English language instruction and also coordinate the classroom support provided by the instructional aides. Monitoring the IEPs and all special education procedures is the primary responsibility of the special educator. Only one team of teachers has ventured into co-teaching thus far. For the most part, the special educator takes the role of support provider and goes into the core classes on a rotating schedule to provide assistance to students and teachers.

When they planned this model of inclusion for MCMS, the special and general education teachers were concerned about students' lack of basic reading and math skills. They believed they could provide adequate modifications and supports to assure students' participation in content area classes but were concerned that students would not get the individualized skills development they needed within the context of the classroom instruction. The teachers decided they would try to integrate basic skill instruction into the general education classrooms and create both formal and informal opportunities to pull students out for individualized instruction. The special educators received training in integrating basic skill instruction into in-class support. This included training in making adaptations as well as integrating basic skill instruction into study skills. They monitor students' progress and provide reading skills instruction whenever they are in the regular classes with the students. However, they also agreed that the special educator would attend the language arts classes and provide reading and writing instruction within small groups or individual instruction sessions during this class time. Most of the language arts classes are using writing process instruction (see Chapter 7) and focus on the state-mandated core literature in reading instruction. The class format allows for students to break into work groups or do individual learning tasks. It is during this time that special education teachers work with students on reading and writing skills development.

Mathematics instruction presented additional challenges for the MCMS teachers. Since math instruction is largely skills-based, the teachers believed it would be impossible to heterogeneously group students and make adaptations for students with special needs. Over half of the students with disabilities had adequate skills to function in the regular classroom with simple accommodations such as use of calculators, extra time for tests, and modified assignments. The staff created a special education math class at each grade level for those students with serious mathematics difficulties. The IEP team makes the decision as to which option is appropriate for individual students. Some of the students with disabilities will be placed in the special math classes for all three years of middle school.

An additional opportunity for basic skills development occurs via the use of technology. Computers are available for all students after school, but a few computers are set aside for the students served in special education. Students use these computers for computer-assisted instruction in reading, writing, or mathematics or use them to complete their homework assignments. There are reading, writing and math instructional software programs that provide a wide array of skill instruction. These computers are also equipped with software designed to provide extra support for students with learning disabilities or other reading and writing difficulties.

CLEARVIEW HIGH SCHOOL

The teachers and staff at Clearview High School implemented a tiered model of inclusive education two years ago at the urging of the school board and a group of concerned parents. At the time, there was a great deal of resistance among the teachers, who were fairly satisfied with their existing model of special education. Now, most of the teachers openly support their inclusion program and feel that their initial fears and concerns have been addressed. As they began to develop their plan for inclusion, one of the major concerns of both the special and general education teachers was the wide range of skills and needs of the students served in special education. Some students they could see fitting quite well into inclusion. These students had some reading and writing abilities and, with support and modifications, could probably be successful in subject area classes. However, the teachers felt there were other students whose needs would not be met in the general education classroom and who would probably not experience success. These students either had extremely low academic scores and lacked the basic skills to participate fully in regular classes or they had significant behavior problems that were likely to be disruptive to the classroom and could not be addressed in this context. The teachers, administrators, and staff at Clearview High School adopted a tiered model of inclusion that would allow varying levels of participation of students based on their strengths and needs. They have maintained a continuum of services in the type and intensity of special education support provided. They have built in flexibility so that students may be moved easily from one tier to another as the class demands or their needs change.

Their three-tiered model is based on the intensity of support needed by the student. The first tier is for students who need minimal support, and the majority of students with disabilities are served in Tier 1. These students have some basic reading and writing skills and receive minimal in-class support from the special educator assigned to them. Support is provided through collaboration between the special education teacher and the subject area teachers. For each student served in Tier 1 in each class, the subject area teacher is responsible for managing peer support, providing some in-class support, and implementing any necessary minor modifications. In addition, the general education teacher provides a weekly grade report that includes subject-area grades, progress toward IEP goals, and a behavior report, if appropriate, to the special education teacher. The special education teacher is responsible for monitoring students' progress, consulting with the classroom teachers regarding modifications and meeting with the students at least once a week. If a teacher requests it, the special education teacher may attend the subject area class on a weekly basis to provide in-class support or to consult with the teacher and student together. Students served in this tier may attend a help session one period per day where they can get help with daily assignments or study skills as needed.

The second tier provides a medium intensity of support for students and offers inclusion for the core classes. Students served in Tier 2 usually attend one period per day of intensive skill development and an additional period of assistance with class assignments, both serviced by special education teachers. Students are placed in regular classes for most core subjects and in-class support is provided several times per week by the special education staff. In addition, the special education and general education teachers work together to develop appropriate modifications or to plan specific in-class support. If students do not maintain a class grade of "C" or better in the their core classes, they may be moved to the next tier for more intensive instruction. Because two periods per day are given to special education services, students in this plan usually do not have elective classes. The special education teacher works with the students and parents to assist students in developing interests and skills in other ways such as community center classes or afterschool sports. In a few cases, students have been placed in elective classes, such as music, to allow them to develop in this area of strength, and they have found another way to provide support that would normally be available in one of the special education periods.

Students in the Tier 3 receive the highest intensity of special education support and are included in general classes for only two or three periods per day. Their inclusion classes are selected by determining the areas in which the student most needs to develop a knowledge base (e.g., science, social studies) and the areas in which the student is most likely to experience success among peers. The focus is on building knowledge and on developing social competence. During the periods assigned to special education support, the student receives intensive skill development in basic academic skills, functional life skills, and employment-related skills. In addition, students may attend a transition program one period per day in which they learn important employment skills. The special education staff is primarily responsible for the intensive skill instruction, consulting with the classroom teachers to develop modifications and in-class supports (e.g., peer reader, peer notetaker), and for coordinating with other services such as the transition program. The modifications implemented in the subject area classes tend to be more extensive and more tailored to individual students.

At any tier, students may participate in an afterschool support program. As in Mid-City Middle School described above, computers are available for computer-assisted instruction or for use in completing class assignments. Volunteer and paid assistants are also available to provide help with homework or to read aloud to students from their textbooks. The afterschool program also works with community services to assist students in developing employment skills and outside skills or interests. We will look more closely at some of the classes and services at Clearview High School later in the chapter.

SECONDARY SCHOOL DEMANDS AND CHALLENGES FOR STUDENTS AND TEACHERS

Challenges Students Face

Students with high-incidence disabilities face extraordinary obstacles as they enter the secondary setting. In addition to the normal adolescent struggles, students with high-incidence disabilities encounter unique academic and social challenges simply because they have disabilities. A successful inclusion program at the secondary level should be structured to address these challenges through academic, social, and behavioral supports.

Academic Demands. Students with learning disabilities often feel overwhelmed by the literacy demands of middle and high school (Schumm, Vaughn, & Saumell, 1992, 1994). More so than in elementary school, reading and writing difficulties have a pervasive effect on how students fare in their classes. While most secondary students adapt to the demand to read and write in more volume and complexity, students with literacy-related disabilities find themselves losing ground. In fact, students with reading-related learning disabilities report that they continue to experience difficulty with literacy skills beyond adolescence and into adulthood and many do not finish high school (Adelman & Vogel, 1991; Rogan & Hartman, 1990; Schumaker & Deschler, 1992).

For students with disabilities, adjustment to secondary schools is complicated by an increasing gap between their own academic abilities and the academic demands of the classroom (Algozzine, O'Shea, Stoddard, & Crews, 1988; Warner, Alley, Deschler, & Schumaker, 1980). As students with disabilities move through the middle and high school grades, they encounter increasingly complex concepts and materials delivered by teachers who are primarily concerned with content delivery. Early in middle school, teachers assume students have mastered the basic reading and writing skills necessary for effective learning, and they expect students to read and complete assignments independently. Along with difficult subject matter, students must comprehend more abstract and elaborate ideas, concepts, and vocabulary. A significant portion of school learning is delivered through written text (Zigmond, Levin, & Laurie, 1985). Through the grades, the volume and complexity of reading assignments increases and students must produce more complex and more substantial written work. Textbooks in upper grades can be "inconsiderate," or "reader-unfriendly" with few aids to guide and assist the reader (Armbruster & Anderson, 1988).

Looking beyond the classroom demands, national educational organizations have highlighted the national and world demand for literacy skills as we become a more technologically advanced society (e.g., National Education Goals Panel, 1995; Snow, Burns & Griffin, 1998). Secondary students today are under increased pressure to be able to compete in a global economy and workplace. This means advanced technological skills as well as the ability to communicate in written and spoken language.

We believe that a successful secondary academic program for students with disabilities must be well rounded to address a complex set of academic needs. First and foremost, it must include intensive instruction in reading and writing. Students must learn effective study strategies for mastering difficult material. Furthermore, students must learn to access sources of support and assistance, including assistive technology.

Situational Demands. When students move from elementary to secondary settings, they find themselves in a completely different milieu. Secondary schools and classrooms are different from elementary settings structurally, academically, and socially (Harter, Whitesell, & Kowalski, 1992; Wigfield, Eccles, MacIver, Reuman, & Midgley, 1991). Students must interact with a greater number of teachers and peers, and, as individuals, they are "small fish in a larger sea." The nature of classrooms changes, too. Teachers in secondary schools are often more content-focused than elementary teachers. They not only have higher academic expectations for students, but also expect students to be more responsible and self-reliant. Secondary teachers report that they do not have the time or the opportunity to give personal attention to individual students (Schumm, Vaughn, Haager, McDowell, Rothlein, & Saumell, 1995; Haager & Simon, 1997). They often lack the skills, knowledge, and desire to make adjustments or accommodations to address individual student needs (Schumm & Vaughn, 1991, 1992; Schumm et al., 1995). Thus, students with disabilities who have become accustomed to the supportive environment of an elementary classroom find the secondary classroom and teachers to be quite different.

Challenges of Adolescence. The social milieu of school also changes. Adolescence is a time of increased social pressure, self-doubt, and uncertainty. We can probably all remember a time in our adolescence when someone was singled out and ridiculed by classmates for a seemingly small infraction or misstep. Perhaps it was even ourselves, and we can remember the momentary importance of the event, the feeling that we could not return to school under any circumstance, and the constant fear that we would inadvertently do something again to provoke a repeat occurrence. Generally, adolescence brings a time of extreme sensitivity as students grapple with identity issues (Berndt, 1979, 1982; Hamburg, 1974). In addition to these adolescent worries, students with reading difficulties fear being put on the spot by having to read aloud in class or being asked to answer a question they cannot read or understand (Haager & Simon, 1997; Lavoie, 1989). Early adolescence is marked by general declines in grade point average, self-esteem, and motivation (Seidman, Allen, Aber, Mitchell, & Feinman, 1994), indicating a difficult developmental period for most individuals. While students with learning disabilities have general self-esteem patterns similar to those without disabilities, research indicates that they often have lower self-concepts with regard to their academic skills (Vaughn & Haager, 1994a, 1994b). These, then, are added challenges for students who are experiencing literacy difficulties as they enter the secondary inclusive setting. Not only are they feeling isolated due to their academic difficulties, they are also struggling with the need to "fit in." Students with disabilities dislike the idea of receiving special assistance or of being singled out in any way.

Social Demands. Secondary students face tremendous social challenges, too, as they develop networks of friendship and support. Students with broad peer support find help with both academic and social situations. Having positive peer influences can make a tremendous difference in students' overall school success. Students with learning and behavior problems, however, do not always have positive social experiences in secondary school settings. They often come face to face with their differences as they struggle not only for academic survival, but also to find their place in the social milieu of a large middle or high school. For some students with disabilities, the social circle is the only place where they find success (Upham & Trumbull, 1997). Other students, however, struggle to navigate through a complex social web made more difficult by socially related aspects of their disabilities. Having a network of social support can make the difference between success and failure for students with disabilities.

Adolescence represents a transition period from childhood to adulthood. During this developmental period, students go through physical, biological, psychological, and social changes. Most students go through periods of social awkwardness during adolescence. Having and maintaining appropriate social skills is critical to school success (Berndt, 1982; Wentzel, 1991). The complex social contexts of middle and high schools pose significant challenges for students with high-incidence disabilities, especially if they have significant behavioral or social difficulties. Upon entering middle school, students changing from class to class find that each class may have a distinct social context, with distinct social expectations. Students must navigate social opportunities, behavioral expectations, and academic demands in each class as well as outside of class. Experiencing serious social difficulties can impede a student's academic success and quality of life (Deshler, Ellis, & Lenz, 1996).

Social difficulties may take many forms. Some students may be extremely withdrawn, afraid to take social chances or to reach out to new people. Some may be loud and inappropriate, while others appear to be socially awkward, never quite knowing what to say or when to laugh. Whatever the manifestation, these students need assistance in developing a positive social support network to be successful in an inclusive secondary setting. A successful secondary inclusion program must consider students' social and emotional well-being and must provide appropriate social support to help students maneuver this tumultuous developmental period.

Challenges Teachers Face

What, then, are the challenges special education teachers face when they teach students with disabilities in secondary inclusive settings? There are several issues that must be taken into account when planning instruction and support. Some of these issues are larger ones that impact the structure of the school and all classrooms and require schoolwide consensus. Others must be worked out with individual teachers and students.

Evaluation and Grading. The main whole-school issue relates to the nature of secondary education. Especially in high school, teachers and students are required to adhere to uniform standards and regulations that govern the curriculum. Grading is central to this issue—there is generally a schoolwide policy for grading. Most states require competency testing as part of the evaluative procedure. How do students with disabilities fit into these standards and evaluative procedures? How should students performing below grade level be evaluated and graded? Should students with disabilities be included in competency testing? Should they receive a regular diploma? School, district, and state policy documents may include answers to these questions. Providing individual support and assistance without violating school policy and procedures is an issue that must be addressed by those involved. Certainly, guidance from administrators may help to clear this issue up. Our experience is that, when it is not openly addressed, misconception and misunderstandings are likely to result. Classroom teachers and other students may question why some students receive "help" with classwork, how the students receiving help could receive passing grades, and why others who are failing do not receive help. Parents and students may have difficulty understanding grades—either failing grades due to a policy that students with disabilities adhere to grading standards or passing grades that are earned with supports and modifications provided. They might also wonder why students are graded leniently in one class and stringently in another. Because of the potential for confusion, this issue is best addressed through dialogue within the school's governance channels; that is, faculty meetings, committees, or governing councils.

Competency Testing. More and more states are adopting standards and competency testing to evaluate students. In secondary settings, students may be required to pass certain tests to move on in grades or even to exit high school. These kinds of tests have absolute standards, and students with disabilities may have difficulty passing. Earning a high school diploma may be tied to passing a test. Federal and state laws allow for students to have accommodations when taking such tests, but even with accommodations such as extended time, many students with disabilities have difficulty passing. This poses challenges for teachers in several ways. First, the special education teachers often take responsibility for preparing students for tests, and this is yet another task to fit into a busy schedule. Added pressure may come from families, or teachers may feel the students' performance reflects on their teaching. It is important for teachers, students, and families to have a clear plan in mind for test preparation.

Balancing Curriculum Support and Skills Development. A similar challenge for secondary inclusion teachers is that of balancing subject area support with skill development. It is important for students to be successful in content area classes, and they often need a great deal of support to do so. Secondary special educators coordinate in-class adaptations, read textbooks aloud, help with assignments, administer adapted tests to students, and provide study skills assistance in order to help students experience success in their classes. However, the need to provide intensive instruction in basic skills (reading, writing, and mathematics) is also tremendous. If students do not develop these basic skills, they will never be able to reduce their need for subject-area support or develop important life skills. On the other hand, an imbalance in the other direction—overemphasizing skills instruction and ignoring content-area support—leads to segregated programs as we have had in the past. This excludes students from access to the core curriculum and the motivation that comes from interesting topics, building important knowledge bases in subject areas, and developing peer networks.

To a certain extent, basic skills can be taught within the context of supporting students in content area classes. However, we believe that it is also important to provide direct instruction for a short period of time each day to develop literacy skills. A balanced instructional program in secondary schools would give adequate attention to both content area support and basic skill development. This is indeed a tremendous challenge for the secondary special educator.

How does the secondary inclusion specialist fit skill instruction in with the overall school and classroom structure? This may or may not be a schoolwide issue. Some secondary inclusive schools develop schoolwide inclusion practices and procedures that include intensive individualized instruction. For example, the two high schools described earlier in the chapter adopted inclusive education schoolwide and made explicit plans for how specialized instruction would take place. At Mid-City Middle School, literacy instruction takes place primarily in the language arts classes. At the other school, Clearview High School, there is at least one period set aside for intensive skill instruction for those students who need it. At some schools, the decision of how inclusion takes place is made on a case-by-case basis. Special educators develop arrangements and procedures with individual classroom teachers that fit with the structure of each classroom. The special educator may go in and do small group instruction in one class and co-teach the whole group in another. When a specified plan is not in place, special educators find themselves carving out opportunities to provide intensive instruction. Of course, the danger in "carving out" time for intensive instruction is that it may never take place—other needs and events may take priority. We believe that, especially for students with significant reading and writing difficulties, a schoolwide plan that provides allocated time for intensive skill development as well as support in content area classes works best.

Teacher Resistance to Inclusion. Special educators working in secondary settings report that other teachers often present the greatest challenges. Secondary content teachers often have negative initial reactions to the idea of inclusion. They are less likely to make adaptations and may even feel it does the student a disservice (Schumm et al., 1995). What causes secondary teachers to be resistant to an inclusion model? There may be several reasons.

First, teachers may be resistant to change in general. The structure of a secondary school setting is complex and teachers have many responsibilities. They may teach five or six periods and may have as many as 150 students on their rosters. The sheer number of students in a middle or high school leads to depersonalization of the environment. The secondary environment is typically a "well-oiled machine" with routines and rules that influence teachers' daily activities. Some teachers will resist anything that would cause a major shift in their responsibilities and routines. The teacher's resistance may be a matter of resisting change in general or it may be specific to having a special education teacher come into the classroom. Sharing the classroom domain with another professional is a new concept in middle and high schools. It may be uncomfortable at first for both the general and special educators.

Second, secondary teachers are more likely to resist the idea of making adaptations for individual students (Schumm & Vaughn, 1991, 1992; Schumm et al., 1995). Some believe it is not their job to accommodate students with disabilities and may respond with such comments as, "I am a science teacher, not a special educator." Such teachers are *content-focused* rather than student-focused. Their instruction and planning are driven by content standards and "getting through the book." These teachers view making individualized adaptations as detracting from their real purpose, that of delivering content. Some secondary teachers believe it is inherently wrong to make adaptations because it does not prepare students for the "real world" beyond high school (Schumm & Vaughn, 1992). They believe they do students a disservice to modify the standards.

Another point of resistance is the idea that, in an inclusive model, classroom teachers would be responsible for teaching reading skills or learning strategies—this is outside of their curriculum responsibilities. Secondary teachers do not perceive it as within their roles to teach specific reading skills or to teach students how to learn within the content area (Schumaker & Deshler, 1987). Others would like to be more helpful with individuals in their classes but lack the time and opportunity to work with students (Schumm & Vaughn, 1992). Secondary content teachers often have thirty to forty students in each class for five periods a day. Giving special attention to specific students is beyond their capacity, and individual support should be the primary responsibility of the special educator. However, students with disabilities should have access to any special help that is available to other students, such as afterschool or lunchtime tutoring. Most secondary schools that have adopted an inclusive model have been explicit about establishing teachers' roles. A critical element of success is organizing the special education teachers' roles to include providing individual student support and being available as consultants to the other teachers.

General classroom teachers may be resistant to inclusion because they have had negative experiences with mainstreaming students with disabilities. They may have personal feelings about being responsible for teaching students with disabilities in their classes and may believe that it will reflect negatively on their performance if the student does not do well. This is particularly true for students with behavior problems (Schumm & Vaughn, 1991, 1992). Teachers may not feel it is within their job responsibility to teach students with disabilities and may comment, for example, "If I had wanted to be a special educator, I would have done so."

Probably the most difficult teacher barrier to overcome is that of having low expectations for students with disabilities. General education teachers (and many special educators, too) have inherent beliefs that these students are incapable of learning the secondary curriculum. Having low expectations leads to a self-fulfilling prophecy as teachers communicate low expectations in both explicit and implicit ways to students. For example, a teacher may believe she is being sensitive to a student by not calling on him so as not to embarrass him, but the act of ignoring the student communicates the message that the teacher believes the student is incapable of answering (Lavoie, 1989). It is important to have reasonable but ambitious expectations for students.

Coordination with Other Professionals. Another challenge special educators face in a secondary inclusion model is the enormous task of coordinating with various teachers, special programs, and support personnel. Of course, this is a big job in an elementary program as well, but coordination in a secondary setting requires being informed about all aspects of secondary routines, programs, and curricula. Secondary inclusion teachers are likely to collaborate with more general education classroom teachers than at the elementary level. They may work with teachers they hardly know. In addition, there are more special programs to interface with, such as vocational education and transition programs.

Challenging Student Characteristics. Secondary special educators also must be able to address specific student challenges. As students move into and through the secondary grades, their needs change. Learning difficulties complicate the typical social and emotional issues of adolescence for students with disabilities. Adolescents are very aware of their differences in abilities and characteristics and those with disabilities may be very self-conscious in the classroom. During adolescence, students with disabilities often become more passive and lack motivation. Secondary special educators that we have worked with claim that battling student passivity is their greatest challenge. Many adolescent students give up at this point in their school career. Other students may develop intense behavioral or emotional challenges. Discipline problems and emotional problems such as depression and eating disorders are more prevalent in secondary students with disabilities (Bender, 1999). It is important to be aware of students' social and emotional needs and develop strategies for engaging students in planning and implementing goal-directed instruction.

Curricular Challenges

Academic Standards. Increasingly, schools are adopting higher academic standards and graduation requirements. The demand for literacy skills increases dramatically in middle and high school classrooms where students must keep pace with literature books, textbooks, and written assignments designed to deliver an increasingly complex and diverse curriculum (Ellis & Friend, 1991; Schumm et al., 1995). National and state initiatives push for increasing the academic rigor of our schools. What are the implications for inclusion at the secondary level? How will students with disabilities fare in a standards-driven academic program?

Recent educational reform movements have led to more rigorous academic standards for learning. Students in many states must pass competency examinations to receive a high school diploma. How then, can teachers be responsive to individual students' academic and behavioral difficulties while being responsible and accountable for achievement standards? This is often a school's argument against inclusion. When schools tackle this issue at the outset, their inclusion efforts are more likely to succeed. Shriner, Ysseldyke, and Thurlow (1996) describe schools' possible responses to the establishment of standards and the inclusion of students with disabilities. First, a school may decide to adopt separate standards for special education students. Some feel that establishing separate standards limits the opportunities of students with disabilities. They are less likely to have access to rich learning opportunities or the opportunity to perform at their highest capacity. This certainly works against the very grain of inclusive education. A second possible option for setting standards is to establish a single set of standards but accept a range of performance levels for individuals or groups of students. Thus, students are evaluated against their own personal baseline with, perhaps, a minimal performance goal in mind. A third option is to use standards as a means of examining schoolwide or statewide average performance and develop alternative means for evaluating the performance of students with disabilities, for example, allowing students to demonstrate their achievement in a portfolio format. Last, these authors present the IEP as a set of standards specifically designed to meet students' individual needs. Thus, students with disabilities may be evaluated according to the goals and objectives on their IEPs. When the IEP is carefully planned and designed to address the core curriculum, students with disabilities are evaluated equitably against appropriate standards.

Other Curricular Issues. Students with disabilities cite the inflexibility of the curriculum as a challenge in secondary programs (Lovitt, Plavins, & Cushing, 1999). Secondary teachers often find it difficult to modify the curriculum for individual students because there is a certain amount of rigidity in the content and standards. It is often difficult to discern the critical concepts without making significant compromises in the academic standards. Many secondary courses have sophisticated vocabulary and complex conceptual knowledge that is difficult for students with disabilities. Pacing is another issue. Content area instruction often moves at a fast pace and presents challenges for the student with disabilities and for the special education teacher trying to provide support.

Regardless of these curricular challenges, it is important to remember the underlying purpose of making the core curriculum accessible to students with disabilities. Public schools have a legal responsibility to engage students with disabilities in the core curriculum. IDEA states that, to the extent possible, students with disabilities should be learning in the general education curriculum alongside their peers. Additionally, we have to remember that the content area curriculum provides much of our cultural literacy. The secondary curriculum provides core knowledge that we consider essential for adult life. Common knowledge with which we operate comes from the core literature and content area curriculum. For example, when someone describes an acquaintance as a real

"Romeo," how many of us would fail to connect with the Shakespeare tale? Box 10.1 describes a helpful tool for co-planning content instruction.

INCLUSION PRACTICES AND ROLES OF TEACHERS IN SECONDARY SETTINGS

In reality, there are as many models of inclusion as there are inclusive schools. As school districts or regions adopt models of inclusion, they become fine-tuned by those involved at each school site, resulting in slight, or large, differences from school to school. There are three basic models of secondary inclusion: co-teaching, collaborative consultation, and teaming. It is really better to think of these as components of, or instructional arrangements in, inclusive education because many schools include elements of each model in their own

BOX 10.1
FROM RESEARCH TO PRACTICE

Schumm, Vaughn, and Leavell (1994) developed the Planning Pyramid to guide teachers' thinking while planning for *all* students in heterogeneous classes. This idea was later developed into forms for use in co-planning. Vaughn, Bos, and Schumm (2003) developed the Unit Planning Pyramid and the Lesson Planning Pyramid. Co-planning forms help teachers think about what content will be learned by all students, what content will be learned by most students, what content will be learned by some students, and how activities will be adapted for the students with special needs included in the general education classroom. These Planning Pyramids and their accompanying Planning Forms provide ideal templates for organizing co-planning in inclusion classrooms.

The Unit Planning Form is used by teachers to record the target concepts to be learned within a unit. The base of the pyramid represents those concepts that are the most important. These concepts tend to be broader and more general than concepts at succeeding levels. The next highest level of the pyramid represents information considered to be next in importance, such as additional facts, extensions of base concepts, related concepts, and/or more complex concepts. The top level of the pyramid represents information considered to be supplementary. This information is more complex and/or detailed and will be mastered by the fewest students in the classroom. The form also includes space to record materials and resources that will be needed, instructional strategies and adaptations for students with special needs, and how learning will be evaluated.

The Lesson Planning Form is similar to the Unit Planning Form in that teachers first identify the concepts to be taught to all, most, and some students. Additional space is provided for recording materials, evaluation procedures, in-class and homework assignments, and the instructional agenda.

When using these forms during co-planning sessions, general education and special education teachers can note in parentheses after each item which teacher will be responsible for that aspect of instruction.

Sources: Schumm, Vaughn, & Leavell (1994); Vaughn, Bos, & Schumm (2003).

inclusion plan. Let's examine how individualized instruction might occur within each type of instructional arrangement.

Co-Teaching

Ms. Milford is a special educator at Clearview High School, described earlier in this chapter. She works primarily with students in Tier 1, or those requiring minimal support. For two periods each day, Ms. Milford co-teaches in social studies classes in which students on her roster are scheduled. There are several reasons why she co-teaches in these and not other classes. First, the content area teacher was interested in trying this instructional arrangement, so she had a willing partner. She also had a working knowledge of social studies and felt quite comfortable in a teaching role in this content area. In addition, Ms. Milford was primarily concerned with improving her students' reading and writing skills. She saw these skills as critical to the students' success in high school and, later, in the work force. Social studies seemed to her to be dependent on students' literacy skills, and she thought it would be a perfect opportunity to contextualize and reinforce the instruction she was providing in the skills instruction class for students in Tier 1. Ms. Milford had worked as a consultant teacher in social studies teacher Mr. Graves's class before, and she was comfortable with his teaching style and classroom structure. She was sure they would be compatible co-teachers. The co-teaching began as an experiment when she and Mr. Graves met to discuss the progress of their shared students. They had both learned of co-teaching as a means to facilitate inclusion at a district inservice session. She was eager to try it, and Mr. Graves was interested in trying out other roles in the classroom. He was worried about relinquishing his teaching time and control of the class but felt it would be a good experience for him to take on the role of consultant and support teacher from time to time. They agreed to co-plan and rotate the whole-class teaching by topic areas. When one is in the teacher role, the other is in a support role. Both acknowledge that they are not experts at both roles. Ms. Milford is still primarily responsible for assessment and monitoring and is the special education consultant. Mr. Graves is still the content expert and oversees the classroom management. However, both agree that their teaching effectiveness has increased by exchanging roles. After a few months, Mr. Graves believed he had a deeper understanding of the learning process and individual students' needs. He has developed confidence in his ability to develop adaptations and to think of in-class supports for students. Ms. Milford has earned the respect of the class as a teacher, and the students do not see her presence as a stigma. The most positive result has been the sense of community that has developed in the class. By working together to provide teacher and peer support for students, the class has begun to work together toward the same end.

Collaborative Consultation

Collaborative consultation is a term that has been widely used to describe a model of inclusion for students with learning disabilities. In this model, a specialist, such as the special educator, serves as a consultant for the classroom teacher regarding specific students. Likewise, the classroom teacher serves as a consultant with expertise in the workings of the classroom and observations of specific students while they are in her class. Thus, the "collaborative" part of it is that the two teachers work together to provide support services for the student in the general education classroom. As consultants with separate knowledge bases, they both contribute their expertise to educating students with special needs. Collaborative consultation occurs primarily behind the scenes, while teachers plan and consult outside of class. Consultation is mainly focused on developing adaptations and specific techniques for making required learning accessible to the students. This does not preclude the special educator from going into the class to provide in-class support for students, but it is not inherent in our definition of collaborative consultation.

Ms. Sullivan, at MCMS, the middle school described at the beginning of this chapter, provides a good example of collaborative consultation. She is assigned to seventh grade and works with content area teachers who have students who are served by special education in their classes. Remember that specific reading and writing skills are taught primarily in the language arts classes at this school. However, all teachers are expected to integrate ongoing reading and writing instruction into their content area instruction. Ms. Sullivan gave two 1-hour inservice presentations for the seventh-grade teachers at the beginning of the year. First, she gave ideas on how to integrate reading and writing instruction into the content areas, specifically for students with special learning needs. She helped them understand how important it is for these students to receive ongoing, contextualized instruction. The classroom teachers understood it was not their *primary* responsibility to teach basic literacy skills, but that they should provide what instruction they could and continually reinforce students' basic skills. Ms. Sullivan emphasized how important it would be for the teachers to communicate with her so that she could follow up on this skill building with students in their language arts classes. The classroom teachers would primarily provide incidental instruction. For example, when they had an in-class writing assignment, the teacher might provide suggestions for improving students' written answers, such as reminding them to use appropriate punctuation or encouraging them to elaborate on their ideas. She might also help them to organize their ideas into an outline or visual map before writing. In the second session, Ms. Sullivan helped the teachers develop accommodations and adaptations for students. She helped them to devise strategies for making difficult text accessible to students, including such ideas as breaking a long passage into smaller, comprehensible parts, using paired reading strategies, and introducing key words prior to reading. Some teachers thought giving students additional time to complete tasks might be beneficial. They discussed adaptations of tests and assignments and shared ideas that had worked in the past.

Ms. Sullivan worked with them to develop a monitoring system that would allow the students, parents, special education teacher, and classroom teachers to be informed of student progress and needs. All students in this school are required to carry notebook binders and write down their assignments. Ms. Sullivan designed a special assignment page for the students receiving support services to keep in their notebooks. The sheet had spaces for writing assignments in each subject daily and would be signed by teachers to acknowledge that the assignment had been written correctly. Parents would sign acknowledging that they have seen the work to be done. There were spaces for writing notes back and forth as well. For students who had behavior goals to work on, these spaces allowed teachers to write notes about the student's behavior in class. They discussed eventually fading out the required signatures as students became independent with the procedures.

Following the inservice sessions, Ms. Sullivan maintained ongoing communication with the teachers, students, and parents. She observed students in each content area class at least once a week. She had a checklist for teachers to fill in grades and to write notes about behavior or academic skills. The teachers became accustomed to filling these out and sticking them into her box every Friday. She met twice a week with each teacher to discuss students' progress and to troubleshoot any problems. And there were problems. Two students were consistently receiving failing grades despite modifications and supports. With one student, Ms. Sullivan was able to work out a satisfactory arrangement of additional accommodations, reduced assignments, and more parent involvment. With the other student, however, this was not possible. After much consultation with the student, teacher, and parents, Ms. Sullivan reluctantly arranged for a schedule change to try a different teacher for the student.

You can see that Ms. Sullivan provides a great deal of support for students via the classroom teachers. She has worked to help them to feel empowered to assist students in classes. By serving as a consultant for the content area classes, she is able to focus her instructional time for literacy skills in the language arts classes.

Teaming

Teaming, or including the special educator in a team effort to teach students with disabilities in an inclusive setting, is similar to the collaborative consultation described above. In a teaming approach to inclusion, the special educator participates as an equal partner in a team of teachers to plan and implement inclusion.

In fact, Ms. Sullivan also participates in the middle school teams at MCMS. You may recall that the teachers at this middle school are organized into teams that include the language arts, social studies, science, and math teachers to provide a more personalized and nurturing school environment for students. The MCMS teams also include the special education teacher. Each team teaches a cohort of students that rotate among these teachers. Teaming allows the teachers to plan together, coordinate and integrate their curriculum, work out scheduling, and, most importantly, to discuss individual students and address their specific needs. Ms. Sullivan participates as a team member on each of the three seventh-grade teams at the school. Ms. Sullivan's primary role is to provide consultation and support for the teachers regarding the students with disabilities. Attending the meetings keeps her informed about upcoming topics and events in each class. She is able to work with the group together to discuss students' needs and strategies for assisting them in class. Through the team meetings, she gathers information and involves the teachers in monitoring and writing IEP goals. She also provides informal assistance with other students who are having difficulty but are not receiving special education services. Her participation in the team has added a dimension of support for all students and the teachers have come to appreciate her expertise.

Direct Instruction in Classroom Context

No matter what model of inclusion a school adopts, teachers must decide how to provide direct instruction in literacy skills. Given that secondary students with learning disabilities typically experience serious reading and writing difficulties, and that they are most likely to be included in general education classes with high demands for literacy skills for the majority of the school day, this is a critical instructional need. Though many advocate for infusing skills instruction within the in-class support structure (e.g., while assisting students with classwork), we believe that short periods of direct, intensive instruction in reading and writing skills provides for optimal growth in students' skills.

The two schools described in this chapter have chosen different means of providing intensive instruction. At MCMS, the special education teachers provide literacy instruction within the inclusive language arts classes. The language arts classes use a workshop approach to teaching reading and writing. This means that, much of the time, the students are working independently or in small groups on reading or writing tasks. The classroom teacher and the special educator do not really team teach, rather they each carry out their distinct role in the class. The classroom teacher directs the whole-group activities, facilitates discussions, conferences with students, and teaches mini-lessons. The special educator works with individuals and small groups, conferences with students, teaches mini-lessons, and conducts assessment of individual student progress. Both teachers cover the same topic areas and core literature. Most of the class time is given to reading and writing workshop wherein students select their own books or write on their own. When the class reads a literature selection as a whole class activity, the students with special needs often join in but with support and adaptations.

At Clearwater High School, intensive skill instruction occurs during the period designated for special education instruction. All students have at least one period when they are not included with the general classes, but receive specialized instruction. The teachers and parents who participated in planning felt it was important to provide a time during the day for students to work closely with the specialist. The special education teachers organize their instructional time to address the skills of highest priority for each student. They realize the value of contextualizing instruction and often use reading passages from students' content area textbooks to illustrate concepts or skills. However, the intent of this period is not to assist with homework or class work. Instruction is based on ongoing diagnostic assessment and specifically addresses students' IEP goals. Instruction may occur individually or in small groups, depending on the students' current needs. To maintain interest and to avoid students "burning out" on drill activities, the instruction is fast-paced and activities change frequently. They divide the time between two or three skill areas per day (e.g., decoding, comprehension, sentence construction, spelling). Student progress is monitored on charts so that students may visualize their own successes.

Essential Elements of Secondary Inclusive Programs

In Chapter 1 we described what we believe are the essential elements of an inclusive model. Such elements as collaboration and community building are essential whether you are working in an elementary or secondary setting. In this section, we describe how some of these elements might occur in a secondary setting. We also describe some additional elements that we see as unique to the secondary setting.

The General Education Environment. Adopting an inclusive model may mean that some changes must take place in the general education environment to make it more responsive to individual students' needs. Schools that have offered an inclusive program for several years report this as a positive and welcome change (Dingle, Falvey, Givner, & Haager, 2004). Following are some specific aspects of how to change the general education environment.

Collaboration. Collaboration is an essential ingredient of an inclusive general education classroom. Whether the special educator is co-teaching or consulting behind the scenes, there must be a commitment to professional collaboration to ensure that students meet their learning goals and are successful in the general education environment. What does this look like in the secondary setting? Middle and high schools are often large, and teachers may not have close proximity or access to each other. Special educators may even have to get to know teachers they have only met in passing. It may be necessary in a secondary setting to formalize some of the collaborative activities by establishing regular meeting times, organizing subject area work groups or teams, and establishing a written communication system.

Establishing a Sense of Community. People generally feel more comfortable learning in an environment in which they feel supported and engaged. It is important for students with learning and behavioral challenges to feel they are part of a community. It is important to establish a classroom climate in which it is safe to allow others to provide support and in which it is acceptable to make mistakes or to learn differently. Establishing a positive and supportive classroom climate must begin with the teacher. Setting the tone for the class from the outset is important. In a classroom community, we must teach students to respect learning and to support each other in this endeavor. Such activities as setting personal learning goals and maintaining work portfolios are examples of ways to promote respect for learning. Recognizing students' accomplishments is another way of promoting a positive classroom climate. See Chapter 5 for more ideas about positive classroom management.

Students feel supported in schools that have a general sense of community. MCMS, the middle school described at the beginning of the chapter, went through a long process of community building as parents, teachers, administrators, students, and community leaders came together to plan and reorganize the school. The result was a sense of pride in the school community as well as a sense of belonging to something important. There are no formulae for attaining such a state, but we believe it will facilitate the development of an inclusive program.

Acceptance of Student Diversity. Diversity in the classroom is more than race or ethnicity. Students with and without disabilities have a wide range of abilities, interests, and needs. Therefore, a supportive general education classroom should accommodate and accept students' varying needs and abilities. General education teachers are required by law to accommodate a student's disability, but the attitude with which it is done can make a tremendous difference in the student's learning. Successful classrooms that we have observed are those in which the teacher acknowledges students' differences without negative comment or tone of voice. For example, a middle school teacher that we observed openly acknowledged her own challenges in spelling. She stopped mid-sentence while writing on the overhead projector and said aloud, "I'm not sure I spelled that right. You know I'm not a very good speller. We all have our strengths and weaknesses." This exemplifies the approach she takes with her students. She says she feels better about discussing students' learning challenges when she also openly recognizes their strengths. At another time she said about a student with a learning disability to his work group, "When you work out your assignment, think about each person's strengths. Ben, maybe you would like to do your research in this book because it is a topic you really know something about and this book is pretty readable." Ben was not upset about her offering an easy to read book or acknowledging his reading difficulties, because she also recognized his strength.

Establishing Peer Support. Peer support within the general education classroom is a delicate issue at the secondary level. Students with disabilities typically do not want to share their challenges with other students. They are mortified by the possibility that others may learn of their "condition." However, nondisabled students can be quite understanding and helpful given the right classroom conditions and facilitation by an understanding and tactful teacher.

Peer tutoring is one option for utilizing peers to support content area learning (see Chapter 4 for more information about how to implement this). Peer tutoring can be implemented in varying degrees of formality, ranging from a teacher spontaneously asking one student to help another with a specific concept to a set routine and formal arrangements for tutor training and methods. Notetaking assistance is one type of peer support that is often used in secondary classes. Some teachers purchase NCR paper that automatically creates a copy to give to the student needing assistance. Others provide ready access to a photocopy machine for the students.

Many middle and high schools now have peer mentors or peer leaders. These students learn valuable leadership skills as they encourage and assist students who are at risk in some way. Students with disabilities may benefit from such a program. In interviews conducted by one of the authors of this text with middle students who had just transitioned from the elementary school, the single greatest fear expressed by students was getting lost or not knowing the expected routine or rules in the new school. One student reported having to come to school during the summer to practice the physical route from class to class. Even then, he said he got lost several times. Further problems occurred when he had to go to his locker between two classes and he had not rehearsed the route that would take him by his locker. He got lost and was unable to ask for help. He simply went home because he could think of no other solution. Another student reported feeling uncomfortable during lunch when students had free time. He didn't want to go outside with the other students because he didn't know anyone and felt unable to join in. He waited in the hallway for over a half hour every day for several weeks. These are instances in which a peer mentor could be very helpful. Peer mentors might facilitate movement into and out of activities or might introduce students who seem to be having difficulty with making social contacts. They might also check on students daily or weekly.

Providing Options for Demonstrating Competence. We believe that students with limited or emerging skills in some areas (such as academics) need opportunities to demonstrate their strengths in other areas. All students have areas of strength, and it is from these that they develop their identities. Adolescence is a time in which students are learning about and establishing their identities. One challenge for students with learning and behavioral problems is having opportunities to develop areas of strength. Students with learning challenges often spend more time than other students on their schoolwork. Yet, during middle and high school, it is important for these students to develop important life skills that lead to later careers and adult pursuits. In the next chapter on transition planning, you will see how important this is.

Shared Responsibility for Student Learning. A recent popular book stated that it takes a village to raise a child. In our perspective of an inclusive secondary program, it takes a school, and perhaps a community, to support students with disabilities. Inclusive schools make a commitment to ensuring that all students learn. This means teamwork and shared responsibility. The IEP team is based on this concept and nowhere is it as important as it is in the secondary setting. With multiple social and academic forces working on students, team planning is essential to ensuring student success. The student is of course the first and foremost member of the responsible parties. With family and community support, special and general education teachers must work together to provide the needed support.

Professional Development. We discussed professional development in Chapter 1 as an important component for a successful inclusive school. General and special education teachers who engage in ongoing professional development develop the processes, routines, and skills for implementation of inclusive practices. For many secondary teachers, this is an important factor in fostering the right attitude toward making the necessary changes. Teachers who have not had experience in an inclusive setting may not be unwilling to move to an inclusive model, but they may lack the ability to envision it. Through ongoing planning and professional development, teachers learn to adjust.

Special Education Services. Students who are in special education receive special education services, regardless of where actual instruction takes place. These services can be the accommodations that are made to instruction or to the curriculum, the planning that is involved in preparing for instruction, the behavior modification strategies that are implemented in order to be able to provide instruction, or the extra support provided to help the student to learn at his or her maximum potential.

Provide a Range of Service Options. Students with mild disabilities have very unique needs. Even those who may be classified with the same category of disability may not require the same services in order to achieve their maximum learning potential. It is important that a teacher does not create a standard mold into which each exceptional student is expected to fit. Each student must be monitored on an ongoing basis to determine what services are appropriate, ranging from simple consultation with a special education teacher to collaborative teaching to a separate learning environment for most of the daily instruction.

Teach Teachers to Teach Students, Not Just Subjects. Secondary education teachers are trained to specialize in particular subject areas. While this makes them highly skilled professionals in their areas of expertise, they may tend to see their role in the classroom as an expert in a subject area rather than an expert instructor. While elementary education majors are taught primarily how to teach, secondary education majors focus more on the subject that they will be teaching. Because of this, some secondary education teachers may not have as much training in teaching to various learning styles, adapting curriculum to fit the needs of the students, or teaching to the student as a whole person rather than just the part that is seated in that classroom.

Establish Opportunities for Skill Development. Regardless of what class the student is in at the time, there are certain skills that should always be in development, particularly in special education students. These students should always be developing their reading and writing skills. Additionally, students should be developing critical-thinking and problem-solving skills. It is important that the IEP goals for students are implemented into whatever lesson is being taught; these skills often cross over and go beyond the scope of particular subjects.

Provide Support for Core Curriculum. Support for the core curriculum can take place during actual instruction. A teacher may work directly with the student either one-to-one or in a small group to provide more direct instruction or further explanation of subject matter. Students may also provide support in the form of cooperative learning or peer tutoring. The student may be allowed to move through the curriculum at a slower pace in order to be able to learn the same things that are being taught to the rest of the class. Modified materials may be provided to help the student with disabilities access the curriculum. The curriculum may be adapted to be on a level that is realistically achievable for the student.

These are all modifications that take place during actual instruction. Some support takes place behind the scenes. Support can be provided in the form of collaborative planning with the general education teacher on how instruction can be provided to students with disabilities. When the special education teacher serves as a consultant, he or she aids in the creation or collection of supplemental materials that will support the curriculum and make it more accessible to diverse learners. In addition, the special education teacher may meet with the students in a small group or one-to-one to discuss individual difficulties in the subject areas. Discussions of how to apply general study skills and strategies to specific areas of instruction can be beneficial in improving their ability to learn the curriculum.

Coordinate Services. When students with disabilities are placed in inclusion settings, teachers may not be aware of what services they are to be receiving. One of the roles of the special education teacher should be to work with the student and the general education teachers to coordinate services. If modifications or adaptations are to be made, teachers may need assistance implementing such measures into the classroom. Each teacher who is working with the student should be provided with a copy of the student's goals and objectives from the IEP to be sure that these goals are being included into plans for instruction. Additionally, strategies and timelines for meeting these goals should be provided by the special education teacher.

Engage in Co-Planning. If special education teachers and general education teachers plan for instruction together, the plans can be based on both expertise in subject matter and expertise in presenting material to various learners. Both the selection of goals and objectives to be taught and the decision as to what activities are to be used for instruction should be planned with the needs of all students in mind. If the subject area teacher is not assisted in planning for making the information accessible to all students, he or she is less likely to make such efforts a priority. Co-planning should take place on a regular basis, depending on the level of need.

Build Flexibility into the Model. It is important to realize that even the best of plans will not necessarily work out as planned. The most important aspect of a plan is that it is not set in stone. Things will go wrong. Students will not necessarily master material at the pace or sequence that a teacher might expect. If the model of services is rigid, it is likely to break down at the first glitch. It is important to maintain flexibility to allow for differences in learning rates of various students as well as unforeseen interruptions throughout the school year. Middle and high school classes are frequently subject to changes due to activities such as assemblies, standardized tests, and field trips. This may cause a break in the flow of learning that may lead to the need for additional time for the student to get back on track.

Schedule Time for Collaboration. Secondary education teachers are extremely busy people. Between class sizes and the amount of paperwork that students turn in at this level, if collaborating is left to take place during spare time, it will not likely take place at all. Standard teacher planning time is often fully utilized just for planning for regular instruction. If teachers are forced to collaborate with special education teachers on their own time, or in place of their time to plan for the class as whole, they will either cease to collaborate or become highly resentful of the extra work involved in meeting the needs of the special education students. It is important that time is made available to these teachers for collaboration, as this is an integral part of successful inclusion.

Use Effective Discipline and Behavior Support Strategies. Regardless of the label that is put on special education students, by the time they get to middle and high school, many of these students have some sort of behavioral or emotional issues that can interfere with their learning. This is often caused by years of failure at academics, low behavioral expectations placed upon them, or poor role models in special education classes. Part of the role of the special education teacher is to provide the general education teacher with support in handling these issues.

Behavior management is best accomplished in a proactive manner. By engaging in positive classroom management, many behavior problems can be prevented before they start, therefore avoiding unnecessary or unsuccessful discipline. Three basic premises to remember in implementing positive classroom management (adapted from DiGiulio, 2000) include that (1) students who feel successful are seldom behavior problems; (2) to feel successful, students must actually be successful, (3) to actually be successful, a student must first do something of value.

These premises can help to explain why so many special education students are behavior problems, particularly in the secondary grades. After years of being unsuccessful in the classroom, struggling to complete tasks that they are aware have been watered down to fit lower expectations, these students simply have no reason to behave. When students feel value in the work that they are doing and believe that their teachers believe in them, behavior problems disappear and there is little need for discipline at all.

Provide Social Support. Another side effect of years in the special education system are often problems with socialization. As stated earlier in the chapter, these years are socially challenging for all students. Students who have exceptionalities often have an even more difficult time fitting in or reading social cues. Combine this with the low self-concept that many of these students often have due to years of being unsuccessful in school, and a real need for support becomes apparent.

Some students with disabilities need to be explicitly taught social skills that are second nature to other students. These are best taught in a private setting where their peers will not be aware that such instruction is occurring. Role-playing and practicing scripts for social situations can be helpful for students.

Family Support for Learning. The family is typically less involved in the special education process as the students reach the older grades. Unfortunately, the need for family support and a team approach does not decrease as the child ages, it is just not as often present. Because many families are often detached, the team approach becomes that much more essential. A support system of teachers, counselors, and other role models within the school will provide the student with a network of adults to turn to. This team should also work on keeping open lines of communication with family members and continually pursuing increased parental involvement. The team should be available to families as a resource to provide information about services.

Preparation for Adult Life. A key element of the secondary special education program is planning for adult life. Transition planning should begin in the early middle school years and become more specific as the student gets older. The overall goal of any instruction should be preparing the student to function as independently as possible, because most students' support ends at graduation. The special education teacher should work with the student on setting realistic career and educational goals. The level of support that students receive should gradually be decreased as appropriate throughout the high school years to help the students to become more autonomous.

LITERACY INSTRUCTION IN SECONDARY INCLUSIVE SETTINGS

By the time students with mild disabilities reach adolescence, most have already received years of remedial instruction in basic literacy skills. Yet, most adolescents with learning disabilities or behavior disorders continue to experience serious reading and writing difficulties well into the secondary grades and even into adulthood (Bender, 1985; Deshler, Schumaker, & Lenz, 1984; Deshler, Warner, Schumaker, & Alley, 1983; Gregory, Shanahan, & Walberg, 1985; Mercer, 1997; White, 1992). When you consider the increased demand for literacy skills in secondary settings, it is easier to understand the high dropout rate of 40 to 60 percent for adolescents with learning disabilities or behavior disorders. What, then, can we do to increase students' reading and writing skills and better prepare them for the challenges of secondary classrooms?

Contextualizing Reading and Writing Instruction

In the early years of instruction, students are learning to read and write. At some point, the focus of instruction shifts to reading and writing to learn; that is, instruction that specifies how to use reading and writing skills to facilitate learning. Secondary students with reading and writing difficulties need explicit instruction in strategies that help them use their reading and writing abilities. Students must learn how to use their literacy skills to learn in content area classes as well as in lifelong learning. They need to view reading and writing as a means for learning rather than as the end in itself. As students go through the secondary grades, their reading and writing load increases as textbooks and written assignments become the major sources of learning. Students need to become efficient at taking in and producing written information. It is important for adolescents to think of reading and writing as tools that are useful in their daily lives. For many students, adolescence is a time of questioning—questioning authority and world order, questioning their own place in the world, questioning the value of learning. As one author's daughter expressed while doing a page of dividing decimals for homework, "This is really stupid! When am I ever going to have to divide decimals in my life?" It certainly is easier to point out the utility of being able to read and write than it is to justify dividing decimals.

Contextualizing reading and writing instruction is one way to help students see the importance of reading and writing. When skills are developed within the context of learning for content area classes, students are able to apply their skills directly to required reading or written assignments. For example, using a required social studies chapter to instruct students in finding the main idea allows the students to see a direct link between the skill and its application. Using science vocabulary words to illustrate a strategy for decoding is another example. Instruction in paragraph construction might occur in the context of assisting a student with a written assignment for another class. Earlier in the chapter we discussed the dilemma of balancing skills instruction with subject area support to help students succeed in classes. The idea of contextualizing literacy instruction helps resolve this dilemma. Here, the idea is to integrate the two efforts by addressing specific skills while helping students with classwork.

Because special educators are expected to document their instruction related to IEP goals and objectives and to monitor students' progress toward the goals, it is helpful to document this type of instruction. Keeping a charting system or other type of log helps to keep track of instruction and student progress. This helps the teacher to see the instruction as having a long-term benefit: that is, working toward IEP goals rather than short-term tasks such as helping with today's assignment.

Assessment to Guide Instruction in Reading and Writing

In this section, we will discuss some assessment strategies and tools that will assist the special educator and classroom teacher in planning appropriate reading and writing instruction. Effective special educators are equipped with an array of strategies, tools, and techniques to determine students' specific instructional needs. Assessment should be ongoing, dynamic, and tailored to suit the individual and the subject area of interest. Standardized assessment instruments generally are not very useful in planning instruction. Mostly, they provide a score or set of scores that tell us how the individual is performing as compared to a normative sample. However, a few standardized assessment tools do provide instructionally relevant information in addition to the normative data. These will be mentioned as appropriate, but primarily this section will illustrate curriculum-based and authentic means of assessment.

Direct Observation of Reading and Writing. Most seasoned reading specialists and special education teachers will ask a new student to read aloud and to provide a writing sample as one of the first means of gathering information about a student's abilities. Further information may be gathered by observing the student in various types of learning tasks over a few days' time. The teacher may observe a student in social studies class during a reading task and may collect a written work sample. Observation during a different class may confirm or disconfirm any clues gathered previously or may reveal patterns of reading and writing difficulties. This is a rather informal, yet informative, way to ascertain important diagnostic information. To document this type of data gathering, teachers often use checklists to guide their observation. Figure 10.1 illustrates a reading checklist used

Student's Name ____________________ Date ____________________

Name of Observer ____________________ Class ____________________

Oral Reading Habits	**Yes**	**No**	**Notes:**
Uses conversational tone	___	___	
Reads rhythmically	___	___	
Keeps his or her place while reading	___	___	
Stays focused while reading	___	___	
Reads at an acceptable rate	___	___	
Repeats words or sentences	___	___	
Uses finger to mark place	___	___	
Attends to punctuation	___	___	
Attempts to decode unknown words	___	___	
Miscues common words	___	___	
Attempts to self-correct mistakes	___	___	
Appears calm while reading	___	___	
Completes assigned text	___	___	

Comments:

FIGURE 10.1 Reading Checklist

with middle and high school students. There are many informal checklists in schools as well as published materials. Teachers often make up their own or use those they have borrowed from another teacher.

Checklists are an easy way to assess basic reading abilities. Because they are quick and easy, teachers can be documenting student progress on a checklist without the knowledge of the students. Checklists are easy to create and can be tailored to be broad or specific. A teacher can create a checklist to find out information about various aspects of reading ranging from behaviors exerted during reading time to information recalled from a reading passage. The same checklist can be used over the course of time by marking the date on a new column each time it is used. This affords teachers the opportunity to chart student progress.

Ongoing observation is also useful for monitoring students' progress. When teachers observe students using specific skills repeatedly over time, they check off the skills on a checklist or record sheet and date it to indicated mastery. It is not necessary to always use a test or construct an artificial task to document mastery. Teachers' observations are valid sources of information.

Informal Assessment of Reading. There are several ways to conduct an informal assessment of reading in secondary settings. By observing a student reading, the teacher is able to learn about an individual student's strengths and needs in word recognition, reading rate and fluency, and comprehension. However, the teacher should be aware of the potential for a secondary student to resist reading aloud. By the time students are in secondary settings, most of their reading is done silently. Secondary students, especially those with reading difficulties, may feel awkward reading aloud for the purpose of assessment. One way to avoid this is to conduct the assessment in an isolated area completely away from other students. Explaining the purpose of the reading task may help to ease students' concerns; they are more likely to participate if rapport has been established and the student has a sense of trust.

Many reading specialists and special educators use *informal reading inventories* (IRIs) to assess students' reading skills. This is a very useful and instructionally relevant assessment tool. The IRI allows the teacher to conduct an *error analysis,* or analyze the nature and frequency of students' errors in reading. It also provides a means for determining reading levels of students in order to place them in graded materials. There are several commercially available IRIs, such as Burns' and Roe's *Informal Reading Inventory* (1989) and Leslie's and Caldwell's *Qualitative Reading Inventory* (1990). IRIs contain two to three passages at each reading level, usually 100 words long for ease of scoring, and accompanying comprehension questions. Most also include graded word lists to be used for assessing word recognition level and for deciding where to begin with the reading passages. The teacher may assess oral or silent reading ability, but only oral reading provides clues to students' word recognition difficulties. The passages may also be used for assessing listening comprehension. Most IRIs include scoring forms to record students' responses and to determine reading level. The IRI can be given in one sitting, beginning with word lists to assess word recognition and to determine a starting level for the graded passages. When a student's word reading falls below a set criterion, usually 70 percent, the word lists are stopped. The entry level for the reading passages is one grade level below the highest word list read successfully. However, if a student struggles with a reading passage, the teacher should drop to a lower passage or, if the student breezes through a passage, the teacher may want to skip ahead. IRIs can become tedious when the entry level is not determined easily. For oral passage reading, the teacher records the type of errors (see the error analysis section below) and counts the number of words read correctly. Usually a score of 85 to 100 percent is considered the student's *independent reading level,* 75 to 85 percent is considered the student's *instructional reading level,* and below 75 percent is considered *frustration level,* or the level of difficulty at which a student would experience frustration due to lack of meaningful reading. Each IRI may use different criteria, so the teacher should consult the teacher instructions. Some teachers like to assess both oral and silent reading. This is why the IRIs usually contain two to three passages at each level. Other teachers may use the passages for an indication of oral word recognition and use only silent reading for the passages. In this instance, you lose information about how the student reads words in context, but you may save time. It is up to the teacher to determine the time allotted for the task and how important the oral reading information is.

An alternative to using commercially prepared IRIs, which are often artificial, or removed from authentic secondary reading tasks, is to collect passages at a few different levels of difficulty. Some teachers will mark off a 100-word passage for ease of determining percentage of words read correctly and will score directly on a photocopied passage. Others will ask the student to read for a short time and just conduct an error analysis (see next section), make notes about fluency and rate of reading, and will ask comprehension questions. This more informal method provides equally useful information, provided the teacher has the experience and awareness of reading levels to identify passages at different levels of difficulty.

We have one cautionary note about using informal reading assessments. Whether using a commercially available IRI or an informal assessment from reading passages at different levels, we encourage teachers to note students' strengths as well as weak skill areas. The Burns and Roe IRI (1989) scoring sheet offers the teacher spaces for indicating student strengths as well as weak areas. Knowing students' strengths helps teachers to make instructional decisions about subject areas or tasks that students may be able to do independently in an inclusive classroom. This information is just as valuable as knowing the weak areas that need remediation. It is also a healthy teacher practice to continually focus on students' strengths as well as needs. This influences teachers' attitudes and teacher–student interactions in positive, growth-oriented ways. Teachers who attend to and discuss students' errors and weaknesses continually give the student the message that he or she is "flawed" or incompetent.

Error Analysis. Given the cautionary note above about examining students' strengths, we still must have an efficient means of examining students' reading or writing errors in order to tailor instruction to suit students' needs. *Error analysis,* often referred to as *miscue analysis* in reading, provides such a method. Error analysis involves categorizing or typing students' errors, looking for patterns or consistencies that may be addressed in instruction. Some students with reading difficulties consistently misread words, substituting a word for the correct one. This is called a *substitution* error and may indicate that the student is not looking at the whole word when reading but is relying on beginning letters or sheer guesswork to figure out words. Some students may insert words that are not there, or make *insertion* errors. Another type of error is an *omission*, or leaving out a word. A *reversal* is reading words in an incorrect order. Students may not attempt an unknown word, and this is scored as a *nonresponse*. In this case, the teacher should supply the word so that the student may continue to gain meaning from the text. Figure 10.2 shows each of these types of reading errors and how they would be scored. The scoring system in Figure 10.2 is one that we have used. Of course, there are variations of it in use, and teachers should use a system that is familiar or comfortable. The important point is to be systematic in the manner of scoring so that you can go back to an assessment at a later date and still understand the types of errors that were made.

Progress Charts. Perhaps even more important than how much students know right now is how much progress they have made. This is especially true in the case of students with disabilities: What they are able to do compared to their peers may not seem like a success story; the success is in comparing themselves now to themselves earlier this school year. Progress charts show records of what the student is accomplishing over time. Results can be placed on a graph to get an actual picture of improvement.

Spontaneous Writing Samples. An authentic form of assessment is the use of actual writing samples that students have produced. This provides real evidence of what they are able to do. Students with disabilities often have anxiety about being assessed, probably because they have a history of performing poorly on tests and are well aware of this. Often a truer indication of their abilities lies in the actual writing that they put forth in class. This is not limited to writing for their language arts class, but rather any class in which they are writing (and as stated earlier, all students should have writing opportunities in all classes).

The following sentences are excerpted from passages that were read by seventh graders with learning disabilities. For each sentence below, the handwritten responses indicate the teacher's record of the student's responses.

Type of Error	Sentence with teacher's record marks
Substitution	Mark fell off the dock and went in the ~~water~~. (wait)
Insertion	The captain called out ↑ to the first mate. (loud)
Omission	The air was thick with ~~black~~ smoke.
Reversal	. . . in a calm manner
Hesitation	// When the scout shouted, . .

FIGURE 10.2 Error Analysis of a Reading Passage

Building Reading Skills

In this section, we will discuss instruction to improve students' reading skills in secondary inclusive settings. Instruction for individual students should always be based on assessment data and should directly address students' identified areas of need. Thus far in this chapter, we have built a case for approaching skills instruction in two ways: (1) embedding it in content area instruction in the inclusive classroom and (2) providing intensive, in-depth skills instruction in short periods of time, either in the inclusive classroom or in another, more private, setting.

When skills instruction is embedded in content area instruction, it does not mean that it should be happenstance, or incidental, instruction. Rather, it should be planned and deliberate in its focus on IEP goals and objectives. For example, a special educator may decide to focus on the specific comprehension skill of recognizing cause-and-effect relationships for a one-week period. When reading the social studies textbook, the teacher may assist the student in charting the events that are causes and those that are the effects. The same could be done in science or in literature reading in language arts. The special educator should document the instruction and chart the student's progress in a lesson plan book or teacher log.

For students with serious deficits in reading and writing skills, we advocate for at least one period per day of intensive, skill-building instruction. Though it is possible for this to be done in the inclusive setting, as the middle school described at the beginning of the chapter does in language arts classes, there are often barriers to providing intensive, skills instruction in a typical general classroom. This type of instruction is best done either one to one or in a very small group. It also requires intense concentration. It is often difficult to pull students aside in an inclusive classroom and to remove the distractions of the normal classroom events. It is also embarrassing to some students to be pulled aside to work on specific skills, particularly when it requires reading aloud or sounding out words. Even in the middle school described above where skills instruction for the students with special needs occurs in the language arts classes where they are doing Readers' and Writers' Workshop, the special educator pulls individual students into an isolated spot where they can have some privacy for short periods of time. This does not occur every day, nor for the entire period. The teachers have created two separated areas of the room, in opposite corners, where they do individual conferencing with students. They can maintain eye contact with the entire class, while talking privately with individual students.

Phonological Skills Development. While phonological skills development typically is mastered in the early elementary grades, for many students with reading disabilities, this is a process that is still glaringly deficient when they reach the upper grades. Many middle and high school students with disabilities lack the ability to "sound words out" or "spell it like it sounds." Phonological skills are best taught through direct instruction, but it is a difficult task to teach phonics to older students in a way that is age appropriate and not embarrassing to the student who already has little confidence in his or her reading abilities.

One strategy that has been found to work with older students is the use of alliterations (McCormick, 1999). These are sentences in which most words begin with the same sounds: for example, *Mark made many men mix milkshakes.* The use of alliterations draws attention to letter sounds yet still leaves room for the lesson to be adapted to the age level of the students. Another strategy is to use the lyrics of songs to point out rhyming sounds at the end of words.

For students who are lacking decoding skills, rather than teaching them to decode using words that are clearly "babyish" or intended for younger readers, one strategy is to use nonsense words and syllables (Baker & Irwin, 1989). These words should be words that are spelled as they sound and can initially be monosyllabic. If the students are aware that the words are nonsense words, they will be less likely to focus on trying to guess what the word says and will actually try to use decoding skills to read the words. Examples include words such as "ag," "stig," "saft," "lep," and can get as complex as "confatrigation."

In addition to activities such as these, it is still important to directly teach consonant and vowel sounds. Also, special letter combinations such as "kn," "gh," and "wr" should be explicitly taught as exceptions to the rules. Word walls can be used around a special education resource room that list words in word family groups. In inclusive settings, this might be transferred onto a notebook-page-size laminated insert for students to keep in their notebooks as they travel from class to class. Graphics can be used next to words to help students recognize them, but it is important that these pictures are not drawn at a level that represents an elementary classroom. Magazine pictures or certain computer graphics are more appropriate. High interest materials should be selected for practice activities. Middle and high school students would (and rightfully so) be offended by typical phonics workbooks that were designed by picture selection and font style for kindergarten and first-grade classrooms.

Vocabulary Development. One of the main components of being able to read is to understand what the words on the paper mean. By developing vocabulary, what is being read will have understandable meaning to the students and therefore will be more readily read. McCormick (1999) has developed three conclusions about vocabulary instruction:

1. Instruction should combine several methods for presenting meanings. By combining tasks such as providing the definition, providing context clues, and providing examples, there is an increased likelihood of a complete understanding being obtained.
2. Instruction should include activities that actively involve students in sorting out relationships between words. Mere memorization of definitions is not enough to have deep processing of word meanings. Students must be aware of both denotative and connotative meanings of words.
3. Students must be repeatedly exposed to words and encounter them while they are reading to truly understand them.

It is not enough to merely present students a list of vocabulary words each week and then test them on Friday. They must actually work with these words, see these words in print, process these words, and study relationships between these and other words. An example of one way to involve students in the study of words is through the use of a vocabulary packet (see Figure 10.3). This is an example of an assignment that a high school teacher distributes to her students each Monday. The students then complete each of the tasks listed by Friday. The words are chosen from the literature that the students will be exposed

Weekly Vocabulary Assignment

Check off each box as you complete the assignment, and turn all of your work in on Friday with this sheet stapled to the front.

Copy your words here.

________________________ ________________________

________________________ ________________________

________________________ ________________________

________________________ ________________________

________________________ ________________________

______ (20 points) Write the dictionary definition for each word.

______ (15 points) Write each word in a meaningful sentence.

______ (10 points) List a synonym for each word if appropriate.

______ (10 points) List an antonym for each word if appropriate.

______ (10 points) Write each word five times.

______ (20 points) Create a short story using all of this week's words plus ten words from previous weeks.

______ (15 points) Write each word on flashcards with definitions on the back. (Use these cards to study your words and keep them in your box after the test.)

______ Total points

Sample Critical Reading Activity

Introducing the New Sport Speedster
Voted Car of the Year by the New Press
Sleek, gorgeous styling
Goes from 0–60 in 3.5 seconds
Available in red, yellow, and black
The sweetest car you'll ever drive
Truly a must-have!

FIGURE 10.3 Vocabulary Packet

(continued)

Use the advertisement above to answer the following questions:

1. What is the **purpose** of this advertisement?

____

____

2. List three **facts** about the Sport Speedster.

____

____

a) ______________________________

b) ______________________________

c) ______________________________

3. List three **opinions** about the Sport Speedster.

a) ______________________________

b) ______________________________

c) ______________________________

4. Create two more fact statements and two more opinion statements about the Sport Speedster

Facts	Opinions
______________	______________
______________	______________
______________	______________

5. Is an advertisement a good way to get all of your information about a product? Explain why or why not.

____

____

____

____

____

____

FIGURE 10.3 Continued

to during that week. The words used are not forgotten on Friday, but rather they are kept in active use throughout the remainder of the school year.

Reading Comprehension. In order to comprehend what they are reading, students must be able to understand each sentence that is read as well as paragraphs as a whole. They must be able to take the information from the paragraph and summarize it in their minds so that the important points of the entire reading passage can be understood and remembered. To make passages more comprehensible to students, certain strategies should take place before, during, and after the reading of text.

By the time students reach the upper grades, they have the benefit of life experience to draw upon. If the teacher can teach her students to activate and utilize their prior knowledge when approaching a reading passage, this life experience can actually help the students to understand what they are reading. This is a strategy that should take place before the text is read. The title, heading, or first sentence should be read, and then whatever prior knowledge students mention should be activated. Students need to be taught to use this strategy on their own whenever they read. By already having some ideas present about a topic, the ability to recognize ideas and use context clues should increase.

In addition to activating prior knowledge, many of the strategies discussed in Chapter 9 of this textbook can be utilized in the intensive reading classroom. These strategies ensure that the student is actively participating in the reading process. By developing questions, predicting, summarizing, and clarifying, students are forced to comprehend the reading. Reading passages can either be from the text that is assigned in subject area classes or from special reading books designed to be at the instructional reading level of the student while still being of high interest to older learners. One example of such a series is the *Developing Reading Strategies* series published by Steck Vaughn.

Critical Reading. There is more to reading than simply reading and understanding what has been read. Baker and Irwin (1989) define critical reading as "analyzing and evaluating the ideas expressed in the text." One skill that critical readers have is the ability to distinguish fact from opinion and reality from fiction. Additionally, they are able to make judgments about the credibility of the material and detect things such as propaganda, fallacies of reasoning, and emotionally laden words. Critical readers can determine the author's purpose for writing and evaluate what has been written.

Critical reading skills are particularly important in secondary education due to the types of text that students are often exposed to, as well as many of the types of questions on standardized tests at that level. Additionally, critical reading skills enable the student to thoroughly understand and evaluate text. Of course, these skills are particularly difficult for students with disabilities because it is hard to be thinking critically about what is being read when struggling to merely decode or understand the words on the page. Students with little expertise in reading often assume that everything they read must be true and sensible.

Critical reading skills must be explicitly taught to these students. Some good materials to use with older students include newspapers and magazine articles. Particularly useful are advertisements, editorials, and classifieds. Have students look for facts first and then determine which statements are opinions. Students can also determine the author's purpose for writing and evaluate what they think of what is written. Keep in mind that students' evaluations of what they have read may vary, and it is essential that various ideas and answers are encouraged and accepted as correct. Critical reading is a good way for students to develop critical thinking skills in general and it is important not to limit the creativity or ingenuity of their answers. For a sample critical reading activity to use with older students, see Figure 10.3.

Literature. In the secondary schools, most language arts classes today use literature-based instruction. That is to say, the concepts that are being taught about the English language are done in the context of literature that is being read as a class. Many school districts have established guidelines for the number of books that students are expected to read each semester. Since the recommended reading list contains books that are on grade level for the student, it is often very challenging for the student with disabilities to be able to read and understand such books. There are a few ways that the special education teacher can help a student to overcome this obstacle.

One way that a student can read the same book as his or her nondisabled peers is to find an adapted version of the text. Many famous books are available on reading levels ranging from grade 2 through grade 5. Steck Vaughn publishes a complete line of classic novels at the third- and fourth-grade reading level. For severely delayed readers, this can be one way to provide access to the same stories, but obviously a drawback is that at this reading level, they are missing much of the vocabulary and text structure that is present in the actual stories.

Another option is to have the book read on tape. Many books are already available on tape through Books for the Blind. Any book, however, can be read onto a tape by a teacher, aide, or other willing party. For many students, hearing the book on tape and reading along in their copy will make accessing the literature more feasible. It is important while using this strategy that the text is used in conjunction with the recording.

Finally, the same literature can be used (although the reading level may be well above frustration for the student) with intensive support from the special education teacher. Either in a very small group or one-to-one, the teacher and student can read the book together (the teacher will probably have to do most of the reading aloud with the student), stopping very frequently and implementing various decoding, vocabulary, and reading comprehension strategies such as the ones discussed in this textbook. The advantage to this option is that the student is exposed to the same text as his or her peers, but this will only work if it is truly an intensive remedial situation.

Reading for Memory. Since most of the information taught in secondary settings is presented through text, it is essential that older readers be able to remember what they have read in order to appropriately learn the material. The small group intensive reading setting is the ideal place to teach students strategies to use while reading that help them to remember the information.

Highlighting is a strategy that all older learners should employ when reading text. Many students have trouble highlighting selectively. This strategy is useless if the wrong information (or in many cases all of the information) is highlighted. In order to effectively highlight, students should be taught to read through the passage one time first. Then they are to reread and begin underlining only key ideas from sentences rather than the complete sentence. Use different color highlighters for the passage with one color representing the main idea and another color for important details about that concept. Since most students are not allowed to highlight directly in textbooks, be sure that photocopies of the sections that will be read are provided so that students can highlight on these copies while they are in your class.

Another strategy that older learners should all be employing while reading for memory is notetaking. Like highlighting, this strategy will be ineffective if the students do not take notes on the *important* details. One system that can help students to realize which details are important is the use of power notes. Similar to outlining, numbers are used to represent levels of detail. Power 1 details are the main ideas. Power 2 details support power 1s, power 3s support power 2s, and power 4s support power 3s. To teach this concept, it is easier to begin with words preselected by the teacher rather than starting with the actual text. An example of levels of power is as follows:

Power 1 Clothing
  Power 2 shirts
    Power 3 sweatshirt
    Power 3 blouse
  Power 2 pants
    Power 3 jeans
      Power 4 Calvin Klein jeans
    Power 3 slacks
      Power 4 Levi's Dockers

Once the student has mastered organizing individual words, begin with simple text and work your way up to sections from actual textbooks.

Building Writing Skills

Writing skills should not be isolated from reading skills, rather they should be taught together. The two most important aspects to developing writing skills are to provide students with exposure to and opportunities for writing. This is a skill that truly needs to be practiced. Also, direct instruction of the mechanics of writing is necessary. Writing is covered in great depth in Chapter 7, but we include it here to focus exclusively on secondary instructional issues.

Opportunities for Writing. Students should be given opportunities to write in all areas of instruction. The more practice students have at writing, the more their writing will improve. Any written assignments for subject-area classes should be seen as opportunities to develop the writing skills of students with disabilities. In an intensive remedial class, students should be given opportunities to practice various types of writing.

Journals are a great place to enable students to practice writing without fear of receiving poor grades for scarce writing abilities. Even at the high school level, nonwriters can use pictures and invented spellings to begin putting ideas onto paper. It is through continued exposure to writing that students will become confident enough to put words on paper.

Learning logs also provide students with opportunities to practice writing. Learning logs are different from journals in that logs are directly related to topics that the student is learning rather than simply as an open arena for writing. They can be used in every subject area and provide an opportunity to students to reflect on what they have learned. It can also be used as a safe place for students to jot down questions about things they did not understand that they would prefer to discuss with the teacher in a more private moment.

At the secondary level, it is inevitable that research papers will be assigned in various subject areas. Such assignments could be the basis of some of the writing in the special education class. The special education teacher can help the students develop their writing skills while they are putting their ideas together for such papers. This writing should take place in various formats: prewriting, writing the first draft, revising, editing, and publishing.

Writing Mechanics. Although students should be given the opportunity to write freely, and without fear of dreaded red marks across the page, there is still the need for direct instruction in writing mechanics. One of the best ways that students can learn about writing mechanics is by reading many different examples of well-written work.

Direct instruction is also necessary in teaching the proper form of writing. Many students with disabilities need to be explicitly taught how to write properly. Oftentimes, these students have little confidence in their ability to write and are apprehensive to even put words on the paper. By providing the student with strategies and structured support, they will gain this confidence and hopefully transfer these skills into independent writing in all subject areas.

Literacy-Related Strategy Instruction

Strategic Reading. When students are strategic readers, they are able to utilize the reading strategies that they have been taught in order to help them to read and understand text. They utilize metacognitive strategies and are aware of their purpose for reading.

Writing Strategies. For many students, the biggest problem they face when writing is the feeling of not knowing where to begin. Providing the student with prompts for paragraphs and essays can help students to overcome that feeling and begin putting their thoughts on paper. To assist students in writing paragraphs, they should be taught how to use a structured paragraph model and the transition words used to tie all of the thoughts together.

Structured Paragraph Model. This model teaches students to write a five-sentence paragraph. The first sentence is the introductory sentence and is usually the main idea or topic sentence. Then the student writes three sentences that are details to support the introductory sentence. Finally, the student closes the paragraph with a conclusion statement, which usually restates the main topic of the paragraph and wraps up the ideas.

To make an essay out of this model, students follow the same format as they would a paragraph, only instead of five sentences, they create five paragraphs. The first paragraph is the introductory paragraph that introduces what the essay will be about. The second, third, and fourth paragraphs are the body of the essay, which contains the details of the writing. The fifth paragraph is a conclusion paragraph that ties all of the ideas together.

While this model can be a useful to tool for beginning writers, it is by no means intended to be used as a restriction for students who are able to write in other ways. It should also be phased out as students become stronger writers. This is not a strategy intended to be used permanently in students' writing.

Transition Words. For students who are unsure how to start their sentences or how to make sentences flow together into complete paragraphs, transition words are a tool that can be quite useful. These words are usually the first word in a sentence. Once the student has the first word written, she will often find it easier to put the rest of her thoughts down on paper. Transition words can also make a list of sentences seem to hang together as a paragraph. Read the sentences that follow: *Roll the dough out onto a pan. Spread sauce over the dough. Sprinkle cheese on top. Place it in the oven. Bake it for 20 minutes. You have pizza.* While the reader can understand the thoughts, they become more meaningful and interesting with the use of transition words. Read the sentences again: *First, roll the dough out onto a pan. Next, spread sauce over the dough. After that, sprinkle cheese on top. Finally place it in the oven and bake it for 20 minutes. Then, you have pizza!* Most students will recognize the words that are used as transition words, and in fact use them when they speak. Providing them with a list of such words, and perhaps even hanging them on the wall in the special education classroom will remind them to use these words as cues for writing paragraphs. Examples of words to include in such a list are as follows:

SAMPLE OF TRANSITION WORDS

First	During	Because
Second	Since	To begin with
Next	While	Later
Then	In Conclusion	Earlier
Finally	An example is	At that time
Last	Also	Due to this
Before	Another example is	In spite of that
After	Additionally	Regardless

Transfer of Skills to Other Settings. Once students are using these reading and writing strategies effectively in the special education setting, it is important that they are able to take the skills and carry them over to all areas of instruction. One example of such necessity is Alex. He is a high school student with severe reading and writing disabilities. In his intensive remedial reading course, he learned how to use transition words and the five-sentence paragraph structure frame to develop essays. He must have written nearly twenty essays for his special education teacher during the second semester, yet he failed the essay portion of each of his final exams. When his special education teacher questioned Alex on his poor results, he told her, "But Miss, you know I don't know how to write essays." When she reminded him of all the essays that he had written for her, he replied, "Oh, I didn't write essays for you. I just filled in your sentence structure frames." Although this teacher was successful in obtaining essays from Alex, she was unsuccessful in teaching Alex how to transfer his new abilities—which really made his new skills unimportant. Only once the connection is made how to apply these skills to subject areas are they truly of value to the special education student.

Personalizing Literacy Instruction

Aside from being relevant to the subjects that students are studying, the material being used to provide literacy instruction must be relevant to the student on a personal level. By the time students reach the upper grades, they continuously ask the question, "Why do I need to learn this?" If there is no good answer to that question, then there may not be a good reason to be teaching it, particularly to a learner who needs to put forth more effort than most while learning. If the material is meaningful to the student, he or she will be motivated to put such effort forth.

Determining Students' Needs. For many high school students, the focus on academics is related to developing skills for college. While many students with disabilities do go on to successful college careers, it is important to realize that this is not the goal (nor should it be) for every student. As each student is unique, it is important to realize just what the purpose of instruction is when working with special education students. On the IEP of secondary education special education students, there are areas that talk about plans for after high school. It is important to incorporate this area by setting outcome based goals in literacy instruction (life skills, job skills, academic skills, etc.).

Individualizing Instruction. Just as each student in special education has an individualized education plan (IEP), the instruction that is provided for the student should also be individualized. While the same curriculum may be used to guide lesson plans for the entire class in the inclusion classroom, it is important that each student is receiving instruction that is appropriate to his or her specific needs and goals.

Monitoring Students' Progress in Literacy Instruction

Student progress in literacy instruction should be consistently monitored. This allows the teacher to always be providing instruction at an appropriate level. Students learn best at the instructional level. Since it is hoped that this level would improve as the year goes on, it is important to be aware of student progress.

While it is not feasible to be constantly using IRIs or error analyses, there are ways to be monitoring progress consistently. The use of portfolios shows at a glance how the quality of student work has changed throughout the year. Progress charts provide measures of performance at a glance.

Perhaps even more important than any of these assessment tools, however, are the informal observations made by you as a teacher, or the student herself on a daily basis. You both can see when she is able to complete a task that she was having trouble with before. You can recognize when she is decoding words without prompting or writing in paragraphs without having to refer to the sentence structure mold. You can tell by her reflections in her learning log of how her confidence in her ability to read and write are improving. The method used to monitor student progress is not as important as the fact that it is monitored, and instruction is appropriately adjusted on an ongoing basis to always be appropriate to the specific and immediate needs of the student.

REFERENCES

Adelman, P., & Vogel, S. (1991). The learning-disabled adult. In B. Y. L. Wong (Ed.), *Learning about learning disabilities* (pp. 563–594). San Diego, CA: Academic Press.

Algozzine, B., O'Shea, D.J., Stoddard, K., & Crews, W. B. (1988). Reading and writing competencies of adolescents with learning disabilities. *Journal of Learning Disabilities, 21*, 154–160.

Armbruster, B. B., & Anderson, T. H. (1988). On selecting "considerate" content area textbooks. *Remedial and Special Education, 9*, 44–52.

Baker, I., & Irwin, J. W. (1989). *Promoting active reading comprehension strategies: A resource book for teachers.* Englewood Cliffs, NJ: Prentice-Hall.

Bender, W. N. (1985). Differential diagnosis based on task-related behavior of learning disabled and low-achieving adolescents. *Learning Disability Quarterly, 8*, 261–266.

Bender, W. N. (1999). Learning disabilities in the classroom. In W. N. Bender (Ed.), *Professional issues in learning disabilities: Practical strategies and relevant research findings* (pp. 3–26). Austin, TX: Pro-Ed.

Berndt, T. J. (1979). Developmental changes in conformity to peers and parents. *Developmental Psychology, 15*, 608–616.

Berndt, T. J. (1982). The features and effects of friendship in early adolescence. *Child Development, 53*, 1447–1460.

Burns, P. C., & Roe, B. D. (1989). *Informal reading inventory* (3rd ed.). Boston: Houghton Mifflin.

Deshler, D. D., Schumaker, J. B., & Lenz, B. K. (1984). Academic and cognitive interventions for LD adolescents: Part I. *Journal of Learning Disabilities, 17*, 108–117.

Deshler, D. D., Warner, M. M., Schumaker, J. B., & Alley, G. R. (1983). The learning strategies intervention model: Key components and current status. In J. D. McKinney & L. Feagans (Eds.), *Current topics in learning disabilities* (Vol. 1, pp. 245–283).

DiGiulio, R. C. (2000). *Positive classroom management: a step-by-step guide to successfully running the show without destroying student dignity* (2nd ed.). Thousand Oaks, CA: Corwin Press.

Dingle, M., Falvey, M., Givner C. C., & Haager, D. (2004). Essential special and general education teacher competencies for preparing teachers for inclusive settings. *Issues in Teacher Education, 31*(1), 35–50.

Ellis, E. S., & Friend, P. (1991). Adolescents with learning disabilities. In B. Y. L. Wong (Ed.), *Learning about learning disabilities* (pp. 505–561). San Diego, CA: Academic Press.

Gregory, J. F., Shanahan, T., & Walberg, H. (1985). Learning disabled 10th graders in mainstreamed settings. *Remedial and Special Education, 6*(4), 25–33.

Haager, D., & Simon, S. B. (1997, April). *Transition from elementary to middle school: Social and academic support for students with learning disabilities.* Paper presented at the Annual Conference of the Council for Exceptional Children, Salt Lake City, UT.

Hamburg, B. A. (1974). Early adolescence: A specific and stressful stage in the life cycle. In G. V. Coelho, D. A. Hamburg, & J. E. Adams (Eds.), *Coping and adaptation* (pp. 101–124). New York: Basic Books.

Harter, S., Whitesell, N. R., & Kowalski, P. (1992). Individual differences in the effects of educational transitions on young adolescents' perceptions of competence and motivational orientation. *American Educational Research Journal, 29*, 777–808.

Lavoie, R. D. (1989). *Understanding learning disabilities: How difficult can this be? The F. A. T. City Workshop.* PBS Video. (For information call 1–800–424–7963.)

Leslie, L., & Caldwell, J. (1990). *Qualitative reading inventory*. Glenview, IL: Scott Foresman.

Lovitt, T. C., Plavins, M., & Cushing, S. (1999). What do pupils with disabilities have to say about their experience in high school? *Remedial and Special Education, 20*, 67–76, 83.

McCormick, S. (1999). *Instructing students who have literacy problems.* Upper Saddle River, NJ: Merrill.

Mercer, C. D. (1997). *Students with learning disabilities* (5th ed.). Upper Saddle River, NJ: Prentice-Hall.

National Council on Education Standards and Testing. (1992). *Raising standards for American education.* Washington, DC: U. S. Government Printing Office.

National Education Goals Panel. (1995). *The national education goals report 1995: Executive summary.* Washington, DC: U. S. Government Printing Office.

Rogan, L., & Hartman, L. D. (1990). Adult outcome of learning disabled students ten years after initial follow-up. *Learning Disabilites Focus, 5*, 91–102.

Schumaker, J. B., & Deshler, D. D. (1987). Implementing the regular education initiative in secondary schools—A different ball game. *Journal of Learning Disabilities, 2*, 36–42.

Schumaker, J. S., & Deschler, D. D. (1992). Validation of learning strategy interventions for students with learning disabilities: Results of a programmatic research effort. In B. Y. L. Wong (Ed.), *Learning about learning disabilities* (pp. 563–594). San Diego, CA: Academic Press.

Schumm, J. S., & Vaughn, S. (1991). Making adaptations for mainstreamed students: General classroom teachers' perceptions. *Remedial and Special Education*, *12*, 18–27.

Schumm, J. S., & Vaughn, S. (1992). Planning for mainstreamed special education students: Perceptions of general classroom teachers. *Exceptionality*, *3*, 81–98.

Schumm, J. S., Vaughn, S., Haager, D., McDowell, J., Rothlein, L., & Saumell, L. (1995). General education teacher planning and adaptations for students with diverse learning needs: What can students with learning disabilities expect? *Exceptional Children*, *61*(4), 335–352.

Schumm, J. S., Vaughn, S., & Leavell, A. (1994). Planning Pyramid: A framework for planning for diverse student needs during content area instruction. *The Reading Teacher, 47*, 608–615.

Schumm, J. S., Vaughn, S., & Saumell, L. (1992). What teachers do when the textbook is tough: Students speak out. *Journal of Reading Behavior*, *24*, 481–503.

Schumm, J. S., Vaughn, S., & Saumell, L. (1994). Assisting students with difficult textbooks: Teacher perceptions and practices. *Reading Research and Instruction*, *34*, 39–56.

Seidman, E., Allen, L., Aber, J. L., Mitchell, C., & Feinman, J. (1994). The impact of school transitions in early adolescence on the self-system and perceived social context of poor urban youth. *Child Development*, *65*, 507–522.

Shriner, J. G., Ysseldyke, J. E., & Thurlow, M. L. (1996). Standards for all American students. In E. L. Meyen, G. A. Vergason, & R. J. Whelan (Eds.), *Strategies for teaching exceptional children in inclusive settings* (pp. 53–80). Denver, CO: Love.

Snow, C. E., Burns, M. S., & Griffin, P. (1998). *Preventing reading difficulties in young children.* Washington, DC: National Academy Press.

Upham, D. A., & Trumbull, V. H. (1997). *Making the grade: Reflections on being learning disabled.* Portsmouth, NH: Heinemann, 1997.

Vaughn, S., & Haager, D. (1994a). Social assessments with students with learning disabilities: Do they measure up? In S. Vaughn & C. Bos (Eds.), *Research issues in learning disabilities: Theory, methodology, assessment, and ethics* (pp. 276–309). New York: Springer-Verlag.

Vaughn, S., & Haager, D. (1994b). The measurement and assessment of social skills. In G. R. Lyon (Ed.), *Frames of reference for the assessment of learning disabilities: New views on measurement issues* (pp. 555–570). Baltimore, MD: Paul H. Brookes.

Vaughn, S., Bos, C., Schumm, J. S. (2003). *Teaching exceptional, diverse, and at-risk students in the general education classroom* (3rd ed.). Boston: Allyn and Bacon.

Warner, M. M., Alley, G. R., Deshler, D. D., & Schumaker, J. B. (1980). *An epidemiology study of learning disabled adolescents in secondary schools: Classification and discrimination of learning disabled and low-achieving adolescents* (Research Report No. 20). Lawrence: University of Kansas Institute for Research in Learning Disabilities.

Wentzel, K. R. (1991). Social competence at school: Relation between social responsibility and academic achievement. *Review of Educational Research, 61*, 1–24.

White, W. J. (1992). The postschool adjustment of persons with learning disabilities: Current status and future projections. *Journal of Learning Disabilities, 25*, 448–456.

Wigfield, A., Eccles, J. S., MacIver, D., Reuman, D. A., & Midgley, C. (1991). Transitions during early adolescence: Changes in children's self-esteem across the transition to junior high school. *Developmental Psychology, 27*, 552–565.

Zigmond, N., Levin, E., & Laurie, T. (1985). Managing the mainstream: An analysis of teacher attitudes and student performance in mainstream high school programs. *Journal of Learning Disabilities, 18*, 535–541.

CHAPTER ELEVEN

TRANSITION SERVICES FOR STUDENTS WITH HIGH-INCIDENCE DISABILITIES IN INCLUSIVE SETTINGS

RICHARD ROSENBERG
Whittier Union High School District
Whittier, California

MARY FALVEY
California State University, Los Angeles

Go confidently in the direction of your dreams.
Live the life you have imagined.
—Henry David Thoreau (1817–1862)

KEY CONCEPTS

- Transition services are mandated by federal law and are meant to assist students with disabilities as they transition from school to adulthood.
- Transition planning includes planning for instruction, community, employment, and daily living.
- The transition planning should foster students' sense of empowerment to guide their own lives and futures, but it should also involve the collaborative efforts of family members and professionals.
- Transition planning is based on students' interests, dreams, strengths, and abilities.

FOCUS QUESTIONS

1. What are the transition needs of students with high-incidence disabilities?
2. What is required by law in developing transition plans? How does this process fit into the IEP process?
3. What are the components of an Individualized Transition Plan?
4. What are effective strategies for special educators in facilitating transition services in an inclusive secondary setting?

Julio is a senior at a comprehensive inclusive high school in an urban school district. He was referred and identified as a student with mild mental retardation in second grade. He lives at home with his older sister, mother, and stepfather. His father was in prison for most of his elementary and middle school years and has no contact with him at this time. The family moved to Los Angeles from Mexico when Julio was 1 year old.

Julio has excellent personal relationship skills, and his English and Spanish communication skills are low-average. His disability manifests itself in the areas of math, reading, and writing (both in English and Spanish). At this time, Julio is fully included at his neighborhood high school. He is determined to be the first in his family, including his extended family, to have a high school diploma; however, it will take enormous effort on his part, as well as the efforts of his teachers and his family, to make this dream come true.

Julio has a very sweet and contagious smile that will help him throughout his life. Julio has said many times to his teachers, "I come from the neighborhood, and I want to get out of the neighborhood," meaning that he views his neighborhood as a deterrent to his future success. The Dean of Students describes Julio as a "young gentleman who is rough around the edges; however, with positive support and models he will be okay."

Julio is enrolled in school five of six periods a day. He is taking math, English, science, social studies, and metal shop. Julio receives support in his math, English, social studies, and science classes with a teacher or paraprofessional from the special education department collaboratively teaching with the general education teacher. Julio is provided with highlighted materials from his textbooks in order for him to understand the main points. In addition, material requiring extensive reading skills has been provided to him on tape. With regard to math, Julio is provided with a calculator, a laminated copy of the formulas utilized, and a multiplication chart.

Julio has been participating in the Work Ability project. The Work Ability project assists students to obtain and maintain part-time employment and become eligible for services from the California Department of Rehabilitation in preparation for leaving the school district. Julio worked at KB Toys during his junior year, then the Country Harvest Café. He is still at Country Harvest, with periodic support from the job coach.

Julio brought his stepfather to the last IEP meeting and the team discussed how well Julio is doing at school. However, concerns were shared about his involvement in gang activities. Julio asked for help to "get out" of the gang, because he said he fears for his safety sometimes. As a result, Julio's stepfather agreed to bring him to and pick him up from school to minimize his opportunity for contact with the gang affiliations and activities. Julio shared that his most significant goals in the future are to get a job, have a family, and make enough money to support his family. As Julio said, "I want a LIFE." In addition, the IEP team will do whatever is necessary to assist Julio in reaching his goal of earning a diploma and making good decisions in the community so he can get a job, stay alive, and be successful. Julio is currently passing all of his classes with Bs and Cs, and with an additional year, it appears he will successfully complete the requirements for a high school diploma.

Students like Julio are benefiting from a process mandated by federal law called *transition planning,* where students, their families, teachers, and others meet long before they are about to exit the public schools and begin planning their future. This planning process involves developing academic, social, and work experiences for students so that they can reach their goals. Transition was defined in 1994 by the Council for Exceptional Children, Division on Career Development and Transition, as the following:

> Transition refers to a change in the status from behaving primarily as a student to assuming emergent adult roles in the community. These roles include employment, participating in post-secondary education, maintaining a home, becoming appropriately involved in the community, and experiencing satisfactory personal and social relationships. The process of enhancing transition involves the participation and coordination of school programs, adult agency services, and natural supports within the community. The foundations for transition should be laid during the elementary and middle school years, guided by the broad concept of career development. Transition planning should begin no later than age 14, and students should be encouraged, to the full extent of their capabilities, to assume a maximum amount of responsibility for such planning. (Halpern, 1994, p. 116)

Transition services were developed in order to facilitate the movement from school to adult life for all students who have Individualized Educational Plans (IEP). The intent of transition services is to assure that students receive the opportunities necessary to be prepared for adult life. In addition, students and their families must become knowledgeable of the services and supports available as students transition from school to adult life.

The purpose of this chapter is to define successful transition for students with mild to moderate disabilities, identify the guiding principles that facilitate successful transition, and to provide specific strategies for designing and implementing transition plans to prepare students for adult roles.

DEVELOPMENT OF TRANSITION SERVICES

One of the first references to supporting youth with disabilities to work occurs in 1928 (Descoeudres, 1928). Working in Belgium, she identified that society's responsibility was to help youth with disabilities find jobs and to supervise, aid, and advise them in other aspects of living. Later, in 1943, John Duncan of England discovered that many jobs in the community might be appropriate for those of low intelligence because they demanded more concrete cognitive skills. As a result, he was able to add these concrete job skills to a curriculum in England for those who were slow learners.

Concurrently, some professionals began developing methods for assisting those with disabilities in acquiring occupational skills. In the United States in 1941, Richard Hungerford developed a series of trade-like journals called Occupational Education. The journals provided step-by-step instruction for teaching skills in sewing, service occupations, light industry, and various unskilled and semi-skilled jobs that Hungerford highlighted as appropriate for students with mental retardation.

Legal Mandates

In the 1960s, the United States Congress passed the Vocational Education Act of 1963, which specified that persons with disabilities could be included in ongoing vocational education along with their peers without disabilities. The intent was to enable students with disabilities to learn work skills from experts in the field. In 1968, Congress passed the Vocational Educational Act Amendments, which provided for 10 percent of the funds for vocational education to be set aside to serve youth with disabilities. The major impact and impetus for "Transition," as we know it today, came with the passage of Public Law 94-142, the Education for All Handicapped Children Act (1975). This law mandated that states would lose federal funds for special education services if they did not support students with disabilities in regular vocational education programs.

In 1977, Hoyt defined career education as "an effort at refocusing American education and the action of the broader community in ways that will help individuals acquire and utilize the knowledge, skills, and attitudes necessary for each to make work a meaningful, productive, and satisfying part of his or her way of living" (p. 5). Then, in 1984, Madeline Will, as Director of the Office of Special Education and Rehabilitation services, led the transition movement that expanded the foundation laid in the development of career education into the realm of adult community services for individuals with disabilities. The transition movement at this time began to prepare people with disabilities not only for work, but also for community living. In addition, during her administration such innovations as supported employment and job coaching were initiated to expand the notion of career education. The goal was to prepare students to leave the public schools and be able to live, work, and recreate in their home community with necessary supports (Will, 1983, 1984).

In 1990, the Individuals with Disabilities Education Act (IDEA) was passed, as a reauthorization and expansion of PL 94–142. The following services and support were mandated for all school aged students with disabilities:

> A coordinated set of activities for a student, designed with an outcome oriented process, which promotes movement from school to post-school activities, including post-secondary education, vocational education, integrated employment (including supported employment), continuing and adult education, adult services, independent living, or community participation. The coordinated set of activities shall be based upon the individual student's needs, taking into account the student's preferences and interests, and shall include instruction, community experiences, the development of employment and other post-school adult living objectives, and when appropriate, acquisition of daily living skills and functional evaluation. (PL 101-476, 20 U.S.C. 1401[a][19])

This law emphasized the need for all transitional services and support to be individualized and reflect the dreams and desires of the student. The process must be outcome oriented, which implies that some form of assessment would be necessary. In addtion, the law calls for instruction and community experiences that would allow the student to receive services in five major areas:

1. Instruction: How is the student to be provided educational opportunities?
2. Community: How will services allow the student to function in the "real-world" community?
3. Employment: How will services result in a career or vocation for the student?
4. Daily Living: How will the services assure the student has as many skills as possible to address his or her own personal care/grooming and hygiene?
5. Functional evaluation: How will progress monitoring evaluate the student's competence, full or partial participation at job sites, and modifications that may be necessary?

Legal Provisions

Transition services were strengthened in 1997 when the Individuals with Disabilities Education Act (IDEA), 1997, was re-authorized. Currently, according to federal mandates, every IEP team for students 14 years of age and older must consider transition services and supports needed by the student. The student must be invited to the IEP meeting to address transition services. Agencies that may be able to assist the student and family during this transition are invited to participate in the meeting. Some of the agencies may not be required to attend until the student is ready to leave school; others should participate every year. Collaboration and coordination is key to successful outcomes for all students with IEPs as they move from school to adult life.

Beginning at least one year before a student reaches the age of maturity under the resident state's law (at age 18 in most states), the student's IEP must include a statement that indicates the student has been informed of his or her rights. The students' rights must be explained and presented to them in a format that is meaningful to the students, just as parents' rights have been previously provided to them. In addition, it is the responsibility of the schools to assure the student is knowledgeable about entering into contracts, eligibility for the draft, and other responsibilities as an adult in society.

In addition to IDEA (1990 and 1997), there are several other federal mandates that provide impetus for the provision of transition services and supports. In 1992, the Rehabilitation Act Amendments, Public Law 102-569, provided people with disabilities the opportunity to obtain vocational and independent living help, as needed. In 1990, the Americans with Disabilities Act was passed into law, essentially forbidding employers from discriminating against employees and prospective employees with disabilities. This law also requires that employers provide "reasonable accommodations" to enable individuals with disabilities to perform their jobs.

STRATEGIES FOR SUCCESSFUL TRANSITION

Students reaching high school graduation or culmination often have difficulty adjusting to life after high school. Some go on to college, some pursue employment, some have dropped out before they even reach this stage; others seem to flounder with undefined goals and direction. Some students are living with the consequences of their poor decisions related to employment, the use of drugs and/or alcohol, involvement with gangs, and/or teenage pregnancy. For students with disabilities, this situation often brings on even more challenges, disruptions, and negative consequences. Substantial research exists indicating that for students with disabilities, the transition from school to post-school settings is often met with unsuccessful employment, living dependent on others, having low self-esteem, and generally not being satisfied with their lives (Dunn, 1996; Edgar, 1987; Evers, 1996; Sitlington, 1996).

We may think of successful school programs as directly linked to students' success once they have completed school. In 1994, Louis Harris and Associates conducted a survey regarding the employment of people with disabilities and found the following:

- Two-thirds of Americans with disabilities between the ages of 16 and 64 are not working.
- The overwhelming majority of unemployed people with disabilities in the working-age population want to work.
- Adults with disabilities who are working are employed in a range of occupations, 16 percent are in professional or managerial positions or are proprietors; 14 percent are service workers; 13 percent are clerical or sales workers; 12 percent are unskilled laborers or farmers; while 7 percent are skilled craftspeople.
- Most adults with disabilities who are working or are willing and able to work (i.e., 69%) do not need special equipment or technology in order to perform effectively at work.

- Americans indicated that their attitudes toward integrating people with disabilities into all aspects of life, including employment, are more open and positive than ever before.

School to Adult Connection

Effective transition services and supports must be designed to prepare students with disabilities to live, work, and recreate in adult roles within the community. A strong link must be made in all areas of the curriculum in order to ensure successful adult functioning. There has been a significant push in both general and special education to better prepare students for the real world. Recently, in a publication by the Association for Supervision and Curriculum Development, Penn and Williams (1996) described the need to integrate vocational and academic instruction for all students. They stated:

> For thousands of years people have learned in the "real world." We learned to fish in oceans and streams; we learned to build igloos in the snow; we learned to plant in the fields; we even learned assembly-line work in factories. Over the past 100 years however, we have created artificial environments in which people are supposed to do the bulk of their learning. (Penn & Williams, 1996, p. 5)

Preparation throughout the School Years

Preparation Should Be Longitudinal and Occur over Time. This is the first guiding principle for successful transition. Although IDEA 1997 requires that from the age of 14, all students' transition needs must be explicitly stated in their IEPs, this does not imply that building critical life skills should wait until students are 14 years old. On the contrary, there are logical steps to successful transition that begins in preschool. Educators must begin preparing students in preschool by teaching such critical concepts as responsibility, sharing, cooperation, and other related skills. In elementary school, students must be exposed to various career roles while continuing to develop the special skills began in preschool. Elementary students begin to build an understanding of good work habits; learn to appropriately interact with peers, teachers, and other school personnel; and are assigned chores in the classroom and at home. In middle school, students might have part-time jobs in their neighborhoods, develop hobbies or special interests that can begin to build career options, become aware of their own strengths and needs, and be provided with direct connections between the core general education curriculum and career options. High school then becomes the opportunity to provide specific and comprehensive transition planning directly related to each student's transition goals.

Transition Planning Should Develop Students' Sense of Empowerment. The process of transition planning must provide students with a sense of being in control of their own learning and future. To the extent possible, students must be in a position to plan their futures, with the input and guidance of their teachers, counselors, vocational personnel, parents, and others, as appropriate. Too often in the past, students with disabilities have been handed a transition plan that others thought would be appropriate for them; students were excluded from the process of developing a transition plan intended to direct their lives. A sense of empowerment through involvement can assist the student in developing the very critical skills of self-determination, needed in every adult role.

The Transition Plan Should Involve Person-Centered Planning. This means a transition plan should be based upon students' strengths, interests, and preferences, not preferences or beliefs of others. Transition plans that reflect what the student does well and based upon what the student is motivated to learn are more likely to be achieved. Person-centered planning is a means of exploring the students' dreams and desires and channeling those to academic strengths. The process was developed to ensure that the plans developed were truly the students' (Falvey, Forest, Pearpoint, & Rosenberg, 1994). For example, the student is asked to identify his or her strengths, interests, and preferences.

Transition Planning Must Involve a Collaborative Team. A team of people who have expertise in the transition planning process, as well as those who have experience with the student, are key to successful transition planning. The primary participants of the collaborative transition team might include:

- Student
- Student's family and friends
- General education teachers
- Special education teachers
- Guidance counselors
- Vocational counselors
- Prospective employers
- College and university personnel
- Vocational rehabilitation counselors

There are many activities that special educators can utilize as they address the transition needs of students in both secondary and post-secondary programs. Figure 11.1 provides a listing of some the activities and skills that could be integrated into the core curriculum and/or developed as individual units of instruction to assist students to successfully transition from school to adult roles in the community.

Special educators often serve as case managers for students with disabilities as they go through the transition years. The competencies needed by special educators serving as case managers have been identified and validated in a study conducted by DeFur and Taymans (1995). This study found the following competency domains to be critical knowledge and skills of those special education staff serving as transition case managers.

- Philosophical and historical considerations of transition and employment of students with disabilities
- Knowledge of agency and system changes involved in transition and supported employment of students with disabilities
- Professionalism, advocacy, and legal issues in transition

SCHOOL-BASED TRANSITION ACTIVITIES:

Enroll in a variety of vocational classes

Visit the career/college center

Enroll in an regional occupational training program (ROP) class

Apply to adult education classes

Contact technical school

Investigate enrollment in apprenticeship program

Visit a community college

Obtain community college application

Contact college support services center assessment and/or available services

Obtain four-year college application and catalog

Contact military recruiting office

COMMUNITY-BASED ACTIVITIES:

Explore/join clubs, sport teams, performing arts

Explore community services offered by the city (dances, trips, sports)

Participate in clubs, hobbies, sports, work, religious activities, community services

Access/utilize bus schedule information—ride bus

Apply for Dial-A-Ride

Apply for MTA bus pass

Utilize taxi service

Know bicycle/pedestrian safety rules

Enroll in driver's education

Apply for driver's license

Investigate car insurance cost and coverage

Develop car purchase savings plan

Apply for I.D. card

Apply for medical insurance

Apply for SSI, if appropriate (Supplemental Security Income)

Become aware of available support services and community resources

Apply for assistive technology as appropriate (TDD, V-Tech, books on tape, assistive communication devices

EMPLOYMENT-BASED ACTIVITIES:

Develop job-related skills (work habits, job applications, resumes, attendance, etc.)

Participate in career awareness activities (career day)

FIGURE 11.1 Activities Needed to Successfully Transition to Adult Roles

(continued)

Apply to volunteer
Make appointment with unemployment office or One-Stop Center
Investigate age-appropriate employment (babysitting, paper route, etc.)
Apply for full-time employment
Apply for part-time employment
Apply for State Department of Rehabilitation
Obtain duplicate social security card
Obtain copy of birth certificate
Obtain copy of green card/work permit
Apply for supported employment program

RESIDENTIAL-LIVING– AND COMMUNITY-LIVING–BASED ACTIVITIES:

Identify role and responsibilities
Explore all alternatives for living options (home, relative, friend, group homes, marriage, etc.)
Explore independent living options
Understand written agreement (rental, utilities, etc.)
Explore supported living options
Complete housekeeping chores
Sort clothing, operate washer and dryer
Learn to cook and prepare food
Plan to shop and prepare a meal
Learn to shop
Calendar school and/or personal events
Schedule appointments
Use clock/watch
Use money
Open checking/savings account
Utilize banking services (ATM card)
Learn to call 911
Take messages
Call directory assistance
Set up monthly budget
Use a public phone
Maintain appropriate grooming skills
Use appropriate manners
Explore savings account options

FIGURE 11.1 Continued

- Working with others in the transition process
- Development and management of Individualized Transition Plans
- Curriculum, instruction, and learning theory for preparing students for adult life
- Assessment of skills needed for adult life
- Career counseling and vocational theory
- Vocational assessment and job development
- Job training and support
- Transition administrative functions
- Program evaluation and research of transition services and programs

TRANSITION PLANNING PROCESS

Planning transition services cannot be done in isolation but must reach beyond the school boundaries and into the community. Planning must also involve the exploration of the student's strengths, interests, hopes, and dreams. Transition planning assists students and families to think about life after high school and identify long- and short-range goals. High school experiences should be developed to ensure that students gain the skills and connections they need to achieve those life goals they want after school. The content of the Individualized Transition Plan (ITP) is made up of two major functions, the assessment and the action plan. The assessment function should include

- Students interests, desires, and plans for the future.
- Current levels of performance in academic, social, employment, and community functioning skills.

The action plan function of the transition plan should consist of

- Post-school goals so that individualized instructional objectives can be defined and implemented.
- Designation of responsible persons for implementation of the transition goals and objectives with timelines.
- Identification of accommodations needed to support the student's attainment of transition goals and objectives.
- Dates and methods for reviewing the progress the student is making toward meeting their transition goals and objectives.

ITP Assessments

There are several assessment formats that are particularly useful for building the action plan part of the ITP. Following is a description of a variety of assessment formats that have been used to obtain the necessary information to build a meaningful and relevant action plan in the ITP.

Person-Centered Planning Tools. The goal of person-centered planning is to break the model of describing an individual in terms of disability, IQ, and services, and move to individualized desires, dreams, and needs of the student and his or her family. Person-centered planning begins with the student and uses his or her circle of friends and supporters who come together as needed to explore the future and the current situation of getting to the future (Falvey et al., 1994). The process focuses on the students' strengths and dreams. With students who are unclear of their future, the team process provides the individual with ideas and support.

Some students may not demonstrate their strengths through standard testing of reading, writing, and arithmetic. For those students, Gardner's multiple intelligence theory (Gardner, 1983), which is widely embraced in schools, gives educators and families a set of concepts for describing students' unique strengths and needs. Students can have skills in many of the eight areas, including verbal-linguistic, math-logic, spatial, bodily-kinesthetic, musical, interpersonal, intrapersonal, and naturalistic intelligences. For example, students may have strengths in interpersonal intelligence and not in body-kinesthetic.

The person-centered planning meeting may either be a separate meeting or may be orchestrated as a part of the IEP process/meeting. The general process with person-centered planning would be to have the team address the following questions:

- Who is the student?
- What are his or her strengths and interests?
- What are his or her dreams for the future?
- What are nightmares for the future?
- How do we prepare for the future to reach the dreams and avoid the nightmares?
- What is the specific plan for the future?
  - What are the activities?
  - Who is going to assist?
  - What are the timelines?
- When will there be a followup to this meeting?

Figure 11.2 provides a sample of the person-centered planning process.

As you can see from Angie's planning process, using a person-centered process assists the person in transition to identify his or her interests and strengths and plan for the future. Individuals discover and organize their preferences, interests, needs, hopes, and dreams. The students' existing and future supporters align their activities with the students' dreams and needs. The process is designed to allow students to feel empowered, even if they do not want to do what the "parents" or "school" wants them to do. Cultural, economic, and social factors are central to the planning process.

Student Portfolios. Student portfolios are helpful when developed throughout middle school and carried on to the high school level. The purpose of a career planning portfolio is to assist the student, family, and staff to appreciate the diverse experiences a student has had throughout the school years. This is the beginning of a career resume. The portfolio may consist of interest inventories, job sites toured, hands-on experiences shared, evaluation data, pictures of career/vocational situations, as well as written summaries for each year's vocational/career experience.

Who is Angie and where does she want to be after school?

June 3rd 3:00-4:30

We meet at Angie's house to share and discuss Angie's future, exploring what her life may look like when she is 25, the family's dreams and nightmares, and then explore a timeline from tenth grade summer through until Angie leaves school.

Present:

Angie
Dad—Fernando
Mom—Marina
Sister—Carolina
Job Developer—Alicia acting as an interpreter also
Vocational Counselor/Facilitator—Richard

Angie is the second child in a large family. She has always been an active child with sports as a strength; however, her academic performance has been a challenge. She has some communication difficulties and stubborn behaviors that have been a problem from time to time. Angie has support staff, additional teacher support, or instructional assistant support in all of her classes. Her strengths are in her physical abilities.

Everyone knows that Angie wants and needs her grades to be high enough to be able to play sports. Her strengths are in the area of sports, and the support she needs for academic performance was emphasized at the meeting. Both parents are working, and English is their second language, which sometimes makes it difficult for Angie to complete her homework at home. The New Horizon program, an afterschool support service, is available to all students to assist with homework. Angie has utilized this service from time to time. An additional area of concern that has been addressed is Angie's social activities and being too social in the community.

Angie is very excited about her junior year, playing sports, and then getting ready for community college. If she goes to college she will be the first one in her whole family.

Where Does Everyone See Angie at 25?

Carolina sees Angie as a school teacher, she sees her sister as being very smart and wanting her to have a good job. She felt that she may enjoy sports as a means to deal with her learning disability. Dad stated that he wanted Angie to be as independent as possible by 25, but he was very clear that she will be at home with her sister until they get married. He has a vision for her going to college and that makes him very proud. He is worried about how she will get support in college.

FIGURE 11.2 Angie's Person-Centered Plan

(continued)

Dad stated he felt that Angie likes to be involved in sports—academics are hard for her—and she likes to be active and doing things. Dad stated that he wanted to be sure that Angie would be able to reach her dreams and understands the importance of her being able to "stick to it."

Mom stated she felt Angie was brilliant but the school never figured out how to help her. Mom feels that she can do whatever she really wants. She sees her getting married by 25.

Dreams for Angie:

Angie wants to be in sports for high school and community college. At this time she states she wants to be a childcare director when she grows up. She likes the boys and wants to have a family.

Carolina's dream is that Angie could have a good job and have a good education.

Dad's dream is for better and easier means to acquire the academic skills she needs; he also wants Angie to be independent and would like Angie to be as independent as possible with regards to making good social decisions and having "good" friends.

Mom's dreams are that Angie has friends and is surrounded by a circle of friends and is able to reach her dreams. Mom wants her to go to college, and whatever the family can do to support that they want to help. They realize they do not have the academic skills but they will do whatever they can.

Nightmares:

Angie's nightmare is NO SPORTS. Her other nightmare is that she not get married and not be able to have a family.

Carolina does not want her sister to get in trouble with guys or gangs.

Dad stated he was worried about another "bad" boyfriend. Dad wants to know how to make sure she can play sports this year.

Mom was worried about her friends and attitude and is concerned that Angie may have a drinking problem that no one wants to talk about.

Brief History:

At 9 years Angie had a high fever and had to be hospitalized.
Her reading skills and math skills have been low since middle school.
Angie has allergies that may keep her home from school.

Gifts That Angie Brings with Her:

Strong-willed
Communicative
Affectionate
Love
Attractive
Sense of humor
Sensitive
Good looking
Picks up on feelings, etc.

FIGURE 11.2 Continued

Future:

Summer school to be able to make up credits.
Fully included as a true member of the Whittier High Cardinal's campus.
The presence of staff and individual support who can support Angie all day long.
Angie be given the opportunity and skills to acquire "good" friends.
The family will continue to be a strong advocate for Angie and hope their desires and dreams come true.
High school diploma (Dad recognized and acknowledged that there will be a HUGE amount of work for Angie to stay focused).

Discussed that transition to community college.
Enrolling in the Department of Rehabilitation.
Explore Alanon and programs for teens who show some potential drinking problems.
Respectfully facilitated and submitted,

FIGURE 11.2 Continued

Commercial and Teacher-Made Assessments. The assessment process is important to obtaining individualized information for the students. This is also an opportunity to establish a relationship with a student as he or she transitions to adult life. Some commercial evaluation instruments that have proven to be efficient and effective are described below.

The *Becker Reading Free Interests Inventory* (Becker, 1981) is a forced-choice evaluation system. For each item, the student chooses one of the three pictures of diverse employment and job-related activities reflecting his or her preferences. The inventory is then scored with highest ranked job interests. This is good for students who are nonreaders and is also helpful in establishing rapport with students. The inventory may open a discussion with a student about future planning.

The *Interest Determination, Exploration and Assessment System* (IDEAS) (Johansson, 1996) is also an interest inventory. The student needs to be able to read at the sixth-grade level in order to complete the inventory independently, but may also have assistance. In addition, it may be administered either individually or in a small group. For each statement, the individual ranks his or her response from "strongly dislike" to "strongly like," or "indifferent." IDEAS has an accompanying comprehensive workbook that will assist the individual and staff to identify career options, explore sample jobs, and

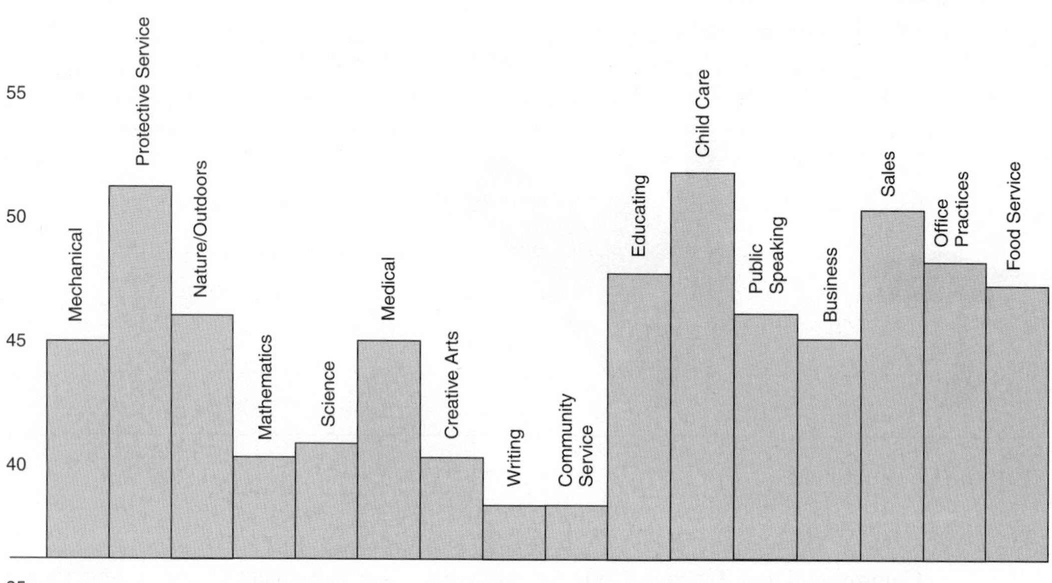

FIGURE 11.3

use the Dictionary of Occupational Titles (DOT). An example of the IDEAS assessment is provided in Figure 11.3 for Angie, the student previously described.

Another commercially available instrument that is useful is the *Self-Directed Search* (SDS) (Holland, 1996). The booklet will assist an individual to find jobs that most closely match his or her interest. The booklet starts with some open-ended questions and then moves into more yes/no questions. The total of the yes responses are utilized to identify the student's possible job matches. At the end of the assessment, the individual is asked to rate his or her own interest in mechanical, scientific, artistic, teaching, sales, and clerical work. This instrument requires a sixth-grade reading level, is self-administered, and when scored, reflects the student's job interests. Those with poor reading skills may take this questionnaire with assistance.

The *Adaptive Behavior: The Street Survival Skills Questionnaire* (SSQQ) (Linenhoker & McCarron, 1983) is utilized to determine a student's current life skills. It must be administered one-on-one, and it may be computer scored. The score reflects the student's performance in the areas of basic concepts; functional signs; tool identification and use; domestic management; health, first aid, and safety; public services; time; money; and measurement. Since pictures are used, the literacy demands are minimal, although the student's ability to communicate clearly is required.

Teachers often create their own checklists to evaluate a student's history and future regarding work and work skills. Figure 11.4 contains a sample of a teacher created interview to explore jobs and job interest.

Before starting the interview explain the ITP process to the student. The purpose of this interview is to get a quick overview of the student so that the ITP case manager can make informed decisions as to what instruments and ongoing evaluations to utilize. This is a brief interview and also acts as an ice breaker activity.

Is there any job(s) you have thought you would like to do or would be good at?

____

What kind of work do you do at home? (yard, dishes, pet care, baby sitting, cleaning, cooking, etc.)

____

What do you do for fun when you are not in school? (hobbies, sports, clubs, leisure time activities)

____

Special talents, skills—something about yourself an employer would like?

____

What are some ways a person can go and find a job?

____

What are some things an employer might look for when hiring?

____

Name as may jobs as you can.

____

What have been your favorite school courses?

____

What courses would you like to take?

____

FIGURE 11.4 Initial Interview

(continued)

What courses do you not want to take?

____

Work History

Employer	Job Title
Duties	Length
Employer	Job Title
Duties	Length
Employer	Job Title
Duties	Length

When you finish school, what do you want?

Study a trade?

____

Go to work?

____

Go to college?

____

OTHER?

____

What is your current method of transportation? Walking, bicycle, bus, family, car, DL#

____

What kind of working conditions do you think you would like? (inside, outside, clean, alone, lots of people, loud, quiet, physically active, etc.)

____

OTHER information

____

____

____

FIGURE 11.4 Continued

Developing the Individualized Transition Plan

With the assessment information collected informally and formally, it is time to draft an ITP. The ITP should be a living document that reflects the student's strengths, needs, and interest, as well as family and school dynamics that may have an impact on the future. The ITP as the action plan must reflect reachable goals, reasonable timelines and the person(s) responsible for carrying out the ITP. Figure 11.5 shows Angie's ITP.

The team meeting for the IEP each year may look and feel different. During middle school, the effort of the IEP team may be to ensure that the student is developing an understanding that he or she has an IEP and has unique learning style and needs. Middle school can be time to address the range of options that are available in many high schools and to prepare to be successful at high school.

During high school, the team will include general and special education staff that support the students, related services provided by the school (e.g., vocational counselor, speech therapist, social worker), and outside agencies that may be assisting the student and family at the time. This team must work collaboratively together. The transition goals of the first two years of high school are to learn what it means to be at high school and start to identify career options. The school personnel and programs that can provide supports to students in planning for their transition from school to adult roles are

- Skill training vocational education.
- General education and special education.
- Work experience career counseling.
- Career centers.
- Life skills training.
- Work training.
- Adult education opportunities.
- Regional occupational program or trade technological training opportunities.
- Night school program.

Generally, by tenth grade, students, their families, and staff are able to make some projections as to whether the student will be completing a traditional four-year program with a diploma and going on to continuing education or seeking employment. If the student needs additional years at high school to complete the diploma—and that is critical to the student as in Julio's situation in the scenario presented at the beginning of this chapter—school personnel should make necessary arrangements. The student may be moving on to a job or participating in a transition program for students beyond high school age. The last years at high school should include the general and special education staff who will support the student and family to identify ongoing supports for the student following school. The option may be the Department of Rehabilitation, adult school, trade schools, college, and/or university. A number of individuals may qualify for ongoing support from community agencies. The Department of Rehabilitation can offer the following services:

- Service coordination (case management).
- Job placement training and support.

Individualized Transition Plan – Action Plan

NAME:	Angie	**AGE:**	16 yr. 10 mos.
BIRTHDATE:	1-30-83	**GRADE:**	10
SCHOOL:	Whittier High School	**SOCIAL SECURITY:**	111-22-3333
GUARDIAN(S):	Fernando and Marina	**HS CREDITS:**	45.00
PROJECTED GRADUATION:	June 2001		

ASSESSMENT INFORMATION

The following information was used in completing the ITP by Vocational Coordinator

- [x] Review of Cumulative Record and IEP
- [x] Initial Interview with Student
- [ ] Preemployment Evaluation
- [x] In-depth Student Interview
- [x] Parent Interview
- [ ] Reading Free Interest Inventory
- [ ] Tyler Vocational Card Sort
- [ ] Rhodes Modification - Tyler Card Sort
- [x] IDEAS
- [x] Self Directed Search - Form E
- [ ] Differential Standards Skills List
- [ ] Street Survival Skills Questionnaire
- [ ] Adaptive Behavior Scale
- [ ] Observation

Soc. Sec. Card	Yes	N/A	Dept. of Rehab	Yes	No	06-01	Cheryl Duran
Drivers License	No	06-00	Regional Center	No	No	N/A	N/A
California ID	No	N/A	Soc. Sec. (SSI)	No	No	N/A	N/A
Bus ID	No	N/A	EDD	No	No	N/A	N/A
Birth Certificate	Yes	N/A	Dept. of Mental Health	No	No	N/A	N/A
Resume	No	06-00	Dept. of Soc. Services	No	No	N/A	N/A
Other			Other				

WORKER CHARACTERISTICS
A=Acceptable U=Unacceptable Q=Questionable

A Dependability
A Motivation to Work
A Perseverance
A Works Independently
A Speed and Accuracy
A Stamina
A Adaptability to Change
A Problem Solving
A Communication
A Work Quality
A Work Production

Community Access **Indicate Yes or No**

N Drives
Y Uses public transportation
Y Uses bicycle/walks
Y Uses community resources (bank, stores)
Y Uses recreational facilities

SELF ADVOCACY SKILLS
Indicate Yes or No

Y Requests assistance when needed
Y Expresses needs
Y Identifies disability in functional terms
Y Appropriately assertive
Y Accesses resources

EMPLOYMENT
Angie stated that she is interested in childcare occupations. The IDEAs and SDS interest inventories were administered to identify Angie's interests. The results were as follows:

IDEAS that Angie had a very high interest in childcare, then protective services and sales. The people business was a high interest of Angie.

FIGURE 11.5 Angie's ITP

SDS also demonstrated a high interest in the Dictionary of Occupational Titles that reflect school and childcare related jobs.

SUMMARY/ITP ASSESSMENT: Angie was referred to have an Individualized Transition Plan (ITP) developed with Richard Rosenberg, Vocational Counselor, and Michelle Mohoff, Vocational Technician, from Career Connections. Informal interviews were conducted with Angie, a person-centered meeting with her family at the house and staff at Whittier High School to assess Angie's interests and future plans.

GENERAL IMPRESSIONS
Angie is a 15-year-old sophomore at Whittier High School. She currently has 45.00 of 220.00 credits required to graduate, and is not on track to graduate. Angie qualifies for special education services because of a specific learning disability due to significant discrepancies between aptitude and achievement. Her educational strengths include being a visual-kinesthetic learner and having good reading comprehension. Her educational needs include improving verbal and written performance, structuring written work, completing work on time, and increasing vocabulary. Some social and community skills and concerns were identified during the assessment process and need to be discussed. The two major areas were friends that Angie is associating with at times and a potential substance-abuse problem.

INSTRUCTION
Angie reported that she is interested in taking courses involving childcare. She stated that she is interested in attending a community college. Angie is currently taking the World of Children course at Whittier High School.

COMMUNITY EXPERIENCE
Angie participates in many activities; she enjoys hanging out with friends, and she was previously on the Whittier High School basketball team, but had to drop due to her grades. Angie stated that next year she is interested in trying out again for basketball and also for softball and tennis.

SCHOOL LIVING OPTIONS
Goals have been set for Angie in order for her to obtain the skills and responsibility involved in independent living. She currently has a somewhat realistic idea of the costs and expenses involved in independent living.

Michelle J. Mohoff
Vocational Technician

Richard L. Rosenberg, Ph.D.
Vocational Counselor

Individualized Transition Plan

Long-Range Goals Desired Post-school Outcome	Activities/Objectives	Person/Agency Responsible	Time Line	Date Met
1. INSTRUCTION [X] Vocational training objective	1. [X] Enroll in vocational education class (keyboarding, woodshop, photography)	1. Angie/VC	1. 06-00	1.
[X] Part time college objective	2. [X] Visit high school career/college center	2. Angie/VC	2. 06-00	2.
[X] Adult education/ROP classes objective	3. [X] Enroll in ROP class	3. Angie/VC	3. 06-00	3.
[X] Visit and enroll in community college	4. [X] Visit community college	4. Angie/VC	4. 06-01	4.
	5. [X] Obtain community college application form and school catalog	5. Angie/VC	5. 06-00	5.
	6. [X] Contact college support services center • Assessment • Available services	6. Angie/VC	6. 06-00	6.

FIGURE 11.5 Continued

(continued)

2. COMMUNITY EXPERIENCE				
[X] Leisure/recreation activities with family and friends	[X] Explore/join clubs, sports teams, performing arts at school Participate in two or more activities: clubs/hobbies/sports/work religious activities community services	1. Angie/VC	1. 06-00	1.
[X] Participate in drug and alcohol prevention programs	[X] Explore project Info and the Alanon and school age program for alcohol abuse.	2. Angie/VC	2. 06-00	2.
B. Transportation				
[X] Drive	[X] Enroll in drivers education [X] Apply for drivers license [X] Investigate car insurance cost and coverage [X] Develop car purchase savings plan	1-4 Angie and family VC	2. 06-00	1. 2. 3. 4.

Long-Range Goals Desired Post-school Outcome	Activities/Objectives	Person/Agency Responsible	Time Line	Date Met
3. EMPLOYMENT				
Employment	1. [X] Develop job-related skills	1. Angie/VC	1. 06-00	1.
	2. [X] Participate career awareness (e.g.: career fairs, workshops, etc)	2. Angie/VC	2. 06-00	2.
	3. [X] Visit school career center	3. Angie/VC	3. 06-00	3.
	4. [X] Apply for part-time employment	4. Angie/VC	4. 06-01	4.
	5. [X] Apply to Department of Rehabilitation (DR)	5. Angie/VC	5. 06-00	5.
4. DAILY LIVING SKILLS (if appropriate)				
Domestic	1. [ ] Complete housekeeping chores	1. Angie/Family	1. 06-00	1.
	2. [ ] Sort clothing, operate washer and dryer	2. Angie/Family	2. 06-00	2.
	3. [ ] Learn to prepare a simple meal	3. Angie/Family	3. 06-00	3.
	4. [ ] Plan to shop and prepare a meal	4. Angie/Family	4. 06-00	4.
	5. [ ] Do comparison shopping	5. Angie/Family	5. 06-00	5.
Time Management	1. [X] Calendar school and personal events	1. Angie/Family	1. 06-00	1.
	2. [X] Schedule appointments	2. Angie/Family	2. 06-00	2.
	3. [ ] Use clock/watch	3. Angie/Family	3. 06-00	3.

FIGURE 11.5 Continued

Long-Range Goals Desired Post-school Outcome	Activities/Objectives	Person/Agency Responsible	Time Line	Date Met
A. Post-school Living Options				
[X] Independent	1. [X] Continue living in family home	1. Angie/Family	1. 06-02	1.
	2. [X] Identify role and responsibilities within living situation	2. Angie/Family	2. 06-02	2.
	3. [X] Explore alternative living options (relative, friend, group homes, etc.)	3. Angie/Family	3. 06-02	3.
	4. [X] Explore independent living options	4. Angie/Family	4. 06-02	4.
	5. [X] Understand written agreement (rental, utilities, etc.)	5. Angie/Family	5. 06-01	5.
Other				
If services are not required, please indicate reason:				

FIGURE 11.5 Continued

- Psychological and other assessments to qualify for support.
- Assistive technology.
- Career counseling.
- Supported employment assessment.
- Supported employment opportunities.
- Ongoing training and book reimbursement as needed and appropriate.
- Interpreting and facilitation as needed.
- Assistance with accessible transportation as needed.

While in high school as well as after high school, "Job Clubs" can be made available as a training and support group for individuals who are in the process of acquiring and maintaining employment. Job Clubs are a means for peers to work together with a facilitator to create and push each other through both peer support and peer pressure to develop resumes and interviewing skills, as well as maintaining employment. They generally consist of a group of two to fifteen students meeting as often as weekly and as infrequently as monthly. The structure varies from group to group. Students with and without disabilities work together to be prepared to obtain and maintain employment. Job Club participants might develop daily, weekly, or monthly assignments for the time between meetings. Some high school offer this within the traditional curriculum, at lunch, after school, or during the summer. Job Clubs might develop the following activities:

- Participating in career exploration activities.
- Recruiting guest speakers from jobs relevant to the specific group.

- Preparing to pick up job applications.
- Preparing to complete job applications.
- Preparing for job interviews (role-play mock job interviews).
- Preparing a resume.
- Preparing career passport, a simple clear form to take to job site to assist in filing out job application.
- Participating in agreements (formal and informal).
- Exploring advanced training options: adult school, community college, trade tech, college, university, private training programs.
- Linking with department of rehabilitation or other support organizations and agencies as needed/identified.

As students progress from school to the adult world, the options continue to expand. For those students who do not complete high school graduation requirements after the "typical" four years, most school districts provide transition programs for students 18 to 22 years of age on a high school campus, or in the community, or at a college/adult school center.

For those students going on to community colleges and universities, transition planning has proven to be beneficial. Students with mild to moderate disabilities often possess average or above average intelligence, which should make the transition to colleges and universities a viable option. This option has increased for students with learning disabilities, although it is still not accessed by enough students. It is critical that during high school years, for those students who are pursuing this option following high school, that students, their families, counselors, and teachers pay special attention to college entrance credit requirements so students are completing a program that specifically prepares them for that environment. Determining whether a college or university provides the following would be helpful to the student pursuing post-secondary education:

- A coordinator of services for students with disabilities.
- Assessment, evaluation, and diagnostic services to determine the needs of students with disabilities.
- Pre-admission advisement.
- Counseling services.
- Students' skills support.
- Remedial and basic education.
- Modified administration procedures.
- Guidance in structuring the student's workday.
- Student groups that facilitate making friends.
- Access to early registration procedures.
- Assistance with class scheduling.
- Job placement centers/services.

In addition, the student must be able to identify the accommodations needed during high school academic classes so he or she can advocate for those same accommodations, if needed, while attending college and/or university classes. Some of the more common accommodations used by students with learning disabilities in college and university settings are:

- Obtaining a notetaker, audiotape lectures.
- Sitting in the front of the room.
- Using visual aids and other handouts.
- Using a laptop computer.
- Meeting with professor to obtain clarification of assignment.
- Having rough drafts evaluated.
- Requesting extra time for writing assignments, tests.
- Hiring an editor to proof and edit papers.
- Requesting distraction-free settings for tests and examinations.
- Requesting an alternate forum of the response format of a test.
- Requesting the textbook on tape.
- Requesting extra time to complete a program (i.e., taking fewer classes each term than other students).

UNDERSTANDING RIGHTS AND SELF-ADVOCACY

Within the transition process one of the major areas proven to be necessary is that of self-advocacy. A person's ability to advocate for what he or she truly wants after leaving school, not just pleasing one's parents or teachers, is crucial. Many of the students have not had opportunities to dream and explore all options for their future.

Self-advocacy is the ability to speak up and have support in the process from others as the student becomes more independent. School and transition programs often have self-advocacy groups that are either facilitated by peers and/or an outside nonbiased facilitator. The goal is for the students to feel comfortable in sharing their concerns and issues and become confident in advocating for their desired outcomes. Participants in self-advocacy groups work on their own or with a partner to be able to

- "Speak" for themselves.
- Solve problems and make decisions.
- Know rights and responsibilities.
- Contribute to the community.
- Accept one's differences.
- Deal with labels and prejudices.
- Increase self-awareness.
- Solve common problems.

Some feel that self-advocacy sometimes is a threat to teachers and parents, when in reality, it is one of the best skills students can learn. Adults with mild to moderate disabilities who have developed the skills and confidence to speak for themselves are at a distinct advantage over those who have not. Self-advocacy not only requires the knowledge of one's disability and needs, it also requires effective social and communication skills to share this information with employers, co-workers, and others. Research has shown that many people with disabilities are reluctant to share information about their disabilities (Greenbaun, Graham, & Scales, 1996). Skilled communicators need to know if, when, and under what conditions should they describe their disability (Gerber, 1992). As students develop better self-advocacy skills and employers adhere to the nondiscriminatory provisions under ADA, the needs of adults with mild to moderate disabilities will be more appropriately addressed in work and school settings.

REFERENCES

Americans with Disabilities Act (ADA). (1990). PL 101–336, 42 U.S.C S 12101 *et seq.*

Becker, R. L. (1981). *Becker Reading Free Interests Inventory*. Columbus, OH: Elbern Publications.

Descoeudres, A. (1928). *The education of mentally defective.* E. F. Row, Trans. Boston: D. C. Heath.

DeFur, S., & Taymans, J. (1995). Competencies needed for transition specialists in vocational rehabilitation, vocational education, and special education. *Exceptional Children, 62*(1), 38–51.

Dunn, C. (1996). A status report on transition planning for individuals with learning disabilities. *Journal of Learning Disabilities, 29,* 17–30.

Edgar, E. (1987). Secondary programs in special education: Are many of them justifiable? *Exceptional Children, 53,* 555–562.

Evers, R. B. (1996). The positive force of vocational education: Transition outcomes for youth with learning disabilities. *Journal of Learning Disabilities, 29,* 69–78.

Education for All Handicapped Children Act. (1975). PL 94–142, 20 U.S.C. SS 1400 *et seq.*

Falvey, M. A., Forest, M., Pearpoint, J., & Rosenberg, R. (1994). Building connections. In J. S. Thousand, R. A. Villa, & A. I. Nevin (Eds.), *Creativity and collaborative learning: A practical guide to empowering students and teachers* (pp. 117–138). Baltimore, MD: Paul H. Brookes.

Gardner, H. (1983). *Frames of mind: The theory of multiple intelligences.* New York: Basic Books.

Gerber, P. J. (1992). At first glance: Employment for people with learning disabilities at the beginning of the Americans with Disabilities Act era. *Learning Disabilities Quarterly, 15*(4), 330–332.

Greenbaum, B., Graham, S., & Scales, W. (1996). Adults with learning disabilities: Occupational and social status after college. *Journal of Learning Disabilities, 29*(2), 167–173.

Halpern, A. S. (1994). The transition of youths with disabilities to adult life: A position statement of the Division on Career Development and Transition, Council for Exceptional Children. *Career Development of Exceptional Individuals, 17*(2), 115–124.

Harris, L., and Associates (1994). *The ICD survey II: Employing disabled Americans.* Washington DC: National Organization on Disability.

Holland, J. L. (1996). *Self-directed search.* Odessa, FL: Psychological Assessment Resources.

Hoyt, K. B. (1977). *A primer for career education.* Washington, DC: U.S. Government Printing Office.

Hungerford, R. (1941). The Detroit plan for the occupational education of the mentally retarded. *American Journal of Mental Deficiency, 46,* 102–108.

Individuals with Disabilities Education Act (IDEA). (1990). PL 101–476, 20 U.S.C. SS 1400 *et seq.*

Individuals with Disabilities Education Act (IDEA) Amendments. (1997). PL 105–17, 20 U.S.C. SS 1400 *et seq.*

Johansson, C. B. (1996). *The interest determination, exploration, and assessment system.* Minneapolis, MN: National Computer Systems.

Linenhoker, D., & McCarron, L. (1983). *Adaptive behavior: The street survival skills questionnaire.* Dallas, TX: McCarron Dial System.

Penn, A., & Williams, D. (1996). *Integrating academic and vocational education: A model for secondary schools.* Alexandria, VA: Association for Supervision and Curriculum Development.

Rehabilitation Act Amendments. (1992). PL 102–569, 29 U.S.C. S 701 *et seq.*

Sitlington, P. L. (1996). Transition to living: The neglected component of transition programming for individuals with learning disabilities. *Journal of Learning Disabilities, 29,* 31–39, 52.

Vocational Education Act (1963). PL 88–210, 26 U.S.C. 5(1964).

Vocational Education of Act Amendments of 1968, PL 90–576, 26 U.S.C. 1262 (c), 1263(b), (F), (1970).

Will, M. (1983). *OSERS programming for the transition of youth with disabilities: Bridges from school to working life*. Washington, DC: U.S. Department of Education.

Will, M. (1984). *Supported employment services: An OSERS position paper.* Washington, DC: U.S. Department of Education.

INDEX